The *Encomenderos* of New Spain, 1521–1555

THE
Encomenderos
OF NEW SPAIN, 1521–1555

Robert Himmerich y Valencia
Foreword by Joseph P. Sánchez

University of Texas Press, Austin

Copyright © 1991 by the University of Texas Press
All rights reserved
Printed in the United States of America

First paperback printing, 1996

Requests for permission to reproduce material from this work should be sent to Permissions, University of Texas Press, Box 7819, Austin, Texas 78713-7819

∞ The paper used in this publication meets the minimum requirements of American National Standard for Information Sciences—Permanence of Paper for Printed Library Materials, ANSI Z39.48-1984.

Publication of this work was assisted in part by a grant from the Spanish Ministry of Culture as a part of their Program for Cultural Cooperation between Spain's Ministry of Culture and United States Universities.

Library of Congress Cataloging-in-Publication Data
Himmerich y Valencia, Robert, 1932–
    The encomenderos of New Spain, 1521–1555 / by Robert Himmerich y Valencia; foreword by Joseph P. Sánchez. —1st ed.
        p.   cm.
    Originally presented as the author's thesis (Ph. D.)—University of California, Los Angeles, 1984.
    "Publication of this work was assisted in part by a grant from the Spanish Ministry of Culture as part of their Program for Cultural Cooperation between Spain's Ministry of Culture and United States Universities"—T.p. verso.
    Includes bibliographical references (p.   ) and index.
    ISBN 0-292-73108-6 pbk.
    1. Encomenderos—Mexico—History—16th century. 2. Encomiendas (Latin America)—History—16th century. 3. Mexico—History—Conquest, 1519–1540—Biography. 4. Mexico—History—Spanish Colony, 1540–1810—Biography. 5. Encomenderos—Mexico—Biography. I. Title.
F1230.H56 1991
972'.02—dc20   90-44785

To Eva Valencia de Himmerich,
and to Marc

Contents

Foreword	ix
Preface	xiii
Acknowledgments	xv

Part One: The *Encomenderos* as a Group

1. Introduction	3
2. The *Encomenderos'* Backgrounds: Regional Origins, Social Standing, and Experience	18
3. Cities and *Encomiendas*	35
4. The Integration of the *Encomenderos* into Local Society: Patterns of Association through Marriage, Officeholding, and *Encomienda* Sharing	63
5. Comparisons and Conclusions	86

Part Two: The Individual *Encomenderos*

Introduction	109
The Biographies	113

Appendixes

A. Roster of First Conqueror *Encomenderos*	267
B. Roster of Conqueror *Encomenderos*	271
C. Roster of *Poblador Antiguo Encomenderos*	276
D. Roster of *Poblador Encomenderos*	278
E. Roster of Indian *Encomenderos*	282
F. Citizenship of the *Encomenderos*	283
G. Methodological Essay	298
Notes	305
Glossary	316
Bibliography	318
Index	323

Tables

1. Governments of New Spain, October 1524 to November 1535 — 14
2. Overall Emigration from Spain to the Indies before and after 1520 — 20
3. Origins of the *Encomenderos* of New Spain — 21
4. *Encomenderos* from Extremadura — 25
5. Callings of the *Encomenderos* — 28
6. Experience of the *Encomenderos* in the Indies to 1521 — 32
7. Time of Arrival of the *Encomenderos* in New Spain — 33
8. Chronology of Spanish Settlement — 38
9. Residence and Origins of *Encomenderos* — 40
10. Origins of *Encomendero Vecinos* of Mexico City — 44
11. *Hidalgo Encomenderos* — 45
12. Distances between *Encomiendas* and Residences — 54
13. *Encomiendas* per *Encomendero* — 55
14. Distribution of *Encomiendas* According to Seniority — 55
15. *Encomienda* Succession — 56
16. Family Representation in Government — 73
17. Marriages between *Encomendero* Families — 75
18. Remarriage of Widows of *Encomenderos* by Region — 80
19. Marriages of Daughters of *Encomenderos* by Region — 81
20. *Encomienda* Sharing by Region of Origin — 82
21. Comparative Chronology of the Two Thrusts of Spanish Conquest — 90
22. Comparison of the Regional Origins of the Conquerors of Mexico and Peru — 93
23. Comparison of Social Standing and Occupation of Conquerors of Peru and Mexico — 95
24. Comparison of New World Experience of Conquerors of Mexico and Peru — 96

Maps

1. Iberian Regions and Provinces — 19
2. Extremadura — 23
3. Settlements in New Spain — 37
4. *Encomienda* Concentration — 53
5. *Encomiendas* of the Cervantes Family — 66
6. Conquest Routes — 88

Foreword

The present study fills an important and somewhat empty niche in the history of colonial Mexico for the period 1521 to 1555. Unlike colonial Peru, the *encomienda* in Mexican history has received limited attention from historians. Further, the present study is much more biographically comprehensive than the now-classic works on the *encomienda* in Mexico, principally those by Silvio Zavala, Charles Gibson, Leslie Byrd Simpson, and José Miranda. Indeed, the aforementioned authors, especially Simpson in *The Encomienda in New Spain: The Beginnings of Spanish Mexico (1950)* and Zavala's *La Encomienda Indiana* (1935), tended to concentrate, almost exclusively, on the legal aspects of the *encomienda* in Mexico. Similarly, Miranda's *La función económica del encomendero de los orígenes del regimen colonial de Nueva España, 1525–1531* (1965) featured the legal and economic aspects of the *encomienda*. In *Tlaxcala in the Sixteenth Century* (1952) and *Aztecs under Spanish Rule* (1964), Gibson presented important and new social patterns as they developed relative to the conquest of Tenochtitlan and its aftermath. These works, however, did not focus on synthesizing the lives of *encomenderos* as does the present study.

Robert Himmerich y Valencia has painstakingly culled through most of the secondary, and some of the available primary sources, resulting in a pioneering effort to identify the first *encomenderos* (recipients of *encomienda* grants) of New Spain. More needs to be done in this area of research to complete other biographical sources as well as the genealogical implications of the *encomienda* in colonial Mexican history and culture. Himmerich y Valencia's prosopographical study examines the founding 506 *encomenderos* in Mexico following the conquest of Tenochtitlan. The work attempts to show patterns of *encomienda* ownership and distribution by tying biographical data about the *encomenderos* to the *encomiendas* they held. The only other study in which a similar approach has been taken is Lockhart's *Men of Cajamarca* (1972). Although Lockhart dealt with a smaller group than the present study, he emphasized biographical data about the early founders of Peru rather than analysis of the *encomiendas* in their possession.

Unlike Himmerich y Valencia, Lockhart was able to derive biographical information from notarial records in Peru. In Mexico, unfortunately, a great fire in the seventeenth century destroyed most of the notarial records for the period 1521 to 1555, thus limiting Himmerich y Valencia's research efforts. Undaunted by the dearth of primary sources that the notarial documents could have provided, Himmerich y Valencia scoured every available source, primary and secondary, for the biographical data contained herein. An excellent detailed summary of the known surviving corpus of such documents was published by Agustín Millares Carlo and José I. Mantecon, "El Archivo de notarias del departamento del Distrito Federal," in *Revista de Historia de América* (vol. 17, 1944: 69–118). Likewise, certain archival sections of the Archivo General de la Nación in Mexico City are rich in information regarding *encomiendas*, but contain little that is not already known about the lives of *encomenderos*. Therein lies one of the distinctions between Lockhart's and Himmerich y Valencia's works. The former's work is biographical, in part by design, but also because of an emphasis on notarial documentation concerning *encomenderos* rather than historical documentation related to *encomiendas*; while the latter contains a greater amount of information about *encomiendas* in relation to their owners. The primary reason for this is the existence of lists of Mexican *encomiendas* made during the colonial period that have since been published in modern historical literature. Silvio Zavala, France V. Scholes, Charles Gibson, and Peter Gerhard are the most important scholars to have done so. As much as these scholars achieved, however, they did not consolidate and analyze the data, which would have been, indeed, an overwhelming task. The task of gathering the voluminous scattered, fragmentary, and seemingly disparate data and subjecting it to Clio's critical microscope, so to speak, has been left to Himmerich y Valencia.

The present study follows the prosopographical methodology used by European historians and improved upon by researchers of colonial Latin American history, among them, Peter Boyd-Bowman, James Lockhart, and David Brading. Indeed, Himmerich y Valencia, who began this study under the direction of James Lockhart at the University of California at Los Angeles (UCLA), has emulated his mentor's work in both methodology and approach. Himmerich y Valencia has done for Mexico what Lockhart did for Peru; that is, produce for the first time an important reference tool for scholars working on the early colonial period of Mexico. Given its parallels, in terms of its pioneering results, with such standard works on Mexican colonial history as those by Agustín Millares Carlo, Ignacio Rubio Mané, Peter Gerhard, Francisco A. de Icaza, Peter Boyd-Bowman, Arthur S. Aiton, Donald Chipman, Manuel Orozco y Berra, Francisco Fernández del Castillo, and others, the present study appears destined to become a classic.

This study is essentially divided into two parts. Part One is an examination of the *encomenderos* of New Spain as a group. Himmerich y Valencia analyzes their places of origin, their social characteristics, their arrival and activities in the Indies, the number and location of their grants, their residence patterns, and, to an extent, the pattern of succession to their *encomiendas* under Spanish law and practice. Part Two contains biographical entries for each *encomendero* included in this study. The 506 biographical accounts not only identify the *encomenderos* of New Spain during the first generation following the fall of Tenochtitlan but also provide a compilation of much personal information about them otherwise scattered among a number of sources.

The present study complements much of what has been written concerning the *encomienda* and *encomenderos* in Mexico and sheds considerable light on the origins of our Pan-American heritage throughout the Americas. As an institution, the *encomienda* was instituted wherever feasible in the Spanish Empire, and *encomenderos*, as conquerors and investors, influenced the development of North and South America. Furthermore, the Christopher Columbus Quincentennial in 1992 will evermore serve to mark our Pan-American heritage that began as an encounter between two worlds: Indian America and Europe.

Joseph P. Sánchez
Director
Spanish Colonial Research Center
National Park Service
University of New Mexico

Preface

This book is the result of an inquiry into the social history of Spanish Mexico, and especially the tenure of the first generation. It was during this period that the conventions of the society were established, the hinterland of Mexico City inventoried, and a portion of the wealth of this new Spanish kingdom distributed among those who risked life and fortune to enhance their respective estates. Spaniards in America during these early years were more pragmatic than idealistic; they fully realized that the true wealth of this recently uncovered part of the world was its native population and not necessarily the precious metals and gems that were nonetheless hoped for. The reward for their efforts was the much sought after *encomienda*—the right to the tribute of an indigenous polity. Not every polity was assigned to individual Spaniards, however, for a large portion of the native population was reserved for the crown and the ecclesiastics.

The study is divided into two parts, with Part One based on data contained in Part Two. Whereas Part Two focuses on specific individual lives and attempts, to some degree, to show uniqueness, Part One combines those with like attributes to ascertain general characteristics and processes. This work deals with a group of individuals who crossed the Mexican scene over a period of thirty years or more, their main common characteristic being simply that they were *encomenderos* at some time during these three decades.

There is a great deal of systematic information on *encomenderos* and *encomiendas* in this present study, going beyond the invaluable contributions of Charles Gibson and Peter Gerhard. It brings together, consolidates, and analyzes for the first time disparate and scattered material on the 506 individuals known to be *encomenderos* present during New Spain's founding generation.

Acknowledgments

A work of history is neither the Alpha nor the Omega, but rather hopes to contribute to a better understanding of the past. As such it should invite new themes of inquiry rather than stand as the final authority on the topic at hand. The literature of the early years of Spanish presence in Mexico is extensive and distinguished and it is here that I wish to express my appreciation for the contributions of all the historians of colonial Mexico. Bernal Díaz del Castillo, France V. Scholes and Eleanor B. Adams, Charles Gibson, and Peter Gerhard, though, have made this particular study possible. I am particularly indebted to Professor James Lockhart who focused my interest in the social history of the early years of Spain in America and directed my graduate studies at the University of California, Los Angeles, and Professor Thomas O. Flickema, then of California State University, Fullerton, who, by example and enthusiasm, showed this one time telecommunication engineer that there was life beyond Ohm's Law.

Dr. Joseph P. Sánchez of the U.S. National Parks Service Spanish Colonial Research Center at the University of New Mexico, Professors Robert Kern of the University of New Mexico and Félix Almaráz, University of Texas, San Antonio were most supportive of my efforts to publish this manuscript. The good office of the Spanish Colonial Research Center also provided material and other intangible support that cannot be accurately quantified. It is here that I wish to thank Mrs. Edwina Abreu of the Center for her off-duty accomplishments in making order and sense out of my notes, corrections, additions, and deletions that constituted the draft with which she worked; and to recognize the encouragement, wise counsel, and support provided by colleagues Susan Schroeder, Linda Hall, and William Broughton; and for Fray Padre Alfred Brichta-López, O.P., a very special thank you.

I especially appreciate the efforts of the University of Texas Press and the support of the Program for Cultural Cooperation between Spain's Ministry of Culture and United States Universities, coordinated by Professor Antonio Ramos-Gascon. Thank you both, and of course my special gratitude to the Spanish Ministry of Culture for its recognition of this work.

And to Eva, my wife, who has participated in every step of this project, I am thankful.

PART ONE

The *Encomenderos* as a Group

CHAPTER ONE

Introduction

The 506 individuals known to have held *encomiendas* in New Spain during the first generation of Spanish presence in Mexico are the subjects of this study. The *encomenderos* as a group are crucially important to the understanding of the early years of Spanish Mexico because the wealth generated by the *encomiendas* served as the engine that drove the society. This was all the more so because the capture of Tenochtitlan and subsequent expeditions failed to produce the anticipated mineral riches. Since nearly all wealth in New Spain during the first generation of Spanish domination originated in one way or another with the natives, it follows that those controlling the Indians in reality dominated all aspects of society.

The time span of this study, 1521 to 1555, in addition to corresponding roughly to the time of dominance of the first generation of Spaniards in New Spain, embraces both the flowering and the eclipse of the *encomienda* as an all-encompassing, quasi-estate form at the very center of Hispanic society. The period has additional significance as an epoch of foundation when lasting social and political characteristics of the colony took shape. The first decade, between the capture of Tenochtitlan in August 1521 and the arrival in 1531 of the second Audiencia, was a dynamic time that often bordered on chaos. While many of those who took part in the conquest, reinforced by new arrivals from the Caribbean and Europe, were exploring the length and breadth of Mesoamerica, New Spain went through a succession of governors who often failed to act in the best interest of all concerned. Relative stability was established by the second Audiencia (arriving in 1531 as just seen), and then continued under viceroys don Antonio de Mendoza (1535–1550) and don Luis de Valesco (after 1551). Two major forces affected the *encomenderos* during the time limits of this study. The first was growing political pressure on the *encomiendas* as increased Spanish immigration allowed the crown to begin implementing its policies aimed at restricting the institution. The other was demographic pressure, as the aboriginal population of the central Mexican region fell from its preconquest level of perhaps 22 million inhabitants to a number estimated at less than 3 million by midcentury.[1]

Conventions and Vocabulary of the Study

The *encomienda*, as apparently perceived by the early recipients in Mexico, was a grant to a Spaniard of the Indians of a prescribed indigenous polity, who were to provide the grantee (the *encomendero*) tribute in the form of commodities and service in return for protection and religious instruction (neither of which were given, in many cases). Land was not a formal component of the *encomienda*, although the *encomendero* often acquired separate grants of land in the vicinity of the Indian community. Hernando Cortés made the initial assignments and reassignments of *encomiendas* in Mexico, being succeeded in that capacity by subsequent governors, the Royal Audiencia, and finally the viceroy. Assignment of rural land as well as city lots was initially within the authority of the *cabildos* (municipal councils).

The municipality in New Spain reflected Spanish urban-centered modes of organization where each city dominated a surrounding hinterland and served as the focus for all economic, social, political, and ecclesiastical activities. The political body ruling, representing, legislating, and adjudicating for the city was the *cabildo*. The *cabildo*, dominated in the early years by *encomendero* families, had jurisdiction over the assignment and reassignment of *solares* (urban house lots), *huertas* (suburban tracts for orchards, vineyards, and vegetable gardens), and *estancias* and *caballerias* (rural tracts for raising horses, cattle, sheep, pigs, or for the cultivation of cereal crops). It also licensed and inspected all business and artisanal activities, and let contracts for municipal services as well as publishing an official—but often ignored—price list for goods and services offered in the municipality. *Cabildo* offices included *regidores* (councilmen), *alcaldes* (magistrates), *alguaciles* (constables), the *alcaide* (jail warden), *procuradores* (legal representatives), the *escribano* (city clerk), the *pregonero* (town crier), and the *portero* (doorman). The office of *regidor* was a proprietary royal appointment that could be bequeathed or sold, subject to crown approval. *Regidores* "elected" the remaining officers at the first annual meeting in January as well as letting contracts for the various municipal services. The number of *regidores* on a *cabildo* depended on the municipal charter; as a general rule *ciudades* (cities) had twelve, *villas* (towns) eight, and *pueblos* (villages) four.

In the sixteenth century, Spanish names and orthography varied a great deal, not only from modern usage, but with the writer and the occasion. In this study names have been modified to conform with the usage of the twentieth century and otherwise standardized so that the same individual will always have the same appellation. For example, Xuárez has been rendered as Suárez, Ximénez as Jiménez, and Ynojosa as Hinojosa, and where a variation in the form (as opposed to the orthography) of a given name appears, for example, Antón and Antonio, Hernán and Hernando, the difference is resolved by writing Antón(io) and Hernán(do). In other instances the same individual may have used or have been referred to by two altogether different given names. Initially I often took the names to identify two separate individuals, but when evidence overwhelmingly established that I was dealing with only one person, the issue was resolved by indicating the least used variant in parentheses together with the more commonly used form. The same solution was adopted when an individual had two different surnames.[2]

The spelling and pronunciation of Mexican place-names have endured a succession of modifications over the past four hundred years. The spelling herein generally follows that used by Gerhard in his *A Guide to the Historical Geography of New Spain* except where the *encomienda* name survives as a present-day location, in which case the current identification is also shown.[3] Gerhard was also used as a guide in locating *encomiendas*, together with current maps, aeronautical charts, and atlases.[4] Because "Tenochtitlan" for the most part was replaced by "México" within fifteen years after the conquest as a designation for the capital of New Spain, this study refers to the latter simply as Mexico City. The use of "Tenochtitlan" is reserved for specific reference to the preconquest Aztec capital. The identification of other centers of Spanish population is further amplified in Chapter 3.

The *encomenderos* of New Spain and the officials who granted *encomiendas* paid great attention to distinctions based essentially on a particular individual's time of arrival in New Spain, and one who studies them must do the same. The basic division between "conqueror" and "settler" as used in Icaza is a convenient point of departure; it makes a distinction between those who arrived before and after the establishment of the first Audiencia in Mexico City in 1528, suggesting that date as the end of the conquest period in the narrower sense.[5] Another effort toward categorizing the conquerors suggests that those who were present at the fall of Tenochtitlan in 1521 were designated *conquistadores de México* and those who arrived after the siege and took part in subsequent actions prior to the arrival of the first Audiencia were *conquistadores de Nueva España*.[6] The presumption here is that the post-first Audiencia arrivals were *pobladores* (settlers), even though many of them earned a claim to an *encomienda* through *entrada* service in Oaxaca, Michoacán, and Jalisco.[7]

Yet another scheme for classifying *encomenderos* is suggested by conventions taken from the *Actas de cabildo* when assigning city house lots.[8] Herein the majority of those who were members of Cortés' original *entrada* are identified as *primeros conquistadores*, and those who arrived after the capture of Mexico City but had been in the Indies prior to its capture are referred to as either *conquistadores de Nueva España* or *pobladores antiguos*. Working out the implications of these terms, I have established the following four categories, which are used throughout the study:

First conqueror—A member of the original Cortés *entrada* that passed muster at Cozumel and again at the founding of Veracruz. The actual number of first conquerors may never be known, but a figure near 400 seems acceptable, with 383 identified by name with some degree of certainty. Perhaps 200 of this group survived, 135 becoming *encomenderos*.

Conqueror—A member of subsequent *entradas* and individual shiploads of reinforcements who arrived in New Spain in time to take part in the siege and capture of Tenochtitlan. The largest group of conquerors sailed from Cuba under Pánfilo de Narváez, but other captains and outfitters included Miguel Díaz de Aux, Francisco de Garay (Garay did not arrive in New Spain until 1523 but members of his unsuccessful 1519 and 1520 *entradas* to Pánuco joined the Cortés force), Diego de Camargo, Luis Ponce de León, Francisco Salcedo, and others. Estimates of the number of surviving conquerors range from 400 to 600. Some 360 have been identified with certainty, and of this number 178 became *encomenderos*.

Poblador antiguo—A resident of the Indies prior to the capture of Tenochtitlan who moved to New Spain thereafter, but within the first decade after 1521. There is no record of how many persons fit this description, but thirty-two received *encomiendas*.

Poblador—One who arrived in New Spain after the capture of Tenochtitlan, but had no previous residence in the Indies. Of the thousands who arrived in the second quarter of the century, only 158 became *encomenderos:* some by *entrada* service, others by purchase, still others by virtue of social status, but the majority by marrying an *encomendera*.

Not only time of arrival but also social standing was important in the allocation of *encomiendas*. Placing an *encomendero* in his correct niche in sixteenth-century Mexico's social pecking order is often a vexing exercise, especially when attempting to determine just who was an authentic *hidalgo*. There is no problem in the case of high nobles entitled *don*; such folk were quite rare in the early years. Perhaps a half dozen spent time in New Spain during the second quarter of the century, of whom only three—don Luis de Castilla, don Luis de Guzmán Saavedra, and don Tristán de Luna y Arrellano—became *encomenderos*.[9] There were no titled nobles among the 345 *encomenderos* who arrived in the Indies before the capture of Tenochtitlan.

The qualifications for being considered an *hidalgo*, an honorific word used by Spaniards for a broad spectrum of society from high nobles to lesser gentry, were undergoing quick change during the time period studied here. All of the *encomenderos* acquired some claim to gentry status by virtue of holding a grant of Indian tributaries. This study, however, identifies as *hidalgos* only those who were acknowledged by contemporaries to have held such status prior to departing from Europe.

There is no foolproof test for identifying *hidalgos*. One must proceed mainly by measuring certain symptoms against each other, especially in borderline cases and with those for whom genealogical information has not survived. Among such symptoms are the role the individual conqueror played in the conquest as well as in the postconquest political milieu, and the deference shown him by contemporaries. Those who retained positions of authority and trust, particularly when an outstanding record of achievement in the conquest is lacking, did so more because of status than ability. The presumption must be that royal officials and nonconqueror members of a *cabildo* were *hidalgos*. Conqueror *regidores* who acquired perpetual appointments to the *cabildo* at the very least had a probable claim to noble descent and could afford to go to the expense of creating adequate legal proof of their status. The nature of marriage partners, whether of the *encomendero*, his children, or his widow, is another significant criterion (see Tables 17, 18, and 19, and the accompanying discussion in Chapter 4). Again one must make subjective decisions, however, since mutually advantageous marriages between those with *encomiendas* and those of noble descent often provided the means to upgrade plebeian status. The posterior editing of the genealogical record has also, unfortunately, muddled the true status of a number of *encomenderos*. Further significant criteria for determining nobility are *encomienda* retention and succession in the face of the difficulties of the postconquest years; the truly noble *encomenderos* retained their grants at the expense of the less wellborn. Bernal Díaz del Castillo provides yet another tool for the identification of gentry through his references to "persons of quality," but he concerns himself primarily with those who were his companions along with Hernando Cortés. In the end, however, his comments lose a degree of credibility when he observes that "we were for the most part *hidalgos*, although some were not of such clear lineage as others, for all cannot be alike in this world, either in rank or in virtues."[10] The final determination of just who were the *hidalgos*, then, is subjective, based on my assessment of an individual's name, parents, relations, and associates, the deference shown him by contemporaries, the offices he held, the awards he received, and the degree of their retention by his heirs.

The reader will find liberal use of Spanish Mexican *encomienda* terminology in the present study. The basic word for an Indian town or city state was *pueblo*. The Spaniards called the center of government and tribute collection within an indigenous state (and hence *encomienda*) its *cabecera* (a distinction not made by the Indians themselves). The name of the *cabecera*, the Indian state, and the *encomienda* were normally all the same. The Spaniards were quite confused between constituent parts of the Indian entity and separate more or less dependent *pueblos*, so they applied a battery of terms somewhat indiscriminately: *sujeto, barrio, estancia, visita*, and *dependencia*. *Sujeto* and *dependencia* were both general terms for *pueblo* subdivisions. A *barrio* was usually a lesser division within or contiguous to the main pueblo, but in some instances the term was synonymous with *estancia*, which usually referred to an outlying settlement. (In an entirely different meaning, an *estancia* could be an agrarian enterprise owned by a Spaniard.) A *visita* was a stop on the circuit of a parish priest, be he regular or secular, and could be a *pueblo, barrio, estancia, sujeto*, or *dependencia*.

Vecino and *casa poblada* are two other terms that require definition. The term "*vecino*" or "citizen" was used quite loosely in New Spain, usually indicating that one owned or maintained a house and property in a given location (normally a Spanish municipality), had been in the immediate area for perhaps a year, and had indicated an intention to stay permanently. A few of the *encomenderos* were considered *vecinos* of two or even three cities, while others were involuntary *vecinos* of remote outposts while actually residing elsewhere. Although citizenship often required formal application to a municipal council and affirmative action by the latter, responsibilities were often treated rather casually. An *encomendero* often actually resided where he could best enjoy the perquisites of his station, and this was where he established his *casa poblada*, literally "peopled house," being his establishment and headquarters. (Most of the time the *encomendero*'s citizenship and the location of the establishment coincided.) Ideally the *casa poblada* was a large house, preferably managed by a Spanish wife, where a number of relatives, guests, and Spanish employees were maintained, catered to by a staff of black slaves and Indian servants.

Spanish money of the sixteenth century can often be a confusing topic. The primary unit in New Spain was the *peso*, a coin that contained eight silver *reales* or gold *tomines*, but the *ducat* was the preferred unit of money in Spain. The basic denomination of account, however, was the *maravedí*, especially favored by merchants and treasury officials for keeping record because of the variable quality of precious metals smelted in America. Accordingly, a "*peso* of good gold" was valued at about 450 *maravedís*, a *ducat* about 375. At any rate, the *maravedí* served as the least common denominator even though it never existed as an actual coin. Money is referred to herein as it appears in the sources, be it peso, ducat, or maravedí.

The Rise and Decline of the *Encomienda* in New Spain

The discovery, conquest, and settlement of New Spain was a continuation of Spanish activity in the Caribbean basin. After Columbus' first landfall, however, twenty-five years elapsed before the trading and slaving voyages of Francisco Hernández de Córdoba and Juan de Grijalva established beyond doubt, in 1517 and 1518, that continental North America was not just another island.[11] Furthermore, there was no immediate rush to populate the islands of the Caribbean. Reports of conditions in the region made by disheartened returnees to Spain were not such as to attract vast numbers of settlers. Only a few more than 200 Europeans were in the Indies until 1502, most of them on the island of Hispaniola. By 1512, ten years after Comendador frey Nicolás de Ovando's 1502 entourage had reportedly added 2,500 to the region's Spanish population, and even after Puerto Rico and Cuba had been occupied, there may have been hardly more than a thousand permanent European settlers in the Indies. After seven more years, when Hernando Cortés was organizing his 1519 *entrada*, the total non-Indian population of the Caribbean basin could not have much exceeded 5,000, of which number perhaps 1,000 were residents of Cuba.[12]

Cortés' initial force, composed of 300 or so residents of Cuba and about 200 veterans of the Grijalva expedition quartered on Cuba, seriously disrupted the local economy when it departed. Not only did nearly one-third of the Spanish population leave, but larders and storerooms were emptied to provision the *entrada*. Cuba became the assembly point for the Antilles, serving as a magnet for those already in the other Caribbean colonies as well as attracting a number of new immigrants directly from Europe as soon as reports from Mexico were announced. Within fourteen months Pánfilo de Narváez, a veteran with some twenty-two years of experience in the Indies, assembled another 1,400 men under the sponsorship of Diego Velázquez, Cuba's governor, and departed for Mexico, where they quickly became part of Cortés' force. The latter, after absorbing the followers of Narváez and succeeding shiploads of independently organized reinforcements, while at the same time having suffered casualties and left some members behind at Veracruz, probably totaled about 1,400 men—conceivably as much as 25 percent of the European population of the Indies.[13] The economic potential of this market redirected commercial activity to Veracruz, further disrupting established trade patterns in the region.[14]

The large body of conquerors now in Mexico expected, and before long received, *encomiendas* as their principal reward, or at least all the more prominent of them did, so it would be well to say a few words here about the *encomienda* as an institution. During the Caribbean period a practice had gradually evolved out of the needs of the local Spaniards and governmental officials' grudging adjustment to those needs. The government had originally not intended to use the moribund Spanish *encomienda* tradition at all in rewarding immigrants, but the Hispanic tradition of dividing newly acquired territories among its conquerors proved too strong to be resisted. What emerged in the Caribbean was a system whereby each Indian political entity under its traditional leadership was granted to a Spaniard deemed deserving because of his prominence and early arrival in the area. The ruler, or *cacique*, using his normal powers, channeled to the grantee whatever his people were accustomed to give or do in the way of tribute. In the Caribbean this was work only, not products. This grant was called a *repartimiento* and in this context can be defined as an apportionment of native service. Today we call such a grant an *encomienda*, although that term was in fact very slow to take hold. From a very early time, however, the holders of grants were called *encomenderos*. Land was not part of the grant, although *encomenderos* usually acquired separate land grants near the area of their *encomiendas*. The basic nature of the institution in any given area was determined by the needs, numbers, and expectations of the local Spaniards in interaction with the characteristics of local indigenous groups. At a distance, uncomprehending crown officials were hostile to the *encomienda* and were forever issuing directives aimed at limiting or even abolishing it, while officials in the Indies tried to mediate between the positions of the settlers and the crown.[15]

The *encomenderos* of New Spain, with the exception of the *pobladores* coming directly from Spain, were familiar with the Antillian *encomienda*, and a number of them had held grants of Indians in one of the Caribbean colonies. Those who took part in the conquest of New Spain were fully aware of the tug-of-war concerning the institution, with the efforts of those in the Indies to retain it and the crown's desire to abolish it.[16] This in no way dimmed the conquerors' zeal. While it is impossible to know exactly what an *entrada* recruiting pitch was like, most surely it held out the promise of *encomiendas* for the participants.

An appreciation of royal sentiment against rewarding more *encomiendas* in the Indies can be recognized in the letter from the *cabildo* of Veracruz to the king, dated 10 July 1519. The communication, written shortly after Cortés organized the municipality as a step toward legitimizing his venture, implies partial agreement with Charles V's stated intention of abolishing the *encomienda* but attributes the institution's evil effect in the Indies to bad management by local governors.[17] There can also be little doubt that the signers of this document cited the evils of the *encomienda* only in the hope of expediting royal sanction for their extralegal, if not illegal, venture. Members of the Cortés *entrada* must have understood that possessing Indians was in fact the wealth of the Indies, and that the acquisition of Indians justified the expense and effort of participating in an *entrada*. Liquid wealth in the form of precious metals, while always an inducement, was still more anticipated than realized. Cortés and his more affluent companions in the enterprise were or had been *encomenderos* in the Indies and would surely have been loath to relinquish the social status and economic advantage that accrued from the position. To others an *encomienda* was an opportunity to enjoy social and economic upward mobility.

The high-sounding statement in the *cabildo's* July 1519 letter, conceding that authority to assign Indians to conquerors should be reserved to the king, was circumvented shortly after the capture of Tenochtitlan. Cortés explained in his third letter to Charles V, dated

15 May 1522, that the demands of the conquerors to recoup their expenses was great because their shares from the division of the treasure acquired from the Indians still left them in debt. In order to prevent the enslavement of the natives, he was forced to "deposit" the chiefs and their subjects in the care of certain Spaniards until such time as the king should see fit to confirm or to void the grants. Such action was further justified as a means to save the crown the expense of the conquest and the maintenance of a garrison in New Spain. Tribute received from the Indians would repay the costs incurred in mounting the *entrada* and would provide for the support of the conquerors as they continued to explore the new dominion.[18]

The assignment of *encomiendas* after the establishment of Mexico City and as part of continuing explorations and conquests in New Spain left Charles V temporarily outmaneuvered. Regardless of the terminology used, Indians had already been assigned to perhaps three hundred of those who took part in the conquest, together with a few veterans of the Indies who arrived during the consolidation of Mexico City. That number represented about 40 percent of the total survivors of the force that captured the city and perhaps as much as 6 percent of the European population of the Indies. For a few years Cortés, having taken the lion's share of Indians and booty for himself, was possibly the richest man in the New World. He was politically and militarily in a very strong position, yet, ever aware of his king's apprehension about creating a new and dangerous nobility, in his correspondence he would wait until the last paragraph to announce his actions concerning the assignment of *encomiendas*, and even then only by oblique reference. Finally, in October 1523, Cortés received specific authority to award and to reassign *encomiendas*.[19] This authority was extended from time to time and exercised by those governing the colony until the issuance of the New Laws in 1542.[20]

The assignment of native lords and their subjects to the conquerors established the social and economic base of the colony. Cortés' assignment and reassignment of *encomiendas* invariably elicited charges of favoritism, perhaps in part true, but he was acting in a sixteenth-century tradition. Like any governor, Cortés moved to consolidate his power base by the means he had available. If an award of Indians would repay debts, well and good. Assigning Indians to the follower of an adversary could create an ally, or at least a neutral. Those who replaced Cortés in authority during his absence from Mexico City between October 1524 and June 1526 were much less moderate in their actions.

Normal attrition, for causes that included death and departure from the region, required reassigning up to thirty grants in any given year. By the time serious political upheavals began in late October 1524, at least a third of the Indians had experienced one change of *encomendero*. A number of *encomienda* reassignments for purely political purposes were made between November 1524 and June 1526 by the four royal officers in the capacity of acting governors. They were Tesorero (treasurer) Alonso de Estrada, Contador (accountant) Rodrigo de Albornoz, Veedor (inspector) Pero Almíndez Chirinos, and Factor (business agent) Gonzalo de Salazar. Nuño Beltrán de Guzmán, as president of the first Audiencia between January 1529 and January 1531, also reassigned a number of *encomiendas* for purely political reasons. Table 1 lists the tenure of the governing officials during this period of flux. During each of the unsettled periods the thrust was against Cortés and his close supporters, all holding inordinately large grants. The beneficiaries of the reassignment made by the co-lieutenant governors and by the first Audiencia were for the most part upper-echelon folk. There was relative stability after Cortés returned from Honduras and during his suspension, as well as during the nearly two-year governing tenure of Alonso de Estrada. The second Audiencia, after voiding the assignments of the first Audiencia, concentrated on enhancing the crown's position. Most *encomiendas* which vacated by death or departure at that time escheated. A few initial assignments were made to correct blatant injustices.

Although the *encomienda* of New Spain was patterned upon that of the Caribbean, it of course differed to the extent that conditions differed. Indigenous Mexican political units were much larger and, hence, so were the *encomiendas* of New Spain, which initially provided each of the three hundred or so *encomenderos* with thousands of tributaries. In Mexico, giving tribute in kind was a well-established indigenous tradition, so commodities were added to labor among the benefits accruing to the *encomenderos*. Demographic catastrophe soon reduced the population of the Caribbean islands to the point that indigenous political units were no longer viable, and the *encomienda* practically ceased to exist within a generation after impact. In the heartlands of Mexico severe population loss ensued, but fell short of destroying the viability of the units on which the *encomiendas* were based, although in peripheral low-lying areas the destruction was nearly as great as in the Caribbean, with the same result: the quick disappearance of the organized units and the *encomiendas* on which they were based. The *encomenderos* of New Spain like their predecessors often held land grants in the areas of their *encomiendas*, the first of these awards were made as

Table 1. Governments of New Spain, October 1524 to November 1535

Prior to October 1524	Hernando Cortés (governor, captain general, and justice)
24 October 1524 to 29 December 1524 (co-lieutenant governors)	Contador Rodrigo de Albornoz Tesorero Alonso de Estrada Licenciado Alonso de Zuaso (justice)
29 December 1524 to 25 February 1525 (co-lieutenant governors)	Veedor Pedro Almíndez Chirinos Factor Gonzalo de Salazar Licenciado Alonso de Zuaso (justice)
25 February 1525 to 19 April 1525 (co-lieutenant governors)	Rodrigo de Albornos Pedro Almíndez Chirinos Alonso de Estrada Gonzalo de Salazar Licenciado Alonso de Zuaso (justice)
19 April 1525 to 23 January 1526 (co-lieutenant governors)	Pedro Almíndez Chirinos Gonzalo de Salazar Licenciado Alonso de Zuaso (justice)

Zuaso was ousted as co-lieutenant governor and justice and imprisoned on 23 April 1525. Almíndez Chirinos and Salazar then became de facto co-justices. On 25 August 1525 they also became de facto co-captains general.

23 January 1526 to 15 June 1526 (co-lieutenant governors and captains general)	Rodrigo de Albornoz Alonso de Estrada

Bachiller Juan de Ortega, *alcalde mayor* of Mexico City, served as justice from 23 January 1526, but did not share in the government.

15 June 1526 to 4 July 1526	Hernando Cortés

early as 10 October 1525, and they too took a large part in mining enterprises, but in the latter case there was a great difference. On the islands, gold mining had been the principal use of Indian tribute labor. In New Spain, the low-lying placer gold areas that were the colony's principal economic asset in the bulk of the time period of this study were mainly located at great distances from the highland populations in *encomienda*. For this reason and because of the feeling that it had been above all gold mining, which destroyed the *encomiendas* of the Caribbean, in New Spain gold mining was not a standard legal use of *encomienda* labor. Instead *encomenderos* used Indian slaves allegedly taken in just wars of conquest (those who refused to submit to Christianity and Spanish dominion when given the opportunity), or used *encomienda* Indians illegally. Despite the lack of an open direct labor tie to gold mining, *encomenderos* still

Table 1. (continued)

4 July 1526 to 20 July 1526 (residencia judge)	Licenciado Luis Ponce de León (died 20 July 1526)
1 August 1526 to 23 February 1527 (residencia judge)	Licenciado Marcos de Aguilar (died 23 February 1527)
23 February 1527 to 22 August 1527 (co-lieutenant governors)	Alonso de Estrada Gonzalo de Sandoval
22 August 1527 to 1 January 1529	Alonso de Estrada
1 January 1529 to 12 January 1531 (First Audiencia)	Nuño Beltrán de Guzmán, president; Licenciado Diego Delgadillo, judge; Licenciado Juan Ortiz de Matienzo, judge
12 January 1531 to 14 November 1535 (Second Audiencia)	Licenciado Sebastián Ramírez Funeleal, president; Licenciado Francisco de Ceynos, judge; Licenciado Alonso Maldonado, judge; Licenciado Vasco de Quiroga, judge; Licenciado Juan de Salmerón, judge
From 14 November 1535	Viceroy don Antonio de Mendoza

Note: With the exception of first conqueror Gonzalo de Sandoval, the lieutenant governors were royal treasury officers of New Spain, and their sole experience in the Indies had been in Mexico. Of the Audiencia members, only Judge Licenciado Juan Ortiz de Matienzo had governmental experience in the Indies. He had spent six years in Santo Domingo and nine years in Cuba before his arrival in Mexico City.

managed to dominate the industry. The overall result was the creation of social, economic, and political complexes, which were far larger, better developed, and more permanent than those associated with the *encomienda* in the Caribbean.

Under these conditions, the *encomienda* was for a time New Spain's master institution. It was the source of great wealth and power for the *encomenderos*, the centerpiece of Spanish urban society, and the primary link between that society and the indigenous societies on which it drew. The *encomienda* was not to go unchallenged, however. The most obvious pressure upon it was the drastic fall of Indian population totals even in the highlands. Epidemic disease reduced the population of central Mexico by millions in the 1520s and 1530s, and the most devastating blow came with the plagues of the period 1545 to 1548; the estimated three million indigenous people left in central Mexico by the end of that time were but a fraction of those alive at first contact with the Spaniards.

As demographic loss mounted, the campaign of the crown to limit the *encomienda* continued. The New Laws of 1542 would in their original form have practically meant the end of the institution, not only removing its labor rights and subjecting tribute in kind to a schedule, but halting succession. The political climate in New Spain was such that the laws were at first ignored, but as immigrants continued to pour in and new bases for the Spanish economy were discovered (principally silver mining), it became possible to put more and more of the legislation into effect. After 1544 Viceroy Mendoza promulgated the New Laws. Enforcement of the ban on personal service tribute began in 1549. Henceforth obligatory Indian labor would be allotted temporarily to Spaniards through a political authority outside the encomienda, whether it be the *corregidor* of the district or special *juez repartidor* (administrator of draft labor). Tribute collected by the *encomenderos* was now limited to commodities, and even these were to be established by an official inspector in proportion to the number of tributaries. Under the new system the profitability of the *encomienda* was tied closely to a plummeting Indian population.

Historians of previous generations who asserted that these measures reduced the *encomenderos* to crown pensioners and deprived the *encomienda* of importance in the country's further development greatly overstated the case. They ignored the fact that the *encomenderos* had private social and economic networks which did not depend on the legal aspects of the *encomienda* grant; the *encomenderos* responded to the new conditions by putting emphasis precisely on the informal aide of their estates. Even under the new system, *encomenderos* got their share and often more than their share of draft labor by striving to have a family member appointed as *juez repartidor* or through discrete arrangements with an *encomienda cacique*. Enforcement of all the new measures tended to be supremely slow and lax, above all in outlying districts. Moreover, the right to succeed by inheritance, after many challenges, was largely preserved through the sixteenth century. Thus the *encomenderos* did not easily fade away, and though the formal benefits of the *encomienda* gradually became relatively insignificant, holding an *encomienda* continued to confer prestige, wealth, and influence in other ways. For example, the important Valley of Toluca was still dominated by *encomienda*-holding families based in Mexico City as late as 1580–1600.[21]

Nevertheless, it remains true that the actual tribute benefits of the *encomienda* in New Spain were in serious decline after mid-sixteenth century and that new elements—miners, officials, agricultural entrepreneurs, and merchants—joined the *encomenderos* at the apex of Spanish Mexican society. Moreover, if the noblest and most powerful of the *encomendero* families managed to survive, many lesser *encomenderos* fell by the wayside. By 1555 the golden age of the *encomienda* of New Spain was over.

CHAPTER TWO

The *Encomenderos'* Backgrounds: Regional Origins, Social Standing, and Experience

The *encomenderos* of New Spain mirrored the society that produced them; they included natives of the major Spanish cities and many smaller communities as well as some of the European foreigners who took part in aspects of Spanish life (especially seafaring). Representatives of almost all of the callings and occupations recognized in the social order held title to grants of Indian tributaries at one time or another during the first two decades of the Spanish occupation. The farther one was from nobility, the more difficult it was to acquire and then to retain an *encomienda*. But as important as social rank was in the assigning of *encomiendas*, an individual's time of arrival and experience in the Indies were perhaps even more so.

Each of the larger regions of the Iberian peninsula, shown in the upper part of Map 1, as well as six non-Spanish principalities and kingdoms, were claimed as places of origin by the *encomenderos*. The provincial borders presented in the lower projection are modern administrative and political conventions and are provided merely to assist in locating the often small and obscure places where the *encomenderos* were born. While those from the same regions often sought each other out and associated closely, regionality was but one of the social factors linking *encomenderos* in New Spain. Equally significant points of contact were family ties, through both blood and marriage, and simple friendships that developed during years of joint campaigning in the Indies. The strongest professional, business, and social bonds developed between those sharing a number of such factors, but especially among those sharing experience in the Indies.

Many of those responsible for the conquest of Mexico left Spain during the period of discovery and initial colonization, before the social and political turmoil attendant upon the coronation of Charles I and his election as Holy Roman Emperor. The record of licenses granted for individuals to leave Spain before 1520 and after that date

THE *ENCOMENDEROS'* BACKGROUNDS 19

Map 1. Iberian Regions and Provinces

Table 2. Overall Emigration from Spain to the Indies before and after 1520

Region	1493–1519[a] (%)	1520–1539[a] (%)	1493–1550[b] (%)
Andalusia	39.7	32.0	34.6
Extremadura	14.1	16.6	15.8
New Castile	8.8	12.0	11.7
Old Castile	18.0	17.6	17.3
León	7.5	7.6	7.3
Biscay	4.4	4.5	4.5
Other Spain	4.9	5.5	5.1
Foreign countries	2.6	4.2	3.7
Total	100.0%	100.0%	100.0%

[a] Peter Boyd-Bowman, *Indice geobiográfico de cuarenta mil pobladores españoles de América en el siglo XVI*, vol. 2 (Mexico City: Editorial Jus, 1968), pp. ix f.
[b] ———, "Patterns of Spanish Emigration to the Indies Until 1600," *Hispanic American Historical Review* 56 (1976): 585.

reflect changes that can be attributed to the widening circle from which emigration was drawn. The changes as shown on Table 2, though relatively small, reflect emigration trends and serve to give context to Table 3. It should be remembered that these data are for those who were issued licenses to leave Spain. The proportion actually arriving in America would be essentially the same, although only about 80 percent of the individual emigrants in the Indies can be located in the Seville listings (see note 12, Chapter 1 above).

The regional distribution of the *encomenderos* of New Spain bears a resemblance to that of Table 2, but there are some differences. Table 3 presents the number of *encomenderos* from each region, showing the number of awards by category (first conqueror, conqueror, *poblador antiguo* and *poblador*) and listing percentages of the total that each group received. It is natural to assume, and rightly so, that Andalusia, the region with the ports of departure, would provide the largest share of emigrants and therefore the greatest number of *encomenderos*. Seville, Spain's largest city and most populous province, was claimed, along with the port city of Huelva, as the home of 18 percent of the *encomenderos*. The remaining Andalusian provinces accounted for another 6 percent of the *encomenderos*, giving the sons of this region title to over one-fourth of the *encomiendas* granted in New Spain. As can be seen, however, Andalusians did not do well compared to their numbers; they repre-

Table 3. Origins of the Encomenderos *of New Spain*

Region	Indians	First Conqueror	Conqueror	Poblador Antiguo	Poblador	Total
Andalusia		39 (28.9%)	42 (23.6%)	9 (28.1%)	38 (24.0%)	128 (25.3%)
Extremadura		24 (17.8%)	20 (11.2%)	8 (25.0%)	27 (17.1%)	79 (15.6%)
New Castile		6 (4.4%)	9 (5.1%)	4 (12.5%)	15 (9.5%)	34 (6.7%)
Old Castile		16 (11.9%)	30 (16.8%)	8 (25.0%)	16 (10.1%)	70 (13.8%)
León		13 (9.6%)	11 (6.2%)	— (—)	17 (10.8%)	41 (8.1%)
Biscay		6 (4.4%)	6 (3.4%)	— (—)	2 (1.3%)	14 (2.8%)
Other Spain		8 (5.9%)	14 (7.8%)	— (—)	12 (7.6%)	34 (6.7%)
Foreign countries		6 (4.4%)	9 (5.1%)	2 (6.3%)	2 (1.3%)	19 (3.8%)
Unknown origin	3	17 (12.6%)	37 (20.8%)	1 (3.1%)	29 (18.3%)	87 (17.2%)
Totals	3 (.6%)	135 (26.7%)	178 (35.2%)	32 (6.3%)	158 (31.2%)	506 (100%)

sented about 39 percent of the people in the Indies prior to 1520 and 32 percent thereafter (Table 2), but in New Spain they received less than 26 percent of the grants overall and contributed only slightly more than 24 percent of the *poblador encomenderos*. The seemingly below average rate of reward can be attributed at least in part to the Andalusian maritime and commerical population, not an insignificant number during the period. Sailors, considered base people and the dregs of society, were not generally in contention for *encomiendas*, and merchants normally did not perform the requisite combat duties to be eligible for consideration. Then too, since Andalusians were most highly represented in the very early years in the Indies, their seniority established them in the older colonies and many had neither the desire nor the need to go elsewhere. Their home region, already the most prosperous in Spain, was also first to benefit financially during the years immediately after contact. Andalusia was thus able to both retain talented men as well as to accommodate many of those who were successful in the Indies. As a final note, an analysis of surnames of those claiming Andalusian origin suggests that a number of their families had come recently from other Spanish regions. The south of Spain continued to be a crossroads for the mobile population of Iberia.

Extremadura and its emigrants remain a subject of interest if only because the conquest leadership of Mexico, Guatemala, and Peru came from the area. As conventionally defined, however, Extremadura is far too complex a region to serve as a basis for social analysis, and the present-day provincial units of Badajoz and Cáceres do not reflect sixteenth-century tensions, rivalries, and associations. Regional loyalties of the period centered on a city and perhaps its hinterland, an area usually much smaller than a modern Spanish province. This was especially true for relatively remote and insular Extremadura. As shown in Map 2, Extremadura is divided into two geographical regions defined by natural features. First, provincial Cáceres-Trujillo on the north occupied perhaps one hundred miles of Tagus River watershed west of the Montes de Toledo, and mountain ranges on both the south and the north provided natural boundaries that created a basin perhaps eighty miles across. Major communities in northern Extremadura included Cáceres, Trujillo, Alcántara, Coria, and Plasencia. Second, almost one hundred and fifty miles of Guadiana River drainage bounded by the Sierra Morena on the south and the Sierras San Pedro and Guadalupe on the north defined another natural basin, larger than that of Cáceres. In the sixteenth century it contained three subdivisions. Badajoz dominated the western reaches of this valley and provided a name for one of them. To the east were four closely associated communities in an area often referred to as La Serena. Mérida, a river crossing and road junction city, is the westernmost, some thirty miles from Cortés' Medellín. Just a few miles east of Medellín is Don Benito, and close by is Villanueva de la Serena. The third subdivision of southern Extremadura, the Maestrazgo de León, was on the northern side of the Sierra Morena and straddled the Seville-to-Salamanca road. These regions were not, however, absolutely separate entities. The citizens of each cooperated as well as competed with their neighbors in bordering regions. For example, those from Alcántara often were more closely associated with those from Badajoz than with citizens of Cáceres.[1]

THE *ENCOMENDEROS'* BACKGROUNDS

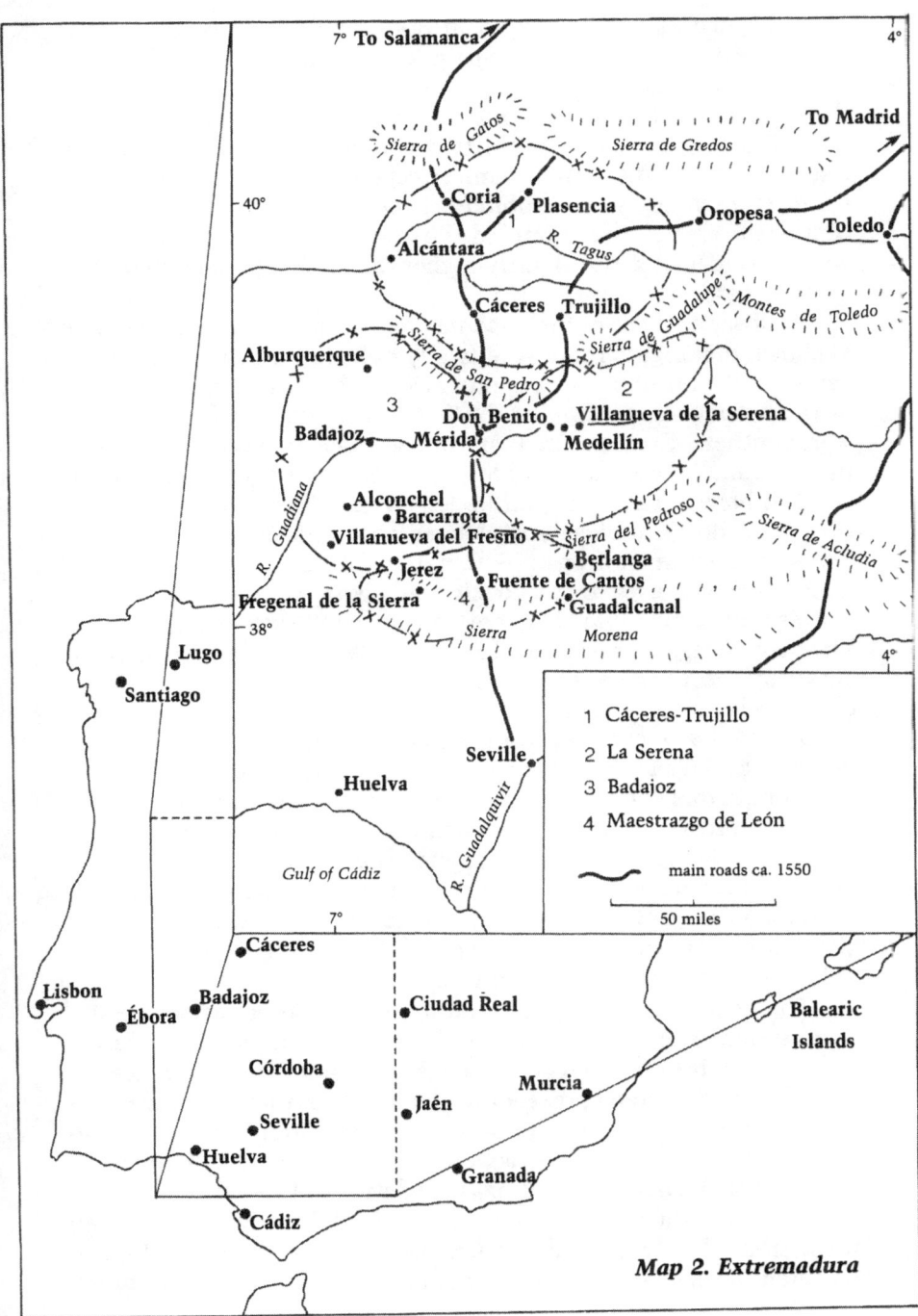

Map 2. Extremadura

Extremadura was the regional homeland of nearly 16 percent of the *encomenderos* of New Spain; data from Table 2 for both before and after 1520 suggest that those from the region received about the same percentage of *encomiendas* as their percentage of emigration. Table 3, however, shows that conquerors, with but slightly less than 10 percent of their number becoming *encomenderos*, were underrepresented, while *pobladores antiguos*, with over 28 percent were greatly overrewarded. First conquerors and *pobladores* were rewarded at a rate slightly higher than the regional emigration percentages.

A closer analysis of the *encomenderos* from Extremadura (Table 4) shows the origins more specifically. Cáceres, a major population center of the northern region, provided but three *encomenderos*, all of them conquerors. Two of the five *encomenderos* from Trujillo were brothers, Gonzalo and Juan Jiménez. Gonzalo was with Cortés in 1519, and Juan joined his brother the following year when he arrived in New Spain with Pánfilo de Narváez. The three *pobladores* from Trujillo were closely associated with Cortés. Maese Manuel Tomás arrived in New Spain with native Trujilloan Francisco de las Casas, one of Cortés' many cousins, and both were members of the Cortés household.[2] Juan de Hinojosa associated with another Cortés kinsman, Diego Becerra de Mendoza of Mérida. Neither of them survived the ill-fated 1533 Pacific coast expedition that Becerra commanded.

The majority of those from the Badajoz area became *encomenderos* by taking part in the capture of Mexico City, eleven of them as first conquerors and the other four arriving with reinforcing groups. Two of Cortés' relations, first conqueror Juan Jaramillo de Salvatierra of Villanueva de Barcarrota and *poblador antiguo* Alonso Valiente of Medina de las Torres, originated in this area. Pedro de Alvarado and his brothers Jorge and Gonzalo dominated the Badajoz city faction. The opportunist first conqueror Rodrigo Rangel was the only Cortés retainer or ally from this city.

The Order of Santiago's Maestrazgo de León, a sparsely populated mountainous region in southern Extremadura, was closely associated with commercial interests in Seville. Like the Cáceres-Trujillo and La Serena areas, only about half of the Maestrazgo natives took part in the capture of Mexico City. Both of the first conquerors originating in the area were from Fregenal de la Sierra. One of them was Francisco de Terrazas, a relation of Cortés.

It is when the La Serena area is discussed that loyalties between those from closely defined districts become most obvious. None of La Serena's six or seven main communities, save Mérida, had much

Table 4. Encomenderos *from Extremadura*

Area	First Conqueror	Conqueror	Poblador Antiguo	Poblador	Total
Cáceres-Trujillo					
Alcántara	1	—	2	—	3
Arroyomolinos	—	1	—	—	1
Cáceres	—	3	—	—	3
Coria	1	—	—	1	2
Coria de Galisteo	1	1	—	—	2
Guadalupe	—	—	—	1	1
Montánchez	—	—	—	1	1
Plasencia	1	—	—	—	1
Santa María de Trebejo	—	—	—	1	1
Trujillo	1	1	—	3	5
					20
Badajoz					
Alconchel	2	—	—	1	3
Badajoz	5	2	1	1	9
Jerez de Badajoz	—	—	—	2	2
Villanueva de Barcarrota	1	1	—	—	2
Villanueva del Fresno	—	1	—	—	1
Badajoz area	3	—	1	—	4
					21
La Serena					
Don Benito	—	—	—	1	1
Guareña	—	—	—	1	1
Medellín	4	1	1	4	10
Mérida	—	2	1	1	4
Puebla de Alcocer	—	—	—	1	1
Villanueva de la Serena	—	1	—	1	2
					19
Maestrazgo de León					
Berlanga	—	2	—	—	2
Burgillos del Cerro	—	—	—	1	1
Fregenal de la Sierra	2	—	—	—	2
Fuente de Cantos	—	—	—	1	1
Llerena	—	—	—	2	2
Ribera del Fresno	—	1	—	—	1
Segura de León	—	—	—	1	1
Villafranca de los Barros	—	1	—	—	1
					11
Extremadura					
Locale not stated	2	2	2	2	8
Totals	24	20	8	27	79

significance in the sixteenth century, and fewer than half of the *encomenderos* from the area took part in the conquest. But Medellín, on the Guadiana River, close to the geographic center of the area (as well as being the birthplace of Hernando Cortés), was also hometown to ten of the nineteen La Serena *encomenderos*. Half of the *encomenderos* from the area were in some way closely associated with Cortés. At least five were related to Cortés in one fashion or another, three more were members of his household, an additional two, first conquerors Gonzalo de Sandoval and Andrés de Tapia—both from Medellín—were staunch allies. It is this reality that elicited Bernal Díaz del Castillo's comment that Cortés limited his favors to those from Medellín.[3]

Extremaduran preeminence in first generation New Spain (and Peru for that matter) can be further rationalized with two complementary themes. Recruitment for America seemed to follow concentric waves emanating from Seville, and much of Extremadura was covered by the first wave. Secondly, Extremadura was relatively poor even in the best of times. Those seeking opportunities were quick to respond to what could be anticipated in America over what was known to accrue from military service in Spanish campaigns in Europe.

Encomenderos from both Castiles, excepting the *pobladores antiguos*, were underrepresented when their numbers are compared to overall emigration percentages. If political revenge is to be considered a factor in *encomienda* eligibility, those from Castile were likely targets, because Cuban governor Diego Velázquez de Cuellar, Cortés' one-time patron and later archenemy, was a native of Segovia in Old Castile. A number of his relatives, countrymen, and followers arrived in New Spain as members of the Narváez *entrada*. Although a few from the Castiles received exceptional grants, many were ignored by each of the officials empowered to assign *encomiendas*, in addition to Cortés himself, so that it appears that their lack of recognition was due to reasons other than the whims of the conquest commander.[4] Like their counterparts from Andalusia and Extremadura, *pobladores antiguos* from both Castiles were well rewarded, 50 percent better than emigration figures would suggest. Such a statement cannot stand without qualification, however. Most, if not all, *pobladores antiguos* came to New Spain by invitation and would not have made the move without assurance of bettering an economic status enjoyed in the islands of the Caribbean.

Encomenderos from León, the Basque country, the rest of Spain, and the foreigners fared better than the emigration totals would suggest, provided they arrived in the Indies prior to 1520. *Pobladores* (those who arrived after the capture of Mexico City) from León and the rest of Spain also received better than average recognition, while the Basques and foreigners appear to have been left out. The total of natives from these regions, however, did not amount to one-quarter of the *encomenderos.*

Eighty-four *encomenderos* left no record of European origin. Perhaps 10 percent can be identified tentatively as foreigners just by surname.[5] Others have surnames taken from Iberian toponyms, but considering the geographical mobility during the four decades prior to the capture of Mexico City, a number of them could be at least a generation removed from a family seat. One could perhaps divide those with unknown origins among the various categories in accordance with the proportions attributed to each of the regions for those of known origin and come close to an accurate numerical estimate, but this does not match specific individuals with particular regions. The unknown homelands will remain unknown until such time as new references are uncovered.

Comment is in order concerning the three Indians awarded *encomiendas.* Two of them were daughters of Moctezuma and were given grants in accordance with what Cortés determined to be their patrimony. Both doña Leonor and doña Isabel were kept well married (that is, to Spaniards), and each of their several husbands acquired separate grants. The women, however, maintained an independent *encomendera* status and were deferred to as surviving native royalty, meaning that they fit into the social scheme somewhere between the Spaniards and the rest of the surviving native nobility. The other native *encomendero,* using the Spanish name Juan Sánchez, was an Indian governor from Oaxaca. He was awarded an *estancia,* changed to *cabecera* status when assigned in 1536. Sánchez appears to have been strongly Hispanicized.

Just where the individual *encomendero* fit into Spanish society is often unclear. In two-thirds of the cases studied, there is scant record to establish what the *encomendero* did prior to coming to Mexico.[6] Table 5 shows the social/occupational status of each of the categories of those who received grants of Indians in New Spain. Most appear to have been versed in the commerce of the day as well as being able to hold their own in the use of weapons. A man of arms was more readily accepted as a potential *hidalgo* than was a man of affairs or a professional, although one could easily combine all of these qualities. Some were obviously *hidalgos,* while a number were from tax-paying families who nevertheless made oblique reference to noble relatives or ancestors. Professionals—notaries, medical practitioners, and accountants—and most artisans were identified

THE *ENCOMENDEROS* AS A GROUP

Table 5. **Callings of the Encomenderos**

Calling	Indians	First Conqueror	Conqueror	Poblador Antiguo	Poblador	Total	
Hidalgos		18	20	7	41	86	(17.00%)
Merchants		1	3	2	—	6	(1.19%)
Professionals[a]	—		15	4	14	33	(6.52%)
Artisans		8	6	2	4	20	(3.95%)
Tratantes[b]	—		2	—	—	2	(.39%)
Military[c]		7	1	—	—	8	(1.58%)
Mariners		4	3	—	1	8	(1.58%)
Miners		2	2	—	—	4	(.79%)
Interpreters		3	1	—	1	5	(1.00%)
Not stated	3	92	125	17	97	334	(66.00%)
Total	3	135	178	32	158	506	(100.00%)

[a] Includes the *mayordomo* of the *cabildo* and the bishops.
[b] An innkeeper and a muletrain owner.
[c] Those who had specific skills useful in combat: cannoneers, archers, crossbowmen, and musicians. All of these skills were primarily non-combat trades; i.e., the cannoneers were founders, and the musicians were teachers and entertainers, all being at the artisan level.

by functioning in accordance with their training (although there are exceptions). Members of the medical profession acquiring *encomiendas* were, for the most part, involved in activities other than medicine. Three of the five were primarily merchants, another a member of Cortés' staff, and the fifth, the *protomédico* (an official authorized to inspect and license other medical practitioners) served as a *regidor* in Puebla.[7] While there were a number of men of affairs—merchants, shippers, and managers—among the *encomenderos*, few declared themselves as such because to do so would permanently identify their social status, thereby precluding future upward mobility. Yet their associations and their transactions indelibly marked them as businessmen. One must, however, admit that the first generation of *encomenderos*, regardless of calling, had to be men of affairs to some extent in order to exploit the potential of their holdings, since in the early years relatively few managers were available for hire.

There were few *hidalgos* in the Indies prior to the subjugation of the Mexicans in 1521, and those with the title of *don* were even rarer. Each of the *encomenderos* had some claim to gentry or lower nobility by virtue of holding a grant of Indian tributaries, but at best only about one in five were acknowledged gentry or nobility when they left Spain. As discussed in Chapter 1, determining just who the *hidalgos* were is a subjective exercise that involves assessing the role the individual played in the society, the deference shown him by contemporaries, offices acquired, marriage partner, and perhaps most significant, *encomienda* retention and succession. An *hidalgo* who survived the siege and capture of Mexico City was *prima facie* eligible for an *encomienda*. Sixteen of the first conquerors were considered *hidalgos* upon arrival in Mexico, as were twenty of the conquerors and seven of the *pobladores antiguos*. Their total represents one-eighth of the *encomenderos* who arrived in the Indies before 1521. An indeterminable number of this group had been elevated to *hidalgo* rank while in the Indies, so the proportion of true gentry was even less. Their contributions in various Caribbean campaigns had been acknowledged through awards of Indians. Twenty-five percent of the *encomenderos* arriving after the capture of Mexico City came directly from Spain as *hidalgos*. Three of this group, don Luis de Castilla, don Luis de Guzmán Saavedra and don Tristán de Luna y Arellano, were the only first-generation *encomenderos* entitled "don" by birthright.

Although declared merchants were numerous in the Caribbean and later in New Spain, only six received *encomiendas*, and all of them arrived in the Caribbean before the capture of Mexico City. Closely associated with the merchants were the mariners—ship owners and pilots—who actively pursued merchandising in support of the conquest of New Spain. The combination of merchants and mariners constituted less than three percent of the *encomenderos*.

Notaries were by far the most numerous of the *encomenderos* with professional training. Their number, thirteen, outshadowed the five medical practitioners receiving awards. Two lawyers and the bishops of Mexico City and Antequera were the remaining professionals. The bishops were not *encomenderos* per se, but held the grants in the name of their respective cathedral chapters for the support of religious houses and charitable institutions.[8]

Tratantes, the marginal entrepreneurs on the fringes of commercial activity, were distinguished from merchants by the type of goods they sold and the scope of their operations. They served as petty dealers in the local retail markets and lacked connections with wholesale companies outside the area. Some augmented these retail activities by operating inns and taverns, and yet others provided transportation services. Not unexpectedly, both of the *tratantes* among the *encomenderos* received very small grants in remote areas of New Spain. Alonso Cano, who owned a muletrain, was an eleven-year veteran of the Indies before joining the Narváez *entrada*. He was assigned a village near his residence in Villa Alta. Innkeeper Gonzalo Rodríguez de la Magdalena was a *vecino* of Puebla, his small grant forty-five miles distant.

The importance of combat communicators, that is, the trumpeters and the drummers, can best be appreciated by considering the size of the *encomiendas* each received. Of the two trumpeters with the Cortés *entrada*, one received an *encomienda* of eighty-five *estancias* and *barrios*; the other, half the tribute from ten *estancias* and forty *barrios*. The trumpeter who joined from the Narváez *entrada* was assigned a *cabecera* with ten *estancias*. The drummer, a veteran of Italian campaigns, had 4,300 tributaries in six *estancias* at Axacuba, near Tula.[9] Because of the vital role they played on the combat field, musicians must be considered along with others who had more traditional military skills, such as artillerymen, archers, and crossbowmen. The two gunners received large *encomiendas*, one supporting twenty-five Spaniards in his Mexico City *casa poblada*. The archer and the crossbowman, having skills in less demand, were not so well rewarded, nor, in the case of the archer, so soon.[10]

While it is difficult to establish a definite niche in the social organization of New Spain for the interpreter, there is no questioning the value and importance of such a person, especially a trustworthy one with talent. An *hidalgo* served as interpreter for the Royal Audiencia, and the others so identified were included as members of various *entradas*. It seems that the office of interpreter, especially for the Audiencia and the *cabildo*, was honorific, with the actual linguistic work done by more plebeian types and Indians. Each interpreter apparently received his reward more in accordance with his social standing and political affiliation than with his contributions.[11] In addition to the declared official interpreters, a number of individual *encomenderos* either learned to function in the language of their Indians or hired Spanish administrators who could do so. The skill was necessary if the *encomienda* was to be profitable.

Mining was a venture in which most *encomenderos* invested, and mineral deposits near Indian communities held in *encomienda* were a definite asset. If the *encomienda* was not well located in this respect, one exploited the next best resource available, the labor of *encomienda* Indians and slaves—both black and Indian—in mining companies in distant locations. While the majority of *encomenderos* derived a part of their income from mining and formed companies with non-*encomendero* miners, few were themselves considered miners. Only four holders of grants were so identified at the time.[12]

Antigüedad, that is, seniority, was perhaps the most valuable asset an *encomendero* could claim, especially if he lacked some remote claim to nobility. The veteran campaigner of the Indies was looked to for leadership and advice, and given deference due to his experience, in much the same way twentieth-century members of military organizations follow the lead of those wearing campaign ribbons and hashmarks, despite contrary orders from commanders who lack "foxhole time." Experience was a sought-after quality during the organization and execution of *entradas*, both in the Caribbean and in New Spain after the capture of Mexico City. Bernal Díaz del Castillo frequently compares the first conquerors and those who came afterwards, referring to the latter in less than flattering terms.[13] One did not need much combat experience, however, to become a veteran. Survival without disgrace was often the sole qualification.

The *encomenderos* of New Spain registered seniority dating from as early as 1497, as shown in Table 6, with three arriving in 1500 or before.[14] The most senior first conquerors were in the group Ovando led in 1502 to Santo Domingo. One-fifth of those who became *encomenderos* were in the Indies by 1514, five years before the Cortés *entrada* formed and sailed. Most of them acquired *entrada* experience in Santo Domingo, Panama (1509), Puerto Rico (1510), Cuba (1511), and Puerto Rico again in 1512. A number of those arriving in the Indies in 1515 later gained their first experience with Francisco Hernández de Córdoba (1517) and with Juan de Grijalva the following year. By mid-1521 two-thirds were veterans and felt justified in demanding the rewards due experienced conquerors.

Well over half of our *encomenderos*, the first conquerors and conquerors, arrived in New Spain by 1520, with Cortés, Narváez and others. As seen earlier, *encomenderos* arriving after the capture of Mexico City are categorized as *pobladores antiguos*—those with experience in the Indies—and *pobladores*—those without it. Immigration peaks for these groups, reflected in Table 7, coincide with the 1522–1523 arrival of the royal treasury officers, the entourage that came with the 1523 return of Francisco de Montejo and Diego de Ordaz from Spain with glad tidings for Cortés and his conquest companions, and the 1528 and 1530 groups that accompanied the first and second Audiencias. It is interesting to note that only five persons who received *encomiendas* during the time period of this study can be identified with certainty as having arrived after 1531.[15] The importance of seniority is reinforced by these data. Clearly, the ear-

THE *ENCOMENDEROS* AS A GROUP

Table 6. Experience of the Encomenderos *in the Indies to 1521*

Year Arrived in the Indies	First Conqueror	Conqueror	*Poblador Antiguo*	Total
1497	—	1	—	1
1498	—	—	—	—
1499	—	—	1	1
1500	—	1	—	1
	0	2	1	3 (.88%)
1501	—	—	—	—
1502	4	4	—	8
1503	—	—	—	—
1504	3	—	—	3
1505	1	1	1	3
	8	5	1	14 (4.06%)
1506	—	1	—	1
1507	1	—	1	2
1508	—	4	5	9
1509	2	2	1	5
1510	4	6	2	12
	7	13	9	29 (8.40%)
1511	3	1	2	6
1512	5	3	4	12
1513	3	2	3	8
1514	13	10	6	29
1515	2	—	—	2
	26	16	15	57 (16.52%)
1516	5	5	—	10
1517	14	11	2	27
1518	56	6	—	62
1519	—	69	2	71
1520	—	3	1	4
1521	—	4	—	4
	75	98	5	178 (51.59%)
Unknown	19	44	1	64
	19	44	1	64 (18.55%)
Totals	135	178	32	345 (100.00%)

THE *ENCOMENDEROS'* BACKGROUNDS

Table 7. Time of Arrival of the Encomenderos in New Spain

Year Arrived in New Spain	Indians	First Conqueror	Conqueror	*Poblador Antiguo*	*Poblador*	Total
1519[a]		135	—	—	—	135
1520[b]		—	174	—	—	174
		135	174			309 (61.07%)
1521		—	4	7	5	16
1522[c]		—	—	3	17	20
1523		—	—	6	27	33
1524[d]		—	—	3	16	19
1525		—	—	4	8	12
1526		—	—	1	11	12
1527		—	—	3	12	15
1528[e]		—	—	1	17	18
1529		—	—	2	2	4
1530[f]		—	—	1	8	9
1531		—	—	—	2	2
		—	4	31	125	160 (31.62%)
1532		—	—	—	—	
1533		—	—	—	—	
1534		—	—	—	—	
1535[g]		—	—	—	2	2
1536		—	—	—	1	1
1537		—	—	—	1	1
1538		—	—	—	1	1
		—	—	—	5	5 (0.99%)
Unknown	3	—	—	1	28	32 (6.32%)
Totals	3	135	178	32	158	506 (100.00%)

[a] Cortés.
[b] Narváez and others.
[c] Arrival of royal treasury officers.
[d] Return of Montejo and Ordaz.
[e] First Audiencia.
[f] Second Audiencia.
[g] Viceroy Mendoza.

lier one arrived in a new region, the better one's chances were for receiving an award. Two-thirds of the *encomiendas* went to those who took an active part in the capture of Mexico City, and half of these conquerors were veterans of one or more of the Caribbean campaigns.

Yet despite this emphasis of early arrivals, the *encomenderos* constituted a broad selection from Spanish society. It may appear that the middle to upper echelons of the social order were overrepresented, but some *encomenderos* are known to have been of humble status, and this number would doubtless rise appreciably if the sources were better. Each of the Spanish regions and several European countries outside Spain contributed individuals to the *encomendero's* ranks. All callings, professions, and occupations necessary to operate a society in the Spanish style were to be found among the group. One can, then, safely state that the *encomenderos* of New Spain mirrored the society that produced them.

CHAPTER THREE

Cities and *Encomiendas*

The order in which its conquerors and settlers established New Spain was ultimately a reflection of Spanish urban-centered modes of organization. In the Spanish scheme each city dominated a surrounding hinterland, which had no other political body to rule, represent, and adjudicate for it than the city's *cabildo*. The wealthy and high-ranking were based in the city, even though their estates and economic base might be predominantly rural. Social, economic, ecclesiastical, and indeed all hierarchies stretched from the highest-ranking members in the city down to the lowest ranking out in the country.

In the Indies these city-centered districts were reproduced in such a way that urban dominance was even greater than in Spain. The *encomienda* took the place of the various kinds of estates existing in the Spanish homeland. The local indigenous states or provincial units went in *encomienda* to a certain number of Spaniards who became principal founders and citizens of a Spanish city established in the middle of the region. The whole initial purpose of the city was to serve as a headquarters for the *encomenderos*, who both kept the Indian hinterland peaceful and received its tributes. In South America, indeed, the very word *vecino* was for many years after the conquest synonymous with *encomendero*. The *encomendero* had the legal obligation of setting up residence in the city within whose jurisdiction his *encomienda* fell. There he would affect as luxurious a life style as his financial condition would allow, supporting a number of relatives, retainers, and other Spaniards in his *casa poblada*.

In areas of the Indies with sedentary Indians, then, the normal picture was that of widely spaced Spanish cities, quite autonomous, dominated by the *encomenderos* of the district, containing the vast majority of all Spaniards, and connected to the subordinated Indian hinterland of the city's district through the *encomiendas* into which the district was divided.[1]

Such a setup did come into existence in New Spain as one would expect, but it was much affected by the country-wide dominance of Mexico City as the initial focus of all Spanish activity. Mexico City was the preferred place of residence and the seat of the highest governmental authorities as well as the center of New Spain's ecclesiastical and commercial worlds and the hub of the country's communications. It retained this status long after the other cities had grown in size and economic importance and could, in some cases, be considered quite well-developed regional centers in their own right. As late as 1538, when other Spanish population centers (Puebla, Antequera, and Colima, for examples) were thriving, the Mexico City *cabildo* retained jurisdiction as the capital or *cabecera* of New Spain and exercised authority over districts not specifically assigned to other Spanish municipalities.[2]

The result was that, for many purposes, the Spaniards acted as though New Spain were not a set of independent city jurisdictions but a single district, the hinterland of Mexico City. Above all, although both law and custom dictated that an *encomendero* be a *vecino* of the city in whose jurisdiction his *encomienda* belonged, in New Spain many *encomenderos* managed to be citizens of Mexico City regardless of the fact that their grants were located in other jurisdictions.[3] (In a certain number of cases, *encomenderos* residing outside the jurisdiction of their grant were *vecinos* of cities other than Mexico City. A few also varied from the normal pattern by avoiding Spanish cities altogether and making their residences wherever their estates could best be managed, even if it meant living within the area of the grant itself.[4])

In addition to other reasons for urban foundations, a city with its *cabildo* was a legal entity required by the conquerors in order to be able to conduct any business with the crown. Municipalities founded prior to the capture of Mexico City (Veracruz and Segura de la Frontera at Tepeaca) served as necessary but transient means to such ends. The successful siege of Tenochtitlan established Mexico City as the capital of New Spain, and this development reoriented the two extant municipalities, drastically reducing their status. Other major Spanish urban centers came into being as New Spain's regions of economic promise were uncovered. Located among dense native populations, they attracted sizable numbers of *encomendero vecinos*, but none of them ever posed a serious threat to the dominance of Mexico City. Other settlements, established as strategic outposts in less economically viable locations, attracted few *vecinos* and fewer still who were *encomenderos*. Often the only resident citizens were those who were under direct orders to maintain the outpost.

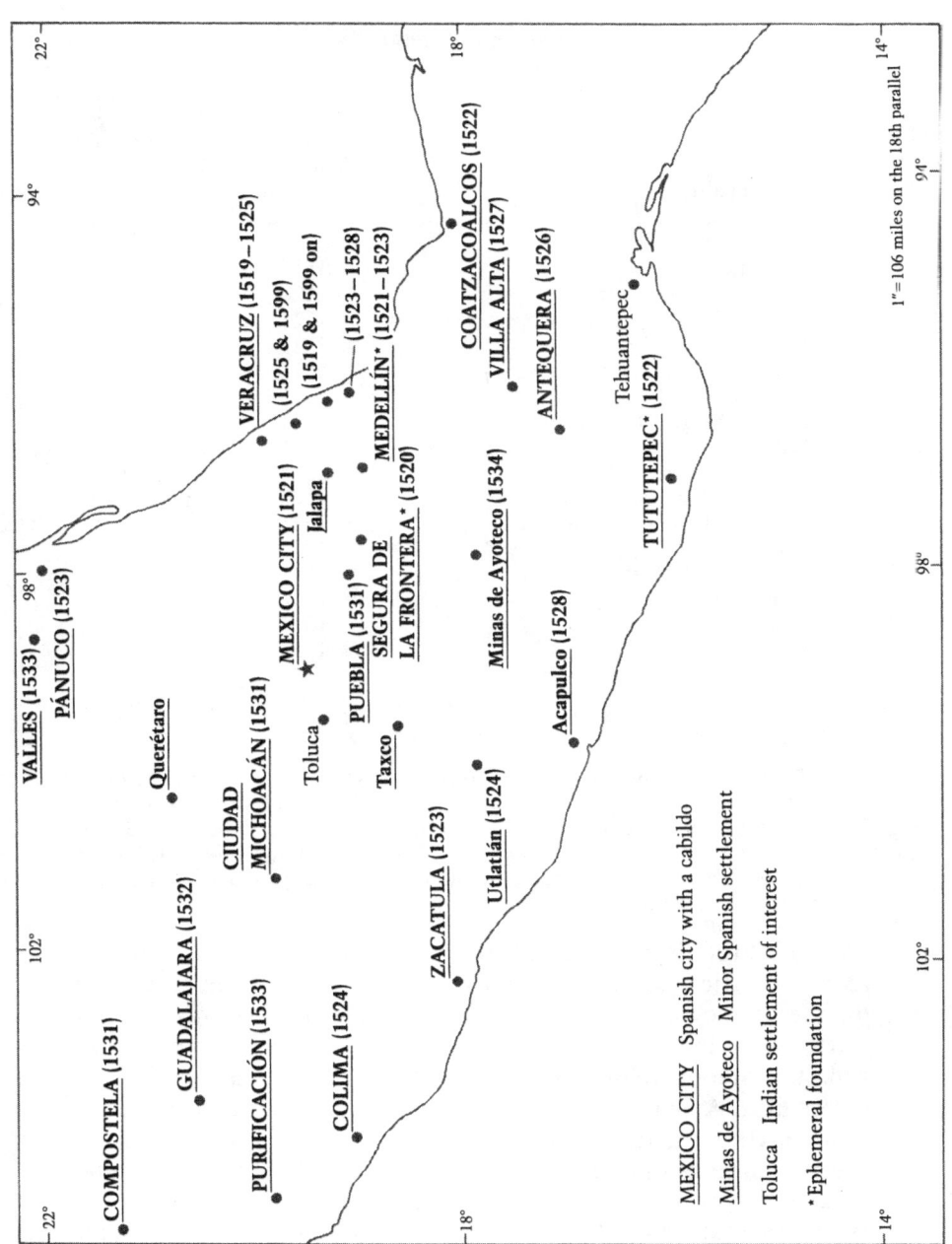

Map 3. Settlements in New Spain

THE ENCOMENDEROS AS A GROUP

Table 8. Chronology of Spanish Settlement

Municipality	When Founded	Known Encomendero Vecinos to 1550
Veracruz	1519	11*
Segura de la Frontera	1520	—
Mexico City (founded at Coyoacán)	1521	248
Medellín	1521	1
Coatzacoalcos (Espiritu-Santo)	1522	10
Zacatula (La Concepción)	1523	17
Pánuco (Santisteban del Puerto)	1523	38
Colima	1524	40
Antequera (Oaxaca)	1526	32
Villa Alta (San Ildefonso)	1527	18
Villarreal (Chiapas)	1528	1
Puebla	1531	37
Ciudad Michoacán	1531	9
Guadalajara	1532	7
Purificación	1533	1
Valles	1533	4
Total		474

*Three of the fourteen one-time *vecinos* moved to other cities. While not municipalities, Utlatlan (1524), Acapulco (1528), Jalapa (ca. 1530), and Guaxuapa (1534) each had one *encomendero vecino*, while Minas de Ayoteco (1534) had two. Three *encomenderos* were *vecinos* of Guatemala and one of Honduras. Twenty-two left no record of place of citizenship. There are 506 known *encomenderos* in all for the period.

The chronology of municipal founding shown in Table 8 permits an appreciation of the speed with which a small number of *encomenderos* moved to dominate the vast area of New Spain. These settlements and the time of founding are also presented on Map 3, and the roster of *encomendero vecinos* of each city and settlement is provided in Appendix F. Segura de la Frontera did not survive as a municipality, and the founding *vecinos* of Veracruz for the most part became citizens elsewhere as the promise of Mexico was revealed. Mexico City was an early and lasting magnet. Only those new municipalities that had extensive exploitable sedentary native populations attracted a significant number of *encomendero vecinos*. A detailed discussion of each of these settlements will put the residence pattern of the *encomenderos* of New Spain into perspective.

Veracruz, the first of New Spain's early municipalities, was founded as Villa Rica de la Veracruz in April 1519 at Ulúa, a sandspit across the bay from the present city. The establishment of the municipality was the first step toward legitimizing Hernando Cortés as an authority independent of Diego Velázquez de Cuéllar, the governor of Cuba. After a month the *villa* was relocated thirty-five miles to the north along the coast to serve as a rear-guard garrison during the conquest activities inland. It was here that Cortés posted the sick, wounded, and otherwise noneffective members of the *entrada* under the protection of a rear-guard initially commanded by Pedro de Ircio, a native of Logroño. The officers of the municipal government, however, moved inland along with Cortés. For a time Veracruz was a mobile municipality, smiliar in many respects to a military staff headquarters. By mid-1525, with a reconstituted municipal government, the site of the town was moved again. Its location this time was a place now called La Antigua, halfway between the original and second locations. It was not until the end of the sixteenth century that Veracruz was moved to its fourth site, the present one. In all its locations Veracruz maintained strategic significance as the official port of entry for New Spain, but its climate and distance from the center of all activity in Mexico City made a less than desirable place of habitation for European settlers.[5]

Fourteen *encomenderos* were *vecinos* of Veracruz during the time frame of this study, three of whom later became citizens of either Mexico City or Puebla. Few if any of the *encomenderos* were full-time residents, however. Of the remaining *encomendero vecinos*, conqueror Miguel de Zaragoza and Francisco de Rosales, natives of Zaragoza and Burgos respectively, were declared merchants. *Hidalgo vecinos* were Diego Marmolejo and Alvaro Saavedra Cerón. The latter, a relative of Cortés, died at sea ca. 1527 on a return trip from the Molucca Islands. Pedro de Sepúlveda, a blacksmith and town founder, had moved to Mexico City by the late 1520s. *Poblador antiguo* Alonso Valiente, a relative and employee of Cortés, was also an early *vecino* here while simultaneously holding citizenship in nearby Medellín as well as Mexico City. He ultimately held dual citizenship in Mexico City and Puebla. Although not declared a merchant, Valiente was heavily involved in commerce, both for himself and for Cortés. (Table 9 shows the origins of the *encomenderos* of all New Spain in relation to the places where they were *vecinos*. Also see Appendix F, citizenship.)

Segura de la Frontera, like Veracruz, was founded to provide a legal channel for specific events. Established as Villa Segura de la Frontera at Tepeaca (twenty miles east of where Puebla was to be) in

Table 9. Residence and Origins of Encomenderos*

Vecino of	Andalusia				Extremadura				New Castile			
	FC	C	PA	P	FC	C	PA	P	FC	C	PA	P
Acapulco	—	—	—	—	—	—	—	—	—	—	—	—
Antequera	3	1	—	2	1	3	—	—	1	—	—	1
Ayoteco (Chiautla)	—	—	—	1	—	—	—	—	—	—	—	1
Cd. Michoacán	1	—	—	1	—	2	—	3	—	—	—	—
Coatzacoalcos	—	—	—	—	1	—	—	—	—	—	—	1
Colima	4	4	1	1	2	1	2	—	—	—	—	2
Guadalajara	—	1	—	2	—	—	—	2	—	—	—	2
Guaxuapa	—	—	—	—	—	—	—	—	—	—	—	—
Jalapa	—	—	—	—	—	—	—	—	—	—	—	—
Medellín	—	—	—	—	—	—	—	—	—	—	—	—
Mexico City	21	22	5	22	13	11	3	7	4	4	2	7
Pánuco	1	2	3	1	—	1	—	5	—	1	—	—
Puebla	4	8	—	1	2	2	2	1	—	3	—	—
Purificación	—	—	—	1	—	—	—	—	—	—	—	—
Utlatlan	—	—	—	—	—	—	—	—	—	1	—	—
Valles	1	—	—	1	—	—	—	1	—	—	—	—
Veracruz	1	1	—	2	—	—	—	1	—	—	—	—
Villa Alta	1	1	—	2	1	—	—	3	—	—	—	1
Villarreal (Chiapas)	—	—	—	—	—	—	—	—	—	—	1	—
Zacatula	2	1	—	2	1	—	—	1	1	—	1	—
Guatemala	—	—	—	—	1	—	—	—	—	—	—	—
Honduras	—	—	—	—	—	—	—	1	—	—	—	—
Not stated	—	1	—	—	2	—	1	2	—	1	—	—
Subtotals	39	42	9	39	24	20	8	27	6	10	4	15
Totals		129				79				35		

July 1520, this settlement provided the municipal services necessary for the administration of the *entrada* after the Spaniards were expelled from the Mexican capital and during preparations for the siege. The *villa* was moved two years later, with newly designated *vecinos*, to Tututepec near the Pacific Ocean, ninety miles southwest of Antequera. Later the same year the *vecinos* abandoned the site and moved again, this time to Huaxyacac near Antequera, where the *villa* charter was extinguished.[6] It was not possible to establish a roster of the *encomendero vecinos* of this municipality.

Tenochtitlan, after being reduced to rubble and resurrected as the Spanish Mexico City, became a typical capital. The third municipality founded in New Spain, its location was as much symbolic as

CITIES AND *ENCOMIENDAS* 41

Table 9. (continued)

	Old Castile				León				Biscay				Other Spain			
FC	C	PA	P	FC	C	PA	P	FC	C	PA	P	FC	C	PA	P
1	3	—	1	1	2	—	1	—	—	—	—	1	2	—	1
—	—	—	—	—	—	—	1	—	—	—	—	1	—	—	—
—	1	—	—	—	—	—	1	—	—	—	—	—	—	—	1
2	2	1	—	—	—	—	1	1	—	—	—	—	2	—	—
—	1	—	—	—	—	—	—	—	—	—	—	—	—	—	—
—	1	—	—	—	—	—	—	—	—	—	—	—	—	—	—
6	19	5	11	7	6	—	10	5	4	—	2	6	6	—	5
1	1	—	3	—	1	—	1	—	1	—	—	—	—	—	—
1	1	1	—	2	—	—	—	—	1	—	—	—	1	—	1
—	—	—	—	—	—	—	—	—	—	—	—	—	—	—	—
—	—	—	—	—	—	—	—	—	—	—	—	—	—	—	—
1	1	—	—	1	—	—	—	—	—	—	—	—	1	—	—
—	—	1	—	—	—	—	2	—	—	—	—	—	—	—	3
—	—	—	—	—	—	—	—	—	—	—	—	—	—	—	—
—	1	—	—	1	—	—	—	—	1	—	—	—	1	—	—
2	—	—	—	—	—	—	—	—	—	—	—	—	—	—	—
—	—	—	—	—	—	—	—	—	—	—	—	—	—	—	—
1	—	1	—	1	1	—	—	—	—	—	—	1	1	—	—
15	31	9	15	13	10	—	17	6	7	—	2	9	14	—	11
	70				40				15				34		

pragmatic. By building a Spanish city on the ruins of the capital used by the Triple Alliance, the conquerors created a monument to their mastery over the former lords of Mexico in terms understood by the natives and eased the way for the continuation of many preconquest mechanisms. It is not surprising that nearly half (48 percent) of the *encomenderos* became *vecinos* of Mexico City, since as a group they replaced the native imperial elite. Just as Tenochtitlan had been the political, social, and economic center of preconquest Mexico, the Spaniards quickly gave Mexico City the same role in postconquest New Spain.

A concentration of nearly one-half the *encomendero* population of New Spain invites analysis, and analysis suggests that the Mex-

42   THE *ENCOMENDEROS* AS A GROUP

Table 9. (continued)

Foreign Countries				Unknown Origin				Totals				Total Encomendero Vecinos
FC	C	PA	P	FC	C	PA	P	FC	C	PA	P	
—	—	—	—	—	1	—	—	—	1	—	—	1 (0.2%)
2	—	—	—	1	4	—	—	11	15	—	6	32 (6.3%)
—	—	—	—	—	—	—	—	—	—	—	2	2 (0.4%)
—	—	—	—	—	—	—	—	2	2	—	5	9 (1.7%)
—	—	—	—	1	1	—	3	2	2	—	6	10 (2.0%)
—	3	—	—	—	5	—	6	9	17	4	10	40 (7.9%)
—	—	—	—	—	—	—	—	—	1	—	6	7 (1.3%)
—	—	—	—	—	—	—	—	—	1	—	—	1 (0.2%)
—	—	—	—	—	—	—	—	—	1	—	—	1 (0.2%)
—	—	—	—	—	1	—	—	—	1	—	—	1 (0.2%)
3	3	—	—	10	12	—	5	75	86	15	69	246 (48.6%)
—	—	1	1	—	4	—	10	2	11	4	21	38 (7.5%)
1	1	—	—	1	3	—	—	11	20	3	3	37 (7.3%)
—	—	—	—	—	—	—	—	—	—	—	1	1 (0.2%)
—	—	—	—	—	—	—	—	—	1	—	—	1 (0.2%)
—	—	1	—	—	—	—	—	1	—	1	2	4 (0.8%)
—	—	—	—	1	1	—	—	4	4	—	3	11 (2.2%)
—	—	—	1	—	1	—	1	2	2	1	13	18 (3.6%)
—	—	—	—	—	—	—	—	—	—	1	—	1 (0.2%)
—	1	—	—	2	1	—	—	7	6	1	3	17 (3.4%)
—	—	—	—	—	—	—	—	3	—	—	—	3 (0.6%)
—	—	—	—	—	—	—	—	—	—	1	—	1 (0.2%)
—	—	—	—	1	2	—	5	6	6	2	7	21 (4.2%)
6	8	2	2	17	36	—	30	135	178	32	158	503 (99.4%)
	18				83				503			Indians 3 (0.6%)
												506 (100%)

Note: Two of the Indian *encomenderos* were *vecinos* of Mexico City. The citizenship of the other is not known.

*FC = first conqueror; C = conqueror; PA = *poblador antiguo*; P = *poblador*

ico City contingent very closely reflected *encomendero* emigration trends, but not necessarily the general emigration pattern (see Table 10). Mexico City *vecino* representation by region of origin falls within three percentage points, plus or minus, of that for all the *encomenderos* of New Spain. The only variation greater than 3 percent is for *encomenderos* whose region of origin cannot be identified with certainty. The lower percentage of unknown origins for Mexico

City than for the overall *encomendero* population of New Spain is doubtless a result of the concentration of record-generating agencies in the capital. Few *encomendero vecinos* could leave their birthplace unrecorded for long in Mexico City (although twenty-seven were successful in doing so).

As the social, economic, administrative, and political hub of New Spain, Mexico City did not fail to attract most of the *hidalgos* in the kingdom, regardless of place of origin, as shown in Table 11. Seventy-one percent of the *hidalgo encomenderos* were *vecinos* of Mexico City. The most numerous contingent originated in Andalusia; of their New Spain total of twenty-five, over 80 percent (twenty-one) were *vecinos* of Mexico City. Slightly more than one out of five (20.5 percent) of all the *encomenderos* from Andalusia were *hidalgos*. *Hidalgos* from Extremadura, on the other hand, seemed to shun Mexico City. Only seven of the sixteen *hidalgos*, representing slightly less than 44 percent, were *vecinos* of the capital. *Hidalgos* from other Spanish regions, although some of the contingents were small, had from 66 to 81 percent of their number near the seat of power. Nearly half (48.2 percent) of the *hidalgo encomenderos* arrived after the capture of Mexico City. While many of them took part in subsequent campaigns, others did not participate directly in the conquest.

Medellín, founded in 1521 near present-day Córdoba shortly after the capture of Mexico City, came into being as a strategic security site. Originally established to protect the road between Veracruz and Mexico City, it was moved to the Caribbean coast south of present-day Veracruz two years later when the native threat had ceased to exist. In the new site Medellín partially replaced the port of Veracruz until that *villa* was moved to a location more accessible to the sea. By 1528 the *cabildo* of Medellín had been dissolved, and the town had but a few full-time European residents. The population would swell, however, when ships arrived. There appear to have been two full-time *encomendero* residents of Medellín. Conqueror Bartolomé Román was a *vecino*, while the other resident *encomendero*, until his death in 1527, was a Mexico City *vecino*, first conqueror Alvaro Maldonado.[7]

Densely populated Coatzacoalcos, 345 miles east-southeast of Mexico City, was an area of interest to Cortés from an early time. Its occupation began as soon as the Narváez threat to the *entrada* was averted. In 1520 Juan Velázquez de León and Rodrigo Rangel, in charge of a force of 120, were detached to settle the area, but were recalled as the situation in Mexico City deteriorated. Coatzacoalcos, about twenty-five miles from the birthplace of Cortés' interpreter

Table 10. Origins of Encomendero Vecinos of Mexico City

Region	Encomendero Vecinos of Mexico City	Encomendero Vecinos of New Spain	General Emigration*
Andalusia	70 (28.2%)	129 (25.3%)	34.6%
Extremadura	34 (13.7%)	79 (15.6%)	15.8%
New Castile	17 (6.9%)	35 (6.7%)	11.7%
Old Castile	41 (16.4%)	70 (13.8%)	17.3%
León	23 (9.3%)	40 (8.1%)	7.3%
Biscay	11 (4.4%)	15 (2.8%)	4.5%
Other Spain	17 (6.9%)	34 (6.7%)	5.1%
Foreign countries	6 (2.4%)	18 (3.8%)	3.7%
Mexico (Indians)	2 (.8%)	3 (.6%)	—
Unknown	27 (10.9%)	83 (16.6%)	—
Totals	248 (100%)	506 (100%)	100.0%

*From Table 2.

doña Marina, was thought to be rich in gold deposits. After the Mexican capital fell, the region became the destination of Gonzalo de Sandoval, who established Espíritu Santo there in May 1522, and assigned *encomiendas* throughout Tabasco to his followers. The assignments were later confirmed by Cortés. Bernal Díaz del Castillo, a founding *vecino* of Espíritu Santo, for a time held some 16,000 tributaries in *encomienda* in the area. He later became a *vecino* and *regidor* of Santiago de Guatemala, retaining title to one grant near Espíritu Santo. Seven *encomenderos* were *vecinos* of the region, living either in Espíritu Santo on the Coatzacoalcos River or at Santa María de la Victoria 124 miles east-northeast on the Caribbean coast. Santa María was established in 1519 but occupied only sporadically. By 1531 the Coatzacoalcos jurisdiction was drastically reduced, its population and territory reassigned to Veracruz, the Marquesado del Valle, Chiapas, and Tabasco.[8]

Motivation for Zacatula's founding in 1523 on the south coast of Mexico was slightly different than for settling Coatzacoalcos. In addition to finding an extensive native population centered 240 miles west-southwest of Mexico City and placer gold in the Balsas River drainage, Cortés felt the site appropriate for shipbuilding, an activity that had commenced the previous May. In 1524, a number of the region's early residents were drafted to help in the settlement of Colima, where some of Zacatula's founding *vecinos* received *encomiendas*. The roster of *vecinos* who remained in Zacatula has not survived. Many of the Zacatula grants were reassigned by the acting governors, and in 1526 the whole region was reappropriated by Cortés for himself. Both the first and second Audiencias made reassignments during their respective tenures. Gold production declined, as did native population, leaving eighteen *encomendero vecinos* in Zacatula by the 1540s.⁹ Seven each of the first conquerors and conquerors held grants nearby, as did one *poblador antiguo* and three *pobladores*.

While Gonzalo de Sandoval was bringing Coatzacoalcos under control and Rodrigo Alvarez Chico was occupied on the Pacific Coast in the Zacatula region, Cortés moved to consolidate his questionable claim over Pánuco, 210 miles northeast of Mexico City. The region had been visited in 1519 by Alonso Alvarez de Pineda, in the employ of Jamaica's governor Francisco de Garay. Alvarez returned to colonize the area the following year but was driven off by Huastecan natives. Expedition survivors were incorporated into the reorganized Cortés *entrada* and took part in the siege and capture of Mexico City.¹⁰ Cortés effected an overland conquest in early 1523 and established Santisteban del Puerto on Río Pánuco with the customary *alcaldes, regidores,* and other officers. One hundred footmen and thirty horsemen of this force were assigned *encomiendas*.¹¹ A number of these grants were reassigned by the acting governors be-

Table 11. Hidalgo Encomenderos

Origin	Hidalgo Vecinos of Mexico City	Hidalgo Vecinos Elsewhere	Total Hidalgos	Total Encomenderos
Andalusia	21 (80.7%)	5 (19.3%)	26 (29.5%)	128 (25.3%)
Extremadura	7 (43.7%)	9 (56.3%)	16 (18.3%)	79 (15.6%)
New Castile	7 (77.7%)	2 (22.3%)	9 (10.2%)	34 (6.7%)
Old Castile	13 (81.2%)	3 (18.8%)	16 (18.3%)	70 (13.9%)
León	5 (71.9%)	2 (28.6%)	7 (7.9%)	41 (8.1%)
Biscay	4 (80.0%)	1 (20.0%)	5 (5.6%)	14 (2.8%)
Other Spain	2 (66.6%)	1 (33.4%)	3 (3.4%)	34 (6.7%)
Foreign countries	2 (66.6%)	1 (33.4%)	3 (3.4%)	19 (3.8%)
Mexico (Indians)	2 (66.6%)	1 (33.4%)	3 (3.4%)	3 (.6%)
Unknown	—	—	—	84 (16.5%)
Totals	63 (71.6%)	25 (28.4%)	88 (100.0%)	506 (100.0%)

tween 1524 and 1526 and again after 1527, when Nuño Beltrán de Guzmán governed the region as a separate province. The Guzmán grants were revoked and a redistribution was made by the second Audiencia when Pánuco was reunited with New Spain. Thirty-eight *encomenderos* were *vecinos* of Pánuco, of whom more than half (58 percent) were *pobladores*.[12]

While the Pánuco issue was being resolved, Gonzalo de Sandoval departed Coatzacoalcos with some 100 followers, twenty-five of them mounted. After a 700-mile march they helped subdue an uprising in Zacatula and then occupied Colima, establishing a *villa* there in mid-1524. Sandoval had acquired a force equal to his own from Zacatula, 140 miles to the east-southeast, to campaign in Colima. The customary officials were designated and *encomiendas* were assigned to 25 horsemen and 120 footmen.[13] Of this number, only 34 can be identified with certainty. The remaining seven known *encomendero vecinos* of Colima acquired the status by marrying widows or daughters of the original grantees.

The settling of Antequera (Oaxaca) was a stormy affair carried out over a five-year period. The Valley of Oaxaca, first visited in 1520, was subdued a year later by Francisco de Orozco. Cortés then laid claim to the entire region for himself. In 1522 the *vecinos* of Segura de la Frontera, New Spain's second municipality, were moved from the original site near Tepeaca to Tututepec (97 miles southwest of Antequera). Tututepec, proving to be less than rewarding, was abandoned shortly thereafter. Its residents and *vecinos* resettled at Huaxyacac, the site of present-day Ciudad Oaxaca, but were expelled by Cortés' agents shortly after their arrival. In 1525 the acting governors once again resettled the site, in the center of Cortés country, then requested and received a royal charter for a settlement to be called Antequera. Upon his return from Honduras, Cortés again had the settlers expelled. In 1529, the first Audiencia established the settlement yet again, satisfying the conditions of the royal charter.[14]

Antequera and the Indian town of Oaxaca were contiguous settlements, the latter serving as the center of the Marquesado administration. Antequera, the Spanish town, was the home of some of the *encomenderos* and a center of royal government. Apparently in the attempt to insure a measure of royal influence within the Marquesado del Valle, Antequera was redesignated a *ciudad* in 1532 and five years later became the seat of a bishopric. This community also had strategic significance as a Spanish town astride the main route from Mexico City to Tehauntepec, Chiapas, and Guatemala. Other way stations on this road were Puebla, Tehuacan, and Huajuapan, each sixty to seventy-five miles apart.

Thirty-two *encomenderos* were *vecinos* of the main Oaxaca settlement, which will henceforth be referred to here as Antequera. Those associated with Cortés in one capacity or another preferred to be identified as *vecinos* of Oaxaca, the others as *vecinos* of Antequera. A plurality of the *encomenderos* of Antequera, fifteen, were conquerors, followed by eleven first conquerors and six *pobladores*. There were no *poblador antiguo encomendero vecinos* here. Furthermore, only four of the *vecinos* were from Extremadura, two of them natives of Mérida. One of the remaining Extremadurans was a native of Cáceres, the other from the Maestrazgo de León. The four *hidalgos*, one a first conqueror and the others conquerors, were each from different Iberian regions. Only *hidalgo* conqueror Gonzalo de Robles, a native of Mérida, was from Extremadura. The others, first conqueror Juan Núñez Sedeño and conquerors Jerónimo de Salinas and Melchor de San Miguel, were natives of Madrid, Zaragoza, and Valladolid, respectively.

Villa Alta, also called San Ildefonso de los Zapotecas, was founded in 1527 after a successful pacification drive under Gaspar Pacheco and Diego de Figueroa, two previous campaigns against the mountain Zapotecs having been less than successful. Four more efforts (1533, 1550, 1552, and 1570) were necessary to bring a definitive end to Indian resistance in the province. Eighteen of the twenty to thirty *vecinos* of Villa Alta were *encomenderos*, and nearly three out of four were *pobladores*. Only two each of the first conquerors and conquerors settled here, along with one *poblador antiguo*. Not one *hidalgo* was a *vecino* of Villa Alta. Eight of the *encomenderos* claimed Andalusia and Extremadura as their homeland, with four originating in each region. Luis de Berrio, who arrived in New Spain in 1526 as a perpetual *regidor* of Mexico City and then sold the post, was the first *alcalde mayor*, appointed ca. 1529 by the first Audiencia. During his tenure in office he remained a *vecino* of Mexico City and *encomendero* of a grant in Michoacán.[15]

Puebla, when founded in 1531, was not to be an *encomendero* center, supposedly, but became a quite normal city anyway. The few *hidalgos* and many Basques and foreigners point to Puebla's plebeian origins, but not markedly so. Whatever the stated reasons for the founding, the city above all satisfied the economic and social needs of New Spain.[16] Puebla was a welcome stopping place on the route between Veracruz and Mexico City, and also points south. In addition, the surrounding terrain was ideally suited for the production of European agricultural goods, and there was a large but relatively unexploited and unassigned labor force nearby at Tlaxcala. *Encomenderos* who were *vecinos* of Mexico City or other places and had grants near Puebla quickly capitalized on the opportunity to live in a Spanish city nearer their Indians and to exploit the agricultural potential of the area.

The municipality, founded as Puebla de los Angeles in 1531 by perhaps as many as sixty householders, had thirty established *vecinos*, six or seven of them *encomenderos*, by August of the year of foundation. Within a few months of founding, a serious flood forced the abandonment of the original site. A new location was designated and occupied in November 1532 by twelve of the original *vecinos*, plus twenty-one new settlers. By 1534 eighteen of the eighty-one *vecinos* were *encomenderos*. Toward mid-century, thirty-seven *encomenderos*, or nearly 8 percent of all those with grants in New Spain, had become *vecinos* of Puebla. Eleven of them were first conquerors, twenty conquerors, and three each were *pobladores antiguos* and *pobladores*. Four of them—conquerors García de Aguilar, Diego de Holguín, Pedro de Meneses, and *poblador antiguo* Francisco de Montalvo—had convincing credentials as *hidalgos*.

A disproportionate number of the *encomendero vecinos* of Puebla were from Andalusian provinces (36 percent as compared to 25.4 percent for Andalusian *encomenderos* in general; see Table 3). The 18 percent with Extremaduran origins, almost equally divided between Badajoz and Cáceres, were slightly above the general *encomendero* emigration from that region. New Castile was also slightly overrepresented (7.6 percent to 6.5 percent), as were the Basques (5.1 percent to 2.8 percent), and the foreigners (5.1 percent to 1.3 percent). Old Castile (7.6 percent to 13.9 percent), León (5.1 percent to 7.9 percent), and other Spanish regions (5.1 percent to 5.4 percent) were underrepresented. Only slightly more than 10 percent of Puebla's *encomendero vecinos* left no record of their European origins, as compared with 17 percent for the general *encomendero* immigration.

The remaining ten communities had but twenty-seven *vecinos* who were *encomenderos* of New Spain, distributed unequally among them. Four settlements, Ciudad Michoacán, Guadalajara, Purificación in New Galicia, and Villarreal, Chiapas (in the jurisdiction of Guatemala), were fully chartered municipalities, and the remaining six places where *encomenderos* lived were sites of economic activity. Guadalajara had seven *vecinos* who were *encomenderos* of New Spain. Purificación, like Medellín, was founded for strategic reasons. Nuño de Guzmán ordered its founding in 1533 as a security outpost, but in reality it served as a boundary marker between New Galicia and New Spain—and was well within the sphere of Colima. The sole *vecino* with an *encomienda* in New Spain during the time frame of this study, *hidalgo poblador* Juan de Villaseñor

Orozco from Andalusia, served there under orders and perhaps duress. He claimed to be a *vecino* of Ciudad Michoacán in the 1540s but actually lived in the area of one of his *encomiendas*, some forty miles from Pátzcuaro.[17] Likewise one of New Spain's *encomenderos* was a *vecino* of Villarreal, Chiapas. Neither of these settlements was consistently subject to all aspects of New Spain's government during the period studied. Utlatlan, an indigenous community 170 miles southwest of Mexico City on a tributary of the Balsas River, was the residence of conqueror Isidro Moreno, the only *encomendero vecino* there. Conqueror Juan de Arriaga was the sole *encomendero vecino* of the Indian area Guaxuapa, present Huajuapan de León, a way station 145 miles southeast of Mexico City on the main route to Antequera, Chiapas, and Guatemala.

Pobladores Juan Larios, a notary, and Bartolomé de Valdés, both of whom had been *encomenderos* earlier, were *vecinos* of Minas de Ayoteco (also called Chiautla), some ninety miles south and east of Mexico City. This site became significant in silver production in the late 1530s and 1540s, and Larios held the office of clerk of the mines there.

Acapulco, established as a shipbuilding settlement in 1528, was an insignificant place with few residents until the commencement of the Manila trade in the 1570s. Its only *encomendero vecino* during the early years was Cristóbal de Monresín, who held a grant forty miles east of the settlement.

Jalapa, like Acapulco, survived for economic reasons but because of the royal dye monopoly rather than shipbuilding. Later it served as a warehousing center, its climate less destructive to goods in storage than at Medellín or Veracruz on the Caribbean coast. From the early 1530s Jalapa was also the site of a Franciscan doctrinal center. Within a few months after the arrival of the Narváez *entrada*, the region had been nearly depopulated by a smallpox epidemic. Its estimated 30,000 tributaries at contact were reduced to 639 by the end of 1521.[18] Jalapa's sole *encomendero vecino* was conqueror Melchor de Arévalo from Avila.

Ciudad Michoacán, the municipal ancestor of present-day Morelia, was established in fits and starts on three different sites, and its permanent location was not consolidated until after the time frame of this study. Around 1524 Cortés assigned *encomiendas* in the region around Lake Pátzcuaro, and Franciscan friars came on the scene shortly thereafter. The initial group of Spanish residents, which arrived ca. 1522, was ordered away for service in Zacatula and then later in Colima. The first municipality was founded ca. 1529 at Tzintzuntzan, seat of the native government, under instructions from the first Audiencia. Vasco de Quiroga was instrumental in the 1533 elevation of the *villa* to *ciudad* status, the charter naming the settlement Granada. Five years later both the Spanish and the Indian *cabildos* relocated from Tzintzuntzan to Pátzcuaro, on the south side of the lake. Miffed because Quiroga had not informed him of the move, Viceroy Mendoza changed the name of the city from Granada to Ciudad Michoacán and ordered it moved thirty-five miles northeast to Guayangareo, the present site of Morelia. Quiroga accepted the name change but not the new location. His reference to Ciudad Michoacán means the Pátzcuaro site, while when Mendoza and subsequent viceroys refer to Ciudad Michoacán they mean the Guayangareo location. The Spanish *cabildo* finally made the move from Pátzcuaro to Guayangareo in 1576 and Valladolid, a name assigned the city in a 1537 *cedula*, became the popular identification.[19]

In spite of the high-level bickering, Ciudad Michoacán had little to attract Spanish settlers other than being an Indian administrative center and a way station on the Guadalajara-Colima route; only nine *encomenderos* were *vecinos*, of whom two each were conquerors and first conquerors. Five were *pobladores*. Three of them, *pobladores* Juan de Alvarado, Francisco Morcillo, and Juan de Villaseñor Orozco, were *hidalgos*. Villaseñor had been an unwilling *vecino* of Purificación, New Galicia. He was married to doña Catalina Cervantes (de Lara), one of Comendador Leonel de Cervantes' six daughters.

Valles, in the Pánuco region, was founded in 1533 as Santiago de los Valles by Nuño Beltrán de Guzmán even though (or perhaps because) Cortés had already claimed the region for himself. By 1534 the second Audiencia voided the Guzmán grants and offices and assigned *encomiendas* not taken for the crown to residents of Valles. Record of four of these *encomenderos* survives. One was a first conqueror, another a *poblador antiguo*, and the remaining two *pobladores*. Two of the four, Portuguese *poblador antiguo* Alvaro de Ribera and *poblador* Diego Cortés from Badajoz, were *hidalgos*. The other two were first conquerors Alonso Navarrete and a black, Juan de Villanueva, both from Granada. Valles continued to be a backwater, but did have twelve Spanish and mestizo families ca. 1560.[20]

Thus within thirteen years of the capture of Mexico City New Spain was essentially occupied. *Encomenderos* held grants throughout the length and breadth of the country. A number of towns and cities had been founded, primarily as headquarters for *encomenderos*. Yet as we have already seen, the location of an *encomienda* did not always correspond to the place where the *encomendero* resided or was a *vecino*. A clause of the standard investiture order prior to the enforcement of the 1542 New Laws obligated the *encomendero* to be a resident of and maintain a *casa poblada* in the *cabecera* of the province in which his *encomienda* lay, as well as attending the annual muster to present his arms and horse(s) for inspection.[21] The intention was clearly to keep *encomenderos* in the vicinity of their grants. Reference to province did not create much of a problem in Spain, where the few remaining *encomiendas* were in Granada, a district not more than 100 miles in its largest dimension. But New Spain, if considered a single province, was larger than the entire Iberian peninsula. It measured roughly 700 miles east to west and over 400 miles north to south. During the third of a century that is the time frame of this study, New Spain developed provincial subdivisions, although Mexico City retained its status as capital and was overwhelmingly the most important city. For this time period, political, economic, and social arguments can be made for considering New Spain as a single province, albeit quite large, and Mexico City as its *cabecera*. If so, *encomenderos* could feel justified in maintaining their citizenship there. Almost half of them did just that, many having been *vecinos* since the foundation of the city. Contributing to the selection of Mexico City as a favored residence, in addition to climate and the already cited attractions, was the fact that a number of *encomenderos* held more than one grant, and this central location eased administration.

A strong relationship exists between nascent provincial boundary lines, geographical features, precontact cultural areas, and effective radius of *encomienda* control. While extant data preclude an accurate determination of the size of each *encomienda*, the exact income derived from it, or the specifics of its administration, one can still establish that *encomenderos* generally resided in places within reach of their *encomiendas*. Circles drawn with seventy-five mile radii (about a three-day march) centered on the *encomendero* headquarters of Mexico City, Puebla, Antequera, Villa Alta, Pánuco, Valles, Zacatula, and Colima, as shown on Map 4, suggest the relationship above, and enclose more than half of the *encomiendas* of *vecinos* of the respective cities.

The area enclosed in the overlapping circles centered on Mexico City and Puebla includes most of the Nahuatl-speaking heartland once directly subject to the Triple Alliance in Tenochtitlan. The Zacatula *encomienda* region, limited to the Pacific drainage, was also a Nahuatl-speaking area. Colima, a relatively short distance to the west-northwest of Zacatula, included Otomis as well as Nahuatl speakers. That these people shared a common language and were tributaries of the Triple Alliance helped mark them for early interest and exploitation by the Spaniards. Although the Pánuco-Valles complex, occupying a tropical coastal plain bounded on the west by a mountain barrier, was a Huastecan language area not controlled by Tenochtitlan, it was destined for early conquest for political reasons. Cortés had to dominate the region in order to preclude entry by Francisco de Garay, who had a much stronger legal claim to the area. The densely populated Antequera-Villa Alta region of Zapotec and Mixtec people was also defined by surrounding mountains. It shared a common boundary with the Mexico City-Puebla complex to the northwest.

These various areas were similar in that at contact each supported a large sedentary agricultural population, had reasonably well-defined natural boundaries, and used a common regional language. In each, the Spaniards established an administrative and population center within three days' march of the bulk of the native population. *Encomendero vecinos* abounded where there was a concentration of Indians. Where Indians survived in numbers, lasting Spanish population centers prevailed. The settlements at Zacutula and in the Pánuco-Valles complex failed with native depopulation.

Table 12 illustrates the assertion made above that over half the *encomiendas* were within seventy-five miles of the places where the respective *encomenderos* resided and claimed citizenship.[22] Approximately 20 percent were less than twenty-five miles distant, and almost four out of ten were closer than fifty miles. Grants less than seventy-five miles from residence were close enough for relatively quick access by the *encomendero* or his agent, and also close enough to permit effective use of natives for personal tribute service in support of the *casa poblada*, gardens, and farms (in spite of subsequent regulations against each activities).[23] Included in Table 12 are those *encomenderos* who for whatever reason chose to live within the area of their grants, shunning Spanish urban life.[24] *Encomiendas* within seventy-five miles of place of residence appear to have been retained under either personal or closely supervised administration. Being accessible made these 397 grants, representing nearly 52 percent of the *encomiendas*, more exploitable and therefore more valuable. One can also establish zones with a 76- to 150-mile radius of Spanish cities and more than 151 miles distant. The former category includes about 25 percent of the *encomiendas*, the latter slightly more than 20 percent. A grant more than three days travel or seventy-five miles distant required the use of either a resident administrator or extended periods of residence in an Indian community for its effective management.

The topic of distance between residence and grant leads to dis-

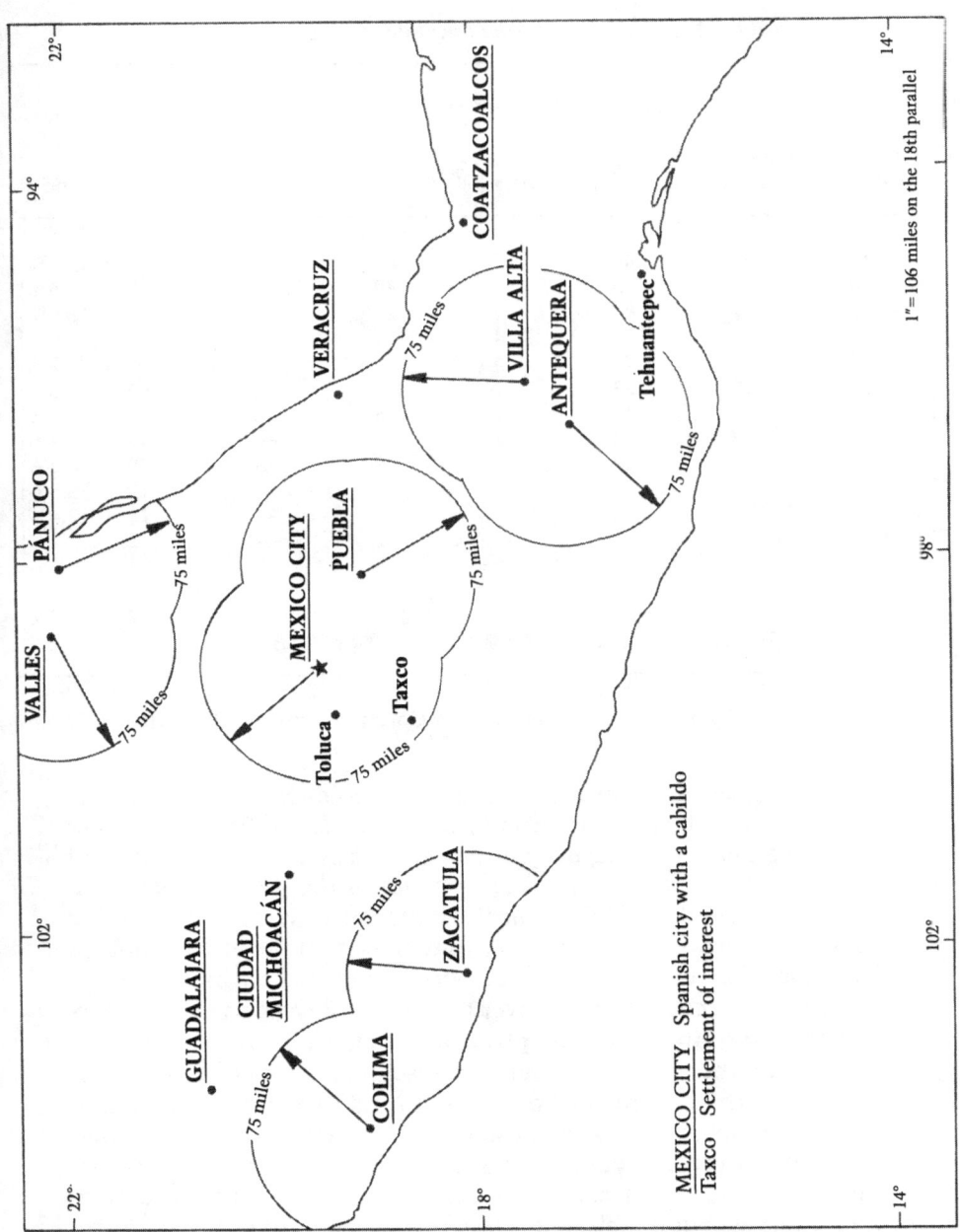

Map 4. Encomienda Concentration

Table 12. *Distances between* Encomiendas *and Residences*

Distance in miles	Encomienda Assigned to					Total Encomiendas
	First Conqueror	Con- queror	*Poblador Antiguo*	*Poblador*	Indian	
Up to 25	31	40	10	64	2	147 (19.2%)
26– 50	39	63	7	39	2	150 (19.5%)
51– 75	37	38	5	20	—	100 (13.0%)
76–100	20	28	4	14	—	66 (8.6%)
101–125	12	23	4	19	1	59 (7.7%)
126–150	19	23	1	23	—	66 (8.6%)
151–175	6	14	1	8	—	29 (3.8%)
176–200	7	14	2	17	—	40 (5.2%)
201–250	14	24	2	8	—	48 (6.3%)
251–300	6	5	1	7	—	19 (2.5%)
301–400	6	3	—	9	—	18 (2.4%)
401 plus	1	—	—	1	—	2 (.2%)
Unknown	5	7	2	8	1	23 (3.0%)
Totals	203 (26.5%)	282 (36.8%)	39 (5.1%)	237 (30.8%)	6 (.8%)	767 (100.0%)

Note: Does not include *encomiendas* held by Cortés or Nuño de Guzmán.

cussion of another aspect of *encomienda* holding, that of multiple *encomiendas*. The distribution of *encomiendas* in Table 13 shows that *encomenderos* assigned but one grant represented 66 percent of the total. They held not quite 44 percent of the *encomiendas*, and nearly three out of five of these grants were within seventy-five miles of stated residences. Thirty-four percent of the *encomenderos* had more than one grant, and this group held slightly more than 56 percent of the *encomiendas*, over 53 percent of which were seventy-five miles or more from the place of residence. Those holding two grants averaged one distant and one close-in *encomienda*. *Encomenderos* with three grants had one close-in and two distant *encomiendas*, a scheme shared with those with four, five, or more holdings.

Another way of examining the distribution of *encomiendas* is to measure the seniority categories against single and multiple assignments. As shown in Table 14, more than 84 percent of the *pobladores antiguos* held but one *encomienda*, followed by *pobladores* with nearly 70 percent, first conquerors with 64 percent, and conquerors with just under 62 percent. The two categories of conquerors thus

CITIES AND ENCOMIENDAS

Table 13. **Encomiendas *per* Encomendero**

Number of Encomiendas	Encomenderos	Encomiendas	Within 75 Miles	Beyond 75 Miles
1	335 (66.2%)	335 (43.6%)	197 (58.8%)	138 (41.2%)
2	107 (21.1%)	214 (27.9%)	106 (49.5%)	108 (50.5%)
3	37 (7.3%)	110 (14.4%)	48 (43.6%)	62 (56.4%)
4	18 (3.6%)	72 (9.4%)	30 (41.6%)	42 (58.4%)
5 or more	9 (1.8%)	36 (4.7%)	16 (44.4%)	20 (55.6%)
Totals	506 (100.0%)	767 (100.0%)	397 (51.8%)	370 (48.2%)

Note: Does not include *encomiendas* held by Cortés or Nuño de Guzmán.

Table 14. **Distribution *of* Encomiendas *According to Seniority***

Number of Encomiendas	First Conquerors	Conquerors	Pobladores Antiguos	Pobladores	Indians	Total
1	86	110	27	110	2	335
2	35	45	3	24	—	107
3	9	12	1	15	—	37
4	1	10	1	5	1	18
5 or more	4	1	—	4	—	9
Totals	135	178	32	158	3	506

had a higher proportion of multiple *encomiendas* than the two categories of *pobladores*. *Pobladores antiguos* came off worst, the vast majority holding a single grant, whereas in all other categories the number of multiple holders approached or somewhat exceeded a third. Conquerors led the percentage and overall number of multiple *encomiendas*. Over 38 percent had more than one grant, with 68 holding 171 *encomiendas*. But holding more than one *encomienda* did not always indicate more wealth. It often required two grants to produce the income required to be a viable *encomendero*. Those with three or more *encomiendas*, however, were generally among the highest ranking. They were all *hidalgos*, and their *encomiendas*, along with other offices, sustained them well. We must remember that there was great variety among those holding a single grant. In some instances the tribute generated by a single *encomienda* was a

Table 15. Encomienda Succession

Heir	First Conqueror	Conqueror	Poblador Antiguo	Poblador	Indian	Total
Son	52	70	17	54	4	197 (25.7%)
Widow						
widowed	12	8	1	13		34
remarried	6	15	1	8		30
to son	4	9	—	5		18
to daughter	3	5	—	1		9
	25	37	2	27		91 (11.9%)
Daughter	12	15	1	9	1	38 (5.0%)
Daughter dowry	2	7	3	5	—	17 (2.2%)
Mother	1	—	—	—	—	1 (.1%)
Brother	—	2	—	—	—	2 (.2%)
Nephew	1	1	—	—	—	2 (.2%)
Niece dowry	—	—	—	1	—	1 (.1%)
Sold	6	6	1	4	—	17 (2.2%)
Reassigned	32	21	8	32	—	93 (12.2%)
Escheated	30	32	8	44	1	115 (15.0%)
Unknown succession	43	89	—	61	—	193 (25.2%)
Totals	204	280	40	237	6	767 (100.0%)

princely amount. *Poblador antiguo* Diego Suárez Pacheco, the father of Cortés' first wife, received half the tribute from Cholula, an *encomienda* with perhaps 100,000 tributaries ca. 1528. Representing the opposite extreme was tailor Martín Rodríguez, also a *poblador antiguo*, who had a reported thirty tributaries in an *encomienda* 300 miles distant before it reverted to the crown in 1535.

A father's desire to provide for his family after his death was as strong among the sixteenth-century *encomenderos* as it is for any father today, if not stronger. Yet in spite of often extraordinary efforts to hold onto an *encomienda*, only slightly more than 45 percent of the grants are known to have stayed in the family line beyond the initial recipient. Overall, nearly 15 percent of the *encomiendas* of our *encomenderos* reverted to the crown during the period under study, and slightly more than 12 percent were reassigned (succession in a fourth of the cases is unknown). Table 15 shows *encomienda* succession, and while there are few real surprises, some things are worthy of note. Succession by an *encomendero*'s widow was close to 12 percent for all but the *pobladores antiguos*, whose lower rate of 5 percent doubtless reflects more than anything else their advanced age. In more than one-third of the cases (34 percent), sons or daughters inherited. Conqueror's widows were almost twice as likely to remarry as the widows of either first conquerors or *pobladores*, but the children of the widow had a greater chance to inherit. The implication is that the widows of conquerors were younger and their husbands had more tenuous claims to the grants.

Twenty-five percent of all *encomiendas* were inherited by a son, with few exceptions the oldest son. The rate was higher for the *pobladores antiguos*, who were succeeded by sons over 43 percent of the time. The average rate of succession by a daughter was about 5 percent, with lower rates for female offspring of *pobladores* and *pobladores antiguos*.

The giving of *encomiendas* in dowry invites discussion because such disposition, with eighteen occurrences during the period (seventeen daughters and one niece received *encomiendas* in dowry) not only falls outside the generally accepted understanding of legal succession, but also appears counterproductive. Any division of an estate diminishes it, a consideration especially cogent at a time of declining native population. A few preliminary comments are in order, however. All of the *encomiendas* given in dowry in New Spain identified during this study were transferred during the tenure of Viceroy don Antonio de Mendoza. One-third of the dowries transferred the entire holdings of the *encomendero* to the recipient or to her spouse. Five of the eighteen dowries went to natural daughters, three of these transferring the total tributary holdings of the father.²⁵ Dowries in the remaining instances effectively divided *encomienda* holdings between the daughter and another heir, be it a son, a daughter, or a widow.

The actual mechanics of transferring an *encomienda* in dowry are vague, for no complete chain of documents showing inception, petition for renunciation, and reassignment of a particular grant has been uncovered. Partial documentation, however, gives some notion of the process. For example, in December of 1537, in a document recorded by Mexico City notary Martín de Castro, *poblador* Gregorio de Saldaña, in arranging for the marriage of his daughter María to Bartolomé de Perales, namesake son of a *poblador antiguo*, conceded a one-third part of Mecatlan, its *estancias, sujeto*, and the services and tributes thereof to help sustain the marriage.²⁶ Missing in this chain of events is the petition presented to the viceroy whereby Saldaña actually renounced one-third of his *encomienda* in favor of his daughter, and the specific reply to the petition. We also do not know what costs were incurred to insure a positive response to the request. A condensed affirmation of such a petition, taken from a report sent to the crown, acknowledges the dowry of Antonia de Avila for her marriage to Gonzalo de Salazar and states in part that upon renunciation by Alonso de Avila, the *encomendero* to that point, Viceroy Mendoza granted half of Matlactonatico and Xuxupango in *encomienda* to Antonia de Avila and Gonzalo de Salazar, her husband.²⁷

Succession by anyone other than a widow, son, or daughter required special consent, and record of succession by a female heir prior to the arrival of the second Audiencia has yet to be found. Furthermore, the Audiencia approved female succession only in cases where the social rank of the woman was felt to justify such action.²⁸ Viceroy Mendoza approved a unique succession in 1540 when he permitted the widow and the mother of first conqueror Antonio Gutiérrez de Almodóvar, a Mexico City *vecino* and native of Ciudad Real, to inherit jointly. Mendoza also approved the inheritance of half of first conqueror Diego de Ordaz's vast holdings by a nephew, but only after four years of litigation did the nephew assume the title. An example of a brother inheriting came when Juan Pérez de Herrera succeeded as *encomendero* of his brother's half of a jointly held grant. Both were conquerors, as was their father. The half which Pérez de Herrera inherited was later taken for the crown by the second Audiencia. Around 1550 Cristóbal Moreno succeeded his brother, Pedro de Simancas, inheriting one of his two *encomiendas*. The other grant escheated. An example of *encomienda* succession being tied to dowry arrangements other than for a daughter is shown in the case of Alonso de Paz, a member of the Cortés entourage. Around 1540 Paz gave all of his *encomiendas* (half the tribute from three grants and all of a fourth) to his niece in dowry. The viceroy sanctioned the transaction, and Paz then returned to Spain, where he married. Within two years he was back in Mexico City, requesting a replacement for the status and income he had relinquished.

The sale of *encomiendas*, although not a common practice, does not appear to have been considered absolutely illegal in New Spain as it was in Peru; perhaps it was viewed in the same light as the disposition by sale of any other office.[29] Even so, only slightly more than 2 percent of our *encomiendas*, most of them with relatively few tributaries, were disposed of by sale. *Encomienda* sellers were equally divided between first conquerors and conquerors, with six sales each. Only one *poblador antiguo* sold his grant, while four *pobladores* were sellers. As can be expected, *pobladores* were the most frequent buyers, purchasing ten of the grants. Conquerors were buyers in four transactions, first conquerors and *pobladores antiguos* the buyers in two transactions each.[30] The earliest recorded *encomienda* transfer by sale occurred sometime before 1532 when first conqueror Francisco Gutiérrez sold Moyutla, a grant near Santisteban del Puerto in Pánuco with fewer than 250 tributaries, to *poblador* Gregorio de Saldaña, Nuño de Guzmán's legal advisor.

As in the case of transferring an *encomienda* in dowry, no documents describe fully the actual steps taken during the sale of a grant or how payment was made. Sufficient indirect evidence exists, however, for the mechanics of the process to be surmised.[31] After parties to the transaction reached an agreement, agents sought informal approval from the Audiencia, and after 1536 from the viceroy. Armed with the informal approval of the sale, the parties then had a notary put the agreement in writing, setting forth the description of the grant to be sold, the conditions of the sale, and the payment, all in separate documents. These instruments, combined with a petition for formal recognition of the sale and the transfer of the title to the *encomienda*, were then submitted for approval, undoubtedly accompanied by a prenegotiated monetary consideration for certain officials. Thereupon the Audiencia, and later the viceroy, reassigned the *encomienda*. The lenient attitude towards transferring *encomiendas* by sale apparently resulted from local interpretation of instructions provided by the crown in 1525 for the Caribbean islands and again in 1536 for New Spain. The latter is often referred to as the Law of Succession.[32] By treating *encomiendas* as property because they could be inherited, one can easily see why *encomenderos* as well as royal officials saw fit to transfer grants through donation, sale, or other means. It is the wording of Article 35 of the New Laws, published in 1542 and selectively promulgated and enforced from 1544 forward, that specifically recognizes what was occurring and orders its prohibition.[33] Viceroy Mendoza was still approving transfer of *encomiendas* by sale as late as 1548. Further evidence of grants changing hands in a nontraditional manner is seen in the abstract of holders of *encomiendas* submitted to the crown by Viceroy Velasco in 1564 wherein a number of *encomiendas* were reassigned to new holders by the viceroy upon renunciation of ownership by the old holder.[34]

Reassignment (unrelated to sales) and escheatment were tools that the Audiencias and the viceroy used in walking the line between the clamoring of unrewarded and underrewarded worthies and the efforts of the crown to recoup *encomiendas*. Of the sixty-two first-conqueror grants vacated (that is, not assigned to an heir on the death of a holder) during the period, slightly over half were reassigned, the remaining thirty reverting to the crown. For vacated conqueror grants, escheatment predominated over reassignment by a rate of three to two, indicating that a number of these *encomenderos* had less than unimpeachable claim to their grants. The reassignment-escheatment ratio for vacated *poblador* grants matched that of the conquerors. The *pobladores antiguos*, like the first conquerors, relinquished half of their unclaimed grants to reassignment, the other half to escheatment. Contributing to the number of grants that went to the crown was the factor of native depopulation; the crown was the ultimate holder of *encomiendas* with no Indians.

The *encomiendas* of New Spain were organized into regional complexes, each with a Spanish city in the center of a ring of reachable *encomiendas*. Referring back to Map 4, one can see that there were only four such complexes.[35] Excepting for Mexico City-Puebla, by far the largest complex, each of the lesser complexes had approximately the same number of *encomendero vecinos*; Pánuco-Valles had forty-two, Colima-Zacatula fifty-eight and Antequera-Villa Alta fifty. Roughly 90 percent of the *encomiendas* assigned to *vecinos* of the cities in the center of these rings were within the seventy-five miles range. We can use Antequera as an example of the complexes other than Mexico City-Puebla. Only four of Antequera's thirty-two *encomenderos* holding one grant had to travel farther than seventy-five miles to their grants, and of those four, two had to go only ten or so additional miles. All of those with more than one *encomienda* (slightly more than one-third of the total) had at least one grant within the seventy-five mile range.[36] For the most part, those with *encomiendas* more distant than seventy-five miles had been assigned the grants prior to moving to Antequera.

The scheme of four separate major complexes was obscured, however, by several factors. First, *encomenderos* could and did retain grants in the jurisdiction of one region after moving to and becoming *vecinos* of the major city in another regional complex. Nearly one-fourth of the *encomendero vecinos* of cities other than Mexico City had more than one grant, and a few had three or more *encomiendas*. Above all, about 48 percent of the *encomenderos* of New Spain were *vecinos* of Mexico City, and almost half of this number had more than one *encomienda*. (The proportion of grants within seventy-five miles was correspondingly less for the Mexico City *vecinos*.) Because of the assignment of multiple *encomiendas*, often at great distances from each other, and the concentration of *encomenderos* in Mexico City, then, New Spain, to an extent, acted as one large complex.

During the first generation in New Spain about half those who took part in and survived the original conquest, plus a few senior veterans of the Indies arriving after the capture of Tenochtitlan, received more than two-thirds of the *encomienda* grants distributed. Close to half the *encomiendas* assigned during the period of this study were within the sphere of Mexico City and Puebla (that is, seventy-five miles or less), while the remaining grants fell within the other three major indigenous population centers, nearly equally divided between them. The proportion of *encomendero vecinos* in each of these complexes generally reflects the number of readily accessible grants.

The ongoing conflict between the king and the *encomenderos* concerning succession was not totally resolved during the period because of modification, selective interpretation, and unequal enforcement of royal decrees by the Audiencia, the viceroy, and even the Council of the Indies in Seville. Traditional succession, wherein the *encomienda* would be inherited directly by a son, was realized in only one out of four instances. Widows succeeded more often than previously believed (12 percent of the successions), and one-third of them retained the status of *encomendera*. The remaining two-thirds of the *encomiendas* that initially went to widows were eventually divided between children of the deceased *encomendero* and second husbands. *Encomiendas* given in dowry approximated the number of *encomiendas* sold, each representing slightly more than 2 percent of the successions. That *encomiendas* could be disposed of legally through sale or donation, especially to natural daughters, most tellingly reflects the proprietary attitudes towards these grants held by both the *encomenderos* and the provincial authorities. Even so, through the offices of the Audiencias and the viceroy, the crown directed over 25 percent of the successions during the period by either reassigning vacated *encomiendas* to the underrewarded or by taking title for the crown through escheatment. The balance was tilted in favor of escheatment, but only by a few percentage points.

CHAPTER FOUR

The Integration of the *Encomenderos* into Local Society: Patterns of Association through Marriage, Officeholding, and *Encomienda* Sharing

Neither the individual biographies presented in Part Two below nor the general analysis developed above in Chapters 2 and 3 more than hint at the complex patterns of social integration manifested by the *encomenderos* of New Spain between 1521 and 1555. It was a dynamic period, full of change, a generation that started with what seemed like promise for all and ended with rewards for only a few, at least in terms of tribute income. As we have seen, the crown sought to recover *encomiendas* and to restrict new assignments of Indian tributaries. For new grants, late arrivals bearing noble credentials were given precedence over those who risked all in the conquest. As the sixteenth century wore on, the loss of Indian population in the succession of plagues placed the viability of the whole *encomienda* system in serious question.

A number of *encomenderos*, perhaps realizing from an early time that the *encomienda* was a transitory base, sought to cement positions within the social structure of New Spain by creating associations with peers that would transcend and outlast outside threats, creating a thread of interlocking familial continuity through intermarriage and dowry agreements, followed in some cases by the establishment of entails to insure estate longevity. *Encomenderos* hoped to amass a fortune adequate to attract a wife with an impressive dowry and found a family in style. Without a large dowry, a woman could not marry well. Many of those conquerors who were married faced the challenge of providing dowries for several daughters. The situation was initially burdensome, but also offered the possibility of multiplying valuable connections within *encomendero* society.

This was the case with Leonel de Cervantes, a Comendador of the Order of Santiago and native of Seville who came to the Indies in 1519.[1] His title gave him an enviable status despite his apparent lack of funds in the early years. Having used the Narváez *entrada* to reach New Spain, Cervantes quickly sided with Cortés. Before the capture of Mexico City and the initial distribution of *encomiendas*, wherein Cervantes received a grant, he requested and received license to return to Spain for his family. By 1524 he was back in Mexico City with his wife, Leonor de Andrada, his son Alonso, and five daughters who all carried the title *doña*. A sixth daughter was born in New Spain. Within a few years Cervantes acquired a second *encomienda* near his original grant.

Cervantes was successful in finding suitable mates for his daughters. In 1524, shortly after the Cervantes family arrived in New Spain, doña Ana de Cervantes married conqueror Alonso de Villanueva Tordesillas from Badajoz. He, like the Comendador, had arrived in Cuba and had come to New Spain with Narváez. Villanueva held Ocelotepec, thirty miles north of Cervantes' *encomienda*, plus another grant northeast of Mexico City, both grants having been assigned him by Cortés. Doña Catalina de Cervantes de Lara married *poblador encomendero* Juan de Villaseñor Orozco from Vélez (Andalusia), and lived on one of his *encomiendas* north of Lake Pátzcuaro. Doña María de Cervantes married first conqueror Pedro de Ircio, a native of Logroño. He had served as a captain under Gonzalo de Sandoval during the siege and capture of Mexico City, and was a *vecino* there. Although he left no record of it, it is highly doubtful that he did not hold an *encomienda*. One with his record and recognition could be expected to have been well rewarded; further, he would not have been considered a suitable mate for a Comendador's daughter without a grant.

Doña Isabel de Lara, probably the oldest of the six daughters, had married Alonso de Aguilar y Córdoba in Spain, prior to the move to Mexico City. She and Alonso were members of the Cervantes entourage that made the transatlantic trip in 1524. Aguilar received two *encomiendas* about forty miles south of the Comendador's grants, west and south of Mexico City. After Aguilar died ca. 1535, doña Isabel married first conqueror Alonso de Mendoza. When Mendoza died in turn, she married a *poblador* known only as Licenciado Alemán, from Lepe, Huelva. Alemán ultimately acquired title to both the *encomiendas* doña Isabel held; one she inherited from her mother, the other from her second husband.

In 1536 doña Luisa de Lara, perhaps the next to youngest of the Cervantes daughters, married *poblador* Juan de Cervantes Casaus. He had arrived in New Spain in 1524 with an appointment as royal factor for Pánuco, a post he held as long as the salary was paid from the royal treasury. He relinquished the office when the income was to be determined by the tribute collected, a less than promising prospect as the population of the Caribbean coastal plains diminished. Cervantes then became a *vecino* of Mexico City. His *encomiendas* were north-northeast of the capital.

The Comendador's youngest daughter, doña Beatriz de Andrada, was born in New Spain. She became the second wife of first conqueror Juan Jaramillo de Salvatierra, a native of Badajoz and the *encomendero* of Xilotepec. His first wife had been doña Marina, the native interpreter of the conquest. At the time of the marriage doña Beatriz could not have been past her teens; Jaramillo was at least thirty years her senior. She inherited the *encomienda* after Jaramillo's death ca. 1543. When doña Beatriz married don Francisco de Velasco, the viceroy's brother, in the early 1550s, half the *encomienda* went to doña María Jaramillo, Juan's daughter by doña Marina.

Cervantes' only son, Juan (Alonso) de Cervantes, received Atlapulco, an *encomienda* halfway between Mexico City and Toluca, as a marriage portion for his match with (doña?) Catalina de Zárate in the 1530s.

When Comendador Cervantes died in 1550, his family was receiving tribute income from at least thirteen *encomiendas* in four indigenous culture areas west, southwest, and northeast of Mexico City. The closest grant was about forty miles from the capital. The total count of tributaries assigned to this family can be roughly estimated as in excess of 40,000 in 1550. *Encomiendas* of the extended Cervantes family are located on Map 5.

All of Cervantes' daughters married proper *hidalgos*, one having done so before leaving Spain and then remarrying twice in New Spain as she survived in turn her first and second husbands. Considering initial unions only, three daughters married *pobladores*, two first conquerors, and one a conqueror. Three of the matches were with Andalusians; two from the family's home of Seville, and the third from Vélez, a place-name found in eastern Andalusia. All of the Andalusians were *pobladores*. The other three daughters married men who had taken part in the conquest, two of them members of Cortés' original *entrada* and one who had joined Narváez along with the Comendador. Two of the conquest veterans were from Badajoz, the other from Logroño. Cervantes' son was married to a Zárate, a name with roots in northern Spain.

If there is any factional preference in Cervantes' alliances, it is in support of Cortés, even though son-in-law *poblador* Juan de Cervantes Casaus functioned in Pánuco throughout the shifts in political winds. He received his original appointment as royal factor for the Garay colony and stayed on in that capacity under both Cortés

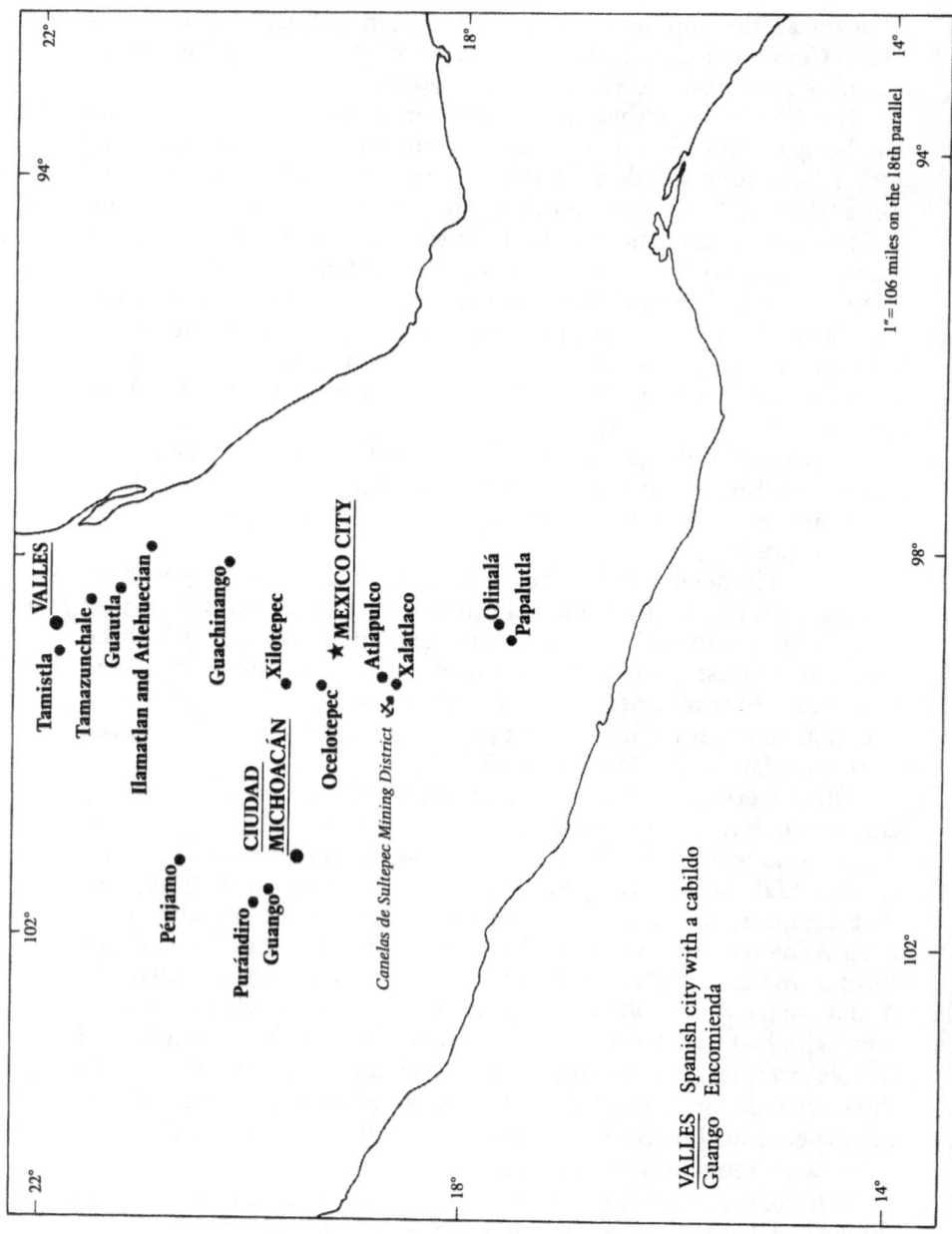

Map 5. Encomiendas of the Cervantes Family

and Nuño de Guzmán. In fact, he was a *residencia* witness for Guzmán. *Poblador* son-in-law Juan de Villaseñor Orozco received his Michoacán *encomiendas* from Cortés and then later served with Guzmán in New Galicia without jeopardizing his holdings. Perhaps the successful survival of the Cervantes family was due in large part to its nobility and consequent ability to remain above the partisan maneuvering of the middle and late 1520s. However, Cervantes' grandson, Baltasar de Aguilar, the son of doña Isabel and Alonso de Aguilar, was involved with the second Marqués del Valle in the abortive mutiny of 1566 and lost his *encomiendas* as a result.

The family also enjoyed a degree of influence in local Mexico City government. Comendador Leonel de Cervantes was *alcalde ordinario* during all of 1525, *regidor* for the first three weeks of 1526, and then *alcalde ordinario* again until mid-June of the same year. This was all during the musical-chairs tenure of the acting governors (see pages 14–15, Chapter 1 above). He was *alcalde ordinario* again in 1534. Cervantes' son-in-law, Alonso de Villanueva Tordesillas, was *regidor* in 1527, 1544, and 1550. Another son-in-law, Alonso de Aguilar, was *alcalde ordinario* in 1535. Future son-in-law Juan Jaramillo de Salvatierra was *regidor* from 3 June 1524, *alcalde ordinario* upon Cortés' return from Honduras in mid-1526, and again in 1539. He then automatically became *alcalde de mesta* for 1540.[2] (The significance of family representation in the *cabildo* is shown on pages 4 and 5, Chapter 1 above.) As we have seen, another son-in-law, Juan de Cervantes Casaus, had been the royal *factor* for Pánuco until early 1533.

Members of this extended family have left scant record of business activity concerning the *encomiendas* that they held. Alonso de Aguilar, perhaps the most aggressive of the lot, was in a gold mining partnership with first conqueror *encomendero* Andrés Núñez of Salamanca. Núñez shared Tequixquiac, forty miles north of Mexico City, with ship's carpenter first conqueror Martín López. Núñez provided 100 Indian slaves, with their equipment, and Aguilar contributed what was necessary to feed, house, and clothe them while working in the Chilapa mining region near Aguilar's *encomienda*. They shared the profit after deducting the royal fifth and minting charges, with three-fifths of the net going to Núñez. Juan de Villaseñor Orozco shared a mining claim in the "Canelas de Sultepec" silver district with miner Ruiz Martínez, but no details are available concerning the management of the partnership.

The example of the Cervantes family is exceptional only in that the Comendador was possessed of such high rank and so many offspring. Those who were best connected could carry out the general patterns of behavior with more consistency and elaboration, and they have also usually left the best written record of themselves.

Another set of family alliances among the upper group revolves around royal treasurer Alonso de Estrada (who claimed to have been a natural son of King Ferdinand) and his wife doña Marina Gutiérrez Flores de la Caballería, who had some successes and some failures.[3] They, together with a son and five daughters, were the nucleus of a large entourage that arrived in New Spain from Ciudad Real in 1523. Daughter doña Luisa married first conqueror Jorge de Alvarado within the year. Not many years thereafter daughter doña María married *poblador* don Luis de Guzmán Saavedra, a native of Seville, who arrived in New Spain in 1525, and doña Francisca married *poblador* Alonso de Avalos Saavedra. In mid-August 1528 Estrada was negotiating a marriage between his son, Juan Alonso de Estrada, and a daughter of Ciudad Real *vecino* and *regidor* don Lope Fernández de Treviño. Juan Alonso's marriage portion included Estrada's office of perpetual *regidor* in Ciudad Real and rents from property in the same city that amounted to $2,500 per year. For reasons not revealed, the marriage did not take place, and Juan Alonso entered the Dominican order.

A year after Estrada's death in 1530, his widow doña Marina succeeded in arranging a match between number three daughter doña Ana and *poblador* Juan Alonso de Sosa from Córdoba, who had been appointed royal treasurer to replace Estrada. Sosa's father had been the governor of Tierra Firme in the 1520s. Estrada's youngest daughter, doña Beatriz, married Francisco Vázquez de Coronado in 1535, shortly after he arrived in New Spain as a member of Viceroy Mendoza's entourage. Doña Marina then became the guardian of three grandchildren when doña María and Luis de Guzmán died ca. 1540. Bartolomé de Estrada, Estrada's natural son by Ana Rodríguez Anhaifa, became a secular priest in Mexico City.

The noble mates for the daughters Estrada came from three different Iberian regions, with Andalusia predominating. Doña Ana's spouse was from Córdoba, and doña María's don Luis came from Seville. His parents were don Fernando de Saavedra, Count of Castellar, and doña Catalina de Guzmán. Jorge de Alvarado, who married doña Luisa, was a native of Badajoz, and Francisco Vázquez de Coronado, married to doña Beatriz, came from Salamanca. The husband of doña Francisca was also a native of Badajoz.

As might be expected, *encomiendas* granted and acquired by the husbands of these five women were impressive. They collectively held as many as eighteen grants, fourteen of these staying under family control into the second and succeeding generations. The three grants assigned to Juan Alonso de Sosa (doña Ana's husband) reverted to the crown in 1544 under the enforcement of the New Laws because the original assignment had been made to him as a perquisite of his office as royal treasurer. In all likelihood his salary and other benefits from the treasury office were increased to offset the loss of tribute from the *encomienda*. Perhaps the greatest inconvenience was the loss of personal service from the residents of Coatepec, only twenty miles east of Mexico City. Don Luis de Guzmán Saavedra (doña María's husband) did not become an *encomendero* until Viceroy Mendoza assigned him Tilantongo in late 1535, ten years after his arrival in Mexico City. Francisco Vázquez de Coronado (doña Beatriz's husband) bought the rights to half of Teutenango, thirty-one miles southwest of Mexico City, and Cuzamala. Doña Beatriz brought half of Tlalpa in dowry to the marriage. Only Jorge de Alvarado (doña Luisa's husband) was an *encomendero* by virtue of being a first conqueror. Of his grants, the closest to Mexico City was Xochimilco, fifteen miles to the south-southeast. Alonso de Avalos Saavedra (husband of doña Francisca) shared the Provincia de Avalos with a brother who was a *regidor* of Puerto de Caballos, Honduras.

This family also had representation in public office. Alonso de Estrada arrived in New Spain as the royal treasurer and alternated as acting governor during the unsettled period between late October 1524 and June 1525 (see pages 16 and 17, Chapter 1 above). He was co-governor with Gonzalo de Salazar from February to August 1527 and then governor of New Spain until relieved by the first Audiencia in January 1529. Shortly after Estrada's death in 1530 he was replaced as royal treasurer by Juan Alonso de Sosa. Within a few months Sosa, as we have seen, married Estrada's daughter doña Ana. Sosa received an appointment as perpetual *regidor* of Mexico City and served in that office in addition to being royal treasurer in 1538, the same year that his brother-in-law Francisco Vázquez de Coronado became a *regidor*. Vázquez de Coronado continued as *regidor*, serving in 1539, 1542, and from 1545 until his death in 1554. In 1536 Sosa's sister, doña Juana de Sosa, became the bride of *poblador* and *regidor* don Luis de Castilla, a relative of the Marqués' second wife, doña Juana de Zúñiga. He served as her escort when she came to New Spain in 1530. Castilla's record as a *regidor* suggests relative independence from any particular political faction. Jorge de Alvarado and don Luis de Guzmán Saavedra appear to have eschewed public office.

Estrada's son-in-law and successor in office, Juan Alonso de Sosa, was the only member of the extended family, other than Estrada himself, to leave a record of actively pursuing business interests, and this was restricted to silver mining ventures in Taxco and Sultepec. Sosa held a quarter interest in a Sultepec venture with Segovia native and Mexico City *regidor* Lope de Samaniego, conqueror Juan de Burgos of Seville, who served as *alcalde ordinario* for three terms, and miner Diego Logroño. Samaniego sold his quarter interest in the company to miner Gabriel Ruiz in March 1537 for $4,125. None other than Hernando Cortés bought a quarter interest, for $12,000, in another Sultepec venture that also involved Sosa and the miner Logroño. During this same time frame Sosa paid $1,500 for a thirty-man Indian slave gang to work a claim near Taxco.

Estrada's cousins from Ciudad Real, *pobladores antiguos* Juan and Luis de la Torre, *poblador* Alonso de la Torre, and their sister doña María, must also be included as members of the extended family. Juan and Luis had arrived in the Indies in 1508 with don Diego Colón; after fifteen years in Santo Domingo performing (according to themselves) various duties for the crown, they joined the 1523 Estrada entourage as it passed through on the way to New Spain. Alonso and doña María were also members of the entourage, having joined it in Spain. Juan served as *regidor* on the Mexico City *cabildo* in 1525 and 1528 and as *alcalde ordinario* in 1526, 1527, and 1532. Luis was *regidor* in 1526 and 1527 and *alcalde ordinario* in 1528, 1538, and 1544. Luis also held the office of *alcalde de mesta* for 1539 and 1545.

Turning to a third family empire, first conqueror Bernaldino Vázquez de Tapia, a native of Oropesa, Toledo, and perpetual *regidor* of Mexico City, maintained a lower profile than did Comendador Cervantes and Alonso de Estrada, but he more than any other individual maintained the continuity of the *cabildo* of Mexico City, serving as *regidor* from 1524 to 1559. Vázquez was also an interim *alcalde ordinario*, finishing the unexpired terms of two incumbents who died in office. He influenced a segment of the *cabildo* through the men who married his nieces. Fellow first conqueror Antonio de Carvajal, a *regidor*, had married a niece of Vázquez de Tapia, doña Catalina de Tapia, in Spain before the conquest. When she died Carvajal married doña María de Olid y Viedma, another Vázquez de Tapia niece. Vázquez also arranged for doña María's sister, doña Isabel Vázquez, to marry *poblador regidor* Bernardino de Albornoz, a namesake nephew of the royal accountant. By the second half of the sixteenth century, the Vázquez de Tapia family was one of the most illustrious and best entrenched in all New Spain.

Conqueror Francisco de Orduña, a notary, was for a while in a position to exert influence in local government through arranged marriages. Two of his six daughters were married to members of the *cabildo* and three others wed prominent persons in Mexico City. One son-in-law, Jerónimo de la Mota, was *alcalde ordinario* seven times during the period and also served as a *regidor* one year. Francisco de Santa Cruz, another son-in-law, spent ten consecutive years in the *cabildo* as a *regidor* and then, after an absence of eight years, served as *alcalde ordinario*, followed by a term as *alcalde de mesta* (magistrate for common grazing land).

How extended families aimed for political influence can be seen in a limited way in Table 16. The Estrada family held the office of royal treasurer throughout the period and had representation in the Mexico City *cabildo* sporadically until 1545 and regularly thereafter, with Francisco Vázquez de Coronado exercising his office as *regidor* on a full-time basis. Comendador Leonel de Cervantes and his family took an active part in local government during only fourteen years of the period under consideration. Bernaldino Vázquez de Tapia, however, held office year in, year out, and the same was true for the husbands of his nieces who were also *regidores*. The Vázquez de Tapia influence builds during the early years; by 1541 it represents a solid 25 percent of the *cabildo* membership, and often 50 percent of the attendance. There is more to the Vázquez de Tapia dominance in the *cabildo* than can be presented in a chart. Not only did Vázquez de Tapia, Albornoz, and Carvajal hold perpetual position as Mexico City *regidores*, they faithfully exercised the offices held. A review of *Actas de Cabildo*, Volumes I through VI, shows that no other individuals were so regular in attendance. It is doubtful that such diligence was necessary to protect the positions they enjoyed in Mexico City society and government.

There were other consistent *regidores* in the *cabildo*. Worthy of note were Gonzalo Ruiz and Ruy González, but no more family coalitions developed. No individual or alliance even closely challenged the contributions of Bernaldino Vázquez de Tapia and his clique. The viceroy, the Audiencia, and the Marqués de Valle exerted social, political, and economic power through their own respective agencies. Vázquez de Tapia let his weight be felt through the *cabildo*.

But *encomenderos* sought to protect and to perpetuate themselves as a group in addition to forming cliques within the group. Within ten years after Mexico City had been captured, much of what was to remain New Spain had been explored and inventoried. Wealth in the form of mineral deposits, agricultural products, and Indian tribute had to be developed, and in order to be meaningful, had to be consistently forthcoming as well as abundant. This meant that new wealth had to be generated and what existed had to be divided into fewer portions. *Encomenderos* had to consolidate their holdings as best they could through family alliances.

During the time frame of this study at least 163 marriages took place, in addition to the matches arranged by the Estrada, Cervantes, Vázquez de Tapia, and Orduña families cited above, in which at least one party was or was to be an *encomendero*. In perhaps two-thirds of these marriages both parties were from *encomendero* families. Table 17 presents the data organized by category of seniority and relationship of the bride to an *encomendero*. Only twenty-one (15.7 percent) of the first conquerors married or remarried during the period of the study. While representing over 26 percent of all *encomenderos*, they contributed slightly more than 23 percent of the daughters for marriage within the group. Forty-eight percent of the widows who remarried had been spouses of first conquerors, and six out of eight of the nieces who married *encomenderos* in New Spain had uncles who accompanied the original Cortés *entrada*. First conquerors were twice as prone to marry a fellow *encomendero*'s daughter or niece as they were a widow, and first conquerors only married nieces of other first conquerors.

Conquerors enjoyed a slightly higher percentage of marriages and remarriages during the same period than first conquerors, and their wives were four times as likely to be daughters of *encomenderos*, primarily fellow conquerors, than to be widows. The conquerors were also party to marriages with four of the eight sisters presented for marriage. By the same token, conquerors supplied half the sisters who married, plus forty-seven of the eighty-six (54.6 percent) daughters contracting marriages with *encomenderos*. Seventeen of the thirty-two marriages were between conquerors and the daughters, sisters and widows of fellow conquerors, eight with kin of first conquerors, and six with those of *pobladores*, while one daughter of a *poblador antiguo* was matched with a conqueror.

As can be seen in Table 17, *pobladores antiguos* were the least active in the nuptials game. *Pobladores*, however, were involved in over 62 percent of all the marriages, though representing but 32 percent of the *encomenderos*. This group of 97 out of a total of 156 *pobladores* married 52 daughters of *encomenderos*, 37 (74 percent) of the widows and half (four each) of the sisters and the nieces, while contributing but 16 percent of the brides.

These data, for the most part, reinforce conclusions stated elsewhere in this study. *Pobladores antiguos* were on the average older men; except for one individual, they were seeking not wives, but rather brides for their sons and suitable matches for their daughters.

Table 16. Family Representation in Government

	1523	1524	1525	1526	1527	1528	1529	1530	1531	1532	1533	1534	1535	1536	1537	1538	1539	1540	1541	1542	1543	1544	1545	1546	1547	1548	1549	1550	1551	1552	1553	1554	1555
Estrada Family																																	
Alonso de Estrada	T	AG	AG	T	CG	G	T	T	—	—	—	—	—	—	—	—	—	—	—	—	—	—	—	—	—	—	—	—	—	—	—	—	—
Juan Alonso de Sosa	—	—	—	—	—	—	—	—	T	T	T	T	T	T	T	T	R	T	T	T	T	T	T	T	T	T	T	T	T	T	T	T	T
Francisco Vázquez de Coronado	—	—	R	AO	AO	R	—	—	—	—	—	—	—	—	R	R	R	R	—	R	—	R	—	R	R	—	—	—	—	—	—	—	—
Juan de la Torre	—	—	—	R	AO	AO	—	—	—	—	—	—	—	—	—	—	—	—	—	—	—	—	—	—	—	—	—	—	—	—	—	—	—
Luis de la Torre	—	—	—	R	R	AO	—	—	—	—	—	—	—	—	AO AM	AO AM	AO AM	—	—	—	—	AO AM	AO AM	—	—	—	—	—	—	—	—	—	—
Cervantes Family																																	
Leonel de Cervantes	—	AO AO	—	—	—	—	—	—	—	—	AO	—	—	—	—	—	—	—	—	—	—	—	—	—	—	—	—	—	—	—	—	—	—
Alonso de Villanueva Tordesillas	—	—	—	—	R	—	—	—	—	—	—	—	—	—	—	—	—	—	—	—	—	R	—	—	—	—	—	R	—	—	R	R	—
Alonso de Aguilar	—	—	—	—	—	—	—	—	—	—	—	AO	—	—	—	—	—	—	—	—	—	—	—	—	—	—	—	—	—	—	—	—	—
Juan Jaramillo de Salvatierra	—	R	R	AO	—	—	—	—	—	—	—	—	—	—	—	—	AO AM	—	—	—	—	—	—	—	—	—	—	—	—	—	—	—	—
Vázquez de Tapia Family																																	
Bernaldino Vázquez de Tapia	—	R	R	R	R	R	R	R	R	R	R	R	R	R	R	R	R	R	AO R	R	R	R	R	R	R	R	R AO	R	R	R	R	R	R
Bernardino de Albornoz	—	—	—	—	—	—	—	—	—	—	—	—	—	—	—	—	—	—	—	—	R	R	R	R	R	R	R	R	R	R	R	R	R
Antonio de Carvajal	—	R	R	—	R	—	—	—	—	—	AO	—	—	R	R	R	R	R	R	R	R	R	R	R	R	R	R	R	R	R	R	R	R
Orduña Family																																	
Francisco de Orduña	—	E	—	—	R	—	—	—	—	—	—	—	AO	—	—	—	—	—	—	—	—	—	—	—	—	—	—	—	—	—	—	—	—
Jerónimo Ruiz de la Mota	—	—	—	—	R	—	AO	—	—	—	—	—	—	—	AO AM	AO AM	AO AM	—	—	AO AM	AO AM	—	—	AO AM	AO AM	AO AM	AO AM	—	—	—	—	—	—
Francisco de Santa Cruz	—	—	R	R	R	R	R	R	R	R	R	R	—	R	R	—	—	—	—	—	—	—	AO AM	AO AM	AO AM	AO AM	—	—	—	—	—	—	—

T = treasurer; AG = acting governor; CG = co-governor; G = governor; R = regidor; AO = alcalde ordinario; AM = alcalde de mesta; E = escribano

In many respects first conquerors resembled the *pobladores antiguos* but were neither as old nor as successful elsewhere in the Indies. Only 21 of the 135 first conquerors acquired wives during this quarter century, most doing so within a few years after arriving in New Spain, and one-third of the brides were widows. First conquerors and *pobladores antiguos* can probably be best described as the last of the first generation of Europeans in the Indies.[4]

Conquerors, on the other hand, married an appreciably greater percentage of daughters (over 12 percent as opposed to just 8 percent for first conquerors and 3 percent for *pobladores antiguos*) and fewer widows (less than 3 percent compared to 6 percent for first conquerors). They, like first conquerors, represented mature individuals, but as a general rule they had fewer years in the Indies and less *entrada* experience, and were just a few years younger. They engendered more daughters to find suitable husbands for and left fewer widows. Many of this group could well be described as the vanguard of the second generation in the Indies.

If the conquerors spearheaded the second generation, then the *pobladores* were truly the main body. They married over 60 percent of the daughters, 75 percent of the widows, and half each of the sisters and nieces. While none of the *pobladores* took part in the events leading up to the capture of Mexico City, many served in subsequent *entradas* in New Spain. For such service, many were rewarded with *encomiendas*; they were considered more eligible for such an assignment if they had married to indicate a serious intent to remain in the province. What better candidates for brides could be found than the daughters of established *encomenderos*? It must be noted that these young ladies represented the majority of the marriageable European women in the region. All things considered, they were the preferred brides. However, if one's service and credentials were insufficient for an outright grant, there was a better and surer avenue to becoming an *encomendero*, and almost one-fourth (23.6 percent) of the *pobladores* took it. They married widows of established *encomenderos* and either managed the *encomienda* or acquired title to the grant. A number also served as guardians for the minor children of the late *encomendero*.

Such intermarriage between the categories of *encomenderos* does not necessarily lead to conclusions that there was social distance between husbands and wives. The nieces of *hidalgo* first conqueror Bernaldino Vázquez de Tapia married proper *hidalgos*, first conqueror Antonio de Carvajal and *poblador* Rodrigo de Albornoz, as did the daughters of Comendador Leonel de Cervantes. The notion that a plebeian *encomendero* enriched by a grant of *enco-*

		Married					
Encomendero		Daughter of Encomendero	Sister of Encomendero	Widow of Encomendero	Niece of Encomendero	Between Children of Encomenderos	Total
First conqueror	First conqueror	2	—	5	3	—	10
	Conqueror	8	—	2	—	1	11
	Poblador antiguo	—	—	—	—	—	—
	Poblador	1	—	—	—	—	1
		11	—	7	3	1	22
Conqueror	First conqueror	4	—	3	1	—	8
	Conqueror	12	3	2	—	2	19
	Poblador antiguo	1	—	—	—	—	1
	Poblador	5	1	—	—	1	7
		22	4	5	1	3	35
Poblador antiguo	First conqueror	—	—	1	—	1	2
	Conqueror	1	—	—	—	—	1
	Poblador antiguo	—	—	—	—	—	—
	Poblador	—	—	—	—	—	—
		1	—	1	—	1	3
Poblador	First conqueror	14	3	15	2	2	36
	Conqueror	26	1	14	1	1	43
	Poblador antiguo	3	—	2	—	1	6
	Poblador	9	—	6	1	2	18
		52	4	37	4	6	103
Totals		86	8	50	8	11	163

mienda was automatically in a position to attract a noble wife does not always follow. Those who took part in the conquest often as not married widows of their fallen comrades as well as daughters and nieces. *Pobladores*, not necessarily *hidalgos*, were most active in acquiring wives from among the widows, daughters, and nieces of *encomenderos*. In the first instance both conquistador and bride were often ennobled by elevation to *encomendero* status. In the latter, a plebeian groom was like as not ennobled by a marriage with a bride who herself was ennobled by the *encomienda* of a father, uncle, or deceased husband.

While instances of overt efforts to maintain *encomienda* succession within a family or among persons from the same European area can be found, often as not second and even third remarriages give the impression of random choice. The example of first conqueror Alvaro Maldonado *"el fiero"* shows regionality prevailing in remarriage and *encomienda* succession. Maldonado, a native of Salamanca, and his first wife, Juana de Castro, had at least one child, first conqueror Francisco Maldonado, who accompanied his father as a member of the Cortés *entrada*. Juana evidently died in Spain prior to Alvaro's departure. At any rate, he remarried in New Spain to María del Rincón, who came, documents imply, from Medina del Campo, a town less than fifty miles from Salamanca though in present-day Valladolid province. Two of Maldonado's four *encomiendas* were reassigned when he died ca. 1527, and the other two, near Veracruz, were inherited by María. The following year both were taken, one being reassigned while the other escheated. Perhaps three years later María married first conqueror Pedro Maldonado, also from Salamanca, although no direct relationship with Alvaro has been established; Pedro was the *encomendero* of seven *cabeceras* near Jalapa. María succeeded as *encomendera* when Pedro died ca. 1544 and shortly thereafter she married once again, this time to *hidalgo poblador encomendero* Gonzalo Rodríguez de Villafuerte, also from Salamanca. These grants were administered for her by Rodríguez until he died ca. 1575, whereupon they reverted to the crown. By Alvaro, María had a son who became a Franciscan, from the union with Pedro no children, and by Rodríguez a daughter.

Another example of successful *encomienda* retention in spite of remarriage, although with a weaker regional dimension, is that of conqueror Alonso Gutiérrez de Badajoz, who married a daughter of first conqueror Gonzalo Hernández Mosquera from Seville. She inherited the *encomienda*, a *cabecera* with at least sixteen dependencies, when Gutiérrez died ca. 1540. She then married *hidalgo poblador antiguo* Hontañón de Angulo, a native of Seville. After Angulo died she married in 1551 for a third time, to Asturian *hidalgo* Francisco de Temiño. Gutiérrez' granddaughter, María Mosquera, was the *encomendera* after 1597.

Marriage also had a way of alienating *encomienda* ownership, as in the case of conqueror Diego Garrido, a native of Huelva, who became a *vecino* of Colima and was assigned three grants nearby. His wife was Elvira de Arévalo, a daughter of fellow conqueror, *encomendero*, and Colima *vecino* Alonso de Arévalo from Badajoz. This pair had one child, a daughter named Catalina. Garrido died before 1545, and then Elvira married *poblador* Francisco Preciado from Molino de Aragón, Guadalajara, who then acquired title to the *encomienda*. He was succeeded by Juan Preciado, his son by Elvira, while Garrido's daughter Catalina was raised as a ward of a relative, Bartolomé Garrido. In this instance the *encomienda* successor was indeed the descendant of a conquest-period *encomendero* through his mother, although the grant he inherited was initially assigned to his mother's first husband.

A summary of remarriages of the widows of *encomenderos* is shown in Table 18. As can be seen, only five of the widows who remarried did so to men from the same European region of origin as their husbands. Andalusia provided the greatest number of first husbands of widows who remarried, as well as the most second husbands of widows. This is in keeping with the preponderance of emigration from Andalusia, but only three of these fifteen widows married men from that region. First conqueror Pablo Retamales' widow, Inés de Contreras, married *poblador* Diego de Escobedo; both her first and her second husbands were from Seville. Beatriz de Escobedo was the second wife of first conqueror Marcos Ruiz; again both were from Seville. When Marcos died ca. 1543 she remarried another Andalusian, but *poblador* Pedro de Fuentes was from Jerez de la Frontera in the Cádiz region, a town perhaps sixty miles to the south. When first conqueror Pedro Sánchez Farfán died ca. 1536, his widow, María de Estrada, succeeded as *encomendera*. Like Sánchez Farfán, she was a native of Seville, a sister of conqueror *encomendero* Francisco de Estrada. Her second husband was *poblador* Alonso Martín (Partidor) of Carmona, a town in the Seville region some twenty miles to the east and north of the city.

The two remarriages shown for widows from León to men from León involve the same widow in two succeeding marriages, and the example has been cited above in the case of María del Rincón and her three husbands, first conqueror Alvaro Maldonado, first conqueror Pedro Maldonado (who may have been related to Alvaro), and *poblador* Gonzalo Rodríguez de Villafuerte. Each of these men were natives of the city of Salamanca, while María appears to have been from nearby Medina del Campo in Valladolid.

Regionalism can be considered in one more remarriage of a widow. Isabel de Olmos, a daughter of conqueror Francisco de Olmos from Valladolid, married the Basque conqueror Juan de Zamudio in the late 1530s. She was a teenager and he, by that time, was in his forties. When Zamudio died in the 1540s, Isabel married *poblador* Alonso Velázquez from Portillo, Valladolid, the same city of origin as her father.

The 10 percent remarriage rate of widows to men originating in the same area of Iberia was bettered by daughters of *encomenderos*, but not by very much. Only 16 percent (fourteen out of eighty-six) married men from the natal region of the *encomendero* father. As shown in Table 19, Andalusia, Extremadura, and old Castile excepted, mate selection for daughters was almost as random, as far as regionality is concerned, as it was for widows. If the percentage of marriages between persons from the same present-day province or the same city is considered, the rate is even further reduced.

Encomenderos from Old Castile arranged the most marriages between their daughters and their fellows from the region. However, only two of the eight unions were between an *encomendero*'s daughter and a man from the same province or city, and one of these matches was a remarriage of a widow. The example, that of the daughter of conqueror Francisco de Olmos, was cited just above. The other match was between the daughter of conqueror Antonio de Maya and conqueror Juan de Cuéllar Verdugo, both from Segovia.

Of the five Andalusian regional marriages, three were between persons claiming the same province or city. First conqueror Diego de Coria, who married a daughter of conqueror Hernando de Chaves, and the daughter of conqueror Pedro Martín Aguado, married to *poblador antiguo* Juan Acedo, were all from Seville. Catalina Vélez Rascona, a daughter of conqueror García Vélez, married first conqueror Bartolomé Hernández de Nava, both natives of Palos.

Excepting the remarriage of Isabel de Olmos, the above-cited marriages were between men and the daughters of men who had been in the Indies prior to the capture of Mexico City. Two of the husbands were first conquerors, one a conqueror, and the remaining man a *poblador antiguo*. All of the women were daughters of conquerors. Five of the remaining marriages of *encomendero*'s daughters and men from the same Iberian region were also between people who had been in the Indies prior to the Mexico City campaign. Parties to these unions included the daughters of four conquerors and one *poblador antiguo*, who married two first conquerors and three conquerors. The other four daughters of *encomenderos* married *pobladores*.

Encomenderos who had more than one daughter to provide with a suitable dowry could not be choosy and seldom arranged matches with men from the region or province of origin, although there were exceptions. The two daughters of Hernán Sánchez de Hortigoza, who claimed only the region of Old Castile as his place of origin, married *pobladores* from the same region: García de Llerena was from Burgos and Gaspar de Avila from Avila. Only one of the two daughters of *poblador antiguo* Bartolomé de Perales, from Badajoz, married an Extremaduran. The other married a *poblador* from Cádiz, in Andalusia. Notary Francisco de Orduña, a Basque conqueror, married three of his six daughters to men from Burgos who took part in the conquest. Of the six other *encomenderos* who left record of more than one daughter, not one of their daughters married a man from the Spanish region claimed as the father's place of origin. Four of the six were first conquerors, one a conqueror, and the other a *poblador*.

Yet another category to be considered is that of marriages arranged between children of *encomenderos* (see Table 17 above, column "Between Children of *Encomenderos*"). The eleven examples shown, involving twenty or so families, occurred late in the period under study. These unions were primarily between families holding extensive *encomiendas* and can be viewed with some degree of certainty as a means of consolidating the most powerful families. Considerations of prestige and political influence were significant, but most, if not all, of these unions were contracted for specific economic reasons.

Another factor contributing to social integration among *encomenderos* was the sharing of *encomiendas*. As a means to distribute income among the worthy, governors often divided *encomiendas*. A favored justification for such action was that some communities were simply too large for one *encomendero*. While this may have been true, a more compelling reason is that the assignment of a very large *encomienda* to one man could well provide that individual with too great a concentration of power.

The usual *encomienda* division was between two men, but on occasion an exceptionally rich grant would be shared by three or perhaps even four *encomenderos*. In other instances an individual received tribute from fractions of several *encomiendas*. This scheme seemed to provide a way of achieving closer administration in remote areas, that is, the dominant *encomendero* relied on the other to manage the grant. Hernando Cortés used the device at least two

Table 18. Remarriage of Widows of Encomenderos by Region

Origin of Encomenderos Who Left Widows	Origin of Second Mates								
	Andalusia	Extremadura	New Castile	Old Castile	León	Biscay	Other Spain	Foreign Countries	Unknown	Total
Andalusia	3	1	2	2	2	1	2	—	2	15
Extremadura	1	—	—	—	—	—	—	—	1	2
New Castile	—	1	—	2	—	—	—	—	—	2
Old Castile	1	—	—	—	—	—	—	—	—	2
León	—	—	—	2	2	—	—	—	—	4
Biscay	2	—	—	1	—	—	1	—	—	4
Other Spain	3	—	—	—	—	—	—	—	1	4
Foreign countries	2	—	—	—	—	—	—	—	—	2
Unknown	4	1	1	2	2	—	—	1	4	15
Totals	16	3	3	9	6	1	3	1	8	50

Table 19. *Marriages of Daughters of Encomenderos by Region*

Origin of the Encomendero Fathers of Brides	Origin of Mates									
	Andalusia	Extremadura	New Castile	Old Castile	León	Biscay	Other Spain	Foreign Countries	Unknown	Total
Andalusia	5	3	1	2	—	2	2	3	2	20
Extremadura	2	1	1	1	—	—	—	—	1	6
New Castile	2	2	—	—	—	—	—	—	1	5
Old Castile	4	1	—	8	1	2	2	1	2	21
León	2	1	—	—	1	—	—	—	2	6
Biscay	1	—	—	5	—	—	—	—	—	6
Other Spain	—	—	—	2	—	—	1	—	5	8
Foreign countries	—	—	—	—	—	—	1	—	—	1
Unknown	1	5	—	2	1	1	2	—	1	13
Totals	17	13	2	20	3	5	8	4	14	86

Table 20. Encomienda Sharing by Region of Origin

Origin of Encomendero	Sharing Encomendero from							
	Andalusia	Extremadura	New Castile	Old Castile	León	Biscay	Other Spain	Foreign Countries	Unknown	Total
Andalusia	12	5	—	3	3	—	1	—	3	27
Extremadura	—	3	—	1	—	1	1	—	1	7
New Castile	3	—	1	1	—	—	1	—	—	6
Old Castile	4	1	—	2	—	—	—	—	1	8
León	2	—	1	—	—	—	—	—	—	3
Biscay	2	—	—	2	1	—	—	—	1	6
Other Spain	—	2	—	—	1	—	1	1	—	5
Foreign countries	1	—	—	—	—	—	—	—	1	2
Unknown	2	1	1	1	2	—	—	—	5	12
Totals	26	12	3	10	7	1	4	1	12	76

times. He shared one grant near Valles with first conqueror Alonso de Mendoza, a native of his own Medellín. Mendoza also served as a lieutenant governor of Pánuco for Cortés. *Poblador* Juan de Solís shared two grants near Pátzcuaro with Cortés. In both cases the grants were taken from Cortés and his partners by the first Audiencia. It took Mendoza eight years to become an *encomendero* again. Nothing more was heard from Solís.

Assignment of an *encomienda* to more than one individual moved in the direction of satisfying the crown's ambition of reducing the influence of *encomenderos*. A divided grant elicited divisive reporting on one peer's real or imagined wrongdoings concerning *encomienda* administration by the other. It encouraged vertical lines of communication, authority, and loyalty at the expense of mutual camaraderie among *encomenderos* as a group.

Shared *encomiendas* also tended to erode regional and provincial alliances. As shown in Table 20, less than 25 percent (eighteen of seventy-six) of joint grants were held by men from the same region. Although twelve *encomiendas* were shared by Andalusians, only one joint assignment included *encomenderos* from the same present-day province. They were brothers, Fernando and Pedro Villanueva of Jaén. There were, however, several grants shared by natives of the neighboring provinces of Seville-Huelva and Jaén-Córdoba. Local ties were somewhat stronger among those from Extremadura. In addition to the Cortés and Mendoza association cited above, the *poblador* brothers Alonso de Avalos Saavedra and Fernando de Saavedra shared six large *encomiendas* between Pátzcuaro and Guadalajara, collectively known as the Provincia de Avalos. The brothers, like Cortés and Mendoza, were from Medellín. The remaining Extremadurans holding a jointly assigned *encomienda* were conqueror García de Aguilar and first conqueror Francisco de Terrazas, both from Badajoz. The nature of Aguilar's affiliation with Cortés is not certain, but Terrazas was his *mayordomo,* and the Saavedra brothers were cousins. But these three examples represent less than half the shared grants assigned to Extremadurans.

The only joint *encomenderos* from New Castile were *poblador* Treasurer Alonso de Estrada and first conqueror Regidor Bernaldino Vázquez de Tapia, who shared Tlapa equally for a time. Estrada was a native of Ciudad Real, and Vázquez de Tapia came from Oropesa in the Toledo area. The other five from New Castile shared *encomiendas* with people from other regions.

The remaining *encomenderos* sharing grants with men from the same identifiable region were those from Old Castile. Conquerors Alonso de Contreras and Juan de Valdivieso were both from Burgos.

First conqueror Rodrigo Guipuzcoano, a second generation Basque from Valladolid, shared Milpa near Colima with Burgos native *poblador antiguo* Pedro de Santa Cruz. Brothers Ginés and Maya [*sic*] Martín shared a small grant near Pánuco, but their European origin has not been established. The remaining shared *encomienda* assignments appear to have been made with the same disregard of regional origins as the majority of marriages discussed above. The main criterion for joint *encomienda* assignment was clearly not regionality.

A final factor in shared *encomienda* assignment is that of the association of *encomenderos* by type, that is, first conqueror, conqueror, *poblador antiguo*, and *poblador* (excluding grants shared with the crown). The percentage of *encomenderos* party to coassigned grants ranged from slightly less than 20 percent of the *pobladores* to slightly more than 25 percent for first conquerors. The thirty-seven first conquerors who shared grants did so with ten other first conquerors, twelve conquerors, three *pobladores antiguos*, and twelve *pobladores*. Almost half of the forty conquerors party to coassigned grants shared them with fellow conquerors, with the remaining *encomiendas* held jointly with first conquerors and *pobladores* in equal proportions. Only seven *pobladores antiguos* shared *encomiendas;* they shared as many with first conquerors and *pobladores*, and one with a conqueror. The thirty-one *pobladores* shared *encomiendas* almost equally with first conquerors and conquerors (twelve and eleven, respectively), only three with *pobladores antiguos*, and five with fellow *pobladores*.

Thus social integration among *encomenderos* developed quite rapidly in New Spain and by diverse means. European regionalism was subordinated in marriage arrangements, *encomienda* assignments, and business partnerships to more locally oriented ties. Much the same thing was happening in terms of social prestige. It is true that a number of *encomenderos* sought marriages in which they traded a position acquired through conquest and income derived from *encomiendas* for higher lineage and a lesser financial endowment in the bride. But often one sees alliances between *encomendero* families who had only conquest credentials on both sides. The same trend toward using local criteria can be seen in the remarriages of widows as in the matches of the sons and daughters of the *encomenderos*. The practice of fractional *encomienda* assignment further reduced the significance of Spanish regional origins, requiring some sort of economic cooperation between *encomenderos* who arrived in New Spain at different times and under distinct circumstances. New interlocking family complexes were arising, understandable only in local terms, and sometimes topped off by local officeholding. By the end of the time frame of this study many *encomendero* families had built a multidimensional base for themselves which would allow them to retain their position in the country even as the *encomienda* as an institution declined.[5]

CHAPTER FIVE

Comparisons and Conclusions

New Spain and Peru Compared

The *encomenderos* of New Spain were but a part of the developing European presence in America. The conquest of Mexico was an extension of that of Cuba, which in turn was based in Hispaniola. Mexico then served as an intermediate area for the occupation of Guatemala and later, New Galicia. The southwestern corner of the Caribbean basin became another focus of Spanish interest, bringing a division of the exploratory thrust. The occupation of the Columbian-Panamanian coast was roughly contemporaneous with that of Cuba; it was followed by the conquest of Nicaragua at the same time as that of Guatemala from Mexico, and ultimately the occupation of Peru in the 1530s took place while New Galicia was coming under control in North America. The Spanish conquest of America proceeded along two parallel, simultaneous lines of expansion.

The first generation of Spaniards in Mexico thus invites comparison with its counterpart in the conquest of the area to the southeast. Such comparison must, of course, be carefully qualified. The single work on early Peru somewhat comparable to this one is James Lockhart's *The Men of Cajamarca*, which treats the lives of the 168 Spaniards who took part in the capture of the Inca Atahuallpa at Cajamarca on 16 November 1532. Lockhart's work is an in-depth study of a group that was together by design and participated in a single event, whereas the present effort deals with fewer than half the surviving conquerors of Mexico City plus a large number of men arriving in New Spain in the years afterwards. The Peruvianist work treats the complete membership of one conquering group, many of them very important people and most at least briefly *encomenderos*, but contains only a fraction of the total number of Peruvian *encomenderos* of the first generation. The present work is not complete

COMPARISONS AND CONCLUSIONS

on any one group of conquerors but does treat the great majority of the *encomenderos* of New Spain, a much larger number of subjects arriving over a longer period of time. Thus, full-scale comparisons of Mexico and Peru will not be possible until more and more similar works are written. Needed would be a work dealing exclusively with the lives of the conquerors of Mexico City, as well as a study of all the *encomenderos* of early Peru. For the moment, a comparison between the men of Cajamarca and the *encomenderos* of New Spain can give a preliminary notion of some trends in the two major regions of Spanish presence in America.

Similarities between the conquest and settlement of Mexico and Peru are many and are often overshadowed by the few but highly important differences. It is true that there was very little crossover of personnel between the group involved along the two watersheds of conquest, the one to Mexico by way of Cuba and the other to Peru through Central America.[1] These watersheds, as depicted by thrust lines on Map 6, were well established before 1515 and remained intact as routes and spheres of influence throughout the period of this study and long after. Santo Domingo in the time before 1518 was indeed a place for decision, for it was here (except for those already recruited in Spain for a particular destination) that one opted for either Central America or for Cuba. This is not to say that no crossing over took place at all. Conspicuous was the group of some 100 (including Bernal Díaz del Castillo) who, having followed Pedrarias de Avila as members of his entourage from Spain to Darién, left Central America for Cuba shortly after arrival there in 1514.[2] There seem to have been even fewer transfers between watersheds after the capture of Mexico City and prior to the opening up of Peru.[3] Another crossover, but subsequent to Cajamarca and Cuzco, was the invasion of Quito by Pedro de Alvarado and his band of Spaniards from Guatemala in 1534.[4] This infrequent moving between major areas of conquest can be partially explained by the advantages of seniority in any one place, even though it be quite marginal over becoming a later arrival elsewhere. There was very little for the individual to gain by a move unless there were special circumstances. Leaving one's position to join a conquest, once it had commenced, was generally counterproductive; unless one was a close associate of a leader in the new area and responding to an invitation, or chanced to become party to some truly spectacular event, chances of benefitting by relocating were very remote. Furthermore, there was no reason a bonanza could not be found quite close to where one happened to be until exploration proved otherwise.

In addition to depicting the thrust of the two separate water-

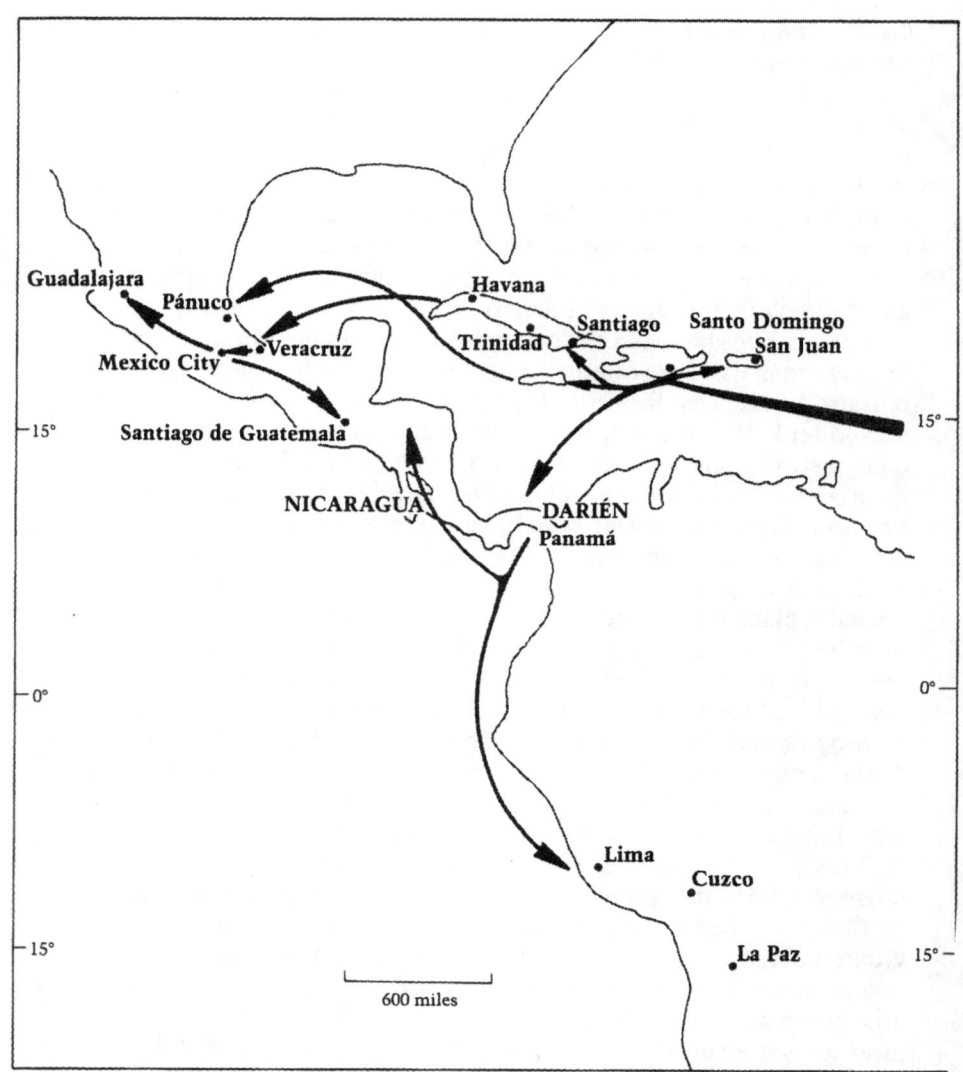

Map 6. Conquest Routes

sheds of Spanish conquest, Map 6 also illustrates relative distances from Santo Domingo to Peru and to Mexico. Prevailing Caribbean winds and ocean currents permitted direct sailing to both Veracruz and the north coast of Panama regardless of the time of year, with the latter closer to Santo Domingo by nearly 1,000 miles. This difference in distance meant from six to ten fewer days at sea under favorable conditions when enroute to Panama. However, those going to Mexico City faced only a week to ten days of overland travel to reach the destination, whereas those who opted for Peru had to endure an additional 1,600 miles at sea in the Pacific, bucking head winds and sailing against the current. This could mean as much as from forty-five to sixty additional days of travail before journey's end, and even more time and effort when the destination was inland. The trip to Mexico City was overall much quicker, easier, and less dangerous. As a consequence, Mexico City fell under much closer crown scrutiny than did Peru. Natural conditions also limited communications between Mexico and Peru along the Pacific coast. One indeed had to be motivated to leave one watershed of conquest for the other in the early years. The thrust lines of conquest became separate maritime, administrative, and commercial routes preventing other than occasional direct interaction between Mexico and South America.

The chronology of the conquests of Mexico and Peru adds weight to the notion that they were separate though parallel phenomena. Table 21 presents a chronology of landmark events of the two conquests, as well as indicating a comparison between the careers in the Indies of the respective leaders, Hernando Cortés and Francisco Pizarro. Both arrived in Santo Domingo in the very early days of the Caribbean experience, Pizarro preceding Cortés by some two years. Pizarro's seven-year stay in Hispaniola is shrouded, although it is known that his uncle, Juan Pizarro, was in the Indies at the same time.[5] Family connections, being from Cáceres-Trujillo like the governor, and maturity (he was about 24 years old when he first arrived in the Indies) stood Pizarro in good stead in consideration for positions of trust and command. Cortés, also from Extremadura, though from a somewhat different subregion, had his gentle birth and education to propel him ahead in spite of his youth. Ultimately both Pizarro and Cortés benefitted from seniority in the Indies. By the time they seized the opportunity to do great things, each had experience, local connections, a history of holding municipal office, and wealth from *encomiendas* and enterprises, in addition to more intangible assets such as leadership qualities.

Although the leaders of both the Mexican and Peruvian enter-

Table 21. Comparative Chronology of the Two Thrusts of Spanish Conquest

	General	Central America/Peru	Cuba/Mexico
1492–1502	Caribbean islands discovered, Santo Domingo established.		
1502	Comendador frey Nicolás de Ovando of Cáceres arrives with large expedition as governor of Hispaniola; Francisco Pizarro, about 24 years old, a member.		
1504	Hernando Cortés arrives in Santo Domingo at age 19.		
1504–1508		Alonso de Ojeda expeditions to Gulf of Urabá; Pizarro a captain at age 30 in 1508.	
1508	Puerto Rico invested.		
1509	Don Diego Colón arrives with fleet as governor of Hispaniola; Puerto Rico secured; Cortés an *escribano*, *encomendero*, and businessman in Azúa.		
1511			Cuba invested; Cortés a notary for the royal treasurer at 26, becomes *encomendero*, *alcalde* of Santiago de Baracoa, Cuba.
1513		Pacific Ocean sighted, Pizarro present.	Cuba secure.
1514		Pedrarias de Avila expedition to Darién.	100 of Darién colony to Cuba.

Year		
1517		Hernández de Córdoba coasts Yucatan.
1518		Grijalva coasts Yucatan and Gulf Coast to Cabo Rojo [N. of Tuxpan].
1519	Panama capital of Tierra Firme, Pizarro a *regidor* and *encomendero*.	Cortés *entrada* to Mexico.
1520		Narváez *entrada* to Mexico.
1521	Probes into Nicaragua from Panama.	Mexico City secure.
1522		*Entrada* to Coatzacoalcos.
1523	Gil González conquers Nicaragua.	*Entradas* to Zacatula and Pánuco; Pedro de Alvarado to Guatemala.
1524	Probes south toward Peru.	Cortés to Honduras, Colima conquered, acting governor turmoil.
1526	Second Peru expedition.	Cortés returns to Mexico City; Antequera established.
1527	Pizarro on Gallo Island.	Political stability.
1528	Coast of Peru reconnoitered, Pizarro goes to Spain.	Cortés goes to Spain.
1529		First Audiencia arrives.
1530	Pizarro to Panama with title of governor of Peru.	Cortés to Mexico with title of Marqués del Valle.
1531	Peru expedition underway.	Second Audiencia arrives; Nuño de Guzmán to New Galicia.
1532	Mainland Peru campaign; Atahuallpa captured at Cajamarca.	Guadalajara founded.

Table 21. (continued)

	General	Central America/Peru	Cuba/Mexico
1533		Almagro arrives; Atahuallpa executed; treasure distributed; Cuzco entered.	
1534		Cuzco secured; treasure distributed; Quito conquered; Alvarado invades.	
1535		Almagro to Chile.	Viceroy don Antonio de Mendoza arrives.
1536		Indian rebellion.	Cortés' South Sea expedition.
1537		Indian rebellion; civil war; Almagro executed.	Two ships sent for Pizarro relief.
1539		Valdivia to Chile.	Baja California *entrada*.
1540			Cortés to Spain; Vázquez de Coronado to Cíbola.
1541		Civil war; Pizarro assassinated, about 64 years old.	
1544		New Laws promulgated; Gonzalo Pizarro rebellion starts.	New Laws promulgated, but enforcement delayed.
1547			Cortés dies at age 62.

Table 22. *Comparison of the Regional Origins of the Conquerors of Mexico and Peru*

Region	General Emigration to 1550[a]	Encomenderos of New Spain[b]	Men of Cajamarca[c]
Andalusia	34.6%	25.3%	20.2%
Extremadura	15.8%	15.6%	21.4%
New Castile	11.7% ⎫	6.7% ⎫	8.9% ⎫
	⎬ 29.0%	⎬ 20.5%	⎬ 19.0%
Old Castile	17.3% ⎭	13.8% ⎭	10.1% ⎭
León	7.3%	8.1%	8.9%
Biscay	4.5%	2.8%	4.7%
Other Spain[d]	5.1%	6.7%	2.3%
Foreign countries	3.7%	3.8%	1.1%
Unknown	—	16.6%	22.0%
	100.0%	99.4%[e]	99.6%

[a] From Table 2, Chapter 2 above.
[b] From Table 3, Chapter 2 above.
[c] Lockhart, *The Men of Cajamarca*, 28.
[d] Combines Asturias, Galicia, Navarre, Aragón, Murcia, and the Canary Islands.
[e] The three Indian *encomenderos* have been deleted from this total.

prises were Extremaduran, the great majority of their followers were not. Table 22 shows the regional origins of the *encomenderos* of New Spain and the men of Cajamarca as compared with the general emigration to the Indies until the mid-sixteenth century. The emigration figures are based on licenses issued to leave Spain, while the percentages presented for the *encomenderos* of New Spain and the men of Cajamarca are based on the record of those actually on the ground in the Indies. But despite the difference in time, criterion of choice, and data base, some trends can be shown and some tentative conclusions drawn.

Persons from León are nearly equally represented in all three columns. Extremadurans had greater than normal representation at Cajamarca, due primarily to Pizarro's recruiting effort there prior to the Peruvian expedition.[6] General emigration from Extremadura during the 1520s and 1530s was only slightly up from previous decades (compare Table 2, Chapter 2 above). People from both the Castiles were underrepresented as *encomenderos* of New Spain and at Cajamarca when compared to the general emigration. Combining the percentages for these two regions in each column clarifies this underrepresentation. The Basques, though not faring well as *encomenderos* in Mexico, did hold their own in the percentages at Cajamarca. Those from other Spanish regions, as well as foreigners, while more conspicuous in percentages as Mexican *encomenderos*, were less well represented at Cajamarca. Andalusians, because they were in the Indies in greater numbers earliest, tended to remain in the Caribbean areas where they had a stake and as a consequence were underrepresented in both groups of conquerors.

Another basis for comparison, although equally imperfect, is the social standing and occupation of the participants in the two areas of Spanish conquest; such comparison is presented in Table 23. One immediately notices the differing percentages of *hidalgos* at Cajamarca and among the *encomenderos* of New Spain. Some of the difference can be attributed to different sources and procedures; we have seen how subjective a matter the identification of *hidalgos* can be. Insofar as the variance is substantive, it can best be explained as a characteristic of the time of each event. Relatively few *hidalgos* were in the Indies prior to Cortés' Mexican venture because there was little in the way of wealth or position to draw them from Europe. Nearly half (forty out of eighty-six) of the *hidalgo encomenderos* of New Spain were *pobladores*, arriving in the Indies after the region was under control and its potential had been announced to the world. During the ensuing ten years, this potential attracted a number of gentlemen, and as a consequence they have greater representation in Peru. Just a few individuals, Pizarro's brothers in particular, had a great effect on the percentages of *hidalgos* at Cajamarca, since the total group of the men of Cajamarca was little more than one-third the number of persons who were *encomenderos* of New Spain. If the percentage of *hidalgos* who took part in the conquest of Mexico City were known with any degree of accuracy, it would undoubtedly be even lower than that shown for the *encomenderos* of New Spain. Peruvian *encomenderos* during the period of Lockhart's *Spanish Peru*, that is, 1532 to 1560, would undoubtedly show a greater percentage of *hidalgos* than known to have been at Cajamarca. The potential for economic gain that drew *hidalgos* had also attracted specialists in commerce and business, and the Cajamarca roster reflects this. But in Peru as in Mexico, relatively few merchants either wanted or acquired *encomiendas*. Artisans, as well as those with artisan-like military trades, are also underrepresented as Mexican *encomenderos* when compared with the men of Cajamarca, and this too is to be expected. The men of Cajamarca were conquerors and the *encomenderos* of New Spain were reaping the benefit of conquest whether they had participated in the action

Table 23. Comparison of Social Standing and Occupation of Conquerors of Peru and Mexico

Calling	Cajamarca[a]	Encomenderos[b]
Hidalgos	38 (22.6%)	86 (17.00%)
Merchants and businessmen	13 (7.7%)	6 (1.19%)
Professionals	12 (7.1%)	33 (6.52%)
Artisans	19 (11.3%)	20 (3.95%)
Tratantes	—	2 (.39%)
Military	7 (4.1%)	8 (1.58%)
Mariners	2 (1.2%)	8 (1.58%)
Miners	—	4 (.79%)
Interpreters	—	5 (1.00%)
Indians	—	3 (.59%)
Not stated	77 (46.0%)	331 (65.41%)
	168 (100%)	506 (100%)

[a] Lockhart, *Men of Cajamarca*, 32 and 40. I have redistributed the information to conform with the categories used here.
[b] Table 5, Chapter 2 above.

or not. On the other hand, the difference between the two groups may not be as large as it seems; the sources for the economic activities of the Peruvian conquerors are considerably better. Miners, interpreters, and Indians as part of the *encomienda* scene in Mexico would not be represented at Cajamarca, nor were they.

In the matter of New World experience or *antigüedad*, compared in Table 24, the two groups are closely matched when considering those with more than five years of service. There is great divergence, however, for those with fewer than five years time in the Indies. This can be attributed in part to the different time periods and the criteria of choice for the two groups. In part the difference is probably an illusion, since the Peruvian unknowns are probably heavily weighted toward greenhorns. One would not ordinarily expect so many persons of little experience among a cumulative group of *encomenderos*. The situation in New Spain was strongly affected by the large number of persons who arrived in Cuba after Cortés and his original *entrada* departed, then joined Narváez and others, and got to New Spain opportunely.[7] The 158 newly arrived *encomenderos*, representing 31.3 percent of those receiving grants in New Spain, are the *pobladores* who came to the Indies from Europe after the capture of Mexico City. Although a few had "served the crown" else-

Table 24. Comparison of New World Experience of Conquerors of Mexico and Peru

Time in the Indies	Cajamarca	Encomenderos
25 years or more	1 (.6%)	1 (.2%)
20–24 years	7 (4.2%)	10 (2.0%)
15–19 years	2 (1.1%)	8 (1.6%)
10–14 years	14 (8.3%)	44 (8.8%)
5– 9 years	28 (16.7%)	76 (15.1%)
Under 5 years	12 (7.1%)	141 (27.9%)
Newly arrived	37 (22.0%)	158 (31.3%)
Unknown	67 (39.8%)	65 (12.7%)
	168 (99.8%)	503 (99.6%)*

*The three Indian *encomenderos* have been deleted from this total.

where in the Indies as well as in Europe or Africa, a number were assigned *encomiendas* for *entrada* service in Mexico. Others acquired grants because their social status demanded it.

The conquerors of Mexico received only a fraction of the precious metals awarded to either the men of Cajamarca or the conquerors of Cuzco. The initial lack of liquid wealth enhanced the thoroughness of immediate postconquest searches in New Spain and tended to keep the original conquerors in America. Few of the conquerors of Mexico City had the means to return to Spain as did almost half of the group at Cajamarca.[8] While a number of the *encomenderos* of New Spain made plans to return, they did so after nearly twenty years in America. Even though several actually liquidated their holdings, few ended up in Spain. Of the nineteen *encomenderos* leaving record of selling out, four actually left Mexico. One of them, after giving his grant to a niece in dowry, returned to Spain only to marry and then reappear in Mexico City two years later.[9] Conqueror Juan de Burgos sold his *encomiendas* to Francisco Vázquez de Coronado in 1538 but continued his mercantile activities in Mexico for a few years more. By 1547 he had died, never having left New Spain. We do not know what proportion of those who did not receive *encomiendas* returned or went elsewhere after the capture of Mexico City, but since they had even less liquid wealth overall, they too probably stayed in the New World.

Clergyman-conquerors, even though not normally in contention for *encomiendas*, played significant but subordinate roles in both

Mexico and Peru. Further, members of the orders were normally barred from individual shares of the treasure acquired by an expedition, while secular priests generally were not. This does not mean that the regular clergy went unrewarded. Those members of religious orders who accompanied the *entrada* to Mexico, however, were neither so well nor so soon compensated as those who went to Peru. After serving as chief ecclesiastic for the Peru expedition, the Dominican fray Vicente de Valverde received the bishopric of Cuzco (including all Peru). Papal bulls creating the diocese and naming the bishop were promulgated in January 1537, only two or so years after the provisional conclusion of the Peruvian conquest.[10] The regular clergy taking part in the conquest of Mexico received no such recognition. Neither fray Bartolomé de Olmedo, the official chaplain of the *entrada* and a Cortés retainer, nor fray Juan de las Varillas, both Mercedarians, received much more than an acknowledgment of their presence during the campaign. Fray Bartolomé was dead by 1525 and fray Juan, after accompanying Cortés to Honduras, appears to have remained in Chiapas.[11]

Secular clergymen were less restrained in both areas of Spanish conquest. Juan de Sosa, a man "involved in the things of the world" received shares of both silver and gold from the treasure of Cajamarca (although he was not physically present at the capture of the Inca Atahuallpa) and invested his wealth in a disastrous expedition to Veragua as its de facto chief.[12] A man of similar ambition in Mexico was Pedro de Villagrán, one of the two secular priests with Cortés in 1519. He returned to Spain in 1529 and acquired a position on the cathedral chapter of Seville.[13] Another secular clergyman with the original Cortés *entrada*, Juan Díaz from Seville, left no record of his activities after the capture of Mexico City, but it appears that he remained in Mexico City. He had been in the Indies since 1512 and was a member of the 1518 Grijalva expedition.[14] A third conquest-era secular priest in Mexico was Diego Velázquez, a nephew of Cuba's governor. He arrived in Mexico as a member of the Narváez *entrada* and went to Pánuco after the capture of Mexico City. By 1528 he was involved in a partnership with conqueror *encomendero* Pedro Lozano, collecting tithes for several other *encomenderos* from grants some 150 miles south of Mexico City.[15]

That the members of the regular clergy taking part in the conquest of Peru received recognition and honors far beyond what was given their counterparts in Mexico can be attributed to a number of factors, not the least of which is the relative wealth generated during the respective campaigns. The secular clergy responded according to individual drives. Sosa in Central and South America and Villagrán in Mexico used wealth acquired in their respective areas of action to further individual goals. Villagrán, while a less spectacular performer, was ultimately more successful. Diego Velázquez of Mexico functioned in a perfectly acceptable manner for a secular priest of the period. Only Juan Díaz, one of the four secular clergymen identified as such during the conquest, left no record of commercial activity and perhaps limited his activities to his vocation.

A long held belief that widows of *encomenderos* had to remarry or lose the *encomienda* was not borne out in this study inasmuch as only one out of three remarried and those who did more than likely did so as a matter of personal election. Of the remaining two-thirds, more than half held title in their own right, while the rest of the *encomiendas* went to sons or daughters. Then too, the pressure to remarry was not as strong where there was a possible legitimate minor heir. Furthermore, society in Mexico had matured and stabilized to the extent that during the decade before the promulgation of the New Laws there was some concern about the legal niceties of *encomienda* succession. In contrast, Peru during the same period was involved in civil war and Indian rebellion. The conquerors of Peru were not yet too concerned about such matters, since they were still actively competing for control of the new area and its assets.

This leads to what was perhaps the most remarkable difference between the first generation in the two colonies, other than the obvious issue of wealth: the relative tranquility in Mexico as opposed to the fifteen years of strife in Peru. Open rebellion in Mexico was short lived and amounted to little more than a riot when on 19 August 1525 the acting governors, Pero Almíndez Chirinos and Gonzalo de Salazar, attempted to take possession of the Cortés estate after proclaiming that he had died in Honduras. Only Cortés' cousin and *mayordomo*, Rodrigo de Paz, died in this episode, executed after failing in his defense of the absent governor's property. Even the negative influence of Nuño Beltrán de Guzmán was minor when compared to what happened in Peru. The civil wars started after the great Indian rebellion and siege of Cuzco of 1536–1537. The first face-off, known as the War of Salinas of 1537–1538, involved the Pizarros and Diego de Almagro and ended with the defeat and execution of the latter. Three years later the Almagrists assassinated Francisco Pizarro and then controlled much of Peru until defeated in the War of Chupas by Governor Vaca de Castro in 1542. Then in 1544 Francisco Pizarro's brother Gonzalo led a rebellion against the first viceroy, Blasco Núñez Vela, killing him in battle not far from Quito in 1546. Licenciado Pedro de la Gasca, president of the Audiencia, led the force that defeated and executed Gonzalo in 1548, thus ending the major rebellions by senior and powerful individuals. There were two subsequent flare-ups in 1553 and 1554, but nothing of the magnitude of the late 1530s and 1540s. Each of these wars brought on major redistribution of *encomiendas*, a phenomenon without a close Mexican parallel. Peru's wealth and remoteness resulted, apparently, in a far higher rate of *encomienda* turnover than in Mexico.

For the rest, it appears that the conquest and settling of Mexico and Peru were in many respects similar. Conquerors and settlers reflected the general emigration trends of the period. Minor anomalies include an underrepresentation of Andalusians and Castilians in both regions and more Extremadurans in the Peruvian conquering expedition than general emigration data would lead one to expect. Basques were fewer in Mexico, while reflecting the regional emigration average in Peru. Foreigners and persons from other than the major regions in central and southwestern Spain were adequately represented in Mexico but not so frequently encountered in the Peruvian expedition. The higher percentage of *hidalgos* in Peru reflects the time of the event within the overall chronology of the American conquest. The level of experience in the Indies for members of both the Mexico and Peru groups is remarkably similar, even for those with fewer than five years seniority when the *poblador encomenderos* (those coming directly from Europe) are discounted. The outstanding differences between the two watersheds of conquest can be reduced to the disparity in liquid wealth produced during the respective conquests, and the matter of distance from Spain and the Caribbean. Mexico was much nearer and, therefore, subjected to closer control much earlier, yet not as wealthy; both aspects contributed to a less rebellious ambiance. Peru lacked a strong crown influence in the early years and had an abundance of wealth both to motivate and to finance conflict. In the long run the differences in the indigenous populations and geography of the two regions were to become important, but that transcends the present topic.

Summation

Assignment of *encomiendas* based on conquest contributions created a new gentry in New Spain including individuals who, had it not been for the chance of time and place, would never have risen above their plebeian origins. By the end of the period under scrutiny in this study, the *encomenderos* as a group had consolidated and matured with the colony. The truly authentic nobles in Spanish peninsular terms retained social and economic supremacy through recognition often based on status rather than contribution. Many acquired *encomiendas* through royal connections, purchase, and marriage, and in the process they often upgraded otherwise plebeian associates. *Encomienda* society and economy, although centered in Mexico City, derived substantial sustenance from regional areas of native population in Pánuco, Oaxaca, and Colima as well as in the Valley of Mexico. The significance of those outlying areas waned in proportion to the decline in native populations, the low-altitude tropical regions suffering most.

Encomenderos were divided into two basic categories: conquerors (in the broader sense), those who took part in the siege and capture of Mexico City, and settlers, those who arrived later. Of those taking part in the conquest, the "first conquerors" were members of the original Cortés *entrada* and the simple "conquerors" arrived later with Pánfilo de Narváez and other reinforcing captains. Even though there were charges and countercharges as to which group was better rewarded, the number of *encomiendas* assigned per *encomendero* to each group was nearly equal (1.5 *encomiendas* per first conqueror as opposed to 1.57 for each conqueror). What remains to be determined, if it ever can be, is the actual value of each grant. Postconquest arrivals were also divided. The *pobladores antiguos*, a very small number of men who had spent some time in the Indies prior to the capture of Mexico City and provided logistical and financial support to the conquest, were in many respects identical to those who effected the conquest. The *pobladores* were those who arrived in the Indies directly from Europe after the Mexican capital had been secured. The *pobladores antiguos* held fewer grants per *encomendero* (1.25 *encomiendas* per *encomendero*) while the *pobladores* were on par with those who took part in the conquest (1.53 grants per *poblador*). The number of Indian *encomenderos* was insignificant.

European origins of the *encomenderos* generally correspond to general patterns of emigration seen in licenses issued for departure through Seville, Spain's gateway to the Indies. Those from Andalusia were less well represented in the ranks of the *encomenderos* in proportion to the emigration information that survives, but this can be expected when the social rank of many of the emigrants from this region is matched with *encomendero* prerequisites. Most of the sailors claimed Andalusian origins, as did merchants and shipowners. Only those who subordinated these callings during the conduct of the conquest received grants of Indians. Even then, the social standing of a seaman was such that he was normally excluded from consideration for *encomienda* assignment. As a result of Andalusia's location close to the port of exit, those from that region amounted to half or more of the total emigration from 1493 to 1509. Many had become well established in older communities in the Caribbean and were therefore not motivated to chance their positions for possible gains elsewhere. Consequently, Andalusians appear to have been underrepresented in Mexico in general, in the very first years, aside from being disadvantaged in the holding of *encomiendas*. Spaniards from the northern and eastern Iberian regions, Basques, and foreigners were few in number in the Mexican conquest *entradas* and were also quite underrepresented as *encomenderos* of New Spain.

Social standing strongly affected the assignment of *encomiendas*. Eighty-six, or about 17 percent of the *encomenderos* were *hidalgos*. They represented all classes of gentry from a few nobles entitled *don* to marginal *hidalgos* who could barely claim a relationship to a family of worth. Almost half (48 percent) of the *hidalgo encomenderos* arrived in New Spain after the capture of Mexico City as part of the 158 *pobladores* (who constituted about 31 percent of the *encomenderos*). While only about 12 percent of the first conquerors and 11 percent of the conquerors were *hidalgos*, almost 22 percent of the *pobladores antiguos* and over 25 percent of the *pobladores* were gentry. Additionally, several of the acknowledged *hidalgos* were practicing professionals, and most of the remaining professionals had at least vague noble pretentions. One of the professed merchants was a Portuguese nobleman, while the remainder of the merchants were either closely associated with Hernando Cortés or with mariners. Twenty artisans also became *encomenderos*, with over half serving in the conquest. Other *encomenderos* claimed various callings including military occupations, petty trade, mining, and interpreting, while the occupations of over 65 percent are not known. Most of this group surely were not *hidalgos*, but effectively erased the stigma of lower trades and plebeian origins by not identifying themselves with a particular calling. It seems likely that the majority of those failing to record their status were of lower or middling social origin, from families of humble agriculturalists, artisans, or at the most merchants, since had they been close enough to gentry, even to make oblique reference to nobility, they certainly would not have failed to do so.

The main cities of New Spain were founded, and thereby the settlement pattern for Spaniards essentially established, within thirteen years of the capture of Mexico City. All the surviving early Spanish towns and cities were superimposed on extant native population centers except Veracruz. Mexico City was overwhelmingly dominant; during the time frame of this study, 48 percent of the *en-*

comenderos (and 71 percent of the *hidalgos*) were *vecinos* of the capital. Other areas attracting Spanish settlements, including the Colima-Zacatula, the Pánuco-Valles, and the Antequera-Villa Alta complexes, were each centers of dense populations and distinct native cultural groups. Puebla, in this context, is considered within the sphere of Mexico City.

The patterns and conditions of being a *vecino* were different in New Spain when compared to South America and elsewhere in the Indies during the same period. For South America, in particular, the term *vecino* was synonymous in the conquest period with *encomendero*, and the *encomendero* had the legal obligation of residing in the city within whose jurisdiction his *encomienda* fell. The residence pattern in New Spain, however, was much affected by the country-wide dominance of Mexico City as the initial focus of all Spanish activity. It retained such status long after other regional cities had grown in size and importance and could have been considered well developed regional centers in their own right. The result was that for many purposes the Spaniards acted as though New Spain was not a set of independent city jurisdictions but rather a large single district, the hinterland of Mexico City. As a result, some 48 percent of the *encomenderos* claimed to be *vecinos* of the capital of New Spain. In the Peruvian orbit Lima too attracted *encomenderos*, but not, it seems, to the same extent.

We also saw that *encomiendas* tended to concentrate within seventy-five miles of Spanish settlements, a distance reflecting a three-day march for those on foot, or perhaps two days or less on the road for mounted travelers. Of the 767 grants identified in the study, 52 percent were within 75 miles of where the *encomendero* lived, with half the remainder no farther distant than 150 miles. About half the *encomiendas* were within reach of Mexico City, which helped reinforce its position as hub of all Spanish activity and the choice place of residence. Fifteen percent of the *encomiendas* were located at a distance of from 151 to 300 miles from the *encomendero*'s stated residence, and 5 percent were in excess of 300 miles. There were 29 grants more than 400 miles from the *encomendero*'s place of citizenship.

The city in which one was a *vecino* and the distance between where the *encomendero* lived and his *encomienda* were factors tempered by the practice of holding more than one grant of Indians. Fully one-third of the *encomenderos* (171) held more than one grant, and this group held slightly more than 56 percent of the *encomiendas*. Generally those with more than one *encomienda* had one grant within seventy-five miles and the other(s) more distant. The remaining two-thirds of the *encomenderos*, those with one grant, held but 44 percent of the *encomiendas*, and nearly three out of five of these grants were seventy-five miles or closer to where the holder was a *vecino*. When the settlement complexes other than Mexico City-Puebla are considered, this ratio of grants within seventy-five miles increases to about nine out of ten. Thus apparently the early and continued dominance of Mexico City as the *cabecera* of New Spain, dictated by its central location and its position as the political, economic, ecclesiastic, and social hub of the colony, was reinforced by the fact that the assignment of *encomiendas* in more than one jurisdiction permitted the holder the option of selecting where he would be a *vecino*. For nearly half the *encomenderos* of New Spain this meant Mexico City.

Encomienda retention by the family was an often-stated goal, and over two-thirds of the grants falling vacant during the time period of the study went to an heir. Of the nearly one-third that were not inherited, the crown acquired title to one-half through escheatment, and the remainder were either reassigned to awaiting worthies, many newly arrived to the Indies, or, as in the case of seventeen *encomiendas*, sold by the original holder to a new one. The succession pattern is not known for one-fourth of the 767 grants, most of which likely lapsed totally as being in areas of greatest indigenous population loss. Of the 349 *encomiendas* where succession information survives, over half (56 percent) went to a son. Widows inherited 91 (26 percent) of the 349 *encomiendas*, and 34 of these women retained title to the grant while leaving no record of remarrying. Thirty of the ninety-one grants were formally reassigned to second husbands when the *encomendera* remarried. There is no doubt that the second (or next, for a number of these ladies had a succession of mates) spouse in cases where the title was not transferred was in fact the administrator of the *encomienda*. These men often stood as legal guardian of minor children of the previous union. Daughters acquired *encomiendas* in over 18 percent of the successions, including the twelve receiving grants in dowry. Succession outside the normal inheritance scheme included one grant going to a mother, two to brothers, and two to nephews.

Encomienda retention and succession was but a part of the campaign of *encomenderos* to acquire and maintain social and political position. Noble *encomenderos*, some of whom arrived in New Spain as royal officers, moved to consolidate their positions within the social order through marriage contracts, either for themselves or for their children. Royal Treasurer Alonso de Estrada is an example of the successful, while Royal Inspector Pero Almíndez Chirinos is one who did not succeed. Comendador Miguel de Cervantes, not a royal officer, was successful in finding suitable mates for his six daughters. Five of *escribano* Francisco de Orduña's six daughters married influential members of the community, two of them Mexico City councilmen. First conqueror Bernaldino Vázquez de Tapia assured his own position and that of two other *regidores* by matches between the councilmen and his nieces. The three dominated the *cabildo* for much of the period of this study.[16]

In marriage arrangements and in other alliances, locally-oriented connections quickly took precedence over those based on Spanish regional origins. That is, the *encomendero* group and by extension Spanish society in Mexico was quick to consolidate and become a relatively autonomous or self-contained community with its own organization and criteria of rank. Of the fifty remarriages by widows of *encomenderos*, only five cases involved men from the same region of European origin as the first husband. Only 17 percent (fourteen out of eighty-six) of the daughters of *encomenderos* married men from the same European region claimed by the father. There were, of course, partial exceptions. Nearly one-third of the *encomenderos* from Andalusia arranged marriages between their daughters and men from the home region, while almost half of those from Old Castile did so. On the other hand, twelve of the thirteen daughters of *encomenderos* from Extremadura married men from regions other than that of their fathers. Grants shared between two or more *encomenderos* tended to dilute European regional ties further, with fewer than 25 percent of the shared *encomiendas* assigned to men from the same Spanish microregion, and even fewer from the same province.

Finally, this study strongly suggests that the conquest of Mexico, and a little later that of Peru, should not be considered too direct a continuation of the Iberian reconquest. In perspective this meant that even a very young veteran of the final siege at Granada would have been nearly fifty years old were he to have taken part in the capture of Mexico City and over sixty if he had participated at Cajamarca. By the time Mexico was invested, the leadership and the important captains had been in the Indies for some time and for the most part had no combat or administrative experience other than in the Caribbean. The few who were veterans of European wars were combat technicians and not leaders. Furthermore, the Iberian reconquest, especially during the closing years, was dominated directly by the crown and the nobility and had taken on the character of a crusade. The American conquest, by contrast, was secured by entrepreneurs who pursued economic motives.[17] The two major conquest areas, those of Mexico and Peru, while drawing on the same tactical and strategic base in the Caribbean, were separate in time as well as in space. Each built on previous American successes in two unrelated watersheds of Spanish enterprise. Then too, the *encomienda* institution, as modified to fit the Mexican reality, differed almost as much from its Antillian predecessor as the institution in the Caribbean islands differed from the Iberian model. The South American *encomienda* was also tailored to reflect that region. Separate realities were, in essence, mastered by using a common vocabulary of concepts and practices, but differed in order to accommodate local conditions.

PART TWO

The Individual *Encomenderos*

Introduction

Part One of this study discusses the *encomenderos* of New Spain as a group, looking at origins, social characteristics, times of arrival, and where possible, activities in the Indies, the number and location of grants, residence patterns, and *encomienda* succession. All such information is distilled from the following 506 individual biographies. A few of the *encomenderos* were cited in Part One as examples to illustrate particular aspects of the society in which the group lived. As it happens in this type of study, the examples selected are generally those who left a more complete documentary trail and are therefore more visible. Too much emphasis on these few, if not kept in perspective, makes them appear larger than life. Worse yet, it could wrongly appear that the few were following different norms than the rest. And patterns aside, it should be remembered that each of the *encomenderos* was at one time indeed a flesh-and-blood man; part of the intent of this section is to present information that humanizes the period and its actors.

Hernando Cortés, the conqueror and the Marqués del Valle, could easily dominate any discussion of the period. His total holdings, as well as political and economic power, place him in a class distinct from other *encomenderos*. Yet his actions as Marqués del Valle, as discussed for example in G. Micheal Riley's *Fernando Cortés and the Marquesado in Morelos, 1522–1547*, strongly suggest that apart from size, his estate and his procedures were in most respects similar to those of other *encomenderos* of the period. In view of the nearly limitless topic and his in some ways exceptional career, the capsule biography of Cortés (Number 105) addresses only the highlights of his career.

Nuño Beltrán de Guzmán (Number 190) had a short but dynamic trajectory in New Spain. His story is also better told elsewhere, by Donald E. Chipman in *Nuño de Guzmán and the Prov-*

ince of Pánuco in New Spain, 1518–1533. Guzmán's holdings and activities are addressed herein only briefly. The numerous crown *encomiendas* and the administrators thereof, plus grants assigned to ecclesiastical groups and the tributaries of the municipalities, have been left out of consideration entirely. These situations essentially represent the absence of an *encomendero*.

The following 506 individual biographies not only identify the *encomenderos* of New Spain during the first generation after the capture of Tenochtitlan but also provide as much personal data as could be gleaned from a number of sources. Only fragmentary information survives for some of the *encomenderos*; a few have left only a single citation to connect them with a grant of Indian tributaries. For others the data are contradictory. Still others leave sufficient record for one in our time to become fairly well acquainted with these residents of sixteenth-century New Spain.

The temptation to arrange the biographies according to seniority, that is, first conquerors, conquerors, *pobladores antiguos*, and *pobladores*, was suppressed in favor of straight alphabetical order for greater ease of reference. Rosters of each category are provided as appendices, as well as a listing of the place of residence of each *encomendero*.

A word concerning the format of the biographies. Each *encomendero* is alphabetized under the surname most commonly used in the sources. In some cases an individual had more than one surname, or there were variants of the name. The most common or basic surname is set in upper case with the less common form in parentheses, e.g., "Martín de la MEZQUITA (Montesinos). Whenever possible the city or village of European origin is shown, followed by the twentieth-century province shown in parentheses, as in "From: Ecija (Seville)."

Citations for the biographies are abbreviated as follows:

Actas	*Actas de cabildo de la ciudad de México.*
BAGN	*Boletín del Archivo General de la Nación, México.*
Aiton	Arthur S. Aiton, *Antonio de Mendoza, First Viceroy of New Spain.*
Bakewell	Peter J. Bakewell, *Silver Mining and Society in Colonial Mexico: Zacatecas, 1546–1700.*
Boyd-Bowman	Peter Boyd-Bowman, *Indice geobiográfico de cuarenta mil pobladores españoles de América en el siglo XVI.*

Cabeza de Vaca	Alvar Núñez Cabeza de Vaca, *Adventures in the Unknown Interior of America*.
Castro y Tosi	Norberto Castro y Tosi, "Verdadera paternidad de Alonso de Estrada," *Revista de Indias* 8 (1948): 1011–1026.
CDIO	*Colección de documentos inéditos relativos al descubrimiento, conquista y organización de las antiguas posesiones españolas de América y Oceanía*, Series 1.
Cerwin	Herbert Cerwin, *Bernal Díaz: Historian of the Conquest*.
Chipman	Donald E. Chipman, *Nuño de Guzmán and the Province of Pánuco in New Spain, 1518–1533*.
Conway	G. R. C. Conway, "Hernando Alonso, a Jewish Conquistador with Cortés in Mexico," *Publication of the American Jewish Historical Society*, No. 31.
Díaz del Castillo	Bernal Díaz del Castillo, *Historia verdadera de la conquista de la Nueva España*.
Dorantes de Carranza	Baltasar Dorantes de Carranza, *Sumaria relación de las cosas de la Nueva España*.
ENE	*Epistolario de Nueva España, 1505–1818*, Series 2.
Fernández del Castillo	Francisco Fernández del Castillo, *Tres conquistadores y pobladores de la Nueva España*.
Gardiner 1957	C. Harvey Gardiner, *Martín López, Conquistador Citizen of Mexico*.
Gardiner 1961	C. Harvey Gardiner, *The Constant Captain: Gonzalo de Sandoval*.
Gerhard 1972	Peter Gerhard, *A Guide to the Historical Geography of New Spain*.
Gerhard 1979	Peter Gerhard, *The Southeast Frontier of New Spain*.
Gerhard 1982	Peter Gerhard, *The North Frontier of New Spain*.
Gibson	Charles Gibson, *The Aztecs Under Spanish Rule*.
Gómara	Francisco López de Gómara, *Historia general de las Indias y la vida de Hernán Cortés*.
Greenleaf	Richard E. Greenleaf, *Zumárraga and the Mexican Inquisition, 1536–1543*.

Henige	David P. Henige, *Colonial Governors from the Fifteenth Century to the Present.*
Icaza	Francisco A. de Icaza, *Diccionario autobiográfico de conquistadores y pobladores de Nueva España.*
Liss	Peggy K. Liss, *Mexico Under Spain, 1521–1556.*
Lockhart and Otte	James Lockhart and Enrique Otte, eds., *Letters and People of the Spanish Indies, Sixteenth Century.*
Miranda	José Miranda, *La función económica del encomendero en los orígenes del régimen colonial (Nueva España, 1521–1531).*
Nobiliario	La Sociedad de Bibliofilos Españoles, *Nobiliario de conquistadores de Indias.*
Orozco y Berra	Manuel Orozco y Berra, *Los conquistadores de México.*
Pagden	A. R. Pagden, tr. and ed., *Hernán Cortés: Letters from Mexico.*
Pike	Ruth Pike, *Enterprise and Adventure: The Genoese in Seville and the Opening of the New World.*
Protocolos	Agustín Millares Carlo and José I. Mantecón, *Indice y extractos de los protocolos del Archivo de Notarías de México, D. F.*
Recinos	Adrián Recinos, *Pedro de Alvarado: Conquistador de México y Guatemala.*
Relación	*Relación particular y descripción de toda la Provincia del Santo Evangelio que es de la Orden de Sant Francisco en la Nueba España.*
Riley	G. Micheal Riley, *Fernando Cortés and the Marquesado in Morelos.*
Scholes and Adams	France V. Scholes and Eleanor B. Adams, *Relación de las encomiendas de indios hechas en Nueva España a los conquistadores y pobladores de ella—Año de 1564.*
Sauer	Carl O. Sauer, *Colima of New Spain in the Sixteenth Century.*
Simpson	Lesley Byrd Simpson, *The Encomienda in New Spain.*

The Biographies

1. Juan ACEDO
   Poblador Antiguo
   From: Sanlúcar la Mayor* (Seville)
   Parents: Antón García Calvo and Inés Alonso Acedo

   Poblador antiguo Acedo had served in Tierra Firme; he arrived in New Spain ca. 1523 as one of Garay's recruits for the Pánuco colony and later joined Nuño de Guzmán's Nueva Galicia *entrada*. Acedo was a *vecino* and *regidor* of Santisteban del Puerto, Pánuco. His *encomienda* included Tamasuchal and Tanzohol (some distance west of Pánuco; 917 tributaries in 1532), paying up to a claimed $100 per year. Acedo married a daughter of conqueror Pedro Martín Aguado and was the father of one son and two daughters. He was succeeded by his widow before his son came of age.

   *Also known as Sanlúcar de Alpechín.

   (Gerhard, 216; Scholes and Adams, 46; Boyd-Bowman, II, no. 8635, 267; Icaza, I, 238f.; Chipman, 292.)

2. Francisco del AGUILA
   Poblador Antiguo
   From: Avila
   Parents: Diego del Aguila and Juana Guillén

   Aguila arrived in New Spain ca. 1525 after spending some six years in Tierra Firme. He then took part in *entradas* to Nicaragua, Honduras, and Oaxaca before becoming a *vecino* of Villa Alta (Cipotecas). He was probably there under the patronage of Cortés. Malinaltepec, his nearby *encomienda*, a very small grant (so small that Aguila claimed it could not be assessed because there was nothing there to assess), was assigned as a result of his services in the conquest of the Zapotec in Oaxaca. In 1548, however, the *encomienda* consisted of five *barrios*. Aguila was married and maintained a *casa poblada* with arms and horses in Villa Alta. A son of the same name inherited the *encomienda* in the 1560s. By 1597 Malinaltepec was held by Diego Núñez Pinto.

   (Gerhard, 371; Icaza, I, 253; Scholes and Adams, 50; Boyd-Bowman, I, no. 115, 5.)

3. Alonso de AGUILAR (y Córdoba)—
   Hidalgo
   Poblador
   From: Burgillos (Seville)
   Parents: Gonzalo Sánchez and Leonor de Aguilar

   Aguilar arrived in New Spain in 1524 in the entourage of his father-in-law, conqueror Comendador Leonel de Cervantes, when the latter moved his entire household from Spain to Mexico City. He became a *vecino* of Mexico City and was assigned Olinalá (112 miles south of Mexico City; 1,669 tributaries in 1543 and 20 percent fewer by 1570) and Papalutla (20 miles west of Olinalá). Like many of his contemporaries, Aguilar formed companies to mine gold. His wife, doña Isabel de Lara, inherited Xalatlaco (36 miles southwest of Mexico City; considered a "medium" sized grant in 1564) from her mother in the 1560s. Aguilar died ca. 1550 and was succeeded by his oldest son, Baltasar. Olinalá and Papalutla reverted to the crown ca. 1566 as a result of Baltasar's conspiratory involvement with the second Marqués del Valle. Xalatlaco was reassigned to don Luis de Velasco during the 1570s.

(Gerhard, 112, 271, and 322f.; Icaza, I, 193; Scholes and Adams, 36; Boyd-Bowman, II, no. 8148, 253; Protocolos, I, no. 1188, 262 of 19 March 1528.)

4. Francisco de AGUILAR
   Conqueror—?
   From: Castillo de Villa Vega (Palencia)
   Parents: Juan de Aguilar and Magdalena de Manjarrés

Available evidence strongly suggests that this Aguilar arrived in the Indies in 1513 and later took part in the capture of Tenochtitlan. He received the first *caballería* granted by the Cabildo of Mexico City, located near Jalapa. He was later granted a second two leagues from the first on 1 December 1526. These grants were awarded to support an inn on the road between Veracruz and Mexico City. He was a *vecino* of Veracruz and the *encomendero* of one of the towns named Malinaltepec. After his death in the mid-1540s his widow married notary Pedro de Salazar, who served as guardian of Aguilar's four children as well as maintaining his *casa poblada*. Aguilar's oldest son became the *encomendero* when he reached legal age.

(Icaza, II, 86; Scholes and Adams, 50; Boyd-Bowman, I, no. 2437, 86; Protocolos, I, no. 45, 36 of 1 September 1525; Actas I, 57 and 63.)

5. García de AGUILAR
   Conqueror—Narváez
   From: Villafranca (Maestrazgo de León, Extremadura)
   Parents: Gonzalo García and Constanza González Jaramillo

Aguilar joined Cortés in 1520 after serving with Juan de Grijalva (1518) and arriving in New Spain with Pánfilo de Narváez. He established his residence in Puebla and shared Igualtepec and Ayusuchiquilzala (75 miles southeast of Puebla; two *sujetos* and three *estancias*) with Cortés' *mayordomo*, first conqueror Francisco de Terrazas. He married a Spanish woman in 1531 and their only child, a daughter named Juana, was born in 1535. Aguilar died ca. 1570 and was succeeded by Juana and her husband, Felipe de Arellano. Their son, Juan Ramírez, was the *encomendero* in 1604.

(Gerhard, 130f., 164 and 166; Icaza II, 49f.; Boyd-Bowman, I, no. 587, 20; Scholes and Adams, 16.)

6. Jerónimo de AGUILAR—Interpreter
   First Conqueror
   From: Ecija (Seville)

Aguilar, a relative of Licenciado Marcos de Aguilar, came to the Indies early enough to have gone to Tierra Firme with Nicuesa and Balboa in 1509. He was shipwrecked off the coast of Yucatan and was among the Maya from 1511 until he was recovered by the Cortés *entrada* at Cozumel in 1519. His services as an interpreter thereafter were of inestimable value. Aguilar was a *vecino* of Mexico City and an *encomendero* of Molongo and Malila (95 miles north-northeast of Mexico City; 40 *estancias* in 1571) and Sochicoatlan (107 miles north-northeast of Mexico City; 37 *sujetos*), both assigned him by Alonso de Estrada in 1526. Like a number of his contemporaries, Aguilar was trained as a religious but did not take final vows; nor did he marry. As he left no legal heir, his *encomiendas* reverted to the crown when he died in 1531. A natural daughter married Cristóbal Doria (de Oria?) of Sega, Guipúzcoa.

(Gerhard, 184, 186, and 243f.; Bernal Diáz, I, 78f.; Orozco y Berra, 74; Boyd-Bowman, I, no. 3040, 107; Icaza, II, 89f.; *Protocolos*, I, no. 95, 48f. and no. 1052, 238.)

7. **Juan de AGUILAR**
   Conqueror—Ponce de León
   From: Aguilar del Campo (Palencia)
   Parents: Pedro de Solórzano and Mari Díaz de Saldaña

   In Cuba by 1519, Aguilar came to New Spain on a ship owned by Adelantado Juan Ponce de León (under Narváez) and joined the Cortés *entrada* prior to the capture of Tenochtitlan. He became a *vecino* of Colima and acquired nearby Xicotlan, Xonacatlan, and Cuatecomatlan in *encomienda* from conqueror Manuel de Cáceres, a native of Segovia. Cáceres still retained three additional villages from his original grant. The *encomienda* probably had in excess of 1,000 tributaries when Aguilar acquired it, but by ca. 1550 that number had diminished to about 150. Aguilar was married and had seven children, one of them a daughter. He was succeeded by a son, Cristóbal de Solórzano, in 1550. The *encomienda* was still in private hands in 1597.

   (Gerhard, 80; Orozco y Berra, 72; Boyd-Bowman, I, no. 2410, 85 and no. 2911, 103; Icaza, I, 76.)

8. **Gabriel de AGUILERA—*Hidalgo Poblador***
   From: Porcuna (Jaén)
   Parents: Diego de Aguilera and Beatriz de Torres

   Aguilera arrived in New Spain in 1527, became a *vecino* of Mexico City, served in *entradas* against the Chontal and the Zapotec, and was awarded an *encomienda* in the Zapotec region by the first Audiencia. Years later, ca. 1547, he bought the rights to Guazalingo (106 miles north-northeast of Mexico City) from *poblador* Juan Rodríguez. Rodríguez had acquired the *encomienda* from a Diego González (possibly the same as the sacristan conqueror of that name who married in Cuba and by 1547 was a *vecino* of Puebla). At any rate, Aguilera considered the *encomiendas* too poor to support his preferred life style. Married ca. 1537, Aguilera had two sons and two daughters and maintained his *casa poblada*, arms, and horses in Mexico City. He was succeeded in 1569 by his son Diego. A Luis Hurtado de Mendoza was receiving the tribute to Guazalingo in the 1590s.

   (Gerhard, 243f.; Boyd-Bowman, II, no. 5732, 173; Icaza, I, 208.)

9. **Melchor de ALANÉS**
   First Conqueror
   From: Turuel (Aragón)
   Parents: Pedro Alavéz (Alanes) and Teresa Gómez Marín

   Alanés, in Cuba by 1517, was with Grijalva's 1518 expedition before joining the Cortés *entrada* of 1519. He was a *vecino* of Antequera, where he maintained his *casa poblada*, arms, and horse. His *encomienda* was Patlahuistlaguaca, a *sujeto* of Yanhuitlan (75 miles northwest of Antequera). By mid-1564 his grant was considered small, perhaps one-seventh of its original size. Alanés married a daughter of first conqueror Juan Rodríguez de Salas and sired ten children. He was succeeded before 1571 by his son, Francisco de Alanés Avendaño.

   (Gerhard, 285; Scholes and Adams, 19; Boyd-Bowman, I, no. 4255, 140; Icaza, I, 54; Orozco y Berra, 35.)

10. **Juan de ALBORNOZ**
    Poblador
    From: Talavera (Toledo)
    Parents: Rodrigo de Albornoz and Juana de Castro

    Poblador Albornoz arrived in New Spain ca. 1522 and took part in *entradas* to Pánuco and New Galicia, where he was a founding *vecino* of Purificación. By 1524 Cortés had assigned him the *encomienda* of Jacona (150 miles east of Purificación near Zamora in Michoacán). Pero Almíndez Chirinos took the grant for himself the following year. Perhaps the number of tributaries (4,361 in six subject *cabeceras* ca. 1546) was too enticing. Albornoz then became a *vecino* of Oaxaca, where he was *alguacil mayor* and *regidor* and maintained his *casa poblada*, arms, and horses, and made the musters. He also had towns in *encomienda* in Oaxaca, but their identity has been lost.

(Gerhard, 399f.; Boyd-Bowman, II, no. 11100, 331; Icaza, II, 201f.)

11. Rodrigo de ALBORNOZ—*Hidalgo*
Poblador
From: Paradinas (Salamanca)
Father: Bernardino de Albornoza

Albornoz had served as a secretary to emperor Charles V and supported the crown in the Comunero Revolt prior to his posting to New Spain as royal *contador* in 1521. He became a *vecino* of Mexico City upon arrival and served for a time as lieutenant governor. Returning to Spain ca. 1526, Albornoz was back in Mexico City in 1529. As an *encomendero* he received tribute from a number of towns, but his income from this source ended in 1544 under the provisions of the New Laws. His *encomiendas*, while they lasted, included Guasaltepec (260 miles east-southeast of Mexico City), assigned by the first Audiencia and held from 1529 to 1531; Atlatlauca-Totolapa-Tlaycapa (42 miles south-southeast of Mexico City), a grant that was contested by both Cortés and the crown but nonetheless held between 1538 and 1544; Charo (125 miles west of Mexico City), contested by Juan Fernández Infante but held between 1524 and 1526; half of Tlagualilpa (45 miles north of Mexico City); all of Tula; and Cempoala (180 miles east of Mexico City). The last three grants were held from the mid-1530s until 1544. Albornoz was married, had a son and a daughter, and maintained a *casa poblada* in Mexico City. He brought his niece, doña Catalina de Albornoz, to New Spain in 1522 to marry conqueror Pedro de Bazán. Two years later he brought Catalina's brother, Bernardino de Albornoz, who then married doña Isabel Vázquez, a niece of first conqueror Bernaldino Vázquez de Tapia, a Mexico City *regidor*. Bernardino de Albornoz later became a *regidor* of Mexico City.

(Gerhard, 86, 103, 106f., 207, 332 and 363; Boyd-Bowman, II, no. 7356, 227; Icaza, I, 221f. and II, 16 and 22.)

12. Bartolomé de ALCÁNTARA
Poblador
From: Bembibre (León)
Parents: Hernán Martínez and Ana González

Alcántara arrived in New Spain ca. 1523 and served in *entradas* to Pánuco, Cipotecas, Chontales, and Tiltepec. He became a *vecino* of Villa Alta and *encomendero* of Tlapanala, twenty-eight miles to the northwest. It was considered a small grant in 1564. Alcántara was married and had four sons and three daughters. One daughter married Diego Argumendo, a native of Puerto de Santa María near Cádiz, and another married *poblador* Alvaro Manzano of Beas, fourteen miles north of Huelva. Both men were *vecinos* of Villa Alta. Alcántara was succeeded by a son, Daniel, in the 1560s.

(Gerhard, 372; Scholes and Adams, 22; Boyd-Bowman, II no. 5867, 177 and no. 5071, 151; Icaza, I, 256f. and II, 225 and 228.)

13. Juan de ALMESTO
Poblador
From: Seville
Parents: Juan de Almesto Ribadeneyra and Isabel Hernández Guerrero

Although Almesto was a native of Seville, both of his parents were born in León. He arrived in New Spain in 1521, too late to take part in the capture of Tenochtitlan. He joined *entradas* that took him to Michoacán, Colima, Motín, and Jalisco. Almesto and an unnamed brother became *vecinos* of Purificación, Nueva Galicia. He was the first *encomendero* of Popoyutla (63 miles east-southeast of Purificación, near Colima), which consisted of "100 Indians more at war than peace who never provided more than $3." The grant, with all of its shortcomings, must have been too good to renounce, however, because Almesto was succeeded first by a daughter married to Bartolomé Sánchez ca. 1550 and then by his son in the 1560s who by then had evidently come of age. Popoyutla was still in private hands in 1597.

(Gerhard, 80; Boyd-Bowman, II, no. 8709, 269; Icaza, I, 261f.)

14. Pero ALMÍNDEZ Chirinos—*Hidalgo Poblador*
From: Ubeda (Jaén)

Almíndez became a *vecino* of Mexico City upon his arrival in New Spain as inspector of the royal treasury (*veedor*) in 1524. Cortés assigned him the tribute from Tepeaca (87 miles east-southeast of Mexico City; 73 *estancias* in 1580). Alonso de Estrada, as acting governor in 1526, took this income for himself but Almíndez recovered the grant later the same year and continued to hold it until the *encomienda* reverted to the crown under the New Laws of 1542. While acting as one of the co-governors in 1525 Almíndez appropriated for himself the tribute of Xacona (320 miles west of Mexico City near Zamora in Michoacán) from Juan de Albornoz. This same *encomienda* was acquired two years later by Gonzalo de Sandoval and then returned to Almíndez in 1528 when Sandoval departed for Spain. Under the New Laws the crown took these tributes as it did with Tepeaca. Xacona more than likely paid well. In 1546 it still had 4,361 tributaries. There is every indication that Almíndez' return to Spain in 1544 was motivated by losing this income as well as by advancing years.

(Gerhard, 278, 280 and 399f.; Boyd-Bowman, II, no. 5761, 174.)

15. Diego de ALMODÓVAR
Poblador
From: **Almodóvar del Campo (Ciudad Real)**
Parents: Pedro de Almodóvar and Inés Díaz

Almodóvar arrived in New Spain in 1530 and joined Cortés' Baja California *entrada* before becoming a *vecino* of Colima. By 1550 he was the *encomendero* of nearby Aquixtlan. His wife was a daughter of conqueror Antón López.

(Gerhard, 80; Boyd-Bowman, II, no. 3600, 106; Icaza, II, 82.)

16. Hernando ALONSO—Blacksmith
First Conqueror
From: **Niebla (Huelva)**

Alonso was in Cuba in 1515, a member of the Cortés *entrada* four years later, and a founding *vecino* of Mexico City after it had been captured. He was about sixty years old at the time of the siege. Although identified as a blacksmith, Alonso had advanced far beyond the practice of his trade in New Spain. He seems to have had a financial interest in every income-producing venture in Mexico City. He consistently got the slaughterhouse franchise, had pig and cattle raising partnerships, loaned money, invested his *encomienda* Indians in mining partnerships, and worked the real estate market by buying and selling houses and lots. Alonso was the *encomendero* of Actopan (62 miles north of Mexico City, 33 miles north-northwest of Pachuca; 8,000 tributaries in 1570), shared Guaniqueo (160 miles west of Mexico City, 33 miles north-northeast of Pátzcuaro; 44 *estancias* in 1524, 14 *barrios* in 1548) with first conqueror Marcos Ruiz (Rodríguez) of Seville (Juan Mateos was their steward in this *pueblo*), and one-half of Pungaravato (160 miles southwest of Mexico City, 75 miles west of Iguala; 13 *estancias* in 1548), reassigned from Juan Velázquez to Alonso and *poblador* Pedro de Bazán of Badajoz before 1528.

Alonso's first wife was Beatriz de Ordaz, a sister of first conqueror Diego de

Ordaz. They had adult children born elsewhere, living in New Spain. When Beatriz died during the siege (she was a member of the *entrada*), Alonso remarried, but this wife died shortly thereafter. He then married Isabel de Aguilar and with her had a daughter. After Alonso was executed on 17 October 1528 (at age 68) as a relapsed Jew, Isabel married conqueror Juan de la Gama. Actopan appears to have been reassigned to Rodrigo Gómez de Avila. Guaniqueo was taken from the partnership and reassigned to Cortés, and Bazán was given Alonso's share of Pungaravato. Alonso's hasty *auto de fe* and execution suggest motives other than a quest for religious orthodoxy on the part of the authorities in Mexico City. It seems that Alonso had exceeded acceptable limits of upward mobility and had to be taken care of.

Note: Alonso also had the meat concession in Cuba.

(Gómara, 21; Gerhard, 44f., 135f., 345, and 351; Boyd-Bowman, I, no. 894, 209, and no. 1872, 64 and II, no. 5163, 154; Greenleaf, 90f.; Orozco y Berra, 44; Conway, 9–26.)

17. **Rodrigo ALONSO**
    Poblador

Little is known about Alonso other than the presumption that he was a *poblador* and a *vecino* of Colima. He held half of Tenamastlan (52 miles north-northwest of Colima) from 1526 until his death in 1528. The other half was held by conqueror Pedro Gómez. Martín Monje, also a conqueror, was assigned the Alonso share after 1528.

(Gerhard, 60.)

18. **Licenciado Juan Gutiérrez ALTAMIRANO**—*Hidalgo*
    Poblador
    From: Paradinas (Salamanca)
    Parents: Hernán Gutierrez Altamirano and doña Teresa Carrillo

Licenciado Altamirano, thought by some to be at least a distant relative of Cortés, arrived in Cuba in 1524 and served there for two years as a lieutenant governor and *residencia* judge before moving to Mexico City in 1527 and becoming a *vecino* there. In 1529 he represented Cortés in actions before the first Audiencia. His *encomiendas*, thirty to thirty-five miles west-southwest of Mexico City and south of Toluca, included Metepec (five or six *estancias* in 1569), and the paired *cabeceras* of Tepemaxalco and Calimaya. The tribute from these communities was claimed by Cortés but assigned to Altamirano ca. 1527. Between 1528 and 1536 the tribute went in succession to Altamirano, Lope de Samaniego, Cristóbal de Cisneros, and Alonso de Avila. Altamirano was the *encomendero* again from 1536 on. He was Cortés' chief *mayordomo* from 1528 to 1530 and governor of the Marquesado from 1534 to 1536 and again from 1539 to 1549. His first wife was Mencia Maldonado, who bore him at least one child, a son named Juan Altamirano. Around 1530 he remarried in Mexico City, to doña Juana Altamirano of Medellín. Altamirano was succeeded by their son, Hernán Gutiérrez Altamirano, in 1558. *Encomienda* successors thereafter were grandson Juan Gutiérrez Altamirano ca. 1564 and a great-grandson, don Fernando Altamirano y Velasco in 1610. The last named became the first Count of Santiago de Calimaya. Tribute went to his heirs into the eighteenth century.

(Gerhard, 175f. and 271f.; Scholes and Adams, 31; Boyd-Bowman, I, no. 443, 15 and II, no. 7362, 228 and no. 1463, 42; Icaza, I, 186; Riley, 154.)

19. **Gonzalo de ALVARADO**—*Hidalgo*
    First Conqueror
    From: Badajoz
    Parents: Gómez de Alvarado, Caballero de Santiago, and doña Leonor de Contreras

The third oldest of the five legitimate Alvarado brothers, Gonzalo arrived in Santo Domingo in 1510 with three of these siblings and a natural half-brother, went to Cuba in 1518, took part in the conquest of Mexico City with Cortés, and then went in 1524 to Guatemala, where he stayed until 1541 as *alguacil mayor* of Santiago. Gonzalo was the first *encomendero* of Teposcolula (87 miles northwest of Antequera) and held it until it was reassigned in 1529 to Juan Peláez de Berrio, *alcalde mayor* of Antequera.

Note: The Alvarado brothers were from a well-established Badajoz family. Their father, Gómez de Alvarado, was a Caballero de Santiago, and an uncle, Diego de Alvarado, was Comendador de Lobón of the same order. Their paternal grandfather, Juan de Alvarado *"el viejo,"* was Comendador de Hornachos, Order of Santiago. An older half-sister by Gómez' first wife, (doña?) Teresa Suárez de Moscoso, also married a *comendador* of the order. Gómez' second wife, doña Leonor de Contreras, was from Santander. Pedro, the oldest son and a twin sister Sarra were born in 1485, the same year as Hernando Cortés' birth. The other legitimate sons in order of birth were Jorge, Gonzalo, Gómez and Juan *"el mozo."* A natural son, also called Juan *"el viejo,"* died in a shipwreck off Cuba ca. 1520. He appears to have been several years older than Pedro. Although Gómez took part in the capture of Mexico City, he was not assigned an *encomienda* in New Spain. Juan *"el mozo"* received a license on 22 September 1511 to leave Spain; there is no record of his joining his brothers.

(Gerhard, 286; Boyd-Bowman, I, no. 255, nos. 256, 257–260, 10; Orozco y Berra, 75; Recinos, 9–11.)

20. Jorge de ALVARADO—*Hidalgo*
First Conqueror
From: Badajoz
Parents: Gómez de Alvarado, Caballero de Santiago, and doña Leonor de Contreras

Jorge, the second oldest of the Alvarado brothers, arrived in Santo Domingo in 1510, took part in the conquest of Cuba, was with Grijalva on the coast of Mexico in 1518 and, along with three of his brothers (and a half-brother who died during this period), joined with Cortés in the conquest of Tenochtitlan. He then took part in *entradas* to Pánuco, Oaxaca, Tehuantepec, Soconusco, and went on to Guatemala in 1527. Jorge was considered a *vecino* of Mexico City as well as Santiago de Guatemala, where he spent much time managing the affairs of Pedro, his governor brother. At any rate, he was living in Mexico City between August 1536 and April 1537. His *encomiendas* in New Spain included Guaquechula (60 miles southeast of Mexico City, 18 miles north-northeast of Izúcar), Tepapayeca (71 miles southeast of Mexico City, 6 miles northwest of Izúcar), half the tributes from Guazpaltepeque (261 miles southeast of Mexico City, 90 miles south of Alvarado) and Sochimilco (15 miles south-southeast of Mexico City). Guaquechula had about 12,000 tributaries and Guazpaltepeque 80,000 at contact. Sochimilco had perhaps fifteen *visitas* with a total of 5,000 tributaries in 1535. There were but 4,000 total tributaries in the 1560s. Sochimilco had perhaps fifteen *visitas* with a total of 5,000 tributaries in 1535. Tepapayeca was initially assigned to Jorge's brother Pedro. Viceroy Mendoza reassigned it to Jorge's widow, doña Luisa de Estrada, in 1541. She was then a resident of Mexico City. Jorge and doña Luisa had three children—a son don Jorge, and two daughters. Don Jorge succeeded as *encomendero* of all his father's holdings, plus the grant assigned to his mother. He in turn was succeeded in 1563 by a son, also named don Jorge.

(Gerhard, 56f., 86f., 160 and 245; Scholes and Adams, 32; Boyd-Bowman, I, no. 259, 10; Orozco y Berra, 75; Icaza, I, 103f.; *Protocolos*, II, no. 1847, 29 of 4 August 1536 and no. 2277, 124 of 17 April 1537; Recinos, 10f.; *Relación*, 10f.)

21. Juan de ALVARADO—*Hidalgo*
Poblador
From: Badajoz
Parents: Comendador García de Alvarado and doña Beatriz de Tordoya

Alvarado arrived in New Spain ca. 1524, took part in the New Galicia *entrada* with Francisco Cortés in 1530, and became a *vecino* of Ciudad Michoacán, near his *encomienda*, Tiripitio (20 miles east of Pátzcuaro). This award still had eleven or twelve *sujetos* as late as 1594, indicating its substantial size at contact. Tiripitio was originally held by Hernando Cortés but taken for the crown in 1528. Viceroy Mendoza assigned the *encomienda* to Alvarado in 1537. The grant reverted to the crown when he died, still a bachelor, ca. 1550. Alvarado was doubtless related to the four Alvarado brothers, but evidence to establish the connection definitely is lacking.

(Gerhard, 345 and 352; Boyd-Bowman, II, no. 783, 25; Icaza, II, 12f.)

22. Pedro de ALVARADO—*Hidalgo*
First Conqueror
From: Badajoz
Parents: Gómez de Alvarado, Caballero de Santiago, and doña Leonor de Contreras

Pedro was the oldest of the five (four legitimate and one natural) Alvarado brothers who arrived in Santo Domingo in 1510. A younger brother received a license to join them in the Indies the following year. He went to Cuba in 1518 and was joined by his brother Jorge on Grijalva's expedition of exploration along the coast of Mexico. Pedro was captain of one of the four ships, the others being Grijalva, Francisco de Montejo, and Alonso de Avila. All of the Alvarado brothers were members of Cortés' 1519 *entrada*. After the capture of Tenochtitlan, Pedro served in leadership positions in *entradas* to Pánuco and Guatemala before returning to Spain during 1526 and 1527. He was back in Mexico the following year with the title governor of Guatemala, went to Guatemala in 1530, spent 1534 in Peru, was in Guatemala again in 1538 and 1539, and then in 1541 was in New Galicia, where he died. His *encomiendas* in New Spain included Tututepec and Xalapa (210 miles south of Mexico City, 60 miles east of Acapulco), assigned by Cortés in 1522 and reassigned to Diego de Olvera and Pedro Lozano in 1528; Izúcar (75 miles southeast of Mexico City), assigned by Cortés in 1522, impounded by the first Audiencia in 1529 but later restored to Alvarado; Tepapayeca, a *sujeto* of Izúcar, which was reassigned to Pedro's sister-in-law, Jorge's widow, by Viceroy Mendoza in 1541; and Sochimilco (14 miles south-southeast of Mexico City), also awarded by Cortés in 1522. For a while in the 1530s income from these grants went to Pedro's brother Jorge. Pedro was married, but had no children except for a natural daughter by an Indian woman. All of his *encomiendas* in New Spain, other than Tepapayeca, reverted to the crown when both he and his wife died in 1541.

(Gerhard, 149, 160 and 145; Boyd-Bowman, I, no. 260, 10; Orozco y Berra, 75; Icaza, I, 103; Diaz del Castillo I, 58; Recinos, 10f.)

23. Pedro de ARAGÓN—Blacksmith
Poblador
From: Aragón

Aragón went with Pedro de Alvarado to Guatemala in 1524, became a *vecino* of Santiago the same year, and then returned to New Spain to take part in the conquest of the Zapotecs in Oaxaca. He was awarded Iztepexi (228 miles southeast of Mexico City near Antequera), probably ca. 1526. This grant still had five *estancias* in 1548, after various epidemics and emigrations. By 1528 Aragón was a *vecino* of Mexico City. He was succeeded by a son, Juan de Aragón, but by 1554 the *encomienda* was a crown holding.

(Gerhard, 158; Boyd-Bowman, II, no. 12946, 391; Orozco y Berra, 98.)

24. Alonso de ARÉVALO
Conqueror—Narváez
From: Berlanga (Badajoz)
Parents: Licenciado Pedro de Arévalo and Marina Temeño

Arévalo arrived in Cuba in 1517 and held a *repartimiento* there, went with Grijalva in 1518, and used the Narváez *entrada* to get to New Spain to take part in the capture of Tenochtitlan. He then served with *entradas* to Pánuco, Zacatula, and Jalisco. In the 1520s Arévalo was assigned the *encomiendas* of Xolotlan (45 miles southeast of Colima) and Miaguatlan (30 miles northeast of Colima) and became a *vecino* of Colima. He and his wife, Beatriz López, had two sons and a daughter, Elvira. She first married conqueror Diego Garrido and later Francisco Preciado. Arévalo died in 1547; his widow held his grants until 1552, when their son Pedro inherited. The *encomiendas* paid less than $120 per year ca. 1550.

(Gerhard, 193 and 339; Boyd-Bowman, I, no. 314, 12; Orozco y Berra, 57; Icaza, I, 112 and 178.)

25. Melchor de ARÉVALO
Conqueror—Narváez
From: Arévalo (Avila)
Parents: Gonzalo de Toledo and María de Arévalo

Arévalo, apparently no relation to Alonso de Arévalo, had been in the Indies since 1513, and after taking part in the capture of Tenochtitlan was assigned the tributes from Miaguatlan (15 miles north of Jalapa) and Chiconquiauco (20 miles northeast of Jalapa); as well as can be determined, he was also a *vecino* of Jalapa. He was succeeded by his wife, who then married *poblador* Juan Valiente of Medina de Torres (Badajoz). In 1553 Valiente succeeded her and received the tribute until his death in 1580. There was no issue of either marriage.

(Gerhard, 375; Orozco y Berra, 57; Boyd-Bowman, I, no. 106, 5 and II, no. 1583, 45; Scholes and Adams, 44.)

26. Antón(io) de ARRIAGA
Conqueror—Narváez
From: Berlanga (Badajoz)

Arriaga had taken part in the conquest of Cuba in 1511, had been an *encomendero* in Santo Domingo in 1514, and was back in Cuba by 1519. He was a *vecino* of Mexico City before becoming a citizen of Ciudad Michoacán. His *encomiendas* included half of Teozacualco (34 miles west of Antequera, 320 miles east-southeast of his residence), shared with merchant conqueror Juan Ochoa de Lejalde from Guipúzcoa until it was taken by the second Audiencia in 1532, and Tlazazalca (65 miles west-northwest of Ciudad Michoacán), acquired in 1528. He married Ana Quintero and sired four daughters. Tlazazalca reverted to the crown when Arriaga died ca. 1534. Three of the daughters then shared a $100 annual crown pension while the fourth, married to Juan Antonio Branbila, received $50 a year.

Note: Arriaga was referred to as "don Antonio de Arriaga" when issued a grant of land on Río Tacubaya by the *cabildo* of Mexico City to build a grist mill.

(Gerhard, 276 and 327; Boyd-Bowman, I, no. 315, 12; Orozco y Berra, 57; Icaza I, 123 and 126; *Actas*, I, 22 and 73.)

27. Juan de ARRIAGA
Conqueror—Narváez
From: Relanga del Duero (Soria)
Parents: Diego de Arriaga and María de Licano

Arriaga was a *vecino* of Ibonao, Santo Domingo, in 1514. He then went to Cuba and used the Narváez *entrada* to get to New Spain. After the capture of Tenochtitlan he went with Alvarado to Guatemala. In 1534 Arriaga was awarded half the tributes from Guaxuapa (100 miles south-southeast of Mexico City), with the remaining half reserved for the crown. Because of his claimed poverty, Arriaga lived in the *pueblo* with his Spanish wife and four children, two of them sons. He was succeeded by the oldest son, a namesake, in the 1560s. By 1597 the tributes had reverted to the crown.

(Gerhard, 129f.; Boyd-Bowman, I, no. 4202a; Orozco y Berra, 75; Icaza, I, 10.)

28. Bartolomé de ASTORGA
Conqueror—Narváez
From: Astorga (León)

Astorga was in Cuba in 1519, went to Mexico with Narváez in 1520, and later became a *vecino* of Ciudad Oaxaca. He received the tribute from Tonaltepec (83 miles northwest of Antequera) and Zoaltepec (73 miles northwest of Antequera). It is assumed that his wife was Indian because the tribute reverted to the crown when Astorga died ca. 1540. Two daughters are listed. One married *poblador encomendero* Antonio de Villarroel, and the other married notary Rodrigo de Vigil, both *vecinos* of Oaxaca.

(Gerhard, 286; Orozco y Berra, 57; Boyd-Bowman, I, nos. 2187 and 2188, 74; Icaza, I, 252 and II, 82.)

29. Alonso de AVALOS Saavedra—
Hidalgo
Poblador
From: Medellín (Badajoz)
Parents: Pedro López de Saavedra and doña Isabel Alvarez Rengel

Avalos, a 1523 arrival in Mexico City, was a cousin of Cortés and the husband of doña Francisca de Estrada, a daughter of royal treasurer Alonso de Estrada. A *vecino* of both Mexico City and Ciudad de Michoacán, he was, as might be expected, well provided for. His *encomienda*, shared with his brother Fernando de Saavedra, was known as the "Provincia de Avalos." It included Atoyaque, Zayula, Amacueca, Tepeque, Techalutla, Teocuitlatlan (all about 180 miles west of Mexico City) and until 1528, Tacámbaro (60 miles west-southwest of Mexico City). The grants had a reported 10,920 tributaries in 1548, reduced to 3,500 fifty years later. This principality was assigned to Avalos by Alonso de Estrada prior to Avalos' marriage to Estrada's daughter. The tribute was sequestered by the first Audiencia and, with the exception of Tacambaro, returned by the second Audiencia. By the mid-1540s Avalos was married to doña Inés de Rivera, his second wife, and living within the *encomienda*. He was still alive in 1568, a *vecino* of Guadalajara. Avalos was succeeded by a son, don Fernando (also referred to in some documents as Gonzalo) de Avalos, married to doña Mariana Infante Samaniego. She succeeded as *encomendera* and later married Rodrigo de Villegas. The tribute was reassigned in 1606 to Sebastián Vezcaíno. In addition to Fernando de Saavedra, who shared Avalos' *encomienda*, two other brothers, Juan de Avalos Saavedra and Francisco de Saavedra, were also in New Spain, and yet another brother drowned off the coast of Cuba in 1526.

(Gerhard, 240 and 345; Scholes and Adams, 21; Boyd-Bowman, II, nos. 1467 and 1468, 42 and no. 1556, 44; Icaza, II, 4; Castro y Tosi, 1023.)

30. Alonso de AVILA (y Benavides)—
Hidalgo
First Conqueror
From: Monte Albán (Avila)

Avila, one of the four captains of the 1518 Grijalva expedition (the others being Grijalva, Pedro de Alvarado, and Francisco de Montejo) was a founding *vecino* of Mexico City. He had been the *contador* of Santo Domingo from 1511 to 1518, a *vecino* and *regidor* of San Juan from 1514, and also held the Cuban town of Chiapiana in *encomienda*. He was captured by French pirates while on a trip to Spain in 1522 as *procurador* (representative) for Mexico City. His *encomiendas* included Xuxupango (130 miles east-northeast of Mexico City, 88 miles northeast of Puebla) and Matlactonatico (in the vicinity of Papantla, 150 miles northeast of Mexico City), both shared with *poblador* Diego Villapadierna, having been assigned to them by Alonso de Estrada in 1527; Guautitlan (18 miles north of Mexico City); Totomeguacan (67 miles east-southeast of Mexico City, six miles south of Puebla); Tlachichilpa (30 miles west-southwest of Mexico City in the vicinity of Toluca); half of Tlapalcatepec (250 miles west of Mexico City, 65 miles west-southwest of Uruapan), the other half being held by first conqueror Pedro Sánchez Farfán from Seville and conqueror Hernando Ergüeta; and Calimaya-Metepec-Tepemaxalco (28 miles southwest of Mexico City, 6 to 12 miles south-southeast of Toluca). Avila married doña Elvira Guillén in March, 1518, after a clandestine betrothal elicited royal censure; some time later he remarried, to a Juana López. He had a total of eleven children. The Avila share of Matlactonatico and Xuxupango was given in dowry to daughter (doña ?) Antonia when she married Gonzalo de Salazar ca. 1540. Avila's son Antonio, who married doña Isabel de Salazar, succeeded as *encomendero* of Tlachichilpa. Another daughter married Cristóbal de Paredes, a *vecino* of Puebla. Guautitlan, assigned by Cortés, was transferred to Avila's brother, Gil González Dávila (Benavides). Totomeguacan was traded to Alonso Galeote in the 1520s, and the entirety of Tlapalcatepec reverted to the crown in August 1531. Calimaya-Metepec-Tepemaxalco, from the mid-1520s, was claimed in succession by Cortés, Licenciado Juan Gutiérrez Altamirano, Lope de Samaniego, Cristóbal de Cisneros, and Avila, with Altamirano the ultimate winner in 1536. Avila's nephew, Hernán Gómez, was a *vecino* of Colima and lieutenant clerk of the mines under Juan de Cuevas. Avila died in the 1540s.

(Gerhard, 127, 175, 218, 221, 250, 271, and 391; Scholes and Adams, 35; Boyd-Bowman, I, no. 117, 5; Icaza, I, 83 and 143 and II, 356; Orozco y Berra, 36; Díaz del Castillo, I, 26f.; *ENE*, Ser. 2, Vol. I, 31; *Actas*, I, 37; *Protocolos*, I, no. 785, 185 of 10 September 1527.)

31. Francisco de AVILA (Dávila)—
Hidalgo
Poblador Antiguo
From: Seville

Avila arrived in Mexico City in 1524. He had taken part in the 1511 conquest of Cuba and served there as a judge of some sort (*justicia*) as well as being an *encomendero*. Avila became a *vecino* upon his arrival in Mexico City and was elected *alcalde ordinario* on 1 January 1525. His *encomiendas* in New Spain included Los Amuzgos (220 miles south-southeast of Mexico City, 110 miles west-southwest of Antequera; including two *cabeceras* and four *estancias*) and Tulancingo (72 miles northeast of Mexico City, 33 miles east of Pachuca; 13 *estancias* in the late 1500s), shared with first conqueror Francisco de Terrazas of Badajoz, one of Cortés' *mayordomos*. It was considered a large *encomienda* in 1565. Avila married Beatriz de Llanos, also of Seville, and had several children. One daughter married Diego de Santa Cruz, a *vecino* of Veracruz, and another married Juan de Salinas, also of Veracruz. In 1537 he was serving as guardian for the minor children of deceased first conqueror Alonso Giraldo. Avila was succeeded by a son, Hernando, married to a daughter of Licenciado Rodrigo de Sandoval. Hernando in turn was succeeded by a daughter, doña María de Avila, married to don Angel de Villafañe y Alvarado (grandson of Jorge de Alvarado and great-grandson of Alonso de Estrada).

Note: Election to *alcalde ordinario* in 1525 amounted to being nominated by Cortés. The ratification by the *regidores* was automatic, for they too had been appointed by Cortés. Such was not the case when the crown started appointing *regidores*. Avila's granddaughter, doña María, appears to be the first generation to affect the "doña." Her maternal grandmother was doña María de Zúñiga of Valladolid.

(Gerhard, 380, 382, 335, and 337; Boyd-Bowman, I, no. 3249, 113, no. 3684, 124 and II, no. 12206, 364; Scholes and Adams,

25f.; Icaza, I, 201f., II, 45f. and 71; *Actas,* I, 24 and IV, 106.)

32. Gaspar de AVILA Quiñones—
Hidalgo
Conqueror—Narváez
From: Avila
Parents: Pedro de Valderrábano de Avila and doña Isabel de Quiñones

Avila came to New Spain with Narváez after having served in Tierra Firme in 1514 and explored the coast of Mexico with Francisco Hernández de Córdoba. After the capture of Tenochtitlan he joined *entradas* to Pánuco, Oaxaca, Mixteca, Zapotecas, Guatemala, and Chontales. Avila was a *vecino* of Mexico City where he maintained his *casa poblada*, arms, and horses. His *encomiendas* included Guatepec and Cuacuyulican (166 miles south of Mexico City, 3 miles east of Acapulco) and half of Taymeo (116 miles west-northwest of Mexico City, 56 miles southwest of Querétaro; ten named *estancias* in 1558). Taymeo was first held by Diego Hurtado, then acquired by Avila in 1529. It was divided by 1531 and shared with Francisco Quintero, also a conquistador. Avila was married and had eleven children, six of them daughters. He was succeeded ca. 1550 by his son, Pedro de Avila Quiñones.

(Gerhard, 149 and 319; Scholes and Adams, 38; Boyd-Bowman, I, no. 124, 6; Icaza, I, 34.)

33. Gonzalo de AVILA
Poblador
From: Llerena (Maestrazgo de León, Extremadura)
Parents: Juan de Arneda and Juana de Leiva

Avila arrived in New Spain with Garay's 1523 Pánuco *entrada*. He became a *vecino* there a few years later when Nuño de Guzmán assigned him the *encomienda* of Tantomol (40 miles south-southwest of Pánuco). It did not make him wealthy, however, as he claimed (ca. 1547) it only paid $30 to $40 worth of food per year. Avila did not marry, but claimed two natural daughters. Tribute from his *encomienda* reverted to the crown ca. 1569 when Avila died without legal issue.

(Gerhard, 216; Boyd-Bowman, II, no. 1388, 40; Scholes and Adams, 21; Icaza, I, 235.)

34. Juan de AVILA *"el tuerto"*
Conqueror—Narváez
From: Avila
Parents: Pedro Martín Cansino and Isabel Gutiérrez

Avila was in Cuba in 1519, went to New Spain with Narváez in 1520 and, after the capture of Tenochtitlan, was a member of the *entrada* to Pánuco. He was awarded the tribute from Chilguatal (70 miles north of Mexico City, 30 miles northwest of Pachuca; its 1,218 tributaries in the *cabecera* and four *estancias* were considered a small grant in 1564) by Governor Alonso de Estrada after it was taken from Martín Vázquez. Avila became a *vecino* of Mexico City on 4 April 1528. His wife was the daughter of conqueror *encomendero* Juan de Cuéllar. He was succeeded by a son, Juan de Cuéllar Verdugo, who in turn was succeeded by his widow, María de Garao, ca. 1570. Their son, Pablo de Vargas, inherited in 1597.

(Gerhard, 155; Scholes and Adams, 27; Boyd-Bowman, I, no. 125a, 6; Orozco y Berra, 75; Icaza, I, 46f.)

35. Luis de AVILA—Page during conquest
First Conqueror
From: Seville
Parents: Gonzalo de Trujillo and Beatriz Sánchez

Avila was in Cuba by 1517 and served Cortés as his page in the conquest up to the taking of Tenochtitlan. Cortés assigned him the *encomienda* of Xuxupango (130 miles east-northeast of Mexico City, 88 miles northeast of Puebla), but the grant was not confirmed by Alonso de Estrada when he was governor. Instead, in 1527 the *encomienda* was reassigned to Alonso de Avila and Diego de Villapadierna. Avila was married, had seven children and, although initially a resident of Mexico City, was an early *vecino* of Ciudad Michoacán.

(Gerhard, 391; Boyd-Bowman, I, no. 3251, 113; Orozco y Berra, 36; Icaza, I, 68f.; *Actas*, I, 7.)

36. Antonio AZNAR
Conqueror—Narváez
From: Guadix (Granada)
Parents: Beltrán de Aznar and Marina Díaz Ortega, natives of Baeza

Aznar arrived in Cuba ca. 1519 and was with the Narváez *entrada* the following year. After the capture of Tenochtitlan he was a member of *entradas* to Pánuco, Colima, against the Yope; much later, he served with Viceroy Mendoza in Jalisco (1541). He was a *vecino* of Puebla, where he maintained his *casa poblada*, arms, and horses. His *encomiendas* included Puctla (six *estancias* in 1598) and half of Justlaguaca, shared with *poblador* Bartolomé de Valdés of Seville. Both *cabeceras* were 145 miles south of Puebla, 70 miles west of Antequera. By 1548 the crown had taken Justlaguaca and reassigned the tribute to Tristán de Arellano. Aznar was married, had five children, and was succeeded by a namesake son in 1559. By 1570 Puctla was a crown holding.

(Gerhard, 164f., Scholes and Adams, 37; Boyd-Bowman, I, no. 1561a, 53; Orozco y Berra, 57; Icaza, I, 78.)

37. Juanés AZPEITIA
Conqueror—Medel
From: Azpeitia (Guipúzcoa)
Parents: Juan de Barrasueta and Marina de Ricarte

Azpeitia arrived in the Indies by 1516, was in Cuba in 1519, arrived in New Spain with Hernán Medel two weeks after the Narváez mission was neutralized, and then took part in the capture of Tenochtitlan under Cortés. He then participated in the pacification of Pánuco. Ten years later the second Audiencia assigned him Nanaguatlan (253 tributaries in 1532), near Pánuco where he was a *vecino*. The original *encomendero* appears to have been a Juan de Carpetia. By 1547 the tributes amounted to a claimed $20 per year. The grant reverted to the crown ca. 1553, the year Azpeitia died without issue or legal heir.

(Gerhard, 215; Boyd-Bowman, I, no. 1635, 56; Icaza, I, 87; Chipman, 292.)

38. Gutierre de BADAJOZ—Miner
Conqueror—Narváez
From: Cáceres
Parents: Gutierre de Badajoz and Catalina Chaves

Badajoz considered himself a native of Cáceres, but was born in Ciudad Rodrigo (Salamanca). His father served in the wars in Portugal and was in Santo Domingo in 1502. Badajoz arrived in the Indies in 1512, was a miner and *encomendero* in Santo Domingo by 1514, and went to Cuba in 1519 to join the Narváez *entrada* and get to New Spain. There he became a *vecino* of Mexico City and was considered a miner. He held the *encomienda* of Tacolula and Huehuetlan (140 miles south of Mexico City, 52 miles east of Acapulco) and by 1531 had acquired nearby Nexpa, initially assigned to conqueror (?) Antonio de Guadalajara. Badajoz received a coat of arms, dated 15 November 1527. He was succeeded by 1565 by a son, Gabriel de Chaves.

(Gerhard, 149; Scholes and Adams, 18; Orozco y Berra, 76; Boyd-Bowman, I, no. 893, 31 and no. 2579, 91; Icaza, I, 40; *Nobiliario*, 15; *Protocolos*, I no. 238, 79 of 20 November 1525.)

39. Rodrigo de BAEZA
Poblador Antiguo
From: Burgos

Baeza arrived in New Spain and became a *vecino* of Mexico City in 1526. He first came to the Indies in 1509, took part in the conquest of Cuba in 1511, and served there as royal treasurer and accountant until his return to Spain in 1521. Four years later he moved his family to Cuba, then the following year to Mexico City. Baeza was assigned the tributes from Tezontepec (2 *sujetos*; 47 miles northeast of Mexico City, 21 miles south-southeast of Pachuca) and Chila (72 miles southeast of Mexico City, southwest of Izúcar; two *estancias* by 1581). His wife, Mari López de Obregón, was also from Burgos. Records list six children. Of these, Baltasar (born 1522 in Moguer) succeeded Baeza as *encomendero* of Tezontepec by 1548 and then passed it to his son and namesake by 1565. It was a crown possession eight years later, but then was reassigned to Francisco Tello de Orozco, the *encomendero* of record in 1597. Chila was given in dowry to Baeza's daughter Elvira when she married Lorenzo Vázquez Marroquino. Elvira succeeded Lorenzo, and then their son, Agustín Marroquino, received the tribute until his death in 1575, at which time the grant reverted to the crown. Six years later Ana Pérez de Zamora is listed as *encomendera*, and by 1596 the *encomendero* was another Lorenzo Marroquino. Final escheatment took place by 1626. Other siblings of Baltasar and Elvira were Gaspar Carrillo (born in Cuba, 1525), Ana Osorio, Bartolomé Obregón, and Luis Obregón.

(Gerhard, 42 and 210; Scholes and Adams, 28 and 40; Boyd-Bowman, I, no. 668, 23 and II, no. 2334, 65; Icaza I, 199 and II, 324ff.; *Actas*, I, 70.)

40. Cristóbal (?) BARRERA—Trumpeter (?)
Conqueror (?)—?

Shown as a conqueror in some documents, Barrera has not been specifically associated with any of the *entradas* to New Spain. It is assumed that he was a *vecino* of Puebla because two of his daughters married *vecinos* of that city. Barrera received the tributes from Chiapulco (65 miles east-southeast of Puebla, 10 miles north of Tehuacan; 6 *barrios* in 1548, with 400 tributaries listed in 1570).

He had trouble with the Holy Office because he refused to play his trumpet for the opening procession unless paid in advance. Barrera was succeeded ca. 1548 by his oldest daughter, who married Esteban de Carvajal, a *vecino* of Puebla. Another daughter married Juan Ponce, also a *vecino* of Puebla. A Carvajal was listed as *encomendero* as late as 1603, but by 1610 Chiapulco was a crown possession.

(Gerhard, 262ff.; Scholes and Adams, 30; Icaza, II, 14f. and 171; *AGN*, Inq., T42, e.3.)

41. Andrés de BARRIOS—*Hidalgo*
First Conqueror
From: Arcos de la Frontera (Cádiz)

Barrios, a knight of the Duke of Arcos, arrived in Cuba by 1518 and came to New Spain with his in-law Cortés (their wives, Leonor Suárez Pacheco and Catalina Suárez, were sisters). Barrios was a *vecino* and *regidor* of Mexico City in 1524–1526 and 1528, *alcalde ordinario* in 1529 and 1541 and a perpetual *regidor* from 1545. In 1525 Cortés took half of the copious tribute to Meztitlan (85 miles north-northeast of Mexico City; 40 *estancias* in 1548 and 120 dependent settlements with a total of 15,500 tributaries 25 years later) from Miguel Díaz de Aux (the other half remained with conqueror Alonso Lucas from Extremadura) and assigned it to Barrios. Díaz sued and ultimately regained one-third of his original half. Barrios was succeeded ca. 1550 by his daughter, doña Isabel de Barrios, married to don Diego de Guevara. She succeeded don Diego and remarried Diego de Guzmán before 1604. Part of this *encomienda* was still in private hands in the eighteenth century.

(Gerhard, 184ff.; Scholes and Adams, 34f.; Boyd-Bowman, I, no. 1127a, 39 and no. 3266, 114.)

42. Francisco BARRÓN
Poblador

Barrón served with an *entrada* to New Galicia and later acquired Oxitipa (175 miles north of Mexico City in the vicinity of Valles) after it had been successively claimed by Cortés, Nuño de Guzmán, and Guzmán's kinsman, Pedro de Guzmán. He was probably a *vecino* of Mexico City. Barrón was succeeded by his wife, a daughter of Licenciado de la Torre. She then married Pedro de Trejo, who served as guardian for Barrón's four children. Barrón's oldest son, Francisco, inherited when he came of age, ca. 1550.

(Gerhard, 62 and 354; Scholes and Adams, 45; Icaza, II, 25.)

43. Pedro de BAZÁN
Poblador
From: Jerez de Badajoz (Badajoz)

Bazán, arriving in New Spain, ca. 1522, took part in *entradas* to New Galicia, Colima, Mar del Sur, Chiapas, and Coatzacoalcos. By 1528 he shared the tribute of Pungaravato (160 miles southwest of Mexico City; 13 *estancias* in 1548) with first conqueror Hernando Alonso. He acquired Alonso's share after the latter was executed on 17 October 1528 for heresy. Bazán was a *vecino* of Mexico City. He married doña Catalina de Albornoz of Paradinas (Salamanca), the niece of the royal accountant, Contador Rodrigo de Albornoz. Her brother, Bernardino de Albornoz, became a Mexico City *regidor* in 1541. By the time Bazán died and was succeeded by his son Hernando, the tribute amounted to about $500 per year. The *encomienda* reverted to the crown in 1597 when Hernando became a priest. Bazán left daughters by a previous marriage in Spain.

(Gerhard, 135f.; Scholes and Adams, 37; Boyd-Bowman, II, no. 1320, 38 and no. 7355, 227; Icaza, I, 221f.)

44. Diego BECERRA de Mendoza—
Hidalgo
Poblador
From: Mérida (La Serena, Extremadura)

Becerra, associated with and a relative of Cortés, captained one of his ships operating between Tehuantepec and Acapulco during 1532–1533. He acquired the *encomienda* of Chiautla (30 miles south of Izúcar; 6,000 tributaries before 1545) ca. 1527 after it had been held by Alonzo de Grado (1525 to 1527) and Diego de Ordaz (ca. 1521 to 1525). He was also assigned Coatlan-Miaguatlan (40 miles east of Antequera; 57 *estancias* in 1548) by Cortés. This second grant was taken by the first Audiencia when Becerra was accused of being the grandson of a heretic. He was assassinated by Fortún Jiménez, his ship's pilot, in 1533. Chiautla reverted to the crown shortly thereafter, although it was unsuccessfully claimed by Jerónimo López. Coatlan-Miaguatlan was reassigned to Andrés de Monjaraz.

(Gerhard, 108f. and 188; Boyd-Bowman, II, no. 1587, 45.)

45. Juan BECERRA
Poblador
From: Toro (Zamora)

Becerra arrived in Mexico City in 1526 in the entourage of Licenciado Luis Ponce de León. He later took part in *entradas* against the Zapotecs, Mixes, and the Chontales. For his services he was awarded the tribute from the small *encomienda* of Ayacastepec near Villa Alta, where he became a *vecino*. He was succeeded before 1550 by his widow, Inés Corneja, daughter of conqueror Pedro Asencio. Inés then married Francisco de Salazar and had children by him, but by the mid-1560s she was the *encomendera* again. A Martín Méndez was receiving the tributes from this *encomienda* in 1597.

(Gerhard, 370; Scholes and Adams, 51; Boyd-Bowman, II, no. 126621, 381; Icaza. I, 231.)

46. Serván BEJERANO
Conqueror—Camargo
From: Benalcázar (Córdoba)
Parents: Antón de Puelles and Catalina Sánchez Bejerano

Bejerano arrived in the Indies in either 1509 or 1510 and spent some time in Darién and Jamaica before going to New

Spain in 1520 with Camargo and joining the reorganized Mexico City *entrada*. He seems to have been a member of nearly every *entrada* after the capture of Tenochtitlan. Bejerano was a *vecino* of Mexico City, where he served as an employee (*criado*) of Gonzalo de Sandoval. His *encomiendas*, assigned in 1527, included half the tribute from Ocuila (32 miles south-southwest of Mexico City near Cuernavaca; 17 *estancias* in 1548) and all of Coatepec (five miles east of Ocuila; two *estancias* in 1548). Ocuila was taken from conqueror Juan de Morales and divided between Bejerano and conqueror Pedro Ruiz Zamorano of Jaén, another Sandoval retainer. Bejerano was married twice and was the father of eight legitimate children who did not reach adulthood, and two natural children, a son and daughter who did. By 1547 he was succeeded by his second wife, Francisca Calderón, who later married and survived Antonio de la Torre. In the 1560s Francisca married Diego de Ocampo Saavedra, the *encomendero* in 1600.

(Gerhard, 170f.; Boyd-Bowman, I, no. 1374, 47; Icaza, I, 74f.; *Protocolos*, I, no. 619, 158 of 27 June 1527, no. 886, 208 of 14 November 1527 and no. 1038, 236 of 1 February 1528.)

47. **Juan BELLO**
    Conqueror—Narváez
    From: Ciudad Rodrigo (Salamanca)
    Parents: Juan Bello Troche and Leonor Gutiérrez de Cáceres

Bello arrived in Cuba ca. 1517 and sailed with Grijalva's 1518 expedition before arriving in New Spain with Narváez. He served in *entradas* to Higueras, Pánuco, and against the Chontales before becoming a *vecino* of Mexico City. His *encomiendas* included Astatla (340 miles southeast of Mexico City, 40 miles southwest of Tehuantepec; five *estancias* in 1550) and Ixmiquilpan (73 miles north of Mexico City; 4,027 tributaries in 1570). Half the tribute from the latter was taken for the crown in 1535. He was denounced to the Inquisition in 1527 for blasphemy.

Bello was succeeded by a daughter married to Gil González de Avila (also known as González de Benavides), namesake grandson of the conqueror. The crown acquired the entire *encomienda* in 1566 when González was executed for his role in the second Marqués conspiracy.

(Gerhard, 124, 126 and 155; Scholes and Adams, 23; Boyd-Bowman, I, no. 2380, 91; Icaza, I, 35; *Protocolos*, I, no. 369, 107 of 14 February 1527; AGN, Inq. T. I., exp. 8.)

48. **Alonso de BENAVIDES**
    Conqueror—Narváez

Benavides was with Francisco Hernández de Córdoba's 1517 expedition before returning to Cuba to join the Narváez *entrada*. After the fall of Tenochtitlan Benavides, along with Antonio Quiñones and Alonso de Avila, was captured by the French while enroute to Spain to represent the interests of Cortés. Upon his release and return to New Spain, Benavides became a *vecino* of Veracruz and *encomendero* of Mexcaltzinco (76 miles northwest of Veracruz near Jalapa; 1,600 tributaries in the *cabecera* and six *estancias*), as well as having property in Mexico City. He was succeeded by his widow, María de la Torre, who later married Andrés Dorantes de Carranza, who, with Alvar Núñez Cabeza de Vaca, survived the ill-fated Narváez Florida *entrada*. A daughter of the first marriage, Antonia de Benavides, married to Antonio Ruiz de Castañeda, succeeded. Ruiz was listed as *encomendero* in 1580. Maxcalcingo reportedly provided an income of $200 per year ca. 1547.

(Gerhard, 375f.; Scholes and Adams, 34; *Protocolos*, I, no. 991, 228 of 13 January 1528; Icaza, I, 195f.; *Actas*, I, 28; Boyd-Bowman, II, no. 7147, 221; Cabeza de Vaca, 139 and 141.)

49. **Nuño (Rufio/Nuflo) de BENAVIDES**
    Conqueror—?

Benavides, presumed to be a *vecino* of Antequera, received the tribute from Chachuapa, a small *encomienda* 50 miles northwest of Antequera. He was succeeded ca. 1550 by a son, Juan de Benavides, and by 1590 the *encomendero* was a grandson, García de Benavides. Chachuapa was a crown property in 1597.

(Gerhard, 200; Scholes and Adams, 30.)

50. Francisco BERNAL
Conqueror—Narváez

Bernal arrived in New Spain with Narváez and ca. 1522 was assigned Tanchinamol, Mecatlan, and Heusco (all near Valles) in *encomienda*. Mecatlan was reassigned to *poblador* Gregorio de Saldaña ca. 1534. The disposition of Heusco is not known. Bernal still held Tanchinamol, a grant with a 1532 count of 552 tributaries. Bernal was probably a *vecino* of Puebla, 210 miles south of his *encomienda*.

(Gerhard, 355; Orozco y Berra, 76; Chipman, 292f.)

51. Juan BERNAL
Conqueror—Narváez

Bernal arrived in New Spain in 1520 with the Narváez *entrada* and after the capture of Tenochtitlan became a *vecino* of Puebla and *encomendero* of Acatlan (60 miles south of Puebla; five named *sujetos* in 1581). The grant was made in the early 1520s and reverted to the crown when Bernal died in 1532. He left three sons. One died early, another became a friar, and the third, his namesake, received an annual pension of $100 that he claimed was inadequate to sustain his arms and horses. Bernal's widow, Catalina de al Torre, later married conqueror *encomendero* Diego de Colio and had another family.

(Gerhard, 42; Orozco y Berra, 58; Icaza, I, 16f. and 131.)

52. Luis de BERRIO
Poblador
From: Jaén

Berrio arrived in New Spain ca. 1526, established his residence in Mexico City, and acquired the rights to one-half of the tributes of Capula (200 miles west of Mexico City near Pátzcuaro; 12 *estancias* in 1571). This *encomienda* was first held by *poblador* Pedro Núñez, Maese de Roa, before the 1528 joint reassignment to Berrio and Dr. Cristóbal de Ojeda, also *poblador*. In 1533 both halves of the *encomienda* were taken for the crown by the second Audiencia. Berrio, who arrived with an appointment as *regidor* in perpetuity of the Mexico City *cabildo*, sold his seat to first conqueror Pedro Sánchez Farfán for $600 in February 1527. Two years later Berrio was the *alcalde mayor* of Zapotecas (Villa Alta), a first Audiencia appointment.

(Gerhard, 344; Boyd-Bowman, II, no. 5645, 170; *Protocolos*, I, no. 403, no. 404 and no. 405, all dated 2 March 1527, 114f.; *Actas*, I, 123, Minutes of 22 February 1527; also see Lockhart and Otte, 97f.)

53. Juan BEZOS
Poblador
From: Seville
Parents: Cristóbal Bezos and Ana Gómez

In 1526 Bezos arrived in Mexico City with three brothers, all members of the entourage of Licenciado Luis Ponce de León. He became a *vecino* of Mexico City and later took part in the Motín *entrada* Nuño de Guzmán assigned him Ucareo (140 miles west-northwest of Mexico City; two sub-*cabeceras* and 24 *barrios* ca. 1548) in 1529 after it had been taken from Gonzalo Holguín. He received the tribute until the grant was annulled in 1536 by Viceroy Mendoza. Bezos remained a bachelor. He claimed that without an *encomienda* he could not afford the expense of matrimony. Bezo's father was a royal boatswain during the conquest of Santo Domingo and was a ship's captain in the Indies from 1512 to 1529. An uncle took part in *entradas* in Tierra Firme and Santa Marta. Another uncle was Pedro Sánchez Farfán, first conqueror and *regidor* of Mexico City. Bezo's brother Rodrigo married Francisca de Vargas, widow of *poblador* Baltasar de Torquemada, becoming the *encomendero* of Tenacusco and Tantima in Pánuco in the process.

(Gerhard, 319f.; Boyd-Bowman, I, no. 3278, 114 and II, no. 8826, 272; Icaza, II, 313f.)

54. Francisco de BONAL
First Conqueror
From: Salamanca

Bonal is first noted as being in Cuba in 1518 and then as a member of the Cortés *entrada* in 1519. He established his residence in Veracruz and later lived in Puebla. While in Veracruz he served as governor's deputy (*teniente*) in Medellín during 1525 and again in 1529. Bonal's *encomienda* consisted of Guatusco and Istayuca (60 miles southwest of Veracruz, 30 miles southwest of Córdoba; two dependencies in 1560) until 1535, when the tributes reverted to the crown and a *corregidor* was assigned.

(Gerhard, 83; Boyd-Bowman, I, no. 2660, 94; Orozco y Berra, 37.)

55. Juan de BONILLA
Poblador
From: Guadalupe (Cáceres)
Parents: Diego Alonso and Inés de Bonilla

Bonilla arrived in New Spain in 1524. He established his residence in Villa Alta, where he maintained his *casa poblada*, arms, and horses, after taking part in the conquest of the region under Gaspar Pacheco and Diego de Figueroa. His *encomiendas* initially included Amaltepec, half of Guatinicamanes (until 1534), Tetetipac, and Coniltepec, all in the vicinity of Villa Alta. By 1548 all but Amaltepec had reverted to the crown and he was left with a claimed 40 tributaries. Married, Bonilla was succeeded ca. 1565 by a daughter.

(Scholes and Adams, 22; Icaza, I, 230 and II, 262f.; Gerhard, 370.)

56. Gabriel BOSQUE
Conqueror—Narváez
From: Aragón
Parents: Juan Bosque and Catalina Bama

Bosque arrived in New Spain with the Narváez *entrada* of 1520. He had been in Cuba since 1517 and was a member of Grijalva's 1518 expedition. He became a *vecino* of Oaxaca, where he made the annual muster with his arms and horse after taking part in one of the Pánuco *entradas*. Sometime prior to 1550 he acquired the *encomienda* of Tlacotepec (70 miles west of Antequera). This town had been an *estancia* of Tecomastlaguaca, granted by Cortés to first conqueror Francisco Maldonado. Bosque was succeeded by his only son, Juan, married to a daughter of conqueror Santos Hernández (*encomendero* of Petlalcingo, southeast of Izúcar, and *vecino* of Oaxaca). Tlacotepec reverted to the crown before 1597.

(Gerhard, 164; Icaza, I, 47; 10 and 171; Boyd-Bowman, I, no. 5016, 167.)

57. Antón BRAVO—Swordsmith
First Conqueror
From: Fregenal de la Sierra (Maestrazgo de León, Extremadura)
Parents: Antón García Payo and Ana García Bravo

Bravo, identified as a swordsmith in some documents, was in Cuba by 1517 and with Grijalva in 1518 before taking part in the conquest of Mexico as a member of the Cortés *entrada*. He was a *vecino* of Mexico City and as an *encomendero* shared the tributes from Hueypustla (36 miles north-northeast of Mexico City; 3,070 tributaries in 1570) with conquistador Pedro (Garao) Valenciano. Before October of 1528 Bravo and blacksmith Hernando Alonso were mining partners. Bravo married Catalina López de Polanco, widow of sievemaker Juan de Gálvez. He was succeeded ca. 1548 by his son, Antonio Bravo de la Laguna, who supported, for a time at least, his mother and two sisters. The tributes from this *encomienda* ultimately were shared by the Moctezuma heirs and the crown.

(Scholes and Adams, 32; Orozco y Berra, 76; Icaza, I, 11 and 132; Gerhard 296 and 298; Boyd-Bowman, I, no. 352, 13; *Protocolos*, I, no. 600, 154 of 21 June 1527 and no. 731, 179 of 21 August 1527.)

58. Juan de BURGOS
Conqueror—(Medel)
From: Seville
Parents: Francisco de Burgos and Guiomar de Escobar

Burgos spent a number of years on Gomera Island in the Canaries before going to Cuba in 1519 and then late the following year with Francisco Medel to New Spain, where he took part in the conquest. He owned the merchandise and horses transported on Medel's ship. He then became a *vecino* of Mexico City, maintaining there his *casa poblada*, arms, horses, and family. By virtue of his association with Cortés, Burgos' *encomiendas* in 1528 included half of Cuzamala (130 miles southwest of Mexico City; 22 *sujetos* in 1570), shared with *poblador* Diego Rodríguez, Guastepec (18 miles east of Cuernavaca) "in deposit" from Cortés to preclude it from reassignment while the latter was in Spain, and half of Teutenango (14 miles southwest of Toluca), also shared with Diego Rodríguez. Cortés recovered Guastepec in 1531, and Burgos became the sole holder of Cuzamala by 1533. In anticipation of returning to Spain, Burgos sold his rights to Cuzamala and his share of Teutenango to Francisco Vázquez de Coronado in 1538. There is little evidence to show that Burgos ever left New Spain, however. He was active in buying and selling slaves (black, Moorish, and Indian) and horses in the late 1520s and, after becoming a royal accountant, got involved in mining and tithe farming. He died ca. 1547, leaving a daughter, Isabel de Escobar, married to Juan Ramírez of Guadalcanal. Burgos received a coat of arms, dated 1527.

(Scholes and Adams, 28; Icaza, I, 129 and II, 260; Gerhard 291f., 95 and 271; Boyd-Bowman, I, no. 3287, 114; *Protocolos*, I, no. 1221, 267 of 5 April 1527, no. 1498, 318 of 11 September 1528, no. 1503, 318f. of 12 September 1528, no. 1771, 366 of 19 November 1528, and II, no. 2202, 108 of 2 March 1537, no. 2215, 110 of 6 March 1537, no. 2321a, 132 of 18 July 1537 and no. 2476, 171f. of 10 January 1538; *Nobiliario*, 114f.; Díaz del Castillo, I, 476; *Actas*, I, 20.)

59. Fernando BURGUEÑO
Conqueror—Luis Ponce de León
From: Oropesa (Toledo)

Burgueño was in Cuba by 1519 and arrived in New Spain with Luis Ponce de León the following year in time to take part in the siege of Tenochtitlan. His *encomienda* was half of Piastla (103 miles southeast of Mexico City; 9 *estancias* in 1581), shared with conqueror Francisco de Olmos. By 1524 Burgueño had become a *vecino* of Mexico City. Late in 1531 Burgueño's half of Piastla was taken as a crown property. He died in the 1530s while on a trip to Spain to petition for another *encomienda*. He was survived by his widow, Inés Gómez of Oropesa, and their son Pedro. They both became residents in the *casa poblada* of Regidor Antonio de Carvajal. A daughter had already married Juan de Cuenca of Bujalance, Córdoba. Burgueño received a coat of arms dated 25 September 1531, about the same time his *encomienda* was taken.

(Gerhard, 42; Boyd-Bowman, I, no. 4313a, 142; Icaza, I, 132f. and 163; *Nobiliario*, 97; *Protocolos*, I, no. 74, 42ff. of 21 September 1525 and no. 649, 164 of 15 July 1527; *Actas*, 4.)

60. Juan BURIEZO
Poblador

Buriezo, a *vecino* of Colima, became the *encomendero* of Pomayagua and Chapula (both near Colima) by marrying María Villacorta, the widow of the original holder, conqueror Gómez Gutiérrez, before 1550. María, a native of New Spain, was the daughter of conqueror Juan de Villacorta and Ana González. The *encomienda* was passed on to a son of the second union in the 1560s.

(Gerhard, 80; Icaza, II, 266.)

61. Doctor Blas de BUSTAMANTE—
Hidalgo
Poblador
From: Tordehumos (Valladolid)
Parents: Mancio Hernández de Bustamante and Mari González

Bustamante arrived in New Spain and became a *vecino* of Mexico City in 1529, the same year the first Audiencia assigned him the tribute from Tonatico (140 miles northeast of Mexico City near Papantla; two named *estancias*, plus others, before 1570). The second Audiencia reassigned the *encomienda* to Rodrigo de Guzmán ca. 1532. Bustamante occupied himself by teaching Latin and was one of the six founders of the University of Mexico City in 1553. His wife was doña Leonor de Bobadilla, a daughter of the Count of Gomera. They had seven sons and two daughters. Prior to 1547, Bustamante bought the rights to Chimalguacan Atenco (15 miles east of Mexico City; 31 *estancias* in 1579) from conqueror Juan de Cuéllar Verdugo. The family (son Gerónimo from 1570 to 1597 and then granddaughter doña María de Bustamante, married to Felipe de la Cueva) retained the *encomienda* until final reversion to the crown ca. 1670.

(Gerhard, 77 and 219; Icaza, I, 213; Boyd-Bowman, II, no. 12006, 358; Scholes and Adams, 17.)

62. Rodrigo de BUSTAMANTE
Poblador
From: Salamanca
Parents: Alonso de Montalbán and Elena García

Bustamante arrived in New Spain ca. 1526 and associated himself with the Nuño de Guzmán faction in Pánuco, where he became a *vecino*. On 1 February 1529 Guzmán gave him a slaving license authorizing him to collect and sell 50 Indians. By 1533 he was the *encomendero* of Chachapala (48 miles southwest of Pánuco; 281 tributaries in 1532). This grant had reverted to the crown by 1545 for the same reason that other *encomiendas* in the area were abandoned—there were no Indians left to pay tribute.

(Gerhard, 215; Chipman, 226 and 293; Boyd-Bowman, II, no. 7415, 229.)

63. Juan de BUSTO—*Hidalgo*
Poblador
From: Medellín (La Serena, Extremadura)
Parents: Pedro de Busto and doña Catalina de Mendoza of Mérida

Busto arrived in New Spain ca. 1523, probably as a member of Garay's Pánuco venture. His father was a son of Pedro de Busto, cousin of the Count of Medellín. After taking part in the conquest of Pánuco, Yopelcingo, and Mestitlan, Busto became one of the founding *vecinos* of Pánuco, where he maintained his *casa poblada*, arms, horses, and family, and received as yet unidentified *encomiendas*. These grants were suspended upon the arrival of Nuño de Guzmán. He bought the rights to Tancetuco (30 miles south-southeast of Pánuco; 708 tributaries in 1532) from Ramiro de Guzmán ca. 1533. In 1534 Tlacolula (three miles from Pánuco) and Tanchunamol (52 miles west of Pánuco, near Valles) were assigned to Busto through the influence of Cortés as repayment for expenses incurred in the California *entrada* of the previous year. Tlacolula was taken for the crown before 1548 and served as center of a congregation. Tanchunamol reverted to the crown by 1550. Juan de Busto, married to a daughter of conqueror Francisco Rodríguez Magariño, was listed as the *encomendero* of Tancetuco in 1612, but the holder was more than likely a namesake son. Busto's brother Alonso was also a resident of New Spain after ca. 1530.

(Scholes and Adams, 20; Icaza, I, 190f.; Boyd-Bowman, II, no. 1473, 42; Gerhard, 216f. and 355; Chipman, 293.)

64. Cristóbal CABEZÓN
First Conqueror
From: Almagro (Ciudad Real)
Parents: Pedro Cabezón and Elvira Ruiz

Cabezón was in Cuba by 1518 and later joined the Cortés *entrada*. After the capture of Tenochtitlan he took part in the pacification of Zacatula, Colima, and New Galicia. During the 1540s he renounced his first *encomienda* in Colima and bought the rights to half the tributes of Tezcatepec and Tuzantlalpa (twin *cabeceras* 30 miles north of Mexico City, eleven dependencies in 1569) from conqueror Alonso Martín Jaca of Huesca. The other half was held by conqueror Francisco de Estrada from Seville. Cabezón married and maintained his *casa poblada*, arms, and horses in Mexico City. He was succeeded by his son, Gregorio (Gerónimo) de Soto.

(Gerhard, 297; Icaza, I, 8f.; Boyd-Bowman, I, no. 1266, 43; Scholes and Adams, 19.)

65. Juan de CABRA—Miner
Conqueror—Camargo
From: Ciudad Real
Parents: Antón de Cabra and Teresa Ruiz

Cabra arrived in Cuba ca. 1519 and came to New Spain the following year as a member of the Garay *entrada*, joining Cortés before the siege of Tenochtitlan. He became a *vecino* of Mexico City and was assigned the *encomienda* of Nochtepec and Pilcaya (twin *cabeceras* 56 miles south-southwest of Mexico City near Taxco; ten *estancias* total ca. 1570). Cabra used the assets of his *encomienda* plus Indian slaves to mine gold near Taxco as well as in Michoacán and Zacatula. One mining company of Cabra's, together with conqueror Serván Bejerano, involved 150 slaves and the assets of both *encomiendas*. Cabra married María de Herrera ca. 1527. In the 1540s their daughter married Taxco *vecino* Nicolás Chamorro of Medina de Río Seco. Cabra's widow succeeded him as *encomendera* ca. 1550 and later married Francisco Ramírez Bravo. The *encomienda* reverted to the crown before 1597.

(Gerhard, 253f.; Icaza, I, 85f. and II, 88; Scholes and Adams, 35; Boyd-Bowman, I, no 1287, 44; *Protocolos*, I, no. 619, 158 of 27 June 1527 and no. 1058, 239 of 6 February 1528; *Actas*, I, 20.)

66. Manuel de CÁCERES
First Conqueror
From: Segovia
Parents: Gonzalo de Cáceres and María de Oña

Cáceres joined the 1519 Cortés *entrada* after spending a year in Cuba. He took part in the pacification of Colima and then stayed there as one of the first settlers. His *encomiendas*, assigned in the early 1520s, included Tototlan, Tlapistlan, Xicotlan, Xonacatlan, Cuautecomatlan, all in the vicinity of Colima, and Maquilí, 40 miles to the southeast. Xicotlan, Xonacatlan, and Cuautecomatlan were reassigned (sold?) to Juan de Aguilar in the 1530s. The rest of the *encomienda* was inherited by Cáceres' son, Gonzalo de Cáceres, before 1550. Cáceres married Isabel de Monjaraz, a daughter of first conqueror Martín Ruiz de Monjaraz. The couple had another son, and Isabel was pregnant when Cáceres died.

(Gerhard, 80 and 193; Icaza, I, 156f.; Boyd-Bowman, I, no. 2911, 103.)

67. Antón CAICEDO
First Conqueror

Caicedo leaves no trace of his origins in Europe. He was, however, considered a man of wealth, and his rewards and business ventures reflect the fact. A *vecino* of Mexico City, Caicedo held the *encomiendas* of Texcaltitlan (60 miles southwest of Mexico City; 850 tributaries in 1569), Tarecuato-Tepeguacan (230 miles west of Mexico City; 3,000 tributaries of 1522 were reduced to 480 by 1579), Periban and Tinhuindín (235 miles west of Mexico City; 1,539 tributaries and 700 minors in 1569), and one-fourth of Teguacan (135 miles east-southeast of Mexico City; 3,000 tributaries in 1570). It is probable that Caicedo received tribute from some 18,000 Indians per year prior to his death in 1536. The entire set of *encomiendas* was claimed by the crown when Caicedo died, but shortly thereafter Texcaltitlan, Periban, and Tarecuato-Tepguacan were reassigned to his widow, doña Marina Montes de Oca (Montesdoca). She soon married Francisco de Chaves, who was shown as the *encomendero* until 1561. Tributes continued to be awarded to the descendants of both Caicedo and Chaves, depending on the current court ruling. The crown was sole recipient of all the tribute after 1657.

(Gerhard, 261, 268, 315, 387; Díaz del Castillo, II, 488; Icaza, I, 227 and II, 67; Scholes and Adams, 36f.)

68. **Martín de CALAHORRA**—Notary
Conqueror—Garay
From: Calahorra (Logroño)
Parents: Martín Sánchez de Cuñada and Isabel Vera Matute

Calahorra was in the Indies by 1519, went to New Spain with the Garay *entrada*, and after the capture of Tenochtitlan went on to Guatemala. Cortés assigned him the *encomienda* of Tepexoxuma (68 miles southeast of Mexico City near Izúcar; two sub-*cabeceras* and 13 *estancias* in 1548; a "medium" grant in 1565). By 1526 he was a *vecino* of Mexico City, functioning as a notary. He changed his residence to Puebla in 1534, the same year he married a daughter (born in Spain) of conqueror Garcí Hernández. Her brothers were conquerors Juan Pérez de Herrera and Pedro Hernández, and one of her sisters married conqueror Diego de Holguín, also a *vecino* of Puebla. The couple had five daughters and two sons. Calahorra was succeeded in the 1550s by a son, Cristóbal de Acuñada. The *encomienda* stayed in private hands until the 1660s.

(Gerhard, 160f.; Scholes and Adams, 38; Icaza, I, 41f. and 76f.; Boyd-Bowman, I, no. 4960a, 165.)

69. **Alonso CANO**
Conqueror—Ruiz de la Mota
From: Alanís (Seville)
Parents: Alonso Martín Cano and Beatriz Sánchez

Cano arrived in Cuba in 1520, joined the Ruiz de la Mota party and got to New Spain in time to take part in the capture of Tenochtitlan. He then served in *entradas* to Oaxaca, Tehuantepec, Pánuco, Guatemala, Coatlan, and Cipotecas. Cano was awarded the *encomienda* of Temascalapa (three miles north of Villa Alta, considered very small by 1565 standards) and became a *vecino* of Villa Alta For a period in the mid-1530s Cano owned a muletrain, selling part of it in August 1536 for $1,050 to doña Inés de Cabrera, the widow of *poblador antiguo* Juan de la Torre, and merchant Luis de Córdoba. Cano later became *corregidor* of Tlahuitoltepec (20 miles southeast of Villa Alta; $50 annual salary) and by 1547 was an *alcalde ordinario* of Villa Alta. He married Antonia Pérez Carballa, widow of Diego Benítez. Her son by Benítez, Alonso Pérez, married one of Cano's daughters (mestiza ?) by a previous union. Antonia, like Cano, was a native of Seville and came to New Spain in 1538. Cano was succeeded by a son ca. 1564. The *encomienda* reverted to the crown before 1597.

(Gerhard, 327; Icaza, I, 89 and 179; Scholes and Adams, 50; Boyd-Bowman, II, no. 8091, 251, no. 9899, 299 and no. 9909, 300; *Protocolos*, II, no. 1914, no. 1915 and no. 1916, 45 of 9 September 1536.)

70. **Juan CANO**
Conqueror—Narváez
From: Cáceres
Parents: Pedro Cano and Catalina Gómez de Saavedra

Cano was in Cuba by 1519 and arrived in New Spain with Narváez the following year. He claimed that both of his grandfathers served the Catholic Kings in Granada and in Italy. Cano became a *vecino* of Mexico City in 1525 after *entrada* service against the Cipotecas,

Huasteca, and in Michoacán. But strange as it may seem, he did not become an *encomendero* until his 1536 marriage to doña Isabel Moctezuma (he was her fourth husband). He was then assigned Macuilsúchil (85 miles north of Mexico City; 120 dependencies in 1537). The pair had four sons and two daughters. Cano renounced his claim to the tribute from this *encomienda* in favor of their son, Pedro, in 1560, ten years after doña Isabel died. Pedro was succeeded by his daughter in the 1570s. Tributes were paid to the Cano family at least until 1631. The actual number of tributaries is not known, and in spite of Cano's complaint of its poverty because the Indians were Chichimecas, the 1565 evaluation places the income from it in the "medium" category.

(Gerhard, 185 and 186; Scholes and Adams, 17; Icaza, I, 31; Boyd-Bowman, I, no. 909, 32.)

71. Hernando CANTILLANA—
    Shoemaker
    Conqueror—Narváez
    From: Grand Canary Island

Cantillana arrived in the Indies in 1514, was in Cuba five years later, and went to New Spain with the 1520 Narváez *entrada*, accompanied by his two brothers. After being awarded a quarter share of Xilotepec (43 miles northwest of Mexico City; 18,335 tributaries in 1565), Cantillana was joined in 1522 by his son Diego and probably by his wife, Catalina Rodríguez of Seville. Diego went to Spain after Cantillana died ca. 1530, and by the time he returned with his wife and four daughters Xilotepec had been reassigned to first conqueror Juan Jaramillo Salvatierra. Diego was awarded $200 annual pension that continued to be paid to his widow for the support of the daughters. Both of Cantillana's brothers died during the siege of Mexico City. This probably explains why a shoemaker received such a valuable grant, beyond what one of his station could ordinarily expect.

(Gerhard, 383ff.; Icaza, I, 145; Boyd-Bowman, I, no. 1251, 43; *Protocolos*, I, no. 739, 181 of 27 August 1527.)

72. Ginés de CÁRDENAS
    Poblador
    From: Seville
    Parents: Antón Jerónimo and Ana García de Cárdenas

Cárdenas arrived in New Spain in 1522 and established his residence in Veracruz. His first *encomienda*, awarded by Alonso de Estrada, was taken by Nuño de Guzmán, who then assigned him Ucila (132 miles southeast of Puebla). The second Audiencia cancelled the award, primarily because by the early 1530s the area had lost about 90 percent of its contact population. Cárdenas was married, had two sons and, after 1534, maintained his *casa poblada* with arms and horses in Puebla.

(Gerhard, 302; Icaza, II, 171; *Protocolos*, I, no. 1213, 266 of 1 April 1528; Boyd-Bowman, II, no. 8864, 273.)

73. Luis de CÁRDENAS *"el hablador"*
    First Conqueror
    From: Triana (Seville) (?)

Cárdenas is thought to have been a native of Triana, Seville, and may have been a *vecino* of Antequera. He was awarded Tepeucila (45 miles northwest of Antequera) and held it until he departed from New Spain in 1544. This region of Oaxaca experienced a 90 to 95 percent loss of native inhabitants between contact and mid-century.

(Gerhard, 306; Orozco y Berra, 77; Boyd-Bowman, I, no. 4111, 135.)

74. Pedro de CARRANZA—*Hidalgo* (?)
    Poblador Antiguo
    From: Pancorbo (Burgos)
    Parents: Pedro de Carranza and Juana de la Serna

Carranza, one of Cortés' *mayordomos*, is thought to have been a native of Pancorbo in the Burgos area. He arrived in

New Spain in 1522 and became a *vecino* of Mexico City after spending eight years in the Indies. Carranza's *encomienda* included Tepexi (110 miles southeast of Mexico City, 45 miles southeast of Puebla; 2,500 tributaries as late as 1570) and Teguantepec, held "in deposit" from Cortés between 1528 and 1530. This grant had perhaps 10,000 tributaries during the period. Tepexi was vacant by 1537, suggesting that Carranza was dead. It was then reassigned to *poblador* Martín Cortés (not related to Hernando) by the viceroy. Carranza and his Indian wife had two children: a son, Antonio, and a daughter, Ana. Ana married Luis de Valdivieso of Salamanca, a *vecino* of Pánuco.

Note: Carranza, possibly a minor *hidalgo*, used the title *escudero*, although his marriage was not of the type usually associated with gentle birth.

(Gerhard, 281 and 264ff.; Icaza, I, 142 and 151; Boyd-Bowman, I, no. 800, 27.)

75. Juan de CARRASCOSA
Conqueror—Narváez
From: Carrascosa (Cuenca)

Carrascosa was in Cuba the year before joining the 1520 Narváez *entrada*. After the capture of Tenochtitlan he served in the Pánuco *entrada*, becoming a *vecino* there. His *encomienda*, 42 miles west in the vicinity of Valles, granted either by Cortés or Alonso de Estrada, was reduced to two villages by Nuño de Guzmán, with a total of 339 tributaries in 1533. These towns, Tamalol and Cuaguacasco, were reassigned to *poblador* Rodrigo de Orduña when he married Carrascosa's widow in the late 1530s. The *encomienda* was inherited by a daughter of this second union when she married Juan de Navarrete. The tribute was being paid to Rodrigo Navarrete in 1597. The crown was the sole holder after 1643.

(Gerhard, 355; Scholes and Adams, 46; Boyd-Bowman, I, no. 1517, 51; Icaza, I, 203d; Chipman, 293.)

76. Alonso CARRILLO—*Hidalgo*
Poblador
From: Toledo
Parents: Pedro Cuello Carrillo and doña Gerónima de la Dueña

Carrillo arrived in New Spain in 1530 as a member of Cortés' returning entourage and became a *vecino* of Mexico City. He married the widow of first conqueror Bartolomé López in the early 1540s and thereby acquired the *encomienda* rights to Comala and Cecamachantla (290 miles west of Mexico City, near Colima). Carrillo felt the $20 per year income from the 50 tributaries inadequate for a *caballero*, especially since he had to support a wife and four children. Nonetheless, tributes from this *encomienda* were still being paid to a Carrillo in 1597.

(Gerhard, 80; Icaza, I, 215; Boyd-Bowman, II, no. 11229, 335.)

77. Jorge CARRILLO—*Hidalgo* (?)
Poblador
From: Toledo
Parents: Don García de Toledo y Cervatos and doña Isabel Pacheco (?)

Carrillo arrived in Mexico City two days after its capture, too late to be considered a conqueror. He subsequently served with *entradas* to the west and south, receiving the *encomiendas* of Tecucitlan and Chiapa (near Colima) and Amatlan and Motenpacoya (25 miles south-southeast of Colima, but in the province of Motines). These *cabeceras* were about 310 miles west of Mexico City. Carrillo married a daughter of Antonio de Nava (a native of Escalona, Toledo, and a *vecino* of Mexico City), had six children, and maintained his *casa poblada* in Mexico City. His son, Alonso Carrillo, inherited the *encomiendas* in 1553, and then a grandson assumed title in the 1560s. Tribute was still going to the family after 1597.

Note: In the extract of his petition submitted in the 1540s to the viceroy and thence to the crown, Carrillo's parents are given as "don" and "doña," but available records show that neither Carrillo nor his son affected the title, nor was any reference made to either of them using the title. Although a *vecino* of Mexico City, Carrillo did not participate in municipal government at any time during the period. Lacking additional documents, the tentative conclusion of this writer is that an error was made in assembling and handling Carrillo's petition over the centuries and that don García de Toledo y Cervatos and doña Isabel Pacheco are not his parents.

(Gerhard, 80 and 192; Icaza, I, 195; Orozco y Berra, 58; Sauer, 34; Boyd-Bowman, II, no. 11231, 335.)

78. **Antonio de CARVAJAL—*Hidalgo***
First Conqueror
From: Zamora
Parents: Pedro González de Carvajal and Isabel Delgadillo

In the Indies by 1517 and in Cuba a year later, Carvajal joined Cortés, acting as a captain in the conquest. He then served in subsequent *entradas* and became a *regidor* of Mexico City, first appointed by Cortés, and later on a perpetual basis. Carvajal received the *encomienda* of Zacatlan (88 miles northeast of Mexico City; perhaps 3,000 tributaries remaining in 1570). Tribute from Zacatlan was still being paid to a Carvajal descendant in 1750. His first wife was doña Catalina de Tapia, a native of Torralba in the Toledo region. The union produced doña Catalina de Tapia Carvajal, born in New Spain. A second marriage, to doña María de Olid y Viedma, produced seven daughters and one son, Antonio. Both of his wives were nieces of first conqueror and *regidor* Bernaldino Vázquez de Tapia. The sister of the second wife married *regidor* Bernardino de Albornoz. Carvajal maintained a *casa poblada*, arms, and horses in Mexico City. His household included Pedro Burgueño, a son of conquistador Hernando Burgueño who died while on a trip to Spain in an attempt to regain his *encomienda*. Carvajal died ca. 1565.

Note: Boyd-Bowman in no. 4859, 161, lists Carvajal as a native of Toro, a lesser city 15 miles east of Zamora. Carvajal, like a number of first conquerors, testified against Cortés in his *residencia*.

(Icaza, I, 72f.; Gerhard, 391f.; Orozco y Berra, 73; Boyd-Bowman, I, no. 4885a, 162 and II, no. 488a, 342; *Actas*, V, 267 of 9 August 1549.)

79. **Francisco de las CASAS—*Hidalgo***
Poblador
From: Trujillo (Cáceres)

Casas, a cousin of Cortés, arrived in New Spain in 1523, went to Honduras with Olid and returned in 1525 to Mexico City, where he served as a lieutenant governor and *alcalde mayor*. Not until 20 December 1527, however, was he formally received, at his petition, as a *vecino* of Mexico City. He acquired the *encomienda* of Yanhuitlan (190 miles southeast of Mexico City; 16 *sujetos* in 1548) in 1536 after its tribute had been paid to the crown for two years. The first holder is not known. Casas was succeeded ten years later by his oldest son, Gonzalo, married to a daughter of first conqueror Andrés de Barrios. A grandson, Francisco, was the *encomendero* in 1591.

(Gerhard, 286; Orozco y Berra, 38; Scholes and Adams, 25; Boyd-Bowman, II, no 3124, 91; Icaza, I, 212; *Actas*, I, 124.)

80. **Francisco CASCO—untitled lawyer**
Poblador
From: Puebla de Alcocer (La Serena, Extremadura)

Casco, an untitled lawyer (*procurador de causas*), was in New Spain in the mid-1520s but did not become a *vecino* of Mexico City until 1528. In the late 1530s he was assigned the tribute from Papaloticpac (220 miles southeast of Mexico City, near Antequera). The first *encomendero* had been Francisco de Ribadeo, warden of the Mexico City jail. The grant reverted to the crown sometime after 1541.

(Gerhard, 306; Boyd-Bowman, II, no. 1725, 48; *Protocolos*, I, no. 319, 98 of 31 January

1527, no. 999, 229 of 13 January 1528, and no. 1684, 351 of 15 October 1528.)

81. Diego de CASTAÑEDA
Poblador

Castañeda, a ship owner, became a *vecino* of Pánuco and acquired Xicaya (vicinity of Pánuco; 287 tributaries in 1532), replacing first conqueror Juan López de Jimena as *encomendero* sometime before 1532. He also acquired Tamacuiche, Tampasquín, Tamunau, and Tachave (all near Valles) before 1550. Castañeda was succeeded by his widow, Elvira de Salcedo, who then married Jerónimo de Mercado de Sotomayor. Xicaya reverted to the crown ca. 1553. The Valles grants were still held by Mercado in 1569.

(Gerhard, 217 and 355; Chipman, 292; Icaza, II, 260; *Protocolos*, I, no. 1584, 332 of 28 September 1528 and no. 1559, 334 of 30 September 1528.)

82. Rodrigo de CASTAÑEDA—*Hidalgo*
First Conqueror
From: Valle de Carriedo (Santander)
Parents: Juan de Castañeda and Leonor Díaz de Zaballos

A son of a *caballero hidalgo*, Castañeda went to join the Cortés *entrada* after having been a *vecino* of Santo Domingo for five years. After the capture of Tenochtitlan Castañeda served with *entradas* to Michoacán, Pánuco, Zapotecas, and Guatemala. By 1530 he was a *vecino* of Mexico City. He was an interpreter for the first Audiencia, as well as holding the title of royal ensign. Available records suggest that Castañeda went unrewarded, except for a coat of arms granted in 1527, until ca. 1532 when the second Audiencia assigned him the *encomienda* of Puctla (also called Yztayuca, 240 miles east-southeast of Mexico City, 30 miles southwest of Alvarado; three *estancias* in 1570). Castañeda was married and had eight children, six of them sons. He died ca. 1560 and was succeeded by a namesake son. The last *encomendero* before escheatment in 1626 was Castañeda's mestizo grandson, according to Gerhard named Zicotencatl Castañeda.

(Gerhard, 86; Scholes and Adams, 34; Orozco y Berra, 77; Icaza, I, 21; Boyd-Bowman, I, no. 2785, 98.)

83. Alonso de CASTELLANOS
Poblador
From: Sahagún (León) (?)
Parents: Alonso de Castellanos and Juana Becerra

Castellanos arrived in New Spain in 1528. Shortly thereafter he acquired the *encomienda* rights to Yolotepec and Ixcatlan (215 miles south-southeast of Mexico City; a number of *estancias* ca. 1550) as the first holder and became a *vecino* of Mexico City. There is every indication that this *encomienda* provided adequate income in spite of population decline. Castellanos' brother, Francisco, was the treasurer of Guatemala. The *encomienda* was inherited by a namesake son ca. 1565. He was still the *encomendero* in 1597.

(Gerhard, 286 and 290; Scholes and Adams, 49; Boyd-Bowman, II, no. 5963, 180.)

84. Pedro CASTELLAR
Conqueror—Narváez

Castellar, in the Indies early enough to have taken part in the campaigns in Cuba, came to New Spain with Narváez in 1520. After serving in various *entradas* he was awarded the *encomienda* of Xicaltepec (120 miles west of Coatzacoalcos, 75 miles south of Veracruz) and became a *vecino* of Coatzacoalcos. Around 1530 Castellar married doña María de León, daughter of Licenciado Pedro de León and doña Beatriz de Alcocer, both of Seville. Doña María succeeded as *encomendera* by 1548 and then renounced her rights in favor of their daughter, doña Antonia de León, when the latter married Diego Núñez de Guzmán (also known as Diego de Esquivel) in 1560. Núñez was still receiving tribute from Xicaltepec in 1597.

85. Don Luis de CASTILLA—*Hidalgo Poblador*
From: Valladolid
Parents: Don Pedro de Castilla and doña Francisca Osorio

Don Luis, a direct descendant of King Pedro I and doña Juana de Castro, was twenty-eight years old when he arrived in New Spain in 1530 as escort for his relation, doña Juana de Zúñiga, the second wife of Hernando Cortés. There were a number of wives of the conquerors in this entourage. Don Luis had seen military action as a teenager in the Comunero Revolt and later against the French. After arriving in New Spain he served in the pacification of Jalisco. He was granted the *encomienda* of Tututepec (280 miles southeast of Mexico City; perhaps 3,000 tributaries in 1565) in late 1534, at about the same time he became a *regidor* of Mexico City. The grant had once belonged to Cortés, had been taken by Salazar in 1525, recovered the following year, and then held by the crown from 1532 until reassigned to don Luis. Upon her arrival in New Spain in 1536, he married doña Juana de Sosa of Córdoba, a sister of royal treasurer Juan Alonso de Sosa. They had three sons and three daughters. Don Pedro de Castilla, the oldest son, inherited the *encomienda* in 1587, two years after don Luis died at age eighty-three. Tributes were still in private hands in 1801. A daughter, doña Catalina Osorio, married *hidalgo* García de Vega of Llerena (Badajoz) but died shortly thereafter (ca. 1547).

(Gerhard, 380f.; Icaza, II, 7 and 298; Boyd-Bowman, II, no. 12093a, 361, no. 4055, 119 and no. 1453, 41; Scholes and Adams, 19.)

86. Alonso del CASTILLO Maldonado—*Hidalgo*
Conqueror—Narváez
From: Salamanca
Parents: Dr. Alonso del Castillo and Doña Aldonza Maldonado

Castillo, a member of the Narváez *entrada*, became a *vecino* of Mexico City after the campaign ended. He shared the tribute from Igualapa, Ometepec, and Suchistlaguaca (190 miles south of Mexico City; 24 *barrios* and *estancias* in the mid-1500s) with Francisco de Herrera. The *encomienda* was assigned by Governor Alonso de Estrada in 1528. Castillo died before 1547. His half was acquired by Francisco de Orduña who, by 1548, had given it to a daughter, Inés de Velasco, when she married Bernardino del Castillo, son of Lupe Pardo del Castillo and Inés Nieto of Toledo. Income from this *encomienda* amounted to $380 per year in the mid-1540s. By 1565 the shared *encomienda* arrangement had terminated; tribute from Igualapa went to Bernardino del Castillo and that from Ometepec and Suchistlaguaca to the Herrera heir. Igualapa reverted to the crown by 1597. Yurirapundaro (150 miles west-northwest of Mexico City), initially assigned to conqueror Juan de Tovar in 1528, was reassigned to Castillo after 1539. It reverted to the crown six years later, the time of Castillo's death. Castillo's brother, Martín Hernández del Castillo, was also *vecino* of Mexico City.

(Gerhard, 65 and 150; Orozco y Berra, 77; Icaza, I, 203; *Protocolos*, I, no. 204, 72 of 9 November 1525; *Actas*, I, 37; Scholes and Adams, 36; Boyd-Bowman, II, no. 11506, 343.)

87. Juan CATALÁN—Cannoneer
First Conqueror
From: Catalonia

Catalán, an artilleryman in the Cortés *entrada*, was in Cuba by 1518; after the conquest he became a *vecino* of Mexico City. He held the *encomienda* of Tlagualilpa (44 miles north of Mexico City,

11 miles northeast of Tula; one *estancia*) and shared Atitalaquía (40 miles north of Mexico City, nine miles east-southeast of Tula; 2,815 tributaries in four dependencies in 1570) with first conqueror Juan Siciliano from Sicily. Catalán was succeeded in the 1520s by his widow, Ana de Segura, and daughter, Juana de Acevedo. Ana, widowed by Diego Ramón before she married Catalán, was the daughter of notary Francisco de Segura and Antonia Maldonado of Seville. She had been in the Indies since 1514 as an employee (*criada*) in the household of *poblador* Juan de Cervantes. The *encomienda* was taken by the crown in 1536, but Ana received Tlamaco, an *estancia* of Atitalaquía, as a replacement. Ana acquired a third husband, Jerónimo Trías, but remained the *encomendera*. By this time her daughter Juana had married Martín de Bandevena of Brussels (probably yet another foreign gunner). The *encomienda* was inherited ca. 1564 by Ana's son Jerónimo Trías, and reverted to the crown in 1643.

(Gerhard, 295 and 297ff.; Icaza, I, 108f.; Boyd-Bowman, I, no. 5029, 168; Orozco y Berra, 38; Scholes and Adams, 22.)

88. Gonzalo CEREZO—Page during the conquest
Conqueror—Narváez
From: Córdoba
Parents: Hernando Cerezo and Catalina de Torres of Murcia

Cerezo had been in Cuba since 1518, and came to New Spain with Narváez. Once there he served as a page to Cortés and after the capture of Tenochtitlan took part in a number of *entradas*. Cerezo became a *vecino* of Mexico City and acquired the position of *alguacil mayor* of the Audiencia. He held the *encomienda* of Cocula (90 miles south-southwest of Mexico City near Taxco; a medium-sized grant with six or seven *estancias* in addition to the *cabecera* ca. 1579). Cerezo married María de Espinoza and maintained a *casa poblada* with servants, family and friends but left no children. Cocula was claimed by the crown after Cerezo died in 1564, but his widow sued and was able to retain the tribute until 1579, when it reverted.

(Gerhard, 146f.; Icaza, I, 32f.; Boyd-Bowman, I, no. 1391, 47; Scholes and Adams, 17; Orozco y Berra, 58.)

89. Juan CERMEÑO
First Conqueror
From: Palos (Huelva)
Father: Rodrigo de Costa

Cermeño spent a year in Cuba before joining the 1519 Cortés *entrada*. He became a *vecino* of Mexico City early in 1525 after taking part in the first Pánuco *entrada* and was assigned Coatlan and Acuitlapan (75 miles south-southwest of Mexico City near Taxco; ten *estancias* in the late 1500s). Cermeño married a daughter of deceased conqueror Juan Ruiz. His household included a daughter and his mother-in-law, also a native of Palos. Cermeño's brother, a pilot, was hanged in Villa Rica at Cortés' command for demanding to return to Cuba. The *encomienda* was inherited by Cermeño's widow, who then married Diego Pérez de Zamora. Zamora was still the *encomendero* in 1597. Part of the tribute reverted to the crown between 1643 and 1688.

(Gerhard, 253; Icaza, I, 9 and II, 70f.; Boyd-Bowman, I, no. 1904, 66; Scholes and Adams, 27; Orozco y Berra, 38; Actas, I, 25.)

90. Jorge CERÓN Saavedra—*Hidalgo Poblador*
From: Baeza (Jaén)
Parents: Martín Cerón and Marta Martínez de Altamirano

Cerón came to New Spain in 1530 to serve as *maestre de campo* for Cortés' Pacific *entrada*; after the expedition he returned to Spain to bring his family, relatives and household to Mexico City, where he became a *vecino*. Viceroy Mendoza assigned him the *encomienda* of Charo—also called Matalcingo (130 miles west of Mexico City near present day Morelia; 600 tributaries in 1573). The first holder of this grant was *contador* Rodrigo de Albornoz. The cleric Bernardo de la Torre was hired in October 1537 to serve as priest and manager of the grant for an annual salary of $100. Ten years later Cerón's administrator was Juan Ortiz, a native of a small town near Baeza. By the early 1550s Cerón was involved in a mining venture in Zacatecas. Alvaro Saavedra Cerón, Jorge's older brother, was associated with Cortés in the Pánuco and Michocán *entradas*. He was lost at sea in 1527 on a return trip from the Moluccas.

(Gerhard, 106f.; Icaza, I, 171f. and II, 17f.; Boyd-Bowman, II, no. 5519, 166 and II, no. 5573, 168; *Protocolos*, II, no. 1989, 63 of 13 October 1563 and no. 2651, 225 of 14 March 1553.)

91. Juan de CERVANTES (Casaus)—
Hidalgo
Poblador
From: Seville
Parents: Gonzalo Gómez de Cervantes and doña Francisca de Casaus

Cervantes, a knight of Santiago, arrived in New Spain in 1524 with an appointment as royal factor for Pánuco, a position he filled until late 1533 at a salary of 200,000 *maravedís* (ca. 445 *pesos*) per year. While not necessarily an ally of Nuño de Guzmán, he did testify on his behalf at the latter's *residencia*. When his salary from the royal treasury was halted early in 1534, he became a *vecino* of Mexico City. Two years later he married doña Luisa de Lara, a daughter of conqueror Comendador Leonel de Cervantes, also of Seville. They had eight children. His *encomiendas* varied somewhat with the political climate. His half of Guautla (145 miles northeast of Mexico City; 418 tributaries in 1532), shared with *poblador* Andrés de Inero, was assigned him by Nuño de Guzmán in 1529 and was taken and reassigned in the early 1540s. Ilamatlan and Altehuecian (130 miles northeast of Mexico City; 1,650 tributaries in 1565) and Tamazunchale (130 miles north-northeast of Mexico City; 1,164 tributaries in 1532) were assigned by the second Audiencia in 1532. Cervantes was succeeded as *enco-* *mendero* by his oldest son, Leonel, in 1564. Tamazunchale reverted to the crown in 1643. The other two *cabeceras* stayed in private hands until late in the 17th century.

(Gerhard, 133f., 243 and 355; Chipman, 103, 269 and 292f.; Icaza, I, 192f.; Boyd-Bowman, I, no. 3342, 116 and II, no. 8914, 274f.; Scholes and Adams, 18.)

92. Comendador Leonel de CERVANTES—*Hidalgo*
Conqueror—Narváez
From: Seville

Cervantes arrived in Cuba in 1519 and was a member of the Narváez *entrada* of 1520 before joining Cortés. In 1520, after the Noche Triste, he received license to go to Spain to get his family and hence did not take part in the siege and capture of Tenochtitlan. He returned to New Spain in 1524 with his wife, Leonor de Andrada, a son, and five daughters. Another daughter was born in New Spain. Cervantes became a *vecino* of Mexico City and *encomendero* of Atlapulco and Xalatlaco (45 miles southwest of Mexico City). Atlapulco was assigned to his son, Alonso, when the latter married doña Catalina de Zárate. She succeeded Alonso in 1550. Also in 1550 Cervantes' widow, Leonor de Andrada, succeeded and became *encomendera* of Xalatlaco (father and son died the same year). Leonor was succeeded by a daughter, doña Isabel de Lara, who married in succession *poblador* Alonso de Aguilar y Córdoba, first conqueror Alonso de Mendoza, and *poblador* Licenciado Alemán. The other daughters also married well: doña Ana Cervantes, Alonso de Villaseñor; doña Catalina de Cervantes (de Lara), Captain Juan de Villaseñor Orozco; doña Beatriz de Andrada, don Francisco de Velasco; doña María de Cervantes, Captain Pedro de Ircio; and doña Luisa de Lara, *factor* Juan de Cervantes Casaus.

(Gerhard, 271; Icaza, II, 9; Boyd-Bowman, I, no. 3342, 116 and II, no. 8910, no. 8913, no. 8914, 274f., no. 8915, 275 and no. 9460, no. 9461, 288; Scholes and Adams,

30f.; Orozco y Berra, 77; Díaz del Castillo, I, 471.)

93. Francisco CIFONTES
Conqueror—Narváez

In Cuba by 1519, Cifontes came to New Spain as a member of the Narváez *entrada*, and after the capture of Tenochtitlan served with a number of *entradas* before becoming a *vecino* of Colima and *encomendero* of nearby Gualata as well as Aguacatlan 115 miles to the north. Aguacatlan was taken by Nuño de Guzmán in 1530. *Encomienda* income was augmented by a tithe-collecting contract with merchant Antón de Carmona. A daughter married Juan Jiménez of Baena, also a *vecino* of Colima. Cifontes was still *encomendero* of Gualata in 1550.

(Gerhard, 80; Icaza, I, 55 and II, 84; *Protocolos*, I, no. 1663, 347 of 12 October 1528 and no. 1703, 355 of 19 October 1528; Gerhard 1982, 60f.)

94. Pedro CINDOS de Portillo
First Conqueror
From: San Román (León)
Parents: Sebastián de Portillo and Catalina Gómez

In the Indies since 1514, Cindos was in Cuba by 1517 and had been a member of Grijalva's 1518 expedition. With *poblador* Hernando de Salazar from Granada he held the *encomiendas* of Tlatlauquitepec (20 *estancias* in 1548), Xonotla (three *estancias* and seven *pueblos* ca. 1600), and Hueytlapa (21 *sujetos* in 1570, including the sub-*cabeceras* Ixtepec and Ixconyamec). The entirety of the grant was about 150 miles east-northeast of Mexico City. Indications are that Cindos lived in one of these *cabeceras*. He renounced his share of the *encomiendas* when he entered the Franciscan order in 1528, spending the last part of his life as a *doctrinero*.

(Gerhard, 229f., 389, and 391; Icaza, II, 292; Boyd-Bowman, I, no. 2227, 76; Orozco y Berra, 53.)

95. Cristóbal de CISNEROS
Poblador Antiguo
From: Escalona (Toledo)
Parents: Félix de Zayas and Catalina de Cisneros

Cisneros, born in 1494, was in the Antilles at age 20, and in Cuba four years later as a member of the Grijalva expedition of 1518. His 1529 arrival in Mexico City coincided with that of the first Audiencia. In the early 1530s Cisneros was assigned the *encomiendas* of Metepec with six *estancias* and the twin *cabeceras* of Calimaya and Tepemaxalco (about 30 miles southwest of Mexico City, six to 12 miles south-southwest of Toluca), in *encomienda*. Though claimed by Cortés, the grant was held in succession from 1528 by Licenciado Juan Gutiérrez Altamirano, Cisneros, and Alonso de Avila, as well as the crown between 1534 and 1536, when Altamirano recovered it. By then Cisneros had become a *vecino* of Villarreal, Chiapas holding the offices of *corregidor* and *alcalde*.

(Gerhard, 175 and 271; Boyd-Bowman, I, no. 4263, 140.)

96. Juan de CISNEROS *"bigotes"*
Conqueror—Narváez

Cisneros arrived in New Spain in 1520 with Narváez and soon became a *vecino* of Mexico City. He was assigned the *encomienda* of Mayamala (105 miles south of Mexico City, six *sujetos* in 1570) and Tasmalaca (92 miles south of Mexico City, eleven *estancias* in 1570). Around 1533 he married doña María de Medina, daughter of Jerónimo de Medina and doña Rosa (?) of Illescas, and had four sons and two daughters. Cisneros was killed in the Mixtón War of 1542, and his widow became the *encomendera*. She was succeeded by a son, Mateo Vázquez de Cisneros. The *encomienda* was still in private hands in 1688.

(Gerhard, 146 and 148; Icaza, I, 117; Scholes and Adams, 40; Orozco y Berra, 58; Boyd-Bowman, II, no. 10910, 326.)

97. Diego de COLIO
First Conqueror
From: Cabrales (Asturias)
Parents: Pedro Díaz de Palmar and Juana Hernández de Cangas

Colio arrived in Cuba in 1518 and joined the Cortés *entrada* the following year. After the capture of Tenochtitlan he arrived with *entradas* in Jalisco and Guatemala. He was a *vecino* of Mexico City and there maintained his *casa poblada*. He remained a strong supporter of Cortés in spite of the difficulty he had in maintaining his status as an *encomendero*. Colio's half of Guatinchan (95 miles southeast of Mexico City; nine *estancias* in 1580), an *encomienda* shared with first conqueror Juan Pérez de Arteaga of Palencia, was reassigned to Pedro de Alvarado in the mid-1520s. Colio claimed that Cortés said that this was done so that he could have something better. His new *encomienda* included towns near Tehuantepec, 340 miles southeast of Mexico City, but these were taken to complete the grant awarded to Cortés as Marqués del Valle. Colio then bought the rights to another town from Hernando Ruiz de Ovalle, a mining entrepreneur, but this grant was "poor and sterile." Colio was married and had three children, one of them a son.

(Gerhard, 221f.; Icaza, I, 16f.; Boyd-Bowman, I, no. 75, 4.)

98. Alonso de CONTRERAS—*Hidalgo*
Conqueror—Narváez
From: Burgos
Parents: García de Contreras and María de Lerma

Contreras, a member of the 1510 *entrada* to Jamaica, arrived in New Spain with Narváez. After the capture of Tenochtitlan he went to Guatemala and Higueras, where he served as *factor* for Cortés. Later (1531) he served with Nuño de Guzmán in Pánuco. By 1528 Contreras was a *vecino* of Mexico City and shared the *encomiendas* of Tamasola (220 miles southeast of Mexico City near Antequera; 14 *estancias* in 1550) and Cenzontepec (230 miles south-southeast of Mexico City; 200 tributaries in 1570) with conqueror Juan de Valdivieso, also from Burgos. Tamasola was assigned by Cortés, Cenzontepec by the second Audiencia. Contreras was married and had three sons and seven daughters. He was succeeded by a son, García de Contreras, when he died in 1559.

(Gerhard, 200 and 176; Icaza, I, 35f.; Scholes and Adams, 31; Boyd-Bowman, I, no. 686, 24; Orozco y Berra, 78.)

99. Diego de CORIA—Notary
First Conqueror
From: Alcalá de Guadaira (Seville)
Parents: Alonso de Coria and Leonor Rodríguez

Coria came to New Spain with the Cortés *entrada* after spending two years in Cuba. After the conquest he served with various *entradas*, including duty as notary with Francisco Cortés in Colima, before becoming a *vecino* of Mexico City in 1524 and establishing his *casa poblada* with arms and horses. Four years later he was assigned a one-third share of Cicoac (130 miles northeast of Mexico City; 300 tributaries in 32 small *estancias* in 1592), with conqueror Francisco Ramírez from León receiving the remaining tribute. Coria and his wife, a daughter of conqueror (Narváez) Hernando de Chaves, had five children. She was from Mairena de Alcor in the Seville region. He also recognized two natural children. Coria was succeeded in 1560 by a son, Hernando de Coria.

(Gerhard, 118 and 133; Icaza, I, 9f.; Boyd-Bowman, I, no. 2984, 105 and no. 3120, 109; Scholes and Adams, 28; Orozco y Berra, 38; *BAGN*, VIII, 546; *Actas*, I, 3f.)

100. Juan CORONEL
Conqueror—Narváez
From: Seville
Parents: Diego Coronel and Elvira Bernal de Ojeda

Coronel arrived in Santo Domingo in 1508, took part in the conquest of Puerto Rico the following year, and served in

Venezuela and Panama before going to Cuba in 1519. After the capture of Tenochtitlan, Coronel served in a Pánuco *entrada*. He was never on friendly terms with Cortés. Coronel was a *vecino* and *regidor* of Zacatula in 1525, then legal representative (*procurador*) of Medellín. Three years later he was an *alcalde* in Veracruz. By 1536 Coronel was a *vecino* of Mexico City. He was the original *encomendero* of Orizaba (140 miles east-southeast of Mexico City; 1,300 tributaries in 1565) and Jalapa (contemporary Jalapa de Díaz, Oaxaca, 240 miles east-southeast of Antequera). In 1515, in Puerto Rico, Coronel married Elvira Hernández of Ejica. They had six children, three of them daughters. He was succeeded by a son, Matías Coronel, in the 1550s.

(Gerhard, 205 and 302; Icaza, I, 69; Boyd-Bowman, I, no. 3054, 107 and no. 3355, 116; Scholes and Adams, 45; Orozco y Berra, 59.)

101. Diego CORREAS—Mariner
Conqueror—Narváez
From: Santarem, Portugal
Parents: Jimón Rodríguez and María de Correas

Correas was in Cuba by 1519 and came to New Spain with Narváez the following year. He became a *vecino* of Zacatula after serving in *entradas* in that region of Mexico under Pedro Sánchez Farfán and Rodrigo Alvarez Chico. He was assigned the *encomienda* of Mitla, in the vicinity of Zacatula. Correas was married but had no children. He died in the 1550s and was succeeded by his widow, who shortly thereafter married Hernán Martín.

(Gerhard, 394; Icaza, I, 51; Boyd-Bowman, I, no. 5252; Orozco y Berra, 38.)

102. Vicencio CORSO
Poblador Antiguo
From: Calve, Corsica
Parents: Vicente de Angulo and Brigida (?)

After spending three years in the Antilles, Corso arrived in New Spain with the 1523 Garay expedition to Pánuco. He took part in the conquest of Pánuco and stayed on as a *vecino* when assigned the *encomiendas* of Tanzinteyzayula, Tamaos, Tamante, Tanzaquila, and Moyutla (all in the vicinity of Pánuco, with a combined 1532 population of 945 tributaries). He was married and claimed four legitimate and three natural children. His son, Francisco Corso, inherited when Corso died ca. 1553.

Note: There was another Moyutla in the area, assigned to first conqueror Francisco Gutiérrez. He later sold his rights to Gregorio de Saldaña.

(Gerhard, 215; Icaza, I, 236f.; Boyd-Bowman, I, no. 5158, 172; Scholes and Adams, 50; Chipman, 292f.)

103. Diego CORTÉS—*Hidalgo*
Poblador
From: Don Benito (La Serena, Extremadura)
Parents: Alonso Gonzáles and Ana Ruiz

Cortés arrived in New Spain in 1524 and took part in *entradas* to Pánuco, Valles, and Jalisco. He was assigned a very small *encomienda* in the vicinity of Valles (60 tributaries in 1532), where he was a *vecino*. There is no record of heirs.

(Gerhard, 355; Chipman, 293; Boyd-Bowman, II, no. 1089, 33; Icaza, II, 218.)

104. Francisco CORTÉS—*Hidalgo*
First Conqueror
From: Extremadura
A relative of Hernando Cortés

Cortés, in Cuba by 1518, was a member of his kinsman's *entrada* the following year. He was assigned the *encomiendas* of Tecoman, Zalagua, and Tlacatipa, all in the vicinity of Colima, in addition to being named lieutenant governor and *alcalde mayor* of the region in 1524. He vigorously continued the conquest of western New Spain, pushing as far north as Tepic and east from there to Lake Chapala.

Cortés then falls from sight, his *encomiendas* reverting to the crown in 1532.

(Gerhard, 80; Boyd-Bowman, I, no. 5093, 170; Orozco y Berra, 39.)

105. Hernando CORTÉS—*Hidalgo*,
Notary
First Conqueror
From: Medellín (La Serena, Extremadura)
Parents: Martín Cortés de Monroy and Catalina Pizarro Altamirano

Hernando Cortés, born in 1485, received perhaps two years of training in grammar while living in Salamanca with a paternal aunt, Inés Gómez de Paz and her husband, notary Francisco Núñez de Valera (there is no record of his attending the university there). He arrived in Santo Domingo in 1504 at age nineteen and within two years was closely associated with Diego Velázquez. His contributions were recognized with a grant of Indians and an appointment as notary of the *cabildo* at Azúa, a town some fifty miles west of Santo Domingo. That he was an *hidalgo* and literate helped compensate for his tender years. While in Azúa Cortés involved himself as a merchant until joining the Velázquez *entrada* to Cuba in 1511. Although not a captain, he did hold the office of notary for expedition treasurer, Miguel de Pasamonte. Cortés was a founding *vecino* of Santiago de Baracoa (and party to legitimizing Diego Velázquez' break with governor don Diego Colón), the initial Spanish municipality on Cuba, located on the north side of the eastern tip of the island. He shared the Indians of nearby Manicarao with Andalusian Juan Suárez, his future brother-in-law. Before long he was married to Catalina Suárez and in a partnership with merchant Andrés de Duero, as well as an *alcalde* of Santiago.

When Cortés had the opportunity to organize his own *entrada* in 1518, he had all the prerequisites—seniority, political and financial contacts, an estate, *entrada* experience, and a record of holding municipal office. Shortly after results of the Juan de Grijalva expedition became known, Cuba's governor Diego Velázquez approached Cortés on the advice of Duero and others with the proposition that he establish a colony on the mainland. Other senior settlers, some of them relatives of the governor, had already declined the offer because the conditions proposed by Velázquez were unacceptable for one reason or another. With the partnership formed, a license to establish the colony was requested and received from the authorities in Santo Domingo.

Cortés commenced outfitting with his own funds as well as assets Velázquez supposedly provided from the holdings of temporarily absent Pánfilo de Narváez (perhaps in part explaining the interest Narváez had in leading the follow-up *entrada* of 1520). Narváez' funds had already been spent when Velázquez withdrew from the enterprise, whereupon Cortés, still short of capital, sought and received backing from Cuba's merchant community, including former partner Andrés de Duero. By November 1518 Cortés had assembled perhaps 300 followers, six ships, and all the provisions that could be acquired in the area, whereupon he departed eastern Cuba. During the ensuing three months the *entrada* was augmented by an additional 200 men, mostly veterans of the Grijalva expedition, plus additional stores, armament, horses, and five more ships. When the force left western Cuba for the mainland on 18 February 1519, Cortés had effectively stripped the island of its provisions and nearly one-third of its Spanish population.

The *entrada* followed the typical Caribbean pattern—working along the coast of the mainland, probing, raiding, inquiring, and reprovisioning as needed. The effort was aided immeasurably by the early acquisition of two interpreters, repatriated Jerónimo de Aguilar and the Indian doña Marina (Malinche). Founding Veracruz and the establishment of a municipal council was also in keeping with tradition. Through it a vehicle for legitimizing the venture as well as a means to deal directly with the crown was created.

The action also effectively severed political ties with Cuba. Velázquez' attempt to regain control of the *entrada* by sending Pánfilo de Narváez, a very senior man in the region, with orders to arrest Cortés was also in keeping with the ways of the Indies.

The tactics Cortés and his followers used against the various native groups encountered in Mexico also followed established Caribbean practices. Control was often gained by seizing the local ruler during a peaceful gathering, followed by reaching an agreement outlining the form and conditions of the relationship. Combat was still required, especially with dominant regional groups. Secondary communities often served as willing allies and auxiliaries of the Spaniards when it was to their advantage. The timely use of horsemen, footmen, and auxiliaries in various tactical combinations permitted the relatively few Spaniards (Cortés was most effective when his force of Spaniards was fewer than 400) to prevail against vastly superior numbers of Indians. The only significant defeat the *entrada* experienced was when it numbered about 1,400 Spaniards and the entire force, along with auxiliaries, was bottled up in Tenochtitlan (the Noche Triste). European technology, coupled with tactics developed in the Indies, proved devastatingly effective against most native forces. However, deploying the brigantine fleet with its mounted artillery was necessary to terminate the siege of Tenochtitlan, surrounded as it was by water.

Another Caribbean carry-over recognized and used by Cortés was to divide the Indians among the conquerors, even with full knowledge of royal directives to the contrary. The primary differences realized in New Spain compared to the Caribbean had to do with characteristics of the local peoples and environment, not with policy decisions on the part of Cortés. And in keeping with the tradition of the Indies, Cortés, as governor, reserved the best areas and the greatest number of tributaries for himself. His *encomiendas* were located in all of the major regions of New Spain and included over fifty major Indian centers, with conceivably as many as a million tributaries at contact. While it is difficult to determine the exact number of *encomiendas* Cortés held at any one given time (no record survives of grants made to himself), he claimed in 1524 that he held forty-one grants with a reported income of 42,800 gold pesos. These holdings were drastically reduced during the tenure of the acting governors while Cortés was in Honduras (1524–1526) and again after the arrival of the first Audiencia in 1529. Cortés' trip to Spain between 1528 and 1530 resulted in the creation of the Marquesado del Valle de Oaxaca, authorizing him 23,000 tributary vassals in twenty-three *encomiendas* in perpetuity. It is doubtful, however, that Cortés received tribute from so few Indians during his lifetime (in 1569 alone the Marquesado income was $86,000, paid by 60,903 tributaries, in spite of the 23,000 tributary limitation imposed by the Marquesado grant). He employed a battery of legal specialists engaged in constant litigation with the crown over title, tribute, recovery, and restitution, while crown attorneys and inspectors labored as diligently to insure that the Marquesado operated within the limits of the grant.

Like any sixteenth-century governor, Cortés made certain that his kin and supporters received their just rewards. At least eleven of his relatives (eight arriving in New Spain after the capture of Tenochtitlan) from Extremadura and Salamanca became *encomenderos*, and three other relatives, although not *encomenderos*, held important positions in the Cortés estate. No fewer than sixteen of his retainers were also *encomenderos*, half of them taking part in the siege and capture of Tenochtitlan. Six held *mayordomo* positions, directing various parts of the organization. An additional forty retainers not assigned *encomiendas* have been identified, most of them associated with some particular task within the estate. Fully one-fourth of those named worked as members of the legal staff. The others were managers and involved in marketing estate products. Cortés' first chief *mayordomo* was his cousin Rodrigo de Paz from Salamanca (Cortés lived in the Paz household from 1499 to 1501 and more than likely learned his notarial skills from Rodrigo's father, Francisco Núñez de Valera), who was hanged by the acting governors on 16 October 1525. Rodrigo's brother, Francisco Núñez, was Cortés' legal counsel in Spain. Cortés then appointed Licenciado Juan Gutiérrez Altamirano, perhaps a distant relative, to be Paz' successor as chief *mayordomo*.

Cortés was married twice. His first wife, Catalina Suárez, arrived in the Indies in 1509, went to Cuba shortly after it was secured and by 1515 or so had married Cortés, surely by way of cementing an alliance between Cortés and her locally influential relatives. She died shortly after moving to Mexico City in 1522; lacking the *doña* and any illustrious lineage, she would have been a source of embarrassment to Cortés had she lived. She had no children. Cortés' second marriage was arranged when he was rich and famous, on the point of bearing the *don* as Marqués del Valle. His bride was doña Juana de Zúñiga, a daughter of don Carlos de Arellano, Count of Aguilar, and doña Catalina de Zúñiga, of the house of the Count of Béjar. The marriage and Cortés' elevation to Marqués both took place in 1529. The following year doña Juana arrived in New Spain in the company of her relative, don Luis de Castilla. The union produced one son and three daughters. Don Martín married a cousin, doña Ana de Arellano. Doña Juana, the youngest daughter, married don Felipe de Arellano, and doña María the Count of Luna de León. Doña Catalina died as a young girl in Seville. Cortés also acknowledged six natural children: don Martín by the Indian interpreter doña Marina (Malinche); don Luis Cortés y Hermosilla by Elvira de Hermosilla, a native of Trujillo (Cáceres); doña Leonor by the Indian noblewoman doña Isabel Moctezuma (doña Leonor later married Juan de Tolosa, a Basque merhant and Zacatecas mine owner); doña Catalina Pizarro, by a Cuban woman who took the name Leonor Pizarro (doña Catalina married conqueror Juan de Salcedo); and two other daughters by Mexican Indian women.

Cortés died 2 December 1547 in his sixty-second year at Castilleja de la Cuesta near Seville. The Marquesado, an entailed estate, went to don Martín. The remaining children were well taken care of. Each of the daughters, legitimate and natural, had received handsome dowries; the sons worked closely with their legitimate half-brother in the Marquesado.

Note: Relatives who received *encomiendas* were Alonso de Avalos Saavedra (Medellín), Diego Becerra de Mendoza (Mérida), Francisco de las Casas (Trujillo), Francisco Cortés (Extremadura), Juan Jaramillo de Salvatierra (Barcarrota), Alonso Lucas (Extremadura), Alonso de Paz (Salamanca), Pedro de Paz (Salamanca), Fernando de Saavedra (Medellín), Alonso Valiente (Medina de Torres), and Francisco de Villegas (Castillana). Relatives who did not receive *encomiendas* were Marquesado accountant Juan Altamirano (Medellín) and fray Diego Altamirano (Medellín). Retainers with *encomiendas* were Rodrigo de Baeza (Burgos), Domingo de Medina (Guareña), Pedro de la Isla (Seville), Bartolomé de Perales (Medellín), Rodrigo Rangel (Badajoz), Francisco de Terrazas (Fregenal de la Serena), Alonso de Villanueva Tordesillas (Villanueva de la Serena), Francisco de Santa Cruz (Burgos), Serván Bejerano (Córdoba), Diego de Ocampo (Lugo), Francisco de Herrera (Seville), Andres de Barrios (Cádiz), Pedro Gallego (Maestrazgo de León), Jorge Cerón de Saavedra (Jaén), Juan de Salamanca (Avila), Diego de Coria (Seville), and Licenciado Juan Gutiérrez Altamirano (Salamanca).

(Boyd-Bowman, I, no. 445, 16, no. 3162a, 167, and II, no. 10772a, 320; Gerhard, 10, 16f., 52f., 56, 71–76, 88–98, 100–105, 117–120, 141–144, 172–177, 180, 200–203, 208f., 226f., 247–249, 252–255, 264–267, 271, 301–304, 312–314, 321–323, 330f., 335, 357, 363–366, 378f., and 394–396; Díaz del Castillo, I, 55–71,

119–122 and II, 437f.; Gómara, 323–325, 327f., 335f., and 339–341; Riley, 20f., 28f., 68–70, 74, and 110f.; Simpson, 164–167; Pagden, 504.)

106. Martín CORTÉS
Poblador
From: Murcia
Parents: Pedro de Abellán and Beatriz Martín

Arriving in 1524, Cortés took part in *entradas* to Yucatan, Río Grijalva, Guatemala, and Honduras. He then acquired the vacant *encomienda* of Tepexi (45 miles southeast of Puebla; 2,500 tributaries in 1570) under a special contract so that he could establish silk growing there. He was to receive full tribute until 1542 and half the tribute until 1557. All the while Cortés was a *vecino* of Puebla. He died before 1547, and his widow, Teresa Jiménez Arreola, continued to collect the one-half tribute until the grant reverted to the crown in 1550. The couple had a son and a daughter.

(Gerhard, 281; Icaza, I, 224; Boyd-Bowman, II, no. 6681, 204.)

107. Juan de CUÉLLAR—Trumpeter
Conqueror—Narváez
From: Cuéllar (Segovia)

Cuéllar had been in the Indies since 1502, having served as trumpeter for Christopher Columbus on his fourth voyage. In 1511 he took part in the conquest of Cuba, arriving in New Spain in 1520 with Narváez. After the capture of Tenochtitlan he participated in some *entradas*, then became a *vecino* of the capital in 1525. His *encomienda*, Ixtapaluca (20 miles southeast of Mexico City; nine or ten *estancias* on Lake Chalco prior to 1558) was assigned him by Cortés. His wife, Ana Ruiz de Berrio, succeeded him ca. 1545 and then passed the grant to their oldest son, Andrés. They had nine children, five of them daughters. When Andrés died without issue ca. 1565, the *encomienda* was assigned to another son, Martín. Tribute reverted to the crown in 1574 and then was reassigned to don Luis de Velasco.

(Gerhard, 103; Icaza, I, 222; Boyd-Bowman, I, no. 2865, 101; Scholes and Adams, 31; Orozco y Berra, 78.)

108. Juan de CUÉLLAR Verdugo
"el gitano"
Conqueror—Narváez
From: Copeses, Cuéllar (Segovia)
Parents: Cristóbal de Cuéllar and Catalina Verdugo

Cuéllar Verdugo arrived in New Spain with Narváez in 1520 after spending a year in Cuba. He may have been a kinsman of Cuba's governor, Diego Velázquez. He was assigned the *encomienda* of Chimalguacan Atenco (16 miles east of Mexico City; 31 *estancias* on Lake Texcoco in 1579) by Cortés and had the award confirmed by Governor Estrada in 1528. Cuéllar relinquished the *encomienda* by sale to *poblador* Doctor Blas de Bustamante in the 1540s. The transaction was confirmed by the viceroy. A *vecino* of Mexico City since 1529, Cuéllar was married to Ana de Maya, also from Cuéllar. She was the daughter of conqueror Antonio de Maya and Mari Alvarez. They had two children, one of them a daughter who married *encomendero* Juan de Avila.

(Gerhard, 77; Icaza, I, 46f., 61f. and 129f.; Orozco y Berra, 78; Scholes and Adams, 17; Boyd-Bowman, I, no. 2867, 101.)

109. Benito de CUENCA
Conqueror—Narváez
From: Jerez de la Frontera (Cádiz)
Parents: Pedro de Cuenca and Constanza Herrera

Cuenca, born ca. 1495, had been in Cuba since 1516, sailed with Hernández de Córdoba in 1517 and was a member of Grijalva's 1518 expedition before joining the Narváez *entrada* in 1520. He maintained a close relationship with Narváez after the capture of Tenochtitlan. Cuenca took part in the first Pánuco *entrada* and remained there as a *vecino* and *encomendero*. He was assigned the *encomienda* of

Calpan, Tamalol, and Chila (southeast of Pánuco; 420 tributaries in 1532). Cuenca married Beatriz González, had two sons, and maintained his *casa poblada*, arms, and horses in Pánuco. He was succeeded as *encomendero* ca. 1560 by his son, Pedro. Pedro in turn was succeeded by his widow, María de Porras, still receiving the tribute in 1597.

(Gerhard, 215; Icaza, I, 43 and II, 219; Boyd-Bowman, I, no. 1158, 40; Scholes and Adams, 20f.; Chipman, 292f.)

110. Luis de la CUEVA
Poblador

Cueva, the first *encomendero* of Tequecistlan (30 miles west of Tehuantepec; 4,000 tributaries in the 1520s, reduced to 650 by 1580), sold his rights to Tomás de Lamadriz. The only other record that Cueva has left is a notarized acknowledgment dated 11 September 1527 in Mexico City that he owed an Andrés de Escobedo 4 *pesos* and 4 *tomines*.

(Gerhard, 265; *Protocolos*, I, no. 760, 185 of 11 September 1527.)

111. Juan de CUEVAS—*Hidalgo*
Poblador
From: Burgos
Father: Licenciado Alonso de Cuevas of Valladolid

Cuevas arrived in New Spain with the royal treasury officers in 1522 and then took part in various *entradas*, including Vázquez de Coronado's Cíbola venture. He also financed persons who took part in *entradas* elsewhere as well as serving as notary for mines (*escribano de minas*). His deputy in Medellín was Bartolomé Román(o). In 1529 Cuevas became a *vecino* of Mexico City, where he maintained his *casa poblada*. Prior to 1546 he acquired the *encomienda* of Cuitlahuac (22 miles southeast of Mexico City near Xochimilco, its *cabecera* on an island in Lake Chalco; 12 or so *estancias* on the north shore of the lake or on other islands). Cuevas married a daughter of *poblador antiguo* Licenciado Diego Téllez and had a son and two daughters. He was succeeded ca. 1560 by his son Alonso, who was still the *encomendero* in 1606.

(Gerhard, 103f.; Icaza, I, 200; Boyd-Bowman, II, no. 2235, 62; Scholes and Adams, 16; *Protocolos*, I, no. 476, 130f. of 4 April 1527 and no. 1278 of 23 April 1528.)

112. Bartolomé CHAVARRÍN(ia)
Conqueror—Narváez
From: Chavarre, Genoa
Parents: Estanani Delpín and Bartaloma de Negro (sic)

Chavarrín arrived in New Spain as a member of the Narváez *entrada* after having spent a year or so in Cuba. After the capture of Tenochtitlan he took part in various *entradas* before becoming a *vecino* of Colima, where he maintained his *casa poblada*, arms, and horses. In 1528 he was assigned the *encomienda* of Chipiltitlan and Aguacatlan (northwest of Colima). He was married and had seven children, four of them sons. His small *encomienda* was inherited ca. 1550 by a son, Antón Chavarrín.

(Gerhard, 59f.; Scholes and Adams, 52; Icaza, I, 249; Boyd-Bowman, I, no. 5186, 173.)

113. Diego de CHAVES
Poblador

Chaves arrived in New Spain in the early 1520s and became a *vecino* of Colima. He was the original *encomendero* of Tepeguacan (in the vicinity of Colima) and Ayuquila-Zacapal (northwest of Colima). Chaves married Catalina de Viñar, but had no children. The *encomienda* was reassigned to Mateo Sánchez of Salamanca when Chaves died in the late 1520s or early 1530s. In the 1540s a Juan de Salamanca received the tribute from Ayuquila-Zacapal. By 1550 the holder of both grants was Antonio de Ortega, the man who married Chaves' widow. The *encomienda* was still in private hands in 1597.

(Gerhard, 59 and 80.)

114. Francisco DAZA de Alconchel
First Conqueror
From: Alconchel (Badajoz)

Daza was in Cuba perhaps a year before joining the 1519 Cortés *entrada*. Extant records suggest that he was a *vecino* of Puebla and held the *encomienda* of Oxitlan (137 miles southeast of Puebla). The grant reverted to the crown ca. 1535 upon Daza's death.

(Gerhard, 302; Orozco y Berra, 78; Boyd-Bowman, I, no. 221, 9.)

115. Francisco DELGADILLO
Poblador
From: Val de Santo Domingo (Toledo)

After his 1528 arrival in New Spain, Delgadillo took part in the 1530 conquest of New Galicia. In 1533 he became a *vecino* of Guadalajara, where he maintained his arms and horses and, according to his petition to Viceroy Mendoza, supported fifteen to twenty soldiers. By 1541 the *encomienda* of Apozotl (present day Apozol, 65 miles north of Guadalajara; perhaps 325 tributaries in 1548) had been assigned to him. Late in the 1540s he claimed that his Indians were bellicose, would rebel without cause, and that the grant paid but $100 per year, while it cost $300 to maintain a priest in the village. Sometime after 1545 Delgadillo also acquired Atistac (three miles south-southwest of Guadalajara) from the recovered holdings of Nuño de Guzmán. Around 1576 he was succeeded by a son, Luis, who was the *encomendero* until 1595, when the *encomienda* escheated.

(Icaza, II, 266f.; Boyd-Bowman, II, no. 11524, 343; Gerhard 1982, 101f. and 151.)

116. Alonso DÍAZ Carballar (de Carvajal)
Poblador
From: Braga, Portugal
Parents: Diego Alvarez Carballar and Blanca González

Díaz arrived in New Spain ca. 1523 and served with *entradas* in Oaxaca. He became a *vecino* of Villa Alta, where he maintained his *casa poblada*, arms, and horses. By 1560 his *encomienda* was Mayana (50 miles northwest of Villa Alta; six *estancias* that delivered their tribute to Xaltepec). The *encomienda* was also referred to as Andaama, Suchitepec, and Guayatepec, a description that corresponds with an area called Tlazaltepec in 1548. Díaz was married and had two sons and a daughter. He was succeeded ca. 1565 by a son, Juan de Espinoza, who was still the *encomendero* in 1597.

(Gerhard, 371; Scholes and Adams, 22; Icaza, I, 233; Boyd-Bowman, II, no. 13448, 407.)

117. Bernal DÍAZ del Castillo—*Hidalgo*
First Conqueror
From: Medina del Campo (Valladolid
Parents: Francisco Díaz del Castillo, *regidor* **of Medina del Campo, and (doña?) María Díez Rejón**

Díaz, famous for his chronicle, arrived in the Indies as a member of the Pedrarias Dávila entourage to Tierra Firme in 1514 at age twenty-two and moved on to Cuba shortly thereafter. He was a member of the expeditions of Hernández de Córdoba and Juan de Grijalva that coasted Mexican shores during 1517 and 1518. Díaz then joined Cortés' *entrada* the following year. Shortly after the capture of Tenochtitlan, Díaz left Mexico City with an *entrada* led by Gonzalo de Sandoval. Evidently he felt that his family ties to Diego Velázquez would prejudice his opportunities with Cortés (*Historia* I, 26). He then went to Guatemala with Pedro de Alvarado and from 1524 to 1526 was with Cortés again as a member of the Honduras *entrada*. He became a *vecino* of Coatzacoalcos in 1522, about the time Sandoval assigned him Potonchon (15,000 tributaries when assigned), Teapa, Tecomaxiaca (1,000 tributaries when assigned), all in Tabasco, as well as Mechoacan, near Coatzacoalcos. The Tabasco grants were taken for the crown in 1527. Sometime around 1541 Mechoacan was reassigned to a natural daughter, doña Teresa Díaz de Padilla, who then married Juan de Fuentes

Díaz became a *vecino* of Santiago de Guatemala in the 1540s and served many years as a *regidor* there. After settling in Santiago, Díaz married Teresa Becerra, widow of Juan Durán, and fathered eight children (five sons and three daughters). He also claimed two natural children, the one named doña Teresa, and a son, Diego Díaz del Castillo.

Note: Of the many versions of Díaz del Castillo's *Historia verdadera*, two perhaps most faithfully represent the old conqueror's original draft. The copy sent to Spain was finally edited and published in 1632 by fray Alonso Remón of the Order of Mercy and has served as the basis of the European transcriptions, editions, and translations. The copy that remained in America was in the custody of the family in Guatemala, then the Ayuntamiento of Santiago, and is now held by the National Archives of Guatemala. It is this copy that was transcribed by Genero García and published in Mexico in 1904. García's transcription is the source used in this study. Needless to say, there are differences in the transcriptions. Most notable for our purposes here is the genealogical information. For instance, both the *BNE* and García versions identify Díaz' mother as "doña María Díez Rejón" in the introductory pages (vii and xx, respectively). The authenticity of the García version is suspect because he also adds "don" to the name of Bernal Díaz' father, a patent absurdity. The BNE version, however, leaves the father's name unadorned as we would expect while awarding the mother the "doña," and it purports to be a copy of the original manuscript in Guatemala. The evidence favors the mother having actually been a doña. In the García transcription, Díaz, in Chapter I, identifies himself only as "natural de la muy noble e ynsigne villa de medina del canpo, hijo de francisco diaz del castillo, regidor que fue della,..." (*Historia*, I, 4).

(Gerhard, 139; Gerhard 1979, 36, 42, and 45; Boyd-Bowman, I, no. 4511, 149; *ENE*, VI, 35f.; Cerwin, 112ff. and 156f.; Díaz del Castillo, I, xx, 4, and 26.)

118. Diego DÍAZ—Stonemason
Poblador

Díaz arrived in Mexico City ca. 1526. Around 1530 he was assigned Chiconautla (15 miles northeast of Mexico City; four or five *estancias*) by the first Audiencia either to teach his tributaries stonemasonry or as a reward for teaching Indians in general his trade. At any rate, the grant reverted to the crown under the second Audiencia in 1532.

(Gerhard, 226; Icaza, II, 310.)

119. Juan DÍAZ del Real
Poblador
From: Aracena (Huelva)
Parents: Diego Martín del Real and Leonor Martínez

Díaz arrived in New Spain with his first wife Leonor Marín in early 1527 and became a *vecino* of Mexico City on 18 February. He was assigned the *encomienda* of Tlapanaloya, a small grant 29 miles north of Mexico City. After Díaz' first wife died he married Elvira de Hermosilla, one of the first eight Spanish women in New Spain and at one time a companion of Cortés (she bore him one son, don Luís Cortés). When Díaz died in the 1540s, Elvira inherited. She then married Lope Vázquez de Acuña, the son of Contador Antón Ruiz de Contreras and doña Leonor de Acuña of Toledo. Díaz' son, Melchor de Chaves, then inherited and was the *encomendero* from 1564 to 1597. The tribute reverted to the crown after 1643.

(Gerhard, 297; Scholes and Adams, 42; Icaza, II, 20; Boyd-Bowman, II, no. 3162a, 92 and no. 5041, 150; *Actas*, I, 122.)

120. Miguel DÍAZ de Aux
Conqueror—Garay
From: Aux (Huesca, Aragón)
Parents: Juan Díaz de Aux and Isabel Dueso

Díaz outfitted two of his own ships and arrived in New Spain as one of Garay's captains in 1520. He claimed that he brought 150 footmen and twenty horsemen to reinforce the Cortés *entrada*. Díaz had been in the Indies since at least 1510, the year he received a license to be absent from his post as *alguacil mayor* of Puerto Rico to return to Spain to bring his wife, Isabel Carrión (de Cáceres?) to the Antilles. He was in Santo Domingo as a ship's master in 1512 and seems to have participated significantly in the commercial development of the Caribbean basin. After the conquest Díaz became a *vecino* of Pánuco but on 15 April 1524 officially changed his citizenship to Mexico City and continued to be active in trade, although never declaring himself or being referred to as a merchant. His *encomienda* interests were complex and changing. In 1521 Cortés assigned him half of Mextitlan (85 miles north-northeast of Mexico City; 120 *sujetos* with 15,500 tributaries in 1573), shared with Alonso Lucas. Then in 1525 the acting governors reassigned Díaz' share to Cortés' in-law Andrés de Barrios. He recovered one-third of this share through a protracted lawsuit. The tribute so regained was given in dowry to his daughter doña Luisa de Aux when she married Rodrigo Maldonado. The income was specifically treated as a pension in accordance with the judgment of the Council of the Indies. In 1524 Cortés assigned Díaz Tempoal (165 miles north-northeast of Mexico City; 1,120 tributaries in 1532). It was taken away the following year, recovered in 1526 and reassigned by Nuño de Guzmán to Juan de Villagrán. Tepetlaostoc (26 miles northeast of Mexico City; 23 *estancias* in 1570) was held by Díaz during 1527 and 1528. It was reassigned to Gonzalo de Salazar. Díaz had another daughter who has left no record of marriage or acquisition of property. He died in the 1560s, no longer an *encomendero*.

(Gerhard, 184, 216, and 312; Chipman, 292; Scholes and Adams, 35; Icaza, I, 73f.; Boyd-Bowman, I, no. 2062, 70; Orozco y Berra, 69; *Actas*, I, 8.)

121. Juan DURÁN
Conqueror—Narváez
From: Madrid

Durán arrived in Cuba in 1519 and joined the Narváez *entrada* the following year. After serving in various *entradas* he became a vecino of Puebla, where he maintained his arms and horses. Durán was assigned the *encomienda* of Elosuchitlan-Axalyagualco (115 miles east-southeast of Puebla; nine *barrios* in 1548). There were still 250 tributaries here in 1570. He was married and had a daughter. Durán was succeeded ca. 1545 by his widow, who then gave the *encomienda* to their daughter, doña Luisa de Frías, when she married Bernardino de Salas. Doña Luisa outlived him and then married Diego de Cisneros. Tribute from this grant reverted to the crown sometime before 1664.

(Gerhard, 261f.; Icaza, I, 12; Scholes and Adams, 32; Boyd-Bowman, I, no. 2284, 79; Orozco y Berra, 79.)

122. Sebastián de EBORA
Conqueror—Narváez
From: Yelves, Portugal
Parents: Luis Méndez de Basconcelos de Abrio

Ebora, a mulatto who had served in Europe, arrived in Cuba in 1519 and went to New Spain the following year with Narváez. After the capture of Tenochtitlan he served in various *entradas* before becoming a *vecino* and *corregido* in Zacatula, where he had his *casa poblada*, arms, and horses. By 1550 he was assigned nearby Axapoteca in *encomienda*. He was married and had three daughters and a son. Ebora died ca. 1560. His son, Alonso, inherited the grant four years later and held it until 1568.

(Gerhard, 394; Icaza, I, 243; Orozco y Berra, 59; Boyd-Bowman, I, no. 5256, 176.)

123. Andrés de ECIJA
First Conqueror
From: Ecija (Seville)

Ecija was in Cuba by 1518 and joined Cortés the following year. He became a *vecino* of Colima and before 1523 was assigned the *encomienda* of Guacoman (30 miles south of Colima). The grant was a crown holding by the mid-1530s.

(Gerhard, 193; Orozco y Berra, 40; Boyd-Bowman, I, no. 3047, 107.)

124. Hernando de ELGÜETA
(Elqueta, Helgueta, Ergueta)
Conqueror

Elgüeta, a *vecino* of Mexico City by September 1528, had joined Cortés as a horseman in Texcoco in 1520 and served in various *entradas* after the capture of Tenochtitlan. He received one-third of the tributes from Tlapalcatepec (255 miles west of Mexico City near Uruapan; three dependencies in 1570) until the second Audiencia claimed them for the crown in August 1531. Conquerors Alonso de Ávila and Pedro Sánchez Farfán shared the other two-thirds of this grant. Elgüeta received a coat of arms dated 4 December 1529.

(Gerhard, 250; *Protocolos*, I, no. 1516, 320 of 15 September 1528 and no. 1542, 325 of 19 September 1528; *Nobiliario*, 309.)

125. Juan de ESCARCENA (Escacena)
Poblador

Escarcena, probably a *poblador* member of Francisco Cortés' *entrada* through Colima, was the *encomendero* of Izatlan (40 miles west of Guadalajara) by 1530. The initial holders of this grant were two *vecinos* of Colima, receiving it ca. 1524. Escarcena was probably also a *vecino* of Colima. The tribute from Izatlan was going to the crown by 1535.

(Gerhard, 157.)

126. Alonso de ESCOBAR
Poblador
From: Medellín (La Serena, Extremadura)
Parents: Diego de Escobar and Catalina Sánchez Verdugo

In 1526 Escobar, a *vecino* of Veracruz, replaced Rodrigo Martín, the first *encomendero* of Xumiltepec (25 miles east of Cuernavaca; seven *estancias*). Title to this medium-sized grant was disputed by two women, each claiming to be the legitimate widow, when Escobar died in the 1540s. The suit was ultimately won by Francisca de Loaysa. She later married Antonio Velázquez, who became the *encomendero*. Escobar had been to the Indies in 1511 but returned to Spain and married. He then came to New Spain after the capture of Mexico City. He brought his first wife, Isabel de Torres, and their son Juan to Mexico City in 1527.

(Gerhard, 92 and 94; Scholes and Adams, 43; Boyd-Bowman, I, no. 447, 16; *Protocolos*, I, no. 103, 50 of 2 October 1525.)

127. Pedro de ESCOBAR
Conqueror—Narváez

Escobar came to New Spain with Narváez; in time became a *vecino* of Mexico City, where he held the humble post of constable (*alguacil*). He held the *encomienda* of Tetila (90 miles east-northeast of Mexico City; four *estancias* in 1548) until 1535, when it was reclaimed by the crown. He was married to Beatriz Palacios, a *parda* (light mulatto), one of the four Spanish women to accompany the Narváez *entrada*.

(Gerhard, 389f.; Orozco y Berra, 59; *Protocolos*, I, no 124, 55 undated in October 1525.)

128. Juan de ESPAÑA (Spaña)
Poblador
From: Alcañiz de la Frontera (Aragón)
Parents: Pedro Malfeyt España and María de la Foz

España arrived in New Spain with Garay's 1523 Pánuco *entrada* and later became a *vecino* of Coatzacoalcos. Sometime after his first *encomienda* was taken, Viceroy Mendoza assigned España half the tribute from Minzapa (west of Coatzacoalcos), shared with *poblador* Gonzalo Rodríguez de Villafuerte from Salamanca. The first holder of Minzapa was Lorenzo Genovés. España's first wife died before 1547, and his second wife inherited the tribute when he died ca. 1567. The *encomendero* in 1597 was Alonso de Horta.

(Gerhard, 139f.; Icaza, II, 1; Boyd-Bowman, II, no. 10784, 321.)

129. Alonso de ESTRADA—*Hidalgo*
Poblador
From: Ciudad Real

Estrada referred to himself as a natural son of King Ferdinand and a lady of the court, but this parentage is not verifiable. He was a native of Ciudad Real, where he held office as a perpetual *regidor*. Estrada arrived in Mexico City in 1523 as royal treasurer and served often as lieutenant governor during the turbulent period from October 1524 to October 1527, when he assumed full governorship, holding the position until the arrival of the first Audiencia in January of 1529. He became an *encomendero* in 1526 by appropriating for himself the tribute from Tepeaca (87 miles southeast of Mexico City), held by the royal treasury inspector Pero Almíndez Chirinos. Almíndez recovered the grant a few months later. Estrada then acquired Teocalhueyacan (Tlalnepantla, 10 miles north-northwest of Mexico City) from Cortés in 1528. The next year he was assigned one-half of Tlapa (150 miles south-southwest of Mexico City). The other half was held for a time by first conqueror Bernaldino Vázquez de Tapia. Early tribute lists are lacking for Teocalhueyacan, but there were perhaps 4,000 tributaries there in 1570. Estrada's share of Tlapa had 3,901 tributaries in 1548. This income was in addition to his salary as treasurer.

Estrada was married to doña Marina Gutiérrez Flores de la Caballería, also from Ciudad Real. They had two sons and five daughters. Don Luis Alonso inherited the entailed estate in Ciudad Real, and don Juan Alonso (also called José Juan) became fray Juan de la Magdalena after the arranged marriage with a daughter of don Lope Fernández de Treviño of Ciudad Real failed to materialize. Daughters doña Ana, doña Luisa, doña Marina, doña Beatriz, and doña Francisca married respectively treasurer Juan Alonso de Sosa, first conqueror Jorge de Alvarado, *poblador* don Luis de Guzmán Saavedra, *poblador* Francisco Vázquez de Coronado, and *poblador* Alonso de Avalos Saavedra. Bartolomé, a natural son by Ana Rodríguez Anhaifa, became a secular priest.

Estrada died in 1530. His widow inherited Teocalhueyacan. She was succeeded in 1551 by their daughter doña Luisa, widow of Jorge de Alvarado. Grandson don Juan de Villafañe inherited in the 1570s, and great-grandson don Angel de Villafañe was the *encomendero* between 1597 and 1629. The Tlapa share was taken by the second Audiencia, then returned to Estrada's widow by royal order. She gave it in dowry to daughter doña Beatriz when she married Vázquez de Coronado in 1535. It was held for a while in the 1560s by Estrada's granddaughter (married to don Luis Ponce de León), and by 1604 the *encomendero* was a great-grandson, don Francisco Pacheco de Córdoba Bocanegra.

(Gerhard, 247 and 321; Icaza, I, 219f. and II, 4; Boyd-Bowman, II, no. 3661a, no. 3672, no. 3673, no. 3675, no. 3676, no. 3676a, 108, and no. 7617, 235; *Protocolos*, I, no. 1442 and no. 1443, 308 of 31 August 1528; Díaz del Castillo, II, 371; Scholes and Adams, 48; Castro y Tosi, 1011–26.)

130. Francisco de ESTRADA—Merchant (?)
Conqueror—Narváez
From: Seville
Parents: Juan Sánchez de Estrada of Las Montañas

Estrada arrived in the Indies in 1509 with don Diego Colón and was in Cuba a year before joining the 1520 Narváez *entrada*. He became a *vecino* of Mexico City and was assigned one-half of Tezcatepec (a two-site *cabecera* 65 and 36 miles north and northeast respectively of Mexico City; 2,150 tributaries in 1570) and one-half of Tuzantlalpa, a *sujeto* of Tezcatepec. The other half was assigned to first conqueror Alonso Martín Jaca of Huesca. Estrada married twice and had a son and daughter by each wife. By 1547 his daughter Ana had married Luis de Villegas from Segovia. A son was also married. Estrada's sister, María, one of the four Spanish women to accompany the Narváez *entrada*, married first conqueror Pedro Sánchez Farfán. By 1547 Estrada's son Juan (also known as Andrés) had inherited the *encomienda* and was maintaining the *casa poblada*, arms, and horses. He was still receiving the tribute in 1604. Estrada received a coat of arms dated 23 May 1539.

(Gerhard, 297; Icaza, I, 44f. and II, 240; Scholes and Adams, 41; Boyd-Bowman, I, no. 3407 and no. 3408, 117; *Nobiliario*, 311; BAGN, Inq., T. 42, e. 9.)

131. Diego FERNÁNDEZ Nieto
First Conqueror
From: Almeida (Zamora)
Parents: Sebastián and Mari Fernández

Fernández, a native of the Portuguese frontier, was in Cuba by 1518 and joined the Cortés *entrada* the following year. After the conquest and various *entradas*, he became a *vecino* of Mexico City, where he maintained his *casa poblada*, arms, and horses. During the 1540s Fernández acquired half of Turicato (145 miles west-southwest of Mexico City, 45 miles south-southeast of Pátzcuaro; 23 *barrios* in 1570) from *poblador* Antonio de Oliver of Ciudad Real. He was married and had seven children, three of them natural. Fernández was succeeded ca. 1571 by a son, Bartolomé Gallegos. The tributes were going to an *encomendero* of the same name 90 years later (1660), perhaps a grandson. A coat of arms was awarded to Fernández, dated 12 December 1539.

Note: The coat of arms citation states that Fernández was a member of the Narváez *entrada*, but all other references establish him as arriving in New Spain with Cortés in 1519.

(Gerhard, 74 and 76; Icaza I, 64; Scholes and Adams, 20; Boyd-Bowman, I, no. 4825, 160; *Nobiliario*, 233.)

132. Comendador Diego FERNÁNDEZ de Proaño—*Hidalgo*
Poblador
From: Seville
Parents: Juan de Proaño and doña Ana Cervantes

Comendador Fernández arrived in New Spain in 1525 with a royal appointment as *alguacil mayor* of Mexico City, a position he held until 1529. He aligned himself with Nuño de Guzmán and served as one of his captains in New Galicia. After the campaign he returned to Mexico City and served as a *regidor* from 1531 to 1535. Fernández was a *vecino* of Mexico City until ca. 1537, when he moved to Guadalajara, became a *vecino*, and kept his *casa poblada*, arms, and horses. He shared the tributes of Cholula (55 miles east-southeast of Mexico City; 20,000 tributaries in 1530) with Diego Suárez Pacheco, the father of Cortés' first wife. This grant made by the first Audiencia was one of the first revoked by the second Audiencia when it assumed jurisdiction in 1531. Fernández later acquired Xalapa (75 miles north of Guadalajara; 2,269 tributaries in 1548). He also held half of Río de Tepec (110 miles west-northwest of Guadalajara; perhaps 1,000 tributaries in 1548), shared with Hernando Martel. Fernández died sometime between 1556 and 1570 and was succeeded by doña Ana de Corral.

(Gerhard, 114f.; Gerhard 1982, 71f. and 101; Icaza, II, 268f.; Boyd-Bowman, II, no. 9963, 301; *Actas*, I, 95f.)

133. Juan FERNÁNDEZ—Notary
Conqueror—Narváez
From: Seville
Parents: Diego and Catalina Fernández

Fernández was in Cuba a year before joining Narváez in 1520. After the capture of Tenochtitlan he took part in *entradas* to Guatemala, Michoacán, Zacatula, Colima, and Yopelcingo. Fernández became a *vecino* of Colima and the *encomendero* of Giroma (or Ziroma, 30 miles south-southeast of Colima, including Huitzitzila, Totontlan, and Turiaque), assigned apparently by Francisco Cortés, the *alcalde mayor* of Colima. He was still receiving the tribute in the 1560s. Fernández was married and had three sons and a daughter. Giroma was a crown possession by 1597.

(Gerhard, 193; Icaza, I, 45; Boyd-Bowman, I, no. 3468, 119; Orozco y Berra, 59; Sauer, 33f.)

134. Juan FERNÁNDEZ de Mérida
Conqueror—Narváez
From: Mérida (La Serena, Extremadura)
Parents: Bartolomé Sánchez and Elvira Sánchez

Fernández joined the Narváez *entrada* after his 1519 arrival in Cuba. He ultimately became a *vecino* of Antequera and *encomendero* of nearby Ixtlan (a small grant 30 miles northeast of Antequera). Fernández was married and had at least one son and a daughter. There is record of his daughter marrying Juan García Estudio of Seville, also a *vecino* of Oaxaca. His son, Alonso Martín Muñoz, inherited when Fernández died in 1544. This son was in turn succeeded by Fernández' grandson, Juan Fernández de Mérida, the *encomendero* in 1597.

(Gerhard, 49; Scholes and Adams, 33; Icaza, II, 87; Boyd-Bowman, I, no. 482, 17.)

135. Juan FERNÁNDEZ de Ocampo
Conqueror—Narváez
From: Ocampo (Lugo)

Fernández probably arrived in Cuba in 1519 and then joined the Narváez *entrada* the following year, although one list of conquerors (Orozco y Berra) suggests he was with Cortés in 1519. He was assigned Ocotlan and Ospanaguastla in *encomienda*, a small grant near Colima, where he was a *vecino*. Fernández was succeeded ca. 1550 by a namesake son, still the *encomendero* in 1597.

(Gerhard, 80; Scholes and Adams, 22; Boyd-Bowman, I, no. 2246, 77; Orozco y Berra, 59.)

136. Pedro FERNÁNDEZ de Navarrete
Conqueror—?
From: Navarre (?)

Fernández has left few tracks. We do know that he held the *encomienda* of Acayuca (10 miles southwest of Pachuca; a grant that had two *estancias*—San Bartolomé and Santiago—in 1569) and that it passed to his widow doña Ana de Rebolledo, before 1547. It was later transferred to a son, García de Navarrete, who then supported his mother and sisters. The tribute reverted to the crown ca. 1568, when García died without issue.

(Gerhard, 209f.; Icaza, I, 115; Scholes and Adams, 25.)

137. Francisco FLORES
Conqueror—Narváez
From: Encinasola (Huelva)
Father: Juan Flores

Flores arrived in New Spain with the 1520 Narváez *entrada*. He had been in Santo Domingo in 1510 and spent from 1511 to 1519 in Cuba. After the conquest he became a *vecino* of Mexico City, serving as *regidor* there from 1530 to 1536. Flores was the first holder of Iguala (76 miles south-southwest of Mexico City near Taxco; six *estancias* in 1579) until it was taken by the crown ca. 1535. He also held Azuntepec, Zoquitlan, Epustepec,

Olintepec, Tepexistepec, and Necotepec, all Zapotecan communities 300 miles southeast of Mexico City. In 1536 his nephew, Pedro Flores, a *vecino* of Antequera, was administering these grants. Flores married doña Francisca de la Cueva, a daughter of Pedro de San Martín and doña Argenta, both of Ubeda, Jaén. They had one son and four daughters. Flores died in the mid-1540s and was succeeded by his widow. She later transferred the *encomienda* to their son, Francisco Flores de la Cueva, a *vecino* of Antequera. Tribute reverted to the crown ca. 1600.

(Gerhard, 146 and 196; *Actas*, V, 163; Icaza, I, 118; Boyd-Bowman, I, no. 1724, 60; Orozco y Berra, 59; Scholes and Adams, 28; *Protocolos*, II, no. 1999, 65 of 16 October 1536.)

138. Juan FLORES
Poblador
From: **Sanlúcar de Barrameda (Cádiz)**
Father: **Diego de Flores**

Flores arrived in New Spain in 1524 and then joined *entradas* against the Mixe, Chontales, and Cipotecas in what is now northern Oaxaca. By 1547 he was a *vecino* of Zacatula and *encomendero* of half of both Echancaleca and Zapotitlan. These towns, in the vicinity of Zacatula, were supposedly acquired from a Licenciado Alemán. Flores had held another unidentified *encomienda* previously by marrying the widow of an unnamed conqueror *encomendero*, but that grant reverted to the crown when the lady died. He leaves no record of children. His Zacatula *encomienda* probably also reverted to the crown when he died sometime after 1564.

Note: Gerhard states that Flores inherited the grant from a Licenciado Alemán, but neither of the two individuals with this identity left record of being *encomendero* of either grant. One Licenciado Alemán married a daughter of Comendador Leonel de Cervantes (she was the widow of first conqueror Alonso de Mendoza) and succeeded her after 1555 as *encomendero* of Tamistla, near Valles. The other, a tutor for the children of first conqueror Juan Gómez de Herrera, left no record of ever having been an *encomendero*.

(Gerhard, 394; Boyd-Bowman, II, no. 3465, 102; Scholes and Adams, 22; Icaza, I, 176f.)

139. Francisco FRANCO Estrada
Poblador
From: **Ribadecillas (Asturias)**
Father: **Alonso Martín Portillo**

Franco spent three years in Santo Domingo before his 1524 arrival in New Spain. He served with Cortés' Honduras *entrada* and was assigned an *encomienda* there. By 1526 he was back in New Spain, taking part in actions in Oaxaca. Franco became a *vecino* and *regidor* of Villa Alta, where he held nearby Lazagaya in *encomienda*, as well as half of Teotalcingo (15 miles northeast of Villa Alta; five *estancias*). The other half of Teotalcingo was in *corregimiento* with Nestepec. Franco married in 1532, had six children and maintained his *casa poblada*, arms, and horses in Villa Alta. Franco's brother, Alonso Martín Asturiano, was an artilleryman in the conquest. He was a *vecino* of Santiago de Guatemala and later lived in Mexico City. A namesake son was the *encomendero* in 1597.

(Gerhard, 371f.; Icaza, I, 229; Scholes and Adams, 22; Boyd-Bowman, II, no. 3261, 10 and I, no. 91, 4.)

140. Cristóbal de FRÍAS
Poblador

Frías, a *vecino* of Pánuco, acquired Tampachiche (20 miles southeast of Pánuco), Tampuche (vicinity of Pánuco), and Guautla (68 miles south-southwest of Pánuco) in the 1540s. Around 1550 his widow, Isabel de Frías, and a namesake son inherited the *encomienda*. By 1597 Tampachiche was a congregation, and a Juan Ramírez was the *encomendero* of Tampuche. A Frías was still receiving the tribute from Guautla in 1597. The scanty records suggest that Frías had two half brothers in New Spain, Juan and Rodrigo Bezos, as well as three uncles. One of the uncles was first conqueror Pedro Sánchez Farfán.

(Gerhard, 216 and 243; Scholes and Adams, 47; Icaza, II, 313f.; Boyd-Bowman, I, no. 3278, 114.)

141. Alonso GALEOTE García
Conqueror—Narváez
From: Huelva
Parents: Alonso Galeote and Isabel Díaz la Cordera

Galeote joined Narváez as a horseman, then sided with Cortés in 1520. He had arrived in Cuba by 1517 and served with Grijalva the following year. After the capture of Tenochtitlan Galeote served in *entradas* to Pánuco and Tututepec before becoming a *vecino* of Puebla, where he maintained his *casa poblada*, arms, and horses. In the 1520s he acquired the *encomienda* of Totomeguacan (six miles south of Puebla; 644 tributaries in 1548 and 1,000 in 1570) through a trade with Alonso de Avila. Galeote married a Spanish woman and had six sons and five daughters, his wife being pregnant again in 1547. A natural daughter was also a member of the household. Galeote's father, Gonzalo, was a conqueror in Santo Domingo (1502), Cuba, Puerto Rico, Jamaica, and Tierra Firme. Gonzalo and two of Alonso's brothers also took part in the Narváez *entrada* and then followed Cortés for the siege and capture of Tenochtitlan. Galeote died in the 1560s and was succeeded by his son Juan, then by his grandson Alonso Galeote. Tribute reverted to the crown ca. 1610 and was later reassigned to the Moctezuma heirs, who received it until 1801.

(Gerhard, 221; Scholes and Adams, 20; Orozco y Berra, 80; Icaza, I, 81; Boyd-Bowman, I, no. 1763, 61.)

142. Juan Sánchez GALINDO *"el buen jinete"*
First Conqueror
From: Carmona (Seville)
Parents: Antón Sánchez de Rueda and Catalina Domínguez Galindo

Galindo arrived in New Spain as a member of the Cortés *entrada* after having been in the Antilles, Florida, and along much of the gulf coast of Mexico with various expeditions. After the capture of Mexico City he went on *entradas* to Tehuantepec and Oaxaca. In January 1525 Galindo became a *vecino* of Mexico City. He shared half of the *encomienda* of Nestalpa (56 miles north-northwest of Mexico City near Tula; two *visitas* in 1570) with conqueror Pedro Moreno Cendejas, a native of Zaragoza. In 1530 Galindo married Elvira Rodríguez, a daughter of Juan Rodríquez and Mari García of Béjer del Castañar. They had one son and three daughters. Galindo also claimed three natural children. His wife had been brought to Mexico in 1530 by her brother, *poblador* swordsmith Diego Rodríguez, who also brought another sister, a brother, and two sisters-in-law. The sisters-in-law married conquerors Esteban Miguel and Domingo Martín. Galindo died sometime before 1547 and was succeeded by a daughter married to Pedro Valdovinos.

(Gerhard, 322; Icaza, I, 82 and II, 126; Scholes and Adams, 35; Orozco y Berra, 41; Boyd-Bowman, I, no. 3019, 106 and II, no. 7167, 222; *Actas*, I, p. 29.)

143. Pedro GALLARDO—Mariner
Conqueror—Salcedo
From: Lepe (Huelva)

Gallardo had a maritime calling and was serving on Juan de Salcedo's ship when he joined the Narváez *entrada*. He was one of the many who then switched sides to go with Cortés to Tenochtitlan. He was awarded the *encomienda* of Amatlan (225 miles southeast of Puebla near Antequera; 9 *barrios* before 1600). Gallardo became a *vecino* of Puebla and married an Indian woman, by whom he had a son and a daughter. He died ca. 1535, leaving his mestizo children in the care of Gonzalo Carrasco, a *vecino* of Puebla and a native of Las Garrovillas, Cáceres. The *encomienda* reverted to the crown when Gallardo died.

(Gerhard, 188; Icaza, I, 132; Orozco y Berra, 80; Boyd-Bowman, I, no. 1792, 62 and no. 970, 34.)

144. Alvaro GALLEGO
First Conqueror
From: Galicia

Gallego had been an *encomendero* in Puerto Plata, Santo Domingo as early as 1514, arriving in Cuba the year before sailing with the Cortés *entrada*. After the conquest he was assigned the *encomienda* of Chocándiro (145 miles west-northwest of Mexico City on the west end of Lake Cuiseo, Michoacán; nine *estancias* by 1600) and became a *vecino* of Mexico City. Gallego and his wife, Leonor de la Peña, had no children. She succeeded him as *encomendera* when he died ca. 1530. Seven years later Leonor married *poblador* Antón de Silva of Ecija, (Seville), a 1530 arrival in New Spain. After Silva died she married Gonzalo Galván, sometime before 1560. The tribute from this *encomienda* reverted to the crown by 1597. A natural daughter of Gallego married Juan Ortiz, a *mayordomo* for Jorge Cerón Saavedra in nearby Charo, Michoacán. Gallego was awarded a coat of arms, dated 4 December 1529.

(Gerhard, 344f.; Scholes and Adams, 45; Orozco y Berra, 41; Icaza, I, 171f. and 114; Boyd-Bowman, I, no. 5122, 171 and II, no. 8339, 258; *Nobiliario*, 312f.)

145. Benito GALLEGO
Conqueror—Camargo
From: Galicia

Gallego arrived in New Spain with Camargo in time to take part in the capture of Tenochtitlan. After various *entradas* he became a *vecino* of Colima and was assigned nearby Aguacatitlan in *encomienda*. He married, but had no children and was succeeded ca. 1540 by his widow. She then married Diego de Velasco, a native of Seville, who succeeded her in the 1560s. Aguacatitlan was still a private *encomienda* in 1597.

(Gerhard, 80; Icaza, I, 251; Scholes and Adams, 52; Orozco y Berra, 80; Boyd-Bowman, I, no. 5126, 171 and II, no. 10315, 211.)

146. Gonzalo GALLEGO Hernández—Caulker
First Conqueror
From: Alconchel (Badajoz)

Gallego was in Cuba for a year before joining the Cortés *entrada* and, after the capture of Tenochtitlan, became a *vecino* of Coatzacoalcos. He was assigned half of nearby Guazacualco in *encomienda*, plus Guacuilapa, Cosoliacac, Mecatepec, Ocuapa, and half of Agualulco (the additional five towns were from 60 to 70 miles east to east-southeast of Coatzacoalcos). Gallego was married and had a family. He was succeeded ca. 1560 by a son, Gonzalo Hernández and by 1597 by a grandson, Gonzalo Hernández de Alconchel.

(Gerhard, 139; Boyd-Bowman, I, no. 226, 9.)

147. Juan GALLEGO
Conqueror—?

Gallego was a *vecino* of Antequera and, in the early 1520s, received an *encomienda* consisting of Lapaguia, Pilcintepec, Tizatepec, Topiltepec, and Xolotepec (towns 40 miles, plus or minus, southeast of Antequera). He held them until his death ca. 1553, when the crown claimed them. Gallego also bought the rights to half of Atlatlauca (40 miles north of Antequera) from conqueror Juan de Mancilla in 1538. His namesake son inherited this grant and was still the *encomendero* in 1597.

(Gerhard, 54 and 197.)

148. Lucas GALLEGO
   Conqueror—?
   From: Galicia

Gallego was a *vecino* of Mexico City from 1525 and held the *encomienda* of Cuacuacintla (150 miles east of Mexico City near Jalapa; one *estancia* ca. 1550). He and his wife, Catalina Rodríguez, had a number of children. Gallego was succeeded by 1551 by his son Miguel Arias. A grandson, Domingo Gallego, inherited in the 1570s. Cuacuacintla was a crown *encomienda* by 1626.

(Gerhard, 375 and 377; Scholes and Adams, 32; Boyd-Bowman, II, no. 13222, 399.)

149. Pedro GALLEGO
   Poblador
   From: Burguillos del Cerro (Maestrazgo de León, Extremadura)
   Parents: Hernán García Jaramillo and Mayor Gallego de Andrada

Gallego arrived in New Spain in 1523 and became a *vecino* of Mexico City shortly thereafter. During 1528 he became the third husband of doña Isabel Moctezuma and was assigned one-half of the *encomienda* of Iscuincuitlapilco (52 miles north-northeast of Mexico City near Pachuca; 4,000 tributaries in 1570) together with *poblador antiguo* Licenciado Pedro López of Seville. They had one son. Gallego died by 1531, the year that his grant reverted to the crown.

(Gerhard, 44; Icaza, II, 311f.; Boyd-Bowman, II, no. 1041, 31; *Actas*, I, 9.)

150. Juan GALLEGOS
   Poblador
   From: Seville
   Parents: Lorenzo Montesinos and María de Medina

Gallegos arrived in Pánuco in 1523 as one of Garay's recruits, took part in the pacification of the region under Cortés, became a *vecino* of Pánuco, and then went on to the Valles area, where he received an *encomienda*. The grant was taken by Nuño de Guzmán before 1531. Much later (1547–1548) he was awarded the tribute from Tampuche (also referred to as Tanpacal and Tampuxeque, also in the vicinity of Valles). Gallegos married in the early 1530s and had a daughter. He died before 1564 and was succeeded by his widow, who then married Juan Rodríguez. Diego de Salas received the tribute from this *encomienda* between 1569 and 1584.

(Gerhard, 355; Scholes and Adams, 50; Icaza, II, 216f.; Boyd-Bowman, II, no. 9241, 283; Chipman, 183 and 302.)

151. Hernando de GAMBOA
   Poblador

Gamboa acquired the rights to Petatlan (vicinity of Colima) by becoming a *vecino* of Colima and marrying the widow of first conqueror Ginés Pinzón, the original holder, ca. 1550. He was still receiving the tribute in the 1560s.

(Gerhard, 80.)

152. Alonso GARCÍA
   Poblador

García is listed as the *encomendero* of Las Laxas (12 miles south of Pánuco) from 1548 until it was claimed by the crown in 1570. He was more than likely a *vecino* of Santisteban del Puerto, Pánuco.

(Gerhard, 215.)

153. Alonso GARCÍA Bravo—Mason
   Conqueror—Camargo
   From: Ribera del Fresno (Maestrazgo de León, Extremadura)
   Father: Gonzalo García Bravo

García Bravo arrived in the Indies as a member of Pedrarias Dávila's 1514 Darién expedition and later got to New Spain as a member of Camargo's 1520 *entrada* providing reinforcements for Cortés. After the capture of Tenochtitlan he served in a Oaxaca *entrada*. García Bravo was considered adept in measures (*muy buen geométrico*) and is said to have surveyed the layout of Mexico City in 1523. The following year he became a *vecino* of Oaxaca. García Bravo may have held Tepalcatepec (a Chontal village 80 miles south of Antequera) for a period in the mid-1520s and was then assigned Mistepec (70 miles west of Antequera; six *estancias* in 1598), succeeding Martín Vázquez. He married María Núñez, a daughter of conqueror Antonio de Almodóvar del Campo and Violante Núñez. They had one daughter, who married Melchor Suárez. This daughter inherited ca. 1563. A grandson, Lázaro Suárez, was the *encomendero* towards the end of the century. Mistepec became a crown holding ca. 1665.

(Gerhard, 164 and 166; Icaza, I, 55f.; Scholes and Adams, 18; Boyd-Bowman, I, no. 529b, 18 and II, no. 3599, 106; Orozco y Berra, 70.)

154. Bartolomé GARCÍA
Poblador
From: Montánchez (Cáceres)
Parents: Juan García Fleiro and Mari Jiménez

García came to New Spain in 1528 as a member of the Nuño de Guzmán entourage and, after taking part in the conquest of New Galicia, became a *vecino* of Guadalajara and *encomendero* of Mescala (45 miles northeast of Guadalajara; 287 tributaries in 1548 although García claimed but 40 in his petition to Viceroy Mendoza in the mid-1540s). He was married and had four children. The *encomienda* escheated ca. 1570.

(Icaza, II, 167; Boyd-Bowman, II, no. 3003, 87; Gerhard 1982, 136.)

155. Diego GARCÍA Jaramillo
Conqueror—Narváez
From: Badajoz

García Jaramillo arrived in the Indies ca. 1497 and took part in "all of the conquests of the isles." He was a *vecino* of Puerto de Plata, Santo Domingo in 1514, went to New Spain with the 1520 Narváez *entrada*, and by 1523 was apparently a *vecino* of Mexico City. In the 1520s he was assigned Citlaltomagua (160 miles south-southwest of Mexico City near Acapulco; seven *barrios* in 1548 and only two 21 years later), had it taken and then reassigned in rapid succession. García Jaramillo also held the *encomienda* of Zumpango (135 miles south of Mexico City; 15 *estancias* in 1560). He and his wife, Cecilia Lucero, also of Badajoz, had a daughter, doña Ana de Andrada, and at least two nephews in New Spain. Juan Jaramillo *"el mozo,"* of Villanueva de Barcarrota, married doña Ana. The other nephew, Alonso Valiente (a cousin of Cortés), became a *vecino* of Veracruz, Medellín, Mexico City, and ultimately Puebla, and acted as García Jaramillo's business partner in slaving ventures. García Jaramillo died ca. 1546 and was succeeded by his widow, who became the *encomendera*. Citlaltomagua reverted to the crown by 1550, while Zumpango, although claimed by the crown in the 1550s, paid tribute to Cecilia Lucero until 1562. Thereafter a part of the tribute went to a grandson, Cristóbal de Vargas.

(Gerhard, 39, 41, 316 and 318; Boyd-Bowman, I, no. 283, 11 and II, no. 2006, 55; Icaza, I, 220f. and II, 148; *Protocolos*, I, no. 1545, 325 of 19 September 1528.)

156. Hernán GARCÍA
Poblador
From: Triana (Seville)
Parents: Diego Hernández and Catalina Hernández

García came to the Indies in 1526 and arrived in New Spain four years later. By 1547 he was a *vecino* of Colima. He acquired Guazaltepec, a very small grant, sometime after 1547. He married a daughter of Juan Montañés, a conqueror killed by Indians in Michoacán. They had three children. García was succeeded by a namesake son ca. 1564.

(Scholes and Adams, 50; Boyd-Bowman, I, no. 740, 25 and II, no. 10392; Icaza, I, 77.)

157. Juan GARCÍA de Lemos
Poblador
From: Lemos (Coruña)

García arrived in New Spain ca. 1528 after having been a *vecino* of Havana,

Cuba for an unstated period of time and became a *vecino* of Villa Alta. He acquired Iscuintepec, a Zapotec settlement with several dependencies near Villa Alta, as his *encomienda*. Shortly thereafter he was succeeded by a daughter married to Juan de Aldaz Navarro, a native of Peralta, Navarre. When the daughter died, Aldaz succeeded, after which he married Juana Verdugo, a natural daughter of conqueror Francisco Verdugo. The *encomienda* reverted to the crown by 1578.

(Gerhard, 371; Icaza, I, 324; Scholes and Adams, 51; Boyd-Bowman, II, no. 4210, 124 and no. 6752, 206f.)

158. Gaspar GARNICA
First Conqueror
From: Guernica (Biscay)

Garnica arrived in New Spain as a member of Cortés' *entrada* after having been a *vecino* of Santiago de Cuba. He then went to Honduras with Cortés and served there as a *regidor* of Trujillo before returning to and becoming a *vecino* of Mexico City in 1528. Garnica's *encomienda* included half the tribute from Zapotitlan (130 miles southeast of Mexico City near Tehuacan; 2,000 tributaries in 1571), reassigned from Rodrigo de Segura by the first Audiencia in 1530, and half of Tlacotepec (36 miles west-southwest of Mexico City near Toluca; five *estancias* in 1580) assigned by the second Audiencia in 1532 although claimed, unsuccessfully, by Cortés. Garnica shared Tlacotepec with conqueror Alonso de la Serna and Zapotitlan with *encomendera* Catalina Vélez Rascona, a native of Palos (Huelva). She was the heiress of her father, *poblador* (?) García Vélez. Garnica was succeeded by his widow in the 1540s and she by their son ca. 1560. A grandson, Antonio de Garnica, was the *encomendero* in 1600.

(Gerhard, 175, 177 and 216f.; Scholes and Adams, 27f.; Boyd-Bowman, I, no. 4729, 156 and II, no. 5340, 160; Orozco y Berra, 41.)

159. Diego GARRIDO
Conqueror—Narváez
From: Moguer (Huelva)

Garrido was in Cuba by 1519, joined the Narváez *entrada* the following year, and took part in the capture of Tenochtitlan. He became an early *vecino* and *poblador* of Colima, acquiring the *encomienda* of Zapotlanejo and Suchitlan (near Colima) as well as Epatlan (30 miles south-southeast of Colima). Garrido married Elvira de Arévalo, the daughter of conqueror Alonso de Arévalo, and had a daughter, Catalina. He was succeeded before 1545 by his widow. She later married Francisco Preciado, a follower of Cortés and a native of Molina de Aragón (Guadalajara). Preciado became the *encomendero* and in turn was succeeded by a son, Juan Preciado, in the 1560s. Garrido's daughter, Catalina, was raised as a ward of a relative, Bartolomé Garrido.

(Gerhard, 80, 160, and 192; Boyd-Bowman, I, no. 1827a, 63 and II, no. 4691, 140; Icaza, I, 182f.; Orozco y Berra, 60.)

160. Lorenzo GENOVÉS—Pilot/Mariner
First Conqueror
From: Genoa

Genovés was in Cuba in 1518 and probably had been in the Indies for some time. After service with the Cortés *entrada* he was assigned the *encomienda* of Minzapa, near Coatzacoalcos (175 miles northeast of Oaxaca), and became a *vecino* of Oaxaca. His wife Malgarida Ruiz, was a native of Madeira and was considered "old Portuguese." Their one child, a daughter, married Luis de Mazariegos, a *vecino* of Ciudad Real, Chiapas. Genovés was dead by 1547. The *encomienda* was reassigned to Gonzalo Rodríguez de Villafuerte and Juan de España. Genovés' widow then took up residence with their daughter in Chiapas. There is no evidence to establish a relationship between Lorenzo and *poblador* Lucas Genovés other than that they both came from Genoa.

(Gerhard, 139; Icaza, I, 134; Boyd-Bowman, I, no. 5196, 174 and II, no. 13566, 410; Orozco y Berra, 41.)

161. Lucas GENOVÉS
Poblador
From: Genoa

By 1533 Genovés, *vecino* of Pánuco, held the *encomienda* of Chachavala (12 miles northeast of Pánuco). He was married, had two sons, and was succeeded by one of them, named Alonso Genovés de Alvarado. At some time betwen 1564 and 1568, Alonso was in turn succeeded by his widow. Alonso's son, Alonso de Alvarado, was listed as the *encomendero* in 1597. Lucas' widow married another Genoese, Bernaldo Peloso. The *encomienda* was abandoned by 1600.

(Gerhard, 216; Scholes and Adams, 50; Boyd-Bowman, I, no. 5197, 174 and II, no. 13299, 402; Icaza, II, 163.)

162. Alonso GIRALDO—Trumpeter
First Conqueror

Giraldo, probably a *vecino* of Mexico City, was assigned the *encomienda* of Tututepec (110 miles northeast of Mexico City near Pachuca; 85 *estancias* and *barrios* in 1548). He married Francisca de Zambrano and had two sons and a daughter. Giraldo died ca. 1535 while with Cortés on the California *entrada*, and the *encomienda* was then reassigned to Maese Manuel Tomás. *Encomendero* Francisco de Avila served as guardian for his minor children. Tomás' son, Diego Rodríguez de Orozco, who acquired the rights to Tututepec ca. 1548, was still shown as the *encomendero* in 1597. Part of the tribute was still going to a person other than the crown as late as 1697.

(Gerhard, 336; Icaza, II, 64; *Protocolos*, I, no. 1543, 325 of 19 September 1528.)

163. Bartolomé GÓMEZ
Conqueror—?
From: Morón (Seville)
Parents: Antón Sánchez de Ruy Gómez and Mari Hernández

Gómez arrived in the Antilles in 1519 and joined the Cortés *entrada* just before the capture of Tenochtitlan. He became a *vecino* of Mexico City after taking part in *entradas* to Oaxaca, Tehuantepec, and Guatemala. At one time he had *encomiendas* in Guatemala, Oaxaca, and near Mexico City, but by 1547 he held only Tepetitlan (60 miles north of Mexico City near Tula; 10 *barrios* in 1548). Gómez was married and had one son and two daughters. He maintained a *casa poblada*, arms, and horses in Mexico City. A daughter, married to Juan (also called Diego) Azpeitia, succeeded when he died ca. 1564. An Azpeitia heir was the *encomendero* until the tribute reverted to the crown ca. 1643.

(Gerhard, 332 and 334; Scholes and Adams, 22; Icaza, I, 86f.; Boyd-Bowman, I, no. 3135a, 110.)

164. Gonzalo GÓMEZ
Poblador Antiguo
From: Seville
Parents: Merchant Juan Gómez and Beatriz Gómez

Gómez, born in 1498, arrived in the Indies at age 12 with his father. At 16 he was with Pedrarias in Tierra Firme, and ten years later he became a *vecino* of Mexico City, where he maintained his *casa poblada*, arms, and horses. He too, without a doubt, was originally a merchant. Gómez served as *alcalde* in Michoacán, Tamazula, and Zacatula, where he also held citizenship. Around 1528 Alonso de Estrada, while governor, assigned him the *encomienda* of Istapa (also called Etucuaro, 135 miles west-southwest of Mexico City, 42 miles east-southeast of Pátzcuaro; four *estancias* in 1550). Gómez was married, had six children, and was succeeded by a son, Amador Gómez, ca.

1560. The *encomendera* in 1597 was Francisca López de Herrera.

Note: Gómez was the recipient of a number of powers of attorney to collect debts owed to others. He also maintained a close association with merchants Pedro Hernández Parada, Martín de Aranda of Seville, and conqueror Alonso González, a Portuguese *encomendero* who was also identified as a merchant. While in Michoacán (1536) Gómez was the subject of Inquisition investigation for Judaizing.

(Gerhard, 345 and 351; Boyd-Bowman, I, no. 3566, 121 and II, no. 10453, 315; Scholes and Adams, 33; Icaza, I, 201; *Protocolos*, I, no. 830, 198 of 30 October 1527, II no. 2252, 118 of 6 April 1537, and no. 2255, 119 of 7 April 1537; and Greenleaf, 93 and 135.)

165. Juan GÓMEZ de Herrera
First Conqueror

Gómez was with Cortés in 1519 and had become a *vecino* of Zacatula by 1525. He was not an *encomendero* until 1532, when the second Audiencia assigned him half the tribute from Arimao-Pinzándaro (65 miles northwest of Zacatula; 1,200 tributaries in 1565 and completely depopulated by 1743), shared with first conqueror Pedro Ruiz de Requena of Cuenca. Gómez married Elvira de Torres and had five children. A daughter married Miguel de Padilla, who left her in Mexico when he went to Peru. In the 1540s Gómez' widow succeeded him as *encomendera*. Sometime later she remarried, to Juan de San Juan of Baeza. He was the administrator of the grant until Gómez' son, Francisco, came of age and inherited. Tribute reverted to the crown in the 1570s.

(Gerhard, 250ff.; Scholes and Adams, 48; Icaza, I, 140 and 155; Orozco y Berra, 41; *Protocolos*, I, no. 377, 109 of 18 February 1527.)

166. Pedro GÓMEZ
Conqueror—Narváez

By 1526 Gómez, a member of the Narváez *entrada*, was a *vecino* of Colima. He shared the tribute of Tenamastlan (75 miles northwest of Colima; 3,000 tributaries in 1525 and about 800 in 1550) first with *poblador* Rodrigo Alonso until his death in 1528 and then with conqueror Martín Monje of Huelva. Gómez married Leonor de la Torre and by her had at least one daughter, Inés de Eslava. Leonor succeeded Gómez as *encomendera* ca. 1545 and then married Gasper Hurtado from Lepe, who administered the grant until Inés married Juan de Gámez sometime after 1547. At that time Gámez became the *encomendero*.

(Gerhard, 60f.; Icaza, I, 250f. and II, 94f.; Orozco y Berra, 60.)

167. Pierrez GÓMEZ
Conqueror—Díaz de Aux
From: Eindhout, Flanders
Parents: Pierrez Gómez and Catalina Gómez

Gómez arrived in New Spain with Miguel Díaz de Aux in time to take part in the siege and capture of Tenochtitlan. He was in Santo Domingo in 1505, in Tierra Firme eleven years later as a catechist, in Cuba in 1519, and with Díaz de Aux the following year. Gómez became a *vecino* of Mexico City shortly after it was captured and there maintained his *casa poblada*, arms, and horses. He was the first holder of Ayocinapa, also called Izcaytoyac (220 miles south-southeast of Mexico City, a *cabecera* until the congregations of 1598–1604, producing a claimed annual income of less than $200 by 1547). Gómez was married and had seven children, five of them daughters. Sometime before 1547 he was succeeded by a son, Alguacil Mayor Baltasar Mejía Salmerón. Baltasar was the *encomendero* until at least 1604.

(Gerhard, 150f.; Scholes and Adams, 33; Boyd-Bowman, I, no. 5164, 172; Icaza, I, 78f.)

168. Rodrigo GÓMEZ de Avila—*Hidalgo*
Conqueror—*Narváez*
From: Avila

Gómez was in Cuba by 1518, arrived in New Spain with Narváez, was active in *entradas*, and became a *vecino* of Mexico City by 1525. In the 1530s he was assigned the *encomienda* of Actopan—also known as Atucpa, Atocpan, and Otucpa—(65 miles north of Mexico City; 8,000 tributaries in 1570 and 4,000 eleven years later). In the 1520s Actopan had been held by both Hernando Alonso and Juan González de Ponce de León. Around 1538 Gómez gave the *encomienda* in dowry to his natural daughter, doña Beatriz, when she married *hidalgo* Juan Martínez Guerrero of Alcaraz (Albeceta). Between 1589 and 1593 Gómez' grandson, Agustín Guerrero de Luna, inherited, and was the *encomendero* until the tribute reverted to the crown in 1643. There were 1,092 tributaries at this time.

(Gerhard, 44f.; Scholes and Adams, 23; Boyd-Bowman, I, no. 136, 6 and II, no. 144, 6; Icaza, II, 6; *Actas*, I, p. 37.)

169. Alonso GONZÁLEZ de Portugal—
Hidalgo, Merchant
Conqueror—*Narváez*
From: Lisbon, Portugal
Father: Juan Alvarez do Gago

González was in Cuba by 1519 and with the Narváez *entrada* the following year. He became a *vecino* of Mexico City after its capture and was identified as a merchant. His *encomienda* was half of Teupantlan (86 miles southeast of Mexico City near Izúcar; five *barrios* in 1548 and eight in 1570 as a result of congregation), initially shared with conqueror Bachiller Alonso Pérez of Huelva until 1534, then shared with the crown. González married Isabel de Bolaños; by 1547 he had a son and a daughter, and his wife was expecting. He also claimed two natural (mestiza) daughters. Isabel succeeded him as *encomendera* ca. 1560, and a grandson, Diego de Bolaños, inherited ca. 1600. The 1547 income from the *encomienda* was claimed to be but $60.

(Gerhard, 161 and 163; Icaza, I, 46; Boyd-Bowman, I, no. 5262, 176; *Protocolos*, I, no. 23, 29f. of 21 August 1525.)

170. Diego GONZÁLEZ—Merchant (?)
First Conqueror
From: La Parra (Badajoz)

González was in Cuba by 1518 and signed on with Cortés the following year, taking part in the entire Mexico City adventure. In the 1530s he became a *vecino* of Puebla and held the *encomienda* of Guazalingo (120 miles north of Puebla; 265 tributaries ca. 1532). He and his wife, a Cuban native, had one son. He remarried when she died. González relinquished his rights to Guazalingo ca. 1540 in favor of Juan Rodríguez, who sold the grant to Gabriel de Aguilera ca. 1548. González died before 1547.

(Gerhard, 243; Boyd-Bowman, I, no. 518, 18; Icaza, I, 27; Chipman, 292; Orozco y Berra, 42.)

171. Gil GONZÁLEZ de Benavides
(Avila)—Hidalgo
Conqueror—Garay
From: Monte Albán (Avila)

González arrived in the Indies ca. 1514, served in Tierra Firme with Pedrarias, and arrived in Cuba in 1519 by way of Santo Domingo. He then went on to New Spain in 1520 on one of Garay's ships and took part in the capture of Tenochtitlan with his brother, Alonso de Avila y Benavides. González became a *vecino* of Mexico City and was closely associated with his brother, who transferred to him the *encomienda* rights of Guautitlan (15 miles north-northwest of Mexico City; including Huehuetoca, Xaltocan, Zumpango, and other sub-*cabeceras* and over 25 *estancias* in 1570), originally granted by Cortés in the early 1520s. By 1527 González had acquired Guaymeo and Sirándaro (132 miles west-southwest of Mexico City towards Pátzcuaro; ten *su-*

jetos in 1579). He married doña Leonor Alvarado, a niece of Pedro de Alvarado, and had at least one child, a son named don Alonso de Avila Alvarado, who inherited in 1544. The *encomienda* reverted to the crown in August, 1566, when Avila Alvarado was executed for his part in the second Marqués del Valle conspiracy.

(Gerhard, 127f. and 135ff.; Scholes and Adams, 29; Boyd-Bowman, I, no. 137, 6; Icaza, I, 199f.)

172. Gil GONZÁLEZ de Trujillo
Conqueror—?

González, a *vecino* of Pánuco, was assigned Tlanchinolticpac (80 miles southeast of Pánuco; 80 *sujetos* in 1570), probably by Cortés. He was executed by order of Nuño de Guzmán in 1527. The *encomienda* was then reassigned by Guzmán to Andrés de Inero. Between 1531 and 1534 the second Audiencia took the grant from Inero and divided it between Alonso Ortiz and Jerónimo de Medina.

(Gerhard, 184ff.; Chipman, 151ff.; Orozco y Berra, 42.)

173. Jorge GONZÁLEZ
Poblador

González, a *vecino* of Mexico City by 1537, bought Tlapotongo (143 miles northeast of Mexico City near Papantla; 10 tributaries in 1567) from first conqueror Tomás Rijoles in the 1540s and was succeeded by a son ca. 1565. By 1570 the *encomienda* was deserted.

(Gerhard, 219; *Protocolos*, II, no. 2314, 130 of 16 June 1537 and no. 2357, 140 of 9 June 1537; Scholes and Adams, 20.)

174. Juan GONZÁLES Ponce de León
First Conqueror

González was a member of the Cortés *entrada* and later became a *vecino* of Mexico City. In 1522 he received the *encomienda* of Tecama (25 miles northeast of Mexico City, 20 to 30 dependencies ca. 1550). He also held Actopan (65 miles north of Mexico City; 8,000 tributaries in 1548) in the early 1520s. González married Francisca de Ordaz, one of the eight Spanish women who accompanied the *entrada*. They had at least one child before González died in the 1530s. A son, Juan Ponce de León, married Catalina, a daughter of Hernando de Herrera, *relator* of the Audiencia. Juan inherited Tecama ca. 1540 and held it until he was murdered ca. 1553, perhaps by Bernardino de Bocanegra in a conspiracy with Catalina. As a result, the *encomienda* escheated, Catalina was exiled, and their three children—Luis, Juan, and María—were awarded lifetime pensions from the royal treasury. Actopan was later reassigned to Rodrigo Gómez de Avila.

(Gerhard, 226f. and 44; Gibson, 426f.; Greenleaf, 90f.; Icaza, I, 117; Orozco y Berra, 43.)

175. Ruy GONZÁLEZ
Conqueror—Narváez
From: Villanueva de Fresno (Badajoz)
Parents: Alonso González and Catalina Suárez

González arrived in the Indies in 1519, joined the Narváez *entrada* the following year, and took part in the capture of Tenochtitlan. After that event he went on *entradas* to Michoacán before becoming a *vecino* of Mexico City in 1526. González was the original *encomendero* of Tlalcozautitlan (122 miles south of Mexico City; 7,440 tributaries in 1570). His *encomienda* was enlarged in 1528 when Alonso de Estrada, while governor, reassigned to him the tribute from Teutlalco (76 miles south-southeast of Mexico City near Izúcar; 5,060 tributaries in 1555), taken from Cortés grantee Nicolás López de Palacios. The two holdings were about fifty miles apart. A 1531 action by the second Audiencia reassigned half the tribute from Tlalcozautitlan to conqueror Vasco Porcallo and took half the tribute from Teutlalco for the crown. González was an *alcalde ordinario* of Mexico City for 1533 and served as a *regidor* from 1534 to 1550. He had three mestiza daughters, one of whom married Francisco de Nava. When

González died ca. 1559, his half of Tlalcozautitlan reverted to the crown. The half of Teutlalco, claimed by the daughter married to Nava, went to the crown shortly thereafter.

(Gerhard, 112f. and 310f.; Boyd-Bowman, I, no. 591a, 21; Icaza, I, 31f.; Orozco y Berra, 60.)

176. Alonso de GRADO
First Conqueror
From: Alcántara (Cáceres)

Grado, a *vecino* of Buenaventura, Santo Domingo by 1514, was in Cuba four years later and sailed with Cortés in 1519. He was appointed *alcalde ordinario* of Veracruz upon its establishment. Cortés later made him the treasurer of the *entrada* as well as inspector general of the Indians. These duties were in keeping with Bernal Díaz del Castillo's evaluation that Grado was "more suited for business than war." In the early 1520s Grado became a *vecino* of Mexico City and *encomendero* of Chiautla (90 miles south-southeast of Mexico City, 30 miles south of Izúcar; 6,000 tributaries in 1545), reassigned to him from Diego de Ordaz. This assignment seemed to coincide with Grado's marriage to doña Isabel Moctezuma, a match that produced no children. Grado had a natural daughter who married *poblador* Alonso Hernández of Jumela (Toledo). The *encomienda* was reassigned to Diego Becerra de Mendoza when Grado died in 1527.

(Gerhard, 108f.; Icaza, I, 143; Boyd-Bowman, I, no. 852, 30; Orozco y Berra, 42; Díaz del Castillo, II, 449.)

177. Juan GRIEGO
First Conqueror
From: Greece

Griego became a member of the Cortés *entrada* after having spent at least five years in the Indies. He had been a *vecino* of Yaquimo, Santo Domingo, in 1514 and by 1518 was in Cuba, where he married. After the capture of Tenochtitlan Griego went to Guatemala before returning to New Spain in 1528 and becoming a *vecino* of Antequera. He was assigned the *encomienda* of Atoyaquillo (a very small grant 76 miles west-northwest of Antequera). Griego was succeeded ca. 1560 by Pedro Sánchez (a son?), still the *encomendero* in 1597.

(Gerhard, 285 and 287f.; Scholes and Adams, 53; Boyd-Bowman, I, no. 5219, 174; Orozco y Berra, 42.)

178. Sebastián de GRIJALVA
Conqueror—Narváez
From: Cuéllar (Segovia)

Grijalva was in Cuba in 1519 and went to New Spain with Narváez the following year. By mid-1524 he was a *vecino* of Mexico City and later may have been a *vecino* of Antequera. His *encomiendas* included Sosola and Tenexpa (very small grants, 30 miles northwest of Antequera, first held by first conqueror Alvaro Maldonado "*el fiero*" in the 1520s, and Texotepec (also small, 20 miles northwest of Antequera), probably assigned at the same time. He was married and had a son and two daughters. When Grijalva died ca. 1552, Sosola and Texotepec went to his son Antonio de Grijalva, and Tenexpa went to his daughter, doña Rufina, married to *hidalgo* Melchor de Robles, a *vecino* of Oaxaca who was from Almazán (Soria). By 1547 Grijalva's other daughter was a widow with three children. Her husband had been *hidalgo* Clemente de Mederos from Ciudad Rodrigo. Both *encomiendas* were inherited by Grijalva's grandsons.

(Gerhard, 49 and 201; Icaza, I, 151f. and 153; Boyd-Bowman, I, no. 2873, 102; Scholes and Adams, 26; Orozco y Berra, 81; *Actas*, I, 17 and 20.)

179. Antonio de GUADALAJARA
Conqueror—?
From: Guadalajara (?)

Guadalajara was the first *encomendero* of Nexpa, 57 miles east of Acapulco. It was reassigned by the first Audiencia to Gutierre de Badajoz ca. 1531.

(Gerhard, 149.)

180. Lázaro (Alvaro) GUERRERO
Conqueror—Narváez

Probably a vecino of Antequera, Guerrero was assigned the *encomienda* of Tepexicoapan (also called Tepexillo, 70 miles west of Antequera). He was succeeded by a daughter, who married Andrés Tello of Fregenal (Badajoz) before 1547, in which year the tribute amounted to a claimed $150. A grandson of Guerrero, Diego Tello, was the *encomendero* of record from 1597. The grant was a crown *encomienda* by 1664.

(Gerhard, 164; Scholes and Adams, 38; Icaza, II, 12.)

181. Francisco GUILLÉN
Conqueror—?
From: Escacena del Campo (Huelva)
Parents: Alonso Guillén and Estebania Gómez

In Cuba by 1518 or 1519, Guillén was about twenty-five years old when he took part in the capture of Tenochtitlan. He was a member of subsequent *entradas* to Pánuco, Tehuantepec, against the Yope, and to New Galicia before becoming a *vecino* of Mexico City. He shared the tribute from Xicayan (205 miles south of Mexico City, his share of the tribute in 1547 being $134) with conqueror Juan de Tovar. They were the original *encomenderos*. Guillén married ca. 1539 and by 1547 had two sons and a daughter, maintaining a *casa poblada*, arms, and horses in Mexico City. Between 1537 and 1538 Guillén was in a mining venture with the Portuguese miner Antonio Díaz. He was succeeded ca. 1555 by a son, Antonio (also known as Cristóbal) Guillén. The *encomienda* reverted when Antonio died, sometime before 1597. Guillén's daughter married Diego Veedor of Sanlúcar de Barrameda, a *vecino* of Colima.

(Gerhard, 150; Scholes and Adams, 43; Boyd-Bowman, I, no. 1733a, 61; Icaza, I, 83f. and II, 94; *Protocolos*, II, no. 2267, 121 of 12 April 1537.)

182. Rodrigo GUIPUZCOANO (Lepuzcano)
First Conqueror
From: Medina del Campo (Valladolid)
Parents: Osursula [sic] Guipuzcoano, from Biscay, and Catalina González

Guipuzcoano was in Cuba by 1517 and joined the Cortés *entrada* two years later. After various other *entradas*, Guipuzcoano became a *vecino* of Colima and *encomendero* of half of Milpa (65 miles northwest of Colima; 8,230 tributaries in 1525), reassigned from Diego Martín de Mérida in 1528. The other half was assigned to *poblador antiguo* Pedro de Santa Cruz of Burgos. It was claimed that the income from half of Milpa amounted to $40 in 1547. Guipuzcoano was also the *encomendero* of Pascoatlan (near Tecoman, 30 miles south of Colima). Guipuzcoano died before 1547, and his son, Francisco, inherited ca. 1550. By 1560 the *encomendera* of all of Mitla was the granddaughter of Diego Martín de Mérida. Milpa was a crown holding by 1597. There is no record of Pascoatlan after ca. 1550.

(Gerhard, 60 and 80; Scholes and Adams, 53; Boyd-Bowman, I, no. 4516, 149; Icaza, I, 249f.)

183. Alonso GUTIÉRREZ de Badajoz
Conqueror—?
From: Badajoz

Gutiérrez, a *vecino* of Mexico City, was assigned Tianguiztengo (98 miles north-northeast of Mexico City; a *cabecera* with 16 dependencies in 1548). He was succeeded ca. 1540 by his widow, a daughter of conqueror Gonzalo Hernández Mosquera. She remarried in 1551, to *hidalgo* Francisco de Temiño, a veteran of Vázquez de Coronado's Cíbola *entrada*. Temiño was shown as the *encomendero* into the 1570s. María Mosquera, a granddaughter of the original holder, was the *encomendera* after 1597.

(Gerhard, 184; Scholes and Adams, 40f.; Icaza, I, 215f. and II, 312; *Protocolos*, I, no. 787, 190 of 5 October 1527 and no. 1131, 252 of 3 March 1528.)

184. Antonio GUTIÉRREZ de Ahumada
First Conqueror

Gutiérrez, a member of Alvarado's *entradas* subsequent to the conquest, was a *vecino* of Mexico City and *encomendero* of Guatulco (also referred to as Ocotepec, 355 miles southeast of Mexico City, 85 miles west-southwest of Tehuantepec near the ocean; six to eight *estancias* by the 1570s). He shared at least one gold-panning company with *poblador* Pedro de Pantoja, *encomendero* of nearby Cimatlan. Gutiérrez was succeeded ca. 1549 by his son, Diego. Diego's daughter, married to Bernardino López, inherited the *encomienda* ca. 1565. Guatulco was a crown possession by 1597.

(Gerhard, 124f.; Scholes and Adams, 36; *Protocolos*, I, no. 1246, 271 of 16 April 1528.)

185. Antonio GUTIÉRREZ de Almodóvar
First Conqueror
From: Almodóvar del Campo (Ciudad Real)

Gutiérrez was in Cuba at least by 1518, then joined the Cortés *entrada*. He later became a *vecino* of Mexico City and was assigned half the tribute of Mizquiaguala (65 miles north of Mexico City near Tula; one *estancia*) with first conqueror Pablo Retamales of Seville. Gutiérrez married María Corral, widow of conqueror Diego de San Martín, by whom she had had two sons. There were also children of the union with Gutiérrez. When Gutiérrez died ca. 1540, half of his share of the tribute went to his widow, and the other half went to his mother. By 1545 the mother's share had reverted to the crown, leaving María Corral with one-fourth of the tribute. She married again, this time to Juan de Vargas, by whom she had a son and a daughter. She was a widow again by 1547. The remaining Gutiérrez share reverted to the crown during the 1550s.

(Gerhard, 296 and 299; Icaza, I, 184f.; Boyd-Bowman, I, no. 1278, 44.)

186. Diego GUTIÉRREZ Lavado
Conqueror—Garay
From: Seville (?)

Gutiérrez, a *vecino* of Pánuco, acquired Cuzcatlan (45 miles west near Valles) in the 1530s. He was succeeded before 1547 by a daughter married to Juan Sánchez Bermijo, a native of Puebla de Sancho Pérez (Badajoz). The *encomendero* from ca. 1567 to 1604 was a grandson, Alonso Montaño.

(Gerhard, 355; Icaza, I, 238; Scholes and Adams, 47; Boyd-Bowman, I, no. 3598, 122(?) and II, no. 1743m, 49.)

187. Francisco GUTIÉRREZ—
Blacksmith (?)
First Conqueror
From: Villa de Gota (Alcántara, Cáceres)
Parents: Francisco Gutiérrez and Catalina Sánchez Roblada

Gutiérrez was in Cuba by 1518 and with the Cortés *entrada* the following year. For a time prior to 1532 he was a *vecino* of Pánuco and *encomendero* of nearby Moyutla (246 tributaries in 1532, which, however, he sold to Gregorio de Saldaña, Nuño de Guzmán's lawyer. He then became a *vecino* of Zacatula. In the mid-1540s he was still a bachelor, claiming near poverty because of the few Indians he had in Zacatula. He appears to have been working as a blacksmith of sorts, making items for war as well as nails and iron fittings for the region's shipbuilding efforts. By 1550 he was the *encomendero* of Pochutla and half of Chipila, both in the vicinity of Zacatula. Ten years later he was succeeded by a son, also named Francisco. The *encomienda* was a crown holding after 1565.

(Gerhard, 215 and 394; Scholes and Adams, 51f.; Boyd-Bowman, I, no. 5101, 170; Icaza, I, 242f.; Chipman, 262 and 292.)

188. Gómez GUTIÉRREZ
Conqueror—Narváez

Before 1530 Gutiérrez, a member of the Narváez *entrada*, became a *vecino* of Colima and *encomendero* of nearby Pomayagua and Chapula. He married María Gutiérrez de Villacorta, a native of New Spain and daughter of conqueror (Garay) Juan de Villacorta and Ana González. He was succeeded by his widow, who then married Juan Buriezo. María claimed ca. 1547 that the *encomienda* was but a single *estancia* with twenty tributaries. A son María had by Buriezo inherited in the 1560s.

(Gerhard, 80; Icaza, II, 266; Orozco y Berra, 81; Boyd-Bowman, I, no. 2958, 105.)

189. Don Luis de GUZMÁN Saavedra—
Hidalgo
Poblador
From: Seville
Parents: Don Fernán Darias de Saavedra, Count of Castellar, and doña Catalina de Guzmán

Don Luis, the grandson of the Duke of Medina Sedonia, arrived in Mexico City with his brother, don Hernán Darias de Saavedra, and became a *vecino* in 1525. In 1536 Viceroy Mendoza assigned him the *encomienda* of Tilantongo (200 miles southeast of Mexico City; a *cabecera* with five *sujetos* in 1550, eight in 1579 and ten in 1600). His wife was doña María de Estrada, a daughter of treasurer and sometimes governor Alonso de Estrada. They had two sons and a daughter. Don Luis was succeeded ca. 1543 by his second son, don Alonso Saavedra de Estrada y Guzmán. The succession required confirmation by the Council of the Indies because don Alonso was still underage, in addition to not being the first-born son. His grandmother, doña Marina Gutiérrez Flores de la Caballería, stood as his guardian. Don Alonso was the *encomendero* until the grant reverted to the crown in 1566.

(Gerhard, 201f.; Scholes and Adams, 34; Boyd-Bowman, II, no. 9373, 286; Icaza, I, 220; Dorantes de Carranza, 264.)

190. Nuño Beltrán de GUZMÁN—
Hidalgo
Poblador
From: Guadalajara
Parents: Hernán Beltrán de Guzmán and doña Magdalena de Guzmán

So many negative words have been written about Nuño de Guzmán that one can at least wonder if the case against him has been overstated. At any rate, he has left an indelible mark on the history of Mexico. Guzmán was born ca. 1485 (the same year as Cortés and Pedro de Alvarado) and spent his early years closely associated with the Spanish court. During the decade immediately prior to his posting as governor of Pánuco, Guzmán and his next younger brother (he had four brothers and two sisters) were members of Charles V's personal guard (*continuo*). Nuño had also satisfactorily accomplished a relatively delicate diplomatic mission for the king concerning the Bishop of Cuenca. He was about forty years old when he received the appointment as governor of Pánuco, dated 4 November 1525.

Arriving in Pánuco in May 1527, Guzmán soon received the additional assignment of president of the first Audiencia even though he was not a university trained lawyer. He took up residence in Mexico City perhaps in mid-December 1528. In both assignments in New Spain Guzmán, like any ambitious sixteenth-century governor, left his mark. His position was a difficult one. The colony was already polarized. Opposing factions supported Cortés and the various treasury officers who had served as temporary governors. Unrewarded veterans resented the favors given high-born greenhorns. Perhaps much of the resentment of Guzmán stemmed from his being an outsider with no experience in the Indies. His bad reputation in New Spain was such that he sealed the Caribbean ports to prevent other than approved correspondence from leaving the country. Enough unfavorable information did get back to the court that the king moved to curb Guzmán's influence by appointing an entirely new Audiencia with orders to arrest the former court members and to conduct *residencias*.

Guzmán countered this threat to his career by mounting an *entrada* of his own to conquer the area to the north and west of New Spain. In effect he reconquered parts of Michoacán and Jalisco from a handful of Cortés' followers, then blazed new trails in Nayarit and Sinaloa. His reports to Spain were convincing enough that the *residencia* was postponed and Guzmán was appointed governor of New Galicia, perhaps in early 1531. The commission was the doing of Empress Juana and not that of Charles V, who was absent from Spain. She also named Guzmán's older brother, the Franciscan fray Juan de Guzmán, to an influential ecclesiastical position in New Spain, either archbishop or *comisario general* of his order, depending on the source. Juan's departure was deferred on the advice of the Council of the Indies. Their position was that the recall of Bishop Zumárraga and the posting of brothers in such high offices would not be in the best interests of the crown, especially since the differences between Zumárraga and Nuño were unresolved. Juan died without leaving Spain. It was not until after the arrival of Viceroy don Antonio de Mendoza that Guzmán faced the inevitable. After a pleasant time as a guest of the viceroy in late 1536, Guzmán was confined with common criminals and slaves in the Mexico City jail, languishing there for nearly eighteen months while his *residencia* was being held. He was then recalled to Spain, where he spent the rest of his life under house arrest at the Spanish court. He died about 1560. There is no record of Guzmán ever marrying.

During his time in Mexico, Guzmán held perhaps fourteen *encomiendas*, at least four of them taken from Cortés. The Cortés grants have been identified as Chalco (19 miles southeast of Mexico City, a vast province containing many kingdoms, recovered by Cortés in 1531, then surrendered to the crown two years later), Tuspa (240 miles west of Mexico City, northeast of Colima; 20,000 tributaries at contact, went to the crown in 1531), Oxitipa (180 miles north of Mexico City near Valles, reassigned to Pedro de Guzmán), and Tamoín (180 miles north of Mexico City near Valles, reassigned to Francisco de Villegas). Another Guzmán *encomienda* in New Spain was Tampico, on the coast, 215 miles north-northeast of Mexico City. Except for Toluca (32 miles west-southwest of Mexico City), a grant later reassigned to García del Pilar, the other Guzmán *encomiendas* were in New Galicia and reverted to the crown before the province was annexed to New Spain in 1545. They included Cuisco (13 miles southeast of Guadalajara; 6,155 tributaries in nineteen or so subject towns in 1548), Pocintlan (eight miles southeast of Guadalajara; 2,467 tributaries ca. 1548), Atlemaxaque and Tetlan (on the site of Guadalajara; 1,000 tributaries in 1530), Senticpac (160 miles west-northwest of Guadalajara near San Blas; 18,000 tributaries at contact, 1,129 in 1548), Tepic, Tlaxomulco, and Cuyutlan (12 miles southwest of Guadalajara; 3,440 tributaries ca. 1548), Tonalá (eight miles southeast of Guadalajara; 11,000 "persons" in 1530, 5,110 tributaries ca. 1548) and in Sinaloa, the towns of Navito, Culiacan, Guamuchiles, Diabuto, and Colometo (400 miles northwest of Guadalajara; 4,000 tributaries total when reassigned to Cristóbal de Tapia ca. 1545).

Note: Nuño de Guzmán's family, early career, and experiences as governor of Pánuco are treated in Donald E. Chipman's *Nuño de Guzmán and the Province of Pánuco in New Spain, 1518–1533.*

(Chipman, 112–137 and 278–281; Gerhard, 102–105, 216, 330, 338–340 and 354–357; Gerhard 1982, 67f., 90f., 122, 125–127, 139f., 151f., 154f. and 257–261; ENE, I, 95ff; Alonso López de Haro, *Nobiliario genealógico de los reyes y titutos de España.*)

191. Ramiro de GUZMÁN
Poblador

Guzmán, a member of the Nuño de Guzmán entourage, arrived in New Spain in late 1528 and went to Pánuco, becoming a *vecino* there the following year. He was assigned the *encomienda* of Tancetuco (30 miles south-southwest of Pánuco; 708 tributaries in 1532) and served as *alcalde mayor* of Pánuco from 1530 to 1532. He sold his rights to the *encomienda* to *poblador* Juan de Busto in 1533, a name listed on the rolls until 1612.

(Gerhard, 216; Chipman, 241 and 293.)

192. Rodrigo de GUZMÁN
Poblador
From: Portillo (Toledo)
Parents: Alonso Núñez de Guzmán and Juana Ferreira

Guzmán arrived in New Spain in 1528 along with his brother Esteban. Their father, who left Spain with them, died enroute. Guzmán became a *vecino* of Mexico City and ca. 1532 was assigned Tonatico (140 miles northeast of Mexico City near Papantla) by the second Audiencia. A previous assignment of this *encomienda* had been made by the first Audiencia to Doctor (Maestre) Blas de Bustamante. The tribute reverted to the crown in April 1544, when Guzmán departed for Spain.

(Gerhard, 219; Boyd-Bowman, II, no. 11043, 330; Icaza, II, 346f.)

193. Rodrigo de HEREDIA (d'Evia)
Conqueror—Narváez
From: France (?)

Heredia, possibly a native of Evian, France, was a *vecino* of Colima and *encomendero* of Ostutla (45 miles southeast of Colima in Motines). He was succeeded ca. 1550 by his widow, who then married Juan Alcalde. Ostutla was a crown holding by 1580.

(Gerhard, 193; Orozco y Berra, 59.)

194. Bartolomé HERNÁNDEZ de Nava
First Conqueror
From: Palos (Huelva)

Hernández was in Cuba by 1518 and joined Cortés as a member of his personal guard the following year. It is assumed that he was a staunch supporter of Cortés. After various *entradas* Hernández became a *vecino* of Puebla. He held his first *encomienda*, one-fourth of the tribute of Ocuituco (36 miles west-southwest of Puebla; two *barrios*, Tlalnepantla and Tlaltengo, with five *estancias* each) from ca. 1522 to 1528, when it was transferred to Hernán Medel while Hernández went to Spain. After he returned he bought the rights to half of Iztaquimaxtitlan, also referred to as Castilblanco (60 miles northeast of Puebla; two *cabeceras*, and a number of *estancias* in 1569), shared with first conqueror (?) Pedro de Vargas. Around 1525 his wife, Catalina Vélez Rascona, also a native of Palos, inherited half the tribute of Zapotitlan (65 miles southeast of Puebla near Tehuacan; 2,000 tributaries in 1570) from her father, conqueror García Vélez. In 1548 these tributes were reassigned to the original *encomendero*, Francisco Montaño. Hernández and his wife had seven children. She remarried when Hernández died ca. 1540, this time to Francisco de Orduña, also a *vecino* of Puebla. She had two sons and two daughters by Orduña and was again a widow by 1548. A son, Hernando de Nava, inherited the Iztaquimaxtitlan share and was the *encomendero* into the 1570s. By 1597 the tribute was going to Francisco de Nava (another son?) and by 1604 to a grandson, Martín de Nava Guevara.

(Gerhard, 92f., 228ff., and 261f.; Boyd-Bowman, I, no. 1921, 16 and II, no. 5340, 160; Icaza, I, 74f. and II, 15f.; Orozco y Berra, 43.)

195. Cristóbal HERNÁNDEZ Mosquera
First Conqueror
From: Alanís (Seville)
Parents: Gonzalo Hernández Bermejo and Francisca Hernández

Hernández was in the Indies by 1516 and two years later in Cuba, where he and his brother, Gonzalo, joined the Cortés expedition. After service with various *entradas*, Hernández became a *vecino* of Mexico City and *encomendero* of Apazco (40 miles north of Mexico City near Tula; 1,210 tributaries in 1570), receiving the grant in the 1520s. Hernández was married and sired six legitimate sons and a daughter. He also claimed one natural son. By 1547 his daughter, married to Diego Suárez and mother of two, was living at home while Diego was out of the country seeking his fortune. Hernández' brother, Gonzalo, was the *encomendero* of Tornacuxtla, some 30 miles northeast of Apazco. Cristóbal was succeeded by his oldest son, Gonzalo (also possibly Cristóbal or Francisco) Hernández de Figueroa, still the *encomendero* in 1604. Hernández' nephew, heir to the *encomienda* of Tornacuxtla, was also named Gonzalo Hernández de Figueroa.

(Gerhard, 295 and 298; Scholes and Adams, 25; Boyd-Bowman, I, no. 2964, 105; Icaza, I, 13.)

196. Gonzalo HERNÁNDEZ Calvo—Mariner
First Conqueror
From: Palos (Huelva)
Parents: Francisco Calvo and Leonor Hernández

Hernández spent part of his early career in the Indies (Tierra Firme in 1504) as a mariner before going to Cuba in 1518 and joining the Cortés expedition the following year. After the capture of Mexico City and various *entradas* he became a *vecino* of Puebla. By 1547 he was a *regidor* there and maintaining a *casa poblada*, family, arms, and horses. Hernández became *encomendero* of Zultepec (a *cabecera* under the jurisdiction of Texcoco 40 miles north-northwest of Puebla) ca. 1535 by marrying Isabel Muñoz, the widow of original holder Diego Motrico, a Basque. They had a son and a daughter. The title was disputed when Isabel died in the late 1540s. Half of the tribute was transferred to Pedro de Meneses, the *encomendero* of neighboring Tequipilpa, through purchase. Hernández died ca. 1552 and was succeeded by his son, Francisco Calvo. His heirs received tribute until the crown acquired possession ca. 1688. Hernández was awarded a coat of arms, dated 22 April 1535.

(Gerhard, 312f.; Boyd-Bowman, I, no. 1929, 66; Orozco y Berra, 43; Icaza, I, 71; *Nobiliario*, 38ff.)

197. Gonzalo HERNÁNDEZ Mosquera
First Conqueror
From: Alanís (Seville)
Parents: Gonzalo Hernández Bermejo and Francisca Hernández

Hernández arrived in Cuba by 1518 and, with his brother Cristóbal, joined the Cortés expedition the following year. After the capture of Tenochtitlan and subsequent *entradas* he became a *vecino* of Mexico City and *encomendero* of Tornacuxtla (a *cabecera* 65 miles northeast of Mexico City with three *estancias*—considered a small grant in 1564). Hernández married a niece of Pedro de Alvarado and had five children. In his *casa poblada* he also maintained, in addition to his arms and horses, eight natural children, a sister and her child, and a daughter married to *poblador antiguo* Antón (Hontañón de) Angulo (she was also the widow of conqueror Alonso Gutiérrez de Badajoz). He was succeeded by his son, Gonzalo Hernández de Figueroa, and by 1599, a grandson, Juan Pacheco, was the *encomendero*. Tornacuxtla was a crown *encomienda* by 1643.

(Gerhard, 297 and 300; Scholes and Adams, 19; Boyd-Bowman, I, no. 2965, 105; Icaza, I, 42f.)

198. Juan HERNÁNDEZ de Prado
Conqueror—Narváez
From: Galende (Zamora)
Parents: Juan de Prado and María de Prado

Hernández was in Cuba in 1519 and joined the Narváez *entrada* the following year. After the capture of Tenochtitlan and subsequent *entradas* he was assigned the *encomienda* of Guamelula (40 miles southwest of Tehuantepec) ca. 1529 by Nuño de Guzmán and then had the grant taken from him for the crown by the second Audiencia in April, 1531. Hernández' wife and two children remained in Spain, and he acknowledged two natural children in New Spain.

(Gerhard, 124; Icaza, I, 67f.; Boyd-Bowman, I, no. 4842, 161.)

199. Pedro HERNÁNDEZ
Conqueror—Narváez
Parents: Garci Hernández and Elvira Hernández de Herrera

Hernández, his father, and his brother, Juan Pérez de Herrera, were all members of the Narváez *entrada*. The father died shortly after the capture of Tenochtitlan, and his *encomienda*, Epatlan, was divided between the two sons. Epatlan (70 miles southeast of Mexico City near Izúcar; 11 *barrios* in 1548) was shared by the brothers, both *vecinos* of Mexico City, until ca. 1529, when the first Audiencia reassigned Pedro's half to Juan. The second Audiencia revoked the assignment and took the half for the crown. It is assumed that Pedro either died or left for Spain ca. 1529. The brothers also had three sisters in New Spain. One married conqueror Martín de Calahorra, another married *hidalgo* conqueror and *encomendero* Diego de Holguín, and the third married an unknown man who left her a widow.

(Gerhard, 160 and 163; Icaza, I, 41f.; *Protocolos*, I, no. 694, 172 of 27 August 1527.)

200. Santos HERNÁNDEZ "*el buen viejo*"
First Conqueror
From: Coria (Cáceres)
Father: Pedro Hernández

Hernández, called "*el buen viejo*" by Bernal Díaz del Castillo, arrived in Santo Domingo in 1502 and took part in the conquests of Tierra Firme, Cuba, Jamaica, Puerto Rico, Cartagena, and Santa Marta before joining the Cortés *entrada* in 1519. After the capture of Tenochtitlan, Hernández went to Guatemala with Pedro de Alvarado before becoming a *vecino* of Oaxaca, where he maintained his arms and horses. In the 1520s he was assigned the *encomienda* of Petalcingo (a *cabecera* 105 miles northwest of Oaxaca; two *estancias*, Temascalapa and Tepexic, in 1581). He was succeeded before 1569 by a son (?), Francisco Hernández Guerrero, still the *encomendero* in 1597. María de Vera received the tribute as *encomendera* after 1603. By 1630 Petalcingo was a crown possession.

(Gerhard, 42f.; Boyd-Bowman, I, no. 941, 33; Icaza, I, 10f.; Orozco y Berra, 43; Díaz del Castillo, II, 451.)

201. Cristóbal de HERRERA
Poblador

By 1554 Herrera was the *encomendero* of Chinameca and Mistecas (nine *sujetos* in the vicinity of Coatzacoalcos in 1580), as well as a *poblador vecino* of Coatzacoalcos. He was succeeded by a namesake son ca. 1567.

(Gerhard, 139.)

202. Francisco de HERRERA
Poblador
From: Seville
Parents: Pedro Díaz de Villacreces and Constanza Gómez de Herrera

In 1526 Herrera arrived in New Spain and became a *vecino* of Mexico City. Governor Alonso de Estrada assigned him half the tribute from Igualapa (a *cabecera* with ten *estancias* in 1582), Ometepec (a *cabecera* with six subject *pueblos* in 1700), and

Suchistlaguaca (a *cabecera* with eight *pueblos* in 1700), all about 200 miles south of Mexico City and from 90 to 100 miles east of Acapulco. The other half belonged initially to Basque conqueror Francisco de Orduña and then was given in dowry when a daughter married conqueror Alonso del Castillo. About 1547 each share was claimed to provide $380 income annually. Herrera also served as an agricultural *mayordomo* for Cortés and later as an accountant. He had married in Spain, leaving his wife and seven children there while he developed an estate in New Spain. By 1546 three sons and a daughter were in Mexico City. That same year he sent his oldest son to Spain to bring back his wife, their three youngest children, and various nieces. Herrera died before his family could reunite. He was succeeded ca. 1548 by a son, Gonzalo Hernández de Herrera. By 1565 half the tribute from Igualapa was going to the Castillo heirs and the rest to Hernández Herrera. Igualapa reverted to the crown before 1597. Pedro Fajardo was receiving the tribute from Ometepec and Suchistlaguaca at the turn of the century.

(Gerhard, 150f.; Scholes and Adams, 36; Boyd-Bowman, I, no. 9388, 287; Icaza, I, 203; Riley, 69f.)

203. Juan (Francisco) de HINOJOSA
Poblador
From: Trujillo (Cáceres)

Hinojosa arrived in New Spain in 1522, served with various *entradas*, and by 1525 was a *vecino* of Mexico City. Towards mid-1528 he shared the *encomienda* rights to Atlán and Metateyuca (147 miles northeast of Mexico City near Poza Rica) with Juan de Nájera, a native of Logroño. Hinojosa had Juan de Cabrera in his employ to manage his interest in the grant. Later the same year he had a miner, Francisco de Ballesteros, working for him. Both shares of the *encomienda* reverted to the crown when Hinojosa died on the 1533 *entrada* under Cortés' relation, Diego Becerra de Mendoza (Becerra was assassinated at sea by Fortún Jiménez, the ship's pilot). Hinojosa was married to Beatriz Mejía de Tapia of Trujillo and had a son, Francisco, who came to Mexico City ca. 1537. He was a *vecino* there ten years later.

(Gerhard, 118; Icaza, II, 18f.; Boyd-Bowman, II, no. 3165 and no. 3166, 92; *Protocolos*, I, no. 1394, 299 of 12 [*sic*] June 1528 and no. 1518, 321 of 15 September 1528.)

204. Gaspar de HITA
Poblador
From: Hita (Guadalajara ?)

Before 1554 Hita was the *encomendero* of Suchititlan, Guatepec, and Milpancingo (in the vicinity of Coatzacoalcos) and was more than likely a *vecino* of Coatzacoalcos. He was succeeded by a namesake son. In 1597 the *encomendera* was Catalina de Hita.

(Gerhard, 139.)

205. Diego de HOLGUÍN—*Hidalgo*
Conqueror—Narváez
From: Cáceres
Parents: Diego de Holguín and Catalina Alvarez Moraga

Holguín was in Cuba in 1519 and sailed with the Narváez *entrada* on one of Licenciado Alonso Zuazo's ships the following year. He missed taking part in the capture of Tenochtitlan because illness forced him to remain in Veracruz. After being a member of various *entradas*, Holguín became a *vecino* of Puebla, where he was appointed *corregidor* in 1534, and there he maintained his *casa poblada*, family, arms, and horses. His time as an *encomendero* was limited. Cortés, to protect his own interests, "deposited" half the tributes of Yecapixtla (35 miles southwest of Puebla; a *cabecera* with 17 *estancias* in 1570) with Holguín in 1528 when he went to Spain. The other half was "deposited" with Francisco de Solís. The tribute was recovered by Cortés when he returned in 1531 as Marqués del Valle. Holguín married Elvira Herrera, a daughter of conqueror Garci Hernández and had four children, two of them sons. His wife was also a sister of conqueror *encomenderos* Juan Pérez de Herrera and Pedro Hernández. One of her sisters married conqueror *encomendero* Martín de Calahorra, and another was a widow in New Spain. Their oldest daughter married Juan de Jerez "*el mozo.*" He was the nephew of Juan de Jerez "*el tio,*" who replaced Vicente Yañez Pinzón as pilot for Colón. *El tio* was a first conqueror who died in Mexico City in 1520. *El mozo* arrived in Mexico City in 1525.

(Gerhard, 95f.; Icaza, I, 41f. and 65; Boyd-Bowman, I, no. 916a, 325; no. 1168, 40, and II, no. 3365, 98; Orozco y Berra, 82.)

206. Sancho de HORNA
Poblador Antiguo
From: Alcántara (Cáceres)
Parents: Hernán Martín and María Jiménez de Horna

Horna arrived in the Indies in 1512 and got to New Spain shortly after the capture of Mexico City. After service on an *entrada* to the west coast he became a *vecino* of Colima and in the 1520s was assigned *encomienda* rights to Alima, Pochotitlan and Tlacuahuan (all in the jurisdiction of Colima). The tribute from all three had reverted to the crown by 1532.

(Gerhard, 80; Boyd-Bowman, I, no. 854, 30.)

207. Gómez de HOYOS
First Conqueror
From: Medina de las Torres (Badajoz)
Parents: Pedro de Perada and María de Barajas

Hoyos arrived in the Indies with his brother, Alonso de Perada, in 1514 and was with the Cortés *entrada* five years later. After the capture of Tenochtitlan and subsequent *entradas*, in the 1520s Hoyos became a *vecino* of Colima and *encomendero* of Xuluapa (a small grant in the vicinity of Colima). The tribute from Xuluapa reverted to the crown ca. 1550 when Hoyos died. Shortly thereafter the tribute was reassigned to his widow, who received it until her death ca. 1567. Xuluapa then escheated.

(Gerhard, 80; Scholes and Adams, 49; Boyd-Bowman, I, no. 471, 17; Orozco y Berra, 44.)

208. Diego HURTADO de Mendoza
Poblador
From: Madrid
Parents: Rodrigo Hurtado and Inés de Tapia

Hurtado arrived in New Spain ca. 1528 and acquired the *encomienda* of Taimeo (a *cabecera* 56 miles southwest of Querétaro; at least ten *estancias* in 1558). The following year the first Audiencia reassigned the tribute to conqueror Gaspar de Avila Quiñones. Hurtado then took part in the conquest of New Galicia and became a *vecino* of Guadalajara. Around 1548 he bought the rights to Cuzpatlan (40 miles north of Guadalajara; 60 tributaries). He married a daughter of one of the conquerors of Hispaniola and had four children, two of them sons. His *casa poblada* included his mother-in-law and a brother-in-law as well as arms and horses. Hurtado died ca. 1570 and was succeeded by his son Cristóbal, the *encomendero* until 1595.

(Gerhard, 319f.; Boyd-Bowman, II, no. 6305, 193; Icaza, II, 258; Gerhard 1982, 101.)

209. Andrés de INERO
Poblador

Inero arrived in New Spain as a member of Nuño de Guzmán's entourage, became a *vecino* of Pánuco, and shortly thereafter was assigned half the tribute from Guatla (80 miles southwest of Pánuco; 48 tributaries in 1532) and Ilamatlan (85 miles south of Pánuco; 431 tributaries in 1532), shared with *poblador* Juan de Cervantes Casaus of Seville. He was later assigned all of Tlanchinolticpac (90 miles south-southwest of Pánuco; 80 or more *sujetos* in 1573) when Guzmán ordered the execution of conqueror Gil González de Trujillo. All of the tribute from Ilamatlan was going to Cervantes by the mid-1530s; Tlanchinolticpac was reassigned by the second Audiencia to conqueror Alonso Ortiz de Zúñiga and *poblador* Jerónimo de Medina; and by 1540 *poblador* Cristóbal Bezos Frías was the sole holder of Guatla. Inero simply dropped from the scene.

(Gerhard, 133f., 184ff. and 243f.; Chipman, 292.)

210. Juan INFANTE—*Hidalgo*
Poblador
From: Seville

Infante was a *vecino* of Mexico City. In 1528 he was assigned Tzintzuntzan near Lake Pátzcuaro (155 miles west of Mexico City) by Governor Alonso de Estrada; the grant was originally claimed by Cortés. A twenty-five-year-long tug-of-war for possession ended with most of the tribute from this collection of communities going to the crown. The first Audiencia assigned Comanja and Naranja (20 miles north-northwest of Pátzcuaro; 38 *sujetos* in 1523) to Infante, reassigning it from *poblador* Juan de Solís and Cortés. At about the same time Infante claimed Pamacoran (35 miles west-northwest of Pátzcuaro, a former dependency of Tzintzuntzan and a Solís-Cortés grant) and acquired title. The aggregate made a rather large *encomienda* that Infante passed to his son, Juan Infante Samaniego, in 1574. After that Infante's granddaughter, doña Francisca de Estrada Infante Samaniego, inherited. She was married to Diego Fernández de Velasco.

(Gerhard, 344f. and 350ff.; Scholes and Adams, 17; Boyd-Bowman, II, no. 12921, 390; *Protocolos*, I, no. 531, 141 of 4 May 1527.)

211. Bernardino IÑIGUEZ
First Conqueror
From: Santo Domingo de la Calzada (Logroño)

Iñiguez was in Cuba by 1517, becoming the treasury inspector (*veedor*) of the Hernández de Córdoba expedition. He then joined the Cortés *entrada* two years later. After the capture of Tenochtitlan he went to Spain, returning with an appointment as *veedor* of Yucatan. But instead of going to Yucatan, he became a *vecino* of Pánuco and served as treasurer there. He is listed as *encomendero* of Huexutla (65 miles south-southeast; three *estancias* in 1548) between 1527 and 1533. After that the tribute was claimed by Juan Rodríguez and Gabriel de Aguilera. By 1548 Huexutla was a crown holding.

(Gerhard, 144f.; Boyd-Bowman, I, no. 4988, 166; Chipman, 247 and 292; Díaz del Castillo, I, 10.)

212. Martín de IRCIO—*Hidalgo*
Conqueror—Narváez
From: Briones (Logroño)
Parents: Pedro Sánchez de Ircio and María Jiménez de Ribafrecha

Ircio arrived in Cuba in 1519 and sailed with the Narváez *entrada* the following year to join his brother Pedro. He sided with Cortés to take part in the capture of Tenochtitlan. After a number of *entradas*, Ircio became a *vecino* of Mexico City, where he maintained his *casa poblada*, arms, and horses. Cortés assigned him the *encomiendas* of Oapa (95 miles south of Mexico City; six *estancias* in 1570), Tistla (130 miles south of Mexico City; 28 *estancias* in 1570), Huitziltepec (108 miles south of Mexico City; three *estancias* in 1570), and Muchtitlan (100 miles south of Mexico City; 18 *estancias* in 1570). Ircio married doña María de Mendoza, a sister of the viceroy, and had many children. His brother, first conqueror Pedro de Ircio, served as a captain during the Tenochtitlan campaign and married doña María de Cervantes, a daughter of Comendador Leonel de Cervantes. Ircio was succeeded by his daughter, doña María, who married don Luis de Velasco the Younger ca. 1566. The *encomienda* became part of the Marquesado de Salinas.

Note: Pedro de Ircio must also have been an *encomendero*, though there is no record of it.

(Gerhard, 316ff.; Scholes and Adams, 18f.; Orozco y Berra, 44; Icaza, I, 30f.; Boyd-Bowman, I, no. 4959, 164.)

213. Pedro de la ISLA
Poblador Antiguo
From: Seville

In Santo Domingo in 1514 and a *vecino* of Mexico City by 1525, Isla was an employee of Cortés. By 1528 he shared the tributes from Tancítaro (235 miles west of Mexico City, 28 miles west-southwest of Uruapan; 14 *sujetos* in 1580) with fellow Cortés employee, *poblador* Domingo de Medina of Badajoz. Isla's share reverted to the crown before 1531.

(Gerhard, 250f.; Boyd-Bowman, I, no. 3615, 123; *Protocolos*, I, no. 74, 42 and no. 386, 111.)

214. Juan JARAMILLO de Salvatierra—
Hidalgo
First Conqueror
From: Villanueva de Barcarrota (Badajoz)
Parents: Alonso Jaramillo and Mencía de Matos

Jaramillo, the son and nephew of conquerors of Tierra Firme and Española (his uncle was Diego García Jaramillo; his first cousin was *poblador antiguo* Alonso Valiente, also a cousin of Cortés), arrived in Cuba in 1518 and joined Cortés the following year. After the capture of Tenochtitlan, he became a *vecino* of Mexico City and took part in a succession of *entradas*. By 1533 he had acquired full possession of Xilotepec (40 miles north-northwest of Mexico City near Tula; 18,335 tributaries ca. 1565). Previous claimants included Hernando Cantillana, Francisco de Quevedo, and Juan Núñez de Sedeño. Jaramillo's first wife was the Indian interpreter doña Marina, by whom he had a daughter, doña María Jaramillo. When doña Marina died he remarried, this time to doña Beatriz de Andrada.

She was the youngest daughter of Comendador Leonel de Cervantes. Jaramillo was succeeded by doña Beatriz, who then married don Francisco de Velasco, the viceroy's brother. By 1555 half the tribute was assigned to Jaramillo's daughter, doña María, by this time married to don Luis de Quesada. Around 1592 her son, don Pedro de Quesada, inherited this share. Part of the *encomienda* was still in private ownership at the close of the eighteenth century.

(Gerhard, 383f.; Scholes and Adams, 43; Orozco y Berra, 83; Boyd-Bowman, I, no. 588, 20f. and no. 283, 11; *Protocolos*, I, no. 1545, 325 of 19 September 1528.)

215. Juan de JASO "*el viejo*"—Hidalgo
Poblador
From: San Juan del Pie del Puerto (Navarre)
Parents: Musior [sic] Juan Pérez de Jaso and Madama [sic] Graciana de Gorostiaga

Jaso arrived in New Spain in 1523 as a recruit of Francisco de Montejo, bringing with him arms and three horses. Upon arrival, Cortés assigned him the *encomienda* of Guachinago (120 miles northeast of Mexico City; 65 *estancias* in 1571). Shortly thereafter Cortés also reassigned him Cuicatlan (185 miles southeast of Mexico City; four *barrios* and three *estancias* in 1548), taking the *encomienda* from first conqueror Juan Tirado. Jaso went with Cortés to Honduras and then in 1527 became a *vecino* of Mexico City. Within the next two years Cuicatlan and Guachinango were taken by the first Audiencia, the latter being reassigned to conqueror Alonso de Villanueva and the former returned to Tirado. By early 1528 Jaso also shared the tribute from Arimao-Pinzándaro (250 miles west of Mexico City near Uruapan; a *cabecera* with four *sujetos* in 1580) with conqueror Juan Jiménez. This grant was taken by the second Audiencia and reassigned to conqueror Pedro Ruiz de Requena and first conqueror Juan Gómez de Herrera. By 1534 Jaso was no longer an *encomendero* but maintained his *casa poblada*, arms, and horses in Mexico City. His wife was doña María Ponce de León. They had one daughter. Jaso's cousin (?), poblador Juan de Jaso *"el mozo,"* was also a member of Mexico City's elite.

(Gerhard, 118f., 250, 252, 306, and 308; Boyd-Bowman, II, no. 6755, 207; Icaza, II, 21f. and I, 197.)

**216. Juan de JASO *"el mozo"—Hidalgo Poblador*
From: San Juan del Pie del Puerto (Navarre)
Parents: Musior [sic] Martín de Jaso and Madama [sic] Graciana de Aramburu**

Jaso arrived in New Spain in 1527, served as a page to Cortés, and later became a *vecino* of Mexico City, where he maintained a *casa poblada*. He did not become an *encomendero* until ca. 1540, when Xipacoya (42 miles north of Mexico City near Tula; a *cabecera* with two *estancias* in 1548) was transferred to his bride, Isabel Payo, as her dowry. She was a daughter of conqueror Lorenzo Payo, also a member of the Jaso household. Jaso and Isabel had three daughters. She succeeded as *encomendera* sometime before 1597. Part of the tribute from Xipacoya went to a private recipient as late as 1688. An older cousin(?), Juan de Jaso *"el viejo,"* was also a *vecino* of Mexico City.

(Gerhard, 332 and 334; Icaza, I, 197; Boyd-Bowman, II, no. 6756, 207.)

**217. Hernando (Gómez) de JEREZ
Conqueror—Narváez
From: Jerez de la Frontera (Cádiz)**

Jerez arrived in Cuba in 1519 and was a member of the Narváez *entrada* the following year. Shortly after his arrival in New Spain he became an employee of Cortés; by 1524 he was a *vecino* of Mexico City. In that year Cortés assigned him the *encomienda* of Zacapo and Tescalco (180 miles west of Mexico City near Pátzcuaro; a *cabecera* with nine *barrios* in the 1540s). He was later assigned Atlatlauca (33 miles southwest of Mexico City) and Suchiaca (34 miles southwest of Mexico City). Around 1523 Jerez married Ana Rodríguez, also from Jerez de la Frontera, and had one daughter, Juana de Jerez. He was succeeded by his widow ca. 1537. She retained Zacapo and Tescalco and gave them to Juana in dowry when she married *hidalgo* Gonzalo de Avalos of Ubeda, a 1537 arrival in New Spain. Although Ana claimed Atlatlauca and Suchiaca, Viceroy Mendoza assigned the tribute therefrom to the royal mint and then in 1544 to the crown. Zacapo and Tescalco were also crown *encomiendas* in 1597.

(Gerhard, 271, 346, and 353; Icaza, I, 110f. and II, 8f.; Boyd-Bowman, I, no. 1166, 40, II, no. 3386, 99 and no. 5765, 174; Orozco y Berra, 82; Scholes and Adams, 41; *Protocolos*, I, no. 732, 179f. of 22 August 1527 and no. 757, 184f. of 9 September 1527; *Actas*, I, 16.)

**218. Gonzalo JIMÉNEZ
First Conqueror
From: Trujillo (Cáceres)
Parents: Juan Jiménez and Inés Hernández**

Jiménez was in Cuba in 1518 and sailed with the Cortés *entrada* the following year, being then about twenty-five years old. After the capture of Tenochtitlan, a trip to Spain and back, and subsequent *entradas*, Jiménez became a *vecino* of Villa Alta and *encomendero* of Ayacastla (vicinity of Villa Alta; 17 *estancias* in 1548). Around 1533 he was an unsuccessful claimant to Tlacuacintla. He was married, but his wife stayed in Spain until after 1547. A daughter married Juan Gómez of Ontiveros, Avila, also a *vecino* of Villa Alta. Jiménez was succeeded by his widow ca. 1565. She then married Gaspar de Vargas, shown as *encomendero* of Ayacastla from 1570 to 1597.

(Gerhard, 302 and 370; Scholes and Adams, 21; Boyd-Bowman, I, no. 1090, 37; Icaza, I, 180 and 255; Orozco y Berra, 44.)

219. Juan JIMÉNEZ
Conqueror—Narváez
From: Trujillo (Cáceres)

Possibly a brother of first conqueror Gonzalo Jiménez, Juan Jiménez was in Cuba by 1519 and sailed with the Narváez *entrada* the following year. He was a *vecino* of Mexico City between 1525 and 1530 or so and shared the tribute from Arimao-Pinzándaro (240 miles west of Mexico City and southwest of Uruapan; four *sujetos* in 1580) with Juan de Jaso "*el viejo*" from before 1528 until 1532, when the second Audiencia reassigned these *encomiendas* to conquerors Pedro Ruiz de Requena and Juan Gómez de Herrera.

(Gerhard, 250; Boyd-Bowman, I, no. 1091, 37; *Protocolos*, I, no. 233, 78 of 18 November 1525.)

220. Juan JIMÉNEZ de Rivera
First Conqueror
From: Santander

Jiménez was in Cuba by 1518 and joined the Cortés *entrada* the following year. He was assigned the *encomienda* of Teutitlan (208 miles southeast of Mexico City; six *barrios*, five *sujetos*, and one *estancia* in 1548), presumably by Cortés. It was reassigned to the crown by the first Audiencia in March, 1531. Jiménez died before 1547, leaving his widow, Leonor Gutiérrez, a son, and a daughter.

(Gerhard, 306 and 308; Boyd-Bowman, I, no. 2832, 100; Icaza, I, 108.)

221. Martín JIMÉNEZ
Poblador

A *vecino* of Colima, Jiménez was assigned Alcozahui and Mixtlan (vicinity of Colima) in *encomienda* in the 1520s. By 1527 he had formed a one-year company with first conqueror, Hernando de Torres, *encomendero* of Tepecuaculco (25 miles south-southeast of Taxco) and a *vecino* of Mexico City, to exploit mines in Zacatula. A year later he contracted to administer Istapa for *poblador* Cristóbal de Valderrama, Istapa being part of the latter's *encomienda* in southern Michoacán and northern Zacatula. Jiménez was succeeded ca. 1560 by his son Juan. The *encomienda* was still paying tribute to the family in 1597.

(Gerhard, 80; *Protocolos*, I, no. 411, 117 of 4 March 1527, no. 423, 119 of 10 March 1527, no. 1616, 338 of 3 October 1528, and no. 1668a, 348 of 12 October 1528.)

222. Pedro JUÁREZ (Suárez)
Poblador

Around 1528 Juárez acquired the rights to Maravatio (90 miles west-northwest of Mexico City; 1,000 to 1,200 tributaries in 1570) from *poblador* Diego de Ocaña. The tribute reverted to the crown in August, 1550, when Juárez died without legal issue.

(Gerhard, 172.)

223. Tomás de LAMADRIZ
Poblador
From: Lamadrid (Santander)

Lamadriz arrived in New Spain with his wife, María Ramírez (also of Lamadrid, daughter of Gonzalo de Castañeda) in 1524 and became a *vecino* of Oaxaca. He bought the rights to Tequecistlan (88 miles southeast of Antequera; 4,000 tributaries in 1580) from *poblador* Luis de la Cueva and was the *encomendero* until his death ca. 1546. He was succeeded by his widow and then by a daughter, doña Juana de Castañeda, married to Diego de Alavés (son of first conqueror and Antequera *vecino* Melchor de Alavés). A grandson, Melchor de Alavés, was the *encomendero* by 1597. Lamadriz and his wife had two other daughters, doña Ana and doña Juliana Ramírez. Both of them married sons of conquerors and *vecinos* of Antequera.

Note: All three daughters used the title *doña*, but no *hidalgo* connections have been discovered for their father. That the girls took names from the maternal line suggests that Lamadriz' wife had a more illustrious lineage.

(Gerhard, 265f.; Icaza, I, 224; Boyd-Bowman, II, no. 7731 and no. 7733, 239.)

224. Juan LARIOS—Notary
Poblador
From: Navalmorcuende (Toledo)
Parents: Juan Hernández Larios and María Hernández Blanca

Larios arrived in New Spain ca. 1527 with a title as his majesty's notary. As a result of his participation in an *entrada* against the Yope he was awarded the *encomienda* of Copalitas and Cuilutla (62 miles east of Acapulco) by the first Audiencia, only to have it taken by Viceroy Mendoza as a crown holding in 1535. Larios did not marry, probably contributing to the justification for the viceroy's action. He then took up residence at the mines of Ayoteco (Chiautla, south of Izúcar).

(Gerhard, 149; Icaza, II, 341f.; Boyd-Bowman, II, no. 10952, 327.)

225. Diego (Francisco?) de LEIVA
Conqueror—?

Leiva, probably a *vecino* of Antequera, was assigned Centecomaltepec and Tecpa (Chontal villages 85 miles southeast of Antequera) and prevailed against the claims of *poblador* Juan López de Jimena and first conqueror Gonzalo Jiménez for the *encomiendas* of Tlacuacintepec (a *cabecera* with four *estancias* 40 miles north of Antequera) and Tecomaltepec (also a *cabecera* with four *estancias* 45 miles north of Antequera). He married Francisca de la Cueva and had at least one child, a son. Leiva was succeeded in the 1550s by this son, Diego, married to Juana de Cabrera. The succession was unsuccessfully contested by Diego's mother. Diego was succeeded ca. 1565 by his widow, soon remarried to Alonso de Olivares.

(Gerhard, 196f., 302 and 304; Scholes and Adams, 42.)

226. Juan de LIMPIAS Carvajal—*Hidalgo*
First Conqueror
From: Santa María la Mayor (Seville)
Parents: Hernando de Carvajal and Lucía de Limpias

Limpias was in the Indies by 1513, in Cuba five years later, and a member of the Cortés *entrada* in 1519. After taking part in the capture of Tenochtitlan and a succession of *entradas*, he became a *vecino* of the capital and *encomendero* of Otatitlan (220 miles east-southeast of Mexico City, 80 miles south of Veracruz; three *estancias* in 1548). Limpias was married and had several children. He was succeeded ca. 1567 by a son, Juan de Limpias. The *encomendero* of Otatitlan in 1597 was Fernando de Carvajal (a grandson?).

(Gerhard, 86 and 88; Scholes and Adams, 18; Boyd-Bowman, I, no. 3648, 124; Icaza, I, 20; *ENE* I, 41.)

227. Guillén de la LOA—Notary
Conqueror—Garay
From: Vizcaya

Loa arrived in the Indies at least by 1519, joined Garay's 1520 *entrada*, and took part in the capture of Tenochtitlan. By 1525, he was a *vecino* of Mexico City and held the *encomiendas* of Guayacocotla (96 miles northeast of Mexico City; 2,000 tributaries in 1565) and Coyuca (155 miles southwest of Mexico City; 12 *sujetos* in 1579). Coyuca was reassigned after 1533 to Pedro de Meneses. Loa was married to doña Isabel de Alvarado and had three children, one of them a daughter who married Alvaro de Bracamonte. The *encomienda* was divided between doña Isabel and the oldest son, Gómez de Alvarado, when Loa died ca. 1545. Sometime later the widow's half went to a second son, Julián de la Loa. By 1560 both sons were dead. Doña Isabel, now remarried, received half the tribute, and a grandson (a son of Gómez de Alvarado) received the other half. The entire *encomienda* had reverted to the crown by 1594.

(Gerhard, 133f. and 135f.; Scholes and Adams, 44; Icaza, I, 105f. and 212f.; Boyd-

Bowman, I, no. 4788, 158; Orozco y Berra, 69; Actas, I, 38.)

228. Alonso LÓPEZ
Conqueror—Díaz de Aux
From: Córdoba
Parents: Gonzalo López and Mari Gutiérrez

López had been in Santo Domingo some fourteen years before sailing with Miguel Díaz de Aux in the Narváez *entrada* in 1520. After serving in the siege of Tenochtitlan and a number of *entradas*, López became a *vecino* of Colima ca. 1523. He was reassigned Moyutla and Ixtapa (in the vicinity of Colima) from an unknown first holder and then acquired Aguatlan (115 miles north) in Jalisco. López married ca. 1536; he had one son and five daughters, of whom the son and perhaps the two oldest daughters were natural children. By 1547 one daughter had married Hernando de Palencia, a *vecino* of Guadalajara. López was dead by 1547, and the *encomienda* reverted to the crown four years later for lack of a legal heir.

(Gerhard, 80; Icaza, I, 84 and II, 248f.; Boyd-Bowman, I, no. 142a, 48; Orozco y Berra, 62; Gerhard 1982, 60f.)

229. Andrés LÓPEZ de Sevilla
Conqueror—Narváez
From: Seville

López was in Cuba by 1519 and sailed with the Narváez *entrada* the following year. He was undoubtedly a *vecino* of Mexico City. López and *poblador* Antonio Medel, a native of Huelva, were assigned equal shares of the *encomiendas* of Tlaquilpa (48 miles northeast of Mexico City near Pachuca; a large *cabecera* with three *sujetos* in 1580) and Guaquilpa (45 miles northeast of Mexico City near Tlaquilpa; one *estancia* in 1581). The rights to the grants were sold to *poblador antiguo* Licenciado Diego Téllez in the 1540s, about the time that López was active in New Galicia. López and his wife Catalina had two sons, Andrés and Martín, and a daughter also named Catalina. By 1547 the daughter had married Francisco Arlite of "Borgoña la Alta" (France), and both López and his wife were dead.

(Gerhard, 68f. and 209ff.; Scholes and Adams, 39; Boyd-Bowman, I, no. 3656, 124 and II, no. 13145, 397; Icaza, I, 138 and II, 239; Orozco y Berra, 62.)

230. Bartolomé LÓPEZ de Sanlúcar—Archer
First Conqueror
From: Sanlúcar la Mayor (Seville)
Parents: Pedro López, a carpenter, and Isabel Gutiérrez

López was in the Indies by 1512 and in Cuba in 1518, joining the Cortés *entrada* the following year as an archer. He was a *vecino* of Veracruz (Villarrica) subsequent to the capture of Tenochtitlan, but later relocated to Colima. Before 1530 Comala and Cecamachantla (vicinity of Colima; 50 tributaries in 1547) were reassigned to him from conqueror Pedro de Simancas. López died in the mid-1530s and was succeeded by his widow, who in 1537 married *hidalgo poblador* Alonso Carrillo from Toledo. Carrillo acquired title to the grant and was succeeded by a son in the 1560s. Tribute was still being paid to heirs in 1597.

(Gerhard, 80; Icaza, I, 215; Boyd-Bowman, I, no. 3174, 111 and II, no. 11229, 335; Orozco y Berra, 83.)

231. Gonzalo LÓPEZ "el camarero"
Conqueror—Narváez

López, a member of the Narváez *entrada*, became a *vecino* of Mexico City after its capture. Before 1528 he was assigned the *encomienda* of Cuiseo (140 miles west-northwest of Mexico City; 4,379 persons over the age of four years residing in four *cabeceras* and 36 *estancias* in 1548). By 1560 the *encomienda* had reverted to the crown.

(Gerhard, 99; Orozco y Berra, 83; *Protocolos*, I, no. 620, 158 of 28 June 1527.)

232. Jerónimo LÓPEZ—*Hidalgo*, Notary
Conqueror—Narváez
From: Villa Pedroso (Seville)
Parents: Antón López de Viar and Elvira Hernández de la Cuesta

López was in Cuba a year before sailing as a member of the 1520 Narváez *entrada*. In 1526, after participating in the conquest and several *entradas*, López became a *vecino* of Mexico City. He was assigned Tepetitango (300 miles west of Mexico City near Colima) in the 1520s but lost it in 1532, when the second Audiencia took it for the crown. López had gone to Spain, perhaps with intent to remain. He later claimed he went home only to marry. After his return to New Spain Viceroy Mendoza assigned him Axacuba (45 miles north of Mexico City near Tula; 4,300 tributaries in 1570), which had been a crown property for about ten years. López married three times and had six daughters and four sons. One daughter married Pedro Hernández Bota, a *vecino* of Mexico City from Nogales (Soria). López was the clerk of the Audiencia from 1531 to 1534 and a Mexico City *regidor* in 1532, 1533, 1540, 1542, and 1544–1549. He died in 1550 and was succeeded by his oldest son, Jerónimo, who was the *encomendero* until 1608. Jerónimo married doña Ana Carrillo de Peralta from Logroño. Axacuba reverted to the crown in 1688. López received a coat of arms dated 26 June 1530. He maintained a running correspondence with the king concerning activities in New Spain, with much discussion of his poverty and lack of rewards.

Note: López' will is contained in Fernández del Castillo, 227–246 and an inventory of his goods follows. His first wife was Elvira Alvarez de Mendoza, a daughter of Alonso Durán de Mendoza of Trujillo or Medellín. They married on 24 November 1532 and had two daughters who survived. His second wife was Catalina Alvarez of Badajoz, daughter of Juan Zapata and Catalina Núñez. They married 4 September 1536, and she died 15 July 1537 in giving birth to Jerónimo. His third wife was Mencia de Ribera of Nogales (Soria), a widow.

They married on 16 June 1538 and had three sons and four daughters.

(Gerhard, 80, 296 and 298; Scholes and Adams, 24; Icaza, I, 88 and II, 46; Orozco y Berra, 45; *ENE*, II, 107ff., 178ff.; *ENE*, IV, 18ff., 47ff.; *ENE*, V, 4ff., 43ff., 52ff., 64ff.; Fernández del Castillo, 223–331.)

233. Juan LÓPEZ Frías
Poblador

López, perhaps a *vecino* of Coatzacoalcos, was the *encomendero* of Monzapa, Chacalapa, Pechucalco, and Zolcuautla (*cabeceras* in the vicinity of Coatzacoalcos). A person of his name held these *encomiendas* from before 1554 to 1597, but a namesake son more than likely was the *encomendero* during part of the period. Monzapa was held by *encomendera* Catalina del Castillo in 1597, at which time a Juan López also held nearby Cotastan, Cempoala, and Pechucalo. These towns were at one time assigned to conqueror Bartolomé Sánchez.

(Gerhard, 139.)

234. Juan LÓPEZ de Jimena—*Hidalgo*
First Conqueror
From: Jimena (Jáen)

López was in Cuba by 1518 along with his brother Gonzalo, and joined Cortés the following year. He was a founding *vecino* and *alcalde mayor* of Veracruz. Cortés assigned him the *encomiendas* of Ixcatlan (a *cabecera* 50 miles southwest of Veracruz), Otlaquistla (40 miles west of Veracruz), and Xicayan (240 miles north-northwest near Pánuco; 287 tributaries in 1532). López married Francisca de Nava and had three sons and four daughters. He died ca. 1540 and was succeeded by his widow, who became *encomendera* of Ixcatlan. Xicayan had been reassigned to Diego Castañeda ca. 1532. López' son, Pedro de Nava, succeeded as *encomendero* of Otlaquistla ca. 1540 and then in the late 1550s inherited Ixcatlan. By 1566 a grandson, Diego de Nava, was the *encomendero*. In 1628 a great-granddaughter, doña Juana de Nava, was *encomendera* of Otlaquistla and a great-grandson, Diego de Nava, was *encomendero* of Ixcatlan.

(Gerhard, 302, 304, 84, and 217; Scholes and Adams, 33; Boyd-Bowman, I, no. 2142, 73; Icaza, I, 104; Chipman, 292.)

235. Fray Juan LÓPEZ de Zárate—Bishop of Oaxaca
Poblador
From: Oviedo (Asturias)

Bishop López de Zárate arrived in Oaxaca in 1535 and in 1537 was assigned the tribute from Talistaca (six miles east of Antequera; a *cabecera* with three subject *pueblos* and many *estancias* in the eighteenth century) by Viceroy Mendoza. The grant had been claimed by Cortés in the 1530s as part of the Marquesado. In 1544 Talistaca reverted to the crown under the New Laws.

Note: The grant was to the bishop *ex officio*, not personally; it was administered by the cathedral chapter for the support of the cathedral.

(Gerhard, 49 and 51; Boyd-Bowman, II, no. 3250, 10; Simpson, 194, n. 14.)

236. Martín LÓPEZ—Ship's Carpenter
First Conqueror
From: Seville
Parents: Cristóbal Díaz Narices and Estefanía Rodríguez

López was about twenty-six years old when he arrived in the Indies in 1516. He spent a year in Cuba before joining the 1519 Cortés *entrada*. On this and prior occasions he carried significant amounts of merchandise and wine for resale. After helping build the brigantines for the siege of Tenochtitlan, he became a *vecino* of Mexico City and was a member of *entradas* to Pánuco and Jalisco. Cortés assigned López and first conqueror Andrés Núñez of Salamanca equal shares of the *encomienda* of Tequixquiac (a *cabecera* with three *barrios*, 40 miles north of Mexico City). He later acquired a grant of arable land between the *encomienda* area and Mexico City, as well as land near Xilotepec, north of Toluca. López married twice. His first wife, Inés Ramírez of Seville, died before 1529, and in 1533 in Seville he married Juana Hernández. At the same time his father and uncles attained the tax-exempt status given to *hidalgos*. López was the father of ten children, five of them sons. He was succeeded as *encomendero* ca. 1575 by the oldest, Martín López Osorio. A namesake grandson held the grant after 1591. Tequixquiac did not become a crown possession until after 1666. López received three different coats of arms, dated 21 December 1539, 15 May 1550, and 20 May 1551. In spite of his efforts to establish an identity as an *hidalgo*, his contemporaries always referred to him as ship's carpenter Martín López.

Note: C. Harvey Gardiner's *Martín López, Conquistador Citizen of Mexico* focuses on López' contributions and attempts to gain a more "suitable" reward.

(Gerhard, 401f.; Scholes and Adams, 19; Boyd-Bowman, I, no. 3669, 124; Icaza, I, 8; Orozco y Berra, 83; *Nobiliario*, 193f.; *Protocolos*, I, no. 739, 181 of 27 August 1527 and no. 1095, 245 of 17 February 1528; Gardiner 1957; *Actas*, I, 8.)

237. Nicolás LÓPEZ de Palacios
Poblador
From: Zorita de la Frontera (Salamanca)
Parents: Tomás López and Francisca Rodríguez

López arrived in New Spain in 1523 and went with Cortés to Honduras. Upon returning, Cortés assigned him Cuiseo (112 miles south of Ciudad Michoacán; a joint *cabecera* with Huetamo, more than 40 *sujetos* in 1558) and Teutlaco (a *cabecera* with 50 *estancias* in 1569, 220 miles southeast of Ciudad Michoacán near Izúcar). Teutlaco was taken by the first Audiencia in 1529 and reassigned to conqueror Ruy González, later a *regidor* of Mexico City. Cuiseo was taken for the crown by the second Audiencia and then in the 1540s reassigned by Viceroy Mendoza to *poblador* Gonzalo Ruiz, a Mexico City *regidor*. López married in 1532, took part in the 1541 New Galicia *entrada* called the Mixtón War, and by 1547 was a *vecino* of Ciudad Michoacán, where he maintained his *casa poblada*, arms, and horses.

(Gerhard, 135 and 310f.; Boyd-Bowman, II, no. 7673a, 237; Icaza, II, 207; Orozco y Berra, 85.)

238. Licenciado Pedro LÓPEZ—
Protomédico
Poblador Antiguo
From: Seville
Parents: Juan de Jerez and Beatriz López

López arrived in the Indies in 1514, had a *repartimiento* and was holding a municipal office in Puerto Rico two years later, and then moved to Mexico City in 1524. He left shortly thereafter for *entrada* service with Cortés in Honduras. López eventually became a *vecino* and *regidor* of Puebla. Cortés assigned him Chicoloapa (52 miles west-northwest of Puebla, 20 miles east of Mexico City; a *cabecera* with five *estancias* in 1579) and half of Iscuincuitlapilco (86 miles northwest of Puebla near Pachuca; 4,000 tributaries in 1570) with *poblador* Pedro Gállego of Badajoz. Iscuincuitlapilco was taken for the crown by the second Audiencia in April, 1531. López was married twice. His first wife was Ana de Castellanos, his second, Ana de Rivera. Between them he had sixteen children. One daughter married Juan de Toledo, a *vecino* of Oaxaca from Almagro. A son, Gaspar López, inherited when López died ca. 1550. The *encomienda* reverted to the crown when Gaspar died sometime before 1597.

(Gerhard, 77 and 344f.; Scholes and Adams, 26; Icaza, I, 200 and II, 213; Boyd-Bowman, I, no. 3670, 124; *Actas*, I, 27.)

239. Román LÓPEZ
First Conqueror
From: Toro (Zamora)
Parents: Cristóbal López and María de Solís

López was in Cuba by 1518, joined Cortés the following year and took part in the capture of Tenochtitlan, in which he lost an eye. After various *entradas* López became a *vecino* of Oaxaca. In the early 1520s Cortés awarded him the *encomiendas* of Zola (45 miles south-southwest of Antequera; a *cabecera* with 12 *estancias* in 1599), reassigned from first conqueror Bartólome Sánchez, and Istayutla (78 miles southwest of Antequera; a *cabecera* and five *estancias* in 1548). He and his wife, doña Inés de Guzmán, had six children. López died ca. 1565 and was succeeded by a son, don (?) Cristóbal López de Solís. By 1598 the *encomendero* was a grandson, don Juan de Guzmán Sotomayor.

(Gerhard, 72f. and 276f.; Scholes and Adams, 16f.; Boyd-Bowman, I, no. 4865, 161; Icaza, I, 15; Orozco y Berra, 45.)

240. Hernando de LORITA—Notary
Poblador
From: Jerez de Badajoz (Badajoz)
Parents: Bachiller Francisco Guillén and Catalina Méndez

Lorita arrived in New Spain in 1521, just after the capture of Tenochtitlan. He was a member of various *entradas* in Oaxaca, finally becoming a *vecino* of Villa Alta, where he also served as notary, prosecuting attorney, and chief constable for some ten years. He later received an appointment as *corregidor*. Lorita became the *encomendero* of Xareta and other small Mixe towns by purchasing them for an undisclosed amount from the original holder, *poblador* Gaspar Pacheco, on 26 July 1536. He was married and had a natural daughter in his household as well as serving as the guardian of five orphaned daughters of conquerors. Lorita was succeeded in the 1550s by his childless wife.

The *encomendero* of Xareta in 1597 was Diego Dávila.

(Gerhard, 372; Scholes and Adams, 51; Boyd-Bowman, II, no. 1341, 39; Icaza, I, 234f.; *Protocolos*, II, no. 1831, 25f. of 26 July 1536.)

241. Pedro LOZANO
Conqueror—Narváez
From: Coria de Galisteo (Cáceres)

Lozano, who had been in the Indies since 1513, became a *vecino* of Mexico City shortly after it was established as a Spanish city. The second Audiencia assigned him the *encomienda* of Ayutla, Tututepec, and Suchitonalá (185 miles south of Mexico City; a "small" holding in 1565, Ayutla paying $150 in tribute per year ca. 1548). Lozano married María Perales, a daughter of *poblador antiguo encomendero* Bartolomé Perales, and had at least two sons, Francisco and Juan. Lozano was succeeded before 1548 by Francisco. His widow then married *poblador* Diego de Ojeda from Seville, a page to Audiencia Judge Juan Ortiz de Matienzo. His son Juan complained of receiving nothing. Francisco was in turn succeeded by a son, Pedro, before 1597. Pedro was still the *encomendero* in 1626. Not too long after that, however, the crown acquired control of the *encomienda*.

(Gerhard, 149; Scholes and Adams, 24; Boyd-Bowman, I, no. 946, 16 and II, no. 9824, 297f.; Icaza, I, 164f. and II, 156f.; Orozco y Berra, 62; *Protocolos*, I, no. 39, 34f. of 29 August 1525.)

242. Alonso LUCAS—Notary
Conqueror—?
From: Extremadura

Lucas, a relation of Cortés, was initially a *vecino* of Pánuco. Cortés assigned him half of Mestitlan (108 miles south-southwest of Pánuco; 120 dependencies in 1573) with conqueror Miguel Díaz de Aux of Huesca. Lucas then became a *vecino* of Mexico City and served as *escribano de cámara* of the Audiencia. Around 1535 Alonso de Mérida bought Lucas' half of the *encomienda*. Lucas died in the early 1540s, and by 1547 his daughter, doña Violante de Herrera, who was married to Pedro Ortiz de Zúñiga (a son of conqueror Sancho Ortiz de Zúñiga), unsuccessfully sued to recover a portion of the grant. By 1560 half of the tribute was going to the Mérida heirs, one-third to the heirs of *poblador* Andres de Barrios and one-sixth to the heirs of Díaz de Aux.

(Gerhard, 183f. and 185f.; Scholes and Adams, 34; Chipman, 95f.; *BAGN*, XII, 12.)

243. Don Tristán de LUNA y ARELLANO—*Hidalgo*
Poblador
From: Borovia (Soria)
Parents: Don Carlos de Arellano and doña Juana de Avalos

Don Tristán arrived in and became a *vecino* of Mexico City in 1537 at age twenty-three. Shortly thereafter he joined Francisco Vázquez de Coronado's *entrada* to Culiacan and then, in 1541, went on to New Mexico with the Cíbola expedition. He was assigned half the tribute from Justlaguaca (185 miles southeast of Mexico City) and acquired nearby Tecomastlaguaca (five miles distant) after 1548 by marrying Isabel de Rojas, widow of first conqueror Francisco Maldonado, the original *encomendero*. Isabel's first husband was first conqueror Juan Velázquez. The combined 1555 population of these two grants was 6,800 tributaries. Isabel also brought don Tristán nine more *cabeceras* (Achiutla, Atlatlauca, Atoyac-Yutacanu, Cuicuila, Chalcatongo, Mitla, Ocotepec, Tlatlaltepec and Yucucuy-Tlazoltepec), centered fifteen to twenty miles northeast of the other two *encomiendas*. The Justlaguaca share reverted to the crown ca. 1550, leaving don Tristán with the vast Maldonado *encomienda*. In 1551 he was appointed governor of the Marquesado del Valle. Don Tristán was succeeded in 1573 by his son, don Carlos, who was still the *encomendero* in 1597.

(Gerhard, 164f., 285f. and 287ff.; Boyd-Bowman, II, no. 10523, 318; Riley, 91.)

244. Cristóbal de MAFRA
Conqueror—?
From: Portugal (?)

Mafra, a *vecino* of Mexico City, shared the *encomiendas* of Xicayan (240 miles southeast of Mexico City near Antequera), Ayutla (four miles north of Xicayan), and Tetepec (22 miles east-southeast of Xicayan) with conqueror Pedro Nieto. He exploited his portion of the grant in a six-year partnership with Juan de Olaejos that combined the total assets of both parties to mine for gold or profit in other ways. Mafra's half of the *encomienda* reverted to the crown before 1544.

(Gerhard, 381; *Protocolos*, I, no. 1335, 288 of 11 May 1528.)

245. Alvaro MALDONADO "el fiero"
First Conqueror
From: Salamanca

Maldonado was in Cuba by 1518 and, with his son Francisco Maldonado, sailed with the Cortés *entrada* the following year. He was a *vecino* of Mexico City by 1525 and a *regidor* by mid-1526. His *encomiendas* included Sosola and Tenexpa (200 miles southeast of Mexico City near Antequera), managed by Medellín *vecino* Pedro de Villalobos; Xicotepec (95 miles northeast of Mexico City; 23 dependencies in 1570); and Tlaliscoya (210 miles east-southeast of Mexico City near Veracruz; two *estancias* in 1571). Starting in 1525 he and Villalobos had a mining partnership using Indians from Sosola and Tenexpa. Maldonado and his first wife, Juana de Castro, had at least one child, first conqueror Francisco Maldonado. He and his second wife, María del Rincón, also had a son, Cristóbal, who became a friar. Sosola and Tenexpa were reassigned to conqueror Sebastián de Grijalva when Maldonado died in ca. 1527. Xicotepec and Tlaliscoya were inherited by his widow but were taken the following year by Alonso de Estrada, then governor of New Spain. Xicotepec became a crown possession and Tlaliscoya was reassigned to *poblador* Gil de Molina of Fuente de Cantos (Badajoz). By 1534 this grant too had become a crown property under order of the second Audiencia. María del Rincón later married first conqueror and *encomendero* Pedro Maldonado. It is quite possible that Pedro was also from Salamanca, but a relationship between him and Alvaro could not be established with available sources.

(Gerhard, 49, 118, 120, 360, and 362; Icaza, I, 130 and II, 313; Boyd-Bowman, I, no. 2685 and II, no. 1193, 35; Orozco y Berra, 46; *Protocolos*, I, no. 15 and 16, 28f. of 17 August 1525.)

246. Francisco MALDONADO
First Conqueror
From: Salamanca
Parents: Alvaro Maldonado and Juana de Castro

Maldonado was in the Indies in early 1518 as a member of Grijalva's expedition and more than likely had been in the Antilles for some time. The following year he, accompanied by his father Alvaro Maldonado, joined Cortés and served as a captain on the Tenochtitlan and subsequent *entradas*. His service is outlined in his coat of arms citation, dated 18 September 1538. Maldonado was a *vecino* of Mexico City and *encomendero* of Tecomastlauaca (222 miles southeast of Mexico City and west of Antequera; 6,800 tributaries in 1555, nine *cabeceras*—Achiutla with four *barrios* in 1548; Mitla, Atlatlauca, Atoyac-Yutacanu, Cuicuila; Chalcatongo with eight *estancias* ca. 1575; Ocotepec; Tlaltepec; and Yucucuy) in the jurisdiction of nearby Teposcolula and Chicomeaguatepec (280 miles east-southeast of Mexico City and 40 miles southeast of Antequera). It was still considered a large grant by 1565 standards. He married Isabel de Rojas, widow of first conqueror and *encomendero* Juan Velázquez. They had no children although Maldonado did claim a natural son, Alvaro, in Salamanca (Spain) and a natural daughter married to Oaxaca *vecino* Marcos Ruiz de Rojas of Madrid. In August of 1536 Maldonado granted a special power of attorney to don Cristóbal Suárez, accountant at the Spanish Court, to obligate himself for up to 3,000 gold ducats to whomever necessary to acquire a grant in perpetuity of his *encomiendas* and a title as their lord (*señor*) with temporal jurisdiction therein. Maldonado was succeeded ca. 1548 by his widow, who then married *poblador* don Tristán de Luna y Arellano of Borovia (Soria). The *encomienda* went to a son of Isabel and don Tristán.

(Gerhard, 164, 197, and 285; Scholes and Adams, 48f.; *Protocolos*, II, no. 1881, 37f. of 22 August 1536 and no. 1976, 58f. of 10 October 1536; *Nobiliario*, 237ff.; *Actas*, I, 14.)

247. Pedro MALDONADO
First Conqueror
From: Salamanca (?)

Maldonado arrived in Cuba at least by late 1518 and perhaps had spent some years in the Indies. After the capture of Tenochtitlan he became a *vecino* of Veracruz. He held seven *cabeceras* (Almolonga, Atezac with 50 tributaries in 1580, Ocuequila, Mazatlaxot, Pangolutla, Chiltoyac, and Xalcomulco with one *sujeto*), all in the vicinity of Jalapa, 60 miles northwest of Veracruz. Maldonado's wife, María del Rincón, was the widow of fellow first conqueror Alvaro Maldonado of Salamanca, who died in late 1527. They had no children. He was succeeded ca. 1544 by his widow, who then married *poblador encomendero* Gonzalo Rodríguez de Villafuerte, also of Salamanca. Rodríguez' *encomienda* was half of Minzapa in the vicinity of Coatzacoalcos. All of these grants reverted to the crown when Rodríguez died ca. 1575.

(Gerhard, 375ff.; Scholes and Adams, 21 and 37; Orozco y Berra, 46.)

248. Juan de MANSILLA
Conqueror—Narváez
From: Old Castile

Mansilla arrived in Cuba by 1519 and sailed with the Narváez *entrada* the following year. He became a *vecino* of Mexico City before 1525 and served as a *regidor* from 1532 to 1538. Mansilla held the *encomienda* of Tetela (135 miles southwest of Mexico City; 24 *estancias*) and half of Atlatlauca (190 miles southeast of Mexico; 1,000 tributaries in 1560). Both were granted to him by Cortés. He was married and had a daughter who married Juan Rodríguez, a son of Pero Pérez Jarada, conqueror of Cuba, and Isabel Alvarez of Illescas. In 1538 Mansilla sold his rights to Tetela to *poblador* Francisco Rodríguez (Odrero) de Guadalcanal and his share of Atlatlauca to conqueror Juan Gallego. It is presumed that he then returned to Spain.

(Gerhard, 54f. and 291ff.; Scholes and Adams, 19; Boyd-Bowman, I, no. 5066, 169; Orozco y Berra, 83; Icaza, I, 152; *Actas*, I, 36.)

249. Juan de MANZANILLA
Conqueror—Narváez
From: Manzanilla (Huelva)

Manzanilla was in Cuba by 1519 and in New Spain the following year as a member of the Narváez *entrada*. He was initially a *vecino* of Mexico City but later moved to Puebla. By 1532 he was the *encomendero* of Cicapuzalco (112 miles west-southwest of Puebla; 14 *barrios*). Manzanilla married twice and had a son and daughter by each union. His second wife was Leonor de Villanueva, daughter of conqueror Pedro de Villanueva. His father-in-law served as guardian for the minor children when Manzanilla died in 1545. The oldest son, Juan de Caravallar (Manzanilla) inherited the *encomienda*. His sister, doña María de Caravallar, who married Gonzalo de Aguilar (*el Portugués*), claimed succession when Juan died in the 1590s, but the tribute reverted to the crown in 1600.

(Gerhard, 153; Scholes and Adams, 28f.; Icaza, I, 110 and II, 175; Boyd-Bowman, I, no. 1813b, 63; *Protocolos*, I, no. 297, 91 of 5 December 1525.)

250. Alvaro MANZANO
Poblador
From: Beas (Huelva)
Parents: Juan García and Leonor López la Manzana(?)

Manzano arrived in New Spain in 1526 as a member of the entourage of Licenciado Luis Ponce de León, having earlier served twelve years in Melilla, Morocco. He became a *vecino* of Villa Alta and *encomendero* of Tepecpanzacualco, a small *cabecera* in Zapotec country to the northeast. Manzano married a daughter of *encomendero* and Villa Alta *vecino poblador* Bartolomé de Alcántara. He was succeeded by his son Juan ca. 1560; by 1597 his grandson, Juan Manzano de Chaves, was the *encomendero*.

(Gerhard, 372; Scholes and Adams, 51; Icaza, I, 232 and II, 228; Boyd-Bowman, II, no. 5071, 151.)

251. Luis MARÍN—*Hidalgo*
First Conqueror
From: Sanlúcar de Barrameda (Cádiz)
Parents: Francisco de Marín and Marina Bernal Guillén

Marín was from a noble family, of Genoa, where his father was born. Just when he arrived in the Indies is not known, but he was an experienced thirty-year-old man of substance when he joined the Cortés *entrada* in 1519, serving as a captain. Marín became a *vecino* of Mexico City and his *encomienda*, consisting of eight *cabeceras* (Acayuca, Chacalapa, Olutla, Tequecistepec, Tetiquipa, Xaltipa, and Zayultepec), was 350 miles southwest in the vicinity of Coatzacoalcos. Around 1531 he married doña María de Mendoza de Soria in Mexico City; the pair had eleven children. Four of his sons joined the Augustinian order in Mexico City. Extant information suggests that Marín was a close associate of several merchants if not himself in fact a merchant. About 1547 he was succeeded by a son, don Francisco Marín. By the late 1560s don Francisco's sons were receiving the tribute, and by 1597 the *encomendero* was Marín's great-grandson, don Luis Marín.

(Gerhard, 139; Scholes and Adams, 53; Boyd-Bowman, I, no. 1222, 42 and II, no. 10570, 319; Icaza, I, 5f.; *Protocolos*, I, no. 606, 156 of 25 June 1527.)

252. Diego MARMOLEJO—*Hidalgo*
Conqueror—Alderete
From: Seville

After service in Africa, Marmolejo came to the Indies, arriving in New Spain with Alderete in time to take part in the capture of Tenochtitlan. He became a *vecino* of Veracruz and received nearby Ozumacintla and Tlatectla in *encomienda* from Cortés, hiring candlemaker Juan Martínez as administrator of the grant. In the mid-1520s Marmolejo married Francisca Mejía de Villalobos. Francisca inherited when Marmolejo died ca. 1533. She then married *hidalgo* Juan de Miranda of Soria, who had been in Peru and then gone to Florida with Soto. There were no children of either union. When Miranda died in March 1564, the *encomienda* reverted to the crown.

(Gerhard, 363; Scholes and Adams, 44; Boyd-Bowman, II, no. 9584, 292 and no. 10571, 319; *Protocolos*, I, no. 392, 112 of 21 February 1527.)

253. Juan MARTEL
Poblador Antiguo
From: Seville
Parents: Alonso Martel and Juana Gómez

Martel arrived in New Spain with his mother and three sisters ca. 1530 after having lived in Santo Domingo since perhaps 1514. He became a *vecino* of Colima and *encomendero* of nearby Tecolapa by marrying the *encomendera*, the widow of conqueror and initial holder Juan Bautista de Rapalo, in the 1540s. The *encomienda* was a crown holding by 1560.

(Gerhard, 80; Boyd-Bowman, I, no. 3702b, 125; Icaza, I, 250.)

254. Alonso MARTÍN de Jerez
Conqueror—?
From: Moguer (Huelva)
Parents: Cristóbal García Sarmiento and Elvira Martín

Martín arrived in New Spain in time to take part in the capture of Tenochtitlan and later became a *vecino* of Zacatula and *encomendero* of Toliman, a very small grant nearby. Martín married ca. 1535 and by 1547 had two daughters. A son was born later. He was succeeded by this son ca. 1565.

(Scholes and Adams, 52; Icaza, I, 244; Boyd-Bowman, II, no. 5212, 156.)

255. Alonso MARTÍN Jaca (Jara)
First Conqueror
From: Jaca (Huesca)

Martín was in Cuba in 1518, with Cortés the following year, and a *vecino* of Mexico City before 1525. He shared the *encomienda* of Tezcatepec and Tuzantlalpa (twin *cabeceras* 36 miles north of Mexico City; 11 dependencies in 1569) with conqueror Francisco de Estrada. Martín sold his share to first conqueror Cristóbal Cabezon in the 1540s.

Note: Martín Jaca is often shown as "Minxaca" in published transcriptions of documents. The perpetuation of this contraction of surname and place of origin as a unique name in subsequent literature is a misinterpretation of sixteenth-century orthography, when surnames were often abbreviated and capital letters and spacing between words hardly ever used. In that period Martín was invariably written "min" which when joined with Jaca without capital letters or spacing, resulted in "Minxaca," a name form sixteenth-century Spaniards would have immediately recognized as Martín Jaca.

(Gerhard, 297 and 299; Boyd-Bowman, I, no. 2063, 70; Scholes and Adams, 19; *Protocolos,* I, no. 711, 175 of 12 August 1527; *Actas,* I, 26.)

256. Antón MARTÍN Breña
Poblador
From: Coria (Cáceres)
Parents: Sebastián Rodríguez Breña and Leonor García

Martín arrived in New Spain ca. 1523 and later became a *vecino* of Puebla, where he maintained his *casa poblada,* arms, and horses. He held the *encomienda* of Micaoztoc (110 miles east-southeast of Puebla—a very small grant). Martín was married and was succeeded in the 1550s by his widow and after that perhaps by a son named Juan de Vivanco, the *encomendero* of record in 1597.

(Gerhard, 302 and 304; Scholes and Adams, 35; Boyd-Bowman, II, no. 2875, 83; Icaza, II, 15.)

257. Cristóbal MARTÍN Millán de Gamboa
First Conqueror
From: Biscay

Martín, perhaps the natural son of an *hidalgo,* arrived in Santo Domingo in 1502 as a member of Comendador frey Nicolás de Ovando's entourage. After various actions against the natives of Hispaniola, Martín was assigned a *repartimiento* and the title of captain. By 1516 he was in Cuba and two years later sailed with Grijalva's expedition. Martín then joined the Cortés *entrada,* serving as Master of the Horse (*caballerizo mayor*) as well as captain in various actions during and subsequent to the capture of Tenochtitlan. Asuchitlan (135 miles southwest of Mexico City; 1,000 tributaries in 1570) was assigned as his *encomienda.* Martín married María Coronado while in Santo Domingo. They had four children, two of them sons. He was a *vecino* of Mexico City and there maintained his *casa poblada,* arms, and horses. His postconquest activities included the buying and selling of sheep and real estate. The second Audiencia took the *ncomienda* for the crown in July, 1533, and by 1536 Martín was dead. Martín's eldest son, don Gaspar Millán de Gamboa, who married doña María de Viveros, acted very much like an *hidalgo*. An unsuccessful claimant to his late father's *encomienda*, don Gaspar received instead a *corregidor*ship.

Note: The title "*caballerizo mayor*" initially was mainly honorific, an office not really necessary for the *entrada*'s fifteen horsemen, but it became a most necessary office after mustering the assets of the Narváez and other *entradas*. At that time there were 100 horsemen. Francisco Fernández del Castillo published "Información de méritos del capitán Cristóbal Martín Millán de Gamboa y su descendencia" in *Tres conquistadores y pobladores de la Nueva España*.

(Gerhard, 291f.; Orozco y Berra, 80; Boyd-Bowman, I, no. 5301, 177(?); *Protocolos*, I, no. 1006, 230 of 15 January 1528, no. 1220, 167 of 4 April 1528, and no. 1239, 270 of 16 April 1528; Fernández del Castillo, 14, 15, 19 and 143f.; Gómara, 206; *Actas*, I, 20.)

258. Diego MARTÍN de Mérida
Poblador Antiguo
From: Mérida (La Serena, Extremadura)

The presumption is that Martín had been in the Indies since about 1513 and arrived in New Spain shortly after the capture of Tenochtitlan as did his partner, Pedro de Santa Cruz. Both were *vecinos* of Colima and shared the tribute from Milpa (northwest of Colima; 8,230 tributaries in 1525). Martín's share was reassigned to first conqueror Rodrigo Guipuzcoano (Lepuzcano) in 1528.

(Gerhard, 60.)

259. Ginés MARTÍN
Conqueror—Narváez

Martín, a member of the Narváez *entrada*, became a *vecino* of Pánuco and ultimately shared Tamintla (40 miles southwest of Pánuco; 178 tributaries ca. 1533) with his brother Maya.

(Gerhard, 215; Chipman, 293.)

260. Hernán MARTÍN—Blacksmith
Conqueror—?

Martín, other than claiming to be and functioning as a blacksmith, left little record of his roots. A *vecino* of Mexico City, he was briefly the *encomendero* of Macuilsuchil (240 miles southeast of Mexico City; three *estancias* in 1580) and firmly in possession of Malinaltepec (160 miles southeast of Mexico City). He was succeeded ca. 1543 by his widow, who then married *poblador* Bartolomé Tofiño from Seville, a *vecino* of Oaxaca. Tofiño was the *encomendero* until 1564, when the widow again succeeded and remained the *encomendera* until the tribute was reassigned to don Luis de Velasco in the 1570s. Martín was the steward for the hospital and *cofradía* of Santa Vera Cruz in Mexico City.

(Gerhard, 160 and 285; Scholes and Adams, 35; Icaza, I, 254; *Protocolos*, I, no. 1737 and no. 1738, 360f. of 9 November 1528; *Actas*, I, 4.)

261. Juan MARTÍN de Valencia
Poblador
From: Valencia(?)

Martín was the *encomendero* of Xoteapa and Quinamulapa (near Coatzacoalcos) from before 1554 until ca. 1567, when he was succeeded by Luis Guillén.

(Gerhard, 139.)

262. Maya MARTÍN
Conqueror—Narváez

Martín, a member of the Narváez *entrada*, became a *vecino* of Pánuco and ultimately shared Tamintla (178 tributaries in 1532, 40 miles southwest of Pánuco) with his brother Ginés.

(Gerhard, 214; Chipman, 293.)

263. Pedro MARTÍN de Coria
First Conqueror
From: Coria de Galisteo (Cáceres)

Martín was in Cuba by 1518 and a member of the Cortés *entrada* the following year. He was the first holder of the *encomienda* of Petlacaltepec (65 miles east of Antequera) and was probably a *vecino* of Antequera. There is no record of its disposition when Martín died in 1525.

(Gerhard, 127; *Protocolos*, I, no. 135, 57 of 17 October 1525; Boyd-Bowman, I, no. 948, 33.)

264. Rodrigo MARTÍN
Conqueror—?

Cortés assigned Martín the *encomienda* of Xumiltepec (35 miles east of Cuernavaca, seven *estancias* in 1550) shortly after the area was occupied. The tribute was reassigned to *poblador* Alonso de Escobar by the acting governors in 1526.

(Gerhard, 92 and 94.)

265. Pedro de MAYA
First Conqueror
From: Amaya (Burgos)

Maya, initially a *vecino* of Mexico City, later moved to Antequera. By 1525 he was the *encomendero* of Nochistlan (40 miles northwest of Antequera; four *estancias* by 1550). In May of 1528 he contracted with Gonzalo López "to be and reside for us in our name" in Nochistlan. López was to watch the *pueblo* and its market and to carry out other obligations, for which he was to receive $100 per year, paid in thirds.

(Gerhard, 200 and 202; *Protocolos*, I, no. 1349, 290f. of 18 May 1528; Boyd-Bowman, I, no. 634, 22.)

266. Antonio (Hernán) MEDEL
Poblador
From: Palos (Huelva)

Medel was a *vecino* of Mexico City by 1524. He shared Guaquilpa (a *cabecera* with one *estancia* in 1569; 48 miles northeast of Mexico City near Pachuca) and Tlaquilpa (a *cabecera* with three *sujetos* in 1580; three miles to the north of Guaquilpa) with conqueror Andrés López de Sevilla from the 1520s until the 1540s, when both sold out to *poblador antiguo* Licenciado Diego Téllez.

(Gerhard, 68 and 209; Boyd-Bowman, II, no. 5309, 159(?); *Actas*, I, 12; Scholes and Adams, 39.)

267. Hernando MEDEL
Conqueror
From: Palos (Huelva)

Medel was in the Indies by 1516 and in Cuba three years later. He outfitted a ship to accompany the 1520 Narváez *entrada*. Delays caused him to arrive in New Spain two weeks after Cortés had detained Narváez. It appears that Medel became a *vecino* of Mexico City in 1528 when Ocuituco (48 miles southeast of Mexico City; two *barrios* and 10 *estancias* in 1550) was reassigned to him from Bartolomé Hernández de Nava. He was married and sent to Palos for his wife in October in 1528. The *encomienda* reverted to the crown when Medel died ca. 1531. His will was still being probated five years later.

(Gerhard, 92f.; Boyd-Bowman, I, no. 1977, 76f.; *Protocolos*, I, no. 1501, 318 of 11 September 1528, no. 1659, 346 of 10 October 1528 and II, no. 1929, 48f. of 15 September 1536.)

268. Domingo de MEDINA
Poblador
From: Guareña (La Serena, Extremadura)
Parents: Diego González Serrano and Ana Hernández Zambrano

Medina arrived in Mexico City in 1524 as an employee of Cortés. He was first a *vecino* of Mexico City and later became a resident of Ciudad Michoacán, where he maintained his *casa poblada*. By 1528 he shared Tancítaro (63 miles southwest of Ciudad Michoacán near Uruapan;

14 *sujetos* in 1580) with *poblador* and fellow Cortés employee Pedro de la Isla. He employed first conqueror *encomendero* Juan de la Torre to administer his half of the grant. Medina was married and by 1547 had sons and a married daughter. He was succeeded ca. 1569 by a son, Diego Enríquez de Medina. The *encomienda* was a crown possession by 1623.

(Gerhard, 250f.; Icaza, I, 214; Boyd-Bowman, II, no. 1262, 37; *CDIO*, XII, 368; *Protocolos*, I, no. 1523, 322 of 16 September 1528.)

269. Jerónimo de MEDINA *"el viejo"*—
Hidalgo, Notary
Poblador
From: Illescas (Toledo)
Parents: Gonzalo Hernández de Medina and Mari Núñez de la Cámara

Medina, accompanied by his son Jerónimo, arrived in New Spain in 1526 as a member of the Licenciado Luis Ponce de León entourage and became a *vecino* of Mexico City, where he carried out his appointment as a lieutenant governor and inspector. He was also a clerk of the first Audiencia. Shortly after his arrival he was assigned the *encomienda* of Tepexpan (21 miles northeast of Mexico City; 13 *sujetos* in 1580). Later the second Audiencia assigned him half of both Tlanchinolticpac and Cuimantlan (105 miles north-northeast of Mexico City; 80 *sujetos* in 1573), shared with conqueror Alonso Ortiz de Zúñiga, a native of Seville. Later in the decade Medina and Ortiz simplified the administration of the grants: Medina took Tlanchinolticpac and Ortiz Cuimantlan. Medina married doña Ana de Rosa, also from Illescas. Their children included Jerónimo, who married a daughter of conqueror Pedro de Meneses; doña María de Medina, who married Juan de Cisneros; doña Inés de Vargas, who married Comendador Juan Baeza de Herrera; and a daughter who married Juan de la Serna. The elder Medina's brother, Francisco de Medina, had been in the Indies since 1511. Medina died sometime before 1546. Tlanchinolticpac went to his son Jerónimo and then in 1565 to a granddaughter married to Juan de Montejo. Tepexpan had been assigned to doña Inés in dowry in 1538. It went to a grandson, don Jerónimo Baeza de Herrera, before 1597.

(Gerhard, 185 and 274f.; Scholes and Adams, 40f.; Icaza, I, 194 and II, 34; Boyd-Bowman, I, no. 4281, 141 and II, no. 10910, no. 10911, no. 10912 and no. 10913, 326; *Protocolos*, I, no. 534, 141 of 6 May 1527.)

270. Juan de MEDINA—Butler during conquest
First Conqueror
From: Antequera (Málaga)
Parents: Juan de Medina and Catalina Díaz

Medina was in the Indies by 1517 and in Cuba the following year. He sailed with Cortés as his *repostero* (butler?) in 1519. Initially a citizen of Mexico City, by 1530 Medina was a *vecino* of Santisteban del Puerto, Pánuco, and *encomendero* of Texupespa (50 miles southwest of Pánuco, near Tempoal; 288 tributaries in 1532). By 1545 the *encomienda* had reverted to the crown, and Medina's widow, Juana Clavijo, had married conqueror *encomendero* Juan (Leiva) de Nájera.

(Gerhard, 217; Chipman, 292; Boyd-Bowman, I, no. 2354, 81; Orozco y Berra, 46; Icaza, I, 152f.; *Actas*, I, 44.)

271. Héctor MÉNDEZ—Silversmith
Poblador

Méndez came to New Spain as a member of the Nuño de Guzmán entourage, became a *vecino* of Pánuco, and ca. 1528 was assigned the *encomienda* Chiconamel and Tanta (a very small grant near Pánuco). The grant was reassigned to his widow, who then married (ca. 1537) Alonso Audelo of Seville. By 1553 the *encomendero* was Juan Méndez de Sotomayor, Héctor's son. He was still receiving the tribute from this grant in 1597.

(Gerhard, 215; Scholes and Adams, 44f.; Icaza, II, 68f.; Chipman, 197f. and 301; Boyd-Bowman, II, no. 8676, 268.)

272. Teresa MÉNDEZ
Pobladora

Teresa Méndez was either the widow or daughter of the first holder of Miaguatlan and Guatepe (vicinity of Coatzacoalcos). She was the *encomendera* from before 1554 to ca. 1567. By 1600 these *cabeceras*, victims of congregation, were no longer listed.

(Gerhard, 139f.)

273. Alonso de MENDOZA
First Conqueror
From: Medellín (La Serena, Extremadura)
Parents: Alvaro de Mendoza and Catalina López

Mendoza was in Santo Domingo by 1508, *alcalde ordinario* of Santiago de Cuba in 1518, and with Cortés the following year. He became a *vecino* of Mexico City and enjoyed half of the *encomienda* of Tamoín (192 miles north of Mexico City near Valles) with Cortés. Mendoza was also the lieutenant governor of Pánuco under Cortés. The Tamoín grant was taken by Nuño de Guzmán in 1527, and Mendoza received Tamistla (also called Tancuilave, a small community 15 miles east of Valles) in its place. Shortly thereafter Tamistla was reassigned, Mendoza not regaining title until 1537. After 1550 he married doña Isabel de Lara, one of Comendador Leonel de Cervantes' six daughters. She was also the widow of *poblador* Alonso de Aguilar. When Mendoza died shortly thereafter, doña Isabel married *poblador* Licenciado Alemán, who succeeded as *encomendero*. The *encomienda* reverted to the crown when Alemán died ca. 1575.

(Gerhard, 355; Scholes and Adams, 38; Boyd-Bowman, I, no. 456, 16.)

274. Lope de MENDOZA
Poblador

Mendoza, more than likely an *hidalgo*, was in New Spain by 1525 and shortly thereafter became a *vecino* and *alcalde ordinario* of Santisteban de Puerto, Pánuco. He became an *encomendero* in 1527 when Nuño de Guzmán took Metatepec (40 miles south of Pánuco; 1,541 tributaries in 1533) from Francisco Ramírez and reassigned it to Mendoza and Licenciado Pedro de Mondragón. Mondragón died ca. 1530, and Mendoza then received all the tribute. As a deputy and lieutenant governor for Guzmán, Mendoza was able to maintain his position and assets in the region. Around 1537 Mendoza and Marcos Ruiz de Sevilla traded *encomiendas*. Ruiz got Metatepec and Mendoza Epazoyuca (145 miles south-southwest of Pánuco near Pachuca; four *barrios* and four *estancias* in 1580). Mendoza was married to doña Francisca del Rincón, a daughter of Licenciado Antonio Ruiz de Medina, prosecuting attorney of the Audiencia. She succeeded him as *encomendera* in the late 1540s. Epazoyuca was reassigned to don Luis de Velasco when doña Francisca died in the 1570s.

(Gerhard, 67ff. and 216; Chipman, 292 and 301; Scholes and Adams, 31; *Protocolos*, I, no. 210, 74 of 11 November 1525.)

275. Pedro de MENESES—*Hidalgo*
Conqueror—Narváez
From: Talavera de la Reina (Toledo)
Parents: Bernardino de Meneses and doña Gracia de Ulloa (?)

Meneses was in Cuba by 1519 and, at age twenty, a member of the Narváez *entrada* the following year. He served as a page to Cortés during the siege of Tenochtitlan and on subsequent *entradas*. Initially a *vecino* of Mexico City, he moved to Puebla in 1534 and there maintained his *casa poblada*, arms, and horses. With the possible exception of Coyuca (165 miles southwest of Puebla; 12 *sujetos* in 1579), granted ca. 1540, Meneses acquired his *encomiendas* through purchase. He bought Tequepilpa (57 miles north-northwest of Puebla; two *estancias* in 1570) and two-thirds of Cicoac and Chicontepec (128 miles north of Puebla; 300 tributaries in 32 small *estancias* in 1592) from Francisco Ramírez in the 1540s and ca. 1550 respectively. During the 1540s he also bought half of Zultepec (39 miles north-northwest of Puebla, two *estancias* in 1570), next to his holdings at Tequepilpa, from the estate of Isabel Muñoz, who had been the widow of first conqueror Diego Motrico but was married to Gonzalo Hernández Calvo when she died. Meneses was married and had eight children. A daughter, doña Agustina, married Andrés de Loya and another, whose name is not known, married *poblador encomendero* Jerónimo de Medina *"el hijo."* Meneses' brother, Bernardino, was a member of Nuño de Guzmán's entourage. When Meneses died in 1566, Coyuca went to his son, Cristóbal de Soto, then to a grandson, don Rodrigo de Meneses. Doña Agustina de Meneses was the *encomendera* in 1603, and Tequepilpa was divided between don Rodrigo's son, don Germán and doña Agustina. The Cicoac and Chicontepec share went to another son, Pedro Bermúdez de Meneses, then to Licenciado Miguel de Chaves, but by 1597 doña Agustina was the *encomendera* of this grant too. She also inherited the Zultepec share.

(Gerhard, 133f., 135f., and 312ff.; Icaza, I, 41 and 94; Scholes and Adams, 16; Boyd-Bowman, I, no. 4332, 143; Orozco y Berra, 47; *ENE*, I, 95.)

276. Alonso de MÉRIDA
Poblador

Around 1535 Mérida bought conqueror Alonso Lucas' half of Meztitlan (90 miles north of Mexico City near Pachuca; more than 120 dependent settlements in 1573). He was succeeded in the mid-1550s by his son, Francisco de Mérida y Molino, and then by a granddaughter, Mariana de Mérida, married to Francisco de Quintana Dueñas. This share of Meztitlan reverted to the crown ca. 1623. The other half of Meztitlan was held by first conqueror Andrés de Barrios (two-thirds) and conqueror Miguel Díaz de Aux (one-third).

(Gerhard, 184ff.; Scholes and Adams, 34.)

277. Martín de la MEZQUITA (Montesinos)
First Conqueror
From: Seville
Parents: Juan de la Mezquita and Catalina Muñoz

Mezquita was in Cuba by 1518 and with the Cortés *entrada* the following year. After the capture of Tenochtitlan and *entradas* to Guatemala and Oaxaca, Mezquita became a *vecino* of Oaxaca and served there as a *regidor* in 1531. Cortés assigned him Tecuicuilco (24 miles north-northeast of Antequera, a *cabecera* with one *estancia* and three sub-*cabeceras*, one having three *sujetos*) and possibly Cimatlan and Tepecimatlan (15 miles south-southwest of Antequera, 12 *estancias* each). Tecuicuilco was taken for the crown on 30 July 1531. Cimatlan and Tepecimatlan were reassigned to conqueror Jerónimo de Salinas in 1527 but reverted to royal administration after October 1532. Mezquita was still alive ca. 1547, recounting his services and asking for support.

(Gerhard, 71f. and 258f.; Boyd-Bowman, I, no. 3755, 126; Icaza, I, 56f.; Orozco y Berra, 47.)

278. Antón MIGUEL
Conqueror—?

Miguel, a *vecino* of Villa Alta, was *encomendero* of Cacalotepec, a small Zapotec community in the mountains about 15 miles east of Villa Alta. He was married and was succeeded ca. 1550 by a son, Diego Miguel Negrete.

(Gerhard, 370; Scholes and Adams, 51.)

279. Doña Isabel MOCTEZUMA
From: Tenochtitlan
Father: Moctezuma

Doña Isabel married in succession the Aztec emperor Cuauhtemoc, first conqueror Alonso de Grado (died ca. 1527), *poblador* Pedro Gallego (died ca. 1531), and conqueror Juan Cano. Her inheritance from her father included Chapulguacan—also called Macuilsuchil—(125 miles north of Mexico City; nine *estancias* and 54 lesser settlements), Ocoyoaca (recovered ca. 1540 from Antonio Villagómez, 20 miles southwest of Mexico City), Tepexoyuca (28 miles southwest of Mexico City), Cuapanoaya (near Tepexoyuca, southwest of Mexico City), and Tacuba (50 or more *estancias* and *pueblos* in 1593). Tributes were granted in perpetuity to her heirs. Doña Isabel died ca. 1551. Chapulguacan went to don Pedro Cano, her son by Juan Cano. Tacuba was divided between Juan Cano, his sons Pedro and Gonzalo, and doña Isabel's son, don Juan de Andrade (Gallego) Moctezuma, by Pedro Gallego. The grants southwest of Mexico City were divided in like manner. Doña Isabel also had a daughter by Cortés, named doña Leonor Cortés Moctezuma, who married the Basque merchant Juan de Tolosa.

(Gerhard, 184, 186, 247ff. and 271; Scholes and Adams, 29; Liss, 130; Díaz del Castillo, II, 437.)

280. Doña Leonor MOCTEZUMA
   From: Tenochtitlan
   Father: Moctezuma

In 1527 Cortés assigned doña Leonor, doña Isabel Moctezuma's younger sister, the perpetual *encomienda* of Ecatepec (12 miles north of Mexico City; including *cabeceras* Coatitlan and Acalhuacan, formerly under Tlatelolco, plus 10 or 12 *estancias*) as her patrimony. She married Juan Paz in the 1520s and then *poblador* Cristóbal de Valderrama, after Paz died. Doña Leonor succeeded Valderrama ca. 1537 and transferred the tribute to her daughter, doña Leonor de Valderrama y Moctezuma, who was married to Diego Arias de Sotelo. When Arias was exiled in 1568, the *encomienda* went to their son, don Fernando Sotelo de Moctezuma. In 1593 Fernando transferred a third of the tribute to his younger brother, don Cristóbal de Sotelo Valderrama. Don Cristóbal's share was reassigned when he died in 1607, and don Fernando's sons sold the remaining two-thirds eleven years later.

(Gerhard, 266f.; Scholes and Adams, 27.)

281. Licenciado Pedro de MONDRAGÓN
   Poblador

Licenciado Mondragón, a deputy of Nuño de Guzmán, was a *vecino* of Pánuco and shared Metatepec (a *cabecera* 40 miles south of Pánuco; 1,541 tributaries in 1532) with *poblador* Lope de Mendoza. The grant was reassigned to them from Cortés' lieutenant, *alguacil mayor* Francisco Ramírez, in 1527. Mendoza acquired full title to the grant when Mondragón died in 1530.

(Gerhard, 216; Chipman, 292.)

282. Andrés de MONJARAZ—Hidalgo(?)
   First Conqueror
   From: Durango (Biscay)

Monjaraz may have had *hidalgo* lineage through his mother (a great-aunt was doña María Ruiz de Monjaraz). He served as a captain in the Cortés *entrada* after having spent a year in Cuba. Monjaraz held the office of *alcalde ordinario* of Medellín in 1521 and shortly thereafter became Cortés' lieutenant in Oaxaca. He was a *vecino* of Mexico City and *encomendero* of Jaso and Teremendo (170 miles west of Mexico City near Pátzcuaro; 24 *estancias* in 1548). In 1528 he contracted Miguel Mesa and Pedro López Galbito to "be and live" in his Indian pueblos in Michoacán. A brother, Mateo or Gregorio, and an uncle, Martín Ruiz de Monjaraz, were also first conquerors. Another uncle, Andrés, was a conqueror with Juan de Burgos, who arrived with Medel. The *encomienda* reverted to the crown by 1532, and Monjaraz was dead two years later.

(Gerhard, 345 and 351; Boyd-Bowman, I, no. 4719, 156; *Protocolos*, I, no. 1086, 244 of 12 February 1528; Orozco y Berra, 84; Díaz del Castillo, I, 476f.)

283. Mateo (Gregorio) de MONJARAZ—
Hidalgo(?)
First Conqueror
From: Durango (Biscay)

Monjaraz, a brother of Andrés de Monjaraz, was in Cuba by 1518 and with Cortés the following year. By 1527 he was a *vecino* of Mexico City and the first holder of half of Exutla (260 miles southeast of Mexico City, near Antequera). By 1530 he had also acquired half of Coatlan (290 miles southeast of Mexico City, past Exutla; 33 *estancias* in 1548) and Miaguatlan (280 miles southeast of Mexico City near Coatlan; *sujetos* including Almolonga, Cuistla, and Suchitepec). Tributes from Exutla, Coatlan, and Miaguatlan were shared with Alonso de Paz, a relative of Cortés. Other holders of or claimants to this large grant included Diego Becerra de Mendoza, another Cortés kinsman, and Cristóbal de Salamanca. Monjaraz was married and had at least one son, Mateo, who succeeded him in the 1550s. A grandson, Gregorio, was the *encomendero* ca. 1580. The *encomienda* reverted to the crown on Gregorio's death sometime between 1597 and 1609, thus completing the prescribed three lives.

(Gerhard, 49 and 188f.; Scholes and Adams, 26; *Protocolos*, I, no. 613, 157 of 26 June 1527.)

284. Martín MONJE
Conqueror—Narváez
From: Palos (Huelva)
Parents: Alonso Gutiérrez de León and Inés Alonso Monje

Monje arrived in New Spain in 1520 with the Narváez *entrada*, and after service with various subsequent *entradas* became a *vecino* of Colima and *encomendero* of nearby Cueyatlan. Around 1528 he received through reassignment half of Tenamastlan (65 miles northwest of Colima; 3,000 tributaries in 1524, reduced to 800 by 1550) when Rodrigo Alonso, the original holder, died. The other original co-holder was conqueror Pedro Gómez. Monje was married and by 1547 had three daughters, one of marriageable age. He died in the 1560s and was succeeded by a son, Martín Monje de León.

(Gerhard, 60 and 80; Scholes and Adams, 49; Boyd-Bowman, I, no. 1982, 68; Icaza, I, 51f.)

285. Cristóbal de MONRESÍN (Monrosín, Malresín)
Conqueror—?

Little has been uncovered about Monresín other than his probable status as a conqueror, that he may have been a *vecino* of Acapulco, and that ca. 1530 he was assigned one-third of the *encomienda* of Xocutla (40 miles east of Acapulco; a *cabecera* with one *estancia* in 1570). Monresín was in Mexico City in August of 1536 bringing suit for an undisclosed cause against Colima *vecino* Juan de Aguilar and others. He was succeeded ca. 1548 by his widow. By 1570 José de Monresín (a son?) was the *encomendero*. The tribute was paid to Cristóbal de Monresín (a grandson?) between 1597 and 1626, at which time the *encomienda* reverted to the crown.

(Gerhard, 40f.; Scholes and Adams, 49; *Protocolos*, II, no. 1884, 38 of 22 August 1536.)

286. Francisco de MONTALVO—*Hidalgo*
Poblador Antiguo
From: Segovia
Parents: Diego de Montalvo and Mari López de Cuéllar

Montalvo, an eight-year veteran of the Indies, arrived in New Spain forty days after the capture of Mexico City and later joined the 1523 Gonzalo de Sandoval *entrada* against the Yope near Acapulco. He had held an *encomienda* in Cuba. Montalvo's status provided him with posts like lieutenant treasurer in Veracruz and *alcalde* in Puebla, where he was a *vecino* and maintained his family, *casa poblada*, arms, and horses. His *encomiendas* included Aculcingo (70 miles east-southeast of Puebla, 18 miles southwest of Orizaba) and half of Zoquitlan (107 miles southeast of Puebla, 50 miles south-southeast of Orizaba; five *visitas* within 18 miles of the *cabecera* in 1570). Montalvo was married, perhaps twice. When he died ca. 1547 he left a widow and a daughter, but he was succeeded as *encomendero* by a son, Diego. Diego's widow, Juana Ruiz de Bozbuena, was the *encomendera* ca. 1570. Their son, also named Diego, had succeeded her by 1597. The *encomienda* was a crown possession by 1629.

(Gerhard, 205f. and 261ff.; Scholes and Adams, 25 and 48; Boyd-Bowman, I, no. 2928, 104; Icaza, I, 217.)

287. Francisco MONTAÑO
Conqueror—Narváez
From: Ciudad Rodrigo (Salamanca)
Parents: Francisco López and Elvira Montaño

Montaño was in Cuba by 1519 and with the Narváez *entrada* the following year. He served as Pedro de Alvarado's ensign during the siege and capture of Tenochtitlan. After various *entradas* he became a *vecino* of Mexico City, where he maintained his family, *casa poblada*, arms, and horses. Cortés assigned him Tecali (90 miles south-southeast of Mexico City; 3,830 tributaries in 1548), but then reassigned the *encomienda* to Juan Pérez de Arteaga. In the 1520s Montaño also shared the *encomienda* of Iztaquimaxtitlan—also called Castilblanco—(105 miles east-northeast of Mexico City) with *poblador antiguo* Pedro de Vargas, but he sold his half to first conqueror Bartolomé Hernandez de Nava (also known as Diego Muñoz) in 1530. In 1548 Montaño claimed and through litigation successfully acquired half of the *encomienda* of Zapotitlan (125 miles southwest of Mexico City; 10 *estancias* in 1570). He was married and had nine sons and four daughters. His son Pedro succeeded as *encomendero* ca. 1597. Montaño received a coat of arms dated 23 August 1540.

(Gerhard, 228, 255, and 261; Boyd-Bowman, I, no. 2596, 92; Scholes and Adams, 16; Icaza, I, 53; Orozco y Berra, 84; *Nobiliario*, 315f.)

288. Francisco de MONTEJO
First Conqueror
From: Salamanca

Montejo was about forty years old in 1514, when he served with Pedrarias in Tierra Firme. By 1516 he was an *encomendero* in Cuba, and he was one of the captains for the 1518 Grijalva expedition. (The other captains were Grijalva, Alonso de Avila, and Pedro de Alvarado.) He then joined the Cortés *entrada* and after the capture of Tenochtitlan was a *vecino* there in spite of his activities and commissions elsewhere. His *encomiendas* in New Spain included Azcapotzalco (six miles northwest of Mexico City; seven *estancias* and a number of *barrios* in the vicinity of the *cabecera* in 1570), Matlactlan (105 miles northeast of Mexico City; eight *estancias* in 1570), and Chila (110 miles northeast of Mexico City; 20 *estancias* in 1569). In 1525 Montejo married Beatriz Alvarez de Herrera, widow of first conqueror Alonso Esquivel, in Seville. His coat of arms was awarded the following year, dated 8 December 1526. Their daughter, doña Catalina (Beatriz?) de Montejo, who married Licenciado Alonso Maldonado, inherited in 1553. Montejo also had a natural son, Francisco "el mozo," by Ana de León. He led the second conquest of Yucatan and founded Mérida in 1542. Doña Catalina became the *encomendera* when her husband died after 1565. When doña Catalina died in 1582, the tribute reverted to the crown.

(Gerhard, 248f. and 391; Scholes and Adams, 25; Boyd-Bowman, I, no. 2691, 95 and II, no. 9717, 295; Orozco y Berra, 47; *Nobiliario*, 177–180; Díaz del Castillo, I, 27.)

289. Blas de MONTERROSO
First Conqueror
From: Monterroso (Lugo)

Monterroso was in Cuba a year before joining the Cortés *entrada*, and became a *vecino* of Mexico City sometime before 1527. His *encomienda*, a grant that included Ostuma (88 miles southwest of Mexico City near Taxco; 12 or more *estancias* in 1590) and nearby Alahuistlan (15 *estancias* in 1597), was assigned initially by Cortés to a López and then reassigned to Monterroso. He was married and had a daughter, Francisca de Xexa (?), who married Juan del Aguila. A natural daughter married Diego García of Mérida, La Serena (Extremadura). He was a *vecino* of the mines of Zultepec. Monterroso died before 1548 and was succeeded by his widow, who later passed the *encomienda* to Francisca. Francisca's husband was the *encomendero* from 1550 to 1567. The grant reverted to the crown before 1597.

(Gerhard, 152ff.; Scholes and Adams, 35f.; Boyd-Bowman, I, no. 2245, 77; *Protocolos*, I, no. 326, 99 of 1 February 1527; Orozco y Berra, 47; Icaza, II, 121.)

290. Juan de MORALES
Conqueror—Garay
From: Seville
Parents: Diego Morales de la Orden and Ana de Morales

Morales was in Cuba by 1519 and arrived in New Spain the following year on one of the ships sent by Garay to his Pánuco settlement. He joined the Cortés *entrada* in time to take part in the siege and capture of Tenochtitlan, becoming a *vecino* of Mexico City six years later. By the mid-1540s he was maintaining his *casa poblada*, family, arms, and horses in the capital. Cortés awarded Morales Suchitepec (145 miles southeast of Mexico City; paying a claimed $50 per year by 1547) and half of Ocuila (32 miles southwest of Mexico City; 17 *estancias* in 1548) jointly with Serván Bejerano. Sometime after 1527 Morales went to Spain, married Ana de Agüero, and returned to Mexico City. They had no children. Governor Alonso de Estrada reassigned Morales' share of Ocuila to Pedro Zamorano during the time he was in Spain. Ana de Agüero became the *encomendera* of Suchitepec when Morales died ca. 1566. By 1597 it had been reassigned to don Luis de Velasco.

(Gerhard, 130 and 170f.; Scholes and Adams, 19; Icaza, I, 80; *Protocolos*, I, no. 886, 208 of 14 November 1527; Orozco y Berra, 84.)

291. Alonso de MORCILLO
Conqueror—Narváez
From: Seville

Morcillo was in Cuba by 1519 and joined the Narváez *entrada* the following year. Probably a *vecino* of Antequera, Morcillo held the *encomienda* of Chicaguastepec and Iztactepec (with *cabeceras* 75 and 68 miles respectively northwest of Antequera). He and his wife, Catalina García, had no children. She succeeded ca. 1552 and was recognized as the *encomendera*. The grant reverted to the crown ca. 1568.

(Gerhard, 285 and 288; Scholes and Adams, 44; Boyd-Bowman, I, no. 3776, 127; Orozco y Berra, 84.)

292. Francisco MORCILLO—*Hidalgo Poblador*
From: Villanueva de la Serena (La Serena, Extremadura)
Parents: Hernán Sánchez and Elvira González Morcillo

Morcillo arrived in New Spain in 1522 as a member of the household of Luis de la Torre, a *poblador antiguo*, in the entourage of Treasurer Alonso de Estrada. He was then a member of *entradas* of Pánuco and later Michoacán. Initially a *vecino* of Mexico City, by 1547 Morcillo had moved his residence to Ciudad Michoacán, where he maintained his *casa poblada*, family, arms, and horses. Cortés assigned him the *encomienda* of Indaporapeo (46 miles northeast of Ciudad Michoacán; three *sujetos* in 1548). Around 1527 Morcillo married Catalina de Vergara, and both of their children, a son Gaspar and a daughter, married and remained in Ciudad Michoacán. Gaspar married the daughter of *po-*

blador Pedro de Pantoja, and his sister married Miguel de Ribera of Santa Gadea (Burgos). Gaspar inherited the *encomienda* when Morcillo died ca. 1550. A grandson, Alonso de Vargas Morcillo, was the *encomendero* in 1604.

(Gerhard, 345 and 351; Icaza, I, 207f. and II, 162 and 165; Scholes and Adams, 33; Boyd-Bowman, II, no. 2080, 57.)

293. Isidro MORENO
Conqueror—Ponce de León
From: Ciudad Real
Parents: Alonso Moreno de Morillas and Catalina Indo

Moreno was in the Antilles by 1516 and came to New Spain with Luis Ponce de León in 1520 in time to take part in the capture of Tenochtitlan. He was then a member of various *entradas*. Moreno lived in Utlatlan (170 miles southwest of Mexico City in the jurisdiction of Zacatula; 10 *estancias* with 190 tributaries in 1570), one of the *cabeceras* of his *encomienda*. It was here that he maintained his *casa poblada*, arms, and horses. A son, Pedro Jenenes (Jiménez ?) lived in Huizuco (30 miles southeast of Taxco, 117 miles east-northeast of Utlatlan; 15 *estancias* in 1570), his other *cabecera*. Moreno and his wife had four other children, two of them sons. Both *cabeceras* were inherited ca. 1550 by another son, Bernardino (Moreno) de Casasola, still the *encomendero* in 1597. It was not until after 1643 that the crown took possession.

(Gerhard, 146ff. and 292f.; Scholes and Adams, 32; Boyd-Bowman, I, no. 1295a, 44; Icaza, I, 77f.)

294. Juan MORENO
Conqueror—Ponce de León
From: Lepe (Huelva)

Moreno spent at least a year in Cuba before joining the 1520 Juan Ponce de León *entrada*, arriving in New Spain in time to take part in the capture of Tenochtitlan. Cortés assigned him the *encomienda* of Alpizagua (39 miles south-southeast of Teotitlan; two dependent settlements in 1548), but in 1527 Alonso de Estrada, while governor, reassigned the grant to conqueror Jerónimo de Salinas. Moreno's widow, Catalina Rodríguez, petitioned for relief from her poverty ca. 1547.

(Gerhard, 306 and 308; Boyd-Bowman, I, no. 1804, 62; Icaza, II, 72; Orozco y Berra, 84.)

295. Pedro MORENO Cendejas
Conqueror—Narváez
From: Torre Hermosa (Zaragoza)
Parents: Antón Moreno and Catalina Alvarez

Moreno was in Cuba by 1519 and with Narváez the following year. After the capture of Tenochtitlan he was a member of *entradas* to Pánuco and Guatemala. By 1527 Moreno was a *vecino* of Mexico City and *encomendero* of Amatlan, Cuzama, and Sernaca (240 miles east-southeast of Mexico City; four *estancias* in 1570), Acatlan (155 miles east of Mexico City), and part holder of Nextalpa (56 miles north-northwest of Mexico City near Tula; two *visitas* in 1570) with first conqueror Juan Sánchez Galindo. He married and by 1547 had one son. Another son was born some time later. Moreno also acknowledged a natural son and daughter. The Nextalpa share went to a namesake son when Moreno died ca. 1565. By 1597 the *encomendero* was Sebastián Moreno, perhaps a grandson. The remaining grants went to another son, Martín de Mafra, who ca. 1569 added Cintla and Tepetlachaco (in the vicinity of Córdoba) to his holdings. The tribute from all of these *encomiendas* reverted to the crown between 1600 and 1626.

(Gerhard, 83, 86f., 332f. and 375; Scholes and Adams, 16 and 18; Icaza, I, 45; Orozco y Berra, 84.)

296. Sebastián MOSCOSO
First Conqueror
From: Badajoz (province)

Moscoso was in Cuba a year before joining the 1519 Cortés *entrada*. He became a *vecino* of Mexico City, where he maintained his *casa poblada* with "many Spaniards and family." Cortés assigned him *encomienda* rights to Tepexi (40 miles north of Mexico City near Tula; 10 *visitas* in 1570) and nearby Otlazpa (four *sujetos* in 1570). Around 1564 it was considered a very large *encomienda*. Moscoso married an Indian noblewoman (*india principal*) and had two daughters and a son, Juan, who succeeded him ca. 1551. Juan's son, Sebastián de Moscoso, inherited in 1593. Both grants were crown property by 1688.

(Gerhard, 332ff.; Scholes and Adams, 42; Boyd-Bowman, I, no. 312, 12; Icaza, I, 90; Orozco y Berra, 48; *Protocolos*, I, no. 159, 62 of 25 October 1525.)

297. Diego de MOTRICO—
Merchant/Shipowner
First Conqueror
From: Motrico (Guipúzcoa)

Motrico probably had considerable experience in the Indies; we know for certain he was in Cuba by 1518 and a member of the Cortés *entrada* the following year. He was identified as a mariner and later functioned as a merchant in Mexico City, where he was a *vecino*. Motrico was assigned the *encomienda* of Zultepec (34 miles northeast of Mexico City). His wife, Isabel Muñoz, was from Sanlúcar de Alpechnín (Seville); she arrived in the Indies with her parents in 1513. The couple had no children. She succeeded as *encomendera* ca. 1535 and then married first conqueror Gonzalo Hernández Calvo of Palos (Huelva). Succession was disputed when she died in the 1540s. Hernández retained half the grant, and the other part was purchased by conquistador Pedro de Meneses. Hernández was succeeded by his second wife ca. 1552, and their son, Francisco Calvo, became the *encomendero* in the 1560s.

(Gerhard, 312; Scholes and Adams, 44f.; Icaza, I, 71; Boyd-Bowman, I, no. 1645n, 57 and no. 3181, 111; *Protocolos*, I, no. 239, 79 of 20 November 1525; Orozco y Berra, 48.)

298. Juan (Leiva) de NÁJERA *"el sordo"*— Hidalgo
Conqueror—Juan de la Cueva
From: Nájera (Logroño)
Parents: Juan Gaeta de Leiva and Catalina de Leiva

Nájera was in Cuba by 1519 and went to New Spain the following year on a caravel owned by Juan de la Cueva. He arrived in time to take part in the capture of Tenochtitlan, where he lost an ear and was deafened. Nájera was a *vecino* of Mexico City and, when the crown reclaimed the grant, shared the tribute from Atlan and Metateyuca (125 miles northeast of Mexico City) with Juan de Hinojosa. He also unsuccessfully claimed Xilocingo (32 miles north of Mexico City; three *estancias* from 1550 to 1597), a grant held by first conqueror Martín Vázquez. Nájera was married twice and had a total of six sons and four daughters. Three sons went to Peru and one accompanied Nájera on the 1541 Mixtón War campaign in New Galicia under Viceroy Mendoza. His second wife, Juana Clavijo, was the widow of first conqueror Juan de Medina.

(Gerhard, 118 and 401; Icaza, I, 92 and 152f.; Boyd-Bowman, I, no. 4982, 165.)

299. Alonso NAVARRETE—Page during the conquest
First Conqueror
From: Guadix (Granada)
Parents: Alonso Navarrete and Constanza Muñoz

Navarrete was in the Indies by 1516, in Cuba by 1518 and with Cortés as one of his pages the following year. After the capture of Mexico City Navarrete served with *entradas* to Colima, Pánuco, and later to Baja California. It seems that by 1547 he lived in the *cabecera* of one of his *encomiendas* near Valles, where he held Nespa (1,734 tributaries in 1532) and Tauzán (887 tributaries in 1532). Navarrete initially shared Tauzán with Diego de las Roeles, but bought him out ca. 1536. He also shared Tancolol (in the vicinity of Pánuco, 32 tributaries in 1532) with conqueror

Juan de Villagrán from Valladolid and then with Roeles, until the title went to the latter. For a time in the mid-1520s Navarrete may have held Tepeapulco (155 miles south-southeast of Valles, 40 miles northwest of Tlaxcala; 6,000 tributaries in 1570). This grant was claimed by Cortés, reassigned by the acting governors in 1526, and then recovered by Cortés. Navarrete did not marry. All of his holdings reverted to the crown when he entered the Augustinian order in 1555.

(Gerhard, 52f., 216 and 355; Boyd-Bowman, I, no. 1563, 53; Icaza, I, 18; Orozco y Berra, 85.)

300. Juan NAVARRO
Conqueror—Narváez
From: Xulbe (Aragón)
Father: Nicholás Navarro

Navarro was in Cuba in 1519, with the Narváez *entrada* the following year, and served as a crossbowman during the siege and capture of Tenochtitlan. He became a *vecino* of Puebla, where he maintained his *casa poblada*, family, arms, and horses. His *encomiendas* were Guautla (115 miles southeast of Puebla; five *sujetos* in 1581) and Nanaguaticpac (100 miles southeast of Puebla; one *sujeto* in 1581). Navarro was married and had two daughters, one of whom married Melchor Castañón, also a *vecino* of Puebla. He was succeeded by this daughter ca. 1546. By 1597 Navarro's grandson, also named Melchor Castañón, held Guautla, and another grandson (?), Juan Pacheco, was the *encomendero* of Nanaguaticpac.

(Gerhard, 306ff.; Scholes and Adams, 33; Boyd-Bowman, I, no. 5022, 168; Icaza, I, 12f.; Orozco y Berra, 85.)

301. Juan (Antonio) NAVARRO
Conqueror—?

Navarro held the *encomienda* of Zayanaquilpa (12 miles west-southwest of Tula; 680 tributaries in 1570). By 1545 he had been succeeded by his widow, who then married Juan Bautista Marín. Marín, when widowed, married doña Leonor Marín, a daughter of a conquistador (possibly first conqueror Luis Marín). Doña Leonor inherited ca. 1565, but the succession was contested. By 1570 Zayanaquilpa was a crown property.

(Gerhard, 383ff.; Scholes and Adams, 27.)

302. Gómez NIETO
Conqueror—Narváez

Nieto, a *vecino* of Pánuco, held the *encomienda* of Yagualica (57 miles north of Pachuca; 176 tributaries in 1532, 13 *sujetos*, and five *hermitas* in 1569) at least from 1531 to 1533. He replaced Nuño de Guzmán's 1527 appointee, Juan de Torquemada. Yagualica had reverted to the crown by 1545.

(Gerhard, 243f.; Chipman, 292; Orozco y Berra, 64.)

303. Pedro NIETO (Neto)
Conqueror—Narváez

Nieto arrived in New Spain with the Narváez *entrada* and became a *vecino* of Mexico City. He and Cristóbal de Mafra were together the first *encomenderos* of Xicayan and Ayutla (240 miles south-southeast of Mexico City) and Tetepec (245 miles south-southeast of Mexico City). There were ten *estancias* associated with the three *cabeceras*. Mafra's half reverted to the crown ca. 1544. Nieto was succeeded ca. 1570 by a son, Francisco Nieto Maldonado, still the *encomendero* in 1597.

(Gerhard, 381f.; Icaza I, 32; Scholes and Adams, 21; Protocolos I no. 1301, 281 of 28 April 1528.)

304. Andrés NÚÑEZ
First Conqueror
From: Cantalapiedra (Salamanca)
Parents: Andrés Núñez and Leonor Martínez

Núñez was in the Indies in 1510 and Cuba by 1518, joining Cortés the following year. He became a *vecino* of Mexico City and invested Indian slaves in mining ventures. He shared Tequixquiac (40 miles north of Mexico City, three *barrios* in 1579) with first conqueror Martín López, the ship's carpenter. Núñez was married, and one of his daughters married Mexico City *vecino* Gonzalo Portillo, *alcalde mayor* of Zultepec and Zacualpa. She inherited the Núñez share of Tequixquiac when Andrés died ca. 1543. By 1597 the tribute was reassigned.

(Gerhard, 401f.; Scholes and Adams, 41; Boyd-Bowman, I, no. 2599, 92 and II, no. 3627, 107; Icaza, I, 218f.; *Protocolos*, I, no. 1188, 262 of 19 March 1528; Orozco y Berra, 85.)

305. Juan NÚÑEZ Mercado—Page during the conquest
First Conqueror
From: Ciudad Rodrigo (Salamanca)
Parents: Andrés Núñez Mercado of Cuéllar and Leonor de Torres

Núñez was in Cuba by 1518 and joined Cortés the following year, serving as one of his pages. He was a founding *vecino* of Puebla in 1532. Núñez' time as an *encomendero* was rather short. Tecomavaca and Quiotepec (115 miles south-southeast of Puebla near Teotitlan; 3,200 tributaries in 1521—reduced to 400 by 1570) were assigned to him in the early 1520s, probably by Cortés, then taken and made a crown property by the first Audiencia in November 1531. Núñez did not marry. By 1547 he claimed he was sick, nearly blind, and in great need.

(Gerhard, 306f.; Icaza, I, 25f.; Boyd-Bowman, I, no. 2600, 92; Orozco y Berra, 48.)

306. Juan NÚÑEZ Sedeño—*Hidalgo*
First Conqueror
From: Madrid
Parents: Pedro Sedeño and Mari Núñez

Núñez was in the Indies before 1515, an *encomendero* of Havana and holder of a royal office in Cuba. After serving as a member of the Grijalva expedition, Núñez had a shipload of men and provisions commandeered by Diego de Ordaz under orders from Cortés and was induced to join the 1519 venture. Díaz del Castillo describes Núñez as the richest man in the Cortés *entrada*. In addition to his ship and cargo, he brought a mare that foaled enroute and he owned a black slave. Núñez later became a *vecino* of Ciudad Oaxaca, where he maintained his *casa poblada* and held municipal office as inspector and magistrate (*visitador y justicia*). His *encomiendas* included Calpulalpa (33 miles northeast of Antequera; four *barrios* in 1548), Tlaxiaco (90 miles west-northwest of Antequera; eight sub-*cabeceras* with over 100 *estancias*), and a claimed quarter of Xilotepec (18 miles southwest of Tula; 18,335 tributaries in all as of 1565). First conqueror Francisco de Quevedo and conqueror Hernando Cantillana received the tribute from the other three-quarters. Tlaxiaco, originally assigned by Cortés, was taken in 1528 by governor Alonso de Estrada and reassigned to first conqueror Martín Vázquez. First conqueror Juan Jaramillo de Salvatierra was the sole *encomendero* of Xilotepec ca. 1533 and after. Núñez was married and had four children. His son, Pedro, succeeded him as *encomendero* of Calpulalpa ca. 1550. This grant reverted to the crown after 1570.

Note: Another Xilotepec, located seven miles north of Jalapa, was assigned to first conqueror Juan Sedeño in the early 1520s. This grant was taken for the royal dye industry when Sedeño died in the early 1530s.

(Gerhard, 158f., 286, 289, 383ff.; Scholes and Adams, 44; Icaza, I, 29; Boyd-Bowman, I, no. 2310, 79; Orozco y Berra, 48; Gómara, 22; Díaz del Castillo, I, 66.)

307. Pedro NÚÑEZ, Maese de Roa—Surgeon
Poblador
From: Roa (Burgos)
Parents: Alonso Muñoz, Maestre de Roa, and Catalina Bermúdez

Núñez arrived in New Spain in 1525, acquired an *encomienda*, and joined *entradas* to Honduras and New Galicia. Although trained and titled as a medical practitioner, Núñez functioned as a merchant in Mexico City, where he was a *vecino* and maintained his *casa poblada*, arms, and horses. It was some years before Núñez was able to retain continuous title to an *encomienda*. He was the first holder of Acolman (24 miles northeast of Mexico City near Texcoco; 2,564 tributaries ca. 1570) and Capula (160 miles west of Mexico City near Pátzcuaro; 12 *estancias* in 1571). Both were taken from him and reassigned in 1528. Acolman went to first conqueror Pedro de Solís Barrasa and Capula to Dr. Cristóbal de Ojeda, a *poblador*. Around 1536 Viceroy Mendoza assigned him Xiquipilco (30 miles northwest of Mexico City; 23 *estancias* in 1548). This *encomienda* had been a crown possession for at least two years. During the 1540s Núñez also received the tribute from Coacingo (88 miles southeast of Mexico City) amounting to $40, forty turkeys, and forty loads of corn, perhaps as agent for its *encomendero*, first conqueror Diego Quejada, who had returned to Spain in the early 1540s. This grant was a crown possession after 1553. Núñez married doña María de Chaves, a daughter of conqueror Hernando de Chaves. They had three sons and a daughter. He also acknowledged three natural daughters. Núñez' father, Alonso Muñoz, was also a *vecino* of Mexico City. A son, Pedro Núñez de Chaves, succeeded as *encomendero* of Xiquipilco before 1597. The grant became a crown holding between 1643 and 1688.

(Gerhard, 312f., 344, 350f., 175ff. and 160; Icaza, I, 20 and 213f.; Scholes and Adams, 20; Boyd-Bowman, II, no. 2553 and no. 2554, 72.)

308. Diego de OCAMPO
Poblador
From: Lugo (?)

Ocampo was a *vecino* of Mexico City and a wealthy *encomendero*, also serving as a *mayordomo* for Cortés. In the mid-1520s he was assigned Tlanalpa (including the sub-*cabeceras* Oxtoticpac and Talistaca, 35 miles northeast of Mexico City; 700 tributaries in 1570) and Tatatetelco (114 miles east of Mexico City). By 1528 he also held Pochutla and Tonameca (100 miles west-southwest of Tehuantepec), but the tribute reverted to the crown under the first Audiencia in July, 1530. For two years (from 1525 to 1527) he held Tepetlaostoc (26 miles northeast of Mexico City near Texcoco; 3,500 tributaries in 1570—perhaps one-fifth of the original number). This *encomienda* was claimed by Cortés, reassigned by the acting governors to Ocampo, and then taken and reassigned to conqueror Miguel Díaz de Aux. Finally in 1528, governor Alonso de Estrada reassigned Tepetlaostoc to *poblador* Gonzalo de Salazar. By 1550 Ocampo and his son-in-law, Ramiro Arellano, shared the tribute from Tecamachalco (60 miles southeast of Mexico City; 29 *sujetos* in 1580) with Cortés' secretary, Alonso Valiente. Ocampo did not marry in New Spain, nor is there record of his bringing a wife from Spain. He acknowledged three natural daughters, of whom two married well, receiving excellent dowries. One received Tlanalpa when she married Ramiro Arellano. Their son, don Alonso de Arellano, inherited before 1560 and was still the *encomendero* in 1597. Daughter doña María de Ocampo received Ostoticpac when she married Juan Velázquez Rodríguez. Their son, don Alonso Velázquez, inherited before 1597. Both daughters shared in inheriting the tribute from Tatatetelco. There is no record of the dowry given to the third daughter, who married *hidalgo* Cristóbal de Tejadillo. Ocampo died ca. 1552.

(Gerhard, 53, 68, 83, 124, 208, 278, 280, and 312; Scholes and Adams, 39f.; Icaza, II, 153; *Protocolos*, I, no. 1499, 318 of 11 September 1528.)

309. Diego de OCAÑA—Notary
Poblador
From: Seville

Ocaña arrived in New Spain in 1523 and was notary in and a *vecino* of Mexico City two years later. By 1528 he held Maravatio (87 miles west of Mexico City; perhaps 1,800 tributaries in 1570), but the encomienda was taken shortly thereafter when he was accused of being a Jew. Maravatio was then reassigned to *poblador* Pedro Juárez. Ocaña was reconciled by the Inquisition 17 October 1528, the same day first conqueror Hernando Alonso and Gonzalo de Morales were burned for heresy, but he did not recover his *encomienda*. He was married and had one son, Hernán Suárez, who was disinherited after denying that Ocaña was his father.

(Gerhard, 172f.; Boyd-Bowman, II, no. 9819, 297; *Protocolos*, I, no. 1694 and no. 1695, 353 marginal note, of 17 October 1528; *Actas*, I, 55; Greenleaf, 93; Díaz del Castillo, II, 353 and 397.)

310. **Juan OCHOA de Lejalde—Merchant Conqueror—Narváez**
From: **Salinas de Lenis (Guipúzcoa)**
Parents: **Martín de Lejalde and María de Belategui**

Ochoa was in Santo Domingo by 1508, took part in the capture of Puerto Rico the following year, and helped subdue Cuba in 1511. In 1514 Ochoa was a *vecino* of Ilonao, Santo Domingo. Five years later he was in Cuba, and he joined the Narváez *entrada* in 1520. Initially a resident and citizen of Mexico City, Ochoa became an early *vecino* of Puebla. He held in *encomienda* one-half of Teozacualco (160 miles south-southeast of Puebla near Antequera; 1,982 tributaries in 1548), shared with conqueror Antón(io) de Arriaga; Tututepetongo (105 miles southeast of Puebla; five *estancias* in 1548); Guautla (105 miles south-southeast of Puebla); and Tanantepec (120 miles south-southeast of Puebla). He claimed in 1547 that his total income from these grants amounted to but $700. Ochoa was married and had four sons and three daughters. He was succeeded by a son, Juan Ochoa de Lejalde, ca. 1555. The tribute reverted to the crown when Juan died without issue. Ochoa received a coat of arms dated 9 November 1546.

(Gerhard, 276f., 285, and 289; Scholes and Adams, 41f.; Boyd-Bowman, I, no. 1651a,

57; Icaza, I, 14; Orozco y Berra, 85; *Nobiliario*, 205f., *Actas*, I, 4.)

311. **Alonso de OJEDA**
First Conqueror
From: **Moguer (Huelva)**
Parents: **Alonso Hernández de Ojeda and Leonor Pérez**

Ojeda was in Cuba by 1517, with the Grijalva expedition the following year, and a member of the Cortés *entrada* in 1519. After the siege of Tenochtitlan, in which he lost an eye, Ojeda became a *vecino*, *regidor*, and *alcalde* of Villa Alta, where he maintained his *casa poblada*, arms, and horses. He shared the *encomienda* of Tiltepec (near Villa Alta) with fellow first conqueror Rodrigo de Segura. The latter's share reverted to the crown in 1532. Ojeda was married and had six children. His sister Inés, widow of pilot Nuflo Martín, and nephew Martín Alonso were also *vecinos* of Villa Alta. The nephew married a daughter of conquistador Pedro de Rodas and his Andalusian wife. Ojeda died after 1567 and left his estate to a son of the same name.

(Gerhard, 372; Scholes and Adams, 22; Boyd-Bowman, I, no. 1833, 63 and no. 5223, 175; Icaza, I, 18f. and 179 and II, 226; Orozco y Berra, 86.)

312. **Doctor Cristóbal de OJEDA—Surgeon**
Poblador
From: **Seville**

Ojeda was in Cuba ca. 1521 and in Mexico City five years later: Although identified as a surgeon, Ojeda was more a man of business than a medical practitioner. He had close and long associations with *poblador antiguo* merchant Antón de Carmona, also from Seville, and Pedro Núñez, Maese de Roa, another surgeon. Ojeda was a *vecino* of Mexico City, where he was a *regidor* from 10 September 1527 until his departure for Spain in 1531. During the time he was in Mexico City he was the *encomendero* of at least half of Capula (155 miles west of Mexico City near Pátzcuaro; 12 *estancias* in 1571), perhaps with *poblador* Luis de Berrio. In May of 1528 he contracted with García Gómez to administer the *encomienda* for a seventh share of the tribute. The previous holder of Capula was Pedro Núñez. Ojeda returned to Spain in 1531 and was listed as a *vecino* of Seville seven years later. All of Capula's tribute went to the crown after early 1533.

(Gerhard, 344 and 350f.; Boyd-Bowman, II, no. 9823a, 297; *Protocolos*, I, no. 1341, 289 of 13 May 1528.)

313. Antonio de OLIVER—*Hidalgo*
Poblador
From: Ciudad Real
Parents: Luis de Oliver and Catalina de la Torre

Oliver, after his 1523 arrival in New Spain, took part in *entradas* to Villa Alta, Michoacán, and New Galicia. He then became a *vecino* of Mexico City, where in the 1530s he associated closely with merchants by acting as bondsman or collecting for them. In the late 1520s he became the *encomendero* of Turicato (132 miles west-southwest of Mexico City near Pátzcuaro; 23 *barrios* in 1570). In the 1540s half of the tribute was reassigned to first conqueror Diego Fernández Nieto. Oliver was married but had no children. His half of Turicato reverted to the crown when he died ca. 1563.

(Gerhard, 74 and 76; Scholes and Adams, 20; Icaza, I, 193; Boyd-Bowman, II, no. 3718, 109; *Protocolos*, II, no. 2072, 83 of 19 November 1536, no. 2165, 101 of 9 January 1537 and no. 2226, 112f. of 13 March 1537.)

314. Juan Bautista OLIVER
Poblador
From: Palamós (Catalonia)
Parents: Jerónimo de Oliver and Ana Gordia

Oliver arrived in New Spain ca. 1525 and took part in the pacification of the Zapotecas, the Mixe and the Chontal in what is now east-central Oaxaca. He became a *vecino* of Villa Alta when assigned the *encomienda* of Ocotepec (55 miles southeast of Villa Alta). The grant included Quezaltepec, Acatlan, Xuquila, and other Mixe villages. By 1565 Ocotepec was considered a small grant. Oliver married a daughter of conqueror Juan García de Beas and maintained his *casa poblada*, arms, and horses in Villa Alta. He was succeeded ca. 1565 by a namesake son, who was still the *encomendero* in 1597.

(Gerhard, 197; Scholes and Adams, 22; Icaza, I, 228f.; Boyd-Bowman, I, no. 1699, 60 and II, no. 4377, 130.)

315. Francisco de OLIVEROS
Conqueror—Narváez
From: Lisbon, Portugal
Parents: Diego de Oliveros and Ana Bella

Oliveros was in Cuba at least a year before joining the 1520 Narváez *entrada*. He served as falconer to Cortés during the siege and capture of Tenochtitlan. After various *entradas* and numerous business ventures, Oliveros left Mexico City and became a *vecino* of Puebla, where he was a *regidor*, made musters, and maintained his arms and horses. He held the *encomienda* of Zautla (also called Xonacatlan, 75 miles northeast of Puebla; five *estancias* in 1569). Oliveros was married and had six children, two of them sons. The *encomienda* was inherited by a son, Martín, when Oliveros died in the 1550s.

(Gerhard, 229 and 231; Scholes and Adams, 29; Icaza, I, 47f.; Orozco y Berra, 85.)

316. Francisco de OLMOS—Tailor
Conqueror—Narváez
From: Portillo (Valladolid)
Parents: Antón Martínez de Olmos and Isabel de Olmos

Olmos was a *vecino* of Verapaz, Santo Domingo, in 1514; he was in Cuba in 1519, and a member of the Narváez *entrada* the following year. He then served as a member of the Pánuco *entrada* following the capture of Tenochtitlan. Olmos was a *vecino* of Mexico City and there maintained his *casa poblada*, family, and horses. His *encomienda* was half of Piastla (105 miles southeast of Mexico City near Izúcar, nine *estancias* in 1581), shared with conqueror Fernando Burgueño until 1532, when the latter died and his half went to the crown. In 1524 Olmos married Beatriz Bermúdez Velasco, one of the four Spanish women who accompanied the Narváez *entrada*. Their daughter, Isabel de Olmos, married Basque conqueror Juan de Zamudio, and when he died, married *poblador* Alonso Velázquez from Portillo, her father's home town. When Olmos died ca. 1568, the *encomienda* reverted to the crown. An heir, Gaspar de Burgos, sued successfully and recovered the Olmos half of Piastla. He was still the *encomendero* in 1603, but by 1626 the grant was again a crown holding.

(Gerhard, 42f.; Scholes and Adams, 21; Boyd-Bowman, I, no. 4595b, 151f.; Icaza, I, 48 and II, 11f.; Orozco y Berra, 64; *Actas*, I, 39.)

317. Diego de OLVERA
Conqueror—Narváez
From: Utrera (Seville)
Parents: Hernando de Olvera and Antonia de Saavedra

Olvera arrived in Cuba ca. 1519 and joined the Narváez *entrada* the following year. He became a *vecino* of Mexico City in the early 1520s and was the *encomendero* of Tecaxique and Chicaguaso (44 miles north of Mexico City near Tula; two *sujetos* in 1548). He also held Acatlan (132 miles south of Mexico City), Cintla (210 miles south of Mexico City), and Xalapa (200 miles south of Mexico City) from 1528 until they were taken for the crown by the second Audiencia ca. 1532. Olvera married Juana Ruiz and had three sons and four daughters. By 1547 one of the daughters had married Alonso Calvo. Juana succeeded as *encomendera* ca. 1545. She later transferred title to their son, Juan de Olvera. He was the *encomendero* until his death sometime after 1565, at which time the grant escheated.

(Gerhard, 149, 296f., and 299; Scholes and Adams, 42; Icaza, I, 128; Boyd-Bowman, I, no. 4186, 137; *Protocolos*, I, no. 1021, 233 of 17 January 1528.)

318. Cristóbal Pérez de OÑATE—*Hidalgo Poblador*
From: Vitoria (Alava)
Parents: Juan Pérez de Oñate and Osaña González

Oñate was twenty years old in 1524 when he arrived in New Spain and became a *vecino* of Mexico City. The following year Cortés assigned him the *encomienda* of Culhuacan (nine miles south-southeast of Mexico City; 18 *estancias* in 1580). While governor in 1528, Alonso de Estrada reassigned to him the tribute from Tacámbaro (155 miles west-southwest of Mexico City; 18 *visitas* in 1571) from *poblador* Alonso de Avalos Saavedra. Oñate served with Nuño de Guzmán's *entrada* to New Galicia, acquiring one-half of Mascota (90 miles west of Guadalajara), Tepetlatlauca (80 miles west of Guadalajara), Chistique (75 miles west of Guadalajara), and Xalisco (170 miles northwest of Guadalajara, 10 miles south of Tepic). He also served under Viceroy Mendoza in the Mixtón War. About 1547 he and Diego de Ibarra founded Zacatecas. A brother, Juan de Oñate, was also in New Galicia before going to Peru ca. 1537. Oñate's wife, doña Catalina de Salazar, was the daughter of New Spain's treasury officer (*factor*) Gonzalo de Salazar and widow of don Ruy Díaz de Mendoza. They had a number of children. A son, Hernando, succeeded as *encomendero* of the grants in New Spain in 1568, while a namesake acquired title to the *encomiendas* in New Galicia. Alonso de Oñate y Salazar inherited the Zacatecas mines and Juan de Oñate led the New Mexico *entrada* of 1598. The New Galicia holdings escheated in the 1570s, while the tribute from both *cabeceras* in New Spain went to the family until the 1650s.

(Gerhard, 178f., 345, and 352; Gerhard 1982, 87f. and 140; Scholes and Adams, 19; Icaza, II, 355f.; Boyd-Bowman, II, no. 103, 5; Henige, 313.)

319. Diego de ORDAZ—Hidalgo
First Conqueror
From: Castroverde de Campos (Zamora)

Ordaz took part in the capture of Cuba in 1511 and then was a *vecino* of San Salvador on that island for four years. He joined Cortés in 1519 and after the Tenochtitlan campaign was a member of the Honduras *entrada*. He acquired the governorship of Cumaná (Venezuela) in 1531. All this time Ordaz was a *vecino* of Mexico City, holding the office of *alguacil mayor* during 1525 and 1526. He received significant income from the five grants he held at various times. Teutla (180 miles southeast of Mexico City; five *sujetos* and a number of *estancias* in 1548) was assigned him in the early 1520s. Huexocingo (55 miles east-southeast of Mexico City; 30,000 tributaries in 1531) was claimed by Cortés, taken for the crown in 1526, seized by Factor Gonzalo de Salazar in 1528, its tribute paid to the Audiencia judges the following year, and then reassigned to Ordaz in 1530. Chiautla (90 miles southeast of Mexico City; 6,000 tributaries before 1545) was assigned to Ordaz in the early 1520s and reassigned to first conqueror Alonso de Grado ca. 1525. Calpan (44 miles east-southeast of Mexico City; 20,000 to 24,000 tributaries in 1520, 4,876 in 1570) was claimed by Cortés and then acquired by Ordaz in the late 1520s. Chilapa (130 miles south of Mexico City; 4,000 tributaries in 1570) was first held by Cristóbal Flores and Alonso de Grado before Ordaz acquired it in the late 1520s. While returning from Seville in 1532 with 400 recruits for his Venezuela colony, Ordaz died, without issue or spouse. He named a nephew then living in Spain, Diego de Ordaz Villagómez, as his heir. Teutla and Huexocingo reverted to the crown, and the nephew received Calpan and Chilpa. Ordaz was receiving income from at least 60,000 tributaries at the time of his death. His nephew, when he arrived in New Spain ca. 1536, inherited approximately half this revenue. He in turn was succeeded ca. 1578 by his son, Antonio.

(Gerhard, 56f., 108f., 111, 113, 141f., 302, and 304; Scholes and Adams, 17; Icaza, I, 210; Boyd-Bowman, I, no. 4836, 160.)

320. Francisco de ORDUÑA—Notary
Conqueror—Salcedo
From: Orduña (Biscay)
Parents: Juan López de Barriaga and Inés de Velasco

Orduña arrived in New Spain with Salcedo in 1521 and joined the Cortés *entrada* at Texcoco just prior to the siege of Tenochtitlan. He was an early *vecino* of Mexico City, but by 1540 had become a *vecino* and *regidor* of Puebla. The acting governors reassigned Yautepec and Tepoztlan (36 miles south of Mexico City; 5,500 tributaries in 1551) to Orduña and conqueror Francisco Verdugo ca. 1526. Cortés, the original claimant, recovered the tribute in 1531. About 1528 Orduña acquired half of Igualapa (200 miles south of Mexico City; 10 *estancias* at the time of assignment), Ometepec (270 miles south of Mexico City), and Suchistlaguaca (200 miles south of Mexico City), shared with *poblador* Francisco de Herrera. Three years later he was assigned Tecali (44 miles east-southeast of Mexico City near Puebla; 3,830 tributaries in 1548), in lieu of the grant recovered by Cortés. Around 1530 Orduña returned to Spain to bring his wife, son, and six daughters to New Spain. Five of the daughters were soon married: one to conqueror Francisco de Santa Cruz; another to conqueror Jerónimo Ruiz de la Mota; another—named doña Inés de Velasco after her paternal grandmother—to *poblador* Bernardino del Castillo; and the other two to other established members of the community. After his first wife died, Orduña married Catalina Vélez Rascona, widow of first conqueror Bartolomé Hernández de Nava, and had four more children, two of them sons. Catalina brought her seven children by Hernández to the household. Orduña was succeeded by a son, don José, who inherited Tecali ca. 1550. The other three *cabeceras* had already been transferred to daughter doña Inés in dowry when she married Bernardino del Castillo.

(Gerhard, 95f., 149ff., and 255f.; Scholes and Adams, 36; Boyd-Bowman, II, no. 12447, 373 and no. 11504; Icaza, I, 74f., 33, 183, 72, and II, 15; Orozco y Berra, 71.)

321. Cristóbal de ORTEGA
Poblador

Ortega was a *vecino* of Pánuco and *encomendero* of Tantala (52 miles west of Pánuco near Valles; 1,042 tributaries in 1532) and shared nearby Topla (179 tributaries in 1532) with first conqueror Alonso Romero until he acquired Romero's share. He was succeeded by his childless widow, Catalina Maldonado. She then married *poblador* Diego de Torres of Trujillo (Cáceres), who acquired the *encomienda*. Their son, Diego (Pedro) de Torres Maldonado, inherited ca. 1560, some seven years after both of his parents died. He was still the *encomendero* in 1597.

(Gerhard, 355; Scholes and Adams, 47; Chipman, 293; Boyd-Bowman, II, no. 3240, 95.)

322. Bachiller Juan de ORTEGA—Page during conquest
First Conqueror
From: Ecija (Seville)
Parents: Juan Hernández de Arjona and Mari Rodríguez de Ortega

Ortega was in Santo Domingo in 1512, in Cuba by early 1519, and served as one of Cortés' pages during the Tenochtitlan campaign. He became a *vecino* of Mexico City and *encomendero* of Tepozotlan (22 miles north-northwest of Mexico City; 13 *estancias* in 1570). He left no heirs. The *encomienda* reverted to the crown when he died ca. 1546.

(Gerhard, 127f.; Boyd-Bowman, I, no. 3064, 108; Orozco y Berra, 48; *Actas*, I, 26.)

323. Alonso ORTIZ de Zúñiga—*Hidalgo*
Conqueror—Narváez
From: Seville
Parents: Sancho Ortiz de Zúñiga and Ana de Mesa

Ortiz was with Pedrarias in Tierra Firme in 1514; two years later he had become a Cuban *encomendero*. He was with Grijalva in 1518 and then in 1520 joined the Narváez *entrada*. Ortiz served as captain of crossbowmen during the siege and capture of Tenochtitlan. He then became a *vecino* of the capitol, where he had his *casa poblada*. It was not until ca. 1533, when the second Audiencia reassigned Tlanchinolticpac and Cuimantlan (113 miles north of Mexico City; 80 *sujetos* in 1573) in equal shares to Ortiz and *poblador hidalgo* Jerónimo de Medina, that he became an *encomendero*. He married twice and had seven children—four of them legitimate. Ortiz was succeeded in 1568 by a son of the same name. A grandson, also named Alonso Ortiz de Zúñiga was the *encomendero* after 1597. By 1643 the Ortiz share had reverted to the crown.

(Gerhard, 185 and 187; Scholes and Adams, 19; Icaza, I, 34; Boyd-Bowman, I, no. 3826, 128; Orozco y Berra, 64.)

324. Juan ORTIZ
Conqueror—Narváez
From: Huelva

Ortiz, probably a *vecino* of Puebla, held the *encomienda* of Tamaholipa (220 miles north of Puebla near Pánuco) from the 1530s until his death ca. 1547, when the tributes reverted to the crown. He had a *mestiza* daughter living in the *casa poblada* of Puebla *vecino* Gonzalo Díaz de Vargas and another daughter married to Jerónimo Genovés, also a Puebla *vecino*.

(Gerhard, 215; Icaza, II, 168f. and 203f.; Orozco y Berra, 85.)

325. Juan ORTIZ de Matienzo—*Hidalgo*
Poblador
From: Santander (province)
Parents: Diego de Bárcena and doña Isabel de Matienzo

Ortiz came to New Spain ca. 1528, campaigned in Pánuco, where he became a *vecino*, and later went with Cortés to California, where he lost an eye. Ca. 1529 he was reassigned the *encomienda* of Xaltepec (340 miles south-southeast of Pánuco near Antequera, six *barrios* in

1550) from its first holder, Juan de la Torre. Later the second Audiencia again reassigned Xaltepec, this time to *poblador* Angel de Villafañe. By 1547 Ortiz was again receiving tributes, but by virtue of marrying the widow of an unknown *encomendero*. He also stood as guardian for her four children.

Note: Gerhard, p. 201, shows Licenciado Juan Ortiz de Matienzo, a first Audiencia judge, as the *encomendero* of Xaltepec. The negative findings of Licenciado Ortiz' 1532 *residencia* and his return to Spain in disgrace would justify reassignment by the second Audiencia. It is more likely, however, that Cortés made the reassignment from Torre to the younger Juan Ortiz and the second Audiencia made its reassignment based on the relative merits and "qualities" of Ortiz and Villafañe, plus the ongoing efforts to trim the influence of Cortés. Furthermore, had Licenciado Ortiz received Xaltepec as a Nuño de Guzmán/first Audiencia assignment, its reassignment would have been first order business for the second Audiencia, but it would have become a crown property. Instead, the second Audiencia gave the grant to another individual, thus supporting the claim of one-time ownership made by the younger Juan Ortiz in Icaza, I, p. 242.

(Gerhard, 210f.; Icaza, I, 242; Boyd-Bowman, II, no. 7800, 242 and, I, no. 786, 27.)

326. Cristóbal PACHECO
First Conqueror

In the early 1520s Pacheco, a *vecino* of Mexico City, was assigned the *encomienda* of Tochimilco (also called Ocopetlayuca, 54 miles southeast of Mexico City; 3,000 tributaries in 1570). In 1525 he was raising pigs in the area of the grant, making a company for that purpose with conqueror Diego Valadés, the two sharing the increase. Pacheco was married and had a daughter, Beatriz Pacheco de Escobar. He died in late 1525, leaving everything to Beatriz. For a time Beatriz was under the guardianship of Bernardino de Santa Clara, who was supposed to arrange for her marriage when she came of age. The *encomienda* was reassigned in 1527 to conqueror Gonzalo Rodríguez de Ocaña, a member of the Cortés household.

(Gerhard, 329; *Protocolos*, I, no. 167, 64 of 31 October 1525, no. 267, 85 of 28 November 1525 and no. 1212, 266 of 10 October 1528; Orozco y Berra, 85; *Actas*, I, 26.)

327. Gaspar PACHECO—*Hidalgo Poblador*
From: Toledo

A member of the 1525 entourage of Licenciado Marcos de Aguilar, Pacheco, along with his brother Melchor and sons, Alonso and Melchor, took part in the pacification of the Mixteca and Zapoteca in northern Oaxaca. Pacheco and Diego de Figueroa led this 1526 *entrada*. The following year Pacheco was a founding settler, *vecino*, and *alguacil mayor* of Villa Alta, becoming *encomendero* of Xareta, a small Mixe village, plus other villages southeast of Villa Alta near Nexapa. In 1536 he sold his rights to the *encomienda* and, along with his sons, took part in the 1539 conquest of Yucatan. The Pachecos were founding *vecinos* of Mérida, and the elder was *alcalde* there in 1541.

(Gerhard, 195, 367, and 372; Boyd-Bowman, II, nos. 11369 and 11370, 339; *Protocolos*, II, no. 1831, 25f. of 26 July 1536.)

328. Juan PANTOJA
Conqueror—Narváez
From: Medellín (La Serena, Extremadura)
Parents: Pedro Pantoja and Catalina Rodríguez

Pantoja was in Cuba in 1519, arrived in New Spain as a member of the Narváez *entrada*, and served as a captain of crossbowmen during the siege and capture of Tenochtitlan. After various *entradas* in western New Spain, Pantoja became a *vecino* of Ciudad Michoacán and *enco-*

mendero of La Guacana (35 miles south-southwest of Pátzcuaro; three *barrios* in 1570). He was married and father of six daughters and two sons. Pantoja's father, Pedro, a *poblador*, arrived in New Spain in 1522 with Cortés' secretary Alonso Valiente and became a *vecino* of Mexico City. Pantoja died ca. 1565 and was succeeded by a son, Pedro. A grandson, Juan Pantoja, was the *encomendero* in 1600.

(Gerhard, 74 and 76; Scholes and Adams, 18; Boyd-Bowman, I, no. 457a, 16 and II, no. 662, 23; Orozco y Berra, 64.)

329. Pedro PANTOJA
Poblador
From: Alconchel (Badajoz)
Parents: Fernando de Vargas and Leonor Martínez

Pantoja, father of conqueror Juan Pantoja, arrived in New Spain in 1522 with Alonso Valiente, a relative of Cortés and a member of his household. Valiente was from Medina de las Torres, near Pantoja's home. Pantoja became a *vecino* of Mexico City and was assigned Guazacualco (Coatzacoalco, 340 miles east-southeast of Mexico City) and nearby Xaltepec. Later he acquired Cimatlan and Cacalotepec (280 miles southeast of Mexico City, 58 miles southwest of Tehuantepec; six *estancias*), Cortés' Pacific seaport. Pantoja was married to Catalina Rodríguez, but there is no record that she came to New Spain. A daughter married a Gaspar Morcillo, and Pantoja's son Juan was a conqueror with the Narváez *entrada*. Pantoja surrendered his *encomienda* in 1533 and returned to Spain but was back in Mexico City in the mid-1540s. Cimatlan and Cacalotepec remained crown properties. Guazacualco was reassigned ca. 1554 to first conqueror Gonzalo Gallego Hernández Alconchel (from the same town in Spain as Pantoja), and at the same time Xaltepec went to first conqueror Luis Marín.

(Gerhard, 124f.; Icaza, II, 300f. and 165; Boyd-Bowman, II, no. 662, 23 and I, no. 475, 17.)

330. Diego PARDO—Merchant/Miner
Poblador Antiguo
From: Moguer (Huelva)
Parents: Hernán Pardo (from Galicia) and Beatriz Beltrán González

In the Indies in 1517, Pardo was a *vecino* in Cuba just before he came to New Spain in 1523. He first joined an Honduras *entrada* and later served in another against the Yope east of Acapulco. Pardo developed mines in the vicinity of Acatlan (75 miles north-northeast of Acapulco) before going to Jalisco with Viceroy Mendoza in the Mixtón War. A *vecino* of Mexico City and often identified as a merchant, Pardo claimed to maintain an entourage of Spaniards. Governor Alonso de Estrada assigned him the *encomienda* of Cahuatepec (190 miles south of Mexico City, 24 miles east of Acapulco; one *estancia*). The tributes were taken by the second Audiencia but later recovered. He was married, had children and was succeeded in the early 1560s by a son, then by his son's widow, Inés de Leiva. The latter, a resident of New Spain since 1535, was the daughter of Alonso de March (?) and Inés de Leiva of Villalba (Huelva).

(Gerhard, 39ff.; Icaza, I, 206ff.; Boyd-Bowman, I, no. 1225, 42, II, no. 5227, 157 and no. 5401, 162; *Protocolos*, I, no. 1063, 240 of 7 February 1528.)

331. Marcos de PAREDES
Poblador

Paredes, probably a *vecino* of Villa Alta, held the *encomienda* of Zultepec with its two *sujetos*, Zoquio and Tultitlan (24 miles north (?) of Villa Alta, considered very small in 1565) until the 1540s, when he was succeeded by his widow, Francisca de Grijalva. The *encomienda* reverted to the crown after 1567.

(Gerhard, 373; Scholes and Adams, 51.)

332. Lorenzo PAYO
Conqueror–Narváez

Payo, a *vecino* of Mexico City, held the *encomienda* of Xipacoya (40 miles north of Mexico City near Tula; two *estancias* in 1548). He and his wife, Marina Rodríguez, had at least one daughter, and perhaps Marina had a daughter from a previous marriage. Ca. 1540 daughter Isabel Payo married *hidalgo poblador* Juan de Jaso "*el mozo*" and received the *encomienda* in dowry. She was listed as the *encomendera* in 1597. Inés, the other daughter, was living in Santo Domingo in 1528.

(Gerhard, 332 and 334; Icaza, I, 197; Scholes and Adams, 43; *Protocolos*, I, no. 193, 70 of 6 November 1525 and no. 961, 223 of 8 January 1528.)

333. Alonso de PAZ—Notary
Poblador
From: Salamanca
Parents: Nicolás de Paz and Beatriz de Heredia

Paz, a relative (cousin?) of Cortés and member of his household, was a *vecino* of Mexico City in 1525; some twenty years later he had his *casa poblada* there. He shared the *encomiendas* of Miaguatlan (280 miles southeast of Mexico City, south of Antequera; 16 villages before 1548 plus the sub-*cabeceras* Molonga, Cuistlan, and Suchitepec with its four *sujetos* 20 miles further southeast), Coatlan (five miles south of Miaguatlan; 33 *estancias* in 1548) and Exutla (20 miles north of Miaguatlan) with first conqueror Mateo de Monjaraz and was the sole holder of Colotepec (on the Pacific, 330 miles southeast of Mexico City). The entire income from these *encomiendas* was transferred to a niece, the daughter of Paz' sister and conqueror Juan de Salamanca, when she married Audiencia judge Licenciado Diego de Loaisa in the early 1540s. Paz then returned to Spain and married a widow. By 1542 he was back in Mexico City with his wife, her children, and their household. The *encomienda*, however, stayed in the Loaisa line past the third life, well into the seventeenth century.

Note: Paz perhaps shared Coatlan with his brother-in-law, Cristóbal de Salamanca. A Juan García contracted to manage this grant for a year, commencing in April 1528.

(Gerhard, 49 and 188f.; Scholes and Adams, 26; Boyd-Bowman, II, no. 7548, 233; Icaza, II, 257; *Protocolos*, I, no. 1207, 265 of 1 April 1528.)

334. Pedro de PAZ
Poblador
From: Salamanca
Parents: Notary Francisco Núñez de Valera and Inés Gómez de Paz

Paz, Cortés' first cousin as well as a cousin of Alonso de Paz, was also a member of the Cortés household. (Alonso's brother, Rodrigo, served as *mayordomo* for Cortés and was executed by the acting governors on 16 October 1525.) In the 1520s Paz was a *vecino* of Mexico City; in the 1530s he was in Honduras, and then from the early 1540s back in Mexico City. He held the *encomienda* of Atotonilco (75 miles north-northeast of Mexico City near Pachuca; two sub-*cabeceras* and a total of 22 *estancias* in 1571). This grant was assigned by Cortés from his own vast holdings. In 1565, on his death bed, Paz married doña Francisca Ferrer, a lady in waiting to the Marquesa del Valle. She then married Pedro Gómez de Cáceres, a son of first conqueror Andrés de Tapia. Atotonilco was inherited by their son, don Andrés Ferrer de Tapia, before 1597, and was a crown holding in 1643.

Note: Hernando Cortés lived in the home of notary Francisco Núñez de Valera during the two years when he studied in Salamanca (1499–1501). Inés Gómez de Paz was a sister of Cortés' father.

(Gerhard, 335ff.; Scholes and Adams, 16; Icaza, I, 209; Boyd-Bowman, II, no. 7550, 233; Orozco y Berra, 49; *BAGN*, XXI, 149; Gómera, 324.)

335. Maese Diego de PEDRAZA—Surgeon
Conqueror—?
From: Pedraza (Segovia)
Parents: Hernán Pérez de Tiedra and Catalina Sepulveda

Maese Diego arrived in New Spain just prior to the capture of Tenochtitlan after having spent as many as twenty years in Santo Domingo. He became a *vecino* of Mexico City, where he maintained a *casa poblada*, arms, and horses. He also continued as a medical practitioner, in addition to carrying on business, financing purchases of merchandise in wholesale quantities as well as acting as a collector of debts for others. His *encomienda*, Atotonilco (36 miles north of Mexico City near Tula; including *sujetos* Jomiltongo and Tepetitlan and dependency Zacamulpa, with a total of 1,810 tributaries in 1548), was paying $400 at mid-century. Pedraza and his wife, Ana Hernández, had eight daughters and four sons. When he died ca. 1550, he was succeeded by his son, Melchor, who was still the *encomendero* in 1597. The *encomienda* did not revert to the crown until 1688. Maese Diego received a coat of arms dated 28 January 1541.

(Gerhard, 295 and 298f.; Scholes and Adams, 24; Icaza, I, 206; Boyd-Bowman, I, no. 4465b, 147; *Nobiliario*, 242f.; Orozco y Berra, 65; *Actas*, I, 4.)

336. Juan PELÁEZ de Berrio
Poblador
From: Granada

Peláez, the *alcalde mayor* of Antequera, replaced Gonzalo de Alvarado as *encomendero* of Teposcolula (87 miles northwest of Antequera; six *barrios* in 1548) in 1529. His brother, first Audiencia judge (*oidor*) Licenciado Diego Delgadillo, was a vocal adversary of Cortés. After two years Peláez was exiled, and under the second Audiencia the *encomienda* reverted to the crown.

(Gerhard, 286 and 289; Boyd-Bowman, II, no. 4407, 131.)

337. Juan de la PEÑA Vallejo
Poblador
From: Granada
Parents: Notary Diego de la Peña and María de Vallejo

Peña arrived in Mexico City in 1524 to assume the post of assistant *factor* of the treasury and later *alcalde mayor* of the mines at Taxco, where he was also engaged in mining. He was a *vecino* of Mexico City and, after he brought his wife and two children from Spain in 1542, had his *casa poblada*, arms, and horses there. Peña became an *encomendero* in the late 1530s when he purchased the rights to Teticpac (60 miles south-southwest of Mexico City near Taxco; 10 *estancias* before the congregation of 1600) from first conqueror Francisco Quintero. He died ca. 1560 and was succeeded by a son, Juan de Vallejo, who was in turn succeeded in 1566 by his widow, doña Bernardina de Rivera. The *encomienda* was reassigned to don Luis de Velasco before 1586.

(Gerhard, 253f.; Boyd-Bowman, II, no. 4491, 133; Icaza, I, 202; Scholes and Adams, 45.)

338. Rodrigo de la PEÑA
First Conqueror
From: Miranda (Navarre ?)
Parents: Juan de Peña and Catalina de Miranda

Peña arrived in the Indies in 1516, joined Cortés three years later, and after the capture of Tenochtitlan was assigned the *encomienda* of Ucila (78 miles north-northeast of Antequera; two *estancias* in 1548). He was married and had one child, a daughter, who later married Juan Pérez de Villagrán of Valladolid. Ucila was reassigned by Nuño de Guzmán to Ginés de Cárdenas, but by 1534, under the second Audiencia, it had reverted to the crown.

(Gerhard, 302 and 304; Icaza, II, 158; Boyd-Bowman, I, no. 2392, 83 and II, no. 12271, 366; Orozco y Berra, 86.)

339. Bartolomé de PERALES
Poblador Antiguo
From: Medellín (La Serena, Extremadura)
Parents: Andrés de Perales and María Sánchez

Perales came to the Indies in 1512; fifteen years later he moved to New Spain to join the Cortés household. He became a *vecino* of Mexico City in 1528, about the same time that Cortés assigned him the *encomienda* of Tultitlan (17 miles north of Mexico City; four or five *sujetos*). Perales was married twice. His first wife, Mari Jiménez, came to the Indies in 1513. They had at least three children, a son Bartolomé and two daughters. Daughter María first married conqueror Pedro Lozano and when widowed married Diego de Ojeda. The older daughter married Juan de Jerez. Bartolomé married María de Saldaña, daughter of Mexico City notary Gregorio de Saldaña, from Palencia. She received one-third of Mecatalan as her dowry. By 1537 Mari Jiménez had died; Perales then married twice-wed Antonia Hernández, who succeeded as *encomendera* ca. 1540. Shortly thereafter Antonia married her fourth husband, *poblador* Juan de Moscoso of Zafra (Badajoz). Her spouses before Perales had been Miguel de Güemes and Baltasar Rodríguez. Antonia was dead by 1564. Three years later Tultitlan was a crown holding, but it was later assigned to don Luis de Velasco, the younger.

(Gerhard, 148f.; Icaza, I, 122, 164f., 217f. and II, 133; Boyd-Bowman, I, no. 458, 16 and no. 1481, 49; Scholes and Adams, 41; *Protocolos*, II, no. 2452, 164f. of 17 December 1537.)

340. Martín de PERALTA
Poblador

Peralta was a *vecino* of Mexico City; ca. 1536 Viceroy Mendoza assigned him the *encomienda* of Tezuatlan (150 miles southeast of Mexico City near Huajuapan de León; eight *sujetos* that paid a claimed $200 per year ca. 1547). His wife was doña Beatriz de Zayas of Santa Fe (Granada). They had three daughters and a son, the latter born ca. 1524, perhaps in Mexico City. Peralta died before 1546 and was succeeded first by his widow, then by his son, Alonso.

(Gerhard, 130f.; Icaza, I, 221; Scholes and Adams, 40; Boyd-Bowman, II, no. 4592, 137.)

341. Bachiller Alonso PÉREZ
Conqueror—Narváez
From: Trigueros (Huelva)
Parents: Fernando de Trigueros and Inés Sánchez

Pérez arrived in Cuba in 1519 and joined the Narváez *entrada* the following year. His defense of Juan Cansino in a suit against Cortés in 1521 did not seem to detract from his becoming a successful *encomendero*. Pérez served as *letrado* (counsel) for the Mexico City *cabildo* in 1526, the year after he became a *vecino* there. He was assigned Acamistlaguaca (68 miles south-southwest of Mexico City near Taxco; 18 *estancias* in 1569), Tezontepec (64 miles north of Mexico City near Tula; one *pueblo* in addition to the *cabecera*); he and *hidalgo* conqueror Alonso González also shared Teupantlan (78 miles southeast of Mexico City near Izúcar; five *barrios* in 1570). The Pérez share of the latter reverted to the crown ca. 1534 under the second Audiencia. Pérez was married and had five daughters and eight sons. His oldest son, Alonso, married a daughter of *poblador* Diego Gutiérrez de la Caballería, and a daughter married Rodrigo de Mendoza of Medellín, a *vecino* of Puebla. Pérez sent one son to New Mexico with Vázquez de Coronado and three other sons to Peru. He also brought a brother with five sons and two daughters, as well as other brothers, cousins, and uncles to New Spain. He died in the 1550s, succeeded by his son Alonso. By 1597 his grandson, don Alonso Pérez de Bocanegra, was the *encomendero*. The *encomiendas* were crown holdings by 1643.

(Gerhard, 161, 163, 252ff., 297 and 299; Icaza, I, 38ff., 133f. and II, 194; Boyd-Bowman, I, no. 2047, 69f.; Scholes and

Adams, 24 and 50; Orozco y Berra, 86; Actas, I, 12 and 102.)

342. Alonso PÉREZ de Zamora
Conqueror—Medel
From: Santa Marta (Zamora)
Parents: Alvaro Pérez and Catalina Domínguez

Pérez, his father, and his brother Alvaro arrived in New Spain on a ship outfitted by Hernando Medel 15 days after Narváez had been detained by Cortés. He was a *vecino* of Mexico City and received the *encomienda* of Tolcayuca (40 miles northeast of Mexico City near Pachuca; two *barrios* in 1569). Half was taken for the crown by 1525. Pérez was married and had five daughters and six sons. His father was killed during the siege of Tenochtitlan. His brother, the *encomendero* of Mazatlan (18 miles south-southwest of Tehuantepec), was also a *vecino* of Mexico City. A daughter, María, married Adrián de Benavente. Pérez died ca. 1560 and was succeeded by his son, Alonso. By 1643 the Pérez share of Tolcayuca had escheated.

(Gerhard, 210f.; Boyd-Bowman, I, no. 4854, 161; Icaza, I, 85 and 141; Scholes and Adams, 45; Orozco y Berra, 56.)

343. Hernán PÉREZ de Bocanegra (y Córdoba)—*Hidalgo*
Poblador
From: Córdoba
Parents: Bernardino de Bocanegra y Córdoba and doña Elvira Ponce de León

Pérez arrived in New Spain in 1526 from Cuba as a member of the entourage of Licenciado Luis Ponce de León (an uncle?). He became a *vecino* of Mexico City in the mid-1530s after living for a while in Villarreal, Chiapas. Pérez was an *alcalde ordinario* in Mexico City for 1537 and 1543 and *alcalde de mesta* for 1538 and 1544. In 1538 Viceroy Mendoza reassigned Acámbaro (114 miles west-northwest of Mexico City; 4,500 tributaries in 44 *sujetos* in 1570) to Pérez shortly after *poblador* Gonzalo Rioboz, the original *encomendero*, died. Ca. 1535 Pérez married doña Beatriz Pacheco of Trujillo (her mother was a lady in waiting to Queen Juana of Portugal) in Mexico City. They had at least two sons. Pérez was succeeded in the 1550s by a son, don Bernardino Pacheco de Bocanegra. Then ca. 1565 another son, don Nuño de Chaves de Bocanegra, replaced his brother as *encomendero*. This lineage acquired the title of Marqués de Villamayor in 1625.

(Gerhard, 65f.; Boyd-Bowman, II, no. 4004, 117 and no. 3201, 93; Scholes and Adams, 16.)

344. Juan PÉREZ de Arteaga—Interpreter
First Conqueror
From: Palencia
Parents: Antón Pérez de Arteaga from Biscay and Beatriz Pérez

Pérez arrived in Santo Domingo ca. 1502; by 1519 he was in Cuba as a member of Cortés' *entrada*. He served as an interpreter during his early years in New Spain and was supposedly called "Malinche" by many of the natives. Pérez became a *vecino* of Puebla, where he maintained his *casa poblada*, arms, and horses. In the early 1520s Cortés reassigned the *encomienda* of Tecali (20 miles southeast of Puebla; 3,830 tributaries in 1548) to Pérez and conqueror Francisco de Orduña, taking it from Francisco Montaño. Around 1522 Pérez was also assigned half of Guatinchan (15 miles southeast of Puebla; 2,570 tributaries in 1570). The other half of this grant was held in succession by first conqueror Diego de Colio, Pedro de Alvarado, and finally by *poblador antiguo* Alonso de Valencia (Valiente), before reverting to the crown in 1542. Pérez was married twice. His first wife, by whom he had a son and six daughters, was an Indian. His second wife was a daughter of conqueror Francisco de Santa Cruz. One of Pérez' daughters married *poblador* Diego Ramón, *vecino* of Puebla and a native of Utrera (Seville). Pérez was succeeded in the 1550s by his mestizo son of the same name, and then by a grandson. By 1600 a great-grandson, Francisco de Arteaga Pecheco, was the *encomendero*.

(Gerhard, 211f. and 255f.; Scholes and Adams, 48; Icaza, I, 19 and II, 201f.; Boyd-Bowman, I, no. 2489, 87 and II, no. 10485, 316; Orozco y Berra, 50.)

345. Juan PÉREZ de la Gama
Conqueror—Narváez

Pérez was a *vecino* of Puebla until ca. 1537, when he moved to Mexico City. His *encomienda* was three-fourths of the tribute from Cempoala (52 miles northeast of Mexico City; four *barrios* in 1580). The other one-fourth was initially assigned to conqueror Francisco Ramírez but reverted to the crown ca. 1531. By 1540 Pérez had relinquished his rights to the *encomienda* in favor of *poblador* Licenciado Rodrigo de Sandoval and returned to Spain. While in Mexico he married Isabel de Aguilar, widow of first conqueror Hernando Alonso.

(Gerhard, 67f.; Scholes and Adams, 30; Orozco y Berra, 65; Conway, 21.)

346. Juan PÉREZ de Herrera
Conqueror—Narváez
Parents: Garci Hernández and Elvira Hernández de Herrera

Pérez, his father, and his brother, Pedro Hernández, were all members of the Narváez *entrada*. He became a *vecino* of Mexico City and shared the *encomienda* of Epatlan (70 miles southeast of Mexico City near Izúcar; 11 *barrios* in 1548) with his brother Pedro. The grant was initially assigned to their father, but he died before he could take possession. Pérez was married and claimed fourteen children, four of them natural. Six of the fourteen were sons. He also had three sisters in New Spain. One was married to conqueror *encomendero* Martín de Calahorra, another to *hidalgo* conqueror *encomendero* Diego de Holguín, and the third was left a widow by an unnamed husband. Pérez received his brother's share of the *encomienda* through reassignment by the first Audiencia, but had the share taken a few years later. The remaining half was a crown holding by 1570.

(Gerhard, 160 and 163; Icaza, I, 41f.; Scholes and Adams, 21.)

347. Martín PÉREZ de Badajoz
First Conqueror
From: Badajoz

There is no record of when Pérez arrived in the Indies, but by 1518 he was in Cuba and the following year a member of the Cortés *entrada*. He was assigned the *encomienda* of Xalacingo (36 miles northwest of Jalapa; 3,000 tributaries in 1569). Pérez married Juana Rodríguez prior to coming to New Spain; it appears that they had no children. The *encomienda* reverted to the crown ca. 1536 when Pérez died.

(Gerhard, 375f.; Icaza, II, 96; Boyd-Bowman, I, no. 295, 11; Orozco y Berra, 50.)

348. García del PILAR
Conqueror—Narváez

By 1525 Pilar was a *vecino* of Mexico City. His later service as an interpreter under Nuño de Guzmán in Pánuco was considered by many to be notorious, but nonetheless it was rewarded. He held the *encomienda* of Toluca (35 miles west of Mexico City; 5,207 tributaries in 1569) between 1524 and 1526, after it had been taken from Cortés by the acting governors. Cortés later recovered the grant, minus a number of towns as part of the Marquesado. Pilar's natural daughter married Francisco de Cepeda, a *vecino* of Puebla.

(Gerhard, 330f.; Icaza, I, 185; *Protocolos*, I, no. 43, 35 of 30 August 1525; Orozco y Berra, 86; Chipman, 81f. and 224f.)

349. Ginés PINZÓN
First Conqueror
From: Palos (Huelva)
Parents: Francisco Hernández and Catalina Martín la Pinzona

Pinzón was in Cuba by 1518 and joined the Cortés *entrada* the following year. Fellow first conqueror Juan Pinzón may have been related, perhaps a brother. After the capture of Tenochtitlan and subsequent *entradas* he became a *vecino* of

Colima, where he held the very small *encomienda* of nearby Pitatlan. Pinzón was married but had no children. He was succeeded by his widow, who then married Hernando de Gamboa ca. 1550.

Note: A direct relationship to the Pinzón family which was active with the Columbus expeditions and influential in the Antilles from 1492 could not be established but is nonetheless assumed.

(Gerhard, 80; Scholes and Adams, 52; Boyd-Bowman, I, no. 2000, 68; Icaza, II, 232.)

350. Juan PINZÓN
First Conqueror
From: Palos (Huelva)

Pinzón was in Cuba in 1517, a member of Grijalva's expedition in 1518, and with his brother (?) Ginés Pinzón as a member of the Cortés *entrada* the following year. After the capture of Tenochtitlan and subsequent *entradas*, he became a *vecino* of Colima, where in 1526 he acquired, through reassignment from *poblador* Cristóbal de Valderrama, the *encomiendas* of Tecociapa, Atliacapan, Temecatipan, and Xaltepozotlan (in total, very few tributaries). Pinzón married Ginesa López, also from Palos. They had at least one son, Juan, and two daughters. One daughter married Jácome Rolando, a Genoese *vecino* of Pánuco. Another daughter married Juan Gómez of Cáceres, also a *vecino* of Colima. Pinzón died before 1547. He was succeeded by his widow, who was then the *encomendera*.

(Gerhard, 80; Scholes and Adams, 52; Icaza, I, 174, 181, 248 and II, 84; Orozco y Berra, 86; Boyd-Bowman, I, no. 2001, 68.)

351. Pedro de PLASENCIA
Poblador
From: Seville
Parents: Alvaro de Plasencia and Constanza Hernández de Oviedo

Plasencia came to New Spain in 1527 as a youth with the Nuño de Guzmán entourage and was with Guzmán in New Galicia in 1530. He became a *vecino* of Guadalajara, where he maintained his *casa poblada*, arms, horses, and family. His *encomienda* was a part of nearby Contla (ca. 1547 he claimed his share was 100 tributaries). He was married, but no children were claimed, nor was succession indicated.

(Icaza, II, 267f.; Boyd-Bowman, II, no. 9942, 301; Chipman, 136 f.; Gerhard 1982, 79.)

352. Juan de la PLAZA
Conqueror—Garay
From: Valencia

Plaza arrived in New Spain as a member of Garay's 1520 Pánuco venture and they took part in the siege and capture of Tenochtitlan. By 1527 he was a *vecino* of Zacatula and *encomendero* of Cinagua (50 miles north of Zacatula; four *barrios* in 1570). No more information concerning his personal life has been uncovered. It is presumed that he either died or left New Spain ca. 1533, the year Cinagua reverted to the crown.

(Gerhard, 74 and 75; Boyd-Bowman, II, no. 11583, 346; *Protocolos,* I, no. 756, 184 of 7 September 1527; Orozco y Berra, 70.)

353. Vasco PORCALLO
Conqueror—Narváez

Porcallo was a *vecino* of Mexico City by 1525—at least he was there in jail, suspected of having had a hand in the death of Hernando Cabrera. His innocence must have been established, for in the early 1530s the second Audiencia reassigned him half of the *encomienda* of Tlalcozautitlan (130 miles south of Mexico City; 1,970 tributaries in seven sub-*cabeceras,* 41 *estancias,* and numerous *barrios* in 1570). Conqueror Ruy González, a *regidor* of Mexico City, was the original *encomendero* and retained the other half. Porcallo was married, and ca. 1550 a son, Lorenzo Porcallo de Figueroa, succeeded him. A Lorenzo Porcallo was still the *encomendero* in 1611.

(Gerhard, 112f.; Scholes and Adams, 42; *Protocolos*, I, no. 265, 84 of 29 November 1525 and II, no. 2146, 92 of 5 January 1537; Orozco y Berra, 86.)

354. Diego PORRAS
Conqueror—Narváez
From: Arroyomolinos (Cáceres)
Parents: Diego Martínez and Isabel de Porras

Porras was in the Indies by 1512 and in Cuba by 1517 as a member of the Francisco Hernández de Córdoba expedition. He came to New Spain with Narváez and after the capture of Tenochtitlan went on the Pánuco *entrada*. Porras was a *vecino* of Mexico City, where he maintained his *casa poblada*, arms, and horses. He held the *encomienda* of Achachalintla (118 miles east-northeast of Mexico City; including sub-*cabeceras* Chumatlan and Mecatlan plus 21 *estancias* in 1569). Porras was married and had four daughters. He also claimed three natural sons. He was succeeded ca. 1550 by his daughter, María de Porras, who married Juan de Cuenca. By 1600 the tribute was paid to doña Ana María de Porras, a granddaughter, married to Fernando de Tovar. She was a widow and still *encomendera* twenty years later.

(Gerhard, 218f.; Boyd-Bowman, I, no. 871, 31; Icaza, I, 43f. and II, 152; Scholes and Adams, 25; Orozco y Berra, 86.)

355. Francisco PRECIADO
Poblador
From: Molina de Aragón (Guadalajara)
Parents: Juan Preciado and Catalina Ruiz

Preciado came to New Spain ca. 1530 after royal service in Granada, Navarre, and Africa. By 1547 he was a *vecino* of Colima, where he maintained his *casa poblada*. Three years later he became the *encomendero* of Zapotlanejo, Suchitlan, and Epatlan, all near Colima, by marrying Elvira de Arévalo, the widow of conqueror Diego Garrido and daughter of conqueror Alonso de Arévalo. In the late 1540s the income from the grant was $40 a year. The pair had one son and three daughters. Preciado was succeeded in the early 1560s by his son, Juan Preciado.

(Gerhard, 80; Icaza, I, 178; Boyd-Bowman, II, no. 4691, 140.)

356. Diego QUEJADA
Conqueror—Narváez
From: Espinosa de los Moneros (Burgos)
Parents: Diego Quejada and María de Salazar

Quejada was in Cuba by 1518 and with the Narváez *entrada* two years later. He was probably a *vecino* of Mexico City. Cortés assigned him the *encomienda* of Coacingo (88 miles southeast of Mexico City near Izúcar, a small *cabecera* that, by the late 1540s, paid $40, forty turkeys, and forty loads of corn in tribute). He was married and had a daughter. From the time Quejada left New Spain in the early 1540s into the 1550s, the tribute was collected by Pedro Núñez, Maese de Roa. Whether or not any of the tribute went to the support of Quejada's family is not known. The *encomienda* reverted to the crown in 1553.

(Gerhard, 160; Boyd-Bowman, I, no. 744, 25; Icaza, I, 20; Orozco y Berra, 65.)

357. Francisco de QUEVEDO
First Conqueror

In the early 1520s Quevedo, perhaps a *vecino* of Mexico City, was assigned one-fourth of Xilotepec (42 miles north-northwest of Mexico City near Tula; 18,336 tributaries ca. 1565). Other shares were held by conqueror Hernando Cantillana and *hidalgo* first conqueror Juan Núñez Sedeño. Quevedo, who was married, probably died in the 1530s. His widow married Juan Alemán (Henche), a merchant *vecino* of Mexico City from Hozenploze (?), Germany. The entire *encomienda* was reassigned to *hidalgo* first conqueror Juan Jaramillo de Salvatierra in 1533.

(Gerhard, 183ff.; Icaza, I, 166f.; Orozco y Berra, 50; *Protocolos*, II, no. 2216, 130f. of 16 June 1537; Boyd-Bowman, II, no. 12874, 388.)

358. Francisco QUINTERO—Mariner
First Conqueror
From: Huelva

Quintero, an early arrival in the Indies, was initially identified as a mariner. He was in Santo Domingo in 1504, in Cuba by 1518, and with Cortés the following year. Quintero became a *vecino* of Mexico City and was the first *encomendero* of Teticpac (66 miles south-southwest of Mexico City near Taxco; 10 *estancias* when congregated in 1600). Around 1530 he acquired the rights to half of Taimeo (126 miles northwest of Mexico City near Querétaro; 10 *estancias* in 1558), reassigned from conquistador Gaspar de Avila Quiñones. He was also an early holder of Yetecomac (70 miles north of Mexico City towards Tula). In the late 1530s Quintero sold his rights to Teticpac to *poblador* Juan de Peña Vallejo. During July of 1537 he traded his share of Taimeo and Yetecomac to *poblador* Francisco Rodríguez for Rodríguez' share of Petatlan (200 miles southwest of Mexico City near Zihuatanejo) and nearby Xalxucatitan plus $2,100, justifying the trade by claiming that the cold of the Mexico City region was hazardous to his health. Quintero's *encomiendas* reverted to the crown ca. 1548 when he went to Peru.

(Gerhard, 153f., 297, 300, 319f., and 394; Boyd-Bowman, I, no. 1779, 62; *Protocolos*, II, no. 2365, no. 2366, and no. 2367, 141f. of 13 July 1537; Scholes and Adams, 45; Orozco y Berra, 86.)

359. Diego RAMÍREZ—Carpenter
First Conqueror
From: Jerez de la Frontera (Cádiz)
Parents: Alonso Fernández Palomino and Juana Hernández

Ramírez was in Santo Domingo by 1505 and then in Cuba prior to joining the Cortés *entrada* of 1519. He was a *vecino* of Mexico City, where he maintained his *casa poblada*. Ramírez was the *encomendero* of Atengo (63 miles north of Mexico City near Tula, claimed by Ramírez to be very small). He married Ana de Acosta and, although he recognized his natural children and his *casa poblada* was occupied by nieces and a nephew, he left no legal heir other than his widow, who succeeded him ca. 1546. The *encomienda* reverted to the crown when she died in 1556.

(Gerhard, 295; Icaza, I, 11f.; Boyd-Bowman, I, no. 1179, 40; *Actas*, I, 47.)

360. Francisco RAMÍREZ *"el viejo"*
Conqueror
From: León

In 1520 Ramírez was the master of a ship sailing in support of Garay's Pánuco venture, then opted to support the Cortés *entrada* instead after finding the colony in Pánuco deserted. His arrival in New Spain, shortly after Miguel Díaz de Aux landed with his contingent, added 10 horsemen and 40 footmen to the Tenochtitlan campaign. Ramírez' personal entourage included his father, a brother-in-law, a servant, and two black slaves, not to speak of two horses. By the time he joined Cortés he had been in the Indies for 18 years, having arrived in Santo Domingo in 1502 with frey Nicolás de Ovando. By 1514 he was a *vecino* of Azúa, Cortés' starting point in the Caribbean. He was in Cuba in 1519 and sailed in support of Garay the following year. After the capture of Tenochtitlan Ramírez held the post of *alcalde mayor* of Santisteban del Puerto, Pánuco, where he was a *vecino*. He received *encomienda* tribute on a less than regular basis. He was the first holder of one-fourth of Cempoala (either the *cabecera* of Tequipilpan or Zapotlan, 140 miles south-southwest of Pánuco; four *barrios* in 1580), but it was taken for the crown in 1531. Alonso de Estrada, while governor, reassigned him Cicoac (135 miles south of Pánuco; 300 tributaries in 32 small *estancias* in 1592) from Cortés' holdings. Ramírez sold two-thirds of this grant to conqueror Pedro de Meneses in the 1540s, and the other third was assigned to conqueror Diego de Coria. Cortés had assigned Ramírez Metatepec (170 miles south of Pánuco; 1,541 tributaries in six *estancias* plus the *cabecera* in 1530) along with the appointment as *alcalde mayor*, but Nuño de Guzmán reassigned the grant, dividing it between his deputies, Licenciado Pedro de Mondragón (died ca. 1530) and Lope de Mendoza. Marcos Ruiz de Sevilla was the *encomendero* after 1540. In the early 1520s Cortés also assigned Ramírez Tequepilpa (190 miles south of Pánuco). He sold this grant too, to Pedro de Meneses, in the 1540s. Ramírez married Juana de Godoy of Córdoba. She accompanied him to Santo Domingo in 1502 and probably arrived in Pánuco in 1524 with their children, of whom they had at least two. A son Francisco, a *vecino* of Pánuco ca. 1547, was born in Santo Domingo, and a daughter Andrea, first married conqueror Juan Tirado and then when widowed married *poblador* Juan Blázquez. Ramírez died before 1547. He left no *encomienda* to his heirs, having sold his remaining rights in the 1540s.

(Gerhard, 67, 69, 133f., 216, 312f.; Icaza, I, 128f., II, 58 and 116; Chipman, 292; Boyd-Bowman, I, no. 2206, 75 and no. 1417, 48.)

361. Rodrigo RANGEL—*Hidalgo*
First Conqueror
From: Badajoz

Rangel arrived in Cuba in 1518 and was with Cortés the following year, initially as his chamberlain, and then as one of his captains. He was a founding *vecino* of Mexico City, serving as *alguacil mayor* in 1523, *alcalde ordinario* the following year and *regidor* from 1526 to 1529. Cholula (64 miles east-southeast of Mexico City; 40,000 to 100,000 families at contact, 20,000 tributaries in 1531, and 8,114 by 1588 in 35 *estancias* under six *cabeceras*) was reassigned to Rangel (by Cortés?) after having been first assigned to Andrés de Tapia. There is no record of wife or family. He died ca. 1529 of *bubas* (sores, often syphilis). The first Audiencia then divided Cholula between *poblador* Diego Fernández de Proaño and *poblador antiguo* Diego Suárez Pacheco, father of Cortés' first wife. The second Audiencia revoked the assignment in 1531 and took Cholula as a crown *encomienda*.

(Gerhard, 114f.; Boyd-Bowman, I, no. 279a, 11; Orozco y Berra, 87; Díaz del Castillo, I, 65.)

362. Juan Bautista de RAPALO
Conqueror—Narváez
From: Berazy, Genoa
Parents: Bartolomé Grifo and Ana Blanca

Rapalo was in Cuba in 1517, sailed with Grijalva in 1518 along the coast of Mexico, and went to New Spain with Narváez, siding with Cortés before the capture of Tenochtitlan. Later he served with *entradas* to Pánuco, Michoacán, Zacatula, Colima, and Jalisco. Rapalo was *encomendero* of Tecolapa and Totolmaloya (in the vicinity of Colima). He was a *vecino* of Colima, where he maintained his *casa poblada*, arms, and horses. He complained that his *encomienda* consisted of but one *estancia* with 25 Indians. He was married and claimed paternity of six children (four legitimate and two natural). The *encomienda* was divided between his widow, who received Tecolapa, and his son, Juan Bautista, who was assigned Totolmaloya. The widow later married *poblador* Juan Martel. The son's grant was a crown holding by 1553.

(Gerhard, 80; Boyd-Bowman, I, no. 5174, 173; Orozco y Berra, 51; Icaza, I, 52.)

363. Pablo RETAMALES
First Conqueror
From: Seville

Retamales was in Cuba by 1518 and joined the Cortés *entrada* the following year. He became a *vecino* of Mexico City and was assigned half of Mizquiaguala (60 miles north of Mexico City near Tula; one *estancia* in 1569). The other half of the *encomienda* was held by first conqueror Antonio Gutiérrez de Almodóvar of Ciudad Real. Retamales married Inés de

Contreras, who succeeded him as *encomendera* ca. 1536. Inés then married *poblador* Diego de Escobedo, a native of Seville. The *encomienda* was inherited by Retamales' son, Melchor de Contreras, in 1549. He was still the *encomendero* in 1597.

(Gerhard, 296 and 299; Boyd-Bowman, I, no. 3904; *Protocolos*, I, no. 975, 255 of 10 January 1528; Icaza, I, 113f. and II, 138; Scholes and Adams, 45.)

364. Francisco de RIBADEO
Conqueror—Narváez
From: Ribadeo (Lugo)

Ribadeo was in Cuba at least a year before joining the 1520 Narváez *entrada*. By the mid-1520s he was a *vecino* of Mexico City and warden of its jail. He was the first *encomendero* of Papaloticpac (200 miles southeast of Mexico City; seven *estancias* in 1579). In 1525 the acting governors assigned him at least a quarter of Tlapa (140 miles south of Mexico City; 6,802 tributaries in 1548) after taking it from Cortés. Alonso de Estrada, while governor in 1527, again reassigned Tlapa, Ribadeo's quarter going to first conqueror Bernaldino Vázquez de Tapia. Ribadeo married Leonor Osorio of Seville, widow of Basque conqueror Juan de Espinosa, who was killed during the siege of Tenochtitlan. She arrived in Mexico City ca. 1527 in the entourage of Andrés de Barrios' wife. When Ribadeo died in the early 1530s, Papaloticpac was reassigned to Francisco Casco. Leonor then married a third time. She claimed her third husband died of hunger on Cortés' California *entrada*. In 1547 Leonor had three children, but by which mate(s) is not known.

(Gerhard, 306, 308, 321, and 323; Boyd-Bowman, I, no. 2252, 77, no. 4782, 158, and II, no. 9861, 299; *Protocolos*, I, no. 1684, 351 of 15 October 1528; Icaza, I, 141f.; Orozco y Berra, 51.)

365. Alvaro de RIBERA—*Hidalgo*
Poblador Antiguo
From: Algarve, Portugal
Parents: Comendador Vicente Ribero and Catalina Alvarez

Ribera was in Tierra Firme by 1517, traveled between Cuba and Jamaica from 1518 and 1522, and arrived in New Spain as a member of Garay's 1523 *entrada*. He later served with the 1530 Nuño de Guzmán *entrada* to New Galicia. After 1533 Ribera became a *vecino* of Santiago de los Valles, where he maintained his *casa poblada*, arms, and horses, and was the *encomendero* of nearby Tamalacuaco and Tanlocuc. He and his wife, a Spanish woman, had five children. Ribera died ca. 1565 and was succeeded by a namesake son. By 1597 the *encomendero* was his grandson, Diego de Ribera.

Note: Ribera used the usual Spanish form for his own name, but a Portuguese-influenced form for that of his father.

(Gerhard, 355; Icaza, II, 261; Boyd-Bowman, I, no. 5278, 177; *Protocolos*, I, no. 1343, 289 of 14 May 1528.)

366. Tomás RIJOLES (Ecijoles)—
Interpreter
First Conqueror
From: Italy

It is not known when Rijoles arrived in the Indies, but he had been in the region for some time before joining Cortés' *entrada* in 1519. He served as an interpreter during the Tenochtitlan campaign and afterwards. A *vecino* of Mexico City, Rijoles was the *encomendero* of Tlalpotongo (140 miles northeast of Mexico City near Papantla; 10 tributaries in 1567). In the 1540s he sold the *encomienda* to *poblador* Jorge González. Rijoles married Beatriz Fernández of Seville (?), who accompanied him on various *entradas* subsequent to the capture of Mexico City. Their daughter Elvira Fernández was an only child.

(Gerhard, 218f.; Scholes and Adams, 20; Boyd-Bowman, I, no. 5234, 175; Icaza, I, 63f.; Orozco y Berra, 87; *Actas*, I, 115.)

367. Gonzalo RIOBOZ (Riobó) de Sotomayor
Poblador

Rioboz, a member of the Cortés household, became a *vecino* of Mexico City in mid-1524. This same year Cortés assigned him the *encomiendas* of Acámbaro (114 miles west-northwest of Mexico City; 4,500 tributaries in 1570), Araro, and Cinapecuaro (12 miles southwest of Acámbaro; seven *barrios* with perhaps 500 tributaries in 1548). The assignment survived the acting governors, the first and second Audiencias, and Viceroy Mendoza's initial scrutiny. Rioboz left no record of family. When he died in 1538, Acámbaro was reassigned to Hernán Pérez de Bocanegra. Araro and Cinapécuaro reverted to the crown.

(Gerhard, 65f., 318, and 320; *Protocolos*, I, no. 904, 214 of 30 December 1528; *Actas*, I, 18.)

368. Gonzalo de ROBLES—*Hidalgo*
Conqueror—Narváez
From: Mérida (La Serena, Extremadura)
Parents: García de Robles and Inés Gutiérrez de Rueda

Robles was in Cuba by 1519, with the Narváez *entrada* the following year, and after the capture of Tenochtitlan joined the *entrada* under Francisco de Orozco that subdued Oaxaca. He was an original settler and *vecino* of Oaxaca, where he had his *casa poblada*, arms, horses, and family. He held in *encomienda* Apuala (72 miles northwest of Antequera; two sub-*cabeceras*, Apazco and Xocoticpac, and 10 *estancias* among the three centers) and Cuetlahuistla (50 miles northwest of Antequera). Robles was married and had two sons and a daughter. When he died in the 1540s, he was succeeded by his son, García de Robles. After 1580 his grandson, don Juan de Robles, held Xocoticpac and Cuetlauistla, and another grandson, don García de Robles, was the *encomendero* of Apuala and Apazco.

(Gerhard, 285, 287, and 306; Icaza, I, 36f.; Boyd-Bowman, I, no. 500, 17; Scholes and Adams, 24; Orozco y Berra, 87.)

369. Cristóbal RODRÍGUEZ de Avalos—Trumpeter
First Conqueror

Rodríguez, a trumpeter in the Cortés *entrada*, shared Malinalco (26 miles south-southeast of Toluca; 10 *estancias* and 40 *barrios* between 1548 and 1571) with conquistador Cristóbal Romero until 1532, when the Romero half reverted to the crown. He was married and had two sons and three daughters. Rodríguez was succeeded ca. 1542 by his widow, who later married *poblador* Cristóbal Hidalgo of Zamora. Hidalgo served as guardian for the minor children. Rodríguez' son, Cristóbal, was the *encomendero* between 1560 and 1597. By 1604 a grandson, Agustín de Villasana, was the *encomendero*. This half of Malinalco was still in private hands in 1688.

(Gerhard, 170f.; Scholes and Adams, 45; Icaza, II, 14; Orozco y Berra, 87.)

370. Diego RODRÍGUEZ—Swordsmith
Poblador
From: Béjer del Castañar (Salamanca)
Parents: Juan Rodríguez and Mari García

Rodríguez arrived in New Spain as a member of Andrés de Barrios' 1524 entourage and became a *vecino* of Mexico City. There, in partnership with Juan Pérez, he plied his swordsmithing trade; an Alvaro de León was their apprentice for at least 18 months. Rodríguez shared Teutenango (40 miles southwest of Mexico City) and Cuzamala (125 miles southwest of Mexico City; 22 *sujetos* in 1570) with conqueror Juan de Burgos. He was married and in 1528 returned to Spain to bring his wife, three of her sisters, and two of his own sisters and a brother to Mexico City. Rodríguez had a daughter who married Juan de Madrid. His wife's sisters married conquerors who, for a time at least, were *encomenderos*. One of them, Mari Gutiérrez, married first conqueror Esteban Miguel, and another sister married first conqueror Domingo Martín. Neither Miguel nor Martín were *encomenderos*. Rodríguez' sister Elvira married first conqueror Juan Sánchez Galindo, another swordsmith. The second Audiencia reassigned all of Cuzamala to Burgos in 1533, and the Rodríguez share of Teutenango reverted to the crown in 1535. Evidently swordsmithing was a trade of diminishing importance in Mexico City. By 1547 Rodríguez was afflicted with palsy and unable to practice his trade; the slaves awarded him by virtue of his function as swordsmith were dead.

(Gerhard, 271 and 291ff.; Icaza, II, 126 and 123f. and 82; Boyd-Bowman, II, no. 7165, 221; *Protocolos*, I, no. 1466, 312 of 2 [*sic*] September 1528.)

371. Diego RODRÍGUEZ de Valladolid
Poblador Antiguo
From: Castronuño (Valladolid)
Parents: Cristóbal Rodríguez and Inés Rodríguez

Rodríguez had been in the Indies since 1513. From 1528 to 1533, when he left for Spain, he was the *encomendero* of Urapa and Guanaxo (12 miles southwest of Pátzcuaro, perhaps consisting of three *cabeceras*; nearby Istario; Ario, 21 miles to the southwest; and Uredo, 45 miles west-southwest). There is no record of where he was a *vecino*. The *encomienda* was then reassigned to *hidalgo* Juan Alonso de Sosa, the treasurer of New Spain.

Note: There was another *encomendero* Diego Rodríguez, perhaps a conquistador. His unnamed *encomienda* was left to his widow for their children. She then married *poblador* Gabriel Lopéz, a *vecino* of San Miguel, Cuyacán (New Galicia?), who administered the grant until the children came of age (Icaza, II, 238f.).

(Gerhard, 345f. and 350; Boyd-Bowman, I, no. 4481, 148.)

372. Francisco RODRÍGUEZ
Conqueror—?

Rodríguez, a *vecino* of Zacatula by 1531, received half of the *encomiendas* of Petatlan (70 miles south-southeast of Zacatula) and Xalxucatitan (near Zacatula) through reassignment. Six years later he traded these grants plus $2,100 for half of Taimeo (200 miles north-northeast of Zacatula; ten *estancias* in 1558) and Yetecomac (250 miles northeast of Zacatula near Tula; one *sujeto* in 1537) with first conqueror Francisco Quintero, a *vecino* of Mexico City. Rodríguez married Inés Alvarez de Gibraleón and had a number of children. His widow claimed succession as *encomendera* of Taimeo and Yetecomac for herself and the children, but the crown took possession ca. 1550, five years after Rodríguez died. Thirteen years later the *encomienda* was ordered restored to their son, Pedro Sánchez.

(Gerhard, 297, 300, 319f., and 394; *Protocolos*, II, no. 2365, no. 2366, and no. 2367, 142f. of 13 July 1537; Boyd-Bowman, I, no. 1782, 62 (?); Scholes and Adams, 11.)

373. Francisco RODRÍGUEZ de Guadalcanal
Poblador
From: Guadalcanal (Maestrazgo de León)
Parents: Juan González and Isabel Rodríguez

Rodríguez, perhaps a wineskin maker (*odrero*), arrived in New Spain ca. 1528 and became a *vecino* of Mexico City, where he maintained his *casa poblada*, arms, horses, and family. He became an *encomendero* by purchasing Tetela (140 miles southwest of Mexico City; 24 *estancias* in 1538 of natives speaking four different languages—Náhuatl, Cuitlatec, Chontal, and Tepuztec) from conqueror Juan de Mansilla. He was married and by 1547 supported a widowed sister and her marriageable daughter. By 1594 he had been succeeded as *encomendero* by Juan de Silva. Tetela was a crown property after 1688.

(Gerhard, 291 and 293; Icaza, I, 216f.; Boyd-Bowman, II, no. 8502, 263; Scholes and Adams, 19.)

374. Francisco RODRÍGUEZ Magariño
First Conqueror

Rodríguez, a *vecino* of Zacatula, was the *encomendero* of Chilacachapa (140 miles east-northeast of Zacatula near Taxco; five or six *sujetos* in 1570), Cuezala (145 miles east of Zacatula, also near Taxco; two sub-*cabeceras*—Apatla and Tlanexpatla—with 20 *estancias* between the three), Tlacotepec (83 miles east of Zacatula; 13 *sujetos* in 1579) and Chichicuatla (180 miles northeast of Zacatula near Toluca), all granted him by Cortés in the early 1520s. He was married and had four sons and a daughter. The daughter married *poblador* Juan de Busto, a *vecino* of Pánuco. Rodríguez died ca. 1548, and his son, Juan Rodríguez Enríquez Magariño, inherited. The three younger sons, Francisco, Gaspar and Melchor, were placed under the guardianship of Martín de Solís. Juan Rodríguez was succeeded ca. 1565 by his widow, Polonia de la Serna. She was still the *encomendera* in 1597.

(Gerhard, 153f., 271, and 291f.; Icaza, I, 146 and 191; Scholes and Adams, 27; Orozco y Berra, 51; *Protocolos*, I, no. 536, 142 of 8 May 1527; no. 545, 143 of 14 May 1527; no. 875, 206 of 11 November 1527; no. 885; and no. 888, 208 of 14 November 1527.)

375. Gonzalo RODRÍGUEZ de la Magdalena
Conqueror—Narváez
From: Seville
Parents: Alonso García de la Magdalena and Constanza Rodríguez

Rodríguez was in Cuba in 1519 and a member of the Narváez *entrada* the following year. He was initially a *vecino* of Mexico City, but moved to Puebla in 1534, where he maintained his *casa poblada*, arms, horses, and family. By 1547 he was augmenting his income by operating an inn. Rodríguez was reassigned half of the *encomienda* of Quechula (45 miles east-southeast of Puebla; 34 named *sujetos* in 1580) when the original *encomendero*, conqueror Fernando de Villanueva, died. Villanueva's brother, Pedro, held the other half. Rodríguez married an Indian and had five sons and three daughters. He was succeeded in the 1560s by a son, Alonso Coronado (Rodríguez). By 1600 a grandson, Gonzalo Coronado, was the *encomendero*. A coat of arms was awarded to Rodríguez, dated 8 July 1538.

(Gerhard, 278f.; Scholes and Adams, 17; Icaza, II, 13f.; Boyd-Bowman, I, no. 3932, 130; Orozco y Berra, 66; *Nobiliario*, 239f.)

376. Gonzalo RODRÍGUEZ de Ocaña
Conqueror—Narváez
From: Toledo

Rodríguez served as *alguacil de campo* (in charge of camp cleanliness) for the Narváez *entrada* and, after siding with Cortés at Veracruz, was stable master for the Tenochtitlan campaign. After the capture of Tenochtitlan he continued in the employ of Cortés. He was a *vecino* of Mexico City and a *regidor* there in 1527. During 1527 he acquired the *encomienda* of Tochimilco (64 miles southeast of Mexico City; 3,000 tributaries in nine *estancias* in 1570—reduced to 1,200 tributaries by 1588) by reassignment, the original holder, Cristóbal Pacheco, having died two years previous. Perhaps Rodríguez was married. A daughter (natural ?) married *poblador* Gonzalo Hernández Buenos Años of Santos (Badajoz) and received half of Tochimilco in dowry. When Rodríguez died in February 1546, however, the Audiencia determined that there was no legal heir and took the *encomienda* for the crown.

(Gerhard, 329; Icaza, I, 155; Orozco y Berra, 66; *BAGN*, XII, 22.)

377. Gonzalo RODRÍGUEZ de Villafuerte—*Hidalgo*
Poblador
From: Salamanca
Parents: Licenciado Gonzalo de Villafuerte and doña Catalina Ortiz

Rodríguez arrived in New Spain ca. 1528; by 1532 he was a *vecino* of Coatzacoalcos, the locale of his *casa poblada* and family into the late 1540s. Rodríguez shared the *encomienda* of Minzapa (west of Coatzacoalcos) with *poblador* Juan de España, reassigned from first conqueror Lorenzo Genovés. By the 1530s he was married and had a family. By the late 1540s his first wife had died and he remarried, this time to María del Rincón. This was her third union; other husbands were first conquerors Alvaro and Pedro Maldonado, possibly related. The Maldonados, María, and Rodríguez were all from Salamanca. Rodríguez and María had one daughter. María had also succeeded her previous husbands as *encomendera* of their grants, including Almolonga, Atezcac (50 tributaries in 1580), Ocuequila, Pangololutla, Mazatlaxaya, and Xalomulco, although two others were taken from her in 1528. All of these *encomiendas* were some 180 miles northwest of Coatzacoalcos, near Jalapa. Rodríguez' family in New Spain included brothers Miguel Rodríguez de Villafuerte and Juan Rodríguez de Villafuerte. Gonzalo died ca. 1575, whereupon all of the *encomiendas* reverted to the crown—Minzapa more than likely for lack of tributaries, and the others near Jalapa for having completed the third life.

(Gerhard, 139f. and 375ff.; *Protocolos*, II, no. 2640, 222 of 13 January 1552; Icaza, I, 258; Boyd-Bowman, II, no. 7571, 234; Scholes and Adams, 21.)

378. Juan RODRÍGUEZ
Poblador
From: San Martín de Trevejo (Cáceres)
Parents: Francisco Pérez and Mari Rodríguez

Rodríguez arrived in New Spain as a member of the Nuño de Guzmán entourage and became a *vecino* of Santisteban del Puerto, Pánuco. He acquired Guazalingo (88 miles south-southwest of Pánuco; 265 tributaries ca. 1532 and seven *estancias* 16 years later) from first conqueror Diego González sometime after 1533. By 1548 he had sold his rights to the *encomienda* to *poblador* Gabriel de Aguilar. Rodríguez left no record of family. In the 1550s, then a *vecino* of Puebla, he was actively engaged in the black slave trade and tithe farming.

(Gerhard, 243f.; Scholes and Adams, 18; Chipman, 292; Boyd-Bowman, II, no. 3085, 89; *Protocolos*, II, no. 2550 to no. 2554, 193f., all dated 19 October 1551; *ENE*, I, 96.)

379. Juan de RODRÍGUEZ Bejerano
First Conqueror

Rodríguez, perhaps a *vecino* of Mexico City, shared the *encomienda* of Tabaliloca (also called Tabalilpa and San Francisco Tlagualipa, 58 miles north of Mexico City near Tula; one *estancia* ca. 1550) with *poblador* Rodrigo de Albornoz after 1536. It was reassigned to them after an unsuccessful suit for succession by the heirs of first conqueror Juan Catalán, the original *encomendero*. The Albornoz half reverted under the New Laws in 1544. The Rodríguez share reverted after his death two years later.

(Gerhard, 297 and 299; Orozco y Berra, 51; *Protocolos*, I, no. 196, 71 of 8 November 1525).

380. Juan RODRÍGUEZ de Salas—Mason
First Conqueror

Rodríguez was a *vecino* of Mexico City in 1527. He was *encomendero* of

Macuiltianguis (42 miles east-northeast of Antequera; two *sujetos* with about 500 Zapotec tributaries in 1550) and Yoloxinecuila (48 miles north-northeast of Antequera; about 500 Chinantecan tributaries in 1550). Rodríguez contracted Francisco Gutiérrez to administer Macuiltianguis in October 1527. Gutiérrez was to receive one-sixth of the income from the grant for his services. Rodríguez was married and had at least two children. A daughter married first conqueror Melchor de Alanés, a *vecino* of Antequera. Rodríguez was succeeded as *encomendero* by a son, Sebastián de Salas, before 1547. By 1599 his grandson, Cristóbal de Salas, was the *encomendero*. Both grants reverted to the crown by 1647.

(Gerhard, 258f.; Scholes and Adams, 53; Icaza, I, 54 and 252; *Protocolos*, I, no. 797, 192f., dated 11 October 1527.)

381. Juan RODRÍGUEZ de Villafuerte—
    Hidalgo
    First Conqueror
    From: Salamanca
    Parents: Licenciado Gonzalo de Villafuerte and doña Catalina Ortiz

Rodríguez was in Cuba by 1518. The following year he was a member of the Cortés *entrada*, serving first as *maestre de campo* and then as a brigantine captain during the siege and capture of Tenochtitlan. He was initially a *vecino* of Mexico City but by 1528 claimed Zacatula as his residence. In the early 1520s Cortés assigned him the *encomienda* of Mescaltepec (northwest of Acapulco; nine sub-*cabeceras*, one of which was the port of Acapulco, and eleven minor *estancias* in 1569). Rodríguez married doña Juana de Zúñiga and had one daughter, who married García de Albornoz. She inherited the *encomienda* in the 1540s and was listed as the sole *encomendera* from 1587 to 1597. Mescaltepec was a crown holding by 1643. Rodríguez also had two brothers in the Indies, *pobladores* Miguel Rodríguez de Villafuerte and Gonzalo Rodríguez de Villafuerte.

(Gerhard, 39, 41, and 394; Icaza, I, 224f.; Scholes and Adams, 23; Boyd-Bowman, I, 2707, 95; *Protocolos*, I, no. 228, 77 of 17 November 1525 and no. 1155, 256 of 11 March 1528.)

382. Martín RODRÍGUEZ—Tailor
    Poblador Antiguo
    From: Badajoz
    Parents: Diego Rodríguez and Constanza Rodríguez

Rodríguez arrived in the Indies ca. 1512. By 1527 he was a *vecino* of Mexico City, where he was identified as a tailor and functioned as a *tratante* or petty trader. Rodríguez was the *encomendero* of Cozautepec (300 miles southeast of Mexico City, 75 miles south of Antequera; 38 tributaries in 1565 and even fewer in the 1580s) until it reverted to the crown in November of 1535. There was no mention of Rodríguez after this date.

(Gerhard, 72f.; *Protocolos*, I, no. 515, 138 of 26 April 1527; Boyd-Bowman, I, no. 300, 11.)

383. Melchor RODRÍGUEZ
    Poblador

Rodríguez, an interpreter in Pánuco under both Cortés and Guzmán, was a *vecino* of Santisteban del Puerto. He was the *encomendero* of Tantoyuca (an *estancia* of Metatepec 45 miles south of Pánuco; 165 tributaries in 1532), also referred to as Tantoyeque and Tantoyetle. Rodríguez was married and was succeeded by his namesake son before 1564.

(Chipman, 208 and 292; Scholes and Adams, 49f.; Gerhard, 216.)

384. Pedro RODRÍGUEZ de Escobar
    First Conqueror
    From: Alaejos (Valladolid)
    Father: —— de Escobar

Rodríguez was in Cuba in 1517, with Grijalva in 1518, and a member of the Cortés *entrada* the following year. Cortés assigned Rodríguez Ixmiquilpan (35 miles northwest of Pachuca; 4,027 tributaries in

1570) even though he had established his residence in Guatemala. He was married to Beatriz Palacios (?), but she and their children remained in Ciudad Rodrigo, Salamanca. The *encomienda* was reassigned by the acting governors in 1525 because Rodríguez was not present in Mexico, either to administer his grant or to protect his interest.

(Gerhard, 155; Boyd-Bowman, I, no. 4475, 147f.; Icaza, I, 21; Orozco y Berra, 87.)

385. Sebastián RODRÍGUEZ—
Crossbowman
First Conqueror
From: Olveira, Portugal
Parents: Juan Váez and Isabel Rodríguez

Rodríguez was in Cuba by 1518 and served in the Cortés *entrada* as a crossbowman/crossbow maker. He was a *vecino* of Mexico City until 1534, then became a *vecino* and *regidor* of Puebla, where he maintained his *casa poblada*, arms, and horses. Cortés assigned him the *encomienda* of Chocaman and Tozongo (85 miles east of Puebla near Córdoba). By 1547 Tozongo had been reassigned and Chocaman was paying a claimed $120 per year. He and his wife, María de Villanueva, had two children, one of them a son. A daughter married Bartolomé Ponce Bermijo, a native of Lorca (Murcia), who was a *vecino* of Mexico City. Rodríguez died in the 1560s. He was succeeded by his son and then by his son's widow, who remained the *encomendera* until she died in 1606, the year the grant reverted to crown possession.

(Gerhard, 83f.; Scholes and Adams, 26; Boyd-Bowman, I, no. 5280, 177; Icaza, I, 14 and 182; Orozco y Berra, 88; *Actas*, I, 51.)

386. Diego (de las) ROELAS
Poblador Antiguo
From: Seville
Parents: Luis Roelas and María Roelas

Roelas, a 1512 arrival in the Indies, went to Tierra Firme two years later and by 1526 was associated with Diego de Almagro. He then came to New Spain, allied himself with Nuño de Guzmán, and became a *vecino* of Santisteban del Puerto, Pánuco. By 1528 he had Tancolol (vicinity of Pánuco; 32 tributaries in 1532) and Nespa (vicinity of Valles; 1734 tributaries in 1532) reassigned to him in *encomienda*. Four years later he also shared Tauzán (vicinity of Pánuco; 887 tributaries in 1532) with Alonso Navarrete, and in 1534 he acquired Tempoal (45 miles south of Pánuco; 1,120 tributaries in 1532) from Juan de Villagrán. By 1535 Roelas was receiving tribute from over 3,000 Indians. Two years later he sold Nespa and his share of Tauzan to Alonso Navarrete. Roelas married Isabel de Escobar of Seville, the daughter of Francisco de Párraga and Florentina de Escobar. They had no children but did raise two nephews in their household. Isabel succeeded as *encomendera* when Roelas died some time shortly before 1547. The *encomienda* reverted to the crown after her death in 1564.

(Gerhard, 216f. and 335; Scholes and Adams, 46; Icaza, I, 236; Chipman, 292f.; Boyd-Bowman, I, no. 3946, 131.)

387. Bartolomé ROMÁN (Romano)—
Notary
Conqueror—Ponce de León

Román was an early *vecino* of Medellín and *encomendero* of Tepetotutla (85 miles south of Medellín) and Ixguacan (54 miles west of Medellín near Jalapa, 12 *estancias* in 1580). He was married but had no children. In the 1540s he was succeeded by his widow, who by 1551 had married *poblador* Francisco de Reinoso from Bobadilla de Rioseco (Palencia). There were no children of this union either. Reinoso became the *encomendero* when his wife died, sometime before 1564. The *encomienda* reverted to the crown when Reinoso died ca. 1580, having served three "lives."

(Gerhard, 302, 304, 375, and 377; Scholes and Adams, 39; Orozco y Berra, 88.)

388. Alonso ROMERO
First Conqueror
From: San Vicente (Soria)
Parents: Juan and María Romero

Romero was in Santo Domingo by 1512 and a *vecino* of Guahava, Hispaniola, two years later. He was in Cuba in 1518 and a member of the Cortés *entrada* the following year. After the capture of Tenochtitlan Romero became a *vecino* of Veracruz and *encomendero* of Tlacotalpa (assigned by Cortés, 70 miles southeast of Veracruz; five dependencies in 1570) in addition to sharing Topla (280 miles northwest of Veracruz near Valles; 179 tributaries in 1532) with *poblador* Cristóbal de Ortega. He and his wife, Isabel Vélez, had no children. When Romero died in the 1530s, Isabel succeeded him as *encomendera* of Tlacotalpa. The Topla share was acquired by Ortega. Tlacotalpa reverted to the crown when Isabel died in September 1541.

(Gerhard, 355, 360 and 362; Boyd-Bowman, I, no. 4236, 138; Orozco y Berra, 88.)

389. Cristóbal ROMERO
Conqueror—?
From: Lucena (Córdoba)
Parents: Juan Romero and Leonor Gutiérrez

Romero was in the Indies by 1516 and arrived in New Spain in time to take part in the capture of Tenochtitlan. After that he was a member of an *entrada* to Pánuco. Romero became a *vecino* of Mexico City and shared the *encomienda* of Malinalco (40 miles southwest of Mexico City; 10 *estancias* and 40 *barrios* in 1548) with first conqueror Cristóbal Rodríguez de Avalos. By 1533 he was a *vecino* of Guadalajara and *encomendero* of nearby Tequescistlan, Epatlan, and Tepaca (15 to 18 miles northwest of Guadalajara), a result of *entrada* service to New Galicia. In the 1540s Romero bought the rights to Yagualica (30 miles northeast of Guadalajara) from Juan de Alaejos. His share of Malinalco reverted to the crown when he moved to Guadalajara. Romero was married and had nine children, three of them sons. His *encomienda* income, by 1547, was augmented by $100 from the treasury. The rights to Yagualica were given to a daughter ca. 1550 when she married Francisco de Olivares. By 1570 the *encomendero* of the other three grants was a son, Miguel Romero.

(Gerhard, 170f.; Icaza, II, 284 and 286; Boyd-Bowman, I, no. 1477, 49; Gerhard 1982, 79, and 122.)

390. Juan ROMERO
Poblador

Romero arrived in New Spain ca. 1527, perhaps as a member of the Nuño de Guzmán entourage. He became a *vecino* of Pánuco, and Guzmán assigned him the *encomienda* of Coyutla (vicinity of Pánuco; 478 tributaries in 1532, 1547 income a claimed $360—still three *estancias* in 1571). Romero was married and had at least one son. Ca. 1540 he was succeeded by his widow. She soon married Miguel de Arriaga, whom she succeeded; subsequently she married Andrés Moro, a native of Portillo (Toledo) and a *vecino* of Pánuco. Ca. 1550 she retained one-third of the tribute and her son Juan by Romero had inherited the remainder. A Juan Romero (a grandson?) was the *encomendero* in 1597.

(Gerhard, 215; Scholes and Adams, 49; Chipman, 292; Icaza, II, 217.)

391. Francisco de ROSALES—Merchant
Poblador
From: Medina del Pomar (Burgos)
Parents: Ruy Díaz de Rosales and Constanza de Medinilla

Rosales arrived in New Spain after the capture of Tenochtitlan, in either late 1521 or early 1522. He became a *vecino* of Veracruz, where he was a merchant as well as holding office as *alcalde*. Rosales was the *encomendero* of Aticpac and Tenango (80 miles south-southwest of Veracruz). He was married but left no record of children. When he died ca. 1560, the *encomienda* reverted to the crown.

(Gerhard, 301; Boyd-Bowman, II, no. 2497, 70; Icaza, I, 257; *Protocolos*, I, no. 583, 151 of 8 June 1527 and II, no. 2163 of 9 January 1537.)

392. Andrés de ROZAS
First Conqueror
From: Huelgas de Burgos (Burgos)
Parents: Andrés de Rozas and Elvira de Ormienta

Rozas arrived in the Indies in 1512, was in Cuba in 1518, and joined the Cortés *entrada* the following year. After the conquest he became a *vecino* of Mexico City, where he had his *casa poblada*. His *encomienda*, Suchitlan (48 miles north-northwest of Mexico City near Tula; five *visitas* in 1570), was reassigned to him in the early 1520s after being held for a short time by Rodrigo de Salvatierra. He was married and had at least one son and two daughters. One daughter married *poblador* Manuel de Torres of Badajoz and another Alonso Ruiz of Baeza, who was a *vecino* of Antequera and usher of the Audiencia. Around 1565 Rozas was succeeded by a namesake son still the *encomendero* in 1604.

(Gerhard, 332 and 334; Scholes and Adams, 16; Boyd-Bowman, I, no. 768, 26; Icaza, I, 80, 153 and 226; Orozco y Berra, 52.)

393. Alonso RUIZ
Poblador
From: Baeza (Jaén)
Parents: Gonzola Ruiz and Juana Gutiérrez, both originally from Nombela (Toledo) and *vecinos* of Baeza by the 1520s

Ruiz arrived in New Spain in 1529 with the first Audiencia and served as its usher. Initially a *vecino* of Mexico City, he changed his residence to Antequera ca. 1540 when Viceroy Mendoza reassigned Ocelotepec (55 miles south-southeast of Antequera; 25 *estancias* in 1580) to him after the Indians of the *encomienda* killed *poblador* Alonso Martín Rieros (Riberos). the original *encomendero*. Ruiz married a daughter of *encomendero* first conqueror Andrés de Rozas and established a *casa poblada*, arms, and horses in Antequera. He was succeeded ca. 1565 by his son, Andrés Ruiz de Rosas, still the *encomendero* in 1609.

(Gerhard, 188ff.; Icaza, I, 226; Boyd-Bowman, II, no. 5570, 169; Scholes and Adams, 20.)

394. Diego RUIZ
First Conqueror
From: Moguer (Huelva)
Parents: Diego Ruiz and Mari Sánchez

Ruiz was in Cuba at least a year before joining the 1519 Cortés *entrada*. After the capture of Tenochtitlan and subsequent *entradas* he became a *vecino* of Zacatula, where he had his *casa poblada*. Ruiz was *encomendero* of half of nearby Huitaluta and Coyuca by 1550. He was married and had five children, four of them sons. Ruiz died ca. 1564, and by 1568 his son, Juan Ruiz de Mendoza, had inherited. Juan was still the *encomendero* 30 years later.

(Gerhard, 394; Scholes and Adams, 22; Icaza, I, 28f.; Boyd-Bowman, I, no. 1863, 64.)

395. Gonzalo RUIZ—*Hidalgo*
Poblador
From: Moguer (Huelva)

Ruiz arrived in New Spain ca. 1528 with an appointment as perpetual *regidor* of Mexico City; he became a *vecino* and took his seat on the *cabildo* 1 January 1529, serving until 1559. Around 1540 Viceroy Mendoza reassigned him the *encomienda* of Cuiseo (130 miles southwest of Mexico City; 40 to 50 *estancias* ca. 1558). This grant had first been assigned to *poblador* Nicolás López de Palacios Rubios by Cortés, then taken by the second Audiencia for the crown. Ruiz married doña Juana de Torres but had no children. A Fernando Ruiz "*muchacho*" (a nephew?) accompanied Ruiz from Spain and seems to have been a member of the household. There does not appear to be any relationship between Gonzalo and first conqueror Diego Ruiz, even though they both came from Moguer. Doña Juana succeeded as *encomendera* when Ruiz died ca. 1559. When she in turn died, six years later, the *encomienda* reverted to the crown. Cuiseo was soon reassigned to don Luis de Velasco the younger.

(Gerhard, 135f.; Scholes and Adams, 29; Icaza, II, 6; Boyd-Bowman, II, no. 5236 and no. 5237, 157.)

396. Hernán RUIZ de la Peña
Conqueror—?

Before 1526 Ruiz, probably a *vecino* of Colima, was assigned half of the *encomienda* of Autlan (50 miles northwest of Colima). He was married and had a daughter married to Gaspar de Tapia. Ruiz died ca. 1562 and was succeeded by this daughter. The *encomendero* in 1597 was Diego de Tapia, Ruiz' grandson.

(Gerhard, 59; Scholes and Adams, 50.)

397. Jerónimo RUIZ de la Mota (Zárate)—
Hidalgo
Conqueror—Alderete
From: Burgos
Parents: Regidor Pedro de la Mota and Leonor de la Peña

Ruiz arrived in New Spain in March of 1521 as a captain of a ship under Alderete, joined the Cortés *entrada* at Texcoco, and served as a brigantine captain during the capture of Tenochtitlan. He was a *vecino* of Mexico City, where he maintained his *casa poblada* and "did what was necessary." Ruiz was a *regidor* of the city in 1528, *alcalde ordinario* in 1530, 1537, 1542, and 1547; and *alcalde de mesta* in 1538, 1543, and 1548. He was assigned the *encomiendas* of Mitlatonga (205 miles southeast of Mexico City near Antequera; five *barrios* and five *estancias* in 1550) and Chiapa (37 miles northwest of Mexico City; 22 or more *estancias* in 1570). Around 1531 he married a daughter of conqueror Francisco de Orduña and by 1547 had six daughters and five sons. The oldest daughter married *poblador* Juan de Torres, a *vecino* of Puebla and a veteran of Africa. Ruiz died ca. 1560 and was succeeded as *encomendero* by his oldest son, don Antonio de Orduña. By 1597 a grandson with the same name was the *encomendero*.

(Gerhard, 200, 202, 383, and 385; Scholes and Adams, 28; Icaza, I, 72 and II, 202; Boyd-Bowman, II, no. 2364a, 66 and no. 6700, 204; Orozco y Berra, 73; *Actas*, V, 203.)

398. Juan RUIZ de Alanís
Conqueror—Narváez
From: Alanís (Seville)
Parents: Juan Ruiz and Juana Ruiz

Ruiz was in Cuba by 1519 and joined the Narváez *entrada* the following year. He became a *vecino* of Mexico City (?) and probably in the 1530s was assigned half of the *encomienda* of Tehuacán (145 miles southeast of Mexico City; 3,000 tributaries in 1570), shared with the crown. He was married and had children, and ca. 1550 was succeeded by a son, Antonio Ruiz de Castañeda.

(Gerhard, 261f.; Scholes and Adams, 48; Boyd-Bowman, I, no. 2974, 105; Orozco y Berra, 66; *Protocolos*, II, no. 2458, 166 of 29 December, 37.)

399. Marcos RUIZ
First Conqueror
From: Seville
Parents: Andrés Ruiz and Catalina Hernández

Ruiz' initial trip to the Indies was in 1511, his second in 1515. He was in Cuba by 1518 and a member of the Cortés *entrada* the following year. A *vecino* of Mexico City, he was the first *encomendero* of Epazoyuca (52 miles northeast of Mexico City near Pachuca; four *barrios* and four *estancias* in 1580) and shared Guaniqueo (140 miles west of Mexico City near Morelia; 44 *estancias* in 1524) with Hernando Alonso. All of Guaniqueo was reassigned to Cortés when Alonso was executed in

1528 as a relapsed Jew. Toward 1540 Ruiz exchanged Epazoyuca for Metatepec (144 miles north-northeast of Mexico City, 40 miles south of Pánuco; 1,540 tributaries in 1532) with Lope de Mendoza. Metatepec was initially assigned by Cortés to Francisco Ramírez, then reassigned by Nuño de Guzmán to Licenciado Pedro de Mondragón and Lope de Mendoza. When Mondragón died ca. 1530 all of the tribute went to Mendoza. Ruiz remarried after 1538 to Beatriz de Escobar, a native of Seville. He had daughters by a previous marriage. One of them, Juana Ruiz, married *poblador antiguo* Antón (Hontañon) Anguiano of Seville and when widowed married *poblador* Lloriente Jiménez of Ibdes in Zaragoza (or nearby Judes, Soria?). Another daughter married *poblador* Francisco Nieto of Trujillo, a *vecino* of Pánuco. Ruiz' widow succeeded as *encomendera* ca. 1543. She then married *poblador* Pedro de Fuentes of Jerez de la Frontera (Cádiz), who then became the *encomendero*. She and a son by Fuentes inherited in 1560. A Juan Hernández was the *encomendero* in 1597.

(Gerhard, 67, 69, 216, 345, 351; Chipman, 292; *Protocolos*, I, no. 894, 209 of 15 November 1527; Scholes and Adams, 46; Boyd-Bowman, I, no. 3967, 131; Icaza, I, 138, 172, 218; Orozco y Berra, 52.)

400. Martín (Pedro?) RUIZ de Monjaraz—
Hidalgo
First Conqueror
From: Durango (Biscay)
Parents: Martín de Zamallúa and doña María Ruiz de Monjaraz

Ruiz was in Cuba ca. 1518 and, along with two nephews—Captain Andrés and Gregorio Monjaraz—joined the Cortés *entrada*. Ruiz became a *vecino* of Colima, where he was *encomendero* of nearby Nagualapa and Mispan (considered a small grant in 1564). He was married and had five children. By 1547 his daughter, doña Isabel de Monjaraz, was the widow of first conqueror Manuel de Cáceres, a *vecino* of Colima. Another daughter was married to *hidalgo* conqueror and *encomendero* Pedro Zamorano. Ruiz died ca. 1560 and was succeeded as *encomendero* by a son.

(Gerhard, 80; Scholes and Adams, 22; Icaza, I, 17, 37 and 156; Boyd-Bowman, I, no. 4722, 156 and II, no. 2800, 81; Orozco y Berra, 47.)

401. Pedro RUIZ de Guadalcanal
First Conqueror
From: Guadalcanal (Seville)
Parents: Juan Martín de Zepecero and Teresa Arias

Ruiz was in Cuba by 1518 and with the Cortés *entrada* the following year. After the capture of Tenochtitlan he took part in various *entradas* and before 1527 had established himself as a *vecino* of Zacatula, where he maintained his *casa poblada*, arms, and horses. He was assigned the *encomiendas* of La Guaga (62 miles west-northwest of Zacatula; perhaps 28 *pueblos* and *poblezuelos* in 1571) and Coyuca—also called Copula—(135 miles south-southeast of Zacatula in the vicinity of Acapulco). Ruiz was married and had five daughters. The oldest married Francisco de Castrejón. Another married Nicolás de Aguilar from Seville, a *vecino* of Zacatula. The oldest daughter and her husband inherited the *encomienda* after Ruiz died ca. 1533. By 1564 Castrejón was also dead, and his widow succeeded as *encomendera*. When she died ca. 1580 the tribute reverted to the crown, having served the prescribed three "lives."

(Gerhard, 193 and 394; Icaza, I, 28 and 174; Scholes and Adams, 51; *Protocolos*, I, no. 448, 124 of 22 March 1527; Orozco y Berra, 88; Boyd-Bowman, I, no. 3104, 109.)

402. Pedro RUIZ de Requena
First Conqueror
From: Requena (Cuenca)

Ruiz joined the 1519 Cortés *entrada* after spending perhaps a year in Cuba. By 1532 he was a *vecino* of Zacatula and shared the *encomienda* of Arimao-Pinzándaro (65 miles northwest of Zacatula; 1,200 tributaries in 1565 and 18 *sujetos* in 1580) with Juan Gómez de Herrera. The original *en-*

*comendero*s were Juan de Jaso and Juan Jiménez. Ruiz died without issue ca. 1536. His half of the *encomienda* reverted to the crown shortly thereafter.

(Gerhard, 250ff.; Boyd-Bowman, I, no. 1535, 52; Orozco y Berra, 52.)

403. Alvaro SAAVEDRA Cerón—*Hidalgo Poblador*
From: Baeza (Jaén)
Parents: Martín Cerón and Marta Martínez de Altamirano

Saavedra, a cousin of Cortés through his mother's family, arrived in New Spain in 1522, served on *entradas* to Pánuco, Michoacán, and then went to Honduras with Francisco de las Casas. He led a three-ship expedition to the Molucca Islands in 1527 and was lost at sea on the return trip. Saavedra had been a close ally of his cousin, serving as lieutenant governor and *alguacil mayor* of Medellín, although a *vecino* of Veracruz. Cortés assigned him the *encomienda* of Cempoala (24 miles northwest of Veracruz; 20,000 to 30,000 tributaries at contact and only 20 in 1530) from his own holdings. There is no record of wife or children. His brother, Jorge Cerón Saavedra, came to New Spain ca. 1530 and served as *maestre de campo* under Cortés during the Mar del Sur *entrada*. When information concerning Saavedra's death became known, the first Audiencia recovered Cempoala for the crown but later reassigned it to Contador Rodrigo de Albornoz. The grant reverted to the crown under the New Laws in 1544.

(Gerhard, 363 and 365; Boyd-Bowman, II, no. 5573, 168; Icaza, II, 17f.; *Protocolos*, I, no. 1199, 264 of 28 March 1528.)

404. Fernando de SAAVEDRA—*Hidalgo Poblador*
From: Medellín (La Serena, Extremadura)
Parents: Pedro López de Saavedra and doña Isabel Alvarez Rangel

Saavedra, a cousin of Cortés, arrived in New Spain in 1523 and was a member of the Honduras *entrada* the following year. His brothers in New Spain included Alonso de Avalos Saavedra, Juan de Avalos Saavedra, Francisco de Saavedra, and an unnamed brother who drowned off the coast of Cuba in 1526. Saavedra was Cortés' lieutenant governor in Trujillo, Honduras from 1525 to 1527. In 1528 he became a *vecino* of Mexico City but shortly thereafter he departed for San Pedro de Puerto Caballos, Honduras, where he was a *regidor*. He shared Atoyac, Zayula, Amacueca, Tepec, Techalutla, and Teuzutlatlan (250 miles west of Mexico City; 10,920 tributaries in 1548—reduced by two-thirds fifty years later) with his brother Alonso. Fernando's share of the *encomienda* reverted to the crown ca. 1545, probably the year he died.

(Gerhard, 239ff.; Boyd-Bowman, II, no. 1556, 44; Icaza, II, 230; Gómara, 372.)

405. Lope de SAAVEDRA
Merchant
Poblador Antiguo
From: Seville

Saavedra, a *vecino* of Buenaventura, Santo Domingo from 1514, came to New Spain in 1523 with a royal appointment as manager of the estates of the deceased in Pánuco, where he became a *vecino*. By 1527 he was a lieutenant governor there and *alcalde ordinario* of Santisteban del Puerto as well as a merchant and the owner of the San Antonio, a *caravel* in which he later sold half interest to Miguel de Ibarra. Alonso de Estrada, while governor in 1527, reassigned him the *encomienda* of Tuxpan (11 *estancias* plus the sub-*cabeceras* Xalpantipe with 10 *estancias*, Tiguatlan, Tuzapa with 11 *estancias*, and Papantla with 15 *estancias* according to 1548 documents) from the Cortés holdings. Nuño de Guzmán sequestered the *encomienda* for a while in late 1528. Around 1530 the first Audiencia reassigned Tuxpan and the four sub-*cabeceras* to Andrés de Tapia. Saavedra married a daughter of Gonzalo Gómez de Saavedra and doña Leonor de Orellana, also of Cáceres, and became a *vecino* of Antequera. They had two sons and two daughters. He died in 1538, the same year he was referred to the Inquisition for having a first cousin as a concubine.

(Gerhard, 118, 120, 218, and 220; Chipman, 165f.; Icaza, II, 59f.; Boyd-Bowman, I, no. 923a, 32 and II, no. 2787, 81; *Protocolos*, I, no. 898, 213 of 27 December 1528; Greenleaf, 138.)

406. Luis (Lucas) de SAAVEDRA
Poblador Antiguo
From: Alcántara (Cáceres?)
Parents: Gutierre de Saavedra and Teresa de Aldana

Saavedra may have been in the Indies as early as 1511. He was the *encomendero* of Mizantla (80 miles northwest of Veracruz; five *sujetos* in 1569, after the second congregation) at least in 1527 and 1528. Mizantla was a crown possession by 1534.

(Gerhard, 363 and 366; Boyd-Bowman, I, no. 860, 30.)

407. Diego de SALAMANCA—*Hidalgo*
Conqueror—Narváez
From: Salamanca
Parents: Payo Gómez de la Cabeza and Beatriz Barrientos

Salamanca was in the Indies by 1512, in Cuba in 1519 and a member of the Narváez *entrada* the following year. After the capture of Tenochtitlan he was a member of *entradas* to Oaxaca, Tututepec, and Pánuco. By 1547 he was a *vecino* of Mexico City, where he maintained his arms and horses. Around 1524 Cortés assigned Salamanca the *encomienda* of Jalapa (145 miles east of Mexico City; 30,000 tributaries in the early 1520s—reduced to 639 in 1580). Two years later the grant was reassigned because Salamanca had left New Spain for Santo Domingo to find a cure for an illness. He claimed he did not marry because of his poverty but did acknowledge three natural children. The Jalapa *encomienda* was used between 1537 and 1550 to support a royal dye monopoly (*pastel y glasto*).

(Gerhard, 375f.; Icaza, I, 66f.; Boyd-Bowman, I, no. 2720, 95.)

408. Juan de SALAMANCA—Tailor
Poblador
From: Burgos
Parents: Pedro de Salamanca and Teresa de Cisneros

Salamanca arrived in New Spain as a member of Grijalva's 1524 entourage. Shortly after his arrival he was a member of an *entrada* to suppress an Indian revolt near San Juan de los Llanos (Castilblanco). He was identified as a tailor and functioned in commerce at a level somewhere between merchant and *tratante* (petty dealer). By 1527 he was a *vecino* of Mexico City, where he maintained his *casa poblada*, arms, and horses. He received the *encomienda* of Ayuquila and Zacapala (350 miles west-northwest of Mexico City near Guadalajara) through reassignment in the early 1530s, probably by the second Audiencia. Former holders were *pobladores* Diego de Chaves and Mateo Sánchez. In 1536 Salamanca married a daughter of Licenciado Pedro de León and became the father of two sons and two daughters. The *encomienda* was reassigned ca. 1550 to Catalina de Viñar, the widow of the first holder. She then married Antonio de Ortega.

(Gerhard, 59; Boyd-Bowman, II, no. 2365; Icaza, I, 197f.; *Protocolos*, II, no. 1978, 59ff. of 10 October 1536 and no. 2094, 87 of 5 December 1536.)

409. Juan de SALAMANCA
Conqueror—Narváez
From: Fontiveros (Avila)

Salamanca arrived in the Indies in 1510, was a *vecino* of Puerto Real, Santo Domingo in 1514, came to Cuba by 1519, and was a member of the Narváez *entrada* the following year. After the capture of Tenochtitlan Salamanca joined the Pánuco and Honduras *entradas*; by 1528 was a *vecino* of Coatzacoalcos and one of Cortés' retainers. He was the holder of an as yet unidentified *encomienda* near Espíritu Santo in the Coatzacoalcos jurisdication. Salamanca received a coat of arms dated 23 March 1535.

(Boyd-Bowman, I, no. 191, 8; *Nobiliario*, 70ff.; *Protocolos*, I, no. 1266, 275 of 20 April 1528.)

410. Gonzalo de SALAZAR—*Hidalgo Poblador*
From: Granada
Parents: El doctor de Guadalupe and doña Catalina de Salazar

Salazar's parents were members of the court of the Catholic Kings and enjoyed the position of first citizens (*primeros vecinos*) of Granada; Gonzalo had served as a page to Ferdinand and Isabella and later to Queen Juana. He arrived in Mexico City in 1523 as *factor* of the royal treasury and served as a lieutenant governor from 29 December 1524 to 23 January 1526. He was, of course, a *vecino* of Mexico City. As lieutenant governor, Salazar reassigned Taximaroa (92 miles west-northwest of Mexico City; about 2,000 tributaries in 1570) to himself from Cortés' holdings. Alonso de Estrada, while governor in 1528, increased his holdings by reassigning Tepetlaostoc (27 miles northeast of Mexico City; 23 *estancias* in 1570) to him. This grant had been one of the Cortés holdings reassigned by the acting governors to Diego de Ocampo and then to Miguel Díaz de Aux. Salazar had married doña Catalina de la Cadena of Burgos long before he came to New Spain. They had four children born in Spain, two of them sons. One daughter, doña Catalina, married don Ruy Díaz de Mendoza of Baeza (Jaén). The couple arrived in New Spain as members of Viceroy Mendoza's entourage. When don Ruy died, Catalina married Cristóbal de Oñate. The other daughter, doña Francisca, married Cristóbal de Salazar, a veteran of Florida. Their oldest son, Hernando, came to New Spain with his father and was given the office of royal *factor* in 1529 when Salazar returned to Spain. Hernando died the following year; the office was then given to their youngest son, Juan Velázquez de Salazar, who soon after that received Tepetlaostoc, transferred to him by his father. Salazar was back in New Spain by 1538 and resumed the duties of *factor*. He received an appointment as perpetual *regidor* of Mexico City and became a member of the *cabildo* on 1 October 1542. Juan again became *factor*. Salazar was active in the *cabildo* until the end of 1548. He died ca. 1553. Juan succeeded as *encomendero* of Taximaroa and on 20 August 1554 replaced his father as *regidor*.

(Gerhard, 172f. and 312f.; Scholes and Adams, 40; Icaza, I, 198f. and II, 144, 290, and 355f.; Boyd-Bowman, II, no. 4510a, no. 4511 and no. 4513, 134; *Actas*, IV, 306f. and VI, 144f.)

411. Hernando de SALAZAR—*Hidalgo Poblador*
From: Granada
Parents: Gonzalo de Salazar and doña Catalina de la Cadena

Salazar arrived in New Spain in 1523 with his father, the *factor* of the royal treasury in New Spain. He assumed the office of *factor* himself when his father returned to Spain in 1529. A *vecino* of Mexico City from mid-1524, he shared the *encomienda* of Tlatlauquitlpec (113 miles northeast of Mexico City; 21 *estancias* in 1548), Xontla (three *estancias* and seven *pueblos* in 1600), Hueytlalpa and two of its 21 *sujetos*, Ixtepec and Ixconyamec (all 140 miles east-northeast of Mexico City) with first conqueror Pedro Cindos de Portillo of León. On 16 August 1532 Salazar was granted a *caballería* next to Tlatlauquitlpec to raise Castilian plants and trees. He was probably married, but to whom is not known. His share of the *encomienda* reverted to the crown when he died during 1530s. The office of *factor* was assumed by his brother, Juan Velázquez de Salazar.

(Gerhard, 229f. and 391ff.; Boyd-Bowman, II, no. 4511, 134; *Actas*, I, 18 and II, 190.)

412. Juan de SALCEDO
Conqueror
From: Santander

Salcedo arrived in the Indies sometime prior to 1518, the year he was dispatched by Diego Velázquez from Cuba to Santo Domingo to petition for license to settle Pánuco. Salcedo was also the master of a ship that arrived in Veracruz after Narváez' mission had been rendered futile. After the capture of Tenochtitlan Salcedo became a *vecino* of Mexico City; although a *regidor* there for half of 1526 and all of 1527, he was essentially a horse trader who dabbled in the cacao trade and collected debts for others. His *encomiendas* included Tenancingo (40 miles southwest of Mexico City; nine *estancias* in 1548), Zacualpa (60 miles southwest of Mexico City; three sub-*cabeceras* plus 12 or 13 *estancias* in the late 1500s), and Amatepec (85 miles southwest of Mexico City; 1,333 tributaries in the *cabecera* and five *estancias* in 1569, including sub-*cabeceras* Metlatepec and Hueyxagualço, each with 69 tributaries the same year). Salcedo married doña Catalina Pizarro, a natural daughter of Hernando Cortés and a Cuban woman called Leonor Pizarro, and had a son, Pedro. The boy was placed under the guardianship of Martín Zavala when Salcedo died in 1536. Pedro inherited Tenancingo, but the other *cabeceras* reverted to the crown. After ten or so years of litigation, Pedro acquired Zacualpa as well. Pedro's son, Ruy López de Salcedo, was the *encomendero* after 1570.

(Gerhard, 171f., 268f., and 397f.; Scholes and Adams, 26f.; Chipman, 44; *Protocolos*, I, no. 424, 119 of 11 March 1527; no. 454, 125 of 26 March 1527; no. 939, 220 of 7 January 1528; no. 1401, 300 of 21 August 1528; no. 1425, 304 of 26 August 1528; and II, no. 2317, 131 of 16 June 1537; Pagden, 504.)

413. Francisco de SALDAÑA
Poblador
From: Fuente de Cantos (Maestrazgo de León, Extremadura)
Parents: Bartolomé Mateos Saldaña and Leonor García de Carro

Saldaña arrived in New Spain in 1524 and, after *entradas* to Motín, Jalisco, and various areas in Oaxaca, became a *vecino* of Villa Alta, where he maintained his *casa poblada*. He was the *encomendero* of Totolinga (a small grant by 1564 standards, located near Villa Alta). He married Isabel de Carvajal and had a number of children. Although he was succeeded by a son ca. 1560, Saldaña's widow was listed as the *encomendera* in 1597.

(Gerhard, 372; Scholes and Adams, 51; Boyd-Bowman, II, no. 1199, 35; Icaza, I, 230.)

414. Gregorio de SALDAÑA—Notary
Poblador
From: Saldaña (Palencia)

Saldaña arrived in New Spain in 1529 as a member of the Nuño de Guzmán entourage. As a notary he functioned as a *procurador* (untitled attorney) for Guzmán and also seemed to be a successful merchant, importing wine, sugar, silk and other fabrics, and black slaves. Saldaña became a *vecino* of Mexico City in September 1529, about the time he bought a lot there with a house on it. He became an *encomendero* by purchase, acquiring Moyutla (200 miles north-northeast of Mexico City near Pánuco; 246 tributaries in 1532) from first conqueror Francisco Gutiérrez in 1532 and Mecatlan (180 miles north of Mexico City near Valles) from conqueror Francisco Bernal ca. 1534. One-third of Mecatlan was given in dowry to a daughter, María de Saldaña, when she married Bartolomé de Perales, son of *encomendero poblador antiguo* Bartolomé de Perales of Medellín (Badajoz) and employee of Cortés. Saldaña was married twice, but nothing concerning his first wife was found. He died ca. 1548 and was succeeded by his second wife, María de

Campos. She was still the *encomendera* fifty years later.

Note: The legal profession had two levels. *Letrados*, university trained and holding degrees of *bachiller, licenciado* and *doctor*, gave legal advice. The *procuradores* did most of the actual legal work, serving as trial lawyers or special representatives to appear before the crown, the viceroy, or other official bodies. Notaries, with training in the mechanics of legal administration, often served as *procuradores*.

(Gerhard, 215 and 355; Chipman, 262 and 292; Scholes and Adams, 46; Boyd-Bowman, II, no. 7029, 216; *Protocolos*, I, no. 641, 163 of 11 July 1527; no 701. 174 of 8 August 1527; no. 775, 188 of 20 September 1527; no. 1272, 276 of 21 April 1528; and II, no. 1895, 40 of 29 August 1536; no. 2116, 91 of 15 December 1536; and no. 2452, 164 of 17 December 1537.)

**415. Jerónimo de SALINAS—*Hidalgo*
Conqueror—Narváez
From: Zaragoza
Parents: Bernaldo de Salinas and Petronila Garcés**

Salinas was in Tierra Firme with Pedrarias in 1514, in Cuba in 1516, coasted Mexico with Cristóbal de Olid in 1518, and was a member of the 1520 Narváez *entrada*. After the capture of Mexico City he served on *entradas* to Pánuco, Coatlán, and Meztitlan. Initially a *vecino* of Mexico City, Salinas was a founding *vecino* of Ciudad Oaxaca and was ordered by the Audiencia to reside there. He was the original *encomendero* of Tiltepec (50 miles northwest of Antequera) and Xaltepetongo (66 miles north-northwest of Antequera). Cimatlan and Tepecimatlan (15 miles south-southwest of Antequera; 12 *estancias* each) were reassigned to him from first conqueror Martín de la Mezquita ca. 1527, although claimed by Cortés. Both reverted to the crown in October 1532. Around 1527 Salinas was also reassigned Alpizagua (35 miles north-northwest of Antequera) from conqueror Juan Moreno and received these tributes until 1544. By 1547 his *encomienda* income was a claimed $350. Salinas married twice and had an undisclosed number of children. He died ca. 1560 and was succeeded by a son, Agustín, still the *encomendero* in 1597. Tiltepec and Xaltepetongo reverted to the crown ca. 1623.

(Gerhard, 71f., 201, 286, and 301; Scholes and Adams, 53; Icaza, I, 49; Orozco y Berra, 88; Boyd-Bowman, I, no. 4937, 164; *Protocolos*, I, no. 838, 200 of 31 October 1527.)

**416. Juan de SÁMANO—*Hidalgo
Poblador*
From: Santa Gadea (Burgos)
Parents: Hernando de Sámano and Sancha Sánchez de Orpina**

Sámano, a cousin to the king's secretary by the same name, arrived in New Spain with the 1523 Garay *entrada* to Pánuco after royal service in France and during the Comunero Revolt in Spain. By 1528 Sámano was a *vecino* of Mexico City. The following six years were spent in Michoacán. By late 1536 he became *alguacil mayor* of Mexico City and *vecino* there again. He received an appointment as perpetual *regidor* in 1539 and served in that office until 1547, the year his namesake son became the *alguacil mayor*. Sámano maintained a *casa poblada* in Mexico City and was the *encomendero* of Chilchota (230 miles west of Mexico City near Zamora; 800 tributaries in 1561) from 1528 to ca. 1542, when it was claimed by the crown; a cousin, Juan de Ojeda, was its administrator in late 1528. In 1532 Sámano was assigned Cinacantepec (35 miles west of Mexico City near Toluca; 24 *estancias*), a grant unsuccessfully claimed by Cortés. Sámano was married and had seven children, four of them daughters. He was succeeded ca. 1565 by his namesake son and after that by his grandson don Juan de Sámano Turcios, still listed as *encomendero* 50 years later.

(Gerhard, 175, 177, and 327; Scholes and Adams, 30; Boyd-Bowman, II, no. 2572,

73; *Actas,* V, 199f.; *Protocolos,* I, no. 1633, 341 of 6 October 1528.)

417. Antón SÁNCHEZ—Ship's Carpenter
Conqueror—Salcedo
From: Biscay

The preponderance of evidence suggests that Sánchez arrived in New Spain with Salcedo after the initial Pánuco settlement was aborted. Although identified as a ship's carpenter, he was involved in mining activities, carried on petty traffic in merchandise, and for a time served as collector of tribute for crown *encomiendas* in Zacatula, where he was a *vecino*. Zacatula was an early shipbuilding center that would attract one with his skill. His own *encomiendas* included Cacaopisca, Istapa, and Tlautla (30 miles east-southeast of Zacatula)—*cabeceras* that were all but depopulated by the end of the sixteenth century. Sánchez was married and had children. He was succeeded ca. 1550 by a son, Antón Sánchez, still listed as *encomendero* in 1597.

(Gerhard, 394; Boyd-Bowman, II, no. 12555, 376 (?); *Protocolos,* I, no. 80, 45 of 22 September 1525; no. 171, 65 of 30 October 1525; no. 244, 80 of 21 November 1525; no. 738, 181 of 27 August 1527; and no. 1152, 255f. of 10 March 1528.)

418. Bartolomé SÁNCHEZ
First Conqueror
From: Córdoba
Parents: Pedro García and Inés García

Sánchez was in Cuba by 1518 and with Cortés the following year. After the capture of Mexico City he served on *entradas* to Oaxaca and Guatemala, ultimately becoming a *vecino* of Antequera and, after ca. 1550, a *regidor* there. He was granted a coat of arms, dated 18 February 1562. Sánchez was the *encomendero* of a series of marginal grants during his lifetime. His first *encomienda*, Zola (45 miles south-southwest of Antequera; 12 *estancias* in 1599), was assigned to him by Cortés. By 1525 Cortés had reassigned Zola to first conqueror Román Lopéz and in its place assigned Sánchez Cuyotepec (10 miles southeast of Antequera; 1547 income a claimed $90). He was also assigned Cotastan, Cempoala, and Pechucalco (near Coatzacoalcos) in the mid-1520s. Sánchez received the tribute from Popoyutla (vicinity of Colima) by marrying the daughter of the original holder, conqueror Juan de Almesto, in the 1550s. She was his second wife. This tribute was reassigned to her brother in the 1560s. Sánchez received Zoyaltepec (100 miles north-northeast of Antequera) as the result of a 1552 lawsuit. In the 1560s it was divided between the crown and one of Sánchez' sons, and it became a crown holding by 1567. Sánchez had an undetermined number of children from the two marriages. He died ca. 1565 and was succeeded by a son. Only Cuyotepec was retained by the family after 1567. A grandson (?) named Bartolomé Sánchez was the *encomendero* in 1597.

(Gerhard, 49, 72, 80, 139, and 302; Scholes and Adams, 21 and 48; *Nobiliario,* 18f.; Boyd-Bowman, I, no. 1449, 49; Icaza, I, 15f.; Orozco y Berra, 88.)

419. Diego SÁNCHEZ de Sopuerta—Pilot, Mariner
First Conqueror
From: San Martín de Valdeiglesias (Madrid)

Sánchez, although a native of San Martín, had been a *vecino* of Moguer (Huelva) when he left Spain for the Indies ca. 1502. He was in Cuba by 1518 and a member of the Cortés *entrada* the following year. By 1527 Sánchez was a *vecino* of Mexico City and *encomendero* of Talasco (22 miles southwest of Mexico City; two *estancias* and 596 tributaries in 1564). He was married, perhaps to an Indian woman, and had two sons, Miguel and Diego. A niece was the second wife of *poblador* Diego de Segovia. Sánchez's brother, Alonso Sánchez de Sopuerto, also a *vecino* of Mexico City, was a hatmaker. The *encomienda* reverted to the crown when Sánchez died ca. 1534. Each son, however, received an annual pension of $100 from the royal treasury.

(Gerhard, 168f.; Icaza, II, 24f. and I, 157; Boyd-Bowman, I, no. 2348, 81 and II, no. 6415, 196; Protocolos, I, no. 869, 205 of 10 November 1527; no. 1278, 277 of 23 April 1528; and no. 1764, 365 of 17 November 1528; Actas, I, 10.)

420. Hernán SÁNCHEZ (González) de Hortigosa—Notary
Conqueror—Narváez
From: Old Castile

Sánchez arrived in the Indies in 1508 and took part in the capture of Puerto Rico the following year. By 1519 he was in Cuba and then became a member of the 1520 Narváez *entrada*. After the siege and capture of Tenochtitlan, Sánchez occupied himself by collecting debts for transients, dabbled in real estate and, by 1537, was identified as a notary. He was an early *vecino* of Mexico City and *encomendero* of Chiapantongo (64 miles north-northeast of Mexico City; 15 *barrios* distributed among three *estancias* in 1548, reduced to two *estancias* in 1571). With a license obtained in 1525, Sánchez returned to Spain to bring his wife, Leonor Vázquez de Vivanco, and two daughters to Mexico City. One daughter later married *poblador* Gaspar de Avila (Dávila) and the other, María de Pineda, married García de Llerena from Burgos. By 1547 Sánchez was a *vecino* of Zacatula, his *encomienda* 240 miles to the northeast. He died in the 1550s and was succeeded by his widow, who was the *encomendera* until 1562, when Chapantongo reverted to the crown.

(Gerhard, 383 and 385; Boyd-Bowman, I, no. 5064, 169; Icaza, I, 50; Protocolos, I, no. 360, 105 of 12 February 1527; no. 374, 108 of 16 February 1527; no. 461, 127 of 29 March 1527; no. 1052, 238 of 4 February 1528; no. 1168, 258 of 14 March 1528; no. 1293 and no. 1295, 280 of 27 April 1528; no. 1636, 341 of 6 October 1528; and II, no. 1966, 56f. of 3 October 1536 and no. 2369, 143 of 14 July 1537.)

421. Juan SÁNCHEZ—Indian Governor
From: Oaxaca

Around 1536 Sánchez was assigned Tuchitlapilco (85 miles northwest of Antequera), an *estancia* of Guaxuapa elevated to *cabecera* status when awarded in *encomienda*. Guaxuapa had been the *encomienda* of conqueror Juan Tello de Medina until 1534, when half the tribute reverted to the crown and the other half was reassigned to conqueror Juan de Arriaga. When Sánchez died ca. 1568, his *encomienda* reverted to the crown.

(Gerhard, 130.)

422. Mateo SÁNCHEZ—*Mayordomo Poblador*
From: Salamanca
Parents: Antón Merino and María Sánchez

Sánchez arrived in New Spain early in 1527 and by April was under contract as *mayordomo* for conqueror Francisco de Santa Cruz in Tuzantla (85 miles west-southwest of Mexico City; 3,148 tributaries in 1570). By the early 1530s he was a *vecino* of Colima, where he maintained 15 men in his *casa poblada* and was the *encomendero* of Ayuquila, Zacapal, and Tepeguacan (all of these grants were in the Milpa Valley, in the vicinity of Colima and northward), reassigned from *poblador* Diego de Chaves. Sánchez was married, perhaps to an Indian, had two sons, and probably died shortly after 1547. Ayuquila and Zacapal were reassigned to *poblador* Juan de Salamanca in the 1530s, and by 1550 the *encomendera* was Catalina de Viñar, the widow of the original *encomendero*. Tepeguacan was reassigned to Antonio de Ortega shortly before 1550, about the time he married Catalina de Viñar.

(Gerhard, 59, 80, and 173; Icaza, II, 83f.; Protocolos, I, no. 497, 135 of 12 April 1527.)

423. Pedro SÁNCHEZ
Poblador
From: Segura de León (Maestrazgo de León, Extremadura)
Parents: Diego Sánchez and Isabel Rodríguez

Sánchez arrived in New Spain at the same time as the Nuño de Guzmán entourage and became a *vecino* of Santisteban del Puerto, Pánuco. By 1532 he was the *encomendero* of Acececa (30 miles south-southwest of Pánuco; 431 tributaries living in the *cabecera* and two *estancias* ca. 1532). This *encomienda* was a crown holding by 1545.

(Gerhard, 215; Chipman, 292.)

424. Pedro SÁNCHEZ Farfán
First Conqueror
From: Seville

Sánchez was in the Indies by 1513 and in Cuba for a year before joining the 1519 Cortés *entrada*. As a political supporter of Cortés he was rewarded with an appointment as *regidor* of Mexico City, serving from 1525 to 1527. An attempt to purchase a perpetual appointment to the *cabildo* from *poblador* Luis de Berrio was not successful. By 1529 Sánchez had moved from Mexico City and had taken up residence in Toluca. Cortés assigned Sánchez the *encomienda* of Tetela (48 miles southeast of Mexico City, 61 miles east-southeast of Toluca; two *sujetos*—Hueyapa and Nepopozalco—plus at least nine *estancias* with a total of 2,000 tributaries in 1548). Sánchez also shared Tlapalcatepec (240 miles west of Mexico City, 60 miles southwest of Uruapan) with first conqueror Alonso de Avila and conqueror Hernando de Ergüeta until the grant was reclaimed by the first Audiencia, and held Xilotlan, in the same area, until the second Audiencia took it in 1531. He married María de Estrada, the sister of conqueror Francisco de Estrada, shortly after the capture of Tenochtitlan. Also from Seville, she had arrived in Cuba in 1519 and accompanied her brother to New Spain as a member of the Narváez *entrada*. They had no children. Sánchez died ca. 1536, and his widow succeeded him as *encomendera* of Tetela. She later married *poblador* Alonso Martín (Partidor), a vecino of Puebla from Carmona (Seville). Tetela reverted to the crown in 1561 when a contested suit for succession showed no valid heir.

(Boyd-Bowman, I, no. 4003, 132 and no. 3408, 117; *Protocolos*, I, no. 403, no. 404; no. 405, 114f. of 2 March 1527; and no. 1646, 343 of 8 October 1528; *Actas*, I, 201; Gerhard, 80, 250, and 294; Orozco y Berra, 52 and 66.)

425. Gonzalo de SANDOVAL
First Conqueror
From: Medellín (La Serena, Extremadura)

Sandoval was in Cuba at least a year before joining the Cortés *entrada* as a captain in 1519; he remained a close ally of Cortés. After the capture of Tenochtitlan, Sandoval led an *entrada* into the area south and east of Veracruz where he founded Espiritu Santo on the Coatzacoalcos River. He was a *vecino* of Mexico City and held the post (assigned by Cortés) of *alguacil mayor*. While on the *entrada* to Coatzacoalcos, Sandoval assigned himself Guaspaltepec (240 miles east-southeast of Mexico City; 80,000 tributaries at contact, 350 by 1570). Ca. 1527 he acquired Xacona (210 miles west of Mexico City near Zamora; 4,361 tributaries distributed among it and six subject *cabeceras* in 1546—twenty years later 1,185 tributaries). Cortés had assigned it to Juan de Albornoz in 1524, and Pero Almíndez Chirinos took it the following year. Conqueror *encomendero* Serván Bejerano seems to have administered this grant for Sandoval. Family information for Sandoval is lacking, although there is mention of his cousin, Juan de Sandoval, in New Spain. In 1528 Sandoval returned to Spain. The first Audiencia reassigned Guaspaltepec to the *cabildo* of Veracruz and then to Contador Rodrigo de Albornoz. The second Audiencia took it for the crown in 1531, then reassigned half of the tributes to Jorge de

Alvarado. Xacona was reassigned to Almíndez Chirinos in 1528.

(Boyd-Bowman, I, no. 464, 16; Díaz del Castillo, 333–337; *Protocolos*, I, no. 1038, 236 of 1 February 1528; Gerhard, 86f. and 399f.; Orozco y Berra, 52; Gardiner, 1961.)

426. Licenciado Rodrigo de SANDOVAL—*Hidalgo*
Poblador
From: Valladolid

Licenciado Sandoval arrived in the Indies ca. 1527 with his wife, doña María de Zúñiga, and spent about four years in Guatemala as lieutenant governor. By 1531 he was a *vecino* of Mexico City, serving as *fiscal* (public prosecutor) the following year. The pair had four children, three of them sons. Their daughter, doña Jerónima Bautista de Sandoval, married Hernando, a son of *encomendero poblador antiguo* Francisco de Avila. Sandoval's sons were Licenciado Fernando Sánchez de Sandoval, Francisco Sánchez de Sandoval and Rodrigo de Sandoval. One of them died during *entrada* service. Sandoval was the *encomendero* of Cempoala (42 miles northeast of Mexico City; four *barrios* in 1580), acquired from conqueror Juan Pérez de la Gama (de la Riva). He was succeeded ca. 1546 by his son Licenciado Fernando. A grandson, don Luis de Sandoval, was the *encomendero* in 1597.

(Gerhard, 67f.; Boyd-Bowman, II, no. 12206 and no. 12250, 364f.; Icaza, I, 204f.)

427. Melchor de SAN MIGUEL—*Hidalgo*
Conqueror—Narváez
From: Valladolid
Parents: Hernando de San Miguel of Portillo and Catalina Velázquez of Ledesma

San Miguel arrived in the Indies ca. 1514, was in Cuba by 1519, and then became a member of the 1520 Narváez *entrada*. For a while he was a member of Cortés' personal staff, performing duties as a butler or *aide de camp* (*repostero*). San Miguel was initially a *vecino* of Mexico City, receiving a city lot there in 1524. Later he was a founding *vecino* of Antequera, where he maintained his *casa poblada*. He was assigned the *encomiendas* of Tequecistepec (90 miles northwest of Antequera; two *barrios* and three *estancias*) and Nanalcatepec (24 miles northwest of Antequera). San Miguel married María de Godoy and had one son who succeeded him ca. 1560. Shortly thereafter María was listed as *encomendera*. All tributes reverted to the crown after she died in early 1587.

(Gerhard, 286, 288, and 306; Scholes and Adams, 53; Icaza, I, 37f.; Boyd-Bowman, I, no. 4662, 154; Orozco y Berra, 89; *Actas*, I, 7.)

428. Bernardino de SANTA CLARA—Notary and merchant
Conqueror—Narváez
From: Salamanca
Father: Pedro Gutiérrez de Santa Clara

Santa Clara and his brother, Cristóbal Gutiérrez de Santa Clara, arrived in Santo Domingo in 1502. By 1513 Bernardino was in Cuba, where he received an *encomienda*. He and another brother, Antonio de Santa Clara, were the Cuban end of a company that had as its principals Juan Francisco de Grimaldi and Gaspar Centurión, members of the Genoese and New-Christian merchant community in Seville. Seven years later he joined the 1520 Narváez *entrada* as its treasurer. Evidently his merchant brother, Antonio, along with merchants Andrés de Duero and Pedro de Jerez, a trio who had provided $4,000 of the amount Cortés had borrowed to outfit his *entrada*, wanted someone on scene to look after the account, especially after Cortés had severed his association with Cuba.

Santa Clara, a *vecino* of Mexico City, was the original *encomendero* of Teciutlan and Atempa (125 miles northeast of Mexico City; 1,829 tributaries in 1565) and shared Guatlatlauca (96 miles southeast of Mexico City; 800 tributaries in 1570) with a conqueror whose identity has been lost. By the time he came to New

Spain he was a widower with three daughters. One married Fernando de Torres of Seville in the early 1530s. Daughter María Gutiérrez married Hernando de Terrazas, the son of Cortés' *mayordomo*. The third daughter, Magdalena de Santa Clara, went to a convent in Spain. Santa Clara also acknowledged a number of natural children. He had four children—Florentina, Bernardino, Ana, and Inés—by Teresa Cervantes, a Spanish woman; two children—Vicente and María de Santa Clara—by Juliana, an Indian; and a son, Pedro, by another Indian woman. He also served as guardian for Tomás de Airalde, Cristóbal Gutiérrez, and Beatriz Pacheco de Escobar. Santa Clara was to have arranged a suitable marriage for the latter, but record of his efforts is missing. Also within the sphere of his paternal and business influence was a nephew, Francisco de Santa Clara, and a son of a cousin, Bartolomé Rodríguez. Santa Clara's brother, Cristóbal Gutiérrez, went to Peru ca. 1537 after spending thirty years in Santo Domingo, a number of those years as treasurer. Another brother, Antonio de Santa Clara, was the royal founder of metals in Santiago, Cuba, from 1518 to 1530. In spite of the position Santa Clara had carved out for himself in New Spain and the status of his family, his *encomienda* reverted to the crown shortly after he died in early 1538.

Note: His will, dated 6 December 1537, also directed the manumission of two Indian slaves, Sebastián and Antón, after five additional years' service to the Santa Clara heirs.

(Gerhard, 257 and 282; Boyd-Bowman, I, no. 2734, no. 2735 and no. 2736, 96; Icaza, I, 143 and 149; *Protocolos*, I, no. 267, 85 of 28 November 1525 and II no. 2112, 90 of 14 December 1536, no. 2121, 92 of 20 December 1536; no. 2440, 158 of 6 December 1537; and no. 2443, 161f. of 8 December 1537; Orozco y Berra, 67, *ENE*, I, 25 and 28; Gómara, 21; Pike, 50ff.; *Actas*, I, 40.)

429. Francisco de SANTA CRUZ
Conqueror—Narváez
From: Burgos
Parents: Francisco de Santa Cruz and Catalina de Salamanca

Santa Cruz was in Cuba by 1519 and with the Narváez *entrada* the following year. After the capture of Mexico City he became an employee of Cortés, first as a labor overseer and tribute collector (1522–1524), then *mayordomo* of agricultural enterprises (1531–1534), and finally *mayordomo* of the Marquesado sugar mill at Tlaltenango (after 1536). During this time he was a *vecino* of Mexico City, serving as a *regidor* and was *encomendero* of Axapusco (36 miles northeast of Mexico City; about 2,000 tributaries between the *cabecera* and *sujeto* Zacuala in 1570), Tlacamama (228 miles south-southeast of Mexico City), and Tuzantla (80 miles west of Mexico City; 348 tributaries in 1570), all granted by Cortés. Around 1529 Santa Cruz married a daughter of conqueror Francisco de Orduña; they had ten children, seven of them daughters. One daughter was the second wife of first conqueror Juan Pérez de Arteaga. Santa Cruz was succeeded by a son, Alvaro de Santa Cruz, in the late 1550s. The office of *regidor* had been renounced in favor of Francisco Vázquez de Coronado in mid-1538. Tuzantla, involved in a dispute over rights to it with Alonso de Mata and Juana de Ortega, reverted to the crown ca. 1546. The other grants reverted to the crown when Alvaro died in 1569 but were soon reassigned to Viceroy don Luis de Velasco. All were crown holdings by 1600.

(Gerhard, 68, 172, 208, and 381; Scholes and Adams, 23; Icaza, I, 19 and 33; Orozco y Berra, 89; Boyd-Bowman, I, no. 719, 25; *ENE*, I, 142; Riley, 68, 70, and 74; *Actas*, IV, 130–133, 14 June 1538.)

430. Pedro de SANTA CRUZ
Poblador Antiguo
From: Villadiego (Burgos)
Parents: Andrés de Santa Cruz and Mari García

Arriving in the area two months after the capture of Tenochtitlan could be considered a handicap, but it did not prevent Santa Cruz from becoming an *encomendero*. He may have arrived in Santo Domingo as early as 1514, giving him a degree of experience and *antigüedad*. Santa Cruz was a *vecino* of Colima, where he maintained his *casa poblada*, arms, and horses. He shared the *encomienda* of Milpa (72 miles northwest of Colima; 8,230 tributaries ca. 1525) from the early 1520s, first with Diego Martín de Mérida (to 1528), and then with Rodrigo Guipuzcoano. By 1550 he had acquired Contla (in the vicinity of Colima), but with the population decline the total number of tributaries in all of these towns was no more than 1,200 to 1,300. His share was half that amount. Santa Cruz was married and had one son, who succeeded him as *encomendero* before 1564.

(Gerhard, 60 and 80; Scholes and Adams, 53; Icaza, I, 248f.; Boyd-Bowman, II, no. 2605, 74.)

431. Francisco SANTOS
Conqueror—Narváez

Santos was the first *encomendero* of Tlacoloastla and Almoya (10 miles north-northwest of Colima), receiving his grant in the early 1520s. He was probably a *vecino* of Colima. Around 1550 the *encomienda* was divided between two of his sons, each receiving a *cabecera*. The *encomiendas* were still in private possession in 1597.

(Gerhard, 80; Orozco y Berra, 67.)

432. Francisco de SAUCEDO
Poblador
From: Seville (?)

Saucedo probably arrived in New Spain after 1536, established himself as a *vecino* of Zacatula, and ca. 1550 became the *encomendero* of Ciguatlan and Tamaloacan (under the jurisdiction of Zacatula) either through purchase or by marrying the widow of the original holder. By 1558 he was no longer receiving the tribute, and two years later the *encomienda* was a crown holding.

(Gerhard, 394; Boyd-Bowman, II, no. 10096, 305 (?).)

433. Juan SEDEÑO
First Conqueror

Sedeño, a *vecino* of Veracruz, held the *encomienda* of Xilotepec (60 miles northwest of Veracruz near Jalapa; two *sujetos* in 1569) in the 1520s. He married an Indian named Isabel and had three children, Francisco, García, and Beatriz. Beatriz married *poblador* Luis Hernández de Portillo of Guadix, a *vecino* of Veracruz. Xilotepec was taken for the royal dye industry when Sedeño died in the 1530s. His widow received an annual pension of $200 from the royal treasury in lieu of tribute.

Note: Another Xilotepec, located between Tula and Querétaro, was claimed by *hidalgo* first conqueror Juan Núñez Sedeño. His claim was not recognized, and the *encomienda* went to first conqueror Juan Jaramillo de Salvatierra. Núñez was a *vecino* of Oaxaca and still alive in 1547.

(Gerhard, 375; Orozco y Berra, 53; *Protocolos*, I, no. 45, 36 of 1 September 1525; Icaza, II, 160 and 167.)

434. Rodrigo de SEGURA
First Conqueror
From: Seville
Parents: Ruy de Segura and Francisca de Frías

Segura arrived in Cuba ca. 1518 after having served some 20 years in Italy, France, and Africa. He was a member of the Cortés *entrada* and after the capture of Tenochtitlan and subsequent *entradas* became a *vecino* of Puebla, where he maintained his *casa poblada*, arms, and horses. Segura initially shared the *encomienda* of

Ixcatlan (115 miles southeast of Puebla, 24 miles south of Teotitlan; three *sujetos* and one *estancia*—8,000 tributaries at contact and but 300 in 1597) with *poblador* (?) García Vélez of Palos (Huelva) but acquired the Vélez share ca. 1525. He was married but had no legitimate offspring. His widow succeeded as *encomendera* ca. 1565. Ixcatlan reverted to the crown in the 1570s and then was reassigned to don Luis de Velasco in the 1580s.

(Gerhard, 306ff.; Boyd-Bowman, I, no. 4015, 132; Scholes and Adams, 21; Icaza, I, 53f.; Orozco y Berra, 53.)

435. Cristóbal de SEPÚLVEDA
Poblador

Sepúlveda, probably a member of the Nuño de Guzmán entourage, was a *vecino* of Santisteban del Puerto, Pánuco. He held the *encomienda* of Chalchitlan, Tantoin, Chalchiguautla, and Tlapaguautla (all located between Pánuco and Valles; total of 1,934 tributaries ca. 1532). He was married but left no children. Sepúlveda was succeeded by his widow in the 1540s. She then married *poblador* Francisco de Torres from Trujillo, a *vecino* of Pánuco. Torres was listed as the *encomendero* from ca. 1548 to 1573. By 1597 the crown had reclaimed this grant.

(Gerhard, 355; Scholes and Adams, 47; Icaza, I, 241f.; Chipman, 293.)

436. Maestre Martín de SEPÚLVEDA—Builder
Conqueror—?
From: Sepúlveda (Segovia)

Maestre Martín arrived in New Spain prior to the capture of Tenochtitlan and was selected by Cortés to take charge of its reconstruction as *maestre de obras*, based on his professed architectural/construction experience. The effort began in 1522. He was a *vecino* of Mexico City and was exempted from *entrada* service because of his duties, although he did participate indirectly by providing arms and horses for others. Cortés assigned him the *encomienda* of Iscateupa (76 miles southwest of Mexico City near Taxco; nine *estancias* in 1579). Sepúlveda married María de Guzmán and had one son, Baltasar. The *encomienda* reverted to the crown when Sepúlveda died ca. 1535.

(Gerhard, 153f.; Boyd-Bowman, II, no. 8064, 250; Icaza, I, 143f.; Kubler, I, 111f.)

437. Pedro de SEPÚLVEDA—Blacksmith and founder
Conqueror—Narváez
From: Sepúlveda (Segovia)

Sepúlveda was in Santo Domingo in 1514, in Cuba by 1519, and a member of the Narváez *entrada* the following year. He was an early *vecino* of Veracruz, then by 1529 lived in Mexico City, and later was a resident of New Galicia. During the late 1520s he made gunpowder in addition to his metalworking activities. Sepúlveda received half the tribute of Zongolica (75 miles southwest of Veracruz; 770 tributaries living in 13 *estancias* in 1570). He was married and had one daughter who ca. 1545 married Juan Pérez, a *poblador* and *vecino* of Puebla. Pérez was a native of Coimbra, Portugal. Sepúlveda died ca. 1537 and was succeeded by his daughter. She was the *encomendera* until the grant reverted to the crown in the late 1550s.

(Gerhard, 363 and 365f.; Boyd-Bowman, I, no. 2952, 104; Icaza, I, 170; Orozco y Berra, 89.)

438. Alonso de la SERNA
First Conqueror

Serna was in the Indies by 1518 and a member of the Cortés *entrada* the following year. He became a *vecino* of Mexico City and from the early 1520s held the *encomienda* of Zumpaguacan (43 miles southwest of Mexico City; 22 *estancias* in 1548 and 14 in 1580) and nearby Zoquicingo (34 miles southwest of Mexico City; three *estancias* in 1570). By 1532, after Cortés' claim was overruled by the second Audiencia, he and first conqueror Gaspar Garnica of Biscay shared Tlacotepec (36 miles west-southwest of Mexico City; five *estancias* in 1580). Serna was married and had a number of children. He was succeeded after 1564 by a son, Antonio Velázquez de la Serna. Antonio's widow, Isabel de Cardenas, was the *encomendera* by 1595, and two years later Juana de la Cuadra is listed.

(Gerhard, 170f., 175, and 177; Scholes and Adams, 16; Orozco y Berra, 53; *Protocolos*, I, no. 965, 223 of 9 January 1528.)

439. Juan SICILIANO
First Conqueror
From: Nerbin, Sicily
Parents: Micer Francisco Garbin and Madona con Paula (?)

Siciliano was in Santo Domingo in 1502 and in Cuba by 1518, joining the Cortés *entrada* the following year. He became a *vecino* of Mexico City and there maintained his *casa poblada*, arms, and horses. Siciliano shared the *encomienda* of Atitalaquia (44 miles north of Mexico City near Tula; four dependencies) with Juan Catalán. He married while in Santo Domingo and had a son and a daughter. The daughter was married and living in New Spain by 1546. Siciliano's share of the *encomienda* was reassigned by the first Audiencia ca. 1528 and then three years later became a crown holding.

(Gerhard, 295 and 298; Boyd-Bowman, I, no. 5154, 172; Icaza, I, 23; *Protocolos*, I, no. 1098, 246 of 17 February 1528; Orozco y Berra, 77; *Actas*, I, 46.)

440. Pedro de SIMANCAS
Conqueror—Narváez
From: Simancas (Valladolid)

Simancas arrived in Cuba in 1519 and joined the Narváez *entrada* the following year. He became an early *vecino* of Colima, where he held nearby Comala and Cecamachantla in *encomienda*. He also held Coyutla, Xonacatlan, and Amilpa, 55 miles northwest of Colima in the Autlan jurisdiction. Comala and Cecamachantla were reassigned to first conqueror Bartolomé López in the early 1530s. Around 1550 Simanca's brother, Cristóbal Moreno, succeeded him as *encomendero* of the Autlan *cabeceras*.

(Gerhard, 59 and 80; Boyd-Bowman, I, no. 4601, 152; Orozco y Berra, 58.)

441. Francisco de SOLÍS—Cannoneer
First Conqueror
From: San Martín de Valdepusa (Santander)
Parents: Francisco de Solís and Beatriz Suárez

Solís was in Cuba by 1518 and joined the Cortés *entrada* the following year as a captain of artillery. He became a *vecino* and constable (*alguacil*) of Mexico City and there maintained his *casa poblada*, family, arms, and horses. In the 1540s he claimed to be supporting as many as twenty-five Spaniards. Cortés assigned him the *encomienda* of Zacualpa, Tlacotepec, Temoac, and Guazulco (50 miles southeast of Mexico City, considered a "large" grant ca. 1564). He also held nearby Yecapixtla, shared with conqueror Diego de Holguín "in deposit" from Cortés between 1528 and 1531 while the latter was in Spain. Cortés recovered this *cabecera* as part of the Marquesado del Valle grant. Solís was married and had 17 children, four of them daughters. One married conqueror Juan de Villagrán, *encomendero* of Tempoal and Tancolol in Pánuco. Solís died ca. 1546 and was succeeded by a son, Miguel de Solís, still the *encomendero* in 1604.

(Gerhard, 92 and 95; Scholes and Adams, 42; Boyd-Bowman, I, no. 2829, 100; Icaza, I, 6 and 148; Orozco y Berra, 89; *Actas*, I, 7.)

442. Juan de SOLÍS
Poblador

Solís shared the tribute from Comanja and Maranja (20 miles north-northwest of Pátzcuaro; 38 *sujetos* in 1523) with Hernando Cortés, perhaps in a form of title fiction to protect the *encomienda* from reassignment or escheatment while the latter was in Spain. If so, the scheme was not successful. The first

Audiencia reassigned both *cabeceras* to *hidalgo poblador* Juan Infante in 1529.

(Gerhard, 344f. and 351.)

443. Pedro de SOLÍS Barrasa *"tras la puerta"*
First Conqueror
From: Espinosa de los Monteros (Burgos)
Parents: Pedro de Barrasa and Mari Sáez of Redonodo

Solís had his first experience in the Indies with Pedrarias de Avila in Tierra Firme ca. 1514. Five years later he was in Cuba and a member of the Cortés *entrada*. He became a *vecino* of Mexico City and in 1528 *encomendero* of Acolman (24 miles north-northeast of Mexico City; 13,000 tributaries at contact, reduced to 2,564 in 27 *sujetos* ca. 1570). Acolman was reassigned to Solís from Pedro Núñez, Maese de Roa, the original *encomendero*. Solís married a daughter of conqueror Francisco de Orduña ca. 1529 and had eight children, the oldest born in 1532. He died ca. 1565 and was succeeded by a son, Francisco de Solís Orduña. By 1610 a grandson, Francisco Solís y Barrasa, was the *encomendero*. Acolman reverted to the crown ca. 1680.

(Gerhard, 312f.; Scholes and Adams, 16; Icaza, I, 7; Boyd-Bowman, I, no. 745, 25; Orozco y Berra, 89; Díaz del Castillo, II, 449; ENE, I, 142; Actas, I, 37.)

444. Juan Alonso de SOSA—*Hidalgo Poblador*
From: Córdoba
Parents: Lope de Sosa and doña Inés de Cabrera

Royal treasurer Sosa arrived in and became a *vecino* of Mexico City in 1531 after having been in Tierra Firme from 1521 with his father, the governor there. He was reassigned the tribute from Urapa and Guanaxo (160 miles west of Mexico City near Pátzcuaro) in 1533 from *poblador antiguo* Diego Rodríguez de Valladolid and then in 1537 was assigned the tributes from Coatepec (20 miles east of Mexico City), Tonalá (155 miles southeast of Mexico City), and Tenayuca (nine miles north of Mexico City). All of these grants reverted to the crown after the enforcement of the New Laws, pursuant to a clause denying *encomiendas* to royal officials. Sosa was also a *regidor* of Mexico City from 14 June 1538, replacing Juan Velázquez de Salazar, perhaps by purchasing the office. He was not, however, active as *regidor*. During the second half of the 1530s Sosa was deeply involved in silver mining ventures in Taxco and in a company with Cortés exploiting the silver district of Sultepec.

(Gerhard, 77, 130, and 248; Boyd-Bowman, II, no. 3857, 113; Icaza, II, 356f.; Actas, IV, 130; Protocolos, II, no. 2028 and no. 2029, 71 of 7 November 1536; no. 2051, 76 of 20 November 1536; nos. 2064–66, 79f. of 24 November 1536; and no. 2202, 108 of 2 March 1537.)

445. Cristóbal de SOTO
First Conqueror

Soto, a *vecino* of Puebla, was the *encomendero* of Huehuetlan (21 miles south of Puebla; 500 tributaries in 1570) and for a time in 1527 was a lieutenant to royal treasurer Alonso de Estrada in the Río Grijalva region. He married a daughter of *poblador* Alonso Martín (Partidor). In the 1540s Martín served as executor of Soto's will and guardian of his two daughters and son. Soto's son, Luis, succeeded as *encomendero* when he came of age. Shortly thereafter (ca. 1553) Luis was succeeded by his sister, María de Soto, married to Juan de Carbajal. After 1568 María is listed as the sole *encomendera*, receiving the tribute until 1597.

(Gerhard, 282; Scholes and Adams, 24f.; Icaza, I, 112; Protocolos, I, no. 484, 132 of 8 April 1527; Orozco y Berra, 67.)

446. Bachiller Pedro Díaz de SOTOMAYOR
Poblador
From: Seville
Parents: Gonzalo de Sotomayor and Francisca Alonso

Bachiller Sotomayor, as he was often styled, arrived in New Spain in 1523 and established himself as a *vecino* and *regidor* of Pánuco (Santisteban del Puerto). He held the *encomienda* of Pachuca (140 miles southwest of Pánuco; 6,233 tributaries in 1569) until giving it in dowry to his daughter, doña Francisca, when she married *hidalgo* Antonio de la Cadena from Seville. (He had been in the colony since 1523, holding a succession of minor offices.) Viceroy Mendoza then assigned Sotomayor half the tribute from Cuestlahuaca (170 miles southeast of Mexico City; thirteen sub-*cabeceras* and numerous *estancias*). The other half was held by Francisco Verdugo. It was also about this time (1536) that Sotomayor moved to Mexico City. He was married to Leonor de Torres, also of Seville. The Cuestlahuaca share was inherited by Sotomayor's son, Gaspar de Sotomayor, in 1544 and held by him until his death ca. 1579, when it escheated. By 1565 Pachuca had been inherited by doña Francisca's son, Baltasar de la Cadena. He was still the *encomendero* in 1604.

(Gerhard, 210, 285, and 288; Scholes and Adams, 30 and 37; Icaza, I, 225f.; Boyd-Bowman, II, no. 10208, 308.)

447. Diego SUÁREZ Pacheco—*Hidalgo*
Poblador Antiguo
From: Avila
Parents: Juan Suárez de Avila and Leonor Pacheco

The father-in-law of Cortés, Suárez had established himself and his family in Cuba by 1514 and then in 1527 followed them to Mexico City, where he became a *vecino*. Around 1528 the first Audiencia reassigned Cholula (60 miles east-southeast of Mexico City, seven miles west of Puebla; 40,000 to 100,000 tributaries at contact, 20,000 in 1531) from Rodrigo Rangel to Suárez and Comendador Diego Fernández Proaño. Cortés had originally assigned Cholula to Andrés de Tapia. Suárez was married to María de Marcaida, a native of Biscay. They had several children. A daughter Catalina was the first wife of Hernando Cortés. Another daughter, Leonor Suárez Pacheco, married Andrés de Barrios. A son Juan had been in the Indies since 1499 and ca. 1525 moved the Suárez household to Mexico City in advance of Diego himself. Suárez died in 1529. The second Audiencia took all of Cholula for the crown in 1531.

(Gerhard, 114f.; Boyd-Bowman, I, no. 147a, 6.)

448. Juan SUÁREZ—*Hidalgo*
Poblador Antiguo
From: Avila
Parents: Diego Suárez Pacheco and María de Marcaida

Suárez, brother of Cortés' first wife, arrived in Santo Domingo ca. 1499 and was in Cuba in 1511 with the Diego Velázquez *entrada*. He shared an *encomienda* on the eastern tip of Cuba with Cortés. During the mid-1520s he moved his entire household to Mexico City, bringing his own family, his mother, brothers, sisters, nieces, and nephews, but not his father, who remained for a time in Cuba. He became a *vecino* of the capital and established his *casa poblada* there. His father, Diego Suárez Pacheco, rejoined the family two years later. Suárez was assigned the *encomienda* of Tamazulapa (160 miles southeast of Mexico City, seventy miles northwest of Antequera; six *sujetos* in 1548). He was married and the father of two sons and a daughter. Suárez died in the late 1550s and was succeeded by a son, Luis Suárez de Peralta, still the *encomendero* in 1597.

Note: Boyd-Bowman, in I, no. 3638, 123, states that Suárez was from Seville and was a first conqueror. The evidence in Icaza and Gerhard strongly refutes this. There is little doubt, however, that Suárez was indeed a veteran of the Indies and a conqueror of Cuba.

(Gerhard, 285f.; Boyd-Bowman, I, no. 147b, 6; Icaza, I, 75f.)

449. Lorenzo SUÁREZ "el viejo"—
Hidalgo
First Conqueror
From: Ebora, Portugal

By 1514 Suárez was an *encomendero* in Cuba; five years later he joined the Cortés *entrada*. He became a *vecino* of Mexico City and *encomendero* of Tlanocopan (60 miles north of Mexico City near Tula; three dependencies before 1545, with only the *cabecera* remaining after 1569), granted him by Cortés. In the 1520s Suárez married María de Salazar, a member of an *hidalgo* family from Santa Gadea (Burgos); they had one son, Gaspar. The *encomienda* was taken for the crown in the 1540s in fulfillment of an Audiencia sentence; it seems that Suárez had killed his wife (with a grinding stone, according to Díaz del Castillo). Suárez then took up the religious life, dying as a friar before 1547. Tlanocopan was reassigned to Suárez's son Gaspar in the 1550s, and by the mid-1560s the *encomendero* was a grandson, Andrés.

(Gerhard, 297 and 299; Scholes and Adams, 46; Icaza, II, 239; Boyd-Bowman, I, no. 5285, 177 and II, no. 2571, 73; Díaz del Castillo, II, 453.)

450. Andrés de TAPIA
First Conqueror
From: Medellín (La Serena, Extremadura)

In the early 1520s Cortés assigned to Tapia, his close associate and *vecino* of Mexico City, the *encomienda* of Cholula (60 miles east-southeast of Mexico City; 40,000 to 100,000 tributaries at contact, 20,000 in 1531). By 1526 the *encomendero* was Rodrigo Rangel. The following year the first Audiencia divided the tribute between *poblador antiguo* Diego Suárez Pacheco, father of Cortés' first wife, and *poblador* Comendador Diego Fernández Proaño. Cholula was reclaimed for the crown in one of the initial acts of the second Audiencia. Cortés also assigned Papantla (150 miles northeast of Mexico City; 15 *estancias* in 1548) to Tapia, but Alonso de Estrada reassigned it, along with Tuxpan and three other *cabeceras*, to Lope de Saavedra when he was governor in 1528. By 1530, however, Tapia had again acquired Tuxpan, Papantla, and associated sub-*cabeceras*, giving him a total of at least 46 *estancias* in the lowlands of Pánuco. Tapia married doña Isabel de Sosa of Toledo and from then on used the name Andrés de Tapia y Sosa. They had three sons and a daughter. Their second son, don Pedro Gómez de Cáceres, married doña Francisca Ferrer, widow of Pedro de Paz (a relative of Cortés), and acquired Atotonilco, a large *encomienda* (68 miles north of Mexico City; 22 *estancias* in 1571). Tapia's oldest son, don Cristóbal, succeeded him as *encomendero* ca. 1561. Around 1600 don Cristóbal transferred Papantla to his youngest son, don Andrés de Tapia Sosa, but retained the other *cabeceras*.

(Gerhard, 114, 118, 120, 218, 220, and 355f.; Scholes and Adams, 38; Icaza, I, 4f.; Boyd-Bowman, II, no. 11448a, 341; Orozco y Berra, 54.)

451. Francisco de TARIFA
Poblador
From: Seville
Parents: Diego de Tarifa and Inés de Arcos

Tarifa arrived in New Spain with Garay's 1523 Pánuco expedition. After service with various *entradas* he became a *vecino* of Villa Alta and *encomendero* of Santa María de Lachichina (28 miles north-northwest of Villa Alta). He married a daughter of an unnamed conqueror and had three daughters and a son. Ca. 1567 he was succeeded by the namesake son, still *encomendero* in 1604.

(Gerhard, 371; Boyd-Bowman, II, no. 10027, 308; Icaza, I, 256.)

452. Gaspar de TARIFA
First Conqueror
From: Seville

There were three men surnamed Tarifa (first names unknown) in Cuba in 1518; all were from Seville, and all became members of the Cortés *entrada*. One, called *"el de las manos blancas,"* died on the Honduras *entrada*. Another, called *"el de los servicios,"* is not heard from after the capture of Tenochtitlan. In September, 1524, a Gaspar de Tarifa, presumably the third, acquired a lot in Mexico City, where he was already a *vecino*. By 1528 he was the *encomendero* of Chicomesuchil (250 miles southeast of Mexico City; 11 *estancias* in 1548). He was married and had several children. Around 1548 he was succeeded by a son, Diego de Vargas. A grandson, Melchor de Vargas, was the *encomendero* in 1597.

(Gerhard, 158f.; Boyd-Bowman, I, no. 4039, no. 4040, and no. 4041, 133; Scholes and Adams, 28; *Protocolos*, I, no. 1409 and no. 1410, 301f. of 24 August 1528; Orozco y Berra, 89.)

453. Licenciado Diego TÉLLEZ
Poblador Antiguo
From: Córdoba

Téllez arrived in and became a *vecino* of Mexico City ca. 1529 to serve as an attorney in conjunction with the first Audiencia as well as defending Indians before the Inquisition. He also acted as legal counsel for Cortés. It is likely that he had been in Santo Domingo since ca. 1508, spending over twenty years in the Indies before moving his entire household to Mexico City. During the 1540s Téllez bought the rights to Guaquilpa and Tlaquilpa from conqueror Andrés López and *poblador* Antonio Medel. (Guaquilpa—one *estancia* in 1569—and Tlaquilpa—three *sujetos* in 1580—were neighboring *cabeceras* 48 miles northeast of Mexico City, 12 to 15 miles south and southwest respectively of Pachuca). Téllez was married and ca. 1548 claimed eighteen surviving children, eleven of them sons. One was a priest without a pulpit, and the others were on *entradas* from which one did not return. Of his seven daughters, one married notary Juan de Cuevas, another was the first nun in New Spain, and the remaining five were ready to marry but lacked dowries. Téllez died ca. 1560. Guaquilpa went to son Diego and Tlaquilpa to son Manuel. Half of Tlaquilpa was taken by the crown in January 1562 and the Indians, or some of them, were taken to Cempoala to provide labor for building the Tecaxete-Otumba aqueduct and the monastery there.

(Gerhard, 68f. and 209f.; Boyd-Bowman, II, no. 4062, 119; Icaza, I, 200 and 205; *BAGN* Inq., Tomo 37, exp 4 bis.)

454. Juan TELLO de Medina—*Hidalgo*
Conqueror—Narváez
From: Seville
Parents: Luis Tello and doña Isabel de Mechúa

Tello arrived in the Indies ca. 1517 and was a member of the Narváez *entrada* three years later. He was a *vecino* of Mexico City, where he maintained his *casa poblada*, family, arms, and horses. He held the *encomiendas* of Cuyatepexi (145 miles southeast of Mexico City, sub-*cabeceras* including Guaxolotitlan, Miltepec, Suchitepetongo, and Yeitepec—no listing of *estancias*) and the twin *cabeceras* Guaxuapa and Tuctla (150 miles southeast of Mexico City; 15 to 20 *estancias* between the two). Tello was married and had two children. By 1534, Guaxuapa and Tuctla had been taken by the second Audiencia and half of Guaxuapa reassigned to conqueror Juan de Arriaga. A son succeeded him ca. 1546 and by 1560 he had recovered Tuctla and the unassigned half of Guaxuapa. When young Tello entered the priesthood ca. 1566, his mother, now married to Pedro Calderón, became an *encomendera* of Cuyatepexi. Tuctla and the Guaxuapa share again reverted to the crown.

(Gerhard, 129ff.; Scholes and Adams, 29; Icaza, I, 42; Boyd-Bowman, I, no. 3740, 126.)

455. Francisco de TERRAZAS
First Conqueror
From: Fregenal de la Sierra
(Maestrazgo de León, Extremadura)
Father: Bachiller Diego de Terrazas

Terrazas was in Cuba by 1518; he joined the Cortés *entrada* as *mayordomo* and captain of Cortés' personal guard and continued to serve Cortés as one of his *mayordomos* into the 1530s. He was an early *vecino* of Mexico City but did not become a member of the *cabildo* until elected as one of the *alcaldes ordinarios* for 1538. By December of that year he had acquired Juan de Mansilla's seat as *regidor* through a viceregal appointment but failed to obtain ratification of the office by the king. He was out of office at the end of 1541, although he did serve as *alcalde ordinario* again for 1549. Terrazas shared the *encomienda* of Igualtepec (145 miles southeast of Mexico City; *sujetos* including Tamazola, Tlachichilco and Ayusuchiquilazala, plus a number of *estancias*) with conqueror García de Aguilar and that of Tulancingo (72 miles northeast of Mexico City; 13 *estancias* in the late 1500s) with *poblador* Francisco de Avila. Both were assigned him by Cortés, whether as original grants or as reassignments is not known. Terrazas may have been married in Spain; a son, Hernando, was born there, came to New Spain ca. 1532, and later married María Gutiérrez, a daughter of conqueror Bernardino de Santa Cruz. Ca. 1532 Terrazas married Ana de Castro, a widow with five children. They then had three sons and a daughter. He also claimed a natural son (Hernando ?) and two natural daughters, one of whom married Sebastián de Vázquez ca. 1540. A younger sister of Terrazas' wife married first conqueror Hernando de Torres ca. 1538. Terrazas died between 2 and 9 August 1549 and was succeeded by a son, Francisco de Terrazas (the poet).

(Gerhard, 131f., 164, 335, and 337; Icaza, I, 6f. and 148ff.; Boyd-Bowman, I, no. 368, 13 and II, no. 1143, 34; *Actas*, IV, 155f.; Scholes and Adams, 26; Orozco y Berra, 54; *Protocolos*, II, no. 2508, 178 of 15 February 1538.)

456. Juan TIRADO
First Conqueror

In the early 1520s Cortés assigned Tirado, a *vecino* of Mexico City, the *encomienda* of Cuicatlan (190 miles southeast of Mexico City; four *barrios* and three *estancias* in 1548). By 1524 Cortés had reassigned this *cabecera* to *poblador* Juan de Jaso, but ca. 1529 the first Audiencia reversed the action and restored Cuicatlan to Tirado. Tirado married Andrea Ramírez, a daughter of conqueror Francisco Ramírez "el viejo" and had three children, two of them sons. Ca. 1544 the daughter married *poblador* Francisco de Salazar of Piedrahita (Avila). Tirado died in the early 1540s and was succeeded by his oldest son. Around 1545, however, the crown took the *encomienda*, perhaps considering the initial assignment, the reassignment, and the restoration as constituting the "three lives." The younger son, Pedro, sued unsuccessfully for recovery. By 1547 Tirado's widow had married *poblador* Juan Blázquez of Barco de Avila and had two or three more children. Tirado's coat of arms was dated 12 April 1527.

(Gerhard, 306 and 308; Icaza, I, 127f. and II, 241 and 58; Boyd-Bowman, II, no. 447. 16; *Protocolos*, I, no. 235, 78 of 18 November 1525; Orozco y Berra, 54; *Nobiliario*, 127f.)

457. Maese Manuel TOMÁS—Surgeon
Poblador
From: Trujillo (Cáceres)

Tomás arrived in New Spain as a member of Francisco de las Casas' entourage and, although an ally of Cortés, was able to survive the early political turmoil. Perhaps his profession (plus investing his wealth in the form of loans to those in high places) contributed to his success. Tomás was a *vecino* of Mexico City; in the mid-1520s he acquired the *encomienda* of Tututepec (97 miles northeast of Mexico City; 85 *estancias* and *barrios* in 1548 distributed among the *cabecera* and three sub-*cabeceras*; by 1570, 27 *estancias*) through a reassignment from trumpeter first conqueror Alonso Giraldo. His wife, Leonor Rodríguez de Orozco, remained in Spain. They had at least one son, Diego Rodríguez de Orozco, who arrived in New Spain in 1536. By 1547 Tomás had transferred his rights as *encomendero* of Tututepec to his son. Diego was still receiving the tribute in 1597.

(Gerhard, 336f.; Scholes and Adams, 41; Icaza, II, 4f.; Boyd-Bowman, II, no. 3223 and no. 3236, 94; *Protocolos*, I, no. 180, 67 of 4 November 1525.)

458. Baltasar de TORQUEMADA
Poblador
From: Palencia (?)

Torquemada arrived in New Spain ca. 1527 as a member of Nuño de Guzmán's entourage and became a *vecino* of Santisteban del Puerto, Pánuco. Guzmán assigned him Tenacusco and Tantima (twin *cabeceras* 65 miles south-southeast of Pánuco; 655 and 485 tributaries respectively in 1532.) By 1571 Tantima was one of three *estancias* of Tenacusco. Torquemada's marriage with Francisca de Vargas produced no children. He was succeeded ca. 1546 by his widow, who soon married *poblador* Rodrigo Bezos of Seville, a nephew of first conqueror Pedro Sánchez Farfán. Guzmán also assigned Bezo's brother Juan an *encomienda* (Ucareo, southwest of Querétaro). By 1597 Tenacusco had reverted to the crown.

(Gerhard, 217; Scholes and Adams, 46; Icaza, I, 238; Chipman, 292; Boyd-Bowman, I, no. 3278, 114 and II, no. 8826, 272.)

459. Juan de TORQUEMADA—Notary
Poblador
From: Palencia (?)

Torquemada was secretary to Nuño de Guzmán, arriving with the entourage in 1527. In that year he became a *vecino* of Santisteban del Puerto, Pánuco, and the *encomendero* of Yagualica (77 miles south-southwest of Pánuco; 376 tributaries ca. 1532 and 13 *sujetos* and five *hermitas* in 1569) by a Guzmán reassignment from a Domingo Martín. By 1531 the *encomendero* was conqueror Gómez Nieto.

Note: There was a first conqueror Domingo Martín who took part in the conquest of Pánuco and was a *vecino* of Mexico City ca. 1547. He made no claim of ever having been an *encomendero* in Pánuco or elsewhere.

(Gerhard, 243f.; Chipman, 160 and 292; Icaza, I, 23f.)

460. Juan de la TORRE—*Hidalgo*
Poblador Antiguo
From: Ciudad Real
Father: Antonio de la Torre

Torre arrived in New Spain in 1523 as a member of the entourage of his cousin, Treasurer Alonso de Estrada, after having been in Santo Domingo since ca. 1508. He became a *vecino* of Mexico City, serving as *regidor* in 1525 and 1528 and *alcalde ordinario* in 1526, 1527, and 1532. At one time he held four *cabeceras* in *encomienda*, all assigned by Cortés. They included Tepecuacuilco (80 miles south-southwest of Mexico City, 25 miles south-southwest of Taxco; 50 dependencies in 1579), reassigned in the late 1520s by the first Audiencia to Hernando de Torres; Xaltepec (200 miles southeast of Mexico City, 30 miles northwest of Antequera; six *barrios* in 1550), reassigned at the same time to Audiencia judge Licenciado Juan Ortiz de Matienzo; Istlaguaca (40 miles west-northwest of Mexico City, 19 miles north-northwest of Toluca; 12 *estancias* in 1569); and Tenayuca (eight miles north-northwest of Mexico City; an undisclosed number of *estancias*), also held at times by Cristóbal Flores, but a crown possession in 1532. Torres was married to doña Inés de Cabrera and had six children. Son Juan, born ca. 1524 in Mexico City, married doña Isabel de Tovar, a daughter of first conqueror Domingo García de Alburquerque. Juan held an *encomienda* transferred to him by his uncle, Luis de la

Torre. Other identified Torre children are Agustín de Sotomayor and doña María de Godoy. Torre had two brothers and a sister in New Spain: Luis, who had also been in Santo Domingo since 1508, and Alonso and doña María, who departed from Spain as members of Alonso de Estrada's entourage. The families combined in Santo Domingo and all four siblings, with their households, arrived in Mexico City in 1523. Torre died in 1535. Istlaguaca, his remaining *encomienda*, then reverted to the crown. Doña Inés was still living in Mexico City ca. 1547.

Note: Cortés was considered to be a cousin of the Torre family, but the particulars of the relationship have not been discovered; nor has Cortés' relationship to Alonso de Estrada been made clear by extant records.

(Gerhard, 146, 175, 177, 201f., and 248f.; Boyd-Bowman, I, no. 1299 and no. 1300, 44f. and II, no. 3730 and no. 3730a, 110; Icaza, II, 5f. and 35.)

461. Luis de la TORRE—*Hidalgo*
     Poblador Antiguo
     From: Cuidad Real
     Father: Antonio de la Torre

Luis, the older brother of Juan de la Torre, arrived in Santo Domingo in 1508 with don Diego Colón, serving in a series of official positions until he moved his entire *casa poblada* to Mexico City in 1523 as a part of the entourage of his cousin, Alonso de Estrada. His brother Juan, also a *vecino* of Santo Domingo, and younger brother Alonso and sister doña María—newly arrived from Spain—were also in the Estrada party. Torre became a *vecino* of Mexico City, serving as *regidor* in 1526 and 1527, *alcalde ordinario* in 1528, 1538, and 1544, and *alcalde de mesta* for the years 1539 and 1545. He was assigned the *encomiendas* of Paguatlan (24 *estancias* in 1571), Papaloticpac (10 *estancias* in 1571), Tlacuiloltepec (15 *visitas* in 1571), and Acasuchitlan (13 *estancias* in the late 1500s), probably by Cortés. These *cabeceras* extended in a line thirty-five miles long, starting at a point fifteen miles west of Huachinango (80 to 115 miles northeast of Mexico City) and running northeasterly along Río San Marcos. Torre married doña Luisa de Acuña in Santo Domingo. They had no children. Sometime in the early 1540s Torre transferred his rights to Tlacuiloltepec and Papaloticpac to his nephew, Juan de la Torre (the son of his brother Juan). Doña Luisa succeeded as *encomendera* of Acasuchitlan and Paguatlan when Torre died, sometime between 1544 and 1547. The widow later married Lope de Cherinos. By 1597 doña Luisa was still listed as *encomendera*, and nephew Juan had been replaced by his brother, Luis de la Torre.

(Gerhard, 118, 120, 335, and 337; Scholes and Adams, 23 and 37f.; Icaza, I, 198 and II, 5f.; Boyd-Bowman, I, no. 1300 and no. 1299, 44f. and II, no. 3730 and no. 3730a, 110; *Actas*, I, 47.)

462. Hernando de TORRES
     First Conqueror
     From: Jaén (?)
     Parents: Alonso de Torres and Juana Hernández

Torres arrived in the Indies ca. 1513 and was with Cortés six years later. He became a *vecino* of Mexico City and was identified as a miner in association with *poblador* Martín Jiménez, a *vecino* and *encomendero* of Colima. The *encomienda* of Tepecuacuilco (80 miles south-southwest of Mexico City; 50 dependencies in 1579) was reassigned to him from *poblador antiguo* Juan de la Torre in the late 1520s, probably by the first Audiencia. Around 1538 he married Juana de Loaysa of Béjar del Castañar (Salamanca), giving her a dowry valued at $2,500 (a house in Mexico City worth $500, six bars of 19-carat gold, and 18 plates of silver). The dowry was negotiated by Francisco de Terrazas. The pair had a daughter, doña Bernardina de Torres. When Torres died ca. 1546, the *encomienda* was divided between Juana and doña Bernardina, then about seven years old. By 1548 the widow, now called doña Juana, had married *hi-*

dalgo poblador Antonio de Almoguer. By the mid-1550s doña Bernardina had married Pedro de Osorio, been widowed, and before 1565 was married to Luis de Godoy. She was the sole *encomendera* of Tepecuacuilco by 1579, having survived her second husband and her mother. Francisco Enríquez Magariño (a son-in-law ?) received the tribute between 1591 and 1596. After that date Torres' granddaughter, doña María de Godoy, was the *encomendera*.

(Gerhard, 146ff.; Boyd-Bowman, I, no. 2139, 73(?); Icaza, I, 211 and II, 8; *Protocolos*, II, no. 2508, 178 of 15 February 1538; Orozco y Berra, 90; Scholes and Adams, 38.)

463. Juan de TOVAR—Merchant, employee of Cortés
Conqueror—Salcedo
From: Burgos (?)

Tovar and a brother, Cristóbal, appear to have been in Santo Domingo as merchants in 1519. By 1520 Juan was a member of Salcedo's resupply effort to Pánuco. Finding the colony abandoned he joined the Tenochtitlan campaign, serving as one of Cortés' retainers. In 1541 he received a coat of arms acknowledging his efforts. Tovar was a *vecino* of Mexico City and received half the tribute from Tequecistlan (30 miles northeast of Mexico City; two *estancias*), shared Xicayan (180 miles south-southeast of Mexico City) with conqueror Francisco Guillén, and was the sole *encomendero* of Yurirapúndaro (150 miles west-northwest of Mexico City; 1,500 tributaries in 1570) from ca. 1528 to 1539 when it was reassigned to conqueror Alonso de Castillo. Tovar was married and had several children. In the early 1550s he was succeeded by a son, Juan Hipólito de Tovar. This same son was still *encomendero* until 1600.

(Gerhard, 65f., 150f., and 274f.; *Nobiliario*, 55f.; Scholes and Adams, 42f.; Orozco y Berra, 72; *Protocolos*, I, no. 276, 86f. of 1 December 1525 and no. 1520, 321 of 15 September 1529; *Actas*, I, 39.)

464. Rafael de TREJO
First Conqueror
From: Plasencia (Cáceres ?)
Parents: Juan de Toro and María González

Having been in the Indies since ca. 1514, Trejo joined the Cortés *entrada* and later became a *vecino* of Mexico City. He held the *encomienda* of Zacatepec (210 miles south-southeast of Mexico City; 12 *estancias* in 1548). Trejo was married and had a number of children. He was succeeded ca. 1548 by a son, Rafael de Trejo Carvajal, still listed as the *encomendero* in 1604.

(Gerhard, 381f.; *Protocolos*, II, no. 2198, 107 of 1 March 1537; Orozco y Berra, 54; Boyd-Bowman, I, no. 1057, 36.)

465. Diego VALADÉS
Conqueror—Narváez
From: Villanueva de Barcarrota (Badajoz)
Parents: Alonso Valadés and Catalina de Retamosa

Valadés was in Cuba by 1519, arrived in New Spain with the Narváez *entrada*, and ultimately became a *vecino* of Mexico City, where he had his *casa poblada*, family, arms, and horses. He was a Mexico City constable (*alguacil*) in 1526 and *mayordomo* of the *cabildo* in 1533 and 1536. Valadés was the *encomendero* of Tenampulco (115 miles east-northeast of Mexico City in the Pánuco jurisdiction; eight *estancias* in 1548 and only two by 1581); it had a claimed income of $150 in 1547. He was married to Catalina Rodríguez, still in Seville in 1528. By 1547 he claimed six children, four of them natural. At this same time his household included a brother and sister-in-law with their five children, two sisters, and two nieces ready to marry. Another sister was married to *poblador* Luis Daza of Valladolid, and a niece was the wife of *poblador* Baltasar del Salto of Jaén, who claimed in his petition to Viceroy Mendoza that he supported thirty Spaniards in his house. Valadés received a coat of arms dated 29 April 1544.

He died sometime after 1568 and was succeeded by a son, Alonso, who was still the *encomendero* in 1626.

(Gerhard, 389f.; *Nobiliario*, 74f.; Scholes and Adams, 19; Icaza, I, 54f. and II, 43 and 134f.; *Protocolos*, I, no. 167, 64 of 30 October 1525; no. 1640, 342 of 7 October 1528; and II, no. 1951, 53 of 26 September 1536.)

466. Cristóbal de VALDERRAMA
Poblador
From: Valderrama de las Montañas (Burgos)

Valderrama arrived in New Spain in 1523 and immediately joined the Colima *entrada*. He worked his way back to Mexico City, where in 1525 he was a *vecino* and in the employ of accountant (*contador*) of the royal treasury, Rodrigo de Albornoz. Valderrama was the *encomendero* of Tecociapa, Atliacapan, Temecatipan, and Xaltepozotlan (all *cabeceras* in the Colima jurisdiction) until they were reassigned ca. 1526 to first conqueror Juan Pinzón. Two years later Valderrama was assigned Tarímbaro—also referred to as Istapa—(130 miles west-northwest of Mexico City near Ciudad Michoacán; 12 or more *estancias*), hiring Martín Jiménez, a *vecino* of Colima, to administer it. Valderrama also administered Ecatepec (14 miles north-northeast of Mexico City; 10 to 12 *estancias* in the late 1500s) for his wife, *encomendera* doña Leonor Moctezuma, widow of Juan Paz. She received this grant in perpetuity from Cortés in 1527. They had one daughter, doña Leonor de Valderrama y Moctezuma, who received Ecatepec in dowry when she married Diego Arias de Sotelo in the 1540s. She had at least two sons. When Valderrama's widow died, Tarímbaro also went to doña Leonor and Arias. Arias succeeded as *encomendero*. Their son, don Fernando Sotelo de Moctezuma, succeeded when Arias was exiled in 1568. Don Fernando transferred one-third of Ecatepec to his younger brother, don Cristóbal de Sotelo Valderrama, in 1593.

(Gerhard, 80, 226f., 345, and 352; *Protocolos*, I, no. 11, 27 of 15 August 1525; no. 179, 66 of 3 November 1525; and no. 1668a, 348 of 12 October 1528; Scholes and Adams, 27; Boyd-Bowman, II, no. 2591, 74.)

467. Bartolomé de VALDÉS
Poblador
From: Lebrija (Seville)
Parents: Bachiller Bartolomé Ramírez and Beatriz de Valdés

Valdés arrived in New Spain late in 1521 or in early 1522; he appears to have been a person of little talent. He was initially a *vecino* of Mexico City, but by the 1540s he was living in Chiautla (also called Minas de Ayoteco), a mining camp some fifty miles west of Antequera. In the 1520s Valdés had held Justlaguaca with conqueror Antonio Aznar (120 miles south-southeast of Mexico City). By 1550 half of this *cabecera* was the *encomienda* of *poblador* don Tristán de Luna y Arellano and the other half a crown holding. Valdés, however, claimed to be the *encomendero* of Cuiquila (22 miles southwest of his Chiautla residence), another *cabecera* assigned to don Tristán. He was married to a daughter of *poblador* Juan López Pavón from Almodóvar del Campo (Ciudad Real). She, her father, and two sisters had arrived in New Spain in 1528.

(Gerhard, 164f. and 284; Boyd-Bowman, II, no. 8537, 264 and no. 3619, 106; Icaza, I, 253; *Protocolos*, I, no. 71 and no. 72, 41f. of 19 September 1525).

468. Juan de VALDIVIESO
Conqueror—Ruiz de la Mota
From: Valdivieso (Burgos)

Valdivieso, although claiming a Burgos origin, appears to have been related to the house of San Miguel de Aguayo, Santander. The two places in Spain are less than fifty miles apart and Aguayo could well have been considered in the Burgos district in the sixteenth century. He was in Cuba by 1520 and shortly thereafter arrived in New Spain on a ship captained by

Jerónimo Ruiz de la Mota Zárate in the Alderete *entrada*, just in time to take part in the siege and capture of Tenochtitlan. From there he went to Colima, Oaxaca, and Guatemala. By 1525 Valdivieso was living in Colima, but in October of that year he became a *vecino* of Mexico City. Six years later he was *alcalde ordinario* of Oaxaca. Valdivieso was the *encomendero* of Etlatongo (180 miles southeast of Mexico City; seven or eight *sujetos* in 1550) and Guautla (190 miles southeast of Mexico City; three *barrios* in 1550), and he shared the tribute of Tamazola (205 miles southeast of Mexico City near Antequera; 14 *estancias* in 1550) and Cenzontepec (240 miles south-southeast of Mexico City; 11 *estancias* in 1548 and 200 tributaries in 1570) with conqueror Alonso de Contreras, also from Burgos. The first three *cabeceras* were assigned him by Cortés, the remaining by the second Audiencia. Valdivieso was married and had children. A son, Juan Vázquez de Valdivieso, succeeded in the late 1530s when Valdivieso died while on a trip to Spain. This son was still the *encomendero* in 1597.

(Gerhard, 200, 202, and 276f.; Icaza, I, 118f.; Boyd-Bowman, II, no. 2594, 74; Scholes and Adams, 31; Orozco y Berra, 94.)

469. Pedro (Garao) VALENCIANO
Conqueror—Narváez
From: Valencia

Valenciano was in Cuba by 1517 at least. In 1520, in the company of a Bartolomé Porras and his wife, he arrived in New Spain with the Narváez *entrada*. By 1527 he was a *vecino* of Mexico City, dealing in merchandise, associated with Portuguese conqueror Alonso González in raising pigs and growing wheat in the area of his *encomienda*. He shared Huepustla (31 miles north of Mexico City; 3,070 tributaries distributed among the *cabecera* and its three *sujetos*: Tlacuitlapilco, Tianguistongo, and Texcatepec) with first conqueror Antón Bravo of Badajoz. By 1527 he had married Múñez Mancheño Cerrano [sic], the widow of his conquest companion, Bartolomé Porras. They had one daughter, María Garao, who by 1547 was married to *poblador* Juan de Manzanares of Santo Domingo de la Calzada (Logroño), a relative of Licenciado Lorenzo de Tejada, a judge of the Audiencia. Valenciano was succeeded by this daughter ca. 1545. By 1564 she had been widowed and was married to Dr. Frías de Albornoz. Six years later she had been widowed again and remarried, this time to Dr. Ambrosio de Bustamante. Bustamante was listed as the *encomendero* in 1604.

(Gerhard, 296 and 298; Boyd-Bowman, I, no. 4459a, 147; no. 3062a, 108; and II, no. 6129, 187; Scholes and Adams, 32; Icaza, I, 105 and 158; *Protocolos*, I, no. 295, 90f. of 4 December 1525; no. 408, 116 of 3 March 1527; no. 477, 131 of 5 April 1527; and no. 1635, 341 of 6 October 1528.)

470. Alonso VALIENTE
Poblador Antiguo
From: Medina de las Torres (Badajoz)
Parents: Francisco Martínez and María Mejía

Valiente, a relative of Cortés, arrived in Santo Domingo in 1508 with don Diego Colón and from 1509 until 1521 was a *vecino* of Puerto Rico. He, his household, and sixty Spaniards he provisioned arrived in Mexico City four months after its capture. Valiente held a number of appointive offices in addition to acting as secretary to Cortés. His service is recounted in his coat of arms citation of 26 November 1547. In the 1520s Valiente was considered a *vecino* of Medellín, Veracruz, and Mexico City simultaneously. By 1547 he held citizenship in both Mexico City and Puebla. Cortés assigned him the *encomienda* of Tecamachalco (95 miles east-southeast of Mexico City, 39 miles east-southeast of Puebla; 29 *sujetos* in 1580—shown to be a very large grant in a 1564 listing). Valiente's first wife, whom he married while in Puerto Rico, died in the 1530s. He was referred to the Inquisition in 1538 for having said that simple fornication was not a mortal sin. By 1540 he had married Melchora Pellicel Alberrucia, assumed to be the daughter of the Basque merchant Martín de Alberrucia of Tolosa. There was no issue of either union. Around 1560 he was succeeded by Melchora, who soon married Rodrigo de Vivero, a nephew of the viceroy. The *encomendero* of Tecamachalco ca. 1600 was their son, don Rodrigo de Vivero Alberrucia, who in 1627 became the first Conde del Valle de Orizaba.

(Gerhard, 278 and 280; Boyd-Bowman, I, no. 475, 17; Icaza, I, 191f.; Scholes and Adams, 40; *Protocolos*, I, no. 559, 146 of 24 May 1527; no. 1296, 280 of 28 April 1528; and no. 1545, 325 of 19 September 1528; Greenleaf, 135.) '

471. Gonzalo VARELA (Gallegos)
First Conqueror
From: Gamil, Pontevedra (Galicia)
Parents: Juan de Porto de Zodecada and Teresa de Ramil (Gamil ?)

Varela was in Cuba by 1518 and, after taking part in the capture of Tenochtitlan as a member of the Cortés *entrada*, served in the pacification of the west coast. He was a founding *vecino* of Zacatula and lived there until ca. 1546, when he moved to Ciudad Michoacán. Varela held the *encomienda* of Huiztla, a very small grant near Zacatula. He and his wife, *"una mujer muy honrada,"* had one child, Ana de Porras. Ana succeeded Varela in the 1550s and married *poblador* Andrés Hurtado ca. 1560. Ana was still shown as the *encomendera* in 1597.

(Gerhard, 394; Icaza, I, 17; Boyd-Bowman, I, no. 2513, 88; Scholes and Adams, 52.)

472. Francisco de VARGAS—*Hidalgo*
First Conqueror
From: Seville
Parents: Juan de Vargas and Juana Méndez de Valdés

Vargas was in Cuba by 1518 and, after taking part in the capture of Tenochtitlan, served on *entradas* to Pánuco and Colima. He was a *vecino* of Mexico City, where he maintained his *casa poblada "honradamente"* with arms and horses. His career as an *encomendero* was less than consistent. Cortés assigned him Tulancingo (72 miles northwest of Mexico City; 13 *estancias* in the late 1550s), Amatlan (300 miles southeast of Mexico City; beyond Antequera) and Suchitepec (310 miles southeast of Mexico City near Amatlan; four *estancias* in 1550). Shortly thereafter Cortés reclaimed Tulancingo, reassigning it to his *mayordomo* Francisco de Terrazas, and Amatlan, which he gave to Pedro Gallardo, leaving Vargas with Suchitepec, a grant he held until 1537. Nuño de Guzmán assigned Vargas half of Tangitavo (unlocated, but probably in the vicinity of Pánuco) only to have it taken by the second Audiencia in the early 1530s. Vargas was married and by 1547 had two sons and a daughter. His brother, Juan Alonso de Vargas, was a *poblador vecino* of Zacatula, where Vargas himself for a time held the office of *alcalde mayor*.

(Gerhard, 124, 126, 188, 335, and 337; Icaza, I, 22; Boyd-Bowman, I, no. 3260, 144; Orozco y Berra, 90.)

473. Juan Alonso de VARGAS—*Hidalgo Poblador*
From: Seville
Parents: Juan de Vargas and Juana Méndez de Valdez

Vargas arrived in New Spain in 1521 after the capture of Tenochtitlan and took part in the *entradas* to Pánuco, Colima, Motín, Zacatula, and later Jalisco. He became a *vecino* of Zacatula and *encomendero* of Cigua and Tecpan (105 miles east-southeast of Zacatula). Vargas had held Xicayan (vicinity of Pánuco; 287 tributaries in 1532), Caquistle, Ahualulco, Cicaltlan, and Azicatipan (all near Zacatula), one-third of Sayula (168 miles northwest of Zacatula; three *estancias* in 1548) and four *estancias* southeast of Pátzcuaro, but all were reassigned when he took possession of Cigua and Tecpan. Vargas married María Ruiz Saavedra and had eight children, four of them sons. He was still a *vecino* of Zacatula in 1555. His brother, first conqueror Francisco de Vargas, was a *vecino* of Mexico City.

(Gerhard, 217, 240, 242, and 394; Icaza, II, 65f.; *Protocolos*, I, no. 735, 180 of 23 August 1527 and no. 1127, 251 of 28 February 1528; Boyd-Bowman, II, no. 10295, 311; Chipman, 292.)

474. Pedro de VARGAS
Poblador Antiguo
From: Seville
Parents: Alonso Sánchez de la Parra and Florentina de Vargas

Vargas arrived in Santo Domingo in 1505 and after taking part in the pacification of Cuba spent the next eleven years there. He arrived in New Spain three months after the capture of Tenochtitlan and joined *entradas* first to the west coast and then to Pánuco. Vargas was a *vecino* of Mexico City, where he maintained his *casa poblada*, arms, and horses. He shared Iztaquimaxtlan (also called Castilblanco, 90 miles east of Mexico City, 40 miles northeast of Puebla; two *cabeceras* and an undisclosed number of *estancias*) in the early years with conqueror Francisco Montaño and then after 1530 with first conqueror Bartolomé Hernández de Nava. Vargas was married and had one daughter. He transferred his half of the *encomienda* to her in dowry when she married Juan Ortiz de Arriaga in the 1540s. Arriaga was born in Santo Domingo, the son of Diego de Arriaga, a *regidor* of Azúa (where Hernando Cortés began his public and commercial career). Around 1547 Vargas claimed poverty, requesting a *corregimiento* so that he could support himself in his old age.

(Gerhard, 228ff.; Scholes and Adams, 29; Icaza, II, 137 and I, 216; *Protocolos*, I, no. 420 and no. 421, 118f. of 9 March 1527.)

475. Bernaldino VÁZQUEZ de Tapia—
Hidalgo
First Conqueror
From: Oropesa (Toledo)
Parents: Pedro Sánchez Vázquez and doña Marina Alfonsa de Balboa

Vázquez, after the death of his parents, grew up in the households of a paternal uncle, Doctor Pedro Vázquez de Oropesa, and a maternal uncle, don Francisco Alvarez, Bishop of Toro. He arrived in the Indies ca. 1514 with Pedrarias de Avila's Darién expedition and served with him for over two years, acquiring the title of captain. He then went in 1517 to Cuba, where he was given an *encomienda* (*"por mi persona y servicios, me dió y encomendó pueblos e indios"*). Vázquez was with Grijalva coasting New Spain the following year. He sold his Cuban grant to finance his participation as a horseman in the 1519 Cortés *entrada*, serving as a captain and *factor* of the treasury. He was a founding *regidor* of Veracruz, participating in the legal fiction that created New Spain, and later he represented the new province before the crown as one of the *procuradores*. Vázquez was also a founding *vecino* of Mexico City, a Cortés-appointed *regidor* in 1524, and a perpetual *regidor* of Mexico City from August 1528 until 1559. He also served as *alcalde ordinario* in 1541 and again in 1549 as a replacement for deceased incumbents. Cortés assigned him the *encomiendas* of Guamuchitlan (125 miles south-southeast of Mexico City near Tlapa; 2,247 tributaries in 1548 and 16 *estancias* in 1570) and Churubusco, also called Huitzilopochco (five miles south of Mexico City; 11 *barrios* and three *estancias* in 1569). Alonso de Estrada, when governor in 1528, reassigned him one-fourth of Tlapa (135 miles southwest of Mexico City; 6,802 tributaries in 1548 and more than 130 *sujetos* in 1573). Originally claimed by Cortés, this grant was assigned by the acting governors to conqueror Francisco de Ribadeo in 1525. The Vázquez assignment was made after Ribadeo's death in 1527. The first Audiencia exchanged Churubusco for another quarter of Tlapa in 1529, but the second Audiencia took this quarter for the crown in 1534. Churubusco was returned to Vázquez in 1536. Vázquez was married, perhaps twice, and had five children, one of them a daughter. He also claimed natural children and supported a number of nieces, nephews, and retainers in his large household. One niece, doña Isabel Vázquez, married *poblador regidor* Bernardino de Albornoz, namesake nephew of the *contador* (royal treasury accountant) of New Spain. Another niece, doña Catalina de Tapia, married *regidor* first conqueror Antonio de Carvajal. A natural daughter married Ginés Mercado. Vázquez died late in 1559 and was succeeded as *encomendero* by a son with the same name; after 1604 the *encomendero* was a grandson, don Bernaldino Vázquez de Tapia. Diego Arias de Sotelo succeeded Vázquez as *regidor*.

(Gerhard, 322f. and 178f.; Aiton, 90; Icaza, I, 2 ff. and II, 22; Scholes and Adams, 36; Boyd-Bowman, I, no. 4317, 142; II, no. 11488a and no. 11490a, 342; *Actas*, V, 267; Orozco y Berra, 90; Jorge Gurria la Croix, ed., *Relación de méritos y servicios del conquistador Bernaldino Vázquez de Tapia*.

476. Francisco VÁZQUEZ de Coronado—
Hidalgo
Poblador
From: Salamanca
Parents: Juan Vázquez de Coronado and doña Isabel de Luján

Vázquez de Coronado arrived in New Spain in 1535 as a member of Viceroy don Antonio Mendoza's entourage and served in a succession of offices. He was a *vecino* of Mexico City and *regidor* there for the latter half of 1538, 1539, 1542, and from 1545 to 1554. He acquired the *cabildo* position from Francisco de Santa Cruz. In 1538 Vázquez bought the privately held half of Teutenango (31 miles southwest of Mexico City) and Cuzamala (122 miles southwest of Mexico City; twenty-two *sujetos* in 1570) from conqueror Juan de Burgos in 1538. While serving as governor of New Galicia in the early 1540s he shared Aguacatlan, Xala, Amaxaque, Tepuzuacan, Amatlan, Xalcingo, Istimitique, Atengoychan, Cacaluta, and Guaxacatlan (all in a line, 70 to 85 miles west of Guadalajara; perhaps 3,000 total tributaries ca. 1548) with Alvaro de Bracamonte. The Vázquez share reverted to the crown in 1544. He also held Guazamota (60 miles east-southeast of Durango). It was later transferred to the Portuguese *poblador* Gonzalo Martín, a *vecino* of Compostela. His wife, doña Beatriz de Estrada, had received half of Tlapa (140 miles south-southeast of Mexico City; 6,802 tributaries in 1548) in dowry from her mother the year before. Her parents were the late royal treasurer Alonso de Estrada and doña María Gutiérrez Flores de la Caballería. Vázquez and doña Beatriz had a number of children. He was succeeded ca. 1554 by a daughter, doña Isabel de Luján, who married don Bernardino Pacheco de Bocanegra. She in turn was succeeded ca. 1570 by a sister married to don Nuño de Chaves de Bocanegra, don Bernardino Pacheco's brother. Cuzamala had reverted to the crown by 1597. Doña Beatriz was still listed as *encomendera* of half of Tlapa the same year.

Vázquez de Coronado, or simply Coronado in the English speaking world, is best known for his 1540 to 1542 Cíbola *entrada*. He and a force of 285 Spaniards, 225 of whom were mounted, and perhaps 800 Indian auxiliaries supported by a large logistical train trekked nearly 5,000 miles through what is now northwestern Mexico and southwestern United States. The fabled Seven Cities of Cíbola failed to materialize and Vázquez found no mineral riches. His inventory of lands visited did, however, invite subsequent exploration, settlement, and proselytization.

(Gerhard, 271, 291, 321, and 323; Gerhard 1982, 61f., 87–89, and 213; Boyd-Bowman, II, no. 7617, 235.)

477. Martín VÁZQUEZ
First Conqueror
From: Martín Muñoz de las Posadas (Segovia)
Parents: Francisco and Mari Vázquez

Vázquez came to the Indies in 1514 with the Pedrarias expedition to Tierra Firme, was in Cuba two years later, coasted Yucatan with Fernández de Córdoba in 1517, and by 1519 was a member of the Cortés *entrada*. He then served on *entradas* to Pánuco and Colima before becoming a *vecino* of Mexico City. Vázquez was assigned the *encomiendas* of Xilocingo (36 miles north of Mexico City; three *estancias* in 1550), Chicuautla (70 miles north of Mexico City; 1,218 tributaries in the *cabecera* and four *estancias*), and Mistepec (180 miles southeast of Mexico City; six *estancias* in 1598). During 1528 Governor Alonso de Estrada took Chicuautla and Mistepec, reassigning Chicuautla to conqueror Juan de Avila *"el tuerto"* and Mistepec to conqueror Alonso García Bravo. In return, Vázquez was assigned Tlaxiaco (190 miles southeast of Mexico City near Mistepec; eight sub-*cabeceras* and 100 *estancias* in 1548), originally assigned by Cortés to Juan Núñez Sedeño. Vázquez was married to a Cuban woman and had three sons and a daughter by her. He was succeeded ca. 1547 by one of the sons, Francisco Vázquez Lainez. Francisco died during the 1550s, leaving the *encomienda* to his widow and a son, Matías Vázquez Lainez. When Matías died ca. 1600, the *encomienda* reverted to the crown.

(Gerhard, 155f., 164, 166, 286 and 289; *Protocolos*, I, no. 122, 54f. of 11 October 1525; Boyd-Bowman, I, no. 2899, 103; Scholes and Adams, 49; Icaza, I, 104f.; Orozco y Berra, 55.)

478. Benito de VEJER (Bejer)—Drummer
First Conqueror
From: Vejer de la Frontera (Cádiz)

Vejer, a veteran of the wars in Italy, was in Cuba by 1518 and served as a drummer with the 1519 Cortés *entrada*. By 1524 he was a *vecino* of Mexico City. Three years later he was renting a house for a school of dance. Cortés assigned him the *encomienda* of Axacuba (48 miles north of Mexico City near Tula; six *estancias* with 4,300 tributaries in 1570). The second Audiencia revoked this award in the early 1530s and took the *encomienda* for the crown. Axacuba was reassigned by Viceroy Mendoza to conqueror Jerónimo López in 1543. Vejer, married to Ana Gómez, is not heard from after 1528.

(Gerhard, 296 and 298f.; Boyd-Bowman, I, no. 1244a, 42; *Protocolos*, I, no. 368, 107 of 14 February 1525 and no. 510, 137 of 24 April 1527; Orozco y Berra, 90; *Actas*, I, 11.)

479. Alonso VELÁZQUEZ—Notary
Poblador
From: Portillo (Valladolid)
Parents: Hernán Velázquez and Ana Núñez

Velázquez arrived in New Spain ca. 1538 and three years later took part in the pacification of New Galicia under Viceroy Mendoza. He probably became a *vecino* of Mexico City, where he maintained his *casa poblada*, arms, and horses, about the same time he became the *encomendero* of Michimaloya (50 miles north-northwest of Mexico City near Tula; four *visitas* in 1570) by marrying Isabel de Olmos, widow of the original holder, conqueror Juan de Zamudio. She was a daughter of conqueror Francisco de Olmos. Velázquez and Isabel had three children. He died ca. 1570 and was succeeded by Isabel, still the *encomendera* until after 1597.

(Gerhard, 332f.; Boyd-Bowman, II, no. 11983, 357; Icaza, II, 11f.)

480. Francisco VELÁZQUEZ de Lara—
Hidalgo
Conqueror—Díaz de Aux
From: Ayamonte (Huelva)
Parents: Gonzalo Velázquez de Lara of Oviedo and doña Teresa de Ayamonte

Velázquez was in Santo Domingo by 1518 and left quickly for Cuba in 1519 after an unspecified incident. He sailed with Díaz de Aux for Pánuco in 1520 and when that settlement was abandoned joined the Cortés *entrada* for the siege and capture of Tenochtitlan. Velázquez, one of Cortés' many retainers, became a *vecino* of Mexico City, where he had his *casa poblada*, arms, and horses. He maintained a pattern of buying and selling merchandise in $50 to $150 lots, mostly on credit, plus dealing in horses and slaves, both black and Indian. Velázquez was the first *encomendero* of Ixitlan (190 miles east-southeast of Mexico City), a relatively small grant. He was married and had two children. His son, Luis, succeeded as *encomendero* in the 1570s and was still receiving the tribute in 1604.

(Gerhard, 42f.; Icaza, I, 79; Boyd-Bowman, I, no. 1692, 60; Scholes and Adams, 18; Orozco y Berra, 68; *Actas*, I, 13.)

481. Juan VELÁZQUEZ
First Conqueror (?)

Velázquez, a *vecino* of Mexico City, was the first *encomendero* of Pungaravato (122 miles southwest of Mexico City; 13 *estancias* in 1548). He and his wife, Isabel de Rojas, had no children. Velázquez died ca. 1527. In that year the *encomienda* was reassigned, divided between first conqueror Hernando Alonso and *poblador* Pedro Bazán. Bazán acquired full rights when Alonso was executed as a relapsed Jew in 1528. Isabel then married first conqueror Francisco Maldonado, succeeding as *encomendera* of Maldonado's grant when he died. By 1548 the widow, now styled doña Isabel, had married don Tristán de Arellano. He unsuccessfully petitioned for the reassignment of Pungaravato.

(Gerhard, 135f.; Icaza, II, 10f.; *Actas*, I, 13.)

482. Alonso VERDEJO
Poblador Antiguo
From: Villamayor de la Mancha (Cuenca)
Parents: Francisco de Verdejo and Mari Garrida

Verdejo arrived in Santo Domingo ca. 1508 and became a *vecino* and *encomendero* of Concepción. By 1518 he was in Darién, and by 1523 he had become a member of Garay's Pánuco expedition. After dabbling in business ventures in Mexico City, he joined a 1527 *entrada* to Motines and later (1541) went to New Galicia under Viceroy Mendoza. In the mid-1520s he was a *vecino* of Mexico City; then, after acquiring the *encomienda* of Mechia (in the province of Zacatula), he established his *casa poblada* with arms and horses in Zacatula. Verdejo married and had at least one daughter. In the early 1560s he was succeeded by his widow, who then married *poblador* Juan de Castañeda. Mechia was a crown property by 1570.

(Gerhard, 394; Icaza, I, 243f.; Boyd-Bowman, I, no. 1542, 52; *Protocolos*, I, no. 57, 38 of 9 September 1525; no. 334, 101 of 4 February 1527; no. 854, 202 of 6 November 1527; and no. 939, 220 of 7 January 1528.)

483. Francisco VERDUGO—*Hidalgo*
Conqueror—Narváez
From: Cúellar (Segovia)
Parents: Francisco Verdugo and Inés de Cúellar

Verdugo, in Cuba before 1519, arrived in New Spain as a captain with Narváez and quickly sided with Cortés in spite of his relationship (brother-in-law) to Cuba's governor, Diego Velázquez. He became an early *vecino* of Mexico City, serving as *regidor* in 1526 and 1528 and *alcalde ordinario* in 1529. Verdugo went with Nuño de Guzmán to New Galicia and was a *vecino* of Compostela in 1532, but then came back to Mexico City three years later. Cortés assigned him the *encomienda* of Teotihuacan (30 miles northeast of Mexico City; 18 *sujetos* in 1580). On 2 June 1531 Verdugo received a license to operate an inn near this grant. In 1525 the acting governors reassigned Yautepec and Tepoztlan (39 and 30 miles south of Mexico City; 5,500 tributaries in the two *cabeceras* and 19 *estancias* and *sujetos*) from Cortés to Verdugo and Francisco de Orduña, a Basque. Cortés recovered the *encomiendas* in early 1528. From 1537 Verdugo shared Cuestlaguaca (172 miles southeast of Mexico City; 20 to 30 *sujetos* in the late 1500s) with Bachiller Pedro Díaz de Sotomayor. Verdugo married Isabel Velázquez, Diego Velázquez' sister, in Cúellar before leaving for the Indies. Their daughter, Francisca, married Alonso de Bazán prior to 1535, the year that Verdugo moved his household, including daughter and son-in-law, to Mexico City. A natural daughter married *poblador* Juan Aldaz Navarro of Peralta, Navarre. Verdugo was succeeded by Francisca in the 1540s and she by her son, don Andrés de Bazán, in the 1560s. The *encomienda* was reassigned to don Luis de Velasco when Andrés died in 1568, but a brother, don Antonio Velázquez de Bazán, recovered it. Teotihuacan and half of Cuestlaguaca were in the family for two more generations, reverting to the crown after 1658.

(Gerhard, 95, 97, 285, 273ff., and 288; Scholes and Adams, 30; Icaza, I, 196 and 234; Boyd-Bowman, I, no. 2893, 102 and II, no. 7890; no. 7892, 245; no. 3859; and no. 7860, 244; *Actas*, II, 107.)

484. Angel de VILLAFAÑE
Poblador
From: León
Parents: Juan de Villafañe and Catalina Valdés

Villafañe arrived in and became a *vecino* of Mexico City ca. 1525, perhaps as an extension of a merchant family. His father and an uncle had been in Puerto Rico since 1512 as retainers of the Bishop of San Juan. Villafañe became the *encomendero* of Xaltepec (200 miles southwest of Mexico City; six *barrios* in 1550 and eight *estancias* ca. 1600) in 1532. This grant was first held by *poblador antiguo* Juan de la Torre and then by Juan Ortiz de Matienzo before the second Audiencia reassigned it to Villafañe. Ca. 1536 he married doña Inés de Carvajal of Plasencia (Cáceres). They had at least one son, Juan, who succeeded as *encomendero* in 1567. Ten years later the tribute was assigned to don Luis de Velasco.

Note: See discussion under no. 325, Juan Ortiz de Matienzo.

(Gerhard, 201f.; *Protocolos*, I, no. 149, 60 of 20 October 1525; Boyd-Bowman, II, no. 5933, 179 and no. 3027a, 88; Scholes and Adams, 20.)

485. Leonardo de VILLAFELIZ
Conqueror—Narváez
From: Villafeliz (León)

Villafeliz arrived in the Indies in 1514 as a member of the Pedrarias de Avila expedition and came to New Spain as a member of the Narváez *entrada*. He became a *vecino* of Mexico City in September 1524, and was the *encomendero* of Xiquilpa (33 miles west of Zamora; 1,700 tributaries after the epidemic of 1579) from 1528 to 1545, when the tribute reverted to the crown.

(Gerhard, 387f.; *Actas*, I, 19; Boyd-Bowman, I, no. 2234, 76.)

486. Antonio de VILLAGÓMEZ
Poblador
From: Zamora
Parents: Rodrigo de Villagómez and Isabel de Angulo

Villagómez arrived in New Spain in 1522 with his brother Juan. In 1526 he became a *vecino* of Mexico City and *encomendero* of Ocoyoacac (19 miles southwest of Mexico City), a *cabecera* originally held by Cortés and assigned to Villagómez in 1526. No more is heard from him after the *encomienda* was reassigned to doña Isabel Moctezuma as part of Tacuba in the 1540s.

(Gerhard, 271; Boyd-Bowman, II, no. 12794, 384; *Protocolos*, I, no. 1035, 235 of 1 February 1528.)

487. Juan de VILLAGÓMEZ
Poblador
From: Zamora
Parents: Rodrigo de Villagómez and Isabel de Angulo

Villagómez and his brother Antonio arrived in New Spain in 1522. He then served with *entradas* to Oaxaca, the west coast, and later New Galicia and Jalisco. He was a *vecino* of Mexico City, where he maintained a *casa poblada*, arms, and a horse. Villagómez held the *encomienda* of Tamiagua and Tenesticpac (twin *cabeceras* 160 miles northeast of Mexico City with an undisclosed number of *estancias*) until ca. 1570 when the tribute reverted to the crown. By 1587 these *cabeceras* were reassigned to don Luis de Velasco.

(Gerhard, 118 and 120; Boyd-Bowman, II, no. 12795, 384; *Protocolos*, I, no. 139, 58 of 18 October 1525; Icaza, I, 214f.)

488. Juan de VILLAGRÁN
Conqueror—Narváez
From: Villagrán (Valladolid)

Villagrán arrived in Santo Domingo ca. 1508, spent time in Tierra Firme and around the Antilles, and by 1514 was an *encomendero* in San Juan de Maguana, Santo Domingo. He came to New Spain as a member of the Narváez *entrada* and then, after the capture of Tenochtitlan, joined the Pánuco *entrada*, becoming a *vecino* of Santisteban del Puerto and *encomendero* of Tamistla. Nuño de Guzmán then reassigned Tamistla to Alonso de Mendoza and granted Villagrán instead Tempoal (45 miles southwest of Pánuco; 1,120 tributaries in 1532) and a share of Tancolol (vicinity of Pánuco; 32 tributaries in 1532) with first conqueror Alonso Navarrete. Ca. 1534 Tempoal and Tancolol were reassigned by the second Audiencia to Diego de las Roelas, leaving Villagrán with nothing. He was married and had several children. He died in the 1540s, and by 1547 his son, Alonso de Villagrán, was petitioning for a grant for himself and his siblings.

(Gerhard, 216ff.; Icaza, I, 163f.; Chipman, 196 and 292f.; Boyd-Bowman, I, no. 4685, 154.)

489. Gregorio de VILLALOBOS
First Conqueror
From: Almonte (Huelva)
Parents: Diego de Padilla and Teresa de Villalobos, both natives of Jerez de la Frontera

Villalobos arrived in the Indies in 1516, was in Cuba by 1518, and joined Cortés the following year. He was one of those ordered to remain in Veracruz while the rest went on to the capture of Tenochtitlan. He later took part in the pacification of Jalisco under Viceroy Mendoza. Villalobos was a *vecino*, *regidor*, and *alcalde* of Veracruz and later held the same status and offices in Puebla, where he maintained his *casa poblada*, arms, and horses. He was the *encomendero* of Ixguatlan (60 miles west-southwest of Veracruz, 80 miles east of Puebla near Córdoba). After 1527 he married the widow of conqueror Miguel de Zaragoza; the pair had two sons and a daughter, and there was also a niece living in the household. Villalobos died before 1547 and was succeeded by a son. His successor was dead before 1565, and the *encomienda* was then reassigned to don Luis de Velasco.

(Gerhard, 84; Icaza, I, 223f.; Boyd-Bowman, I, no. 1675, 59; Scholes and Adams, 33.)

490. Alonso de VILLANUEVA Tordesillas
Conqueror—Narváez
From: Villanueva de la Serena (La Serena, Extremadura)
Parents: Suárez de Peralta

Villanueva, in Cuba by 1519 and a member of the Narváez *entrada*, entered Cortés' service as a secretary and later served as a gold courier. He became a *vecino* of Mexico City and *encomendero* of Ocelotepec (29 miles west of Mexico City; a number of dependencies), assigned him by Cortés. By 1525 Cortés had also reassigned him Guachinango (87 miles northeast of Mexico City; 65 *estancias* in 1571), taken from Juan de Jaso. He was awarded a coat of arms, dated 24 September 1531. In 1524 Villanueva married doña Ana Cervantes, one of Comendador Leonel de Cervantes' six daughters. They had several children. One daughter married *poblador* Juan López Patino, a native of Jerez de la Frontera and *vecino* of Puebla. Villanueva was succeeded ca. 1550 by a son, Agustín de Villanueva Cervantes, married to doña Catalina de Peralta. Doña Catalina was the *encomendera* after 1597.

(Gerhard, 118f. and 271; Boyd-Bowman, I, no. 599a, 21 and II, no. 8910, 274; Scholes and Adams, 32; Icaza, II, 169f.; Orozco y Berra, 56; *Nobiliario*, 189ff.)

491. and 493. Fernando and Pedro de VILLANUEVA
Conquerors—Ruiz de la Mota
From: Baeza (Jaén)
Parents: Diego de Villanueva and Leonor Rodríguez

The Villanueva brothers, Fernando and Pedro, were in Cuba by 1520, took part in the capture of Mexico City, and served on *entradas* to Pánuco and Oaxaca. Both were *vecinos* of Puebla, sharing the *encomienda* of Quechula (45 miles east-southeast of Puebla; one sub-*cabecera* plus two sub-*cabeceras* shared with nearby Tecamachalco, and numerous *barrios* and *estancias*). Fernando married Isabel Rodríguez and had five sons, the oldest named Melchor. Pedro married a woman with the same name as his mother, Leonor Rodríguez, and also had five children, at least one, a daughter. The brothers Villanueva may have married sisters. Pedro's son, Hernando, married the widow of Cristóbal de Soto (a daughter of Alonso Martín Partidor), and his daughter Leonor was the second wife of Juan de Mancilla. When Fernando died in the 1530s, his share of Quechula was reassigned to conqueror Gonzalo Rodríguez de la Magdalena. Pedro died in the 1560s and was succeeded by a son, Diego de Villanueva. Both received coats of arms. Fernando's was dated 9 January 1535, and Pedro's 17 March 1559. By 1580 the *encomendero* of Pedro's half of Quechula was his grandson, Nicolás.

(Gerhard, 278 and 280; Icaza, I, 88f., 137, 144f., 169f., and II, 175; Boyd-Bowman, II, no. 5585, no. 5569, and no. 5583, 168; Orozco y Berra, 56 and 72; Scholes and Adams, 17 and 33; *Nobiliario*, 19ff.)

492. Juan de VILLANUEVA *"el negro"*
Poblador
From: Granada

Villanueva, after arriving in New Spain in 1526 as a member of the Licenciado Luis Ponce de León entourage, went to Pánuco with Nuño de Guzmán and eventually became a *vecino* of Valles. In the 1540s he was assigned the *encomienda* of Tanzuy (vicinity of Valles; perhaps three *estancias* in 1547). He and his wife, Ana (Antonia) Vázquez, had four children. Ca. 1567 he was succeeded by Ana, who was still the *encomendera* in 1597.

(Gerhard, 355; Icaza, II, 263ff.; Boyd-Bowman, II, no. 4542, 135.)

493. Pedro de VILLANUEVA (see no. 491)

494. Diego de VILLAPADIERNA
Poblador
From: Llerena (Maestrazgo de León, Extremadura)
Father: Diego de Villapadierna

Villapadierna arrived in New Spain in 1522 and immediately joined Cortés' *entrada* to Pánuco, becoming a *vecino* of Santisteban del Puerto. Cortés assigned him the *encomienda* of Taupa (60 tributaries in 1532), but it was taken from him by Nuño de Guzmán. He suffered other indignities as well for supporting his old captain. Alonso de Estrada then gave him half of Matlactonatico (140 miles south of Pánuco; reduced to 16 tributaries by 1626) and half of Xuxupango (150 miles south of Pánuco; eight *sujetos* in 1569, four in 1580) with first conqueror Alonso de Avila. Around 1525 Villapadierna married a conqueror's widow, and the pair had several children. On 22 June 1528 he became a *vecino* of Mexico City. He was succeeded by a namesake son, still listed as *encomendero* in 1597.

(Gerhard, 218, 220, 391, and 393; Boyd-Bowman, II, no. 1456; 41; *Protocolos*, I, no. 546, 144 of 14 May 1527; Icaza, I, 194f.; Chipman, 147f.; Scholes and Adams, 18; *Actas*, I, 172.)

495. Antonio de VILLARROEL (Antonio SERRANO de Cardona)
First Conqueror
From: Medina de Rioseco (Valladolid)
Mother: Leonor de Villarroel (?)

Villarroel arrived in the Indies, probably as a member of Pedraria's Tierra Firme expedition of 1514. He was in Cuba two years later and sailed as a member of Cortés' *entrada* in 1519. He went to Pánuco in 1523, then on to Michoacán, before becoming a *vecino* of Mexico City and *alguacil mayor* in 1525. He changed his name to Serrano de Cardona and presented an appointment as perpetual *regidor* under the new name on 10 September 1528. He participated in *cabildo* business in 1529, 1533, 1536–38, 1540–41, and 1545. In 1525 the acting governors reassigned him the *encomienda* of Cuernavaca (35 miles south of Mexico City; 82 *estancias* in 1532, 15,000 tributaries in 1551 and 70-plus *estancias* in 1570). Cuernavaca was recovered by Cortés in 1531 as part of the Marquesado holdings. Villarroel was married to Isabel de Ojeda. They had no children of their own but did have nephews, nieces, and other marriageable girls in the home. Villarroel died in early 1546, $20,000 in debt.

(Gerhard, 94ff.; Icaza, I, 106f.; *Actas*, I, 182; Boyd-Bowman, I, no. 4560a, 150; Orozco y Berra, 56.)

496. Antonio de VILLARROEL (Villarruel)
Poblador
From: Sahagún (León)
Parents: Francisco Martagón Quirós and María de Villarroel

Villarroel, a 1523 arrival in New Spain, served with *entradas* in Pánuco, against the Zapotecs near Villa Alta, and then at Peñol de Coatlan southwest of Antequera before being assigned the *encomienda* of Totolapa (a Mixe town 48 miles southeast of Antequera). He ultimately became a *vecino* of Antequera and married a daughter of conqueror (Narváez) Bartolomé de Astorga. Astorga was also a *vecino* of Antequera, as well as being a native of León. Villarroel had two sons and was succeeded ca. 1565 by one named Francisco, still the *encomendero* in 1604.

(Gerhard, 197; Icaza, I, 252; Boyd-Bowman, II, no. 5986, 181; Scholes and Adams, 20.)

497. Juan de VILLASEÑOR Orozco—
Hidalgo
Poblador
From: Vélez (Malaga?)
Parents: Alcalde Diego de Burgos and Guiomar de Orozco

Villaseñor arrived in New Spain with his brother, Francisco de Orozco, in the closing days of 1523. The two, with three horses, took part in an *entrada* to Coatlan and then to New Galicia. Francisco is not heard from again. In the early 1530s Juan was ordered to be a *vecino* of Purificación, New Galicia (105 miles southwest of Guadalajara near Autlán), as a member of a security force. Later he was a *vecino* of Ciudad Michoacán, although he claimed he could not afford to reside in the city because of his poor *encomiendas*. He held Guango and Puruándiro (twin *cabeceras* 30 to 40 miles northwest of Ciudad Michoacán; 19 dependencies in 1548), assigned him by Cortés in 1526. In 1544 he received the *encomienda* of Pénjamo (67 miles northwest of Ciudad Michoacán). During the mid-1530s he had a Sultepec mining partnership with Juan Ruiz Martínez. In 1531 Villaseñor married doña Catalina Cervantes (de Lara), one of Comendador Leonel de Cervantes' six daughters. They had five children. He was succeeded ca. 1570 by a namesake son, still the *encomendero* in 1604.

(Gerhard, 167, 345, and 351; Boyd-Bowman, II, no. 12938, 390 and no. 8913, 274; Icaza, I, 188f.; Scholes and Adams, 17f.; *Protocolos*, II, no. 2202, 108 of 2 March 1537.)

498. Francisco de VILLEGAS—*Hidalgo Poblador Antiguo*
From: Castillana (Extremadura)
Parents: Unknown, but a relative of Cortés

Villegas was in the Indies by 1507, spent time in Darién, and then went on to Cuba. By 1520 he was a *vecino* and *alcalde* of Santiago. He arrived in New Spain in 1521, escorting Cortés' first wife, Catalina Suárez. He later saw service on an *entrada* to New Galicia. Villegas was a *vecino* of Mexico City, holding the office of *alcalde ordinario* in 1536 and then *regidor* from 3 August for the rest of the same year. His son, Pedro, was a *regidor* from 1538 to 1553. Cortés assigned Villegas a number of *cabeceras* in *encomienda*. They included Xocotitlan (44 miles west-northwest of Mexico City, 26 miles north of Toluca; two named *estancias* plus a number of others), Atlacomulco (48 miles west-northwest of Mexico City, 32 miles north of Toluca; perhaps 10 *estancias* in 1548), Uruapan (200 miles west of Mexico City; seven *barrios*), sub-*cabecera* Xicalan (vicinity of Uruapan; one *barrio*) and sub-*cabecera* Zirosto (22 miles northwest of Uruapan; 14 *barrios*). He was married and had a number of children and grandchildren. When Villegas died ca. 1552, Xocotitlan and Atlacomulco went to his son Manuel, and before 1593 to a grandson, don Pedro Villegas y Peralta. Both *cabeceras* were crown holdings before 1597. Uruapan and Xicalan went to son Pedro; after 1585 grandson don Martín Villegas was the *encomendero*. Zirosto went to son Francisco, still the *encomendero* in 1604.

(Gerhard, 175, 177, 346, and 352; Icaza, I, 189; Boyd-Bowman, I, no. 5115a, 170; Scholes and Adams, 23f.)

499. Alvaro de ZAMORA—Interpreter
Conqueror—Medel
From: Santa Marta (Zamora)
Parents: Alvaro Pérez and Catalina Domínguez

Zamora, in Cuba by 1519, arrived in New Spain with his father and brother, Alonso Pérez de Zamora, on a ship outfitted by Hernando Medel two weeks after Cortés had neutralized the threat posed by Narváez and alienated his force. After the capture of Tenochtitlan, in which his father was killed, Zamora joined the *entrada* to Tututepec and the south coast. After this he supported himself by interpreting for the Audiencia. By 1525 he was a *vecino* of Mexico City where he kept his arms and horses "at the ready." In 1544 Zamora received the *encomienda* of Mazatlan (360 miles southeast of Mexico City near Tehuantepec; several *estancias*) for his services as interpreter. Ca. 1536 he married a daughter of *poblador* Alonso de Ortega of Portillo, Valladolid; the pair had three children. He was awarded a coat of arms, dated 15 February 1563. When Zamora died ca. 1570, *encomienda* succession was disputed because of the manner and authority by which it was assigned. At any rate, Mazatlan was a crown property by 1580.

(Gerhard, 124 and 126; Icaza, I, 86 and II, 105; Boyd-Bowman, I, no. 4856, 161; Scholes and Adams, 21; *Nobiliario*, 103f.; *Actas*, I, 42.)

500. Francisco de ZAMORA
Conqueror—Narváez
From: Zamora(?)

Little is known of Zamora other than by inference. He was a *vecino* and *regidor* of Antequera in the late 1520s, and by 1525 he had acquired Mitla (40 miles east-southeast of Antequera; eleven *sujetos* in 1580) and Tlacolula (22 miles east-southeast of Antequera; one *estancia* in 1548). Cortés claimed that both *cabeceras* were sub-*cabeceras* of his Cuilapa. Nevertheless, both grants reverted to the crown in 1531, and Zamora is not heard from again.

(Gerhard, 190f.; Orozco y Berra, 68.)

501. Pedro Ruiz ZAMORANO—*Hidalgo*
Conqueror—Narváez
From: Porcuna (Jaén)
Parents: Pedro Ruiz Zamorano and Beatriz Hernández

Zamorano was in Cuba by 1519, went to New Spain with Narváez at age fifteen, and ten years after the capture of Tenochtitlan went with Nuño de Guzmán to New Galicia. He was a *vecino* of Mexico City and there maintained his arms and horses. Zamorano shared Ocuila (32 miles south-southwest of Mexico City near Cuernavaca; 17 *estancias* in 1548—reduced to 14 by 1580) with conqueror Serván Bejerano, the grant having been reassigned to them in 1527 by Alonso de Estrada from Cortés' appointee, conqueror Juan de Morales. During the 1550s Zamorano received through reassignment another Cortés *cabecera*, Ocotlan (260 miles southeast of Mexico City near Antequera; 12 *sujetos* in the 1700s). Zamorano married a daughter of *hidalgo* first conqueror Martín (Pedro) Ruiz de Monjaraz. They had six children. A son, don Nicolás Zamorano de Arrazola, succeeded as *encomendero* ca. 1562. By 1600 a grandson, don Pedro Zamorano, was receiving the tribute.

(Gerhard, 49, 51, and 170f.; Boyd-Bowman, I, no. 2153, 73; Icaza, I, 37; Orozco y Berra, 91, Scholes and Adams, 17; *BAGN*, XII, 28.)

502. Juan de ZAMUDIO
Conqueror—Narváez
From: Zamudio (Biscay)

Zamudio was in Cuba by 1519. After taking part in the capture of Tenochtitlan, he may have been employed by Rodrigo de Paz. He was a *vecino* of Mexico City and the first *encomendero* of Michimaloya (50 miles north-northwest of Mexico City near Tula; four *visitas* in 1570). Zamudio married Isabel de Olmos, a daughter of conqueror Francisco de Olmos, a native of Valladolid. They had no children. She succeeded as *encomendera* in the 1540s and later married *poblador* Alonso Velázquez, also from Valladolid.

(Gerhard, 332f.; *Protocolos*, I, no. 74, 42ff. of 21 September 1525 and II, no. 2178, 104 of 3 February 1537; Boyd-Bowman, I, no. 4820, 159; Icaza, I, 11f.; Scholes and Adams, 35; Orozco y Berra, 91.)

503. Miguel de ZARAGOZA—Merchant
Conqueror—Narváez
From: Zaragoza

Zaragoza was in Cuba by 1517, coasted Mexico with Francisco Hernández de Córdoba, was with Grijalva in 1518, and then came to New Spain as a member of the 1520 Narváez *entrada*. After the capture of Tenochtitlan he warehoused goods for merchants in Veracruz, where he was a *vecino*. Zaragoza was the *encomendero* of Pilopan (70 miles north-northwest of Veracruz near Misantla), Coatepec (50 miles west-northwest of Veracruz near Jalapa; one *estancia* remaining in 1580), and Chilotepec (46 miles northwest of Veracruz near Jalapa; only the *cabecera* remaining in 1580), all assigned by Cortés. He married Beatriz García de la Fuente and had one son named Juan. When Zaragoza died in 1527, Pilopan and Coatepec reverted to the crown. Chilotepec was reassigned to first conqueror Pedro Maldonado. Beatriz married *poblador* Gregorio de Villalobos, also a *vecino* of Veracruz. Juan de Salcedo, a *vecino* of Mexico City, served as tutor and guardian for Zaragoza's son.

Note: Gerhard states that Grijalva ordered a Miguel de Zaragoza to remain in Cempoala in 1518. Neither Bernal Díaz del Castillo nor Gómara register his presence or give information concerning him when the Cortés *entrada* visited Cempoala in 1519, nor does this Zaragoza recount such an adventure in any statement attributed to him.

(Gerhard, 7, 363, 366, 374, and 377; *Protocolos*, I, no. 153, 61 of 23 October 1525; no. 408, 116 of 4 March 1527; and no. 1213, 266 of 1 April 1528; Boyd-Bowman, I, no. 4942, 164 and II, no. 12853, 386; Icaza, I, 107 and 223f.; Orozco y Berra, 68.)

504. Bartolomé de ZÁRATE
Poblador
From: Oviedo (Asturias)
Brother of Juan López de Zárate, Bishop of Oaxaca

Zárate arrived in New Spain in 1523 and left no record of activity until becoming an employee of first Audiencia judge Licenciado Juan Ortiz de Matianzo in 1529. He continued as Ortiz' agent in New Spain until 1538, six years after the discredited judge was arrested and returned to Spain to be tried for excesses while a member of the Audiencia. Zárate was a *vecino* of Ciudad Oaxaca in 1530, then in 1535 a *vecino* and perpetual *regidor* of Mexico City, serving in that capacity until 1539. He received the *encomienda* of Mixquic (24 miles southeast of Mexico City; five *barrios* and six sub-*cabeceras* in 1571). Ca. 1547 it paid $370 worth of roasted garbanzos per year. Zárate was married and had one daughter, Ana, who married Gil Ramírez de Avalos, an *hidalgo* from Baeza (Jaén), with the *encomienda* as her dowry. The crown took it when Ramírez went to Peru in the 1560s. Ramírez' namesake recovered Mixquic by 1570, but ca. 1587 the *encomienda* was reassigned to don Luis de Velasco.

(Gerhard, 103 and 105; Boyd-Bowman, II, no. 225, 10; Icaza, II, 9f.; Scholes and Adams, 43.)

505. Alonso ZIMBRÓN de Vitoria
Conqueror—Narváez
From: Madrid
Parents: Francisco Zimbrón and Mayor de Vitoria

Zimbrón, in the Indies by 1517 and in Cuba two years later, arrived in New Spain as a member of the 1520 Narváez *entrada*. There is some question as to whether or not he served with Cortés in places other than Tututepec, although he claimed to have done so. Zimbrón was a *vecino* of Mexico City in the 1520s; by the mid-1540s he lived in Puebla. His *encomienda*, Censotepec (208 miles southsoutheast of Mexico City; eleven *estancias* in 1548), was in Tututepec and assigned him by Cortés. It was taken ca. 1533 by the second Audiencia and reassigned to conquerors Juan de Valdivieso and Alonso de Contreras. Zimbrón married ca. 1535 and twelve years later had three sons and a daughter.

(Gerhard, 276f.; Boyd-Bowman, I, no. 2326, 80; Icaza, I, 27; Orozco y Berra, 68.)

506. Fray Juan de ZUMÁRRAGA—Bishop of Mexico
Poblador
From: Durango (Biscay)

Zumárraga arrived in New Spain in 1528, the year following his nomination to the post of Bishop of Mexico, but two years before confirmation. This situation perhaps reduced his effectiveness. He went to Spain in 1532 to correct the matter and returned in 1534, fully consecrated as bishop. The following year Viceroy Mendoza assigned him the *encomienda* of Ocuituco (48 miles southeast of Mexico City; 10 *estancias* divided between two *barrios* in 1550). The grant had been held by various combinations of people before 1531, when it was claimed as a crown holding. Ocuituco reverted to the crown under the New Laws in 1544. Zumárraga was elevated to Archbishop of New Spain in 1547 and died a year later at the age of 80.

See note under no. 235, Bishop Juan López de Zárate.

(Gerhard, 92ff.; Boyd-Bowman, II, no. 12398, 371.)

APPENDIX A

Roster of First Conqueror *Encomenderos*

Encomendero	Calling	Residence	Origin
AGUILAR, Jerónimo de	Interpreter	Mexico City	Seville
ALANÉS, Melchor de		Antequera	Aragón
ALONSO, Hernando	Blacksmith	Mexico City	Huelva
ALVARADO, Gonzalo de	*Hidalgo*	Guatemala	Badajoz
ALVARADO, Jorge de	*Hidalgo*	Mexico City	Badajoz
ALVARADO, Pedro de	*Hidalgo*	Guatemala	Badajoz
AVILA, Alonso de	*Hidalgo*	Mexico City	Avila
AVILA, Luis de		Cd. Michoacán	Seville
BARRIOS, Andrés de	*Hidalgo*	Mexico City	Cádiz
BONAL, Francisco de		Puebla	Salamanca
BRAVO, Antón	Swordsmith	Mexico City	Badajoz
CABEZÓN, Cristóbal		Mexico City	Ciudad Real
CÁCERES, Manuel de		Colima	Segovia
CAICEDO, Antón		Mexico City	?
CÁRDENAS, Luis de		Antequera	Seville
CARVAJAL, Antonio de	*Hidalgo*	Mexico City	Zamora
CASTAÑEDA, Rodrigo de	*Hidalgo*	Mexico City	Santander
CATALÁN, Juan	Cannoneer	Mexico City	Catalonia
CERMEÑO, Juan		Mexico City	Huelva
CINDOS de Portillo, Pedro		?	León
COLIO, Diego de		Mexico City	Asturias
CORIA, Diego de		Mexico City	Seville
CORTÉS, Francisco	*Hidalgo*	Colima	Extremadura
CORTÉS, Hernando	*Hidalgo*	Mexico City	Medellín
DAZA de Alconchel, Francisco		Puebla	Badajoz
DÍAZ del Castillo, Bernal	*Hidalgo*	Guatemala	Valladolid
ECIJA, Andrés de		Colima	Seville
FERNÁNDEZ Nieto, Diego		Mexico City	Zamora

GALINDO, Juan Sánchez	Swordsmith	Mexico City	Seville
GALLEGO, Alvaro		Mexico City	Galicia
GALLEGO Hernández, Gonzalo	Caulker	Coatzacoalcos	Badajoz
GARNICA, Gaspar		Mexico City	Vizcaya
GENOVÉS, Lorenzo	Pilot	Oaxaca	Genoa
GIRALDO, Alonso	Trumpeter	Mexico City	?
GÓMEZ de Herrera, Juan		Zacatula	?
GONZÁLEZ, Diego	Merchant (?)	Puebla	Badajoz
GONZÁLEZ Ponce de León, Juan		Mexico City	?
GRADO, Alonso de		Mexico City	Cáceres
GRIEGO, Juan		Antequera	Greece
GUIPÚZCOANO, Rodrigo		Colima	Valladolid
GUTIÉRREZ de Ahumada, Antonio		Mexico City	?
GUTIÉRREZ de Almodóvar, Antonio		Mexico City	Ciudad Real
GUTIÉRREZ, Francisco	Blacksmith	Zacatula	Cáceres
HERNÁNDEZ de Nava, Bartolomé		Puebla	Huelva
HERNÁNDEZ Mosquera, Cristóbal		Mexico City	Seville
HERNÁNDEZ Calvo, Gonzalo	Mariner	Puebla	Huelva
HERNÁNDEZ Mosquera, Gonzalo		Mexico City	Seville
HERNÁNDEZ, Santos		Oaxaca	Cáceres
HOYOS, Gómez de		Colima	Badajoz
IÑIGUEZ, Bernardino		Pánuco	Logroño
JARAMILLO de Salvatierra, Juan	*Hidalgo*	Mexico City	Badajoz
JIMÉNEZ, Gonzalo		Villa Alta	Cáceres
JIMÉNEZ de Rivera, Juan		?	Santander
LIMPIAS Carvajal, Juan de	*Hidalgo*	Mexico City	Seville
LÓPEZ de Sanlúcar, Bartolomé	Archer	Colima	Seville
LÓPEZ de Jimena, Juan	*Hidalgo*	Veracruz	Jaén
LÓPEZ, Martín	Ship's carpenter	Mexico City	Seville
LÓPEZ, Román		Oaxaca	Zamora
MALDONADO, Alvaro		Mexico City	Salamanca
MALDONADO, Francisco		Mexico City	Salamanca
MALDONADO, Pedro		Veracruz	Salamanca
MARÍN, Luis		Mexico City	Cádiz
MARTÍN Jaca, Alonso		Mexico City	Huesca
MARTÍN Millán de Gamboa, Cristóbal		Mexico City	Biscay
MARTÍN de Coria, Pedro		?	Cáceres
MAYA, Pedro de		Antequera	Burgos

MEDINA, Juan de	Confectioner	Pánuco	Málaga
MENDOZA, Alonso de		Mexico City	Badajoz
MEZQUITA, Martín de la		Oaxaca	Seville
MONJARAZ, Andrés de	*Hidalgo*	Mexico City	Vizcaya
MONJARAZ, Mateo de	*Hidalgo*	Mexico City	Vizcaya
MONTEJO, Francisco de		Mexico City	Salamanca
MONTERROSO, Blas de		Mexico City	Lugo
MOSCOSO, Sebastián		Mexico City	Badajoz
MOTRICO, Diego de	Merchant	Mexico City	Guipúzcoa
NAVARRETE, Alonso		Valles	Granada
NÚÑEZ, Andrés		Mexico City	Salamanca
NÚÑEZ Mercado, Juan		Puebla	Salamanca
NÚÑEZ Sedeño, Juan	*Hidalgo*	Oaxaca	Madrid
OJEDA, Alonso de		Villa Alta	Huelva
ORDAZ, Diego de	*Hidalgo*	Mexico City	Zamora
ORTEGA, Bachiller Juan de		Mexico City	Seville
PACHECO, Cristóbal		Mexico City	?
PEÑA, Rodrigo de la		?	Navarre
PÉREZ de Arteaga, Juan	Interpreter	Puebla	Palencia
PÉREZ de Badajoz, Martín		?	Badajoz
PINZÓN, Ginés		Colima	Huelva
PINZÓN, Juan		Colima	Huelva
QUEVEDO, Francisco de		Mexico City	?
QUINTERO, Francisco	Mariner	Mexico City	Huelva
RAMÍREZ, Diego	Carpenter	Mexico City	Cádiz
RANGEL, Rodrigo	*Hidalgo*	Mexico City	Badajoz
RETAMALES, Pablo		Mexico City	Seville
RIJOLES, Tomás	Interpreter	Mexico City	Italy
RODRÍGUEZ de Avalos, Cristóbal	Trumpeter	Mexico City	?
RODRÍGUEZ Magariño, Francisco		Zacatula	?
RODRÍGUEZ Bejerano, Juan de		Mexico City	?
RODRÍGUEZ de Salas, Juan	Mason	Mexico City	?
RODRÍGUEZ de Villafuerte, Juan	*Hidalgo*	Zacatula	Salamanca
RODRÍGUEZ de Escobar, Pedro		Guatemala	Valladolid
RODRÍGUEZ, Sebastián	Crossbowman	Puebla	Portugal
ROMERO, Alonso		Veracruz	Soria
ROZAS, Andrés de		Mexico City	Burgos
RUIZ, Diego		Zacatula	Huelva
RUIZ, Marcos		Mexico City	Seville
RUIZ de Monjaraz, Martín	*Hidalgo*	Colima	Vizcaya
RUIZ de Guadalcanal, Pedro		Zacatula	Seville
RUIZ de Requena, Pedro		Zacatula	Cuenca

SÁNCHEZ, Bartolomé		Antequera	Córdoba
SÁNCHEZ de Sopuerta, Diego	Pilot	Mexico City	Madrid
SÁNCHEZ Farfán, Pedro		Toluca	Seville
SANDOVAL, Gonzalo de		Mexico City	Badajoz
SEDEÑO, Juan		Veracruz	?
SEGURA, Rodrigo de		Puebla	Seville
SERNA, Alonso de la		Mexico City	?
SICILIANO, Juan		Mexico City	Sicily
SOLÍS, Francisco de	Cannoneer	Mexico City	Santander
SOLÍS Barrasa, Pedro de		Mexico City	Burgos
SOTO, Cristóbal de		Puebla	?
SUÁREZ, Lorenzo	*Hidalgo*	Mexico City	Portugal
TAPIA, Andrés de		Mexico City	Badajoz
TARIFA, Gaspar de		Mexico City	Seville
TERRAZAS, Francisco de		Mexico City	Badajoz
TIRADO, Juan		Mexico City	?
TORRES, Hernando de		Mexico City	Jaén
TREJO, Rafael de		Mexico City	Cáceres
VARELA (Gallegos), Gonzalo		Cd. Michoacán	Galicia
VARGAS, Francisco de	*Hidalgo*	Mexico City	Seville
VÁZQUEZ de Tapia, Bernaldino	*Hidalgo*	Mexico City	Toledo
VÁZQUEZ, Martín		Mexico City	Segovia
VEJER, Benito de	Drummer	Mexico City	Cádiz
VELÁZQUEZ, Juan		Mexico City	?
VILLALOBOS, Gregorio de		Puebla	Huelva
VILLARROEL, Antonio de		Mexico City	Valladolid

APPENDIX B

Roster of Conqueror *Encomenderos* *

*The *entrada* leader or outfitter that the conqueror *encomendero* accompanied to New Spain is indicated parenthetically in accordance with the following schema: (A) Alderete; (C) Camargo; (Cu) Cueva; (D) Díaz de Aux; (G) Garay; (M) Medel; (N) Narváez; (P) Ponce de León; (R) Ramírez; (RM) Ruiz de la Mota; (S) Salcedo; and (?) Unknown.

Encomendero	Calling	Residence	Origin
AGUILAR, Francisco de (?)		Veracruz	Palencia
AGUILAR, García de (N)		Puebla	Badajoz
AGUILAR, Juan de (P)		Colima	Palencia
ARÉVALO, Alonso de (N)		Colima	Badajoz
ARÉVALO, Melchor (N)		Jalapa	Avila
ARRIAGA, Antón de (N)		Cd. Michoacán	Badajoz
ARRIAGA, Juan de (N)		Guaxuapa	Soria
ASTORGA, Bartolomé de (N)		Antequera	León
AVILA Quiñones, Gaspar de (N)		Mexico City	Avila
AVILA "*el tuerto*," Juan de (N)		Mexico City	Avila
AZNAR, Antonio (N)		Puebla	Granada
AZPEITIA, Juanés (M)		Pánuco	Guipúzcoa
BADAJOZ, Gutierre de (N)	Miner	Mexico City	Cáceres
BARRERA, Cristóbal (?)		Puebla	?
BEJERANO, Serván (C)		Mexico City	Córdoba
BELLO, Juan (N)		Mexico City	Salamanca
BENAVIDES, Alonso de (N)		Veracruz	?
BENAVIDES, Nuño de (?)		Antequera	?
BERNAL, Francisco (N)		Puebla	?
BERNAL, Juan (N)		Puebla	?
BOSQUE, Gabriel (N)		Oaxaca	Aragón
BURGOS, Juan de (?)		Mexico City	Seville
BURGUEÑO, Fernando (P)		Mexico City	Toledo
CABRA, Juan de (C)	Miner	Mexico City	Ciudad Real
CALAHORRA, Martín de (G)	Notary	Puebla	Logroño
CANO, Alonso (RM)		Villa Alta	Seville
CANO, Juan (N)		Mexico City	Cáceres
CANTILLANA, Hernando (N)	Shoemaker	Mexico City	Grand Canary

CARRASCOSA, Juan de (N)		Pánuco	Cuenca
CASTELLAR, Pedro (N)		Coatzacoalcos	?
CASTILLO Maldonado, Alonso del (N)	*Hidalgo*	Mexico City	Salamanca
CEREZO, Gonzalo (N)		Mexico City	Córdoba
CERVANTES, Comendador Leonel de (N)	*Hidalgo*	Mexico City	Seville
CIFONTES, Francisco (N)		Colima	?
CISNEROS "*bigotes,*" Juan de (N)		Mexico City	?
CONTRERAS, Alonso de (N)	*Hidalgo*	Mexico City	Burgos
CORONEL, Juan (N)		Mexico City	Seville
CORREAS, Diego (N)	Mariner	Zacatula	Portugal
CUÉLLAR, Juan de (N)	Trumpeter	Mexico City	Segovia
CUÉLLAR Verdugo, Juan (N)		Mexico City	Segovia
CUENCA, Benito de (N)		Pánuco	Cádiz
CHAVARRÍN, Bartolomé (N)		Colima	Genoa
DÍAZ de Aux, Miguel (D)		Mexico City	Huesca
DURÁN, Juan (N)		Puebla	Madrid
EBORA, Sebastián de (N)		Zacatula	Portugal
ELGÜETA, Hernando de (?)		?	?
ESCOBAR, Pedro de (N)		Mexico City	?
ESTRADA, Francsico de (N)		Mexico City	Seville
FERNÁNDEZ, Juan (N)		Colima	Seville
FERNÁNDEZ de Mérida, Juan (N)		Antequera	Badajoz
FERNÁNDEZ de Ocampo, Juan (N)		Colima	Lugo
FERNÁNDEZ de Navarrete, Pedro (?)		?	Navarre
FLORES, Francisco (N)		Mexico City	Huelva
GALEOTE García, Alonso (N)		Puebla	Huelva
GALLARDO, Pedro (S)	Mariner	Puebla	Huelva
GALLEGO, Benito (C)		Colima	Galicia
GALLEGO, Juan (?)		Antequera	?
GALLEGO, Lucas (?)		Mexico City	Galicia
GARCÍA Bravo, Alonso (C)	Mason	Antequera	Badajoz
GARCÍA Jaramillo, Diego (N)		Mexico City	Badajoz
GARRIDO, Diego (N)		Colima	Huelva
GÓMEZ, Bartolomé (?)		Mexico City	Seville
GÓMEZ, Pedro (N)		Colima	?
GÓMEZ, Pierrez (D)		Mexico City	Flanders
GÓMEZ de Avila, Rodrigo (N)	*Hidalgo*	Mexico City	Avila
GONZÁLEZ de Portugal, Alonso (N)	*Hidalgo*	Mexico City	Portugal
GONZÁLEZ de Benavides, Gil (G)	*Hidalgo*	Mexico City	Avila
GONZÁLEZ de Trujillo, Gil (?)		Pánuco	?
GONZÁLEZ, Ruy (N)		Mexico City	Badajoz

GRIJALVA, Sebastián de (N)		Antequera	Segovia
GUADALAJARA, Antonio de (?)		?	Guadalajara
GUERRERO, Lázaro (N)		Antequera	?
GUILLÉN, Francisco (?)		Mexico City	Huelva
GUTIÉRREZ de Badajoz, Alonso (?)		Mexico City	Badajoz
GUTIÉRREZ Lavado, Diego (G)		Pánuco	Seville
GUTIÉRREZ, Gómez (N)		Colima	?
HEREDIA, Rodrigo de (N)		Colima	France
HERNÁNDEZ de Prado, Juan (N)		?	Zamora
HERNÁNDEZ, Pedro (N)		Mexico City	?
HOLGUÍN, Diego de (N)	Hidalgo	Puebla	Cáceres
IRCIO, Martín de (N)	Hidalgo	Mexico City	Logroño
JEREZ, Hernando (Gómez) de (N)		Mexico City	Cádiz
JIMÉNEZ, Juan (N)		Mexico City	Cáceres
LEIVA, Diego de (?)		Antequera	?
LOA, Guillén de la (G)	Notary	Mexico City	Vizcaya
LÓPEZ, Alonso (D)		Colima	Córdoba
LÓPEZ de Sevilla, Andrés (N)		Mexico City	Seville
LÓPEZ, Gonzalo (N)		Mexico City	?
LÓPEZ, Jerónimo (N)	Hidalgo	Mexico City	Seville
LOZANO, Pedro (N)		Mexico City	Cáceres
LUCAS, Alonso (?)	Notary	Mexico City	Extremadura
MAFRA, Cristóbal de (?)		Mexico City	Portugal
MANSILLA, Juan de (N)		Mexico City	Old Castile
MANZANILLA, Juan de (N)		Puebla	Huelva
MARMOLEJO, Diego (A)	Hidalgo	Veracruz	Seville
MARTÍN de Jerez, Alonso		Zacatula	Huelva
MARTÍN, Ginés (N)		Pánuco	?
MARTÍN, Hernán (?)	Blacksmith	Mexico City	?
MARTÍN, Maya (N)		Pánuco	?
MARTÍN, Rodrigo (?)		?	?
MEDEL, Hernando (M)		Mexico City	Huelva
MENESES, Pedro de (N)	Hidalgo	Puebla	Toledo
MIGUEL, Antón		Villa Alta	?
MONJE, Martín (N)		Colima	Huelva
MONRESÍN, Cristóbal de (?)		Acapulco	?
MONTAÑO, Francisco (N)		Mexico City	Salamanca
MORALES, Juan de (G)		Mexico City	Seville
MORCILLO, Alonso de (N)		Antequera	Seville
MORENO, Isidro (P)		Utlatlan	Ciudad Real
MORENO, Juan (P)		?	Huelva
MORENO Cendejas, Pedro (N)		Mexico City	Zaragoza
NÁJERA, Juan de (Cu)		Mexico City	Logroño
NAVARRO, Juan (N)		Puebla	Aragón
NAVARRO, Juan (Antonio) (?)		?	?

Name	Occupation	Location	Origin
NIETO, Gómez (N)		Pánuco	?
NIETO, Pedro (N)		Mexico City	?
OCHOA de Lejalde, Juan (N)	Merchant	Puebla	Guipúzcoa
OLIVEROS, Francisco de (N)		Puebla	Portugal
OLMOS, Francisco de (N)		Mexico City	Valladolid
OLVERA, Diego de (N)		Mexico City	Seville
ORDUÑA, Francisco de (S)	Notary	Puebla	Biscay
ORTIZ de Zúñiga, Alonso (N)	Hidalgo	Mexico City	Seville
ORTIZ, Juan (N)		Puebla	Huelva
PANTOJA, Juan (N)		Cd. Michoacán	Badajoz
PAYO, Lorenzo (N)		Mexico City	?
PEDRAZA, Maese Diego de (?)	Surgeon	Mexico City	Segovia
PÉREZ, Bachiller Alonso (N)	Notary	Mexico City	Huelva
PÉREZ de Zamora, Alonso (M)		Mexico City	Zamora
PÉREZ de la Gama, Juan (N)		Mexico City	?
PÉREZ de Herrera, Juan (N)		Mexico City	?
PILAR, García del (N)		Mexico City	?
PLAZA, Juan de la (G)		Zacatula	Valencia
PORCALLO, Vasco (N)		Mexico City	?
PORRAS, Diego (N)		Mexico City	Cáceres
QUEJADA, Diego (N)		Mexico City	Burgos
RAMÍREZ, Francisco (R)		Pánuco	León
RAPALO, Juan Bautista de (N)		Colima	Genoa
RIBADEO, Francisco de (N)		Mexico City	Lugo
ROBLES, Gonzalo de (N)	Hidalgo	Antequera	Badajoz
RODRÍGUEZ, Francisco (?)		Zacatula	?
RODRÍGUEZ de la Magdalena, Gonzalo (N)		Puebla	Seville
RODRÍGUEZ de Ocaña, Gonzalo (N)		Mexico City	Toledo
ROMÁN, Bartolomé (P)		Medellín	?
ROMERO, Cristóbal (?)		Mexico City	Córdoba
RUIZ de la Peña, Hernán (?)		Colima	?
RUIZ de la Mota Zárate, Jerónimo (RM)	Hidalgo	Mexico City	Burgos
RUIZ de Alanís, Juan (N)		Mexico City	Seville
SALAMANCA, Diego de (N)	Hidalgo	Mexico City	Salamanca
SALAMANCA, Juan de (N)		Coatzacoalcos	Avila
SALCEDO, Juan de (S)		Mexico City	Santander
SALINAS, Jerónimo de (N)	Hidalgo	Mexico City	Zaragoza
SÁNCHEZ, Antón de (S)	Carpenter	Zacatula	Vizcaya
SÁNCHEZ de Hortigosa, Hernán (N)	Notary	Mexico City	Old Castile
SAN MIGUEL, Melchor de (N)	Hidalgo	Antequera	Valladolid
SANTA CLARA, Bernardino de (N)	Merchant	Mexico City	Salamanca
SANTA CRUZ, Francisco de (N)		Mexico City	Burgos
SANTOS, Francisco (N)		Colima	?

SEPÚLVEDA, Maestre Martín de (?)	Builder	Mexico City	Segovia
SEPÚLVEDA, Pedro de (N)	Blacksmith	Mexico City	Segovia
SIMANCAS, Pedro de (N)		Colima	Valladolid
TELLO de Medina, Juan (N)	*Hidalgo*	Mexico City	Seville
TOVAR, Juan de (S)	Merchant	Mexico City	Burgos
VALADÉS, Diego (N)		Mexico City	Badajoz
VALDIVIESO, Juan de (RM)		Antequera	Burgos
VALENCIANO, Pedro (N)		Mexico City	Valencia
VELÁZQUEZ de Lara, Francisco (D)	*Hidalgo*	Mexico City	Huelva
VERDUGO, Francisco (N)	*Hidalgo*	Mexico City	Segovia
VILLAFELIZ, Leonardo de (N)		Mexico City	León
VILLAGRÁN, Juan de (N)		Pánuco	Valladolid
VILLANUEVA Tordesillas, Alonso de (N)		Mexico City	Badajoz
VILLANUEVA, Fernando de (RM)		Puebla	Jaén
VILLANUEVA, Pedro de (RM)		Puebla	Jaén
ZAMORA, Alvaro de (M)	Interpreter	Mexico City	Zamora
ZAMORA, Francisco de (N)		Antequera	Zamora
ZAMORANO, Pedro Ruiz (N)	*Hidalgo*	Mexico City	Jaén
ZAMUDIO, Juan de (N)		Mexico City	Vizcaya
ZARAGOZA, Miguel de (N)	Merchant	Veracruz	Zaragoza
ZIMBRÓN de Vitoria, Alonso (N)		Puebla	Madrid

APPENDIX C

Roster of *Poblador Antiguo Encomenderos*

Encomendero	Calling	Residence	Origin
ACEDO, Juan		Pánuco	Seville
AGUILA, Francisco del		Villa Alta	Avila
AVILA, Francisco de		Mexico City	Seville
BAEZA, Rodrigo de		Mexico City	Burgos
CARRANZA, Pedro de	*Hidalgo*	Mexico City	Burgos
CISNEROS, Cristóbal de		Chiapas	Toledo
CORSO, Vicencio		Pánuco	Corsica
GÓMEZ, Gonzalo	Merchant	Mexico City	Seville
HORNA, Sancho de		Colima	Cáceres
ISLA, Pedro de la		Mexico City	Seville
LÓPEZ, Licenciado Pedro	Physician	Puebla	Seville
MARTEL, Juan		Colima	Seville
MARTÍN de Mérida, Diego		Colima	Badajoz
MONTALVO, Francisco de	*Hidalgo*	Puebla	Segovia
PARDO, Diego	Merchant/Miner	Mexico City	Huelva
PERALES, Bartolomé de		Mexico City	Badajoz
RIBERA, Alvaro de	*Hidalgo*	Valles	Portugal
RODRÍGUEZ de Valladolid, Diego		?	Valladolid
RODRÍGUEZ, Martín	Tailor	Mexico City	Badajoz
ROELAS, Diego (de las)		Pánuco	Seville
SAAVEDRA, Lope de (moved from Pánuco)	Merchant	Antequera	Cáceres
SAAVEDRA, Luis de		?	Cáceres
SANTA CRUZ, Pedro de		Colima	Burgos
SUÁREZ Pacheco, Diego	*Hidalgo*	Mexico City	Avila
SUÁREZ, Juan	*Hidalgo*	Mexico City	Avila

TÉLLEZ, Licenciado Diego		Mexico City	Córdoba
TORRE, Juan de la	*Hidalgo*	Mexico City	Ciudad Real
TORRE, Luis de la	*Hidalgo*	Mexico City	Ciudad Real
VALIENTE, Alonso		Puebla	Badajoz
VARGAS, Pedro de		Mexico City	Seville
VERDEJO, Alonso		Zacatula	Cuenca
VILLEGAS, Francisco de	*Hidalgo*	Mexico City	Extremadura

APPENDIX D

Roster of *Poblador Encomenderos*

Encomendero	Calling	Residence	Origin
AGUILAR, Alonso de	*Hidalgo*	Mexico City	Seville
AGUILERA, Gabriel de	*Hidalgo*	Mexico City	Jaén
ALBORNOZ, Juan de		Oaxaca	Toledo
ALBORNOZ, Rodrigo de	*Hidalgo*	Mexico City	Salamanca
ALCÁNTARA, Bartolomé de		Villa Alta	León
ALMESTO, Juan de		Purificación	Seville
ALMÍNDEZ Chirinos, Pero	*Hidalgo*	Mexico City	Jaén
ALMODÓVAR, Diego de		Colima	Ciudad Real
ALONSO, Rodrigo		Colima	?
ALTAMIRANO, Licenciado Juan Gutiérrez	*Hidalgo*	Mexico City	Salamanca
ALVARADO, Juan de	*Hidalgo*	Cd. Michoacán	Badajoz
ARAGÓN, Pedro de	Blacksmith	Mexico City	Aragón
AVALOS Saavedra, Alonso de	*Hidalgo*	Mexico City	Badajoz
AVILA, Gonzalo de		Pánuco	Badajoz
BARRÓN, Francisco		Mexico City	?
BAZÁN, Pedro de		Mexico City	Badajoz
BECERRA de Mendoza, Diego	*Hidalgo*	?	Badajoz
BECERRA, Juan		Villa Alta	Zamora
BERRIO, Luis de		Mexico City	Jaén
BEZOS, Juan		Mexico City	Seville
BONILLA, Juan de		Villa Alta	Cáceres
BURIEZO, Juan		Colima	?
BUSTAMANTE, Doctor Blas de	*Hidalgo*	Mexico City	Valladolid
BUSTAMANTE, Rodrigo de		Pánuco	Salamanca
BUSTO, Juan de	*Hidalgo*	Pánuco	Badajoz
CÁRDENAS, Ginés de		Veracruz	Seville
CARRILLO, Alonso	*Hidalgo*	Mexico City	Toledo
CARRILLO, Jorge	*Hidalgo*	Mexico City	Toledo
CASAS, Francisco de las	*Hidalgo*	Mexico City	Cáceres
CASCO, Francisco		Mexico City	Badajoz
CASTAÑEDA, Diego de		Pánuco	?
CASTELLANOS, Alonso de		Mexico City	León
CASTILLA, don Luis de	*Hidalgo*	Mexico City	Valladolid

ROSTER OF *POBLADOR ENCOMENDEROS*

CERÓN Saavedra, Jorge	*Hidalgo*	Mexico City	Jaén
CERVANTES Casaus, Juan de	*Hidalgo*	Mexico City	Seville
CORTÉS, Diego	*Hidalgo*	Valles	Badajoz
CORTÉS, Martín		Puebla	Murcia
CUEVA, Luis de la		?	?
CUEVAS, Juan de	*Hidalgo*	Mexico City	Burgos
CHAVES, Diego de		Colima	?
DELGADILLO, Francisco		Guadalajara	Toledo
DÍAZ Carballar, Alonso		Villa Alta	Portugal
DÍAZ, Diego	Stonemason	Mexico City	?
DÍAZ del Real, Juan		Mexico City	Huelva
ESCARCENA, Juan de		?	?
ESCOBAR, Alonso de		Mexico City	Badajoz
ESPAÑA, Juan de		Coatzacoalcos	Aragón
ESTRADA, Alonso de	*Hidalgo*	Mexico City	Ciudad Real
FERNÁNDEZ de Proaño, Comendador Diego	*Hidalgo*	Guadalajara	Seville
FLORES, Juan		Zacatula	Cáceres
FRANCO Estrada, Francisco		Villa Alta	Asturias
FRÍAS, Cristóbal de		Pánuco	?
GALLEGO, Pedro		Mexico City	Badajoz
GALLEGOS, Juan		Pánuco	Seville
GAMBOA, Hernando de		Colima	?
GARCÍA, Alonso		Pánuco	?
GARCÍA, Bartolomé		Guadalajara	Cáceres
GARCÍA, Hernán		Colima	Seville
GARCÍA de Lemos, Juan		Villa Alta	Coruña
GENOVÉS, Lucas		Pánuco	Genoa
GONZÁLEZ, Jorge		Mexico City	?
GUZMÁN Saavedra, don Luis de	*Hidalgo*	Mexico City	Seville
GUZMÁN, Nuño Beltrán de		Mexico City	Guadalajara
GUZMÁN, Ramiro de		Pánuco	?
GUZMÁN, Rodrigo de		Mexico City	Toledo
HERRERA, Cristóbal de		Coatzacoalcos	?
HERRERA, Francisco de		Mexico City	Seville
HINOJOSA, Juan de		Mexico City	Cáceres
HITA, Gaspar de		Coatzacoalcos	Guadalajara
HURTADO de Mendoza, Diego		Guadalajara	Madrid
INERO, Andrés de		Pánuco	?
INFANTE, Juan		Mexico City	Seville
JASO "*el viejo*," Juan de	*Hidalgo*	Mexico City	Navarre
JASO "*el mozo*," Juan de	*Hidalgo*	Mexico City	Navarre
JIMÉNEZ, Martín		Colima	?
JUÁREZ, Pedro		?	?
LAMADRIZ, Tomás de		Antequera	Santander
LARIOS, Juan	Notary	Ayoteco	Toledo
LÓPEZ Frías, Juan		Coatzacoalcos	?

Name	Occupation	Location	Origin
LÓPEZ de Zárate, Juan	Bishop	Antequera	Asturias
LÓPEZ de Palacios, Nicolás		Cd. Michoacán	Salamanca
LORITA, Hernando de	Notary	Villa Alta	Badajoz
LUNA y Arellano, don Tristán de	*Hidalgo*	Mexico City	Badajoz
MANZANO, Alvaro		Villa Alta	Huelva
MARTÍN Brena, Antón		Puebla	Cáceres
MARTÍN de Valencia, Juan		Coatzacoalcos	?
MEDEL, Antonio		Mexico City	Huelva
MEDINA, Domingo de		Cd. Michoacán	Badajoz
MEDINA "*el viejo*," Jerónimo de	*Hidalgo*	Mexico City	Toledo
MÉNDEZ, Héctor		Pánuco	?
MÉNDEZ, Teresa		Coatzacoalcos	?
MENDOZA, Lope de		Pánuco	?
MÉRIDA, Alonso de		?	?
MIGUEL, Antón		Villa Alta	?
MONDRAGÓN, Licenciado Pedro de		Pánuco	?
MORCILLO, Francisco	*Hidalgo*	Cd. Michoacán	Badajoz
NÚÑEZ Pedro, Maese de Roa	Surgeon	Mexico City	Burgos
OCAMPO, Diego de		Mexico City	Lugo
OCAÑA, Diego de	Notary	Mexico City	Seville
OJEDA, Doctor Cristóbal de	Surgeon	Mexico City	Seville
OLIVER, Antonio de	*Hidalgo*	Mexico City	Ciudad Real
OLIVER, Juan Bautista		Villa Alta	Catalonia
OÑATE, Cristóbal Pérez de	*Hidalgo*	Mexico City	Alava
ORTEGA, Cristóbal de		Pánuco	?
ORTIZ de Matienzo, Juan	*Hidalgo*	Mexico City	Santander
PACHECO, Gaspar	*Hidalgo*	Villa Alta	Toledo
PANTOJA, Pedro		Mexico City	Badajoz
PAREDES, Marcos de		Villa Alta	?
PAZ, Alonso de	Notary	Mexico City	Salamanca
PAZ, Pedro de		Mexico City	Salamanca
PELÁEZ de Berrio, Juan		Antequera	Granada
PEÑA Vallejo, Juan de la		Mexico City	Granada
PERALTA, Martín de		Mexico City	?
PÉREZ de Bocanegra y Córdoba, Hernán	*Hidalgo*	Mexico City	Córdoba
PLASENCIA, Pedro de		Guadalajara	Seville
PRECIADO, Francisco		Colima	Guadalajara
RIOBOZ de Sotomayor, Gonzalo		Mexico City	?
RODRÍGUEZ, Diego	Swordsmith	Mexico City	Salamanca
RODRÍGUEZ de Guadalcanal, Francisco		Mexico City	Seville
RODRÍGUEZ de Villafuerte, Gonzalo	*Hidalgo*	Coatzacoalcos	Salamanca
RODRÍGUEZ, Juan		Pánuco	Cáceres
RODRÍGUEZ, Melchor		Pánuco	?
ROMERO, Juan		Pánuco	?

ROSALES, Francisco de	Merchant	Veracruz	Burgos
RUIZ, Alonso		Antequera	Jaén
RUIZ, Gonzalo	*Hidalgo*	Mexico City	Huelva
SAAVEDRA Cerón, Alvaro	*Hidalgo*	Veracruz	Jaén
SAAVEDRA, Fernando de	*Hidalgo*	Honduras	Badajoz
SALAMANCA, Juan de	Tailor	Mexico City	Burgos
SALAZAR, Gonzalo de	*Hidalgo*	Mexico City	Granada
SALAZAR, Hernando de	*Hidalgo*	Mexico City	Granada
SALDAÑA, Francisco de		Villa Alta	Badajoz
SALDAÑA, Gregorio de	Notary	Mexico City	Palencia
SÁMANO, Juan de	*Hidalgo*	Mexico City	Burgos
SÁNCHEZ, Mateo	*Mayordomo*	Colima	Salamanca
SÁNCHEZ, Pedro		Pánuco	Badajoz
SANDOVAL, Licenciado Rodrigo de	*Hidalgo*	Mexico City	Valladolid
SAUCEDO, Francisco de		Zacatula	Seville
SEPÚLVEDA, Cristóbal de		Pánuco	?
SOLÍS, Juan de		?	?
SOSA, Juan Alonso de	*Hidalgo*	Mexico City	Córdoba
SOTOMAYOR, Bachiller Pedro Díaz de		Mexico City	Seville
TARIFA, Francisco de		Villa Alta	Seville
TOMÁS, Maese Manuel	Surgeon	Mexico City	Cáceres
TORQUEMADA, Baltasar de		Pánuco	Palencia
TORQUEMADA, Juan de	Notary	Pánuco	Palencia
VALDERRAMA, Cristóbal de		Mexico City	Burgos
VALDÉS, Bartolomé de		Ayoteco	Seville
VARGAS, Juan Alonso de	*Hidalgo*	Zacatula	Seville
VÁZQUEZ de Coronado, Francisco	*Hidalgo*	Mexico City	Salamanca
VELÁZQUEZ, Alonso	Notary	Mexico City	Valladolid
VILLAFAÑE, Angel de		Mexico City	León
VILLAGÓMEZ, Antonio de		Mexico City	Zamora
VILLAGÓMEZ, Juan de		Mexico City	Zamora
VILLANUEVA, Juan de		Valles	Granada
VILLAPADIERNA, Diego de		Pánuco	Badajoz
VILLARROEL, Antonio de		Antequera	León
VILLASEÑOR Orozco, Juan de	*Hidalgo*	Cd. Michoacán	Málaga
ZÁRATE, Bartolomé de		Mexico City	Asturias
ZUMÁRRAGA, Fray Juan de	Bishop	Mexico City	Vizcaya

APPENDIX E

Roster of Indian *Encomenderos*

Encomendero	Residence
MOCTEZUMA, doña Isabel	Mexico City
MOCTEZUMA, doña Leonor	Mexico City
SÁNCHEZ, Juan	?

APPENDIX F

Citizenship of the *Encomenderos*

Vecino of	Calling	Native of
Acapulco—Settled in 1528		
Conqueror		
MONRESÍN, Cristóbal de		?
Antequera (Oaxaca)—Municipality established in 1526		
First Conquerors		
ALANÉS, Melchor de		Aragón
CÁRDENAS, Luis de		Seville
GENOVÉS, Lorenzo		Genoa
GRIEGO, Juan		Greece
HERNÁNDEZ, Santos		Cáceres
LÓPEZ, Román		Zamora
MAYA, Pedro de (from Mexico City)		Burgos
MEZQUITA, Martín de la		Seville
NÚÑEZ Sedeño, Juan	*Hidalgo*	Madrid
RODRÍGUEZ de Salas, Juan	Mason	?
SÁNCHEZ, Bartolomé	*Regidor*	Córdoba
Conquerors		
ASTORGA, Bartolomé de		León
BENAVIDES, Nuño de		?
BOSQUE, Gabriel		Aragón
FERNÁNDEZ de Mérida, Juan		Badajoz
GALLEGO, Juan		?
GARCÍA Bravo, Alonso		Badajoz
GRIJALVA, Sebastián de		Segovia
GUERRERO, Lázaro		?
LEIVA, Diego de		?
MORCILLO, Alonso de		Seville
ROBLES, Gonzalo de	*Hidalgo*	Badajoz
SALINAS, Jerónimo de	*Hidalgo*	Zaragoza
SAN MIGUEL, Melchor de	*Hidalgo*	Valladolid

VALDIVIESO, Juan de (from Colima and
  Mexico City)   Burgos
ZAMORA, Francisco de   Zamora

Poblador Antiguo
SAAVEDRA, Lope de (moved from
  Pánuco)   Merchant   Cáceres

Pobladores
ALBORNOZ, Juan de   Toledo
LAMADRIZ, Tomás de   Santander
LÓPEZ de Zárate, Juan   Bishop   Asturias
PELÁEZ de Berrio, Juan   Granada
RUIZ, Alonso (from Mexico City)   Jaén
VILLARROEL, Antonio de   León
ZÁRATE, Bartolomé (moved to Mexico
  City)   Asturias

Ayoteco (Chiautla)—Settled
ca. 1534

  Pobladores
  LARIOS, Juan   Notary   Toledo
  VALDÉS, Bartolomé de   Seville

Ciudad Michoacán—Municipality
established in 1531

  First Conquerors
  AVILA, Luis de   Seville
  VARELA Gallegos, Gonzalo (from
    Zacatecas)   Galicia

  Conquerors
  ARRIAGA, Antón de   Badajoz
  PANTOJA, Juan   Badajoz

  Pobladores
  ALVARADO, Juan de   *Hidalgo*   Badajoz
  LÓPEZ de Palacios, Nicolás   Salamanca
  MEDINA, Domingo de (from Mexico
    City)   Badajoz
  MORCILLO, Francisco (from Mexico
    City)   *Hidalgo*   Badajoz
  VILLASEÑOR Orozco, Juan de (from
    Purificación)   *Hidalgo*   Málaga

Coatzacoalcos—Municipality founded in
1522

  First Conqueror
  GALLEGO Hernández, Gonzalo   Caulker   Badajoz

  Conquerors
  CASTELLAR, Pedro   ?
  SALAMANCA, Juan de   Avila

Pobladores
ESPAÑA, Juan de		Aragón
HERRERA, Cristóbal de		?
HITA, Gaspar de		Guadalcanal
LÓPEZ Frías, Juan		?
MÉNDEZ, Teresa		?
RODRÍGUEZ de Villafuerte, Gonzalo	Hidalgo	Salamanca

Colima—Municipality founded in 1524

First Conquerors
CÁCERES, Manuel de		Segovia
CORTÉS, Francisco	Hidalgo	Extremadura
EJICA, Andrés de		Seville
GUIPÚZCOANO, Rodrigo		Valladolid
HOYOS, Gómez de		Badajoz
LÓPEZ de Sanlúcar, Bartolomé (from Veracruz)		Seville
PINZÓN, Ginés		Huelva
PINZÓN, Juan		Huelva
RUIZ de Monjaraz, Martín	Hidalgo	Vizcaya

Conquerors
AGUILAR, Juan de	Palencia
ARÉVALO, Alonso de	Badajoz
CIFONTES, Francisco	?
CHAVARRÍN, Bartolomé	Genoa
FERNÁNDEZ, Juan	Seville
FERNÁNDEZ de Ocampo, Juan	Lugo
GALLEGO, Benito	Galicia
GARRIDO, Diego	Huelva
GÓMEZ, Pedro	?
GUTIÉRREZ, Gómez	?
HEREDIA, Rodrigo de	France
LÓPEZ, Alonso	Córdoba
MONJE, Martín	Huelva
RAPALO, Juan Bautista	Genoa
RUIZ de la Peña, Hernán	?
SANTOS, Francisco	?
SIMANCAS, Pedro de	Valladolid
VALDIVIESO, Juan de (to Mexico City, then Antequera)	Burgos

Pobladores Antiguos
HORNA, Sancho de	Cáceres
MARTEL, Juan	Seville
MARTÍN de Mérida, Diego	Badajoz
SANTA CRUZ, Pedro de	Burgos

Pobladores
ALMODÓVAR, Diego de	Ciudad Real
ALONSO, Rodrigo	?
BURIEZO, Juan	?

CHAVES, Diego de		?
ESCARCENA, Juan de		?
GAMBOA, Hernando de		?
GARCÍA, Hernán		Seville
JIMÉNEZ, Martín		?
PRECIADO, Francisco		Guadalajara
SÁNCHEZ, Mateo	*Mayordomo*	Salamanca

Guadalajara—Municipality founded in 1532

Conqueror
ROMERO, Cristóbal		Córdoba

Pobladores
AVALOS Saavedra, Alonso de (from Mexico City)	*Hidalgo*	Badajoz
DELGADILLO, Francisco		Toledo
FERNÁNDEZ de Proaño, Comendador Diego (from Mexico City)	*Hidalgo*	Seville
GARCÍA, Bartolomé		Cáceres
HURTADO de Mendoza, Diego		Madrid
PLASENCIA, Pedro de		Seville

Guaxuapa (Huajuapan de León, Oaxaca)—Settled in 1534

Conqueror
ARRIAGA, Juan de		Soria

Jalapa—Settled ca. 1530

Conqueror
ARÉVALO, Melchor de		Avila

Medellín—Municipality established in 1521

Conqueror
ROMÁN, Bartolomé		?

Mexico City—Municipality established at Coyoacan in 1521, moved to Tenochtitlan in late 1523

First Conquerors
AGUILAR, Jerónimo de	Interpreter	Seville
ALONSO, Hernando	Blacksmith	Huelva
ALVARADO, Jorge de	*Hidalgo*	Badajoz
ALVARADO, Pedro de (also *vecino* of Guatemala)	*Hidalgo*	Badajoz
AVILA, Alonso de	*Hidalgo*	Avila
BARRIOS, Andrés de	*Hidalgo*	Cádiz
BRAVO, Antón	Swordsmith	Badajoz
CABEZÓN, Cristóbal		Ciudad Real
CAICEDO, Antón		?
CARVAJAL, Antonio de	*Hidalgo*	Zamora

CASTAÑEDA, Rodrigo de	Hidalgo	Santander
CATALÁN, Juan	Cannoneer	Catalonia
CERMEÑO, Juan		Huelva
COLIO, Diego de		Asturias
CORIA, Diego de	Notary	Seville
CORTÉS, Hernando	Hidalgo	Medellín
FERNÁNDEZ Nieto, Diego		Zamora
GALINDO, Juan Sánchez	Swordsmith	Seville
GALLEGO, Alvaro		Galicia
GARNICA, Gaspar		Vizcaya
GIRALDO, Alonso	Trumpeter	?
GONZÁLEZ Ponce de León, Juan		?
GRADO, Alonso de		Cáceres
GUTIÉRREZ de Ahumado, Antonio		?
GUTIÉRREZ de Almodóvar, Antonio		Ciudad Real
HERNÁNDEZ Mosquera, Cristóbal		Seville
HERNÁNDEZ Mosquera, Gonzalo		Huelva
JARAMILLO de Salvatierra, Juan	Hidalgo	Badajoz
LIMPIAS Carvajal, Juan de	Hidalgo	Seville
LÓPEZ, Martín	Ship's carpenter	Seville
MALDONADO, Alonso		Salamanca
MALDONADO, Francisco		Salamanca
MARÍN, Luis		Cádiz
MARTÍN Jaca, Alonso		Huesca
MARTÍN Millán de Gamboa, Cristóbal	Hidalgo	Vascongadas
MAYA, Pedro de (moved to Antequera)		Burgos
MENDOZA, Alonso de		Badajoz
MONJARAZ, Andrés de	Hidalgo	Vizcaya
MONJARAZ, Mateo de	Hidalgo	Vizcaya
MONTEJO, Francisco de		Salamanca
MONTERROSO, Blas de		Lugo
MOSCOSO, Sebastián		Badajoz
MOTRICO, Diego de	Merchant	Guipúzcoa
NÚÑEZ, Andrés		Salamanca
ORDAZ, Diego de		Zamora
ORTEGA, Bachiller Juan de		Seville
PACHECO, Cristóbal		?
QUEVEDO, Francisco de		?
QUINTERO, Francisco	Mariner	Huelva
RAMÍREZ, Diego	Carpenter	Cádiz
RANGEL, Rodrigo	Hidalgo	Badajoz
RETAMALES, Pablo		Seville
RIJOLES, Tomás	Interpreter	Italy
RODRÍGUEZ Bejerano, Juan de		?
RODRÍGUEZ de Villafuerte, Juan (moved to Zacatula)	Hidalgo	Salamanca
RODRÍGUEZ, Sebastián (moved to Puebla)		Portugal
ROZAS, Andrés de		Burgos
RUIZ, Marcos		Seville
SÁNCHEZ de Sopuerto, Diego	Mariner	Madrid

SÁNCHEZ Farfán, Pedro (moved to Toluca)		Seville
SANDOVAL, Gonzalo de		Badajoz
SERNA, Alonso de la		?
SICILIANO, Juan		Sicily
SOLÍS, Francisco de	Cannoneer	Santander
SOLÍS Barrasa, Pedro de		Burgos
SUÁREZ, Lorenzo	Hidalgo	Portugal
TAPIA, Andrés de		Badajoz
TARIFA, Gaspar de		Seville
TERRAZAS, Francisco de		Badajoz
TIRADO, Juan		?
TORRES, Hernando de		Jaén
TREJO, Rafael de		Cáceres
VARGAS, Francisco de	Hidalgo	Seville
VÁZQUEZ de Tapia, Bernaldino	Hidalgo	Toledo
VÁZQUEZ, Martín		Segovia
VEJER, Benito de	Drummer	Cádiz
VELÁZQUEZ, Juan		?
VILLARROEL, Antonio de		Valladolid

Conquerors

AVILA, Juan de		Avila
AVILA Quiñones, Gaspar de	Hidalgo	Avila
BADAJOZ, Gutierre de	Miner	Cáceres
BEJERANO, Serván		Córdoba
BELLO, Juan		Salamanca
BURGOS, Juan de		Seville
BURGUEÑO, Fernando		Toledo
CABRA, Juan de	Miner	Ciudad Real
CALAHORRA, Martín de (moved to Puebla)	Notary	Logroño
CANO, Juan		Cáceres
CANTILLANA, Hernando	Shoemaker	Grand Canary
CASTILLO Maldonado, Alonso del	Hidalgo	Salamanca
CEREZO, Gonzalo		Córdoba
CERVANTES, Comendador Leonel de	Hidalgo	Seville
CISNEROS, Juan de		Seville
CONTRERAS, Alonso de	Hidalgo	Burgos
CORONEL, Juan		Seville
CUÉLLAR, Juan de	Trumpeter	Segovia
CUÉLLAR Verdugo, Juan de		Segovia
DÍAZ de Aux, Miguel		Huesca
ELGÜETA, Hernando de		?
ESCOBAR, Pedro de		?
ESTRADA, Francisco de		Seville
FLORES, Francisco		Huelva
GALLEGO, Lucas		Galicia
GARCÍA Jaramillo, Diego		Badajoz
GÓMEZ, Bartolomé		Seville
GÓMEZ, Pierrez		Flanders
GÓMEZ de Avila, Rodrigo	Hidalgo	Avila

GONZÁLEZ de Portugal, Alonso	Hidalgo	Lisbon
GONZÁLEZ de Benavides, Gil (Avila)	Hidalgo	Avila
GONZÁLEZ, Ruy		Badajoz
GUILLÉN, Francisco		Huelva
GUTIÉRREZ de Badajoz, Alonso		Badajoz
HERNÁNDEZ, Pedro		?
IRCIO, Martín de	Hidalgo	Logroño
JEREZ, Hernando (Gómez de)		Cádiz
JIMÉNEZ, Juan		Cáceres
LOA, Guillén de la	Notary	Vizcaya
LÓPEZ de Sevilla, Andrés		Seville
LÓPEZ, Gonzalo		?
LÓPEZ, Jerónimo	Hidalgo	Seville
LOZANO, Pedro		Cáceres
MAFRA, Cristóbal de		Portugal
MANSILLA, Juan de		Old Castile
MARTÍN, Hernán	Blacksmith	?
MEDEL, Hernando		Huelva
MENESES, Pedro de (moved to Puebla)	Hidalgo	Toledo
MONTAÑO, Francisco		Salamanca
MORALES, Juan de		Seville
MORENO Cendejas, Pedro		Zaragoza
NÁJERA, Juan de	Hidalgo	Logroño
NIETO, Pedro		?
OLMOS, Francisco de		Valladolid
OLVERA, Diego de		Seville
ORDUÑA, Francisco de	Notary	Vizcaya
ORTIZ de Zúñiga, Alonso	Hidalgo	Seville
PAYO, Lorenzo		?
PEDRAZA, Maestre Diego de	Surgeon	Segovia
PÉREZ, Bachiller Alonso	Letrado	Huelva
PÉREZ de Zamora, Alonso		Zamora
PÉREZ de la Gama, Juan (from Puebla)		?
PÉREZ de Herrera, Juan		?
PILAR, García del		?
PORCALLO, Vasco		?
PORRAS, Diego		Cáceres
QUEJADA, Diego		Burgos
RIBADEO, Francisco de		Lugo
RODRÍGUEZ de la Magdalena, Gonzalo (moved to Puebla)		Seville
RODRÍGUEZ de Ocaña, Gonzalo		Toledo
ROMERO, Cristóbal (moved to Guadalajara)		Córdoba
RUIZ de la Mota Zárate, Jerónimo	Hidalgo	Burgos
RUIZ de Alanís, Juan		Seville
SALAMANCA, Diego de	Hidalgo	Salamanca
SALCEDO, Juan de		Vizcaya
SÁNCHEZ de Hortigosa, Hernán	Notary	Old Castile
SANTA CLARA, Bernardino de	Merchant	Salamanca
SANTA CRUZ, Francisco de		Burgos

SEPÚLVEDA, Maese Martín de	Builder	Segovia
SEPÚLVEDA, Pedro de (from Veracruz)	Blacksmith	Segovia
TELLO de Medina, Juan	Hidalgo	Seville
TOVAR, Juan de		Burgos
VALADÉS, Diego		Badajoz
VALDIVIESO, Juan (from Colima, then to Antequera)		Burgos
VALENCIANO, Pedro		Valencia
VELÁZQUEZ de Lara, Francisco	Hidalgo	Huelva
VERDUGO, Francisco	Hidalgo	Segovia
VILLAFELIZ, Leonardo de		León
VILLANUEVA Tordesillas, Alonso de		Badajoz
ZAMORA, Alvaro de	Interpreter	Zamora
ZAMORANO, Pedro Ruiz	Hidalgo	Jaén
ZAMUDIO, Juan de		Vizcaya
ZIMBRÓN de Vitoria, Alonso (moved to Puebla)		Madrid

Pobladores Antiguos

AVILA, Francisco de		Avila
BAEZA, Rodrigo de		Burgos
CARRANZA, Pedro de	Hidalgo	Burgos
CISNEROS, Cristóbal de (moved to Villarreal, Chiapas)		Toledo
GÓMEZ, Gonzalo	Merchant	Seville
ISLA, Pedro de la		Seville
PARDO, Diego	Merchant/Miner	Huelva
PERALES, Bartolomé de		Badajoz
RODRÍGUEZ, Martín		Badajoz
SUÁREZ Pacheco, Diego	Hidalgo	Avila
SUÁREZ, Juan	Hidalgo	Avila
TÉLLEZ, Licenciado Diego		Córdoba
TORRE, Juan de la	Hidalgo	Ciudad Real
TORRE, Luis de la	Hidalgo	Ciudad Real
VALIENTE, Alonso (from Veracruz, then to Puebla)		Badajoz
VARGAS, Pedro de		Seville
VERDEJO, Alonso (moved to Zacatula)		Cuenca
VILLEGAS, Francisco de	Hidalgo	Extremadura

Pobladores

AGUILAR, Alonso de	Hidalgo	Seville
AGUILERA, Gabriel de	Hidalgo	Jaén
ALBORNOZ, Rodrigo de	Hidalgo	Salamanca
ALMÍNDEZ Chirinos, Pero	Hidalgo	Jaén
ALTAMIRANO, Licenciado Juan Gutiérrez	Hidalgo	Salamanca
ARAGÓN, Pedro de	Blacksmith	Aragón
AVALOS Saavedra, Alonso de (moved to Guadalajara)	Hidalgo	Badajoz
BARRÓN, Francisco		?
BAZÁN, Pedro de		Badajoz

BECERRA de Mendoza, Diego	*Hidalgo*	Badajoz
BERRIO, Luis de		Jaén
BEZOS, Juan		Seville
BUSTAMANTE, Doctor Blas de	*Hidalgo*	Valladolid
CARRILLO, Alonso	*Hidalgo*	Toledo
CARRILLO, Jorge	*Hidalgo*	Toledo
CASAS, Francisco de las	*Hidalgo*	Cáceres
CASCO, Francisco		Badajoz
CASTELLANOS, Alonso de		León
CASTILLA, don Luis de	*Hidalgo*	Valladolid
CERÓN Saavedra, Jorge	*Hidalgo*	Jaén
CERVANTES Casaus, Juan de (moved from Pánuco)	*Hidalgo*	Seville
CUEVAS, Juan de	*Hidalgo*	Burgos
DÍAZ, Diego	Stonemason	?
DÍAZ de Real, Juan		Huelva
ESTRADA, Alonso de	*Hidalgo*	Ciudad Real
FERNÁNDEZ de Proaño, Comendador Diego (moved to Guadalajara)	*Hidalgo*	Seville
GALLEGO, Pedro		Badajoz
GONZÁLES, Jorge		?
GUZMÁN Saavedra, don Luis de	*Hidalgo*	Seville
GUZMÁN, Nuño Beltrán de	*Hidalgo*	Guadalajara
GUZMÁN, Rodrigo de		Toledo
HERRERA, Francisco de		Seville
HINOJOSA, Juan de		Cáceres
INFANTE, Juan	*Hidalgo*	Seville
JASO "el viejo," Juan de	*Hidalgo*	Navarre
JASO "el mozo," Juan de	*Hidalgo*	Navarre
LUNA y Arellano, don Tristán de	*Hidalgo*	Soria
MEDEL, Antonio		Huelva
MEDINA, Domingo de (moved to Cd. Michoacán)		Badajoz
MEDINA, Jerónimo de	*Hidalgo*	Toledo
MORCILLO, Francisco (moved to Cd. Michoacán)	*Hidalgo*	Badajoz
NÚÑEZ, Pedro, Maese de Roa	Surgeon	Burgos
OCAMPO, Diego de		Lugo
OCAÑA, Diego de	Notary	Seville
OJEDA, Doctor Cristóbal de	Surgeon	Seville
OLIVER, Antonio de	*Hidalgo*	Ciudad Real
OÑATE, Cristóbal Pérez de	*Hidalgo*	Alava
PANTOJA, Pedro		Badajoz
PAZ, Alonso de	Notary	Salamanca
PAZ, Pedro de		Salamanca
PEÑA Vallejo, Juan de la		Granada
PERALTA, Martín de		?
PÉREZ de Bocanegra y Córdoba, Hernán	*Hidalgo*	Córdoba
RIOBOZ de Sotomayor, Gonzalo		?
RODRÍGUEZ, Diego	Swordsmith	Salamanca

RODRÍGUEZ de Guadalcanal, Francisco		Seville
RUIZ, Alonso (moved to Antequera)		Jaén
RUIZ, Gonzalo	Hidalgo	Huelva
SAAVEDRA, Fernando de (moved to Honduras)	Hidalgo	Badajoz
SALAMANCA, Juan de	Tailor	Burgos
SALAZAR, Gonzalo de	Hidalgo	Granada
SALAZAR, Hernando de	Hidalgo	Granada
SALDAÑA, Gregorio de	Notary	Palencia
SÁMANO, Juan de	Hidalgo	Burgos
SANDOVAL, Licenciado Rodrigo de	Hidalgo	Valladolid
SOSA, Juan Alonso de	Hidalgo	Córdoba
SOTOMAYOR, Bachiller Pedro Díaz (moved from Pánuco)		Seville
TOMÁS, Maese Manuel	Surgeon	Cáceres
VALDERRAMA, Cristóbal de		Burgos
VÁZQUEZ de Coronado, Francisco	Hidalgo	Salamanca
VELÁZQUEZ, Alonso	Notary	Valladolid
VILLAFAÑE, Angel de	Hidalgo	León
VILLAGÓMEZ, Antonio de		Zamora
VILLAGÓMEZ, Juan de		Zamora
ZÁRATE, Bartolomé (moved from Antequera)		Asturias
ZUMÁRRAGA, Juan de	Bishop	Vizcaya

Indians

MOCTEZUMA, doña Isabel	Native Nobility	Mexico City
MOCTEZUMA, doña Leonor	Native Nobility	Mexico City

Pánuco—Municipality founded as Santisteban del Puerto in 1523

First Conquerors

IÑIGUEZ, Bernardino		Logroño
MEDINA, Juan de		Málaga

Conquerors

AZPEITIA, Juanés		Guipúzcoa
CARRASCOSA, Juan de		Cuenca
CUENCA, Benito de		Cádiz
GONZÁLEZ Trujillo, Gil		?
GUTIÉRREZ Lavado, Diego		Seville
LUCAS, Alonso	Notary	Extremadura
MARTÍN, Ginés		?
MARTÍN, Maya		?
NIETO, Gómez		?
RAMÍREZ, Francisco		León
VILLAGRÁN, Juan de		Valladolid

Pobladores Antiguos

ACEDO, Juan		Seville
CORSO, Vicencio		Corsica
ROELAS, Diego		Seville

CITIZENSHIP OF THE ENCOMENDEROS

Pobladores

AVILA, Gonzalo de		Badajoz
BUSTAMANTE, Rodrigo de		Salamanca
BUSTO, Juan de	Hidalgo	Badajoz
CASTAÑEDA, Diego de		?
CERVANTES Casaus, Juan de (moved to Mexico City)	Hidalgo	Seville
GALLEGOS, Juan		Seville
GARCÍA, Alonso		?
GENOVÉS, Lucas		Genoa
GUZMÁN, Ramiro de		?
INERO, Andrés de		?
MÉNDEZ, Héctor		?
MENDOZA, Lope de		?
MONDRAGÓN, Licenciado Pedro de		?
ORTIZ de Matienzo, Juan	Hidalgo	Santander
RODRÍGUEZ, Juan		Cáceres
RODRÍGUEZ, Melchor		?
ROMERO, Juan		?
SÁNCHEZ, Pedro		Badajoz
SEPÚLVEDA, Cristóbal de		?
SOTOMAYOR, Bachiller Pedro Díaz de (moved to Mexico City)		Seville
TORQUEMADA, Baltasar de		Palencia
TORQUEMADA, Juan de	Notary	Palencia
VILLAPADIERNA, Diego de		Badajoz

Puebla—Municipality founded in 1531

First Conquerors

BONAL, Francisco de (moved from Veracruz)		Salamanca
DAZA de Alconchel, Francisco		Badajoz
GONZÁLEZ, Diego	Merchant	Badajoz
HERNÁNDEZ de Nava, Bartolomé		Huelva
HERNÁNDEZ Calvo, Gonzalo		Huelva
NÚÑEZ Mercado, Juan		Salamanca
PÉREZ de Arteaga, Juan	Interpreter	Palencia
RODRÍGUEZ, Sebastián (moved from Mexico City)		Portugal
SEGURA, Rodrigo de		Seville
SOTO, Cristóbal de		?
VILLALOBOS, Gregorio de (moved from Veracruz)		Huelva

Conquerors

AGUILAR, García de	Hidalgo	Badajoz
AZNAR, Antonio		Granada
BARRERA, Cristóbal		?
BERNAL, Francisco		?
BERNAL, Juan		?
CALAHORRA, Martín de (moved from Mexico City)	Notary	Logroño

DURÁN, Juan		Madrid
GALEOTE García, Alonso		Huelva
GALLARDO, Pedro	Mariner	Huelva
HOLGUÍN, Diego de	*Hidalgo*	Cáceres
MANZANILLA, Juan de		Huelva
MENESES, Pedro de (moved from Mexico City)	*Hidalgo*	Toledo
NAVARRO, Juan		Aragón
OCHOA de Lejalde, Juan	Merchant	Guipúzcoa
OLIVEROS, Francisco de		Portugal
ORTIZ, Juan		Huelva
PÉREZ de la Gama, Juan (moved to Mexico City)		?
RODRÍGUEZ de la Magdalena, Gonzalo (moved from Mexico City)		Seville
VILLANUEVA, Fernando de		Jaén
VILLANUEVA, Pedro de	*Regidor*	Jaén
ZIMBRÓN de Vitoria, Alonso (moved from Mexico City)		Madrid

Pobladores Antiguos

LÓPEZ, Licenciado Pedro	Physician	Seville
MONTALVO, Francisco de	*Hidalgo*	Segovia
VALIENTE, Alonso (from Veracruz and Mexico City)		Badajoz

Pobladores

CÁRDENAS, Ginés de (moved from Veracruz)		Seville
CORTÉS, Martín		Murcia
MARTÍN Breña, Antón		Cáceres

Purificación—Municipality established in 1533

Pobladores

ALMESTO, Juan de		Seville
VILLASEÑOR Orozco, Juan de (moved to Cd. Michoacán)	*Hidalgo*	Málaga

Utlatlan—Settled in 1524

Conqueror

MORENO, Isidro		Ciudad Real

Valles—Municipality founded in 1533

First Conqueror

NAVARRETE, Alonso		Granada

Poblador Antiguo

RIBERA, Alvaro de	*Hidalgo*	Portugal

Pobladores

CORTÉS, Diego	*Hidalgo*	Badajoz
VILLANUEVA, Juan de		Granada

CITIZENSHIP OF THE *ENCOMENDEROS*   295

Veracruz—Municipality founded in 1519

First Conquerors

LÓPEZ de Jimena, Juan		Jaén
MALDONADO, Pedro		Salamanca
ROMERO, Alonso		Soria
SEDEÑO, Juan		?

Conquerors

AGUILAR, Francisco de		Palencia
BENAVIDES, Alonso de		?
MARMOLEJO, Diego	Hidalgo	Seville
SEPÚLVEDA, Pedro de (moved to Mexico City)	Hidalgo	Segovia
ZARAGOZA, Miguel de	Merchant	Zaragoza

Poblador Antiguo

VALIENTE, Alonso (moved to Mexico City, then Puebla)		Badajoz

Pobladores

CARDENAS, Ginés de (moved to Puebla)		Seville
ESCOBAR, Alonso de		Badajoz
ROSALES, Francisco de	Merchant	Burgos
SAAVEDRA Cerón, Alvaro	Hidalgo	Jaén

Villa Alta—Municipality founded in 1527

First Conquerors

JIMÉNEZ, Gonzalo		Cáceres
OJEDA, Alonso de		Huelva

Conquerors

CANO, Alonso		Seville
MIGUEL, Antón		?

Poblador Antiguo

AGUILA, Francisco del		Avila

Pobladores

ALCÁNTARA, Bartolomé de		León
BECERRA, Juan		Zamora
BONILLA, Juan de		Cáceres
DÍAZ Carballar, Alonso		Portugal
FRANCO Estrada, Francisco		Asturias
GARCÍA de Lemos, Juan		Coruña
LORITA, Hernando de	Notary	Badajoz
MANZANO, Alvaro		Huelva
OLIVER Bautista, Juan		Catalonia
PACHECO, Gaspar	Hidalgo	Toledo
PAREDES, Marcos de		?
SALDAÑA, Francisco de		Badajoz
TARIFA, Francisco de		Seville

Villarreal (Chiapas)—Municipality founded in 1528

    Poblador Antiguo
    CISNEROS, Cristóbal de (moved from Mexico City) — Toledo

Zacatula—Municipality founded in 1523

    First Conquerors
    GÓMEZ de Herrera, Juan — ?
    GUTIÉRREZ, Francisco (moved from Pánuco) — Blacksmith — Cáceres
    RODRÍGUEZ Magariño, Francisco — ?
    RODRÍGUEZ de Villafuerte, Juan (moved from Mexico City) — *Hidalgo* — Salamanca
    RUIZ, Diego — Huelva
    RUIZ de Guadalcanal, Pedro — Seville
    RUIZ de Requena, Pedro — Cuenca
    VARELA Gallegos, Gonzalo (moved to Cd. Michoacán) — Galicia

    Conquerors
    CORREAS, Diego — Mariner — Portugal
    EBORA, Sebastían de — Portugal
    MARTÍN, Alonso — Huelva
    PLAZA, Juan de la — Valencia
    RODRÍGUEZ, Francisco — ?
    SÁNCHEZ, Antón de — Ship's Carpenter — Vizcaya

    Poblador Antiguo
    VERDEJO, Alonso (moved from Mexico City) — Cuenca

    Pobladores
    FLORES, Juan — Cáceres
    SAUCEDO, Francisco de — Seville
    VARGAS, Juan Alonso de — *Hidalgo* — Seville

Guatemala

    First Conquerors
    ALVARADO, Gonzalo de — *Hidalgo* — Badajoz
    ALVARADO, Pedro de (also *vecino* of Mexico City) — *Hidalgo* — Badajoz
    DÍAZ del Castillo, Bernal — *Hidalgo* — Valladolid
    RODRÍGUEZ de Escobar, Pedro — Valladolid

Honduras

    Poblador
    SAAVEDRA, Fernando de (moved from Mexico City) — *Hidalgo* — Badajoz

Residence Not Located

First Conquerors
CINDOS de Portillo, Pedro		León
JIMÉNEZ de Rivera, Juan		Santander
MARTÍN de Coria, Pedro		Cáceres
PEÑA, Rodrigo de la		Navarre
PÉREZ de Badajoz, Martín		Badajoz
RODRÍGUEZ de Avalos, Cristóbal	Trumpeter	?

Conquerors
FERNÁNDEZ de Navarrete, Pedro		?
GUADALAJARA, Antonio de		?
HERNÁNDEZ de Prado, Juan		Zamora
MARTÍN, Rodrigo		?
MORENO, Juan		Huelva
NAVARRO, Juan (Antonio)		?

Pobladores Antiguos
RODRÍGUEZ de Valladolid, Diego		Valladolid
SAAVEDRA, Luis de		Cáceres

Pobladores
BECERRA de Mendoza, Diego	Hidalgo	Badajoz
CUEVA, Luis de la		?
FRÍAS, Cristóbal de		New Spain
JUÁREZ, Pedro		?
MARTÍN de Valencia, Juan		Valencia
MÉRIDA, Alonso de		?
ORTEGA, Cristóbal de		?
SOLÍS, Juan de		?

Indians
SÁNCHEZ, Juan		?

APPENDIX G

Methodological Essay

My first intention was to study the entire Hispanic population of Mexico City during the first generation. Thereby I hoped to provide a social and economic dimension to correspond to the scholarly work done on Mexico in the mature and late colonial periods. Note, for example, that the socially oriented studies in *Provinces of Early Mexico* begin with the second generation after the conquest at the earliest.[1] (Work on the Mexican conquest period is copious and distinguished, but overwhelmingly narrative and institutional.) Contrary to expectations, however, the resources, above all notarial records, seem much scantier for Mexico than for Peru in the conquest period, hardly going beyond what Millares Carlo and José I. Mantecón have summarized and published.[2] More compilation of lists of *encomenderos* and inquiry into their lives has been done, however, for New Spain than for Peru. In studying Spanish individuals in Mexico, I soon found I was studying mainly *encomenderos*. Since the basis existed for a systematic study of this important group nearly in its entirety during the first generation, and the members of the group were so numerous, it was natural that I finally decided to concentrate on *encomenderos* alone. Despite their high status in Hispanic Mexican society, the *encomenderos* are still a quite broad and representative group.

All individuals known to have held an *encomienda* in New Spain during the established time frame have been included in this study. *Encomenderos* were identified in a number of sources, but the primary resources were lists published by France V. Scholes and Eleanor B. Adams, extracts of copies of petitions to Viceroy Mendoza published by Francisco A. de Icaza, and the historical geographies of Peter Gerhard. These sources were augmented by rosters of those who took part in the conquest of New Spain contained in Bernal Díaz del Castillo's history, the accounts published by Manuel Orozco y Berra, and a study on Colima in the sixteenth century by Carl O.

Sauer. Additional detail was provided by *Actas de cabildo de la ciudad de México*, volumes I through VI, the *Protocolos* of Millares Carlo and Mantecón, the *Pasajeros de Indias*, and the two-volume geobiographical index of Peter Boyd-Bowman.[3] By comparing names and holdings of those identified in the sources, a group roster was developed that includes most of the *encomenderos* during the first generation (many names may be missing, but most are probably those of grantees in ephemeral, mainly peripheral districts). Many of the *encomenderos* were listed in several sources, a few in all of them, and some in only one.

The study is divided into two parts, with Part One based on data contained in Part Two. Whereas Part Two focuses on specific individual lives and attempts, to some degree, to show uniqueness, Part One combines those with like attributes to ascertain general characteristics and processes, as well as to define subgroups within the overall group of those who held *encomiendas*. The individual capsule biographies presented in Part Two vary with the amount of source material available for each *encomendero*. For some the documentary trail permits the reconstruction of a rather complete life; for others there are but hints of their time on earth. In many respects this effort echoes *The Men of Cajamarca*, but there are major differences.[4] The *encomenderos* of New Spain are a much larger group, over 500 individuals as compared to 168. *The Men of Cajamarca* treats a group who were together at the same place in a common tactical effort at a crucial point in time. This study deals with a group of individuals who crossed the Mexican scene over a period of thirty years or more, their main common characteristic being simply that they were *encomenderos* at some time during these three decades. Then too, corresponding to the differing nature of the sources, already mentioned, there is less emphasis on economic behavior in the present case, and more on the specifics of the *encomiendas* held and the details of tenure. The unarguable difference between the two groups, however, can be reduced to wealth. *The Men of Cajamarca* addresses the lives of a group who acquired a bonanza of truly monumental proportions; the *encomenderos* of New Spain held an asset of ever diminishing returns.

Sources of the Study

A socially oriented history requires abundant documents of a personal nature to provide the necessary detail on individuals and groups of individuals in the course of ordinary life. Such documents are necessary to show patterns and relationships so basic that people take them for granted and say little about them or are even not fully aware of them, so that only through following and correlating people's actions can they be detected. For the Mexican conquest and the years immediately ensuing, the majority of surviving documents are reports and posturing correspondence sent out of the area of operation during the evolving action and some memoirs written after the fact.

Documents for the early social history of New Spain, however, have had a poor survival rate, except for bits and pieces such as those found in the minutes of municipal councils. Such records for Mexico City survive for the time from 8 March 1524 forward, providing evidence of interaction between society and the institution, but only insofar as individuals chanced to have some particular reason to deal with the *cabildo*. For the most part, such business is limited to petitions for citizenship and assignment of house lots, garden plots, and rural agricultural tracts. It is to the notarial archives that one must go in order to find records of the flesh and bones of day-to-day interaction among individuals. Unfortunately, notarial records have not yet been located for New Spain and specifically for Mexico City from the conquest and immediate postconquest years; the earliest known extant protocols date from August 1525, a full four years after the siege of Mexico City ended.[5] The files of Mexico City notary Juan Hernañdez del Castillo preserve the record of 1,792 transactions in 1,577 folios, with the earliest documents dating from 9 August 1525. There are lacunae from 10 December 1525 to 28 January 1527, and again from 16 November 1527 to 26 December 1527. Hernández del Castillo's records end as of 1 December 1528, although he remained an active notary in Mexico City until ca. 1539.[6] The 749 protocols of Martín de Castro, drawn up between 20 June 1536 and 28 March 1538, and the 108 Diego Ayala instruments for the period 18 October 1551 to 14 March 1553, along with those of Hernández, have been extracted and published by Agustín Millares Carlo and José I. Mantecón. The protocols of Andrés Cabrera and Gaspar Calderón, also notaries of this period, survive and cover various periods between 1543 and 1559 but have not been published.[7] The presumption is that many of the protocols for the formative years of New Spain perished in the great fire of the seventeenth century.

Perhaps the most valuable source of information for tracing the lives of first-generation *encomenderos* of New Spain is Francisco A. de Icaza's *Diccionario autobiográfico de conquistadores y pobladores de Nueva España*, a two-volume compilation of extracts taken from 1,385 petitions submitted by individuals to Viceroy don Antonio de Mendoza between 1540 and 1550. These documents were in the Archivo General de Indias, Papeles e Patronato, and de Simancas. A cursory search in June 1989, however, failed to locate them. From all indications, Mendoza elicited these petitions under the pretext of making certain that deserving persons who took part in the conquest, or were among the early settlers, were adequately rewarded, while in reality taking inventory of individual holdings as a step toward satisfying royal desires to dissolve the *encomienda* system.[8] Although some of these petitions were copies of *probanzas de méritos y servicios* (proofs of merit and service) previously submitted to the crown, the majority were written during the 1540s, after the 1544 promulgation of the New Laws, either confirming the possession of *encomiendas* or requesting replacements for grants relinquished for one reason or another. Other petitions were initial requests for some sinecure based on the contributions of a relative. Unfortunately, the extracts made in the sixteenth century and published by Icaza do not include the complete petition nor the identification of witnesses, if any, or other supporting documents. Icaza's work does, however, identify a number of those who took part in the capture of Mexico City as well as subsequent actions in New Spain. It further shows who the *encomenderos* of the 1540s were as well as others who had held grants in New Spain at an earlier time. Often a less than objective view of the petitioner's activities is presented, while at the same time the value of the *encomienda* held is underestimated. Perhaps the most significant contributions of Icaza's work are bits of information of a personal nature that are generally omitted in traditional accounts. The petitions often identify the petitioner's birthplace, parents, and wife, or at least marital status. Also included are the number and sex of children, often both legitimate and natural, and the name of the spouse's parents. The social standing of the petitioner is occasionally shown and is perhaps the least inaccurate source of this information available.

Efforts made by the crown a generation later (in the 1560s) to identify *encomenderos* and associate them with specific grants further assisted in the research effort. A list of *encomiendas* and the holders thereof was compiled under the direction of Viceroy don Luis de Velasco in response to a royal edict of 31 May 1562 and forwarded to Spain the following year. A revised copy dated 10 June 1564 was submitted when news came that the ship carrying the original had been lost at sea.[9] This document complements Icaza by verifying much of the information regarding *encomiendas* held, as well as indicating succession. The successor, be it a son, daughter, or widow, is often specified along with the generation status of the *encomienda* (first, second, or third "life" since the original grant), plus occasional comment as to the relative worth of the grant. The 1564 roster published by Scholes and Adams amends the 1563 original by indicating in marginal notes those who had died during the year between submissions.

Information on the specific location and often the population of *encomiendas*, plus corroborating data concerning succession, is contained in Gerhard's *A Guide to the Historical Geography of New Spain*. This publication traces the jurisdictional development of New Spain during the entire colonial period, providing precontact background, *encomienda* and *encomendero* identification, changing political and ecclesiastical status, population trends, and bibliographical sources for each of the colonial political subdivisions. Gerhard augments this work with his *The Southeast Frontier of New Spain* and *The North Frontier of New Spain*. The former deals among other things with the historical geography of the Isthmus of Tehuantepec, especially the area that is present-day Tabasco and Chiapas. Although partly going beyond the scope of the present study, nonetheless *The Southeast Frontier* contributes to the identification of grants and holders in the Coatzacoalcos region of New Spain. *The North Frontier* treats the jurisdictional development of the region north of New Spain in a similar manner; as in the case of *The Southeast Frontier*, it generally covers a time frame later than dealt with here.

(Although Yucatan was a region that interested the Spaniards early on, initial inventories showed that it lacked the mineral wealth of some other parts of Mexico. It became a separate political unit under Francisco de Montejo, and attempts to conquer it in 1527–1528 and 1530–1534 were less than successful. The more settled areas were brought under Spanish control in the mid-1540s, just when the jurisdiction of Yucatan was transferred from New Spain to the Audiencia de los Confines, located at Gracias a Dios, Honduras. Even though the crown ordered the region back under the control of New Spain in 1548, and then to the jurisdiction of Guatemala in 1550, word traveled very slowly. None of the *encomenderos* of New Spain were *vecinos* of the early settlements here, and since the region was not being developed until late in the time frame of this study and then under the aegis of Honduras and Guatemala, Yucatan is not included herein. New Galicia, and especially Guadalajara, on the other hand, had a close relationship with the Audiencia and viceroy in Mexico City, and because a number of

Guadalajara's *vecinos* were *encomenderos* of New Spain, that region is treated tangentially in this study.)

Writing the history of a restricted group can be a difficult task unless the members of the group have been fully identified. Group rosters for Mexico in the immediate conquest period must of necessity be composites, because original lists of participants have not survived. Of the foregoing sources, Icaza, Scholes and Adams, and Gerhard have contributed most toward identifying the *encomenderos*. No one individual source contains a complete roster, but perhaps the composite of the three does identify the great majority of those who held grants during the period between 1521 and 1555. Complementary lists are presented in Manuel Orozco y Berra's *Los conquistadores de México* and Bernal Díaz del Castillo's *Historia verdadera de la conquista de la Nueva España*, contributing much qualifying information. These two sources serve especially to identify those who took part in the capture of Mexico City, distinguishing among those who accompanied Hernando Cortés, Pánfilo de Narváez, and the reinforcing captains who arrived over a period of months in 1520 and 1521.

A final reference providing biographical data to flesh out the lives of some seventy-five percent of the *encomenderos* is Peter Boyd-Bowman's two-volume *Indice geobiográfico de cuarenta mil pobladores españoles de América en el Siglo XVI*.[10] Although this index does not provide initial identification of *encomenderos*, it does offer personal information, including birthplace, parentage, and occasionally occupation, concerning those on the composite roster. Boyd-Bowman's index, although following the lead of Cristóbal Bermúdez Plata's *Catálogo de pasajeros a Indias* in using the Seville emigration registers, contains much information gleaned from additional sources.[11]

It is true that this work lacks original archival citations, but there are excellent reasons for this. The study attempts to show patterns by tying biographical data on *encomenderos* to data on the *encomiendas* held. A standard of a kind is provided by the only other study of a somewhat similar nature, James Lockhart's *Men of Cajamarca*. Although it deals with a similar group compared to this study, it has more biographical information but contains very little information about *encomiendas* held. The source of Lockhart's biographical information was primarily notarial records in which the individuals were mentioned. The previously mentioned fire in the seventeenth century presumably destroyed most of the records for the decades under study here. As a consequence, the excellent detailed summary of the main surviving corpus of such documents published by Millares Carlo and Mantecón was used in this study. This lack of documentation seriously limits the amount of detail on the business activities of most of the *encomenderos*.

The Tierras, Indios, Civil, Mercedes, Tributos, Vínculos, and Inquisición sections of the Archivo General de la Nación are rich in information on *encomiendas* but not on the lives of the *encomenderos*. This study has a great deal of systematic information on *encomiendas*, based on the lists of Mexican *encomiendas* made in the sixteenth century and since published, and a modern historical literature taking advantage of and building on those lists. Scholes, Gibson, and Gerhard are the most important scholars here. As much as these scholars achieved, however, they did not consolidate and analyze their data; that is the contribution of this study—to bring together and rationalize a quite stupendous amount of disparate, scattered, although significant material. The archival sections cited above are precisely those that Gibson and especially Gerhard have already combed through for the same purpose. After spending considerable time working in these sections I realized that Gerhard or one of the other scholars usually had the same references, so I opted for published citations, which often give many additional sources. Clearly more could eventually be unearthed, but there is no known unexplored concentration of likely sources. To spend years in low-yield search for individual facts is less significant than to publish a compilation and analysis of the vast amount already worked.

Notes

1. Introduction

1. Woodrow Borah and Shelbourne F. Cook, *The Population of Central Mexico in 1548—An Analysis of the "Suma de visitas de pueblos,"* 109–115, and *The Aboriginal Population of Central Mexico on the Eve of the Spanish Conquest*, 88, discuss the demography of the region at this time.

2. Mateo and Gregorio de Monjaraz proved to be one person, as did Martín de la Mezquita and Martín de la Montesinos. Non-Spaniards often changed their names as they rose in life. One conqueror, Antonio de Villarroel, became Antonio Serrano de Cardona when he received a royal appointment as a perpetual *regidor* of Mexico City. Andrés de Tapia added "y Sosa" to his name when he married doña Isabel de Sosa.

3. Peter Gerhard, *A Guide to the Historical Geography of New Spain*.

4. *National Geographic Atlas of the World; World Aeronautical Chart CJ-24; World Aeronautical Chart CJ-25;* and *Mexico*.

5. Francisco de Icaza, *Diccionario autobiográfico de conquistadores y pobladores de Nueva España*.

6. See Julia Hirschberg, "Social Experiment in New Spain: A Prosopographical Study of the Early Settlement at Puebla de Los Angeles, 1531–1534," 18.

7. An *entrada* is defined as an expedition into unknown and unclaimed territory, whether the result be discovery, conquest, settlement, or all three. It could be formed as a commercial company headed by a few employer-investors with a great number of employees or as a band of self-financed and outfitted men joined together in a venture where each received a share of the gain. Cortés' expedition was an *entrada*, but the term is used especially of the many subsequent and often futile thrusts into peripheral areas.

8. *Actas de cabildo de la ciudad de México*, vols. I–VI.

9. Anton(io) de Arriaga, a conqueror and longtime veteran of the Indies, is shown as "don Antonio de Arriaga" in the Mexico City Cabildo minutes when granted a license in January 1526 to build a grist mill on Río Tacubaya. This is the only reference found associating him with a high title. There is nothing to suggest even ordinary gentry in his genealogy, nor does his wife, Plain Ana Quintero (from maritime Huelva?), contribute to such identification. The title in this case is conceivably an expression of respect for an old veteran, if it is not indeed a clerical or other error.

10. Bernal Díaz del Castillo, *Historia verdadera de la conquista de la Nueva España.*

11. Hernández, a 1511 arrival in the Indies, took part in the conquest of Cuba with Diego Velázquez. Wounds he received during a skirmish with the residents of Potonchán (established as Santa María de la Victoria in 1519, present day Frontera, Tabasco) prompted the termination of the 1517 expedition. Hernández died soon after returning to Cuba. Grijalva, also a 1511 arrival in the Indies and a conqueror of Cuba, was Diego Velázquez' nephew and a lieutenant governor of Cuba.

12. See Leslie Byrd Simpson, *The Encomienda in New Spain,* 30. Simpson uses the Rodrigo de Alburquerque report of 1514 for Hispaniola, placing its population at 1,000. Peter Boyd-Bowman's *Indice geobiográfico de cuarenta mil pobladores españoles de América en el siglo XVI,* xxxvii, shows those who received licenses to leave Spain. Of the approximately 5,500 so licensed by 1519, there is every indication that a number did not even leave Europe after acquiring the license. Of those who did sail, a number did not reach a destination in the Indies for reasons that include death at sea and shipwreck. Then those who survived the trip but died in the Indies as well as those who returned to Spain must be subtracted. The remaining population, based on those having licenses, would be about 3,700. Approximately 20 percent of the *encomenderos* left no record of departing from Spain, so it is conceivable that at least the same percentage of those who made the trip and survived were never listed on any roster or manifest. Hence, the European population of the Indies in 1519 can be estimated speculatively at between 4,500 and 5,000, distributed unequally among six or seven locations. This total does not include the possibly 375 or so sailors in the region.

13. See Bernal Díaz del Castillo, *Historia verdadera,* vol. 1, 354f., 370, 412, and 449. Narváez left Cuba with about 1,400 men, 80 horses, 20 cannon, and 150 crossbows and muskets. Cortés' 1 June 1520 muster at Tlaxcala reflected 1,300, of which nearly 100 were horsemen and 156 armed with muskets and crossbows. All but 200 came with Narváez and the other reinforcing captains and outfitters. In addition to this were 76 men and seven horses left in Tenochtitlan under Pedro de Alvarado. Cortés' force just prior to its expulsion from the Mexican capital, then, amounted to about 1,300 footmen and 100 horsemen. Arms included 180 muskets and crossbows and 24 cannon. The siege of Tenochtitlan began in July of 1520 with 15 horsemen and 420 footmen, over 850 fewer than the initial combined force of the previous month. A constant reinforcement during the following months perhaps doubled the force by the time the siege ended in August 1521.

14. Personal letter, Hernando de Castro to Alonso de Nebreda, 31 August 1520. James Lockhart and Enrique Otte, tr. and ed., *Letters and People of the Spanish Indies, Sixteenth Century,* 24–38.

15. See James Lockhart, "Encomienda and Hacienda: The Evolution of the Great Estate in the Spanish Indies," 415, note; Charles Gibson, *Spain in America,* 50–54; and James Lockhart and Stuart B. Schwartz, *Early Latin America: A History of Colonial Spanish America and Brazil,* 68–71 and 92–96.

16. See Simpson, *The Encomienda.* Chapters 1 through 4 discuss the evolution of the legal aspects of the *encomienda* in the Indies.

17. Hernando Cortés, *Cartas y Documentos,* 27. This, the first of the celebrated five letters from Cortés to the crown, although signed by members of the Cabildo of Veracruz, must be considered a creation of Cortés. It emphasizes the

righteousness of the venture by citing the irregularities of Diego Velázquez and implies that the social and political evils of Cuba resulted from the governor's authority to assign and revoke *encomiendas*. The *cabildo* petitioned the king not to grant such authority, or any other authority, to Velázquez in New Spain.

18. Ibid., 220ff.

19. Ibid., 27, 200, 240f., and *Epistolario de Nueva España*, vol. I, 55f.

20. The legal aspects of *encomienda* assignment, reassignment, authority, and responsibility are extensively discussed in Simpson, *The Encomienda* and Silvio A. Zavala, *La encomienda indiana*. The great majority of the *encomiendas* were granted by Cortés in anticipation of royal authority. If authority had been denied, it would have been up to the king to undertake the politically unpopular action of revoking the grants. Royal authorization for Cortés as governor to assign Indian tributaries to the conquerors was made by decree, delivered to New Spain by returning *entrada* representatives Francisco de Montejo and Diego de Ordás. This order countermanded a previous decree prohibiting *encomienda* assignment and set forth the conditions under which grants were to be made.

21. James Lockhart, "Españoles entre indios: Toluca a fines del siglo XVI," 435–491.

2. The *Encomenderos*' Backgrounds

1. See Lockhart, *Men of Cajamarca*, 28. Lockhart identifies three regional areas of Extremadura: Cáceres-Trujillo on the east, Badajoz on the west and La Serena and the Order of Santiago's Maestrazgo de León on the south. Particulars concerning the *encomenderos* of New Spain suggest the four regional divisions discussed.

2. *Maese* or *maestre* was the title of a master artisan. Maese Manuel Tomás was a master surgeon.

3. Díaz del Castillo, *Historia verdadera*, vol. 2, 246 and 249–251.

4. Ibid., vol. 1, 26. As a relative of Velázquez, Díaz was perhaps justified in joining Sandoval's *entrada* after the capture of Mexico City. Although Gonzalo de Sandoval was from Medellín as was Cortés, it is doubtful that Díaz' family ties would affect his chance of reward under his good friend and new captain. His decision was prudent under the circumstances and in the end proved to be the right one. Two of his five *encomiendas* in New Spain were assigned by Sandoval and confirmed by Cortés. The five grants provided him with the tribute from more than 16,000 Indians.

5. Names that suggest non-Spanish origin include Alonso Giraldo and Hernando de Gamboa. The only other Giraldo identified was a Genoese sailor. Gamboa married the widow of pilot Ginés Pinzón; the association suggests a maritime background, the name perhaps of Portuguese origin.

6. This relates closely to the conquerors of Peru as presented by Lockhart in *Men of Cajamarca*. Mario Góngora's *Los grupos de conquistadores en Tierra Firme*, 70–74, however, lists the recipients of the first division of Indians in Panama (25 October 1519) citing both social standing/occupation and the extent of service in the Indies.

7. Two of the medical men, *pobladores* Doctor Cristóbal de Ojeda and Pedro Núñez, Maese de Roa, associated in a number of merchandising and mining ventures, often included surgeon conqueror Maese Diego de Pedraza, as a partner. Poblador Licenciado Pedro López, the protomédico, was associated with

a hospital, but was also a *regidor* of Puebla. The fifth surgeon *encomendero*, Maese Manuel Tomás, was a member of Cortés' staff and appears to have been as much an administrator as a surgeon.

8. See Simpson, *Encomienda*, note 13, 194.

9. The trumpeters were first conquerors Cristóbal Rodríguez de Avalos and Alonso Giraldo, and conqueror Juan de Cuéllar. The drummer was Benito de Vejer, who, with his wife Ana Gómez, ran a school of dance in Mexico City ca. 1527.

10. Artillerymen were Juan Catalán, who died in the 1520s, and Francisco de Solís. The archer was Bartolomé López de Sanlúcar and the crossbowman Sebastián Rodríguez, from Portugal.

11. Audiencia interpreter first conqueror *hidalgo* Rodrigo de Castañeda received his *encomienda* from the second Audiencia; the much celebrated Jerónimo de Aguilar received forty *estancias* and thirty-seven *sujetos*; Juan Pérez de Arteaga's *encomienda* totaled over 2,500 tributaries. Italian Tomás Rijoles sold his small grant (ten tributaries ca. 1570) in the 1540s. Conqueror García del Pilar acquired an acting governor grant that was recovered by Cortés in 1526. *Poblador* Melchor Rodríguez appears to have been one of Nuño Beltrán de Guzmán's men in Pánuco.

12. Hernando de Torres, Gutierre de Badajoz, and Juan de Cabra are frequently referred to as miners in notarial records, as is swordsmith Antón Bravo.

13. Díaz del Castillo, *Historia verdadera*, vol. 1, 427, 438, 444, 458, 469, and vol. 2, 249–251. Lockhart, *Men of Cajamarca*, 22f. and 145f. tells of similar attitudes in Peru.

14. The senior *encomendero* was Diego García Jaramillo from Badajoz, followed by *poblador antiguo* Juan Suárez (Cortés' brother-in-law) and then conqueror Maese Diego de Pedraza, a surgeon.

15. Awards to persons arriving after 1531 were made by viceroys; the recipients were Francisco Vázquez de Coronado (1535), Bishop Juan López de Zárate (1535), and don Tristán de Luna y Arellano. The remaining two becoming *encomenderos* after 1535 did so by marrying a widow or daughter of an *encomendero*.

3. Cities and *Encomiendas*

1. See Lockhart, "Encomienda and Hacienda," 411–429; Lockhart, *Spanish Peru, 1532–1560*, Ch. 2; Lockhart and Stuart B. Schwartz, *Early Latin America*, Chs. 1, 3, 4.

2. *Actas de Cabildo*, IV, 144.

3. Ibid., pp. 419ff., and Robert S. Chamberlain, "Castilian Backgrounds of the *Repartimiento-Encomienda*," *Contributions to American Anthropology and History*, 28. A general discussion of the terms *vecino* and *casa poblada* is on pages 28 and 29. The primary source identifying the *vecinos* of Mexico City is the *Actas de Cabildo*, a published transcription of the minutes of the Mexico City council. The identification of those coming before this body generally includes citizenship and social standing. The only reason a number of names were entered was as petitioners to become *vecinos*. The *Actas* do not, however, show if or when an individual changed his citizenship to another municipality. Another significant source showing citizenship information is Icaza's *Diccionario autobiográfico de conquistadores y pobladores de Nueva España*. These extracts of petitions presented to Viceroy Mendoza in the mid-1540s frequently identify not only the petitioner's place of origin, but also where he was a *vecino*

at the time of writing, the existence of a *casa poblada*, and the names of *encomiendas* held at that time. Information corroborating data from the *Actas* and the petition extracts comes from *Indice y extractos de los protocolos del Archivo de Notarías de México*, wherein citizenship is stated along with names and often social standing.

4. Jorge de Alvarado, a *vecino* of Mexico City and *encomendero* of New Spain, spent much time in Guatemala during the late 1520s and the early 1530s assisting his brother, Adelantado Pedro de Alvarado. Adelantado Francisco de Montejo, although governor of Yucatan and active in Chiapas and Tabasco, was a *vecino* of Mexico City and held three *encomiendas* in New Spain. The *encomendero* brothers (and cousins of Cortés), Alonso de Avalos Saavedra and Fernando de Saavedra, held a number of grants west of Mexico City called collectively the Provincia de Avalos. Alonso was a *vecino* of Mexico City, Ciudad Michoacán, and Guadalajara, where he lived after the 1540s. Fernando was a *vecino* of Mexico City as well as a *regidor* and *vecino* of San Pedro de Puerto Caballos, Honduras. Juan de Villaseñor Orozco, although a founding *vecino* of Purificación, New Galicia, was a *vecino* of Ciudad Michoacán and claimed to live on his *encomienda* north and east of Lake Pátzcuaro. Also see Marta Hunt, "Colonial Yucatan: Town and Region in the Seventeenth Century," 40. Even though don Zeferino Pacheco was a resident and *vecino* of Mérida, he was the *encomendero* of Tihosuco, a grant 95 miles distant in the jurisdiction of Valladolid.

5. Cortés, *Cartas y Documentos*, 20 ff.; Díaz del Castillo, *Historia verdadera*, 121; and Gerhard, *Historical Geography*, 13, 363ff., and 365.

6. Cortés, *Cartas y Documentos*, 105f.; Díaz del Castillo, *Historia verdadera*, 451; and Gerhard, *Historical Geography*, 49, 278, and 381.

7. Cortés, *Cartas y Documentos*, 269; and Gerhard, *Historical Geography*, 13, 83, 85, and 360.

8. Cortés, *Cartas y Documentos*, 90 and 137f.; Díaz del Castillo, *Historia verdadera*, 407f.; and Gerhard, *The Southeast Frontier*, 8 and 35ff.

9. Cortés, *Cartas y Documentos*, 204 and 212ff.; Gerhard, *Historical Geography*, 393f. and 396; Carl O. Sauer, *Colima*, 9ff.

10. Donald E. Chipman, *Nuño de Guzmán and the Province of Pánuco in New Spain, 1518–1533*, 51ff. and 65.

11. Cortés, *Cartas y Documentos*, 211, and Francisco López de Gómara, *Historia general de las Indias y la vida de Hernán Cortés*, 69f. Cortés went to Pánuco with a force of 150 horsemen, 300 footmen, and 40,000 Mexicans. Of the 130 Spaniards who were assigned *encomiendas* and became *vecinos*, the identity of thirty-eight is known.

12. Gerhard, *Historical Geography*, 212ff.

13. Cortés, *Cartas y Documentos*, 212ff.; Gerhard, *Historical Geography*, 78ff. and 80; Sauer, *Colima*, 10 and 19ff.

14. Gerhard, *Historical Geography*, 48ff.; and Simpson, *Encomienda*, 137 and 194.

15. Gerhard, *Historical Geography*, 367f. and 370.

16. Hirschberg, "Social Experiment in New Spain," 1–33, discusses some of the reasons for the founding of Puebla.

17. A social analysis of the very early years of New Galicia is overdue, although Gerhard does provide some discussion and sources in *The North Frontier of New Spain*, 90–92, 117–121, and 138–143. The three major settlements here by mid-century, Compostela, Purificación, and Guadalajara, had a combined

vecino population of about 150, with perhaps one-half of them *encomenderos*. Both Purificación and Tepic (later renamed Compostela) were visited as early as 1524 by Francisco Cortés, based in Colima. He assigned *encomiendas* in each area to a few members of his *entrada*. These *vecinos* of Colima were replaced as *encomenderos* by followers of Nuño Beltrán de Guzmán after 1531. Compostela was established as Espiritu Santo near present-day Tepic in 1531 by about sixty founding *vecinos* under Francisco Verdugo. The villa was renamed Compostela the following year and moved about twenty miles south in 1540. By 1548 there were perhaps twenty-four *encomendero vecinos* with grants in the area. About half were residing on their *encomiendas*, ten or so in the *villa* and two, Cristóbal de Oñate the younger and Juan Sánchez, were *vecinos* of Guadalajara. Compostela was the official residence of the governor and the Audiencia of New Galicia from 1540 to 1560, when both officially moved to Guadalajara. Another lieutenant of Nuño de Guzmán, Juan Fernández de Ijar, founded Purificación in February 1533. It had a *cabildo* from founding to 1566 when three *corregimientos* were established. Purificación had from eight to twenty-five *vecinos* after 1543 with fourteen known *encomenderos* ca. 1548. During the first ten years after founding in 1531 Guadalajara was relocated three times. There were a reported sixty-three *vecinos* for the fourth and final founding at its present location in October 1541. By 1550 there were between fifty and eighty *vecinos*, perhaps thirty of whom were *encomenderos* of New Galicia. Seven *vecinos* had grants in New Spain, and a few more *encomenderos* of New Galicia were *vecinos* elsewhere. Also see *Relación breve y sumaria de la visita hecha por el Lic. Lorenzo Lebrón de Quiñones, oidor del nuevo reino de Galicia, por mando de su alteza* and José Luis Razo Zaragoza y Cortés, Guadalajara, 12–16.

18. Gerhard, *Historical Geography*, 376.
19. Ibid., 346ff.; and *Epistolario de Nueva España 1515–1818*, vol. 5, 205ff.
20. Gerhard, *Historical Geography*, 354 and 357; Chipman, *Guzmán*, 293.
21. Chamberlain, "Castilian Backgrounds," 28.
22. The total number of *encomiendas* (767) shown in Tables 12, 13, and 15 does not include the forty-one grants claimed by Hernando Cortés nor the fourteen held by Nuño Beltrán de Guzmán. Although both of these large holdings were managed much like typical *encomiendas*, including them introduces unacceptable inconsistencies in the comparisons. Furthermore, four Guzmán grants in New Spain were taken from Cortés, who recovered one as part of the Marquesado grant, three of them reverted to the crown upon the arrival of the second Audiencia, and another was reassigned. Nine of Guzmán's *encomiendas* were in New Galicia and all but one had reverted to the crown in 1545 when the province was reunited with New Spain.
23. Walter V. Scholes, *The Diego Ramírez Visita*. The report of this *visita* and associated correspondence is replete with charges and countercharges concerning tribute abuses.
24. Complete biographies of the six *encomenderos* who claimed non-urban residences are in Part Two. The following synthesizes these experiences. Two who were not married, first conquerors Pedro Cindos de Portillo and Alonso Navarrete, later renounced the world and entered religious orders. Cindos, who arrived in the Indies in 1514, became a Franciscan in 1528 and spent the rest of his life as a *doctrinero*. Navarrete, from Guadix (Granada), arrived in the Indies in 1516. He was an *encomendero* in the Valles region for over twenty years, becoming an Augustinian in 1555. In both cases the *encomiendas* escheated. Con-

querors Juan de Arriaga and Isidro Moreno were both veterans of the Indies, arriving in 1514 and 1516 respectively. Arriaga, a native of Soria in Old Castile, had a Spanish wife and four children, two of them sons. He lived in Guaxuapa, the *cabecera* of his grant, claiming poverty as the reason. Moreno, from Ciudad Real, was also married—perhaps to an Indian woman—and lived in Utlatlan, one of his *cabeceras* in the Zacatula jurisdiction. A son lived in and administered another *cabecera* near Taxco. It appears Moreno lived apart from the urban life by choice. *Poblador* Bartolomé de Valdés from Lebrija (Seville) was also married, but lived in Chiautla (also called Minas de Ayoteco), a short distance from his claimed *encomienda* at Cuquila. It is not possible to determine the true motive of *hidalgo poblador* Juan de Villaseñor Orozco for choosing to live in one of his *cabeceras*. He and a brother arrived in New Spain in late 1523 with money and horses and took part in a number of *entradas*. Villaseñor was a founder but reluctant *vecino* of Purificación for a while, then became a citizen of Ciudad Michoacán. He claimed that both residences were maintained under orders. Nuño de Guzmán directed the Purificación citizenship, Viceroy Mendoza the Michoacán. His wife was a doña, a daughter of Comendador Leonel de Cervantes, and they had four children. Although he claimed poverty as the reason for the decision to live apart, it seems he was perhaps pouting, feeling that neither Purificación nor Ciudad Michoacán amounted to anything compared to Mexico City. Some of the twenty-plus *encomenderos* who left no record of municipal citizenship may also have lived on or near their *encomiendas*.

25. Sources and additional discussion for *encomenderos* who gave all or part of their grants is contained in Part Two in the individual biographies. The following gave *encomiendas* in dowry:

a. Partial renunciation to legitimate daughters: *poblador* Gregorio de Saldaña, first conqueror Alonso de Avila, *poblador antiguo* Rodrigo de Baeza, conqueror Francisco de Orduña, conqueror Miguel Díaz de Aux, *poblador* Bachiller Pedro Díaz de Sotomayor, the widow of Alonso de Estrada, the widow of Hernando (Gómez) de Jerez, and *poblador* Jerónimo de Medina.
b. Partial renunciation to natural daughters: first conqueror Bernal Díaz del Castillo and conqueror Gonzalo Rodríguez de Ocaña.
c. Total renunciation to legitimate daughters: widow of conqueror Juan Durán, conqueror Lorenzo Payo, and *poblador antiguo* Pedro de Vargas.
d. Total renunciation to natural daughters: conqueror Rodrigo Gómez de Avila and *poblador* Diego de Ocampo (gave *encomiendas* to two of his three daughters).

26. Millares Carlo and Mantecón, *Protocolos*, II, no. 2452, 164ff., of 17 December 1537.

27. Scholes and Adams, *Relación*, 35.

28. The widow of Royal Treasurer Alonso de Estrada initially succeeded as *encomendera* of one grant and later acquired another to provide a dowry for a daughter who married Francisco Vázquez de Coronado.

29. Lockhart, *Spanish Peru*, 20.

30. The number of *encomenderos* involved in sales of grants does not match the number of transactions because conqueror Juan de Mansilla sold *encomiendas* to two different persons, conqueror Pedro de Meneses bought grants from different individuals and *poblador antiguo* Diego Téllez bought a jointly held *encomienda* from *poblador* Antonio Medel and conqueror Andrés López de Sevilla.

31. Scraps of such transactions can be gleaned from *Epistolario de Nueva España*, vols. 1 and 2; Icaza, *Diccionario*; Millares Carlo and Mantecón, *Protocolos*; Gerhard, *Historical Geography*; and Scholes and Adams, *Relación*.

32. *Colleción de documentos inéditos relativos al descubrimiento, conquista y organización de las antiguas posesiones españoles de ultramar*, Second Series, IX, 214–226 and X, 322–329.

33. *Colleción de documentos inéditos relativos al descubrimiento, conquista y organización de las antiguas posesiones españoles*, XVI, 376–406; and Simpson, *Encomienda*, 130.

34. Scholes and Adams, *Relación*, 19, contains a typical entry suggesting transfer by sale: "*El pueblo de Tetela está encomendado por el Virrey don Antonio en Francisco Rodríguez de Guadalcanal, poblador, por renunciación que en él hizo Juan de Mansilla, conquistador, que fue primero tenedor.*" Similar language is used in showing the transfer of grants sold by the other sixteen *encomenderos*.

35. The *encomenderos* of New Galicia, if assigned to complexes, must be treated in a different manner. The fourteen *encomenderos* of Purificación are most appropriately included with those of Colima. This frontier settlement is within seventy-five miles of Colima (and over 100 difficult miles from Compostela as well as over 100 miles from Guadalajara), the indigenous people were similar, and the town was purposely founded as far east as possible to establish occupancy in an area already claimed by New Spain. *Encomiendas* assigned to the *vecinos* of Guadalajara and Compostela were limited to sedentary people to the west and south because Guadalajara was within fifteen miles of the southern boundary and less than fifty miles west of the effective eastern boundary of New Galicia. Although *encomiendas* were assigned north of Guadalajara, the *encomenderos* had difficulty exploiting grants of people who lacked the tradition of providing tribute. A complex for the area that included Guadalajara and Compostela would probably be centered halfway between the two locations in the vicinity of Ixtlán del Río. The fifty to sixty *encomenderos* of this complex did not enjoy the same relationship with their tributaries as did their fellows in New Spain. Not only was the indigenous character and level of social development different, but by the time this complex was in a position to develop, the ravages of Nuño de Guzmán's conquest and Viceroy Mendoza's reconquest finished what plagues and other dislocations had begun.

36. The three complexes other than Mexico City-Puebla account for 30 percent of the *encomenderos*, and Mexico City-Puebla 56 percent. Those with no stated residence and those who were *vecinos* of Honduras, Chiapas, Guatemala, and Guadalajara account for just over 5 percent. The remaining 9 or so percent were *vecinos* of Veracruz (2.2 percent) and Coatzacoalcos (2.0 percent) or lived in settlements near or within their *encomiendas* (4.5 percent).

4. The Integration of the *Encomenderos* into Local Society

1. Citations for facts concerning *encomenderos* are given under individual biographies in Part Two.

2. *Actas de cabildo de la ciudad de México*, vol. IV, 111. The office *alcalde de mesta* (magistrate for common grazing land) was established in 1538 to regulate grazing on public land. Outgoing *alcaldes ordinarios* automatically became *alcaldes de mesta*.

3. See Francisco Fernández del Castillo, "Alonso de Estrada: su familia,"

Memorias de la academia mexicana de la historia 1 (1942): 402, and Norberto de Castro y Tosi, "Verdadera paternidad de Alonso de Estrada," 1011–1026. It appears that the claim of royal paternity was such that Estrada himself was the party calling attention to the relationship.

4. Ida Altman, "Conquest and Settlement: Spanish Society in Mexico City, 1525–1555," 2f. Altman qualifies comments in Herman Merivale's *Lectures on Colonization* on generations in colonization. The *pobladores antiguos* and many of the first conquerors had spent as many as twenty years in the Indies prior to embarking with Cortés. They were men of the Indies, long removed from events in Iberia. The conquerors for the most part were recent arrivals in the Indies, many fresh from Europe. They and the *pobladores* who arrived after the capture of Mexico City were not steeped in the traditions of the Indies and constituted a new wave, hence the designation "second generation." As Altman accurately points out, Merivale's position that the first generation was a failure is not totally justified. Those who remained in the Indies were truly the first generation that Merivale describes. The conquerors of Mexico and especially the *encomenderos* were in fact another first generation, but in a new colony. They were anything but failures.

5. José Miranda, *La función económica del encomendero en los orígenes del régimen colonial (Nueva España, 1525–1531)*. Miranda bases his argument that *encomenderos* began diversifying very early by analyzing the 9 August 1525–1 December 1528 notarial records of Juan Hernández del Castillo and *El libro de las tasaciones de pueblos de la Nueva España-Siglo XVI* (Mexico, 1952). Also see A. Millares Carlo and J. S. Mantecón, *Indice y extractos de los protocolos del Archivo de Notarías de México, D.F.*, vols. I and II. Grants and *estancias* and *caballerías* by *cabildo* of Mexico City within five leagues of an *encomienda*, whether to the *encomendero* or another individual, began as early as August 1532. The product of such grants included a type of livestock as well as wheat. These agricultural enterprises employed a small cadre of full-time workers, plus day laborers during planting, harvesting, and roundup evolutions.

5. Comparisons and Conclusions

1. Lockhart, *The Men of Cajamarca*, 107.
2. Díaz del Castillo, *Historia verdadera*, vol. 1, 8. There were too many underemployed gentlemen in a limited and unhealthy area. The group left the isthmus for Cuba with Governor Pedrarias' blessings.
3. See Lockhart, *Men of Cajamarca*, 393ff. Juan de Salinas, a blacksmith from Córdoba who grew up in Jerez de la Frontera (Cádiz), is identified as one of the very few who had spent time in Mexico before moving on to Panama and thence to Peru. His activities and precisely when he was in Mexico are not known with any degree of certainty. At any rate, Salinas was not an *encomendero* in New Spain, nor was he listed on any of the extant rosters for the conquest of Mexico City.
4. Ibid., 15.
5. Ibid., 141.
6. Ibid., 24.
7. Díaz del Castillo, *Historia verdadera*, vol. 1, 56 and 354. Díaz implies that those who accompanied Cortés invested in the *entrada* under the current Caribbean practice, while the Narváez force was financed by Governor Diego Velázquez. This perhaps explains the much larger *entrada* formed in 1520. Be-

sides, Mexico by then had a known rather than hoped-for economic potential. This potential is discussed by merchant Hernando de Castro in a letter dated 31 August 1520 to his senior partner, Alonso de Nebreda. Lockhart and Otte, *Letters and People of the Spanish Indies*, 27–38.

8. Lockhart, *Men of Cajamarca*, 47.

9. *Poblador* Alonso de Paz, a relative of Cortés, transferred his *encomienda* to his sister's daughter when she married *oidor* Diego de Loaisa ca. 1540. He then returned to Spain, married a widow there, and brought her children and their household back to Mexico City two years later. Conquerors Juan de Mansilla and Juan Pérez de la Gama and *poblador* Pedro Pantoja evidently stayed in Spain.

10. Lockhart, *Men of Cajamarca*, 114 and 201–206.

11. John F. Schwaller, "The Secular Clergy in Sixteenth Century Mexico" (doctoral dissertation, Indiana University, 1978), 4ff.; Boyd-Bowman, *Indice geobiográfico*, vol. 1, no. 2738, 96 and no. 4573, 151; Díaz del Castillo, *Historia verdadera*, vol. 2, 277.

12. Lockhart, *Men of Cajamarca*, 465 ff.

13. Schwaller, "Clergy," 4ff. Schwaller also states that Villagrán was granted a coat of arms, although documentation of the award could not be located by this writer.

14. Schwaller, 4; Boyd-Bowman, vol. 1, no. 4573, 117; Díaz del Castillo, vol. 1, 163. Juan Díaz was party to a conspiracy to return to Cuba prior to the destruction of the fleet and the march inland. All the co-conspirators, except Díaz, were convicted for their participation. Two were hanged, one had his feet cut off, and two received 200 lashes each.

15. Millares Carlo and Mantecón, *Protocolos*, vol. 1, 361ff., 10 November 1528.

16. The dependence on genealogical connections for developing these associations is a result of the dearth of notarial records for the period of this study.

17. Miranda, *La fundación económica del encomendero*. Also see Note 5, Chapter 4, above.

Appendix G

1. Ida Altman and James Lockhart, eds., *Provinces of Early Mexico: Variants of Spanish American Regional Evolution*.

2. Millares Carlo and Mantecón, *Protocolos*.

3. France V. Scholes and Eleanor B. Adams, *Relación de las encomiendas de indios hechos en Nueva España a los conquistadores y pobladores de ella—Año de 1564*; Francisco A. de Icaza, *Diccionario autobiográfico de conquistadores y pobladores de Nueva España*; Peter Gerhard, *A Guide to the Historical Geography of New Spain*, *The Southeast Frontier of New Spain*, and *The North Frontier of New Spain*; Manuel Orozco y Berra, *Los conquistadores de México*; Bernal Díaz del Castillo, *Historia verdadera de la conquista de la Nueva España*; Carl O. Sauer, *Colima of New Spain in the Sixteenth Century*; *Actas de cabildo de la ciudad de México*, vols. I–VI; Millares Carlo and José Mantecón, *Protocolos*; and Peter Boyd-Bowman, *Indice geobiográfico de cuarenta mil pobladores españoles de América en el siglo XVI*.

4. James Lockhart, *The Men of Cajamarca*.

5. A notary (*escribano*) was much more than a scribe. He was a person primarily expert in executing documents in correct legal format and as such formed

the backbone of Spanish governmental administration. Thirty-three persons have been identified as notaries in New Spain during the time frame of this study, with fifteen holding *encomiendas* for at least a while. Over twenty of them actively pursued the profession. The following lists were compiled from various sources. An asterisk denotes an *encomendero*. Practicing notaries were: Francisco de Orduña,* Pedro del Castillo, Juan Hernández del Castillo, Hernando Pérez, Hernándo López, Juan de Cuevas,* Martín de Salas, Antonio de Herrera, Jerónimo López,* Antonio de Turcios, Miguel López de Legaspi, Alonso Lucas,* Hernando Sierra, Diego Tristán, Antonio Trujillo, Diego de Isla, Pedro de Mujica, Bartolomé Román,* Hernán Gómez, Martín de Castro, Diego Ayala, Andrés de Cabrera, Gaspar Calderón, and Sancho López de Agurto. Other notaries were Martín de Calahorra,* Juan Larios,* Guillén de la Loa,* Alonzo de Paz,* Bachiller Alonso Pérez,* Gregorio de Saldaña,* Juan de Torquemada,* Alonso Velázquez,* Diego de Ocaña,* and Hernán Sánchez de Hortigosa.* Notaries of the Mexico City *cabildo* were Francisco de Orduña (to 22 May 1524), Pedro del Castillo (26 May 1525 to 31 December 1527), Alonzo Lucas (1 January 1528 to 31 December 1529), Pedro del Castillo (1 January to 28 January 1530), Miguel Lopéz de Legaspi (28 January 1530 to 31 December 1541), Hernando Sierra (1 January 1542 to 6 August 1543), and Diego Tristán (from 6 August 1543). Miguel Lopéz de Legaspi held the office Escribano Mayor del Cabildo from 1 January 1542.

6. Hernández arrived in the Indies ca. 1514 and served as a notary in Santo Domingo from his arrival there until moving to Mexico City in the early 1520s. See Boyd-Bowman, *Indice*, vol. I, no. 3469, 119.

7. Agustín Millares Carlo and José I. Mantecón, "El Archivo de Notarias del departamento del Distrito Federal," *Revista de Historia de América*, 17 (1944): 69–118. The condition of these protocols was bad in the 1940s when Millares Carlo and Mantecón were investigating the archives.

8. A similar ruse was reportedly effected by Ferdinand to acquire a full inventory of persons and property after the 1490 siege and capture of Málaga, as reported by William H. Prescott in his *History of the Reign of Ferdinand and Isabella, the Catholic*, II, 39ff. A similar invitation to disclose was made by the second Audiencia 23 January 1531. See *Actas de Cabildo*, II, 82. Responses to this invitation have not, to my knowledge, been systematically studied.

9. Scholes and Adams, *Relación*, 7ff.

10. See also Peter Boyd-Bowman, "Patterns of Spanish Emigration to the Indies Until 1600," 580–604. Boyd-Bowman reports that volumes III: 1540–1559, IV: 1560–1570, and V: 1580–1600 are typescripts ready for publication. Volume III would have been an asset for investigating the lives of the *encomenderos* who arrived in New Spain during the final fifteen years covered by this study.

11. Cristóbal Bermúdez Plata, ed., *Catálogo de pasajeros a Indias*.

Glossary

alcaide: warden; keeper of the local jail.
alcalde mayor: deputy governor; local magistrate and judge.
alcalde de mesta: magistrate for common grazing land.
alcalde ordinario: municipal magistrate and presiding officer of a municipal council.
alguacil: constable.
alguacil de campo: constable for agricultural property.
antigüedad: seniority.
Audiencia: high court and advisory body to a viceroy or governor; the territorial jurisdiction of such a body.
bachiller: holder of a university degree.
barrio: settlement subordinate to a pueblo, usually within or next to the main settlement; sometimes synonymous with estancia.
bubas: pustules, often associated with yaws or syphilis.
caballería: tract of rural land, normally used for the production of agricultural crops.
caballerizo mayor: master of the horse for an *entrada*, responsible for care, quartering, grazing and provisioning for horses.
caballero: gentleman.
cabecera: administrative center for a political jurisdiction.
cabildo: municipal council; governing body of a diocese.
cacique: Arawakian word brought from the Caribbean meaning hereditary indigenous ruler.
casa poblada: literally "peopled house." Ideally, a large estate headquarters, preferably managed by a Spanish wife, where a number of relatives, guests, and Spanish employees were maintained, catered to by a staff of black slaves and Indian servants.
ciudad: settlement with royally granted privileges. In New Spain such municipalities were authorized twelve councilmen and two magistrates.
cofradía: religious confraternity.
comisario general: a Franciscan having authority over a religious province.
contador: accountant. One of the four royal treasury officials.
continuo: royal body guard.
corregidor: local magistrate and administrator with jurisdiction over an Indian polity.
criado: servant, employee.
dependencia: a settlement subordinate to a *cabecera*.
doctrinero: priest, friar, or catechist, charged with providing Christian training to an indigenous community.

GLOSSARY

entrada: an expedition organized for trade, raid, exploration or conquest.
escribano: a notary. A person primarily expert in executing documents in correct legal format.
escribano de cámara: notary employed by the Audiencia.
escribano de minas: notary assigned to a mining region.
escudero: squire. Entry level of conquest nobility.
estancia: tract of rural land, normally used for grazing animals; settlement subordinate to a *pueblo*, usually some distance from the main settlement.
factor: business agent or representative. One of the four royal treasury officials.
hidalgo: an untitled noble.
huerta: small tract of agricultural land near a Spanish settlement used for garden, orchard, or vineyard purposes.
juez repartidor: royal official charged with assigning tribute labor under the *repartimiento* of the New Laws.
justicia: judge, magistrate; authority to assign magistrates; royal officer with responsibility of supervising judicial matters.
letrado: titled, university trained lawyer.
maestre: master, master artisan, nondegreed medical practitioner.
maestre de campo: senior *entrada* official charged with logistics, camp orderliness, billeting.
maestre de obras: municipal official charged with supervising public works.
mayordomo: manager, chief steward.
odrero: wineskin maker.
oidor: Audiencia judge.
parda, o: mulatta, o.
poblador: settler.
poblador antiguo: first settler.
poblezuela: small settlement.
portero: doorman.
pregonero: town crier.
procurador: untitled lawyer, member of the legal community who performed most of the actual court representation.
protomédico: official authorized to inspect and license medical practitioners.
pueblo: settlement; lowest level of municipal administration.
regidor: municipal councilman.
relator: narrator, reporter.
repartimiento: division, share; allotment of crown-administered tribute labor under the New Laws of 1542.
repostero: butler, valet.
residencia: official investigation of performance while in office conducted by one's replacement.
solar: urban tract of land, building lot.
sujeto: community subject to a *cabecera*.
teniente: lieutenant.
tesorero: treasurer. One of the four royal treasury officials.
tratante: petty merchant, often dealing primarily in trade with Indians.
veedor: inspector. One of the four royal treasury officials.
villa: town; royally chartered municipality with lesser privileges than a ciudad.
visita: settlement on the circuit of a priest or friar.
visitador: investigator.

Bibliography

Actas de cabildo de la ciudad de México. 54 vols. Mexico City, 1880–1916.
Aiton, Arthur S. *Antonio de Mendoza, First Viceroy of New Spain.* Durham: Duke University Press, 1927.
Altman, Ida. "Conquest and Settlement: Spanish Society in Mexico City 1525–1555." Paper prepared for Seminar in Atlantic History and Culture, Johns Hopkins University, 1977.
Altman, Ida, and James Lockhart, eds. *Provinces of Early Mexico: Variants of Spanish American Regional Evolution.* Los Angeles: UCLA Latin American Center Publications, 1976.
Bakewell, Peter J. *Silver Mining and Society in Colonial Mexico: Zacatecas, 1546–1700.* London: Cambridge University Press, 1971.
Benítez, Fernando. *The Century After Cortés.* Translated by Joan MacLean. Chicago: University of Chicago Press, 1965.
Bermúdez Plata, Cristóbal. *Catálogo de pasajeros a Indias.* 3 vols. Seville: Editorial de la Gavidia, 1942.
Borah, Woodrow and Sherburne F. Cook. *The Aboriginal Population of Central Mexico on the Eve of the Spanish Conquest.* Ibero-Americana, no. 45. Berkeley and Los Angeles: University of California Press, 1963.
———. *The Population of Central Mexico in 1548: An Analysis of the "Suma de visitas de pueblos."* Ibero-Americana, no. 43. Berkeley and Los Angeles: University of California Press, 1960.
Boyd-Bowman, Peter. *Indice geobiográfico de cuarenta mil pobladores españoles de América en el siglo XVI.* 2 vols. Bogota: Instituto Caro y Cuervo, 1964, and Mexico City: Editorial Jus, 1968.
———. "Patterns of Spanish Emigration to the Indies Until 1600." *Hispanic American Historical Review* 56 (1976): 580–604.
Cabeza de Vaca, Alvar Núñez. *Adventures in the Unknown Interior of America.* Translated and edited by Cyclone Covey. Crowell-Collier Publishing Co., 1961. Reprinted Albuquerque: University of New Mexico Press, 1983. 3rd printing 1986.
Castro y Tosi, Norberto. "Verdadera paternidad de Alonso de Estrada." *Revista de Indias* 8 (1948): 1011–1026.
Cerwin, Herbert. *Bernal Díaz: Historian of the Conquest.* Norman: University of Oklahoma Press, 1963.
Chamberlain, Robert S. "Castilian Backgrounds of the Repartimiento-Encomienda." In *Contributions to American Anthropology and History.* Vol. V,

no. 25. Washington, D.C.: Carnegie Institution of Washington, 1939; reprint ed., New York: Johnson Reprint Corporation, 1970.
Chipman, Donald E. *Nuño de Guzmán and the Province of Pánuco in New Spain, 1518–1533.* Glendale, Calif.: Arthur A. Clark Co., 1967.
Colección de documentos inéditos para la historia de España. Edited by Martín Fernández Navarrete et al. 112 vols. Madrid, 1842–1895.
Colección de documentos inéditos para la historia de Ibero-América. 14 vols. Madrid, 1927–1932.
Colección de documentos inéditos relativos al descubrimiento, conquista y organización de las antiguas posesiones españolas de América y Oceanía. Series 1. 42 vols. Madrid, 1864–1884.
Colección de documentos inéditos relativos al descubrimiento, conquista y organización de las antiguas posesiones españolas de ultramar. Series 2. 25 vols. Madrid, 1885–1932.
Conway, G. R. C. "Hernando Alonso, a Jewish Conquistador with Cortés in Mexico." *Publication of the American Jewish Historical Society,* no. 31.
Cook, Sherburne F., and Woodrow Borah. *Essays in Population History, Mexico and California.* Berkeley and Los Angeles: University of California Press, 1979.
———. *Essays in Population History, Mexico and the Caribbean.* 2 vols. Berkeley and Los Angeles: University of California Press, 1971 and 1974.
Cortés, Hernando. *Cartas y Documentos.* Introduction by Mario Hernández Sánchez-Barba. Mexico City: Editorial Porrúa, 1963.
Díaz del Castillo, Bernal. *Historia verdadera de la conquista de la Nueva España.* Introduction and transcription by Genaro García. Mexico City, 1904.
Dorantes de Carranza, Baltasar. *Sumaria relación de las cosas de la Nueva España con noticia individual de los descendientes legítimos de los conquistadores y primeros pobladores españoles.* Mexico City, 1902.
[El] libro de las tasaciones de pueblos de la Nueva España-Siglo XVI. Prólogo de Francisco Gonzáles de Cossío. Mexico City, 1952.
Epistolario de Nueva España, 1505–1818. Recopilado por Francisco del Paso y Troncoso. 2nd Series. 16 vols. Mexico City, 1939–1942.
Fernández del Castillo, Francisco. "Alonso de Estrada, su familia." *Memorias de la academia mexicana de la historia* 1 (1942): 398–431.
———. *Tres conquistadores y pobladores de la Nueva España.* Mexico City: Talleres Gráficos de la Nación, 1927.
Foster, George M. *Culture and Conquest: America's Spanish Heritage.* Chicago: Quadrangle Books, 1960.
Gardiner, C. Harvey. *The Constant Captain: Gonzalo de Sandoval.* Carbondale, Ill.: Southern Illinois University Press, 1961.
———. *Martín López, Conquistador Citizen of Mexico.* Lexington: University of Kentucky Press, 1957.
Gerhard, Peter. *A Guide to the Historical Geography of New Spain.* Cambridge and New York: Cambridge University Press, 1972.
———. *The North Frontier of New Spain.* Princeton: Princeton University Press, 1982.
———. *The Southeast Frontier of New Spain.* Princeton: Princeton University Press, 1979.
Gibson, Charles. *The Aztecs Under Spanish Rule.* Stanford: Stanford University Press, 1964.

———. *Spain in America*. New York: Harper and Row, 1967.
Góngora, Mario. *Los grupos de conquistadores en Tierra Firme (1509–1530)*. Santiago de Chile: University of Chile, 1962.
Greenleaf, Richard E. *Zumárraga and the Mexican Inquisition, 1536–1543*. Washington, D.C.: Academy of American Franciscan History, 1961.
Gurria la Croix, Jorge, ed. *Relación de méritos y servicios del conquistador Bernaldino Vázquez de Tapia*. Mexico City: Antigua Librería Robredo, 1953.
Henige, David P. *Colonial Governors from the Fifteenth Century to the Present*. Madison: University of Wisconsin Press, 1970.
Hirschberg, Julia. "Social Experiment in New Spain: A Prosopographical Study of the Early Settlement at Puebla de Los Angeles, 1531–1534." *Hispanic American Historical Review* 59 (1979): 1–33.
Hunt, Marta Espejo-Ponce. "Colonial Yucatan: Town and Region in the 17th Century." Doctoral dissertation. Department of History, University of California, Los Angeles, 1974.
Icaza, Francisco A. de. *Diccionario autobiográfico de conquistadores y pobladores de Nueva España*. Madrid: El Adelantado de Segovia, 1923.
Kubler, George. *Mexican Architecture of the Sixteenth Century*. 2 vols. New Haven: Yale University Press, 1948.
Liss, Peggy K. *Mexico Under Spain, 1521–1556: Society and the Origin of Nationality*. Chicago: University of Chicago Press, 1975.
Lockhart, James. "Encomienda and Hacienda: The Evolution of the Great Estate in the Spanish Indies." *Hispanic American Historical Review* 49 (1969): 411–429.
———. "Españoles entre indios: Toluca a fines del siglo XVI." In *Estudios sobre la ciudad iberoamericana*, 435–491. Edited by Francisco de Solano. Madrid: Consejo Superior de Investigaciones, Instituto Gonzalo Fernández de Oviedo, 1975.
———. *The Men of Cajamarca: A Social and Biographical Study of the First Conquerors of Peru*. Austin: University of Texas Press, 1972.
———. *Spanish Peru, 1532–1560*. Madison: University of Wisconsin Press, 1968.
Lockhart, James and Enrique Otte, eds. *Letters and People of the Spanish Indies, Sixteenth Century*. Cambridge: Cambridge University Press, 1976.
Lockhart, James and Stuart B. Schwartz. *Early Latin America: A History of Colonial Spanish America and Brazil*. Cambridge and New York: Cambridge University Press, 1983.
López de Gómara, Francisco. *Historia general de las Indias y la vida de Hernán Cortés*. Prólogo y cronología por Jorge Gurria Lacroix. Caracas: Biblioteca Ayacucho, 1979.
Martínez Cosío, Leopoldo. *Los caballeros de las órdenes militares en México. Catálogo biográfico y genealógico*. Mexico City, 1946.
Merivale, Herman. *Lectures on Colonization and Colonies*. London: Longman, Green, Longman and Roberts, 1861; reprint ed., New York: August M. Kelly, Publishers, 1966.
Mexico, 1981 ed. Falls Church, Va.: American Automobile Association, 1981.
Millares Carlo, Agustín and José I. Mantecón. "El Archivo de Notarías del departamento del Distrito Federal." *Revista de Historia de América* 17 (1944): 69–118.
———. *Indice y extractos de los protocolos del Archivo de Notarías de México, D.F.* 2 vols. Mexico City: El Colegio de México, 1945–1946.
Miranda, José. *La función económica del encomendero en los orígenes del régi-*

men colonial (Nueva España, 1525–1531). Mexico City: Universidad Nacional Autonoma de México, 1965.
Muro Orejón, Antonio, ed. *Las leyes nuevas de 1542–1543*, 2nd ed. Seville: Escuela de Estudios Hispano-Americanos, 1961.
National Geographic Atlas of the World, 4th ed. Washington, D.C.: National Geographic Society, 1975.
Nobiliario de conquistadores de Indias. Madrid: La Sociedad de Bibliófilos Españoles, 1892.
O'Gorman, Edmundo. "Catálogo de pobladores de Nueva España." *Boletín del Archivo General de la Nación*, XIII, No. 2 to XV, No. 1 (April 1941–January 1944).
Orozco y Berra, Manuel. *Los conquistadores de México*. Mexico City: Editorial Pedro Robredo, 1938.
Otte, Enrique. "Mercaderes burgaleses en los inicios del comercio con México." *Historia Mexicana* 18 (1969): 108–144, 258–285.
———. "Nueve cartas de Diego de Ordaz." *Historia Mexicana* 14 (1964): 102–130, 320–338.
Pagden, A. R., tr. and ed. *Hernán Cortés: Letters from Mexico*. New York: Grossman Publishers, 1971.
Paz y Melia, A. *Nobiliario de conquistadores de Indias*. Madrid: M. Tello, 1892.
Pike, Ruth. *Enterprise and Adventure: The Genoese in Seville and the Opening of the New World*. Ithaca, N. Y.: Cornell University Press, 1966.
Prescott, William Hickling. *History of the Reign of Ferdinand and Isabella, the Catholic*. 3 vols. Edited by John Foster Kirk. Philadelphia: J. B. Lippincott Company, 1902.
Razo Zaragoza y Cortés, Jose Luis. *Guadalajara*. Guadalajara: University of Guadalajara, 1975.
Recinos, Adrián. *Pedro de Alvarado: Conquistador de México y Guatemala*. Mexico City: Fondo de Cultura Económica, 1959.
Relación breve y sumaria de la visita hecha por el Lic. Lorenzo Lebrón de Quiñones, oidor del nuevo reino de Galicia, por mando de su alteza. Guadalajara, 1951.
"Relación particular y descripción de toda la Provincia del Santo Evangelio que es de la Orden de Sant Francisco en la Nueba España (el visitador Lic. Juan de Ovando)." In *Nueva colección de documentos, Vol II*.
Ricard, Robert. *The Spiritual Conquest of Mexico: An Essay on the Apostolate and the Evangelizing Methods of the Mendicant Orders in New Spain: 1523–1572*. Translated by Lesley Byrd Simpson. Berkeley and Los Angeles: University of California Press, 1966.
Riley, G. Micheal. *Fernando Cortés and the Marquesado in Morelos, 1522–1547*. Albuquerque: University of New Mexico Press, 1973.
Sauer, Carl O. *Colima of New Spain in the Sixteenth Century*. Berkeley and Los Angeles: University of California Press, 1948.
Scholes, France V. and Eleanor B. Adams. *Cartas del licenciado Jerónimo Valderrama y otros documentos sobre su visita al gobierno de Nueva España—1563–1565*. Mexico City: José Porrúa e Hijos, Sucesores, 1961.
———. *Información sobre los tributos que los indios pagaban a Moctezuma—Año de 1554*. Mexico City: José Porrúa e Hijos, Sucesores, 1957.
———. *Relación de las encomiendas de indios hechas en Nueva España a los conquistadores y pobladores de ella—Año de 1564*. Mexico City: José Porrúa e Hijos, Sucesores, 1955.

Scholes, Walter V. *The Diego Ramírez Visita*. Columbia: University of Missouri, 1946.
Schwaller, John F. "The Secular Clergy in Sixteenth Century Mexico." Doctoral dissertation. Department of History, Indiana University, 1978.
Simpson, Lesley Byrd. *The Encomienda in New Spain: The Beginning of Spanish Mexico*. 3rd ed. Berkeley and Los Angeles: University of California Press, 1966.
—————. *Exploitation of Land in Central Mexico in the Sixteenth Century*. Ibero-Americana: 36. Berkeley and Los Angeles: University of California Press, 1952.
Vázquez de Espinosa, Antonio. *Compendium and Description of the West Indies*. Translated by C. U. Clark. Washington, D.C.: Smithsonian Miscellaneous Collections, 108, 1948.
Villar Villamil, Ignacio de. *Cedulario heráldico de conquistadores de Nueva España*. Mexico City: Talleres Gráficos del Museo Nacional de Arqueología, Historia y Etnología, 1933.
Winship, George Parker. "The Coronado Expedition, 1540–1542." In *Fourteenth Annual Report of the Bureau of American Ethnology, 1892–1893*. Washington, D.C.: United States Government Printing Office, 1896.
World Aeronautical Chart CJ-24, 4th ed. of 27 December 1979. Washington, D.C.: U.S. Department of Commerce, National Oceanic and Atmospheric Administration National Ocean Survey.
World Aeronautical Chart CJ-25, 3rd ed. of 30 November 1977. Washington, D.C.: U.S. Department of Commerce, National Oceanic and Atmospheric Administration National Ocean Survey.
Zavala, Silvio. *La encomienda indiana*. Madrid, 1935.

Index

Acalhuacan, 196
Acámbaro, 215, 222
Acamistlaguaca, 214
Acapulco, 49, 120, 124, 125, 127, 197
Acasuchitlan, 251
Acatlan, 129, 206, 207
Acayuca, 156, 189
Acedo, Juan, 78, 113
Acevedo, Juana de, 140
Achachalintla, 218
Achiutla, 186, 187
Acolman, 204, 245
Acosta, Ana de, 219
Actas de Cabildo, 71
Actopan, 117, 166
Acuitlapan, 140
Aculcingo, 197
Acuña, doña Leonor de, 151, 251
Acuñada, Cristóbal de, 134
Aguacatitlan, 159
Aguacatlan, 142, 149, 257
Agualulco, 159
Aguatlan, 182
Agüero, Ana de, 199
Aguila, Francisco del, 113
Aguila, Juan del, 199
Aguilar, Baltasar de, 67
Aguilar, Francisco de, 114
Aguilar, Gabriel de, 225
Aguilar, García de, 48, 83, 114, 249
Aguilar, Gonzalo de, 188
Aguilar, Isabel de, 118, 216
Aguilar, Jerónimo de (interpreter), 114–115, 145
Aguilar, Juan de, 115, 197
Aguilar, Marcos de (Licenciado), 114
Aguilar, Nicolás de, 231

Aguilar y Córdoba, Alonso de, 64, 67, 113–114, 141, 194
Aguilera, Gabriel de, 115, 165, 177
Ahualulco, 255
Airalde, Tomás de, 241
Alaejos, Juan de, 228
Alanés, Melchor de, 115, 226
Alanés Avendaño, Francisco de, 115
Alavés, Diego de, 180
Alavés, Melchor de, 180
Alberrucia, Martín de, 255
Albornoz, Bernardino de, 70, 116, 127, 137, 257
Albornoz, doña Catalina de, 116, 127
Albornoz, Dr. Frías de, 254
Albornoz, García de, 226
Albornoz, Juan de, 115–116, 118, 239
Albornoz, Rodrigo de, 13, 75, 116, 127, 140, 225, 232, 239
Alcalde, Juan, 172
Alcántara, 22
Alcántara, Bartolomé de, 116
Alcocer, doña Beatriz de, 138
Alcozahui, 180
Aldaz Navarro, Juan de, 162, 260
Alemán (Henche), Juan, 218
Alemán (Licenciado), 64, 141, 157, 194
Alima, 176
Almagrists, 98
Almagro, Diego de, 98
Almesto, Juan de, 116–117, 237
Almíndez Chirinos, Pero, 98, 103, 116, 117, 154, 239
Almodóvar, Diego de, 118
Almodóvar del Campo, Antonio de, 161
Almoguer, Antonio de, 252
Almolonga, 188, 197, 225

Alonso, Hernando, 117–118, 127, 130, 166, 205, 216, 230, 259
Alonso, Martín, 205
Alonso, Rodrigo, 118, 164, 197
Alonso de Estrada, Juan, 68
Alonso de Sosa, Juan, 68, 69, 139, 223, 245
Alonso de Vargas, Juan, 255
Alpizagua, 200, 236
Altamirano, Juan, 118
Altamirano, Juan Gutiérrez (Licenciado), 118
Altamirano, doña Juana, 118
Altamirano y Velasco, don Fernando, 118
Alvarado, Alonso de, 163
Alvarado, Gómez de, 181
Alvarado, Gonzalo de, 118–119
Alvarado, doña Isabel de, 181
Alvarado, Jorge de, 24, 68, 69, 119, 123, 154, 239, 240
Alvarado, Juan de, 50, 120
Alvarado, doña Leonor, 166
Alvarado, Pedro de, 24, 87, 120, 144, 173, 215
Alvarez, Catalina, 183
Alvarez, don Francisco (Bishop of Toro), 256
Alvarez, Isabel, 188
Alvarez, Mari, 148
Alvarez Chico, Rodrigo, 144
Alvarez de Gibraleón, Inés, 223
Alvarez de Herrera, Beatriz, 198
Alvarez de Mendoza, Elvira, 183
Alvarez de Pineda, Alonso, 45
Amacueca, 122, 232
Amaltepec, 130
Amatepec, 235
Amatlan, 158, 200, 255, 257
Amaxaque, 257
Andaama, 150
Andalusia, 21, 47, 49, 65, 100
Andrada, doña Ana de, 161
Andrada, doña Beatriz de, 65, 141, 178
Andrada, Leonor de, 64, 141
Andrade (Gallego) Moctezuma, don Juan de, 196
Anguiano, Antón (Hontañon), 231
Angulo, Antón (Hontañon de), 76, 173
Antequera, 40, 46, 47, 115, 119, 121–123, 128, 135
Antequera-Villa Alta, 52
Antigüedad, 31, 89, 95

Apatla, 224
Apazco, 173, 222
Apozotl, 150
Aqueduct, 248
Aquixtlan, 117
Aragón, 130
Aragón, Juan de, 120
Aragón, Pedro de, 120
Aranda, Martín de, 164
Araro, 222
Arcos de la Frontera, 126
Arellano, don Alonso de, 204
Arellano, doña Ana de, 147
Arellano, don Carlos de, 147
Arellano, Felipe de, 114, 147
Arellano, Ramiro, 204
Arellano, Tristán de, 125, 259
Arévalo, Alonso de, 77, 121, 162, 218
Arévalo, Elvira de, 77, 162, 218
Arévalo, Melchor de, 49, 121
Arías, Miguel, 160
Arimao-Pinzándaro, 164, 178, 180, 231
Ario, 223
Arlite, Francisco, 182
Arriaga, Antón(io) de, 121, 205, 305
Arriaga, Juan de, 49, 121–122, 238, 248
Arriaga, Miguel, 228
Arteaga Pecheco, Francisco de, 215
Artisans, 94, 101
Asencio, Pedro, 127
Astatla, 128
Astorga, 122
Astorga, Bartolomé de, 122, 263
Asuchitlan, 190
Atahuallpa, 86, 97
Atengo, 219
Atengoychan, 257
Atezac, 188
Atezcac, 225
Aticpac, 228
Atistac, 150
Atitalaquia, 140, 244
Atlacomulco, 264
Atlan, 175, 201
Atlapulco, 65, 141
Atlatlauca, 159, 179, 186–188
Atlatlauca-Totolapa-Tlaycapa, 116
Atlehuecian, 141
Atliacapan, 217, 253
Atotonilco, 212, 213
Atoyac, 232

Atoyac-Yutacanu, 186, 187
Atoyaque, 122
Atoyaquillo, 167
Atucpa, 166
Audelo, Alonso de, 193
Autlan, 230
Aux, doña Luisa de, 152
Avalos, Gonzalo de, 179
Avalos Saavedra, Alonso de, 69, 83, 122, 154, 207, 232
Avalos Saavedra, Juan de, 122, 202, 232
Avila, 49, 79, 113, 124
Avila (y Benavides), Alonso de, 58, 118, 120, 122–123, 125, 128, 143, 153, 158, 165, 239, 263
Avila, Antonia de, 58
Avila, Francisco de, 123, 163, 240, 249
Avila, Gaspar de, 79
Avila (Davila), Gaspar de, 238
Avila, Gonzalo de, 124
Avila, Juan de, 124, 148, 258
Avila, Luis de, 124–125
Avila, doña María de, 123
Avila, Pedrarias de, 87
Avila Alvarado, Alonso de, 166
Avila Quiñones, Gaspar de, 124, 176, 219
Avila Quiñones, Pedro de, 124
Axacuba, 30, 183, 258
Axapoteca, 152
Axapusco, 241
Ayacastepec, 127
Ayacastla, 179
Ayocinapa, 164
Ayuquila, 233, 238
Ayuquila-Zacapal, 149
Ayusuchiquilzala, 114, 249
Ayutla, 186, 187, 202
Azcapotzalco, 198
Azicatipan, 255
Aznar, Antonio, 125, 253
Azpeitia, 125
Azpeitia, Juan, 163
Azpeitia, Juanés, 125
Azua, 145
Azuntepec, 156

Badajoz, 22, 65, 68, 77, 79, 83, 117–120, 178
Badajoz, Gutierre de, 125, 167
Baena, 142
Baeza, Rodrigo de, 125–126

Baeza de Herrera, don Jerónimo, 193
Baeza de Herrera, Juan (Comendador), 153
Baja California, 117, 132
Ballesteros, Francisco de, 175
Balsas River, 44, 49
Bandevena, Martín de, 140
Barrera, Cristóbal, 126
Barrios, Andrés de, 126, 138, 152, 186, 195, 221, 246
Barrios, doña Isabel de, 126
Barrón, Francisco, 126–127
Basque country, 26
Basques, 47, 94
Bautista de Sandoval, doña Jerónima, 240
Bautista Oliver, Juan, 206
Bazán, Alonso de, 260
Bazán, don Andrés, 260
Bazán, Pedro de, 116, 117, 127, 259
Beas, 117
Becerra, Juan, 127
Becerra, Teresa, 151
Becerra de Mendoza, Diego, 24, 127, 167, 175, 197
Bejerano, Serván, 127–128, 133, 199, 239, 265
Bello, Juan, 128
Beltrán de Guzmán, Nuño, 13, 46, 50, 59, 67, 109, 132, 135, 170
Bembibre, 116
Benalcázar, 127
Benavente, Adrián de, 215
Benavides, Alonso de, 128
Benavides, Antonia de, 128
Benavides, García de, 129
Benavides, Juan de, 129
Benavides, Nuño de, 128–129
Benítez, Diego, 134
Berlanga, 121
Bermúdez de Meneses, Pedro, 195
Bermúdez Velasco, Beatriz, 207
Bernal, Francisco, 129
Bernal, Juan, 129
Berrio, Luis de, 47, 129, 205, 239
Bezos, Juan, 129, 158
Bezos, Rodrigo, 158, 250
Bishops, 29
Blacksmith, 39, 117
Blázquez, Juan, 220, 249
Bobadilla, doña Leonor, 132
Bocanegra, Bernardino de, 166
Bolaños, Diego de, 165

Bolaños, Isabel de, 166
Bonal, Francisco de, 130
Bonilla, Juan de, 130
Bosque, Gabriel, 130
Bracamonte, Alvaro de, 181, 257
Branbila, Juan Antonio, 121
Bravo, Antón (swordsmith), 130
Bravo, Antonio, 254
Bravo de la Laguna, Antonio, 130
Bujalance, 131
Burgillos, 113
Burgos, 39, 79, 83, 84, 125, 126
Burgos, Gaspar de, 207
Burgos, Juan de, 70, 131, 196, 222, 257
Burgueño, Fernando, 131, 207
Burgueño, Hernando, 137
Burgueño, Pedro, 137
Buriezo, Juan, 131, 170
Bustamante, Doctor Ambrosio de, 254
Bustamante, Doctor (Maestre) Blas de, 132, 148, 172
Bustamante, doña María de, 132
Bustamante, Rodrigo de, 132
Busto, Juan de, 132, 172, 224
Busto, Pedro de, 132

Caballería, 114
Cabezón, Cristóbal, 133
Cabezón, Francisco, 190
Cabildo, 4, 35
Cabra, Juan de, 133
Cabrera, Andrés, 300
Cabrera, Hernando, 217
Cabrera, doña Inés de, 134, 250
Cabrera, Juan de, 175
Cacalotepec, 195, 211
Cacaluta, 257
Cacaopisca, 237
Cáceres, 22, 47, 125, 134, 152
Cáceres, Gonzalo de, 133
Cáceres, Manuel de, 115, 133, 231
Cadena, Antonio de la, 246
Cadena, Baltasar de la, 246
Cadena, doña Catalina de la, 234
Cádiz, 79, 117
Cahuatecpec, 211
Caicedo, Antón, 133-134
Cajamarca, 86, 94, 96
Calahorra, 134
Calahorra, Martín de, 134, 174, 176, 216
Calderón, Francisca, 128

Calderón, Gaspar, 300
Calderón, Pedro, 248
California. *See* Baja California
Calimaya, 118, 143
Calimaya-Metepec-Tepemaxalco, 123
Calpan, 149, 208
Calpulalpa, 203
Calvijo, Juana, 201
Calvo, Alonso, 207
Calvo, Francisco, 173, 201
Camargo, 128
Campo, Aguilar del, 115
Campos, María de, 235, 236
Canaries (Islands), 131
Canelas de Sultepec, 67
Cano, Alonso, 29, 134
Cano, Juan, 134-135, 195, 196
Cano, don Pedro, 196
Cantillana, Hernando, 135, 178, 203, 218
Capula, 129, 204, 205
Caquistle, 255
Caravallar, Juan de, 188
Caravallar, doña María de, 188
Carbajal, Juan de, 245
Cárdenas, Ginés de, 135, 213
Cardenas, Isabel de, 244
Cárdenas, Luis de, 135
Caribbean, 101
Caribbean basin, 10
Carmona, Antón de, 142, 205
Carpetia, Juan de, 125
Carranza, Pedro de, 135-136
Carrasco, Gonzalo, 159
Carrascosa, Juan de, 136
Carrillo, Alonso, 136, 182
Carrillo, Gaspar, 126
Carrillo, Jorge, 136-137
Carrillo de Peralta, doña Ana, 183
Carrión, Isabel, 152
Carvajal, Antonio de, 70, 75, 131, 137, 257
Carvajal, Fernando de, 181
Carvajal, doña Inés de, 260
Carvajal, Isabel de, 235
Casa poblada, 35, 308
Casas, Francisco de las, 24, 137
Casasola, Bernardino (Moreno) de, 200
Casco, Francisco, 137, 221
Castañeda, Diego de, 138, 183
Castañeda, Gonzalo de, 180
Castañeda, Juan de, 259
Castañeda, Rodrigo de, 138

Castañón, Melchor, 202
Castellanos, Alonso de, 138
Castellanos, Ana de, 185
Castellar, Pedro, 138
Castilblanco, 172, 198, 256
Castilla, don Luis de, 29, 69, 139, 147
Castilla, don Pedro de, 139
Castillo, Alonso del, 175, 252
Castillo, Bernardino del, 139, 208
Castillo, Catalina del, 183
Castillo de Villa Vega, 114
Castillo Maldonado, Alonso del, 139
Castrejón, Francisco de, 231
Castro, Ana de, 249
Castro, Juana de, 76, 187
Castro, Martín de (notary), 58, 300
Castro, Vaca de (Governor), 98
Catalán, Juan, 139–140, 225, 244
Cecamachantla, 136, 182, 244
Cempoala, 116, 216, 219, 232, 237, 240
Censotepec, 266
Centecomaltepec, 181
Centurión, Gaspar, 240
Cepeda, Francisco de, 216
Cerezo, Gonzalo, 140
Cermeño, Juan, 140
Cerón Saavedra, Jorge, 140–141, 159, 232
Cervantes, doña Ana, 65, 141, 262
Cervantes (de Lara), doña Catalina, 50, 64, 141, 264
Cervantes, Juan (Alonso) de, 65, 141
Cervantes, Leonel de (Comendador), 50, 63–65, 67, 71, 74, 113, 141, 157, 177, 178, 262
Cervantes, doña María de, 64, 177
Cervantes, Miguel de (Comendador), 104
Cervantes, Teresa, 241
Cervantes Casaus, Juan de, 64, 65, 141, 176
Charles V, 116
Cíbola, 149, 257
Cicaltlan, 255
Cicapuzalco, 188
Cicoac, 143, 194, 219
Cifontes, Francisco, 142
Cigua, 255
Ciguatlan, 242
Cimatlan, 169, 195, 211, 236
Cinacantepec, 236
Cinagua, 217
Cinapecuaro, 222

Cindos de Portillo, Pedro, 142, 234
Cintla, 200, 207
Cipotecas, 117, 134
Cisneros, Cristóbal de, 118, 123, 142
Cisneros, Diego de, 152
Cisneros, Juan de (bigotes), 142, 193
Citlaltomagua, 161
Ciudad Michoacán, 48–50, 120, 121
Ciudad Oaxaca, 46, 122
Ciudad Real, 58, 68, 70, 83, 133, 155
Ciudad Rodrigo, 125, 128
Clavijo, Juana, 193
Clergyman-conquerors, 96
Coacingo, 204, 218
Coatepec, 69, 245, 265
Coatitlan, 196
Coatlan, 140, 197, 212
Coatlan-Miaguatlan, 127
Coatzacoalcos, 43, 127, 138, 150, 154, 159
Coatzacoalcos River, 44
Cocula, 140
Colima, 44, 46, 49, 51, 77, 84, 100, 115, 117, 118, 121, 123, 125, 131, 133, 136, 142, 144, 149, 162
Colio, Diego de, 129, 143, 215
Colometo, 171
Colón, don Diego, 70, 145
Colonization, 313
Colotepec, 212
Columbus, Christopher, 148
Comala, 136, 182, 244
Comanja, 177, 244
Combat communicators, 30
Comunero Revolt, 116
Conde del Valle de Orizaba, 255
Coniltepec, 130
Conquerors, 6, 100
Conquistadores de México, 6
Conquistadores de Nueva España, 6
Contla, 217
Contreras, Alonso de, 83, 143, 254, 266
Contreras, García de, 143
Contreras, Inés de, 77, 220, 221
Contreras, Melchor de, 221
Copalitas, 181
Copula, 231
Córdoba, 43, 68, 130, 131
Córdoba, Luis de, 134
Coria, 22
Coria, Diego de, 78, 143, 220
Corneja, Inés, 127

Coronado (Rodríguez), Alonso, 224
Coronado, Gonzalo, 224
Coronado, María, 190
Coronel, Juan, 143–144
Corral, María, 169
Correas, Diego, 144
Corso, Francisco, 144
Corso, Vicencio, 144
Cortés, Diego ,50, 144
Cortés, Francisco, 120, 143, 144–145
Cortés, Hernando, 4, 10, 24, 26, 39, 44, 67, 70, 83, 89, 98, 101, 109, 145–147, 235, 246
Cortés, Martín, 148
Cortés Moctezuma, doña Leonor, 196
Cortés y Hermosilla, don Luis, 147
Cosoliacac, 159
Cotastan, 237
Council of the Indies, 61
Count of Gomera, 132
Count of Luna de León, 147
Count of Medellín, 132
Count of Santiago de Calimaya, 118
Coyuca, 181, 194, 195, 229, 231
Coyutla, 228, 244
Cozautepec, 226
Cozumel, 114
Cuacuacintla, 160
Cuacuilco, 252
Cuacuyulican, 124
Cuadra, Juana de la, 244
Cuaguacasco, 136
Cuapanoaya, 196
Cuatecomatlan, 115
Cuauhtemoc, 195
Cuautecomatlan, 133
Cuba, 31, 121, 125, 143, 197
Cuellar, Juan de, 148
Cuéllar Verdugo, Juan de, 78, 124, 132, 148
Cuenca, Benito de, 148–149
Cuenca, Juan de, 131, 218
Cuernavaca, 128, 131, 263
Cuestlahuaca, 246
Cuetlahuistla, 222
Cueva, Felipe de la, 132
Cueva, doña Francisca de la, 157, 181
Cueva, Luis de la, 149
Cuevas, Juan de, 123, 149, 248
Cueyatlan, 197
Cuezala, 224

Cuicatlan, 178, 249
Cuicuila, 186
Cuilapa, 265
Cuilutla, 181
Cuimantlan, 193, 209
Cuiquila, 253
Cuisco, 71, 182
Cuiseo, 184, 229
Cuistla, 197
Cuistlan, 212
Cuitlahuac, 149
Culhuacan, 207
Culiacan, 171
Cuyacán, 223
Cuyatepexi, 248
Cuyutlan, 171
Cuzama, 200
Cuzamala, 131, 222, 223, 257
Cuzcatlan, 169
Cuzco, 87, 96
Cuzpatlan, 176

Chacalapa, 189
Chachapala, 132
Chachavala, 163
Chachuapa, 128, 129
Chalcatongo, 186
Chalchiguautla, 243
Chalchitlan, 243
Chalco, 171
Chamorro, Nicolás, 133
Chapula, 131, 170
Chapulguacan, 195
Charo, 116, 140
Chavarrín, Antón, 149
Chavarrín, Bartolomé, 149
Chaves, Diego de, 149, 233, 238
Chaves, Francisco de, 134
Chaves, Gabriel de, 125
Chaves, Hernando de, 78, 143, 204
Chaves, doña María de, 204
Chaves, Melchor de, 151
Chaves, Miguel de (Licenciado), 195
Chaves de Bocanegra, don Nuño de, 215, 257
Cherinos, Lope de, 251
Chiapa, 136, 230
Chiapantongo, 238
Chiapas, 44, 46, 48, 127, 142
Chiapana, 122

INDEX

Chiapulco, 126
Chiautla, 49, 127, 167, 208
Chicaguaso, 207
Chicaguastepec, 199
Chichicuatla, 224
Chichimecas, 135
Chicoloapa, 185
Chicomeaguatepec, 187
Chicomesuchil, 248
Chiconamel, 193
Chiconautla, 151
Chiconquiauco, 121
Chicontepec, 194, 195
Chicuautla, 258
Chila, 126, 149
Chilacachapa, 224
Chilapa, 67, 208
Chilchota, 236
Chilguatal, 124
Chilotepec, 265
Chiltoyac, 188
Chimalguacan Atenco, 132, 148
Chinameca, 174
Chipila, 169
Chipiltitlan, 149
Chirinos, Pero Almíndez, 13
Chistique, 207
Chocaman, 227
Chocándiro, 159
Cholula, 57, 155, 220, 246, 247
Chontal, 115
Chontales, 116, 124, 127, 128
Chumatlan, 218
Churubusco, 256, 257

Darias de Saavedra, don Hernán, 170
Darién, 87, 127
Dávila, Pedrarias, 150
Daza, Luis, 252
Daza de Alconchel, Francisco, 150
Delgadillo, Diego (Licenciado), 213
Delgadillo, Francisco, 150
Diabuto, 171
Díaz, Antonio, 168
Díaz, Diego, 151
Díaz, Juan, 97, 98
Díaz Carballar (de Carvajal), Alonso, 150
Díaz de Aux, Miguel, 126, 151–152, 186, 195, 204, 234
Díaz de Mendoza, don Ruy, 234

Díaz de Padilla, doña Teresa, 150
Díaz de Sotomayor, Pedro (Bachiller), 246, 260
Díaz de Vargas, Gonzalo, 209
Díaz del Castillo, Bernal, 8, 26, 31, 44, 87, 150–151
Díaz del Castillo, Diego, 151
Díaz del Real, Juan, 151
Díez Rejón, doña María, 151
Don Benito, 22
Don Fernando, 122
Dorantes de Carranza, Andrés, 128
Doria, Cristóbal, 115
Dowry, 63
Duero, Andrés de, 145, 240
Durán, Juan, 152
Durán de Mendoza, Alonso, 183
Dye monopoly, 49

Ebora, Sebastián de, 152
Ecatepec, 196, 253
Echancaleca, 157
Ecija, 110, 114
Ecija, Andrés de, 153
Elgüeta (Ergueta, Ergüeta), Hernando de, 123, 153, 239
Elosuchitlan-Axalyagualco, 152
Emigration trends, 20
Encomendera, 76
Encomenderos, 6, 19, 21, 24, 51
Encomiendas, 3, 4, 10, 12, 13, 16, 17, 35, 51, 52, 58, 59, 61, 64, 79, 83, 99, 102, 115
  assignment, 307
  in dowry, 311
  retention and succession, 29, 57, 103
  terminology, 8
Enríquez de Medina, Diego, 193
Enríquez Magariño, Francisco, 252
Entrada, 305, 313
Epatlan, 174, 216, 228
Epazoyuca, 194, 230, 231
Epustepec, 156
Escarcena, Juan de, 153
Escheatment, 60, 63
Escobar, Alonso de, 153, 192
Escobar, Beatriz de, 231
Escobar, Florentina de, 227
Escobar, Isabel de, 131, 227
Escobar, Pedro de, 153

Escobedo, Andrés de, 149
Escobedo, Beatriz de, 77
Escobedo, Diego de, 77, 221
Eslava, Inés de, 164
España, Juan de, 153–154, 162, 225
Espinosa, Juan de, 221
Espinoza, Juan de, 150
Espinoza, María de, 140
Espíritu Santo, 44
Esquivel, Alonso, 198
Esquivel, Diego de, 138
Estrada, Alonso de, 13, 68–70, 83, 103, 114, 118, 122–124, 135, 136, 154
Estrada, Bartolomé de, 68
Estrada, doña Beatriz de, 257
Estrada, doña Francisca de, 122, 177
Estrada, Francisco de, 133, 154–155, 190, 239
Estrada, doña Luisa, 119
Estrada, doña María de, 170, 239
Etlatongo, 254
Etúcuaro, 163
Extremadura, 22, 47
Exutla, 197, 212

Fajardo, Pedro, 175
Family alliances, 72
Ferdinand, King, 68, 154
Fernández, Beatriz, 221
Fernández, Elvira, 221
Fernández, Juan (infante), 116
Fernández, Juan (notary), 156
Fernández de Mérida, Juan, 156
Fernández de Navarrete, Pedro, 156
Fernández de Ocampo, Juan, 156
Fernández de Proaño, Diego (Comendador), 155, 220, 246–247
Fernández de Velasco, Diego, 177
Fernández Nieto, Diego, 155, 206
Ferrer, doña Francisca, 212, 247
Ferrer de Tapia, don Andrés, 212
Figueroa, Diego de, 47, 130
First Audiencia, 47, 50, 172
First conquerors, 6, 100
Flores, Cristóbal, 208, 250
Flores, Francisco, 156–157
Flores, Juan, 157
Flores, Pedro, 157
Flores de la Cueva, Francisco, 157
Franco Estrada, Francisco, 157
Fregenal de la Sierra, 24, 130

Frías, Cristóbal de, 157–158
Frías, Isabel de, 157
Frías, doña Luisa de, 152
Fuentes, Juan de, 150
Fuentes, Pedro de, 77, 231

Galeote, Alonso, 158
Galeote García, Alonso, 123, 158
Galindo, Juan Sánchez, 158
Gallardo, Pedro, 158–159, 255
Gallego, Alvaro, 159
Gallego, Benito, 159
Gallego, Domingo, 160
Gallego, Juan, 159, 188
Gallego, Lucas, 160
Gallego, Pedro, 160, 185, 195
Gallego Hernández, Gonzalo, 159, 211
Gallegos, Bartolomé, 155
Gallegos, Juan, 160
Galván, Gonzalo, 159
Gálvez, Juan de, 130
Gama, Juan de la, 118
Gamboa, Hernando de, 160, 217
Gámez, Juan de, 164
Garao, María, 254
Garao, María de, 124
Garay, Francisco de, 45, 52
Garbanzos, 266
García, Bartolomé, 161
García, Catalina, 199
García, Diego, 199
García, Genro, 151
García, Hernán, 161
García, Juan, 212
García Bravo, Alonso, 160–161, 258
García de Alburquerque, Domingo, 250
García de Beas, Juan, 206
García de la Fuente, Beatriz, 265
García de Lemos, Juan, 161–162
García Estudio, Juan, 156
García Jaramillo, Diego, 161, 178
Garnica, Antonio de, 162
Garnica, Gaspar, 162, 243
Garrido, Diego, 77, 121, 162, 218
Garrido, Bartolomé, 77, 162
Gasca, Pedro de la, 98
Genovés, Jerónimo, 209
Genovés, Lorenzo, 154, 162, 225
Genovés, Lucas, 162, 163
Genovés de Alvarado, Alonso, 163
Giraldo, Alonso (trumpeter), 123, 163, 250

INDEX 351

Giroma (Ziroma), 156
Godoy, Juana de, 220
Godoy, Luis de, 252
Godoy, María de, 240
Godoy, doña María de, 251, 252
Gold mining, 14, 67
Gomera Island, 131
Gómez, Amador, 163
Gómez, Ana, 258
Gómez, Bartolomé, 163
Gómez, García, 206
Gómez, Gonzalo, 163–164
Gómez, Hernán, 123
Gómez, Inés, 131
Gómez, Juan, 179, 217
Gómez, Pedro, 118, 164, 197
Gómez, Pierrez, 164
Gómez de Avila, Rodrigo, 118, 165
Gómez de Cáceres, don Pedro, 212, 247
Gómez de Herrera, Juan, 164, 178, 180
Gómez de Paz, Inés, 145
Gómez Saavedra, Gonzalo, 232
Gonzales de Portugal, Alonso, 165
González, Alonso, 164, 214, 254
González, Ana, 131, 170
González, Beatriz, 149
González, Diego, 115, 165, 225
González, Jorge, 166, 221
González, Ruy, 71, 166–167, 184, 217
González Dávila, Gil, 123
González de Avila, Gil, 128
González de Benavides, Gil, 165–166
González de Trujillo, Gil, 166, 176, 177
González Ponce de León, Juan, 165, 166
Gonzalo, 24
Governments of New Spain, 14
Grado, Alonso de, 127, 167, 208
Granada, 50
Grand Canary Island, 135
Griego, Juan, 167
Grijalva, Antonio de, 167
Grijalva, Francisca de, 211
Grijalva, Juan de, 9, 31, 115, 121, 145
Grijalva, Sebastián de, 167, 187
Grimaldi, Juan Francisco de, 240
Guachinago, 178
Guachinango, 178, 262
Guacuilapa, 159
Guadalajara, 48, 77, 122
Guadalajara, Antonio de, 125, 167
Guadalupe, 130

Guadiana River, 22
Gualata, 142
Guamelula, 174
Guamuchiles, 171
Guamuchitlan, 256
Guanaxo, 223, 245
Guango Puruándiro, 263
Guaniqueo, 117, 230
Guaquechula, 119
Guaquilpa, 182, 192, 248
Guasaltepec, 116
Guaspaltepec, 239
Guastepec, 131
Guatemala, 46, 48, 86, 119–121, 124, 134
Guatepe, 194
Guatepec, 124, 175
Guatinchan, 144, 215
Guatinicamanes, 130
Guatlatlauca, 240
Guatulco, 169
Guatusco, 130
Guautitlan, 165
Guautla, 141, 157, 202, 205, 254
Guaxacatlan, 257
Guaxolotitlan, 248
Guaxuapa, 49, 121, 248
Guayacocotla, 181
Guayangareo, 50
Guayatepec, 150
Guaymeo, 165
Guazacualco, 211
Guazalingo, 115, 165, 225
Guazaltepec, 161
Guazamota, 257
Guazpaltepeque, 119
Guazulco, 244
Güemes, Miguel de, 214
Guerrero, Lázaro (Alvaro), 168
Guerrero de Luna, Agustín, 165
Guevara, don Diego de, 126
Guillén, Antonio, 168
Guillén, doña Elvira, 123
Guillén, Francisco, 168, 252
Guipúzcoa, 121
Guipuzcoano, Rodrigo, 84, 168, 191, 242
Gutiérrez, Cristóbal, 241
Gutiérrez, Francisco, 59, 169, 226, 235
Gutiérrez, Gómez, 170
Gutiérrez, Leonor, 180
Gutiérrez, Mari, 222–223
Gutiérrez, María, 241, 249

Gutiérrez Altamirano, Hernán, 118
Gutiérrez Altamirano, Juan (Licenciado), 118, 123, 143, 147
Gutiérrez de Ahumada, Antonio, 169
Gutiérrez de Almodovar, Antonio, 58, 169, 220
Gutiérrez de Badajoz, Alonso, 76, 168, 173
Gutiérrez de Caballería, Diego, 214
Gutiérrez de Santa Clara, Cristóbal, 240
Gutiérrez de Villacorta, María, 170
Gutiérrez Flores de la Caballería, doña Marina, 68, 154, 170
Gutiérrez Lavado, Diego, 169
Guzmán, doña Catalina, 68
Guzmán, Diego de, 126
Guzmán, doña Inés de, 185
Guzmán, fray Juan de, 171
Guzmán, María de, 243
Guzmán, Nuño Beltrán de, 170–171
Guzmán, Pedro de, 127, 171
Guzmán, Ramiro de, 132, 172
Guzmán, Rodrigo de, 132, 172
Guzmán Saavedra, don Luis de, 29, 68, 69, 154, 170
Guzmán Sotomayor, Juan de, 185

Heredia, Rodrigo (d'Evia), 172
Hermosilla, Elvira de, 147, 151
Hernández, Alonso, 167
Hernández, Ana, 213
Hernández, Antonia, 214
Hernández, Elvira, 144
Hernández, Garci, 134, 176
Hernández, Juan, 231
Hernández, Juana, 184
Hernández, Pedro, 134, 174, 176, 216
Hernández, Santos (el buen viejo), 130, 174
Hernández Bota, Pedro, 183
Hernández Buenos Años, Gonzalo, 224
Hernández Calvo, Gonzalo, 173, 195, 201
Hernández de Alconchel, Gonzalo, 159
Hernández de Córdoba, Francisco, 9, 31, 124
Hernández de Figueroa, Gonzalo, 173
Hernández de Herrera, Gonzalo, 175
Hernández de Nava, Bartolomé, 78, 172, 192, 198, 208, 256
Hernández de Portillo, Luis, 242
Hernández de Prado, Juan, 174
Hernández del Castillo, Juan, 300

Hernández del Castillo, Martín, 139
Hernández Guerrero, Francisco, 174
Hernández Mosquera, Cristóbal, 173
Hernández Mosquera, Gonzalo, 76, 168, 173
Hernández Parada, Pedro, 164
Herrera, Cristóbal de, 174
Herrera, Elvira, 175
Herrera, Francisco de, 139, 174–175, 208
Herrera, María de, 133
Herrera, Violante de, 186
Hidalgo, Cristóbal, 222
Hidalgos, 7, 27, 101
Higueras, 128
Hinojosa, Juan de (Francisco), 24, 175, 201
Hipólito de Tovar, Juan, 252
Hispaniola, 86, 89
Hita, Catalina de, 175
Hita, Gaspar de, 175
Holguín, Diego de, 48, 134, 174, 175–176, 216, 244
Holguín, Gonzalo, 129
Honduras, 13, 46, 67, 97, 113
Horna, Sancho de, 176
Horta, Alonso de, 154
Hoyos, Gómez de, 176
Huajuapan, 46
Huajuapan de León, 49
Huasteca, 135
Huastecan language area, 52
Huaxyacac, 46
Huehuetlan, 125, 245
Huehuetoca, 165
Huelva, 21, 77, 117, 182
Huepustla, 254
Huesca, 133
Huexocingo, 208
Huexutla, 177
Hueyapa, 239
Hueypustla, 130
Hueytlalpa, 234
Hueytlapa, 142
Hueyxagualco, 235
Huitaluta, 229
Huitzilopochco, 256
Huitziltepec, 177
Huitzitzila, 156
Huiztla, 255
Huizuco, 200
Hurtado, Andrés, 255

INDEX 333

Hurtado, Gaspar, 164
Hurtado de Mendoza, Diego, 124, 176
Hurtado de Mendoza, Luis, 115

Ibarra, Diego de, 207
Ibarra, Miguel de, 232
Ibonao, 121
Icaza, Francisco A. de, 300
Iguala, 117, 156
Igualapa, 139, 174, 208
Igualtepec, 114, 249
Ilamatlan, 141
Indaporapeo, 199
Indians, 27, 95
Inero, Andrés de, 141, 166, 176–177
Infante, Juan, 177, 245
Infante Samaniego, Juan, 177
Iñiguez, Bernardino, 177
Interpreters, 30, 95
Ircio, Martín de, 177
Ircio, Captain Pedro de, 39, 64, 141, 177
Iscateupa, 243
Iscuincuitlapilco, 160, 185
Iscuintepec, 162
Isla, Pedro de la, 178, 193
Istapa, 163, 180, 237, 253
Istario, 223
Istayuca, 130
Istayutla, 185
Istimitique, 257
Istlaguaca, 250, 251
Ixcatlan, 138, 183, 243
Ixconyamec, 142, 234
Ixguacan, 227
Ixguatlan, 261
Ixitlan, 259
Ixmiquilpan, 128, 226
Ixtapa, 182
Ixtapaluca, 148
Ixtepec, 142, 234
Ixtlan, 156
Izatlan, 153
Izcaytoyac, 164
Iztactepec, 199
Iztaquimaxtitlan, 172, 198, 256
Izúcar, 119, 120, 126, 127, 134

Jacona, 116
Jaén, 128, 129
Jalapa, 49, 76, 114, 121, 144, 203

Jalisco, 117, 121
Jamaica, 127
Jaramillo, Juan, 161
Jaramillo, doña María, 65, 178
Jaramillo de Salvatierra, Juan, 24, 65, 67, 135, 178, 203, 218, 242
Jaso, 196
Jaso, Juan de (el mozo), 179, 212
Jaso, Juan de (el viejo), 178–179, 180, 232, 249, 262
Jenenes, Pedro, 200
Jerez, Hernando de (Gómez), 179
Jerez, Juan de, 214
Jerez, Juan de (el mozo), 176
Jerez, Juan de (el tio), 176
Jerez, Juana de, 179
Jerez de Badajoz, 127
Jerez de la Frontera, 77
Jiménez, Fortún, 127, 175
Jiménez, Gonzalo, 24, 179, 180, 181
Jiménez, Juan, 24, 142, 178, 180, 232
Jiménez, Lloriente, 231
Jiménez, Mari, 214
Jiménez, Martín, 180, 251, 253
Jiménez Arreola, Teresa, 148
Jiménez de Rivera, Juan, 180
Jomiltongo, 213
Juárez, Pedro (Suárez), 180, 205
Juez repartidor, 16
Justlaguaca, 125, 186, 253

La Antigua, 39
La Guacana, 211
La Guaga, 231
La Serena, 22, 26
Lake Chalco, 148
Lake Chapala, 144
Lake Pátzcuaro, 49, 64, 177
Lake Texcoco, 148
Lamadriz, Tomás de, 149, 180
Lapaguia, 159
Lara, doña Isabel de, 65, 113, 141, 194
Lara, doña Luisa de, 65, 141
Larios, Juan, 49, 181
Las Laxas, 160
Law of Succession, 59
Lawyers, 29
Lazagaya, 157
Leiva, Diego (Francisco) de, 181
Leiva, Inés de, 211

León, 26, 116
León, Alvaro de, 222
León, Ana de, 198
León, doña Antonia de, 138
León, doña María de, 138
León, Pedro de (Licenciado), 138, 233
Lepe, Huelva, 64
Letrados, 236
Licenses, 19, 306
Limpias, Juan de ,181
Limpias Carvajal, Juan de, 181
Llamatlan, 176
Llanos, Beatriz de, 123
Llerena, 124
Llerena, García de, 79, 238
Loa, Guillén de la, 181
Loaisa, Diego de (Licenciado), 212
Loaysa, Francisca de, 153
Loaysa, Juana de, 251
Logroño, 39, 65
Logroño, Diego, 70
López, Alonso, 182
López, Antón, 117
López, Beatriz, 121
López, Bernardino, 169
López, Gabriel, 223
López, Gaspar, 185
López, Ginesa, 217
López, Gonzalo, 192
López, Gonzalo (el camarero), 182
López, Jerónimo, 127, 183, 258
López, Juana, 123
López, Martín (ship's carpenter), 67, 184, 203
López, Pedro (Licenciado), 160, 185
López, Román, 185, 237
López de Jimena, Juan, 138, 181, 183–184
López de Palacios, Nicolás, 166, 184–185, 229
López de Polanco, Catalina, 130
López de Salcedo, Ruy, 235
López de Sanlucar, Bartolomé, 136, 182, 244
López de Sevilla, Andrés, 182, 192
López de Solís, don Cristóbal, 185
López de Zárate, Fray Juan (Bishop), 184
López Frias, Juan, 183
López Galbito, Pedro, 196
López Osorio, Martín, 184
López Patino, Juan, 262

López Pavón, Juan, 253
Lorita, Hernando de, 185–186
Los Amuzgos, 123
Loya, Andrés de, 195
Lozano, Pedro, 120, 186, 214
Lucas, Alonso, 126, 152, 186, 195
Lucero, Cecilia, 161
Luján, doña Isabel de, 257
Luna y Arellano, don Tristán de, 29, 186, 188, 253

Macuilsuchil, 135, 191, 195
Macuiltianguis, 226
Madrid, 47
Madrid, Juan de, 222
Maestrazgo de León, 22, 47
Mafra, Cristóbal de, 187, 202
Magdalena, fray Juan de la, 154
Maldonado, Alonso (Licenciado), 198
Maldonado, Alvaro, 43, 167, 188
Maldonado, Alvaro (el fiero), 76, 187
Maldonado, Antonia, 140
Maldonado, Catalina, 209
Maldonado, Francisco, 76, 130, 186, 187–188, 259
Maldonado, Mencia, 118
Maldonado, Pedro, 76, 187, 188, 265
Maldonado, Rodrigo, 152
Malila, 114
Malinalco, 222, 228
Malinaltepec, 113, 114, 191
Managers, 28
Mancheño Cerrano, Múñez, 254
Mancilla, Juan de, 159, 262
Manicarao, 145
Mansilla, Juan de, 188, 223, 249
Manumission, 241
Manzanares, Juan de, 254
Manzanilla, Juan de, 188
Manzano, Alvaro, 117, 189
Manzano de Chaves, Juan, 189
Maquilí, 133
Mar del Sur, 127
Maranja, 244
Maravatio, 180, 204, 205
Marcaida, María de, 246
March(?), Alonso de, 211
Marín, don Francisco, 189
Marín, Juan Bautista, 202
Marín, Leonor, 151, 202

Marín, Luis, 189, 211
Marina, doña (malinche), 44, 65, 145, 147, 178
Mariners, 29, 101
Marmolejo, Diego, 39, 189
Marquesado de Salinas, 177
Marquesado del Valle de Oaxaca, 44, 46, 146
Marriages, 79
Marroquino, Agustín, 126
Martel, Hernando, 155
Martel, Juan, 189, 220
Martín, Alonso (partidor), 77, 239, 245, 262
Martín, Domingo, 158, 223, 250
Martín, Ginés, 84, 191
Martín, Gonzalo, 257
Martín, Hernán, 144, 191
Martín, Maya, 84, 114, 191
Martín, Nuflo, 205
Martín, Rodrigo, 192
Martín Aguado, Pedro, 78, 113
Martín Asturiano, Alonso, 157
Martín Breña, Antón, 190
Martín de Coria, Pedro, 192
Martín de Jerez, Alonso, 190
Martín de la Mezquita, 110
Martín de Mérida, Diego, 168, 191, 242
Martín de Valencia, Juan, 191
Martín Jaca, Alonso, 133, 155, 190
Martín Millán de Gamboa, Cristóbal, 190–191
Martín Muñoz, Alonso, 156
Martín Rieros (Riberos), Alonso, 229
Martínez, Juan, 189
Martínez, Ruiz, 67
Martínez Guerrero, Juan, 165
Mascota, 207
Mata, Alonso de, 241
Matalcingo, 140
Mateos, Juan, 117
Matías, Coronel, 144
Matlactlan, 198
Matlactonatico, 58, 122, 262
Maya, Ana de, 148
Maya, Antonio de, 78, 148
Maya, Pedro de, 192
Mayamala, 142
Mayana, 150
Mazariegos, Luis de, 162

Mazatlan, 215, 264
Mazatlaxaya, 225
Mazatlaxot, 188
Mecatepec, 159
Mecatlan, 58, 129, 218, 235
Mechia, 259
Medel, Antonio (Hernán), 125, 172, 182, 192, 248
Medel, Francisco, 131
Medel, Hernando, 192
Medellín, 22, 26, 43, 49, 83, 118, 122, 130, 132, 144
Mederos, Clemente de, 167
Medical, 28
Medina, Domingo de, 178, 192–193
Medina, Francisco de, 193
Medina (el hijo), Jerónimo de, 195
Medina (el viejo), Jerónimo de, 166, 177, 193, 209
Medina, Juan de, 193, 201
Medina, doña María de, 143, 193
Medina de las Torres, 24
Medina de Río Seco, 133
Medina de Torres, 121
Medina del Campo, 76, 78
Mejía de Tapia, Beatriz, 175
Mejía de Villalobos, Francisca, 189
Mejía Salmerón, Baltasar, 164
Méndez, Héctor, 193
Méndez, Martín, 127
Méndez, Teresa, 194
Méndez de Sotomayor, Juan, 193
Mendoza, Alonso de, 65, 83, 141, 157, 194, 261
Mendoza, don Antonio de (Viceroy), 3, 17, 50, 120
Mendoza, Lope de, 194, 196, 220, 231
Mendoza, doña María de, 177, 189
Mendoza, Rodrigo de, 214
Meneses, doña Agustina de, 195
Meneses, Pedro de, 48, 173, 181, 193, 194–195, 201, 219, 220
Meneses, don Rodrigo, 195
Mercado, Ginés, 257
Mercado de Sotomayor, Jerónimo de, 138
Mercantile activities, 96
Mercedarians, 97
Merchants, 28, 29, 94, 101
Mérida, 22, 47, 127
Mérida, Alonso de, 186, 195

Mérida, Mariana de, 195
Mérida y Molino, Francisco de, 195
Mesa, Miguel, 196
Mescala, 161
Mescaltepec, 226
Mestitlan, 132, 186
Metatepec, 194, 196, 220, 231
Metateyuca, 175, 201
Metepec, 118, 143
Metlatepec, 235
Mexcaltzinco, 128
Mexico, 86, 96
Mexico City, 36, 40, 42, 43, 47, 51, 100, 101, 119, 122, 123, 246
Mextitlan, 152
Mezquita, Martín de la, 195, 236
Meztitlan, 126, 195
Miaguatlan, 121, 194, 197, 212
Micaoztoc, 190
Michimaloya, 258, 265
Michoacán, 47, 67, 116, 117, 118, 133, 135
Miguel, Antón, 195
Miguel, Esteban, 158, 223
Miguel Negrete, Diego, 195
Millán de Gamboa, don Gaspar, 191
Milpa, 84, 168, 191, 242
Milpancingo, 175
Miltepec, 248
Minas de Ayoteco, 49
Minzapa, 154, 162, 188, 225
Miranda, Juan de, 189
Mispan, 231
Mistecas, 174
Mistepec, 161, 258
Mitla, 144, 186, 187, 264
Mitlatonga, 230
Mixes, 127
Mixquic, 266
Mixtec, 52
Mixteca, 124
Mixtlan, 180
Mizantla, 233
Mizquiaguala, 169, 220
Moctezuma, 27, 130
Moctezuma (heirs), 158
Moctezuma, doña Isabel, 27, 135, 147, 160, 167, 195–196, 261
Moctezuma, doña Leonor, 27, 196, 253
Molina, Gil de, 187
Molino de Aragón, Guadalajara, 77

Molonga, 212
Molongo, 114
Moluccas Islands, 39, 141, 232
Mondragón, Pedro de (Licenciado), 194, 196, 220, 231
Monjaraz, Andrés de, 196, 197, 231
Monjaraz, Gregorio, 231
Monjaraz, doña Isabel de, 133, 231
Monjaraz, Mateo (Gregorio) de, 197, 212
Monje, Martín, 118, 164, 197
Monje de León, Martín, 197
Monresín, Cristóbal de, 49, 197–198
Monresín, José de, 197
Montalvo, Francisco de, 48, 197–198
Montañés, Juan, 161
Montaño, Alonso, 169
Montaño, Francisco, 172, 198, 215, 256
Montejo, doña Catalina (Beatriz?) de, 198
Montejo, Francisco de, 31, 120, 198
Montejo, Juan de, 193
Monterroso, Blas de, 198–199
Montes de Oca, doña Marina, 134
Montes de Toledo, 22
Monzapa, 183
Morales, Gonzalo de, 205
Morales, Juan de, 128, 199, 265
Morcillo, Alonso de, 199
Morcillo, Francisco, 50, 199–200
Morcillo, Gaspar, 211
Morelia, 49
Moreno, Cristóbal 58, 244
Moreno, Isidro, 49, 200
Moreno, Juan, 200, 236
Moreno, Sebastián, 200
Moreno Cendejas, Pedro, 158, 200
Moro, Andrés, 228
Moscoso, Juan de, 214
Moscoso, Sebastián, 200–201
Mosquera, María, 77, 168
Mota, Jerónimo de la, 71
Motenpacoya, 136
Motín, 117, 129
Motines, 136
Motrico, Diego, 173, 195, 201
Moyutla, 59, 144, 169, 182, 235
Muchtitlan, 177
Multiple encomiendas, 54
Municipal founding, 38
Muñoz, Alonso, 204
Muñoz, Diego, 198

INDEX 337

Muñoz, Isabel, 173, 195, 201
Muster at Tlaxcala, 306

Nagualapa, 231
Nahuatl-speaking heartland, 51
Nájera, Juan (Leiva) de, 175, 193, 201
Nanaguaticpac, 202
Nanaguatlan, 125
Nanalcatepec, 240
Naranja, 177
Narváez, Pánfilo de, 10, 24, 121, 145
Nava, Antonio de, 136
Nava, Diego de, 183, 184
Nava, Francisca de, 183
Nava, Francisco de, 166, 172
Nava, Hernando de, 172
Nava, doña Juana de, 183
Nava, Martín de, 172
Nava, Pedro de, 183
Navarrete, Alonso de, 50, 201–202, 227, 261
Navarrete, García de, 156
Navarrete, Juan de, 136
Navarrete, Rodrigo, 136
Navarro, Juan, 202
Navarro, Juan (Antonio), 202
Navito, 171
Necotepec, 157
Nepopozalco, 239
Nespa, 201, 227
Nestalpa, 158
Nestepec, 157
New Castile, 83
New Galicia, 48, 86, 115, 120, 133, 309, 312
New Laws, 12, 17, 51, 116, 118
New Mexico, 186, 207, 214
New Spain, 86, 102, 110
Nexpa, 125, 167
Nicaragua, 86, 113
Niebla, 117
Nieto, Francisco, 231
Nieto, Gómez, 202, 250
Nieto, Inés, 139
Nieto, Pedro, 187, 202
Nieto Maldonado, Francisco, 202
Noche Triste, 146
Nochistlan, 192
Nochtepec, 133
Notary (escribano), 29, 314
Nueva Galicia, 117

Nun, 248
Núñez, Andrés, 67, 184, 202–203
Núñez, Catalina, 183
Núñez, Francisco, 147
Núñez (Maese de Roa), Pedro, 129, 203–204, 205, 206, 218, 245
Núñez, Violante, 161
Núñez Cabeza de Vaca, Alvar, 128
Núñez de Chaves, Pedro, 204
Núñez de Guzmán, Diego, 138
Núñez de Valera, Francisco, 145, 147
Núñez Mercado, Juan, 203
Núñez Pinto, Diego, 113
Núñez Sedeño, Juan, 47, 178, 203, 218, 242, 258
Núñez Vela, Blasco (Viceroy), 98

Oapa, 177
Oaxaca, 27, 100, 113, 116, 119, 120, 124, 130, 135
Obregón, Bartolomé, 126
Obregón, Luis, 126
Obregón, Mari López de, 126
Ocampo, Diego de, 204, 234
Ocampo, doña María de, 204
Ocampo Saavedra, Diego de, 128
Ocaña, Diego de, 180, 204–205
Ocelotepec, 65, 229, 262
Ochoa de Lejalde, Juan, 121, 205
Ocopetlayuca, 210
Ocotepec, 169, 186
Ocotlan, 156, 265
Ocoyoaca, 196, 260
Ocuapa, 159
Ocuequila, 188, 225
Ocuila, 128, 199, 265
Ocuituco, 172, 192, 266
Ojeda, Alonso de, 205
Ojeda, Doctor Cristóbal de, 129, 204, 205–206
Ojeda, Diego de, 186
Ojeda, Isabel de, 263
Ojeda, Juan de, 236
Olaejos, Juan de, 187
Old Castile, 26, 78, 79, 83
Olid y Viedma, doña María de, 70, 137
Olinalá, 113
Olintepec, 157
Olivares, Alonso de, 181
Olivares, Francisco de, 228

Oliver, Antonio de, 155, 206
Oliver, Juan Bautista, 206
Oliveros, Francisco de, 206
Olmedo, fray Bartolomé de, 97
Olmos, Francisco de, 78, 131, 206–207, 258, 265
Olmos, Isabel de, 78, 207, 258, 265
Olutla, 189
Olvera, Diego de, 120, 207
Olvera, Juan de, 207
Ometepec, 139, 174, 208
Oñate, Cristóbal Pérez de, 207, 234
Oñate, Juan de, 207
Oñate y Salazar, Alonso de, 207
Ordaz, Beatriz de, 117
Ordaz, Diego de, 31, 58, 127, 167, 208
Ordaz, Francisca de, 166
Ordaz Villagómez, Diego de, 208
Order of Santiago's Maestrazgo de León, 24
Orduña, don Antonio de, 230
Orduña, Francisco de, 70, 79, 104, 139, 172, 175, 208, 230, 241, 245, 260
Orduña, Rodrigo de, 136
Orellana, doña Leonor de, 232
Orizaba, 144
Oropesa, 70, 83, 131
Orozco, Francisco de, 46
Ortega, Alonso de, 264
Ortega, Antonio de, 149, 233, 238
Ortega, Cristóbal de, 209, 228
Ortega, Juan de (Bachiller), 209
Ortega, Juana de, 241
Ortiz, Juan, 141, 209
Ortiz de Arriaga, Juan, 256
Ortiz de Matienzo, Juan, 186, 209–210, 260
Ortiz de Matienzo, Juan (Licenciado), 250
Ortiz de Zúñiga, Alonso, 166, 177, 193, 209
Ortiz de Zúñiga, Pedro de, 186
Ortiz de Zúñiga, Sancho, 186
Osorio, Ana, 126
Osorio, doña Catalina, 139
Osorio, Leonor, 221
Osorio, Pedro de, 252
Ospanaguastla, 156
Ostuma, 199
Ostutla, 172
Otatitlan, 181
Otlaquistla, 183
Otlazpa, 201

Otucpa, 165
Ovando, Comendador frey Nicolás de, 9
Oxitipa, 126, 171
Oxitlan, 150
Oxtoticpac, 204
Ozumacintla, 189

Pacheco, doña Beatriz, 215
Pacheco, Cristóbal, 210, 224
Pacheco, Gaspar, 47, 130, 185, 210
Pacheco, Juan, 173, 202
Pacheco de Bocanegra, don Bernardino, 215, 257
Pacheco de Escobar, Beatriz, 210, 241
Pachuca, 117, 123, 124, 126, 195, 246
Padilla, Miguel de, 164
Paguatlan, 251
Palacios, Beatriz, 153, 227
Palencia, 144
Palencia, Hernando de, 182
Palos, 78, 140
Pamacoran, 177
Panama, 31, 89, 144
Pangololutla, 225
Pangolutla, 188
Pantoja, Juan, 210–211
Pantoja, Pedro de, 169, 200, 211
Pánuco, 45, 46, 50, 65, 83, 84, 100, 115, 117, 119–121, 124, 125, 128, 129, 132, 136, 139–141, 144, 157, 169
Papaloticpac, 137, 221, 251
Papalutla, 113
Papantla, 122, 232, 247
Paradinas, 116, 118, 127
Pardo, Diego, 211
Pardo del Castillo, Lupe, 139
Paredes, Cristóbal de, 123
Paredes, Marcos de, 211
Párraga, Francisco de, 227
Pasamonte, Miguel de, 145
Pátzcuaro, 49, 50, 117, 120, 129
Payo, Isabel, 179, 212
Payo, Lorenzo, 179, 211–212
Paz, Alonso de, 59, 197, 212
Paz, Juan, 196
Paz, Pedro de, 212, 247
Paz, Rodrigo de, 98, 147
Pechucalco, 183, 237
Pedraza, Maese Diego de, 213
Peláez de Berrio, Juan, 119, 213
Pellicel Alberrucia, Melchora, 255

Peloso, Bernaldo, 163
Peña, Juan de la, 213
Peña, Leonor de la, 159
Peña, Rodrigo de la, 213
Peña Vallejo, Juan de, 213, 219
Pénjamo, 263
Perada, Alonso de, 176
Perales, Bartolomé de, 58, 79, 186, 214, 235
Perales, María, 186
Peralta, doña Catalina de, 262
Peralta, Martín de, 214
Pérez, Alonso, 134
Pérez, Alonso (Bachiller), 165, 214
Pérez, Juan, 222, 243
Pérez Carballa, Antonia, 134
Pérez de Arteaga, Juan, 143, 198, 215, 241
Pérez de Badajoz, Martín, 216
Pérez de Bocanegra, don Alonso, 214
Pérez de Bocanegra, Hernán, 215, 222
Pérez de Herrera, Juan, 58, 134, 174, 176, 216
Pérez de la Gama, Juan, 216, 240
Pérez de Oñate, Cristóbal, 207
Pérez de Villagrán, Juan, 213
Pérez de Zamora, Alonso, 215
Pérez de Zamora, Ana, 126
Pérez de Zamora, Diego, 140
Pérez Jarada, Pero, 188
Periban, 133, 134
Peru, 86, 98, 120
Petalcingo, 174
Petatlan, 160, 219, 223
Petlacaltepec, 192
Petlalcingo, 130
Piastla, 131, 207
Pilar, García del, 71, 216
Pilcaya, 133
Pilcintepec, 159
Pilopan, 265
Pineda, María de, 238
Pinzándaro, 178
Pinzón, Ginés, 160, 216–217
Pinzón, Juan, 217, 253
Pitatlan, 217
Pizarro, doña Catalina, 147, 235
Pizarro, Francisco, 89, 98
Pizarro, Juan, 89
Pizarro, Leonor, 147, 235
Plasencia, 22
Plasencia, Pedro de, 217

Plaza, Juan de la, 217
Pobladores, 6, 100
Pobladores antiguos, 6, 100
Pochotitlan, 176
Pochutla, 169, 204
Pocintlan, 171
Pomayagua, 131, 170
Ponce Bermijo, Bartolomé, 227
Ponce de León, Juan, 166
Ponce de León, Juan (Adelantado), 115
Ponce de León, Luis (Licenciado), 127, 129
Ponce de León, don Luis, 154
Ponce de León, doña María, 179
Popoyutla, 117, 237
Porcallo, Vasco, 166, 217
Porcallo de Figueroa, Lorenzo, 217
Porras, Ana de, 255
Porras, doña Ana María de, 218
Porras, Bartolomé, 254
Porras, Diego, 218
Porras, María de, 149
Portillo, Gonzalo, 203
Portillo, Valladolid, 78
Potonchon, 150
Preciado, Francisco, 77, 121, 162, 218
Preciado, Juan, 77, 162, 218
Procuradores, 236
Professionals, 27, 101
Protomédico, 28
Provincia de Avalos, 122
Puctla, 125, 139
Puebla, 30, 39, 46, 47, 48, 114, 115, 124, 125, 130, 134, 194
Puerto de Caballos, Honduras, 69
Puerto de Santa María, 116
Puerto Rico, 31, 143
Pungaravato, 117, 127, 259
Purificación, 48, 115, 118

Quechula, 224, 262
Quejada, Diego, 204, 218
Querétaro, 124
Quesada, don Luis de, 178
Quesada, don Pedro de, 178
Quevedo, Francisco de, 178, 203, 218
Quezaltepec, 206
Quinamulapa, 191
Quiñones, Antonio, 128
Quintana Dueñas, Francisco de, 195
Quintero, Ana, 121
Quintero, Francisco, 124, 213, 219, 223

Quiotepec, 203
Quiroga, Vasco de, 50
Quito, 87, 98

Ramírez, Andrea, 249
Ramírez, Diego, 219
Ramírez (el viejo), Francisco, 143, 194, 196, 216, 219–220, 231, 249
Ramírez, Inés, 184
Ramírez, Juan, 114, 131, 157
Ramírez, doña Juliana, 180
Ramírez, María, 180
Ramírez Bravo, Francisco, 133
Ramírez de Avalos, Gil, 266
Ramón, Diego, 140, 215
Rangel, Rodrigo, 24, 43, 220, 246, 247
Rapalo, Juan Bautista de, 189, 220
Rebolledo, doña Ana de, 156
Recruitment, 26
Regional complexes, 60
Reinoso, Francisco de, 227
Relanga del Duero, 121
Remón, Alonso, 151
Repartimiento, 10
Retamales, Pablo, 77, 169, 220–221
Ribadeo, Francisco de, 137, 221, 256
Ribera, Alvaro de, 221
Ribera, Diego de, 221
Ribera, Mencia de, 183
Ribera, Miguel de, 200
Rijoles (Ecijoles), Tomás, 221
Rincón, doña Francisca del, 194
Rincón, María del, 76, 187, 188, 225
Río de Tepec, 155
Río Pánuco, 45
Rioboz (Riobó) de Sotomayor, Gonzalo, 222
Rivera, Ana de, 185
Rivera, doña Bernardina de, 213
Rivera, doña Inés de, 122
Roa, Maese de. *See* Núñez (Maese de Roa), Pedro
Robles, García de, 222
Robles, Gonzalo de, 47, 222
Robles, don Juan de, 222
Robles, Melchor de, 167
Rodas, Pedro de, 205
Rodríguez, Ana, 179
Rodríguez, Baltasar, 214
Rodríguez, Catalina, 135, 160, 200, 211, 252

Rodríguez, Diego, 131, 158, 222–223
Rodríguez, Elvira, 158
Rodríguez, Francisco, 188, 219, 223
Rodríguez, Isabel, 262
Rodríguez, Juan, 115, 160, 165, 177, 188, 225
Rodríguez, Juana, 216
Rodríguez, Leonor, 262
Rodríguez, Marina, 212
Rodríguez, Martín, 57, 226
Rodríguez, Melchor, 226
Rodríguez, Sebastián, 227
Rodríguez Anhaifa, Ana, 68
Rodríguez Bejerano, Juan de, 225
Rodríguez de Avalos, Cristóbal, 222, 228
Rodríguez de Escobar, Pedro, 226–227
Rodríguez de Guadalcanal, Francisco, 223
Rodríguez de la Magdalena, Gonzalo, 30, 224, 262
Rodríguez de Ocaña, Gonzalo, 210, 224
Rodríguez de Orozco, Diego, 163, 250
Rodríguez de Orozco, Leonor, 250
Rodríguez de Salas, Juan, 115, 225–226
Rodríguez de Valladolid, Diego, 223, 245
Rodríguez de Villafuerte, Gonzalo, 76, 154, 162, 188, 225, 226
Rodríguez de Villafuerte, Juan, 225, 226
Rodríguez de Villafuerte, Miguel, 225, 226
Rodríguez Enríquez Magariño, Juan, 224
Rodríguez Magariño, Francisco, 224
Roelas, Diego de las, 201, 227, 261
Rojas, Isabel de, 186, 187, 259
Rolando, Jácome, 217
Román, Bartolomé, 43, 149, 227
Romero, Alonso, 209, 228
Romero, Cristóbal, 222, 228
Romero, Juan, 228
Romero, Miguel, 228
Rosa, doña Ana de, 193
Rosales, Francisco de, 39, 228–229
Rozas, Andrés de, 229
Ruiz, Alonso, 229
Ruiz, Diego, 229, 230
Ruiz, Fernando, 229
Ruiz, Gabriel, 70
Ruiz, Gonzalo, 71, 185, 229–230
Ruiz, Juan, 140
Ruiz, Juana, 207, 231
Ruiz, Malgarida, 162
Ruiz, Marcos, 77, 117, 230–231
Ruiz, Pedro, 128, 180

Ruiz de Alanís, Juan, 230
Ruiz de Berrio, Ana, 148
Ruiz de Bozbuena, Juana, 198
Ruiz de Castañeda, Antonio, 128, 230
Ruiz de Contrares, Antón, 151
Ruiz de Guadalcanal, Pedro, 231
Ruiz de la Mota, Jerónimo, 208, 230
Ruiz de la Peña, Hernán, 230
Ruiz de Manjaraz, doña María, 196
Ruiz de Medina, Antonio (Licenciado), 194
Ruiz de Mendoza, Juan, 229
Ruiz de Monjaraz, Martín, 133, 196, 231, 265
Ruiz de Ovalle, Hernando, 143
Ruiz de Requena, Pedro, 164, 178, 180, 231–232
Ruiz de Rojas, Marcos, 188
Ruiz de Rosas, Andrés, 229
Ruiz de Sevilla, Marcos, 194, 220
Ruiz Martínez, Juan, 263, 264
Ruiz Saavedra, María, 255

Saavedra, don Fernando (Count of Castellar), 68, 83, 122, 232
Saavedra, Francisco de, 122, 232
Saavedra, Lope de, 232–233, 247
Saavedra, Luis (Lucas) de, 233
Saavedra Cerón, Alvaro, 39, 141, 232
Saavedra de Estrada y Guzmán, don Alonso, 170
Sailors, 23
Salamanca, 67, 68, 76, 130, 132
Salamanca, Cristóbal de, 197, 212
Salamanca, Diego de, 233
Salamanca, Juan de, 149, 233, 238
Salamanca, Juan de (conqueror), 212, 233–234
Salas, Bernardino de, 152
Salas, Cristóbal de, 226
Salas, Diego de, 160
Salas, Sebastián de, 226
Salazar, doña Catalina de, 207
Salazar, Cristóbal de, 234
Salazar, Francisco de, 127, 249
Salazar, Gonzalo de, 13, 58, 69, 98, 123, 152, 204, 234
Salazar, Hernando de, 142, 234
Salazar, doña Isabel de, 123
Salazar, María de, 247
Salcedo, Juan de, 147, 235, 265
Saldaña, Francisco de, 235

Saldaña, Gregorio de, 58, 129, 169, 214, 235–236
Saldaña, María de, 214, 235
Salinas, Jerónimo de, 47, 195, 200, 236
Salinas, Juan de, 123
Salto, Baltasar del, 252
Salvatierra, Rodrigo de, 229
Samaniego, Lope de, 70, 118, 123
Samaniego, doña Mariana Infante, 122
Sámano, Juan de, 236
Sámanos Turcios, don Juan de, 236
San Antonio, caravel, 232
San Bartolomé, 156
San Francisco Tlagualipa, 225
San Ildefonso de los Zapotecas, 47
San Juan, Juan de, 164
San Martín, Diego de, 169
San Martín, Pedro de, 157
San Miguel, Melchor de, 47, 240
Sánchez, Antón, 237
Sánchez, Bartolomé, 118, 185, 237
Sánchez, Juan, 27, 238
Sánchez, Mateo, 149, 233, 238
Sánchez, Pedro, 223, 239
Sánchez Bermijo, Juan, 169
Sánchez de Hortigoza, Hernán, 79, 238
Sánchez de Sandoval, Fernando (Licenciado), 240
Sánchez de Sandoval, Francisco, 240
Sánchez de Sopuerta, Diego, 237–238
Sánchez de Sopuerto, Alonso, 237
Sánchez Farfán, Pedro, 77, 123, 129, 144, 153, 155, 158, 239, 250
Sánchez Galindo, Juan, 158, 200, 223
Sandoval, Gonzalo de, 26, 44, 46, 65, 118, 128, 239–240
Sandoval, Juan de, 239
Sandoval, don Luis de, 240
Sandoval, Rodrigo de (Licenciado), 123, 216, 240
Sanlúcar de Alpechín, 113
Sanlúcar la Mayor, 113
Santa Clara, Antonio de, 240, 241
Santa Clara, Bernardino de, 210, 240–241
Santa Clara, Francisco de, 241
Santa Clara, Magdalena de, 241
Santa Cruz, Alvaro, 241
Santa Cruz, Diego de, 123
Santa Cruz, Francisco de, 71, 208, 215, 241, 257
Santa Cruz, Pedro de, 84, 168, 191, 242

Santa María de Lachichina, 247
Santa María de la Victoria, 44
Santa Marta, 129
Santiago, 120, 156
Santiago de Baracoa, 145
Santiago de Guatemala, 44
Santiago de los Valles, 50
Santisteban del Puerto, 45, 59, 113
Santo Domingo, 31, 70, 87, 118, 120, 121, 129, 143, 145
Santos, Francisco, 242
Saucedo, Francisco de, 242
Sayula, 255
School of dance, 258
Secular clergymen, 97
Sedeño, Juan, 203, 242
Segovia, 26, 70, 78, 115, 133
Segovia, Diego de, 237
Segura, Ana de, 140
Segura, Francisco de, 140
Segura, Rodrigo de, 162, 205, 242–243
Segura de la Frontera, 36, 39, 46
Seniority. See Antigüedad
Sepúlveda, Cristóbal de, 243
Sepúlveda, Martín de (Maestre), 243
Sepúlveda, Pedro de, 39, 243
Serna, Alonso de la, 162, 243–244
Serna, Juan de la, 193
Serna, Polonia de la, 224
Sernaca, 200
Serrano de Cardona, Antonio, 263, 305. See also Antonio de Villarroel
Settlers, 100
Seville, 21, 61, 64, 76, 117, 123, 124, 129, 133, 135
Shipbuilding, 49
Shippers, 28
Siciliano, Juan, 140, 244
Siege of Cuzco of 1536–1537, 98
Sierra Guadalupe, 22
Sierra Morena, 22
Sierra San Pedro, 22
Silva, Antón de, 159
Silva, Juan de, 223
Simancas, Pedro de, 58, 182, 244
Sirándaro, 165
Sochicoatlan, 114
Sochimilco, 119, 120
Soconusco, 119
Solís, Francisco de, 175, 244
Solís, Juan de, 177, 244–245

Solís, Martín de, 224
Solís, Miguel de, 244
Solís Barrasa, Pedro de, 204, 245
Solís Orduña, Francisco de, 245
Solís y Barrasa, Francisco, 245
Solórzano, Cristóbal de, 115
Sosa, doña Isabel de, 247
Sosa, Juan Alonso de, 68, 154, 245
Sosa, Juan de, 97
Sosa, doña Juana de, 69, 139
Sosola, 167, 187
Sotelo de Arías, Diego, 196, 253, 257
Sotelo de Moctezuma, don Fernando, 196, 253
Sotelo Valderrama, don Cristóbal de, 196, 253
Soto, Cristóbal de, 195, 245, 262
Soto, Gregorio (Gerónimo) de, 133
Soto, María de, 245
Sotomayor, Agustín de, 251
Sotomayor, Gaspar de, 246
Sotomayor, Pedro Díaz de, 246
Spanish money, 9
Suárez, Catalina, 126, 145, 147, 264
Suárez, don Cristóbal, 188
Suárez, Diego, 173
Suárez, Hernán, 205
Suárez, Juan, 145, 246
Suárez, Lázaro, 161
Suárez, Lorenzo (el viejo), 247
Suárez, Melchor, 161
Suárez de Peralta, Luis, 246
Suárez Pacheco, Diego, 57, 155, 220, 246, 247
Suárez Pacheco, Leonor, 126, 246
Suchiaca, 179
Suchistlaguaca, 139, 175, 208
Suchitepec, 150, 197, 199, 212, 255
Suchitepetongo, 248
Suchititlan, 175
Suchitlan, 162, 218, 229
Suchitonalá, 186
Sultepec, 70

Tabaliloca, 225
Tabalilpa, 225
Tabasco, 44
Tacámbaro, 122, 207
Tachave, 138
Tacolula, 125
Tacuba, 196

Tagus River, 22
Taimeo, 176, 219, 223
Talasco, 237
Talavera, 115
Talistaca, 184, 204
Tamacuiche, 138
Tamaholipa, 209
Tamalacuaco, 221
Tamaloacan, 242
Tamalol, 136, 149
Tamante, 144
Tamaos, 144
Tamasola, 143
Tamasuchal, 113
Tamazola, 249, 254
Tamazulapa, 246
Tamazunchale, 141
Tamiagua, 261
Tamintla, 191
Tamistla, 157, 194, 261
Tamoín, 194
Tampachiche, 157
Tampasquín, 138
Tampico, 171
Tampuche, 157, 160
Tampuxeque, 160
Tamunau, 138
Tanantepec, 205
Tancetuco, 132, 172
Tanchinamol, 129
Tanchunamol, 132
Tancítaro, 178, 192
Tancolol, 201, 227, 244, 261
Tancuilave, 194
Tangitavo, 255
Tanlocuc, 221
Tanpacal, 160
Tanta, 193
Tantala, 209
Tantima, 129, 250
Tantoin, 243
Tantomol, 124
Tantoyeque, 226
Tantoyetle, 226
Tantoyuca, 226
Tanzaquila, 144
Tanzinteyzayula, 144
Tanzohol, 113
Tanzuy, 262
Tapia, Andreś de, 26, 220, 232, 246, 247
Tapia, doña Catalina de, 70, 137, 257

Tapia, Diego de, 230
Tapia, Gaspar de, 230
Tapia Carvajal, doña Catalina de, 137
Tapia Sosa, don Andrés de, 247
Tarecuato-Tepeguacan, 133
Tarifa, Francisco de, 247
Tarifa, Gaspar de, 248
Tarímbaro, 253
Tasmalaca, 142
Tatatetelco, 204
Taupa, 262
Tauzán, 201, 227
Taxco, 70, 140
Taximaroa, 234
Taymeo, 124
Teapa, 150
Tecali, 198, 215
Tecama, 166
Tecamachalco, 204, 254, 262
Tecaxique, 207
Techalutla, 122, 232
Teciutlan, 240
Tecociapa, 217, 253
Tecolapa, 189, 220
Tecomaltepec, 181
Tecoman, 144
Tecomastlaguaca, 130, 186, 187
Tecomavaca, 203
Tecomaxiaca, 150
Tecpa, 181
Tecpan, 255
Tecucitlan, 136
Tecuicuilco, 195
Teguacan, 133
Teguantepec, 136
Tehuacán, 46, 126, 230
Tehuantepec, 46, 119, 127, 128, 143, 149
Tejadillo, Cristóbal de, 204
Téllez, Diego (Licenciado), 149, 182, 192, 248
Tello, Andrés, 168
Tello, Diego, 168
Tello de Medina, Juan, 238, 248
Tello de Orozco, Francisco, 126
Temascalapa, 134, 174
Temecatipan, 253
Temiño, Francisco de, 168
Temoac, 244
Tempoal, 152, 244, 261
Tenacusco, 129, 250
Tenamastlan, 118, 164, 197

INDEX

Tenampulco, 252
Tenancingo, 235
Tenango, 228
Tenayuca, 245, 250
Tenesticpac, 261
Tenexpa, 167, 187
Tenochtitlan, 3, 40, 110, 114, 120, 121, 146
Teocalhueyacan (Tlalnepantla . . .), 154
Teocuitlatlan, 122
Teotalcingo, 157
Teotihuacan, 260
Teozacualco, 121, 205
Tepaca, 228
Tepalcatepec, 160
Tepapayeca, 119, 120
Tepeaca, 36, 39, 117, 154
Tepeapulco, 202
Tepec, 232
Tepecimatlan, 195, 236
Tepecpanzacualco, 189
Tepecuacuilco, 250, 251
Tepecuaculco, 180
Tepeguacan, 149
Tepemaxalco, 118, 142
Tepeque, 122
Tepetitango, 183
Tepetitlan, 163, 213
Tepetlachaco, 200
Tepetlaostoc, 152, 204, 234
Tepetlatlauca, 207
Tepetotutla, 227
Tepeucila, 135
Tepexi, 136, 148, 201
Tepexic, 174
Tepexicoapan, 168
Tepexillo, 168
Tepexistepec, 157
Tepexoxuma, 134
Tepexoyuca, 196
Tepexpan, 193
Teposcolula, 119, 187, 213
Tepozotlan, 209
Tepoztlan, 208, 260
Tepuzuacan, 257
Tequecistepec, 189, 240
Tequecistlan, 149, 252
Tequepilpa, 194, 195, 220
Tequescistlan, 228
Tequipilpan, 219

Tequixquiac, 67, 184, 202
Teremendo, 196
Terrazas, Francisco de, 24, 83, 114, 123, 249, 251, 255
Terrazas, Francisco de (the poet), 249
Terrazas, Hernando de, 241
Tescalco, 179
Tetela, 188, 223, 239
Tetepec, 181, 202
Tetetipac, 130
Teticpac, 213, 219
Tetila, 153
Tetiquipa, 189
Tetlan, 171
Teupantlan, 166, 214
Teutenango, 69, 131, 222, 257
Teutitlan, 180
Teutla, 208
Teutlaco, 184
Teuzutlatlan, 232
Texcaltitlan, 133
Texcatepec, 254
Texotepec, 167
Texupespa, 193
Tezcatepec, 133, 154, 155, 190
Tezontepec, 126, 214
Tezuatlan, 214
Tianguistongo, 254
Tianguiztengo, 168
Tierra Firme, 68, 113, 114, 124, 129
Tilantongo, 69, 170
Tiltepec, 117, 205, 236
Tinhuindín, 133
Tirado, Juan, 178, 220, 249
Tiripitio, 120
Tistla, 177
Tizatepec, 159
Tlacamama, 241
Tlacatipa, 144
Tlachichilco, 249
Tlachichilpa, 123
Tlacoloastla, 242
Tlacolula, 132, 264
Tlacotalpa, 228
Tlacotepec, 130, 162, 224, 243, 244
Tlacuacintepec, 181
Tlacuacintla, 179
Tlacuahuan, 176
Tlacuiloltepec, 251
Tlacuitlapilco, 254

Tlagualilpa, 116, 139
Tlahuitoltepec, 134
Tlalcozautitlan, 166, 217
Tlaliscoya, 187
Tlalnepantla, 172
Tlalpa, 69
Tlalpotongo, 221
Tlaltengo, 172
Tlamaco, 140
Tlanalpa, 204
Tlanchinolticpac, 166, 176, 193, 209
Tlanexpatla, 224
Tlanocopan, 247
Tlapa, 83, 154, 221, 256, 257
Tlapaguautla, 243
Tlapalcatepec, 123, 153, 239
Tlapanala, 116
Tlapanaloya, 151
Tlapistlan, 133
Tlapotongo, 166
Tlaquilpa, 182, 192, 248
Tlatectla, 189
Tlatlaltepec, 186, 187
Tlatlauquitepec, 142, 234
Tlautla, 237
Tlaxcala, 47
Tlaxiaco, 203, 258
Tlaxomulco, 171
Tlazazalca, 121
Tlazoltepec, 150
Tochimilco, 210, 224
Tofiño, Bartolomé, 191
Tolcayuca, 215
Toledo, 70, 136, 151
Toledo, Juan de, 185
Toliman, 190
Tolosa, Juan de, 147, 196
Toluca, 118, 123, 131, 143, 171, 216
Tomás, Maese Manuel, 24, 163, 249–250
Tonalá, 171, 245
Tonaltepec, 122
Tonameca, 204
Tonatico, 132, 172
Topiltepec, 159
Topla, 209, 228
Tordehumos, 132
Tornacuxtla, 173
Toro, 127
Torquemada, Baltasar de, 129, 250
Torquemada, Juan de, 202, 250

Torre, Alonso de la, 70
Torre, Antonio de la, 128
Torre, Bernardo de la, 141
Torre, Catalina de la, 129
Torre, Juan de la, 70, 134, 193, 210, 250–251, 260
Torre, Leonor de la, 164
Torre, Licenciado de la, 127
Torre, Luis de la, 70, 250–251
Torre, María de la, 128
Torres, doña Bernardina de, 251
Torres, Diego de, 209
Torres, Elvira de, 164
Torres, Fernando de, 241
Torres, Francisco de, 243
Torres, Hernando de, 249, 250, 251–252
Torres, Isabel de, 153
Torres, Juan de, 230
Torres, doña Juana de, 229
Torres, Leonor de, 246
Torres, Manuel de, 229
Torres Maldonado, Diego de, 209
Totolapa, 263
Totolinga, 235
Totolmaloya, 220
Totomeguacan, 123, 158
Totontlan, 156
Tototlan, 133
Tovar, Fernando de, 218
Tovar, doña Isabel de, 250
Tovar, Juan de, 139, 168, 252
Tozongo, 227
Tratantes, 29
Trejo, Pedro de, 127
Trejo, Rafael de, 252
Trejo Carvajal, Rafael de, 252
Treviño, don Lope Fernández de, 68
Triana (Seville), 135
Trías, Jerónimo, 140
Tribute, 17
Triple Alliance, 41, 51
Trujillo, 22
Tuchitlapilco, 238
Tuctla, 248
Tula, 30, 116, 140, 169
Tulancingo, 123, 249, 255
Tultitlan, 211, 214
Turiaque, 156
Turicato, 155, 206
Turuel (Aragón), 115

Tuspa, 171
Tututepec, 40, 46, 120, 139, 163, 186, 249, 250
Tututepetongo, 205
Tuxpan, 232, 247
Tuzantla, 238, 241
Tuzantlalpa, 133, 155, 190
Tzintzuntzan, 49, 177

Ubeda, 179
Ucareo, 129, 250
Ucila, 135, 213
University of Mexico City, 132
Urapa, 223, 245
Uredo, 223
Uruapan, 180, 264
Utlatlan, 49, 200

Valadés, Diego, 210, 252-253
Valderrama, Cristóbal de, 180, 196, 217, 253
Valderrama y Moctezuma, doña Leonor de, 196, 253
Valdés, Bartolomé de, 49, 125, 253
Valdivieso, Juan de, 83, 144, 253-254, 266
Valdivieso, Luis de, 136
Valdovinos, Pedro, 158
Valencia, Alonso de, 215
Valenciano, Pedro (Garao), 130, 254
Valiente, Alonso, 24, 39, 161, 178, 204, 254-255
Valiente, Juan, 121
Valladolid, 47, 50, 84, 123
Valladolid, province of, 76
Valle, Second Marqués del, 67
Vallejo, Juan de, 213
Valles, 50, 83, 127, 132
Valley of Mexico, 100
Valley of Oaxaca, 46
Valverde, fray Vicente de, 97
Varela (Gallegos), Gonzalo, 255
Vargas, Cristóbal de, 161
Vargas, Diego de, 248
Vargas, Francisca de, 129, 250
Vargas, Francisco de, 255, 256
Vargas, Gaspar de, 179
Vargas, Juan de, 169
Vargas, Juan Alonso de, 255-256
Vargas, Melchor de, 248
Vargas, Pablo de, 124

Vargas, Pedro de, 172, 198, 256
Vargas Morcillo, Alonso de, 200
Varillas, fray Juan de las, 97
Vázquez, Ana (Antonia), 262
Vázquez, doña Isabel, 116, 257
Vázquez, Martín, 124, 161, 201, 203, 258
Vázquez, Sebastián de, 249
Vázquez de Acuña, Lope, 151
Vázquez de Cisneros, Mateo, 142
Vázquez de Coronado, Francisco, 68, 69, 71, 96, 131, 154, 241, 257
Vázquez de Oropesa, Doctor Pedro, 256
Vázquez de Tapia, Bernaldino, 70, 71, 75, 83, 104, 116, 137, 154, 221, 256-257
Vázquez de Tapia, don Bernaldino, 257
Vázquez de Valdivieso, Juan, 254
Vázquez de Vivanco, Leonor, 238
Vázquez Lainez, Francisco, 258
Vázquez Lainez, Matías, 258
Vázquez Marroquino, Lorenzo, 126
Vecino, 308
Veedor, Diego, 168
Vega, García de, 139
Vejer (Bejer), Benito de, 258
Velasco, don Francisco de, 65, 141, 178
Velasco, Inés de, 139
Velasco, doña Inés de, 208
Velasco, don Luis de, 3, 114, 148, 177, 191
Velázquez, Alonso, 78, 207, 258, 265
Velázquez, don Alonso, 204
Velázquez, Antonio, 153
Velázquez, Diego, 10, 97, 98, 145
Velázquez, Isabel, 260
Velázquez, Juan, 117, 186, 187, 259
Velázquez de Bazán, don Antonio, 260
Velázquez de Cuéllar, Diego, 26, 39
Velázquez de Lara, Francisco, 259
Velázquez de la Serna, Antonio, 244
Velázquez de León, Juan, 43
Velázquez de Salazar, Juan, 234, 245
Vélez (Andalusia), 65
Vélez, García, 78, 162, 172, 243
Vélez, Isabel, 228
Vélez Rascona, Catalina, 78, 162, 172, 208
Venezuela, 144
Vera, María de, 174
Veracruz, 10, 36, 47, 49, 89, 101, 114, 130, 145
Veragua, 97

INDEX 347

Verdejo, Alonso, 259
Verdugo, Francisco, 162, 208, 246, 259–260
Verdugo, Juana, 162
Vergara, Catalina de, 199
Vigil, Rodrigo de (Notary), 122
Villa Alta, 30, 47, 113, 117, 127, 130, 134, 150, 211
Villa Rica de la Veracruz, 39
Villacorta, Juan de, 170
Villacorta, María, 131
Villafañe, Angel de, 210, 260
Villafañe, don Juan de, 154
Villafañe y Alvarado, don Angel de, 123
Villafeliz, Leonardo de, 260
Villafranca, 114
Villagómez, Antonio de, 196, 260–261
Villagómez, Juan de, 261
Villagrán, Alonso de, 261
Villagrán, Juan de, 152, 202, 227, 244, 261
Villagrán, Pedro de, 97, 98, 187
Villalobos, Gregorio de, 261, 265
Villamayor, Marqués de, 215
Villanueva, Diego de, 262
Villanueva, Fernando de, 224, 262
Villanueva, Juan de, 50
Villanueva, Juan de (el negro), 262
Villanueva, Leonor de, 188
Villanueva, María de, 227
Villanueva, Pedro de, 188, 262
Villanueva Cervantes, Agustín de, 262
Villanueva de Barcarrota, 24
Villanueva de la Serena, 22
Villanueva Tordesillas, Alonso de, 65, 67, 178, 261–262
Villapadierna, Diego de, 122, 125, 262–263
Villarreal, Chiapas, 48, 49
Villarroel, Antonio de, 122, 263, 305. See also Serrano de Cardona, Antonio
Villasana, Agustín de, 222
Villaseñor, Alonso de, 141
Villaseñor Orozco, Juan de, 48, 50, 65, 67, 141, 263–264
Villegas, Francisco de, 171, 264
Villegas, Luis de, 155
Villegas, don Martín, 264
Villegas, Rodrigo de, 122
Villegas y Peralta, don Pedro, 264
Viñar, Catalina de, 149, 233, 238

Vivanco, Juan de, 190
Vivero, Rodrigo de, 255
Vivero Alberrucia, don Rodrigo de, 255
Viveros, doña María de, 191

War of Chupas, 98
War of Salinas of 1537–1538, 98
Widows, 98

Xacona, 117, 239
Xala, 257
Xalacingo, 216
Xalapa, 120, 155, 207
Xalatlaco, 113, 141
Xalcingo, 257
Xalcomulco, 188
Xalisco, 207
Xalomulco, 225
Xalpantipe, 232
Xaltepec, 150, 209, 211, 250, 260
Xaltepetongo, 236
Xaltepozotlan, 217
Xaltipa, 189
Xaltocan, 165
Xalxucatitan, 219, 223
Xareta, 185, 210
Xexa, Francisca de, 199
Xicalan, 264
Xicaya, 138
Xicayan, 168, 183, 187, 202, 252, 255
Xicotepec, 187
Xicotlan, 115, 133
Xilocingo, 201, 258
Xilotepec, 65, 135, 178, 203, 218, 242
Xilotlan, 239
Xipacoya, 179, 211
Xiquilpa, 260
Xiquipilco, 204
Xochimilco, 69, 149
Xocoticpac, 222
Xocotitlan, 264
Xocutla, 197
Xolotepec, 159
Xolotlan, 121
Xonacatlan, 115, 133, 206, 244
Xonotla, 142
Xontla, 234
Xoteapa, 191
Xuluapa, 176
Xumiltepec, 153, 192

Xuquila, 206
Xuxupango, 58, 122, 124, 263

Yagualica, 202, 228, 250
Yañez Pinzón, Vincente, 176
Yanhuitlan, 115, 138
Yautepec, 208, 260
Yecapixtla, 175, 244
Yeitepec, 248
Yetecomac, 219, 223
Yolotepec, 138
Yoloxinecuila, 226
Yope, 125, 197
Yopelcingo, 132
Yucatan, 114
Yucucuy-Tlazoltepecl, 186, 187
Yurirapundaro, 139, 252
Yztayuca, 138

Zacamulpa, 213
Zacapal, 238
Zacapala, 233
Zacapo, 179
Zacatecas, 141, 207
Zacatepec, 252
Zacatlan, 137
Zacatula, 44–46, 49, 51, 121, 133, 144, 223
Zacuala, 241
Zacualpa, 235, 244
Zalagua, 144
Zambrano, Francisca de, 163
Zamora, 116, 118, 137
Zamora, Alvaro de, 264
Zamora, Francisco de, 264–265
Zamorano, don Pedro, 265

Zamorano, Pedro Ruiz, 199, 231, 265
Zamorano de Arrazola, don Nicolás, 265
Zamudio, Juan de, 78, 207, 258, 265
Zapata, Juan, 183
Zapotecas, 124, 129
Zapotecs, 47, 53, 113, 115, 120, 127
Zapotitlan, 157, 162, 172, 198
Zapotlanejo, 162, 218
Zaragoza, 39, 47
Zaragoza, Miguel de, 39, 261, 265
Zárate, Bartolomé de, 266
Zárate, doña Catalina de, 65, 141
Zautla, 206
Zavala, Martín, 235
Zayanaquilpa, 202
Zayas, doña Beatriz de, 214
Zayula, 122, 232
Zayultepec, 189
Zimbrón de Vitoria, Alonso, 266
Ziroma, 156
Zirosto, 264
Zoaltepec, 122
Zola, 185, 237
Zolcuautla, 183
Zongolica, 243
Zoquicingo, 243
Zoquio, 211
Zoquitlan, 156, 197
Zoyaltepec, 237
Zultepec, 173, 195, 201, 211
Zumárraga, fray Juan de (Bishop of Mexico), 266
Zumpaguacan, 243
Zumpango, 161, 165
Zúñiga, doña Juana de, 69, 139, 147, 226
Zúñiga, doña María de, 123, 240

www.ingramcontent.com/pod-product-compliance
Lightning Source LLC
Chambersburg PA
CBHW020635230426
43665CB00008B/184